W9-CIA-731

Mal

# 5,500 QUILT
# BLOCK
# DESIGNS

Edited by Nancy E. Sherman

**Library of Congress Cataloging-in-Publication Data Available**

10  9  8  7  6  5  4  3  2  1

Published by Sterling Publishing Co., Inc.
387 Park Avenue South, New York, NY 10016
© 2003 by Maggie Malone
Distributed in Canada by Sterling Publishing
C/o Canadian Manda Group, One Atlantic Avenue, Suite 105
Toronto, Ontario, Canada M6K 3E7
Distributed in Great Britain by Chrysalis Books
64 Brewery Road, London N7 9NT, England
Distributed in Australia by Capricorn Link (Australia) Pty. Ltd.
P.O. Box 704, Windsor, NSW 2756, Australia

BOOKSPAN ISBN 1-4027-1482-3

# Maggie Malone

# 5,500 QUILT
# BLOCK
# DESIGNS

Sterling Publishing Co., Inc.
New York

# Key

| | | | | |
|---|---|---|---|---|
| **AB** | Alice Brooks | | **MLM** | Mary Lee Moynihan |
| **AG** | Alice Gammell | | **MM** | Maggie Malone |
| **AK** | Aunt Kate | | **MoM** | Mountain Mist |
| **AMS** | Aunt Martha Studios | | **NC** | Nancy Cabot |
| **CAM** | Cincinnati Art Museum | | **NCS** | Needle Craft Supply |
| **CaS** | Carlie Sexton | | **NM** | Needlecraft Magazine |
| **CG** | Country Gentleman | | **NP** | Nancy Page |
| **CoM** | Comfort Magazine | | **OCS** | Old Chelsea Station |
| **CR** | Caroline Reardon | | **OF** | Ohio Farmer |
| **CS** | Clara Stone | | **OJF** | Orange Judd Farmer |
| **CW** | Capper's Weekly | | **PAG** | Patchwork Accessories & Gifts |
| **EH** | Ernie Haight | | **PF** | Progressive Farmer |
| **FF** | Farm and Fireside | | **PP** | Prudence Penny |
| **FJ** | Farm Journal | | **PQ** | Patchwork Quilts |
| **GB** | Georgia Bonesteel | | **qac** | quilting.about.com |
| **GC** | Grandmother Clark | | **QC** | Quilt Craft |
| **GD** | Grandma Dexter | | **QEQ** | Quick & Easy Quilting |
| **GH** | Golden Hands | | **QM** | Quiltmaker |
| **GLB** | Godey's Lady's Book | | **QN** | Quilter's Newsletter |
| **HaM** | Harriet Moore | | **QT** | Quilting Today |
| **HAS** | Home Art Studios | | **QW** | Quilt World |
| **HH** | Hearth & Home | | **QWB** | Quilter's Workbook |
| **HHA** | Household Arts | | **QWO** | Quilt World Omnibook |
| **HHJ** | Household Journal | | **RD** | Roy Daniel |
| **HM** | Household Magazine | | **RF** | Robert Frank |
| **HMD** | H.M. Designs | | **RM** | Ruby McKim |
| **IS** | Indianapolis Star | | **RMS** | Ruth M. Swasey |
| **JM** | Judy Martin | | **SD** | Susan Dague |
| **KCS** | Kansas City Star | | **SSQ** | Stitch 'n Sew Quilts |
| **LAC** | Ladies Art Company | | **TFW** | The Farmer's Wife |
| **LBC** | Lockport Batting Company | | **TQ** | Traditional Quiltworks |
| **LCPQ** | Ladies' Circle Patchwork Quilts | | **TQr** | Traditional Quilter |
| **LHJ** | Ladies' Home Journal | | **VJ** | Victoria Johnson |
| **LR** | Lou Rathjen | | **VS** | Virginia Snow |
| **LS** | Lois Smith | | **WB** | Workbasket |
| **LW** | Laura Wheeler | | **WBM** | Workbasket Magazine |
| **MD** | Mrs. Danner | | **WC** | Woman's Century |
| **MJ** | Michael James | | **WD** | Woman's Day |
| | | | **WW** | Woman's World |

# Table of Contents

NINE PATCH PATTERNS
*9*

FOUR PATCH PATTERNS
*91*

FIVE PATCH PATTERNS
*189*

ELEVEN PATCH PATTERNS
*239*

EIGHTEEN PATCH PATTERNS
*245*

TWENTY-FOUR PATCH PATTERNS
*249*

TWELVE PATCH PATTERNS
*253*

TEN PATCH PATTERNS
*257*

EIGHT PATCH PATTERNS
*261*

CIRCLES AND CURVES PATCH PATTERNS
*265*

OCTAGONS, DIAMONDS, AND EIGHT POINT STARS PATCH PATTERNS
*319*

ALPHABET PATCH PATTERNS
*427*

INTERNATIONAL SIGNAL FLAGS PATCH PATTERNS
*431*

I clipped my very first quilt pattern in 1958 from *McCall's Needlework and Crafts* magazine. It was called Lone Star, a five point star set in a pieced circle. I made one block and decided I'd never live long enough to complete a quilt by hand. Nevertheless, quilts continued to catch my eye and I clipped many more patterns. I didn't really start to quilt though until the early 1970s, when I read Barbara Johannah's book, *Quick Quilting*. That book made it begin to seem that it might not take a lifetime to make a quilt after all.

The first quilt I completed was an Ohio Star I made for my brother-in-law. It took only about two weeks to finish. After that, I was hooked. Every quilt pattern I came across was added to my collection, as well as every picture of one. By 1980, I had stacks of magazines everywhere. And I could never remember which magazine it was that contained the pattern I needed. So I began removing the patterns from magazines, organizing them by the number of squares in a block, and filing each type by name in alphabetical order. The file boxes proliferated, but so did the new magazines I bought. I just wasn't gaining on the problem.

As I became more proficient at quilting, I realized I didn't need the entire pattern, just a sketch of it. That was the basis for *1,001 Patchwork Patterns*, but those sketches were all hand drawn and it seemed like an awful lot of time-consuming work to draw pictures of every new pattern I happened upon. As I collected and filed them, I also became aware that some patterns went by more than one name, sometimes as many as five or ten.

Then came the computer. Once I found a decent drawing program, it was child's play to draw the patterns and save them to disk. I got rid of tons of paper. The end result is the book you now hold in your hands.

The patterns are drawn on a grid showing the number of squares to the block. The most basic and most common pattern is the nine patch, a block that is 3 squares by 3 squares. Patterns progress from there to blocks that are 6 squares by

6 squares, 9 squares by 9 squares, and so on. This arrangement also makes it easy to mix and match patterns if desired, as they all draft to the same size block.

To draft a pattern, draw a square the size you want the finished block to be. Divide it into the appropriate number of squares and draw in the lines.

If possible, find grid paper for circles and hexagons. These designs are so much easier to draft when you have the proper grid. You'll find that many octagonal patterns are easier to draw on a circular grid.

If you feel uncomfortable about drawing your own patterns, take this book to a copy shop and have them enlarge your selected pattern. Be aware that there may be some distortion in the enlarging process. Draw a grid over the enlarged pattern, then adjust any lines that do not line up with the grid.

This book gives the name (or names) of each pattern, as well as some of the publications in which the patterns first appeared and the name of the creator, where known (see key on p. 4). Some of the patterns are very old and are copied from holdings in museum collections. Other old patterns were passed along from friend to friend and were not actually published until the 1890s or later. Most of the patterns published in the *Kansas City Star* fall into this category. Readers sent in patterns for publication that had been in their families for 50, 60, even a 100 years. Other publications, designers, and editors relied heavily on patterns from the Ladies Art Company catalogs. The oldest catalog I have was published in 1892 and many of the designs appearing in it have become classics.

I hope you enjoy this book and find it useful for many projects and many, many years.

—Maggie Malone

# NINE
## PATCH
## PATTERNS

3 X 3 GRID

6 X 6 GRID

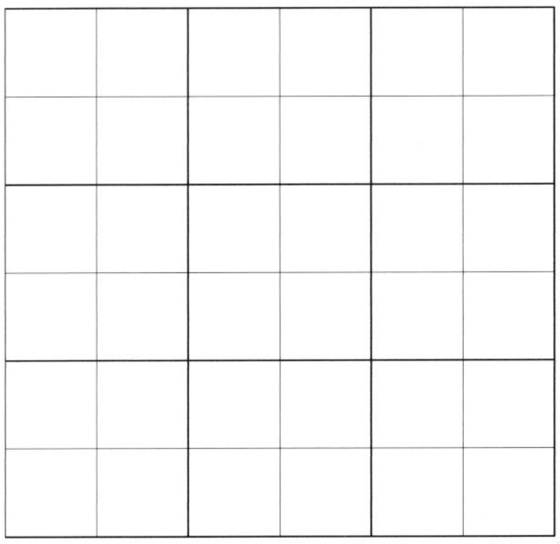

A NINE PATCH PATTERN IS MADE ON A GRID OF 3X3 SQUARES
THESE PATTERNS ARE EASILY SCALED TO ANY BLOCK SIZE DIVISIBLE BY 3

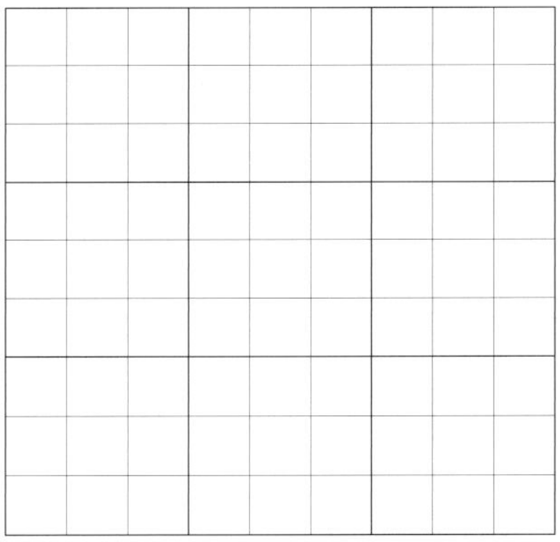

9 X 9 GRID

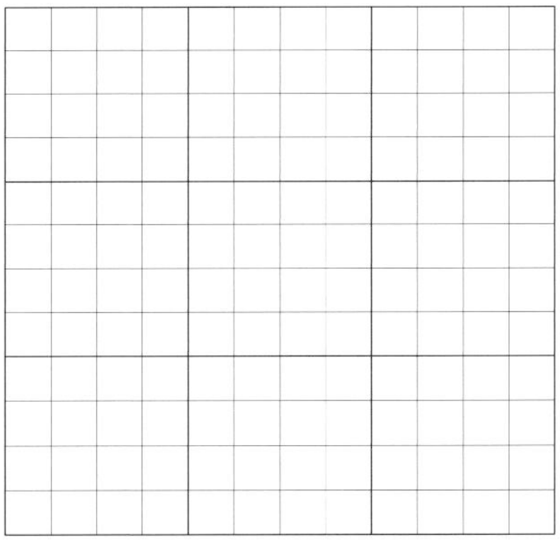

12 X 12 GRID

1   Nine Patch, *OF, 1896*
    Simplex Star, *HH*
    Checkerboard Design,
       *1931*
    Double Nine Patch

2   Nine Patch
    Patience Nine Patch
    Easy Quilt

3   Red Cross

4   Patience Nine Patch

5   H-Square
    Blocks in a Box

6   Bright Hopes
    Twist

7   Hourglass

8   Calico Puzzle, *KCS, 1930*

9   Snowball

10  Snowball Variation

11  Split Nine Patch

12  Split Nine Patch

13  Big O

14  Octagon, *KCS*
    Calico Snowball
    Hour Glasses
    The Marble Floor, *KCS*
    Rob Peter to Pay Paul,
       *CaS*
    Snowballs, *NC*

15  Hourglass

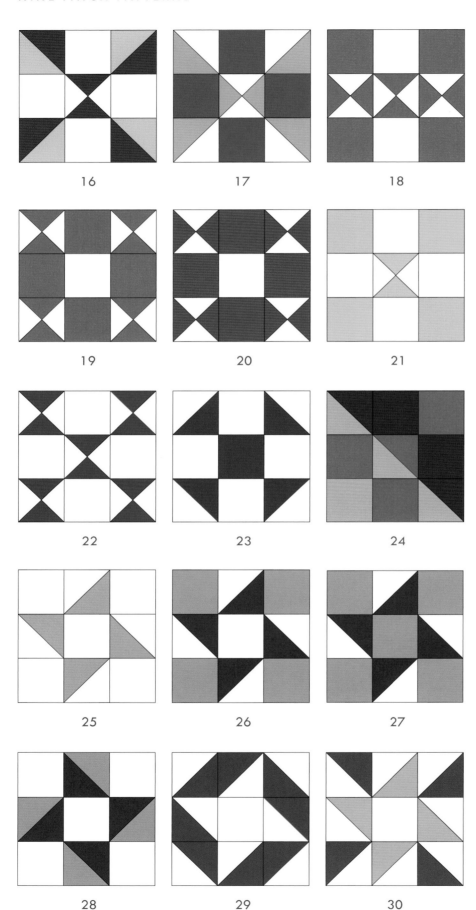

16    Practical Orchard, *LAC*

17    Hour Glass, *CS*

18    Triplet, *KCS*

19    Letter X, *LAC*

20    At the Square, *LAC*

21    Practical Orchard, *LAC*
       Practical Orchard, *NC*,
        *1934*

22    Clown's Choice

23    Shoofly, *LAC*
       Eight Cornered Box,
        *1896*
       Fifty Four Forty or
        Fight, *NC*
       Simplicity, *OCS*
       Fence Row Quilt, *KCS*
       Hole in the Barn Door

24    Straight Furrow
       Nine Patch Variation
       Perkomen Valley

25    Friendship Star

26    The Pinwheel, *KCS*
       Simplex Star, *HH*
       Wings in a Whirl, *KCS*

27    The Lost Goslin', *KCS*

28    New Home

29    Ribbon Star, *NP*

30    Nine Patch Star

31 Indiana Puzzle

32 Eccentric Star

33 Eccentric Star

34 Box, *LAC*

35 Formal Garden
 Eccentric Star, *NC*
 Eccentric Star, *CW*

36 Wandering Star

37 Birds in the Air
 Birds of the Air
 Flock of Geese
 Flying Birds
 Flying Geese

38 Corn and Beans

39 Tree Everlasting
 One Way
 Trip to the Altar
 Wild Geese

40 Windmill

41 Spider, *NC*

42 Cat's Cradle
 Tennessee
 Double Pyramid

43 Double X, *LAC*
 Jacks on Six, *OF, 1894*
 Kindergarten Block
 Old Maid's Puzzle, *1895*
 Three and Six, *NC, 1936*

44 Jack and Six, *NP*
 Tennessee, *NP*

45 Vermont Maple Leaf,
 *WB, 1935*

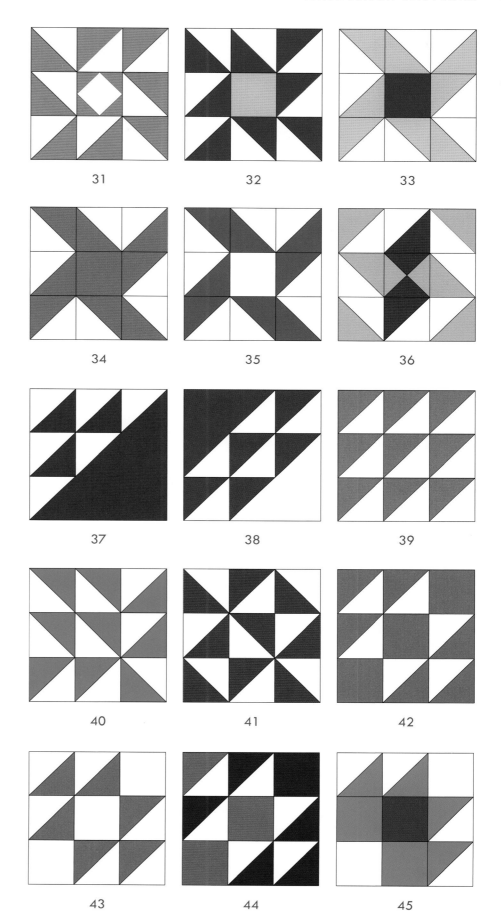

5,500 QUILT BLOCK DESIGNS

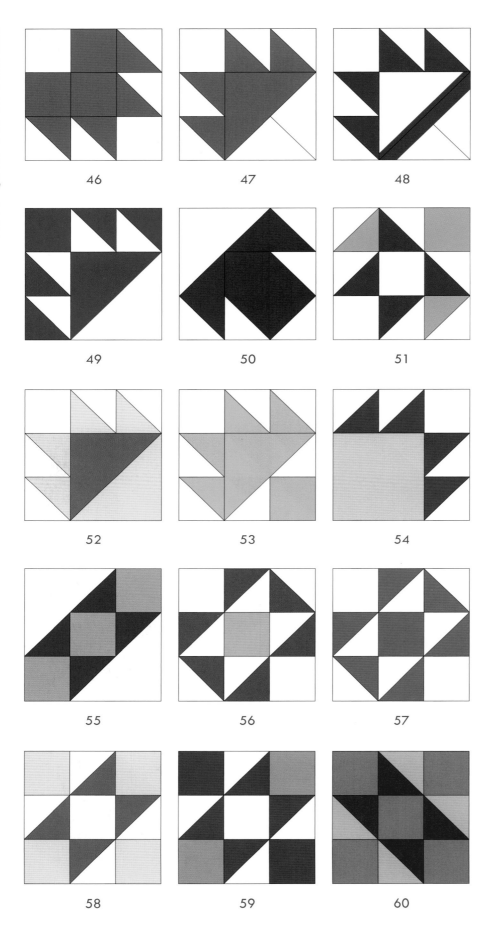

46 Tea Leaf
 Bear Tracks, *NC, 1937*
 Duck's Foot in the
  Mud, *NC*
 Maple Leaf Quilt
 Tea Leaves, *NC*

47 Maple Leaf, *CS*
 Album
 Autumn Leaf, *LW*
 Magnolia Leaf, *CS*
 Poplar Leaf
 Tea Leaves

48 Sawtooth

49 Cactus Bud

50 Tin Soldier "T" Quilt
 Boxed T, *LAC*

51 Darting Birds, *NP*

52 Cake Stand

53 Old Bear's Paw

54 Bear Paw

55 Road to California

56 Split Nine Patch

57 Split Nine Patch

58 Double Hour Glass, *NC,*
 *1933*

59 Contrary Wife, *KCS*

60 Contrary Wife

61 Attic Window
   Garret Window, *NC*

62 Autumn Trails, *MM*

63 Slanted Diamonds, *NC*

64 Spool
   Empty Spool, *NC*
   Love Knot

65 Malvina's Chain, *LAC*
   Aunt Melvernia's
      Chain, *NC*

66 Friendship Name
      Chain, *KCS*

67 Sailboat Block, *KCS*
   Lost Ship, *LAC*
   Victory Boat
   West Wind, *NP*

68 Cobwebs

69 Green River, *NP*

70 Calico Spools

71 Zig Zag Path, *SD*, *1999*

72 Sailboat

73 Northwind

74 Birds in the Air

75 Attic Window
   Shadow Box

61   62   63

64   65   66

67   68   69

70   71   72

73   74   75

5,500 QUILT BLOCK DESIGNS

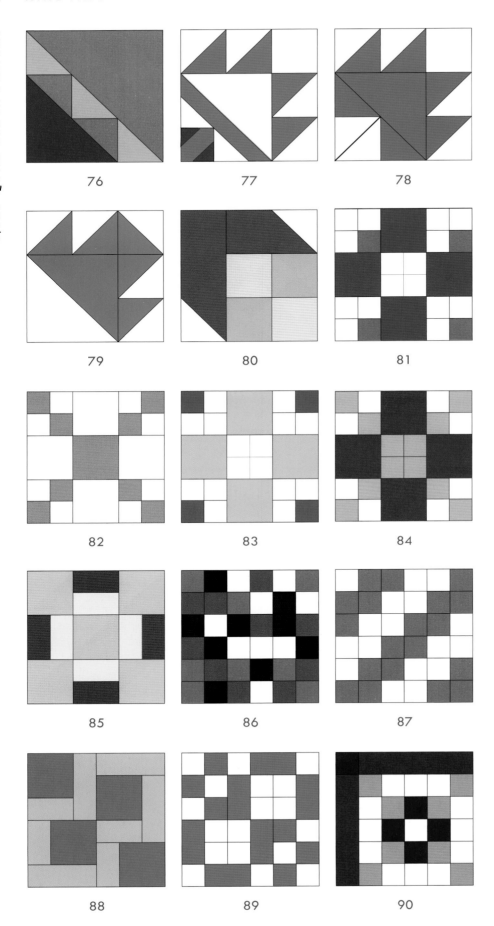

76 · 77 · 78

79 · 80 · 81

82 · 83 · 84

85 · 86 · 87

88 · 89 · 90

76 Golden Stairs

77 Texas Flower, *LAC*

78 Apple Leaf, *KCS*
Maple Leaf

79 Double T, *NP*
Mixed T, *NP*

80 Beginner's Choice

81 Pussy in the Corner,
*GC, 1931*
Puss in the Corner, *NC,
1932*

82 Pennsylvania, *NP*
Criss Cross Quilt, *NP*
Simple Cross
Single Irish Chain, *NC*

83 Homeward Bound

84 Thrifty, *KCS*

85 Unknown

86 Postage Stamp

87 Streak of Lightning

88 Patience Corners

89 Domino
Chained Dominos

90 Nine Patch Plaid

91 Nine Patch

92 Antique Tile Block, *NC, 1938*

93 Interlocked Squares, *KCS*
   Four Part Striped Block, *KCS*
   Spin Wheel

94 Zig Zag

95 Spirit of St. Louis, *NC, 1934*
   Tricolor Block, *NC*

96 Basket Weave

97 London Stairs, *KCS*
   Virginia Worm Fence
   Endless Stairs, *HH*
   Endless Stair, *NC*

98 Roman Square

99 Four H, *KCS*

100 Unknown

101 Edna's Choice

102 Confetti, *TQ*

103 Color Ways

104 Interlocked Squares

105 Roman Squares
    Fence Posts
    Three by Three, *CG*

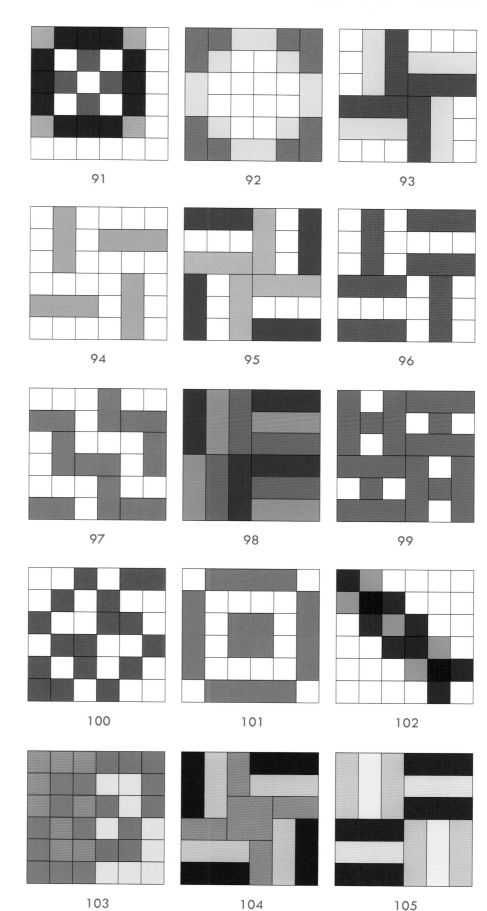

91  92  93

94  95  96

97  98  99

100  101  102

103  104  105

5,500 QUILT BLOCK DESIGNS

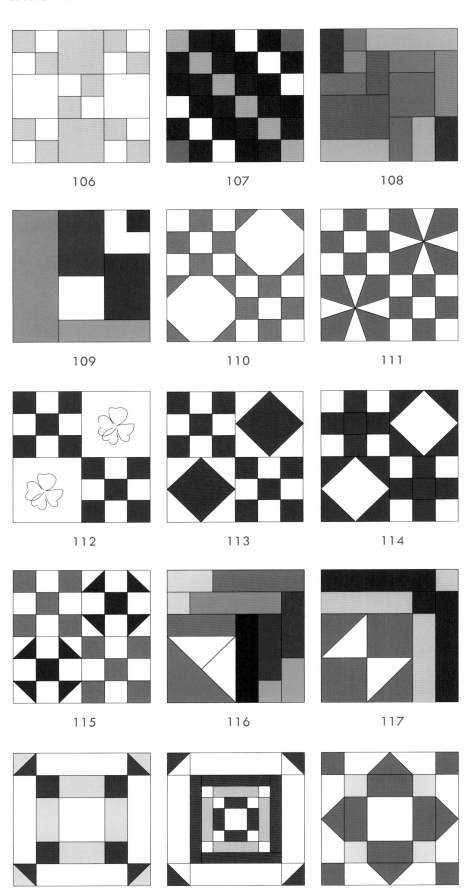

106

107

108

109

110

111

112

113

114

115

116

117

118

119

120

106 Cogwheel

107 No Room at the Inn, *HMD, SSQ, 1984*

108 Patio Tiles, *EH, LCPQ*

109 Becky's Nine Patch

110 Flagstones, *LAC*
Aunt Patsy's Pet, *NC*
Aunt Patty's Favorite, *FJ*
Delaware's Flagstones, *WB*
Dutch Mill
Federal Chain, *NC*
Four and Nine Patch, *NC*
Grandmother Short's Quilt
Improved Nine Patch, *AMS*
New Nine Patch
New Snowball, *HH*
Nine and Four Patch, *DA*
Pullman Puzzle
Snowball
Snowball and Nine Patch

111 Oklahoma Trails and Fields

112 Good Luck Block, *NC*
Lucky Block
Lucky Quilt
Four Leaf Clover, *1935*

113 Snowball

114 Goose Creek

115 Tic Tac Toe, *NP*

116 Cascade Pride

117 Odds and Ends, *LAC*

118 Puss in the Corner, *NC*

119 Yankee Charm, *NC*

120 Quarterfoils, *NC*

121 Fair and Square, *KCS*

122 Boxes

123 Churn Dash, *RM*
   Broken Plate, *NC*
   Double Monkey
      Wrench
   Double T, *HH*
   Dragon's Head, *WW*
   Fisherman's Reel
   Hens and Chickens
   Hole in the Barn Door
   Indian Hammer
   Joan's Doll Quilt
   Lincoln's Platform
   Love Knot
   Ludlow's Favorite
   Old Mill Design, *TFW*
   Picture Frame
   Puss in the Corner
   Quail's Nest
   Sherman's March, *CW*
   Shoo Fly, *NC*
   Wrench

124 Churn Dash

125 Grecian Design, *LAC*
   Grecian Square, *WW*
   Grecian
   Greek Square, *NC*

126 Greek Cross

127 Prairie Queen
   True Blue, *HH*

128 Chained Nine Patch

129 Cups and Saucers, *KCS*

130 Illinois, *HH*

131 Eddystone Light

132 Hidden Star

133 Card Trick

134 No Name Patch

135 Arbor Window

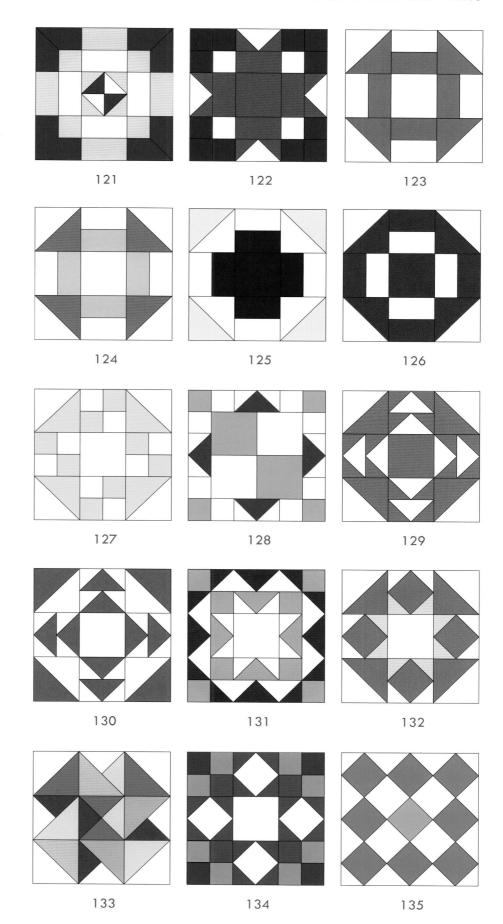

121  122  123
124  125  126
127  128  129
130  131  132
133  134  135

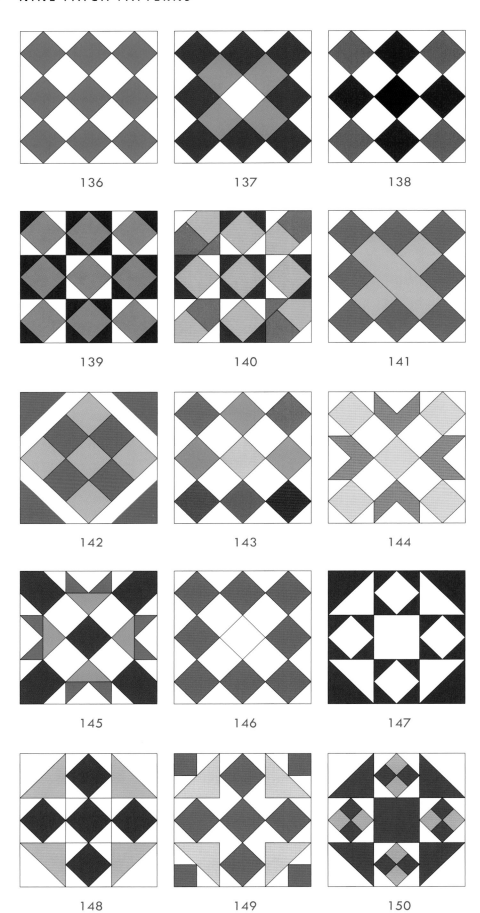

136

137

138

139

140

141

142

143

144

145

146

147

148

149

150

136 Nine Patch

137 Courthouse Square
   Grandmother's Pride,
      *HAS*

138 Checkerboard

139 Montpelier Quilt Block

140 Patchwork Bedspread

141 Album, *KCS*
   Arbor Window, *GC*
   Courthouse Square
   The Cross Patch
   Odd Fellow's Quilt, *OJF*

142 Mayor's Garden, *NC*
   Modern Broken Dish,
      *KCS*

143 Checkerboard
   Nine Patch
      Checkerboard
   Old Mail, *WC*
   The Queen's Favorite,
      *CW*

144 Joy Bells
   Eight Hands Around
   Swing in the Center, *NC*
   Turkey in the Straw, *NC*

145 Swing in the Center,
      *LAC*
   Dumbbell Block
   Mrs. Roosevelt's
      Favorite
   Roman Pavement
   Swinging in the
      Center, *NC*

146 Beggar Block

147 Sawtooth Patchwork,
      *LAC*
   Mrs. Brown's Choice

148 Sawtooth Patchwork
   Five Diamonds

149 Five Spot, *NC*

150 The Pinwheel Quilt,
      *KCS*

151  Cross and Chains, *KCS*

152  Richmond
Aunt Vina's Favorite
Butterfly Quilt Block,
*NC*
Lucy's Four and Nine

153  Jefferson City, *HH*

154  No Name Patch

155  Creole Puzzle, *NC*

156  Fresh Start, *RMS, SSQ,
1983*

157  Robbing Peter to Pay
Paul

158  Arizona, *NP*

159  Crossroads to Jericho,
*HH*

160  Union Squares

161  Double Anchor, *KCS*

162  Mrs. Bryan's Choice

163  Cracker

164  H Quilt

165  Jewel

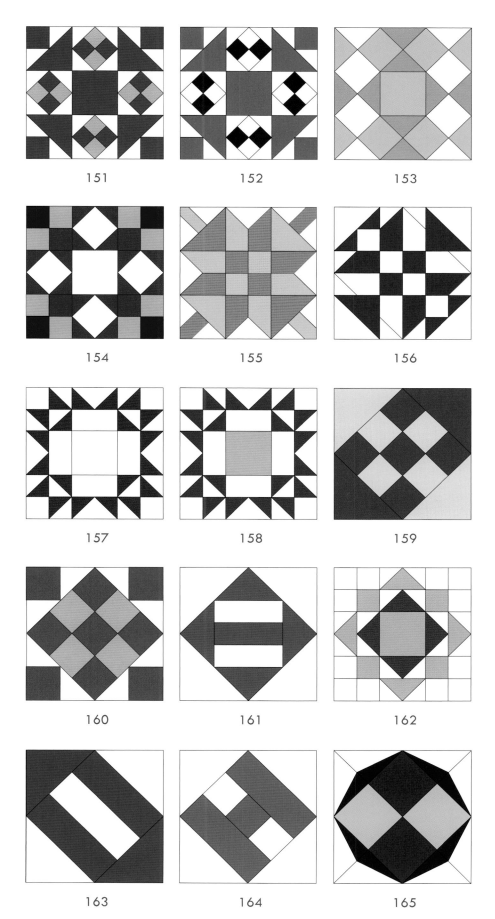

151    152    153

154    155    156

157    158    159

160    161    162

163    164    165

5,500 QUILT BLOCK DESIGNS

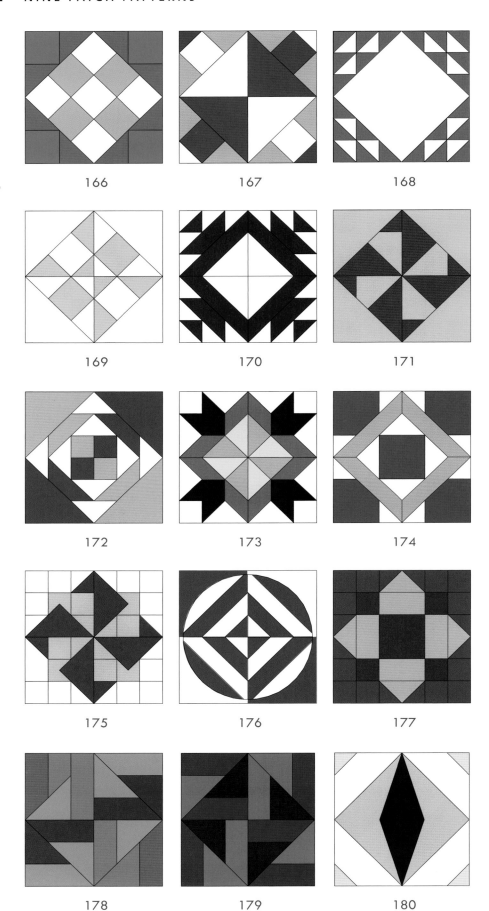

166

167

168

169

170

171

172

173

174

175

176

177

178

179

180

166 Union Square, *NC*
Beacon Light, *NC*

167 Ladies' Aid, *LAC*

168 Carol's Scrap Time
Quilt

169 Storm Signal, *NC*
Hail Storm, *NC*

170 Four Ships Sailing,
*LCPQ*

171 Wheeling Triangles

172 Trees in the Park

173 Weathervane Pinwheel

174 Nine Patch Frame

175 Twisting Star

176 Merry-Go-Round

177 Cornerstone, *KCS*

178 Turnabout Variation

179 Turnabout, *QN*

180 Squares and Diamonds

181 Vines at the Window,
 *NC*

182 Nine Patch Frame

183 The Village Green, *1930*

184 Diamond Star, *LAC*
 A Quilt Mosaic, *KCS*

185 Mother's Choice, *CS*
 Dove at the Windows,
 *MD*
 Fringed Square, *NC*
 Laurel Wreath, *CW*

186 Sandhills Star, *KCS*
 Blossoming Cactus, *NC*

187 A Quilt Mosaic, *KCS*

188 Aunt Sukey's Choice,
 *LAC*

189 Hopscotch, *KCS*

190 Christmas Star, *KCS*

191 Turkey's Dilemma,
 *RMS, SSQ, 1982*

192 Indian Puzzle, *KCS*

193 Love in a Mist

194 Best of All

195 Housewife Quilt Block

181

182

183

184

185

186

187

188

189

190

191

192

193

194

195

196 All Hallows

197 Castle Tower

198 Shaded Compass

199 Cups and Saucers, *KCS*

200 Autumn Maze

201 Diamond Star, *AMS*

202 Weathervane Variation

203 Garden Path

204 Shaded Trail, *KCS*

205 Arrowhead Star, *KCS*
    Laurel Wreath, *GC*
    Many Pointed Star, *NC*
    Michigan Beauty, *CS*
    Modern Star, *GC*
    Star of Many Points,
     *LAC*

206 Sailboat Block

207 Ohio Star
    Eastern Star
    Eight Point Design, *LAC*
    Eight Point Star
    Lone Star
    Shoofly
    Star
    Texas
    Texas Star
    Tippecanoe and Tyler,
     Too

208 Variable Star
    Henry of the West, *NP*
    Lone Star, *NP*
    Star of Hope, *NP*
    Star of the West, *NP*
    Star Spangled
    Texas

209 Flying Crow, *FJ*

210 Mosaic
    Star of Virginia
    Variable Star
    Happy Home, *HH*

211 Four X Quilt
    Four X's

212 Unknown Star

213 Mosaic

214 Squares and
    Diamonds, *KCS*

215 Mosaic, *NP*

216 Silent Star, *KCS*
    Star X
    Old Tippecanoe

217 Swamp Angel, *NC*

218 Midnight Star Block

219 Star X, *NC*

220 Combination Star, *LAC*
    Ornate Star

221 Mystery Flower
    Garden, *AMS*

222 Variable Star
    Aunt Eliza's Star, *HH*
    Ohio Star
    Star of Hope, *NP*

223 Country Farm

224 Braced Star

225 Braced Star

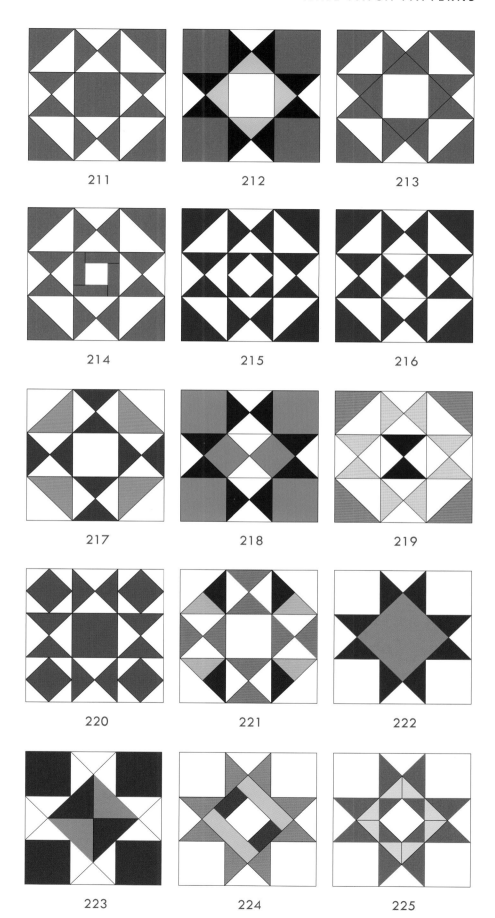

211   212   213

214   215   216

217   218   219

220   221   222

223   224   225

5,500 QUILT BLOCK DESIGNS

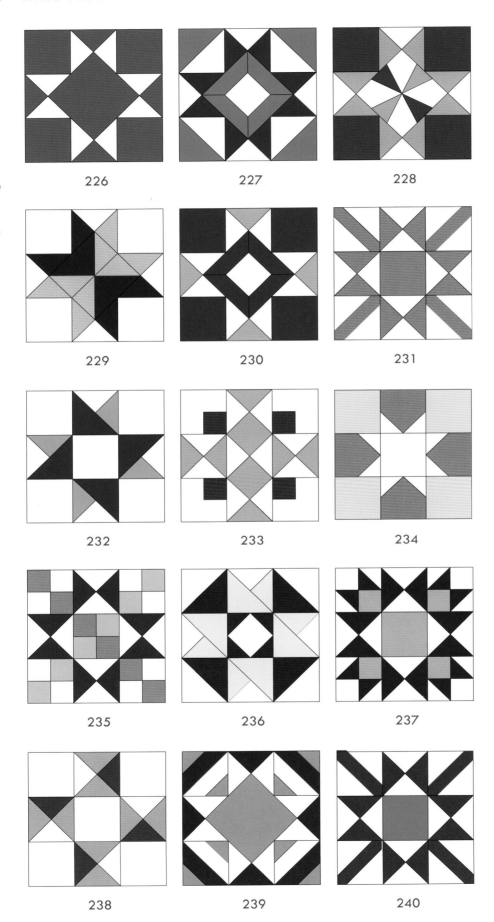

226

227

228

229

230

231

232

233

234

235

236

237

238

239

240

226 Aunt Eliza's Star, *LAC*
   Aunt Lottie's Star, *NC*
   Texas Star

227 Card Basket

228 Sparkling Star Block

229 Right Hand of
   Fellowship, *HH*

230 Friendship Star, *HH*
   Braced Star, *LAC*
   Eliza's Star

231 Turnabout T

232 Twin Star

233 Four Corners

234 Morning Star

235 Chained Star,
   *Margaret Huckeby,
   QN, 2000*

236 Air Castle, *LAC*
   Towers of Camelot, *NC*

237 Honeymoon

238 Stellie

239 Jackknife
   Treasure Chest, *OCS*
   Night and Noon

240 Old Snowflake, *NC*

241 Aunt Dinah

242 Morning Star

243 January Thaw, *TQ*

244 Swamp Patch

245 Ornate Star

246 Four Corners

247 Blocks and Stars

248 Album Star
Friendship Star

249 Salem, *HH*

250 Combination Star

251 Boy's Nonsense, *LAC*
Nonsense, *LAC*
Boy's Fancy
Boy's Playmate, *NC*

252 Jack's Delight

253 Card Basket
Carson City

254 Points Homeward,
*RMS, SSQ*

255 Phoenix

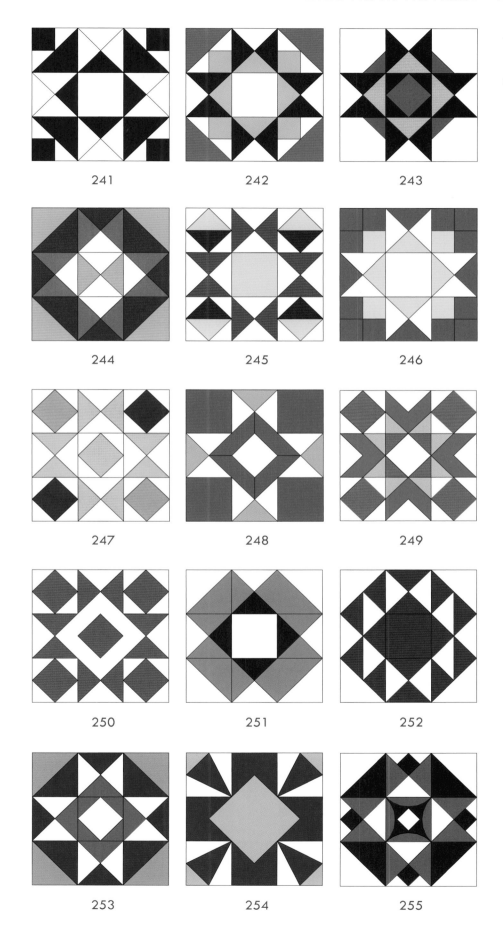

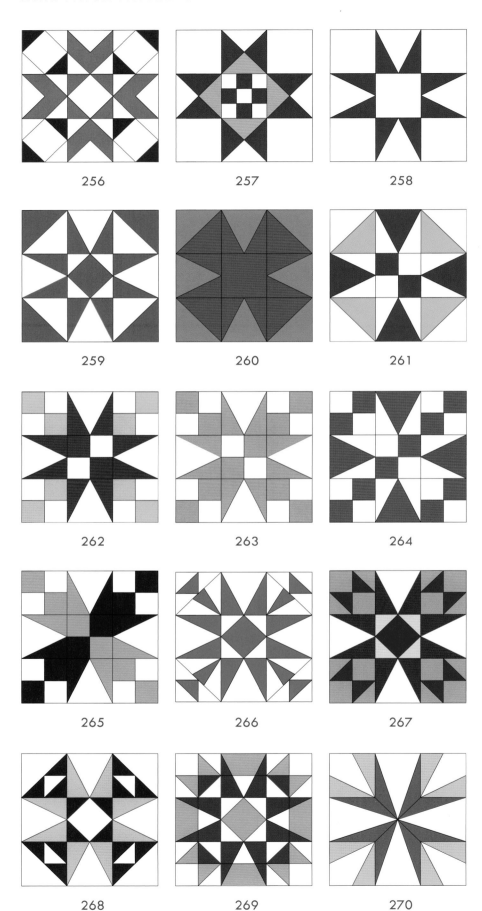

256

257

258

259

260

261

262

263

264

265

266

267

268

269

270

256 Salem

257 Dolly Madison's Star

258 Sun Rays Quilt, *KCS*

259 Doris' Delight, *FJ*
Storm at Sea

260 Eight Pointed Star

261 Judy in Arabia, *Beth Gutcheon*

262 Fifty-Four Forty or Fight

263 Fifty-Four Forty or Fight, *KCS*
Grandma's Star
Nine Patch Star Quilt
Railroad Quilt

264 Garden Walk, *KCS*
Garden Patch
Texas, *NP*
An Old-Fashioned Pinwheel

265 Bird of Paradise

266 Rosebuds

267 Rose Mosaic

268 Panama Star

269 Scattered Points

270 Lily Palm

271 Claws

272 Pineapple

273 Double Z

274 Mayflower

275 Maltese Star

276 1941 9-Patch

277 Eight Pointed Star

278 Straight and Narrow,
    *Beth Schwartz, SSQ*

279 Big T

280 Garden Square

281 Capital T, *LAC*
    Double T, *NP*
    Cut the Corners, *1910*

282 Friendship Quilt, *KCS*

283 Capital T, *HM*
    Double T

284 Imperial T, *LAC*
    Big T, *Dakota Farmer,
    1927*
    Capital T
    Tea for Four, *NP*

285 Double T, *NP*
    Four T Square, *NC*

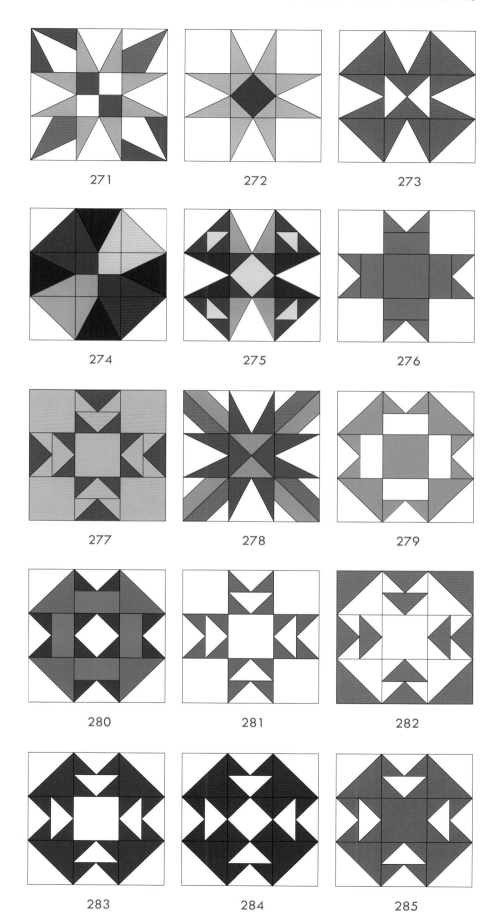

271

272

273

274

275

276

277

278

279

280

281

282

283

284

285

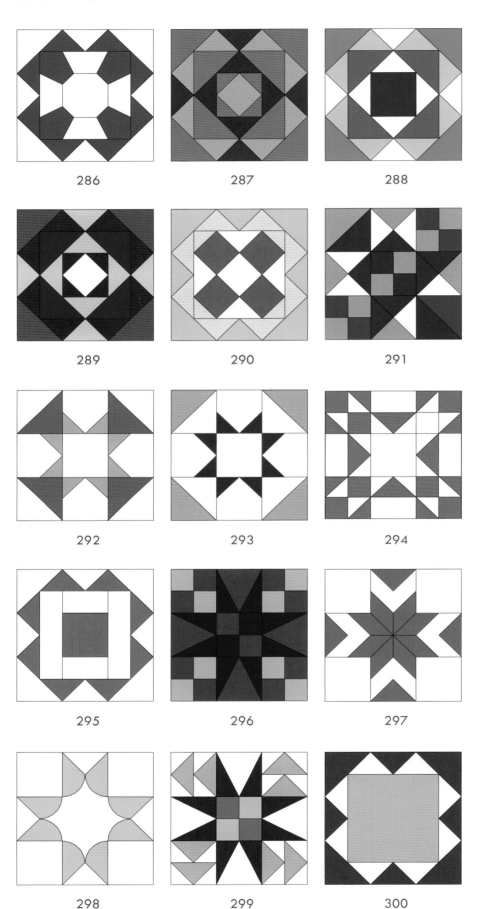

286

287

288

289

290

291

292

293

294

295

296

297

298

299

300

286 Imperial T, *KCS*

287 Boxes

288 Gentleman's Fancy, *LAC*
   Mary's Block, *NC*
   Twenty-four Triangles, *FJ*
   Unnamed, *OF*, *1894*

289 Handy Andy

290 Treasure Box

291 Queen's Petticoat, *1979*

292 A Dandy

293 The Dandy Quilt Block, *1910*

294 Amish Star

295 Prairie Home, *QM*, *1994*

296 Tennessee Waltz

297 Eight Point Star

298 Arkansas Star, *KCS*
   Bursting Star, *HAS*
   Morning Sun, *KCS*

299 Star Geese

300 Country Farm

301 T-Squares

302 Pershing, *NP*

303 Morning Star, *LAC*
Rosebud, *NC*
Virginia, *HH*

304 South Carolina Star

305 Maltese Cross

306 State of Virginia, *HH*

307 Crowning Glory

308 Kansas Star, *KCS*
Crystal Star, *KCS*

309 Lover's Lane

310 Traditional T

311 Sawtooth

312 Sawtooth
Kansas Troubles

313 Lost Ships

314 Lost Ships

315 Tangled Briars

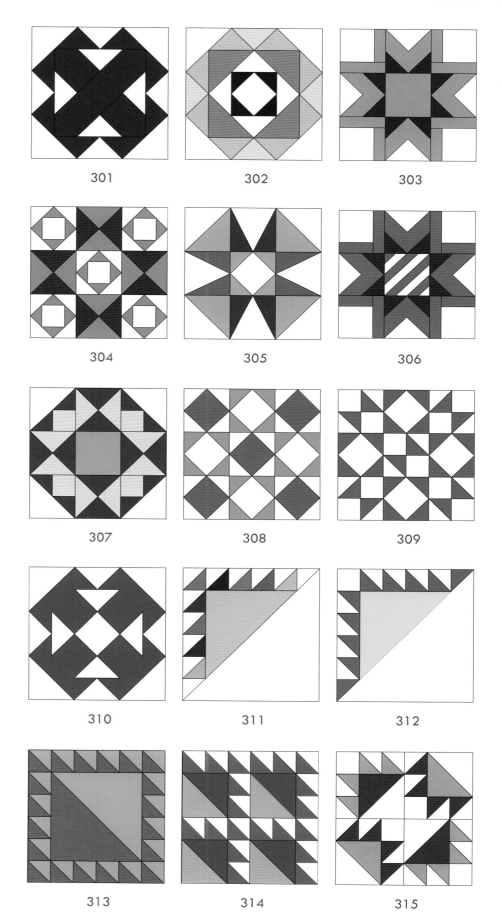

301

302

303

304

305

306

307

308

309

310

311

312

313

314

315

5,500 QUILT BLOCK DESIGNS

316 London Square, *NC*
    City Square

317 Birthday Cake

318 Four Crowns

319 Lady of the Lake, *NC*
    Galahad's Shield, *PF*

320 Star of Spring, *LW*

321 City Park, *QN*
    Crossroads America
    Flower Fields
    Galaxy
    Night Watch
    Under Blue Mountain
      Skies

322 F Patchwork, *1900*

323 Utility Block, *OF, 1896*

324 Pyramids, *NC*

325 Navajo, *LAC*
    Indian Mats, *NC*

326 Mother's Choice

327 Kansas, *HH*

328 Lindy's Plane

329 Union Star

330 Triangles

331  Circling Swallows

332  L Quilt

333  Broken Window, *KCS*

334  The Road to
      Grandma's, *RMS, SSQ*

335  Turnabout

336  Contrary Wife

337  Union Square

338  Wyoming Valley

339  The Original, *NC*

340  Four Crowns

341  Poinsettia

342  Broken Window, *KCS*

343  Thunder and
      Lightning, *NC*

344  Memory, *CS*

345  Pinwheels & Sawtooth

331

332

333

334

335

336

337

338

339

340

341

342

343

344

345

346 King's Crown

347 Joyce's Mystery Block

348 Silver Lane

349 Buzz Saw Charm, *LS,
   QN, 1991*

350 Bride's Puzzle
   Twelve Crowns, *FJ*
   Wedding March,
   *Women's Comfort*

351 Square Dance

352 Large Star Pattern

353 King's Crown

354 Frame

355 Friendship Block

356 Framed Squares, *NP*

357 Star Gardner

358 Union Square, *CW*
   Four Crowns, *KCS, 1933*
   Union, *LAC*
   Union Block, *NC*

359 Maple Leaf

360 Four Crowns

361 Thunder and Lightning

362 Four Winds

363 Double X

364 Wheeling Nine Patch

365 Crown of Thorns

366 Four Winds, *NC*

367 Triangles, *CaS*

368 Queen Victoria's
    Crown

369 Spinning Arrows, *NC*

370 Lightning in the Hills,
    *NC*

371 Dove of Peace

372 Double X, *LAC*

373 Eva's Garden

374 Indian Plume

375 Wagon Tracks
    Jacob's Ladder

361

362

363

364

365

366

367

368

369

370

371

372

373

374

375

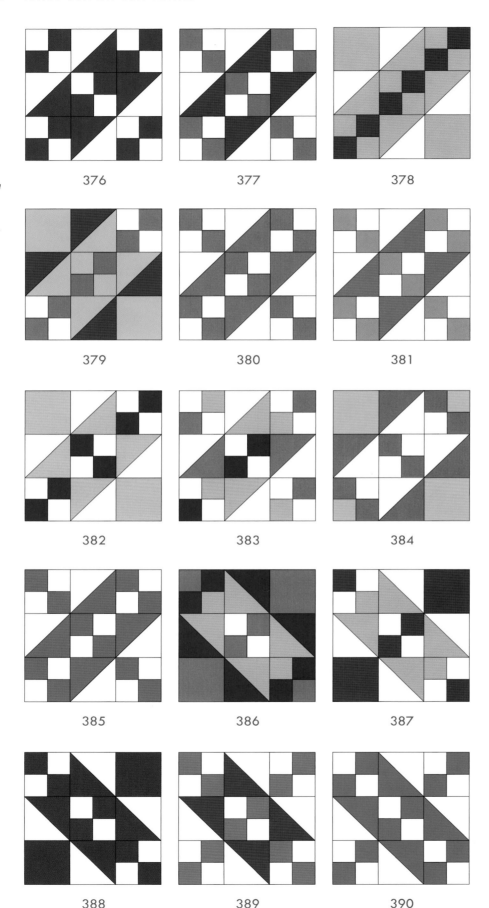

376

377

378

379

380

381

382

383

384

385

386

387

388

389

390

376 Road to Arkansas

377 Jacob's Ladder
Double Hour Glass, *GC*
Stepping Stones
Tail of Benjamin's Kite
Trail of the Covered
   Wagon
Underground Railroad
Wagon Tracks

378 Road to the White
   House

379 Road to the White
   House

380 Going to Chicago, *NP*
Golden Stairs, *NC*
Jacob's Ladder
Off to San Francisco,
   *NP*
Railroad
Road to California
Susie's Fancy

381 Jacob's Ladder

382 Rocky Road to
   California

383 Unknown Silk Block

384 Broken Sugar Bowl,
   *KCS*
Road to the White
   House, *FJ*

385 Railroad

386 Broken Sugar Bowl
Rocky Road to
   California

387 Broken Sugar Bowl

388 Rocky Road to
   California

389 Jacob's Ladder

390 Jacob's Ladder

391  Kelly's Block

392  Railroad

393  Rocky Road to
        California, *LAC*
      Home Queen

394  Steps to the Altar

395  Wagon Tracks
      Pacific Rail Road, *NC*
      Road to Arkansas

396  Foot Prints in the
        Sands of Time

397  Blue Chains, *NC*

398  Tail of Benjamin's Kite

399  Dublin Steps

400  Rocky Road to Dublin,
        *NC*

401  Flying Shuttles, *NC*

402  Hour Glass

403  Hovering Hawks

404  Battle of the Alamo

405  Winged Square

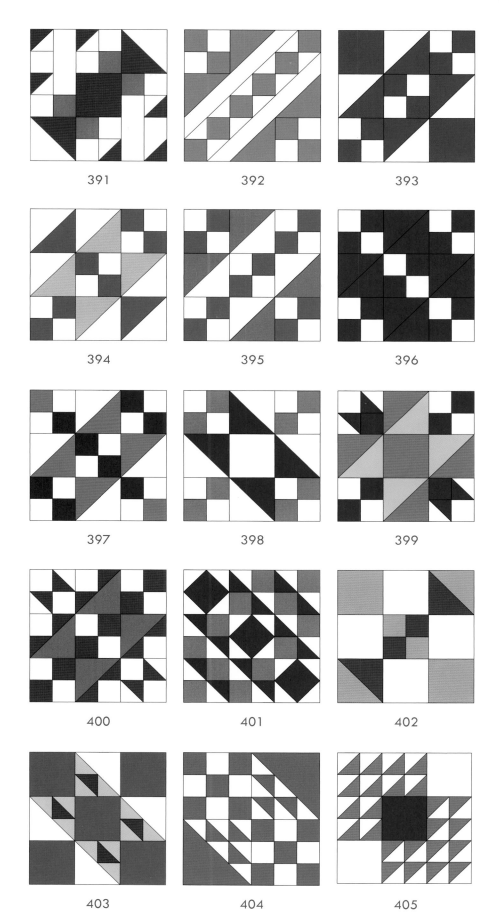

391

392

393

394

395

396

397

398

399

400

401

402

403

404

405

406

407

408

409

410

411

412

413

414

415

416

417

418

419

420

406 Cut Glass Dish, *LAC*
Golden Gates
Prism Block
Winged Square

407 Birds in the Air
Flight of Swallows, *NC*
Flock of Geese
Flying Birds

408 Cat's Cradle
Dove at the Window,
*CoM*
Double Pyramids, *MD*
Flying Birds, *NP*
Harrison, *Dakota
Farmer, 1929*
Harrison Rose, *1930*
Harrison Quilt
Hour Glass, *NP*
Wandering Lover, *HH*

409 Yellow Ribbon, *Cindy
Erwin*

410 Garden Path
Flower Garden Path

411 Spider Legs

412 Wood Lily, *KCS*
Indian Head, *KCS*
St. Elmo's Fire, *NC*

413 Cats and Mice, *LAC*

414 St. George's Cross

415 Linoleum

416 Golgotha
Cross Upon Cross
The Three Crosses

417 Mrs. Fay's Favorite
Friendship Block, *HH*

418 Merry Kite, *LAC*

419 An Arrangement of
Small Pieces, *KCS*

420 Four Squares

421 Aunt Dinah

422 The Chinese Quilt
    Block, *KCS*
    Broken Dishes, *NM*

423 Mystery Block

424 Friendship Block

425 Weathervane, *NC*

426 Owl, *KCS*

427 Ranger's Pride

428 Friendship Quilt, *KCS*

429 Morning

430 Summer Winds, *NP*

431 Welcome Hand

432 Follow the Leader

433 Whirlpool

434 Dove in the Window

435 Broken Wheel
    Block Circle
    Johnnie Round the
      Corner
    Single Wedding Ring
    Squirrel in a Cage
    Wheel

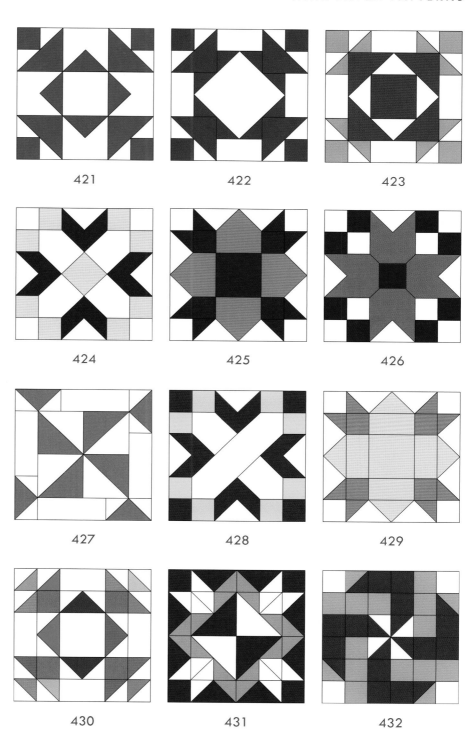

421        422        423

424        425        426

427        428        429

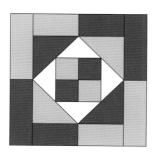
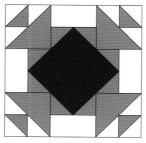
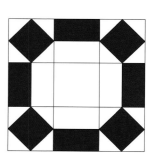

430        431        432

433        434        435

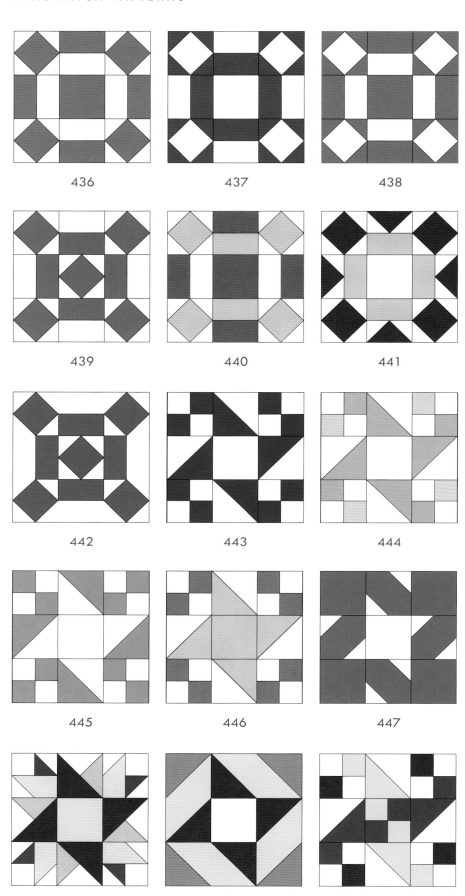

436 Squirrel in a Cage

437 Broken Wheel, *CS*
Mrs. Miller's Favorite

438 Rolling Stone, *LAC*
Letter O, *Dakota Farmer*
Wedding Ring

439 Friendship Quilt

440 New Hampshire Granite Block

441 Rolling Squares

442 Friendship Quilt, *HH*

443 Square and Half Square, *KCS*
Chinese Coin, *AMS*
Crosses and Losses, *QN*
Friendly Hand, *CoM*
Indian Puzzle, *AMS*
Indiana Puzzle, *KCS*
Milky Way, *LAC*
Monkey Wrench, *AMS*
Pinwheels, *NC*

444 Water Wheel

445 Chinese Coin

446 Waterwheel

447 Mississippi, *HH*

448 Sunflower, *QN*

449 Quartered Star

450 Waterwheel

451  Dancing Pinwheels, *NC*

452  Amish Star

453  T Quilt, *LAC*

454  Rolling Pinwheel

455  Mrs. Morgan's Choice,
    *LAC*
    Spinning Wheel

456  Rolling Pinwheel, *NC*
    Pinwheel Star
    Whirling Pinwheel, *KCS*

457  Tunnels

458  Corn and Beans, *LAC*

459  Arkansas Snowflake,
    *KCS*
    Arkansas Star, *KCS*
    The Kite Quilt, *KCS*
    Star Kites, *NC*

460  Carnival, *NC*

461  Mill and Stars

462  No Name

463  No Name

464  President Carter, *QW*,
    *1977*

465  Optical Illusion

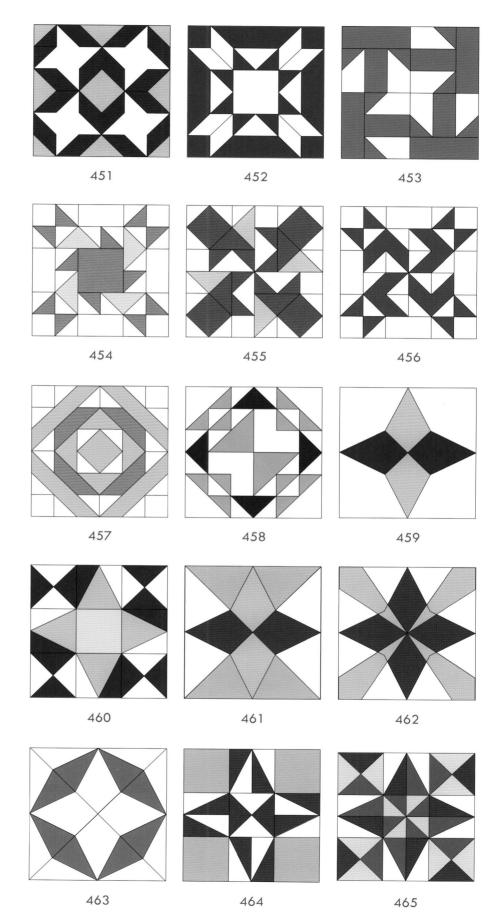

451    452    453

454    455    456

457    458    459

460    461    462

463    464    465

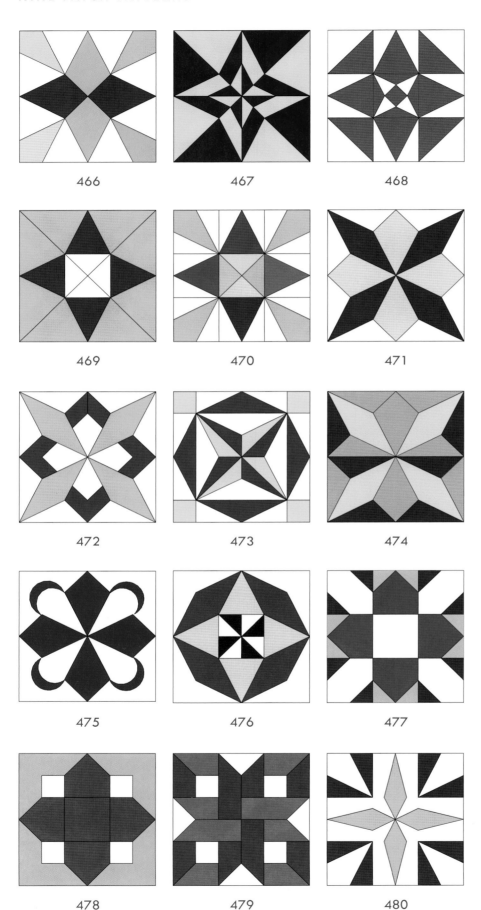

466    Time and Tide
       Four Pointed Star, *KCS*
       Twinkling Stars, *CoM*

467    Night and Day

468    Little Rock Block, *LAC*
       Arkansas Star, *NC*
       Butterfly Block, *NC*
       Sea Star, *NC*
       Star of the Sea, *NC*

469    The Star of Alamo, *KCS*

470    Japanese Scrap Quilt,
       *QT*

471    Skyrocket

472    Barbara Bannister Star

473    Wintery Reflections

474    Century of Progress,
       *KCS*

475    Star and Crescent

476    Rolling Pinwheel

477    Prairie Flower, *NC*

478    Grandmother's Own

479    Endless Ribbon, *SSQ*

480    Guiding Star, *KCS*

481 Victorian Square, *MLM, SSQ, 1982*

482 Lucky Clover, *AMS*

483 Betty's Delight

484 Double Necktie, *LAC*

485 Spools, *LAC*

486 California Chimney

487 Beginner's Choice

488 Oklahoma Twister, *AK*

489 Love and Kisses

490 Tulip Lady Fingers, *LAC*

491 Steps to the Altar, *LAC*
Dish of Fruit, *1896*
Flatiron Patchwork
Strawberry Basket

492 Nosegay, *KCS*

493 Galaxy Star

494 Firecrackers and Skyrockets

495 Maple Leaf

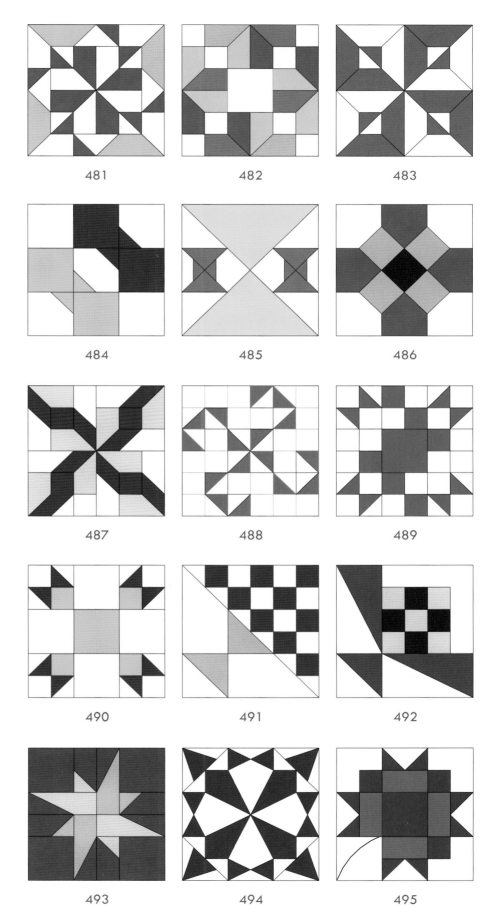

481

482

483

484

485

486

487

488

489

490

491

492

493

494

495

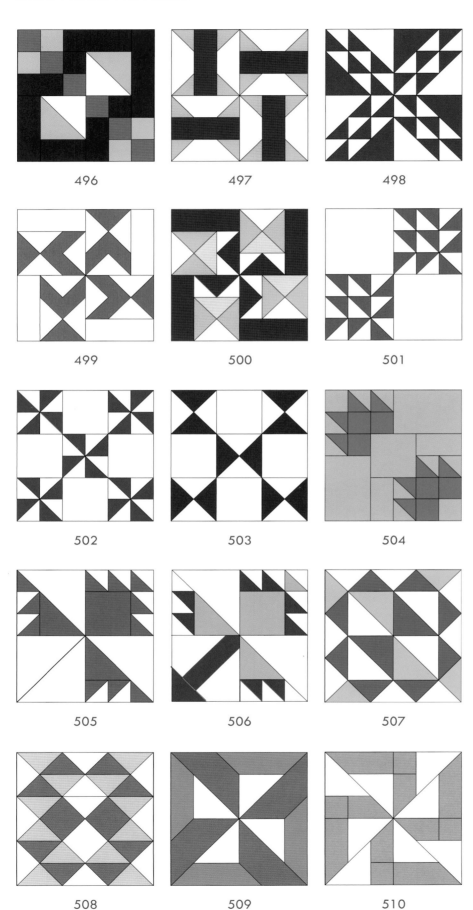

496 Hay's Corner

497 Arkansas Traveller, *LAC*

498 Mosaic

499 Flying Dutchman, *LAC*

500 Flying Dutchman, *NP*

501 Windmill

502 Windmill, *LHJ, 1903*
Clover Leaf
Flutter Wheel, *LAC*
Pin Wheels

503 Flying X

504 Tea Leaf

505 Historic Oak Leaf

506 English Ivy

507 Grandma's Hopscotch, *KCS*

508 Buckwheat

509 Unnamed

510 Good Luck

511 Indian Mats, *NC*

512 Mosaic

513 Colonial Rose

514 Sweet Gum Leaf, *LAC*

515 Love Knot

516 Maggie's Double
    Pinwheel

517 Wedding Bouquet

518 Cats and Mice, *LAC*

519 T-Quartette, *LAC*
    Boxed T, *LAC*
    Mixed T
    Tete-a-Tete

520 Builder's Block, *KCS*

521 Contrary Wife

522 Cedars of Lebanon

523 Mosaic

524 Battlegrounds

525 Rosebud, *LAC*
    Bright Star, *NC*
    Crow's Foot
    Hummingbird, *CoM*
    Maple Leaf, *NC*

511

512

513

514

515

516

517

518

519

520

521

522

523

524

525

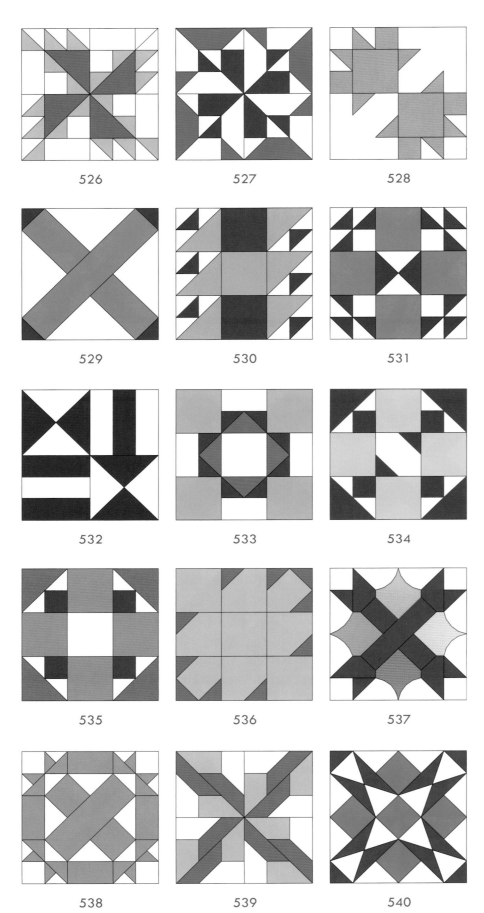

526

527

528

529

530

531

532

533

534

535

536

537

538

539

540

526 Straw Flowers

527 Victoria Square

528 Ozark Maple Leaf, *NP*
Broad Arrow, *FJ*
Maple Leaf Design, *LHJ*
Broad Arrows, *NC*
Arabic Latticework, *QN*
Fig Leaf, *QN*

529 Crosspatch

530 Wampum, *NC*

531 Peaceful Evening

532 Chain and Hourglass

533 Ladies Aid Album, *LAC*

534 New Album, *KCS*
Cedars of Lebanon, *HH*

535 Album

536 Flying Leaves, *NC*

537 Pathfinder

538 Easy Ways

539 Christmas Cheer

540 Augusta, *HH*

541 Gardener's Prize

542 Cookies and Milk,
   *HaM, SSQ, 1983*

543 Japanese Lantern

544 Sparkler

545 Dover, *HH*
   Dover Quilt Block, *LAC*

546 Patch as Patch Can,
   *AMS*

547 Double Tulip

548 Double Pinwheel

549 Whirlaround, *KCS*

550 The Mayflower, *LAC*
   Hard Times Block, *NC*

551 Butterfly

552 Hill and Valley

553 Weathervane and
   Steeple, *NC*

554 Square within Squares

555 Evening's Last

541    542    543

544    545    546

547    548    549

550    551    552

553    554    555

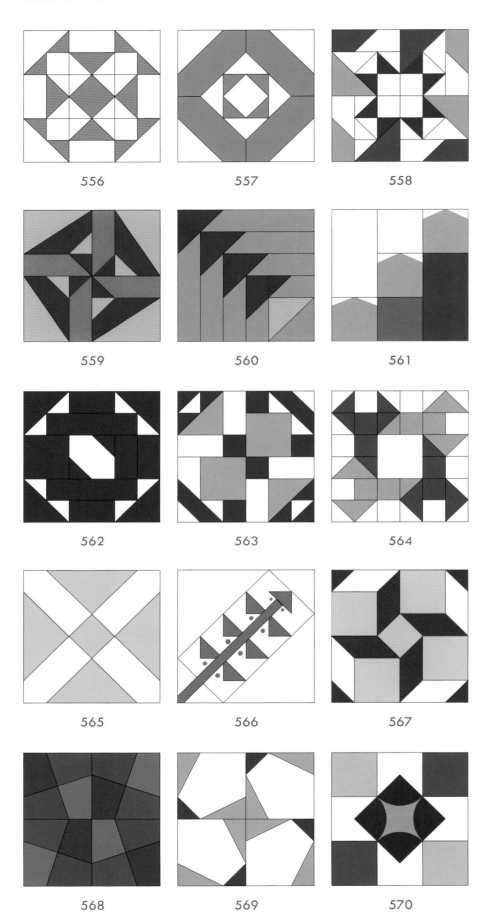

556
557
558
559
560
561
562
563
564
565
566
567
568
569
570

556 State Fair, *NC*

557 A Striped Plain Quilt, *KCS*

558 Rolling Pinwheel

559 My Mistake, *MM*

560 Chicago Geese

561 American Homes, *QW*

562 Cedars of Lebanon, *KCS*

563 Indian Mat, *NC*

564 Crab Claws

565 St. Andrew's Cross

566 Fernberry

567 Whirlaround

568 Broken Rainbows, *NC*

569 Unnamed, *QN*

570 Window Square

571 Shooting Star, *SSQ, 1989*

572 Patchwork Bedspread

573 Double L

574 Ballot Box

575 The Wind Wheel Quilt Block

576 Tandi Whirl Quilt

577 Pennsylvania, *HH*

578 Gretchen

579 Patch as Patch Can

580 Union Star

581 The Sprite, *AMS*

582 Kite, *TQ*

583 Good Fortune

584 Bells

585 The Chief, *LBC*

571

572

573

574

575

576

577

578

579

580

581

582

583

584

585

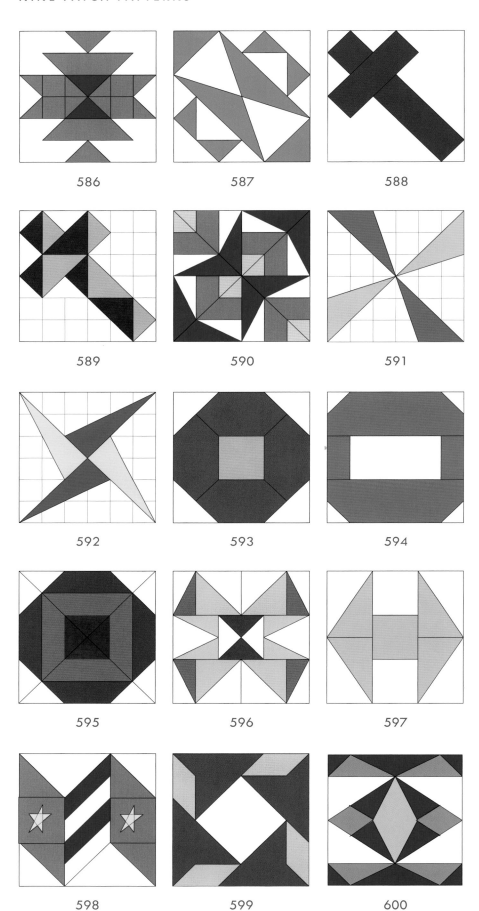

586 Squash Blossom, *QW*

587 Fair Play, *HH*

588 The Cross

589 Cross

590 Flutterbye

591 Twisted Ribbons

592 Wheel of Destiny, *FJ*

593 Wishing Ring, *KCS*

594 American Chain, *OJF*

595 The Kitchen Woodbox

596 Bow

597 The Bobbin, *QN*

598 Stars and Stripes, *NC*

599 Turkish Puzzle

600 Shooting Star

601 Three Kings' Journey, *HMD, SSQ, 1984*

602 Unnamed, *1943*

603 Delaware Crosspatch, *NC*

604 Washington Puzzle, *LAC*

605 Radio Windmill, *KCS*

606 Arabic Lattice, *LAC*

607 Picket Fence

608 Northern Lights

609 Cross Bars and Squares

610 Walking Triangles

611 Plane Thinking

612 Double L

613 Autograph, *CS*

614 Pinwheel Star

615 Heart

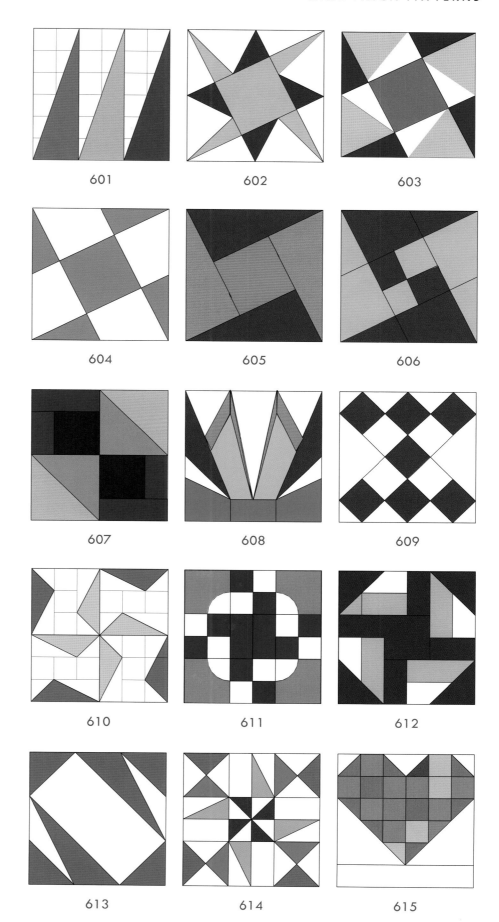

601

602

603

604

605

606

607

608

609

610

611

612

613

614

615

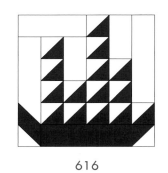

616

617

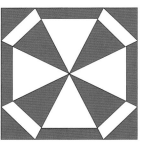

618

619

620

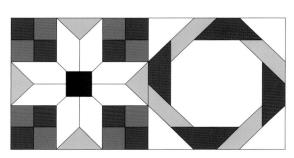

621

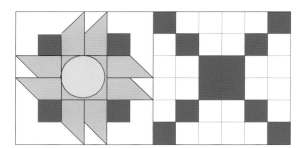

622

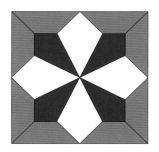

623

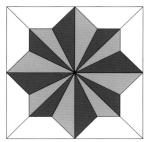

624

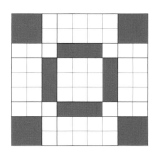

625

616 Voiliers, *LCPQ*

617 Emerald & Topaz, *QN*

618 Spider Web

619 Dutchman's Puzzle
Variation

620 Triangles, *WD, 1943*

621 State Fair Block

622 Star & Web, *SSQ, 1986*

623 Home Again, *FJ*

624 The Whirling Star, *KCS*
Patriotic Star

625 Hand Weave, *LAC*

626 Double Necktie

627 New Four Pointer, *KCS*

628 Puss in the Corner
  Double Nine Patch
  Fundamental Nine
    Patch, *QN*
  Golden Steps, *OCS*
  New Nine Patch
  Single Irish Chain

629 Double Nine Patch
  Dutch Nine Patch

630 Hen and Her Chicks

631 Swastika Patch, *LAC*
  Swastika
  Battle Ax of Thor
  Catch Me If You Can
  Chinese 10,000
    Perfections
  Favorite of the
    Peruvians
  Heart's Seal
  Mound Builders
  Pure Symbol of Right
    Doctrine
  Wind Power of the
    Osages

632 City Streets, *NC*
  Hand Weave

633 Farmer's Puzzle

634 Hand Weave, *NP*
  Handcraft, *NC*
  Handwoven, *NP*
  Interwoven, *NP*
  Over and Under, *NP*
  Strips and Squares, *NP*

635 Bradford Nine Patch

636 Broken Paths

637 Nonsuch, *LAC*

638 Flag In, Flag Out, *KCS*

639 Wedge and Circle

640 Aunt Tryphosa's
  Favorite

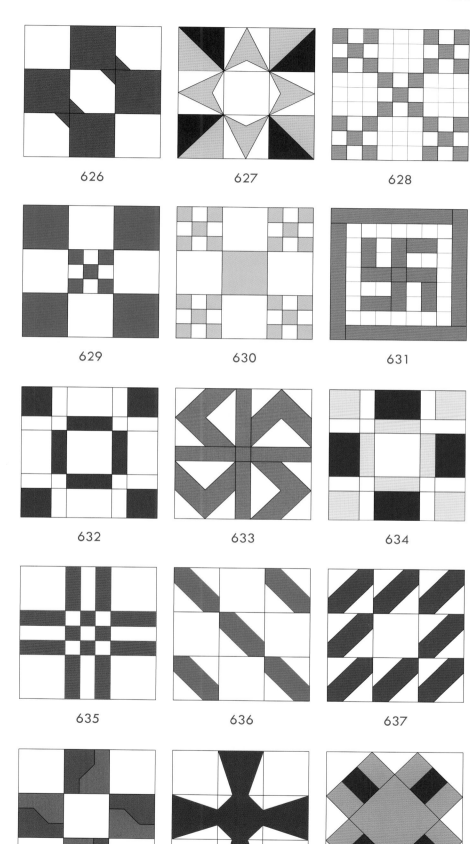

626

627

628

629

630

631

632

633

634

635

636

637

638

639

640

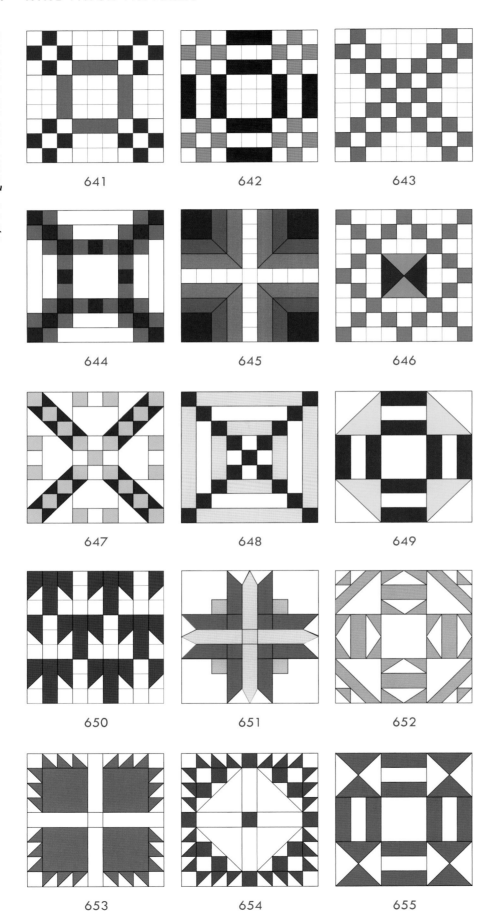

641

642

643

644

645

646

647

648

649

650

651

652

653

654

655

641 Puss in the Corner
Five Patch, *LAC*
Glorified Nine Patch

642 Building Blocks

643 Garden Path

644 Name Unknown

645 City Streets

646 Crosspatch

647 Dublin Chain
New Irish Chain
On the Square, *HH*

648 Alabama, *HH*

649 Golden Gate

650 Mixed T

651 Patchwork Posy

652 Mollie's Choice
Joseph's Coat

653 Premium Star

654 Bear's Den

655 London Roads
Arrow, *AMS*
At the Square, *NP*
Betty's Choice
Colorado's Arrowhead
Fireside Visitor, *CS*
Rope and Anchor, *KCS*

656 London Roads

657 Dolly Madison Star
President's Block

658 Pigeon Toes
Resolutions, *NP*
Turkey Tracks

659 Montana

660 Continental

661 Golda, Gem Star

662 Tile Puzzle

663 Voter's Choice

664 Double Pyramid

665 Independence Square

666 Four Clowns, *NC*

667 Chain & Hourglass

668 Bishop Hill, *NC*

669 Cross Patch, *AK, 1966*

670 Beggar Block, *LAC*
Over and Under Quilt
Design, *NP*

5,500 QUILT BLOCK DESIGNS

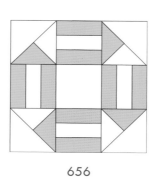

656

657

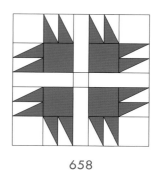

658

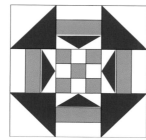

659

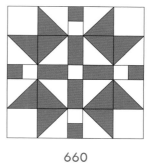

660

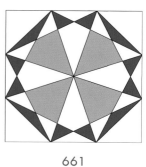

661

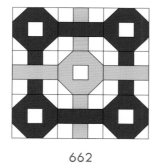

662

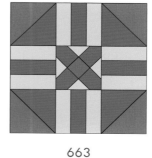

663

664

665

666

667

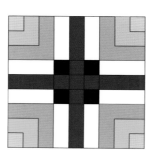

668

669

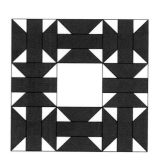

670

671

672

673

674

675

676

677

678

679

680

681

682

683

684

685

671 Beggar's Blocks
Cats and Mice
Spool and Bobbin, *NC*,
*1936*

672 Beggar's Blocks, *NP*

673 Homespun, *NP*

674 Santa Fe

675 Arkansas

676 Goose Tracks

677 Wedding March, *CoM*

678 Emma C

679 All Points

680 Sunburst

681 Crossroads, *NP*

682 Tangled Garters, *LAC*
Crossroads, *NP*
Garden Maze, *NC*
Queen of May, *HH*
Sun Dial, *NC*

683 Mrs. Dewey's Choice,
*HH*

684 Chicago Star, *LAC*

685 Dallas Star

686  Columbian Star, *LAC*

687  Prosperity Block, *NC, 1933*

688  Mona's Choice, *KCS*

689  Windmills All Around

690  Main Street

691  Housewife's Dream

692  Ribbon Star

693  Santa Fe Trail, *NC, 1934*

694  Meeting House Square, *NC*

695  Flying X

696  Nine Patch Variation

697  Winged Nine Patch

698  Love in a Tangle

699  Diamond Plaid Block, *NC*

700  Valley Falls Square, *Arlene Gier, SSQ*

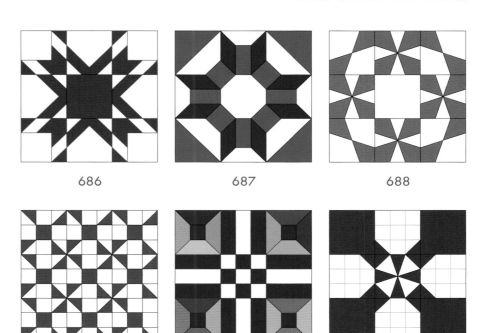

686                    687                    688

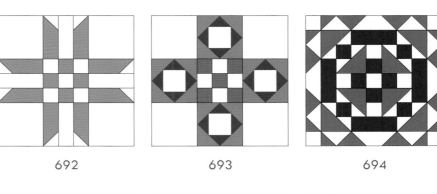

689                    690                    691

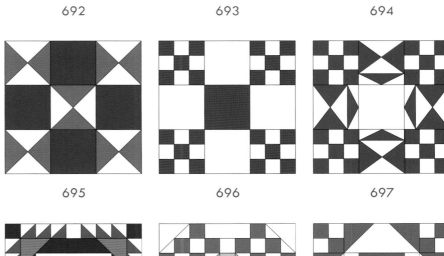

692                    693                    694

695                    696                    697

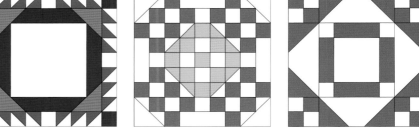

698                    699                    700

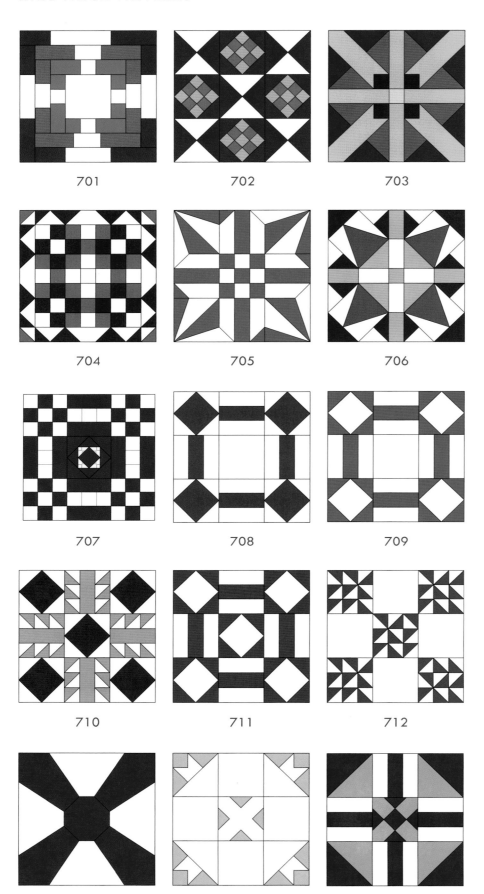

701 · 702 · 703 · 704 · 705 · 706 · 707 · 708 · 709 · 710 · 711 · 712 · 713 · 714 · 715

701 White House Steps, *LW*

702 Kentucky Patch

703 Far West, *NC*

704 Scotch Heather, *NC*

705 Sunburst, *LW*

706 Ladies' Delight, *NC*

707 The Cheesebox Quilt, *CG*

708 Puss in the Corner
Kitty Corner
Tic Tac Toe

709 Blockhouse, *NC*
Kitty Corner

710 Mother's Dream, *NP*
Grandmother's Dream
Turkey in the Straw, *FJ*

711 Peekaboo, *WW*

712 Windmill

713 Adam's Refuge, *SSQ*, *1993*
New Cross and Crown, *CS*

714 Name Unknown

715 Everybody's Favorite, *HH*

5,500 QUILT BLOCK DESIGNS

716 Burnham Square, *LAC*
Hole in the Barn Door,
*QN, 1977*
Star in the Window,
*QN, 1977*

717 Beggar's Blocks
Cats and Mice
The Roman Square

718 Flagstones, *LAC*
New Snowball, *HH*

719 Dewey Quilt Block

720 Skip to My Lou, *QM,*
*1992*

721 Glory Be, *QM, 1992*

722 Starburst

723 Jackson Quilt Block
Miss Jackson

724 Path and Stiles, *NC*
Far West, *NC*
Shoo Fly, *LAC*
Stiles and Paths

725 Duck's Foot in the Mud

726 Missouri Puzzle, *CS*

727 Rolling Stones

728 Royal Star

729 Crow's Nest

730 Water Mill

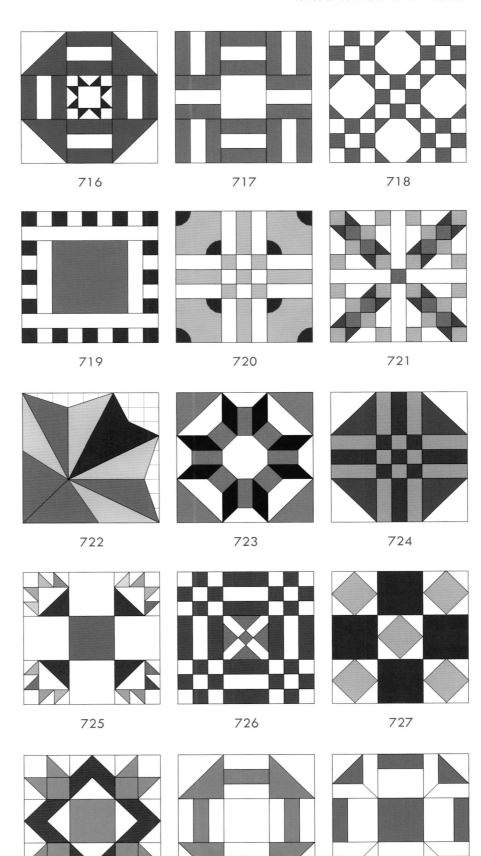

716

717

718

719

720

721

722

723

724

725

726

727

728

729

730

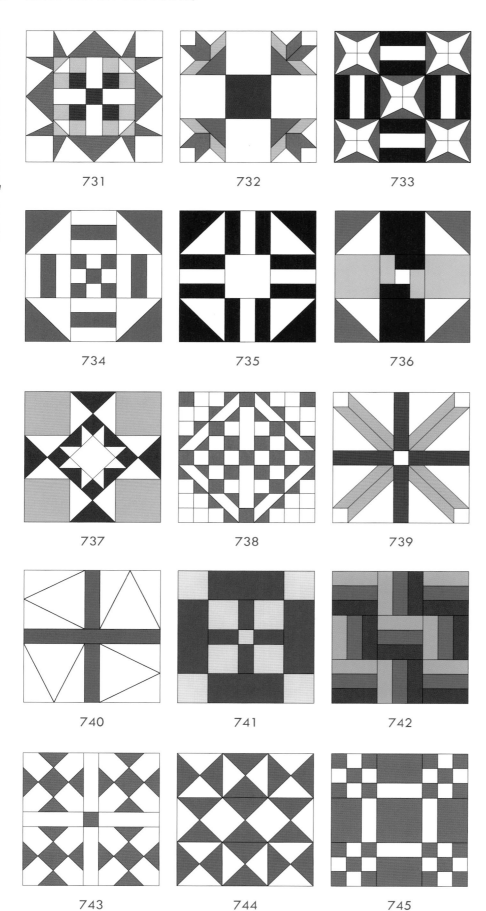

731

732

733

734

735

736

737

738

739

740

741

742

743

744

745

731 Trucker's Dream, *Sandra Copeland*, *1988*

732 Sage Bud, *KCS* Mexican Star

733 Star Spangled Banner

734 New Waterwheel

735 Friendship Quilt

736 Squared Chain

737 Rhode Island, *HH*

738 Medieval Walls, *NC* Medieval Mosaic, *NC*

739 Flyaway Feathers

740 Bowknot

741 The Comfort Quilt, *KCS*

742 The Roman Stripe

743 Bachelor's Puzzle, *CS*

744 Aunt Malvina's Quilt, *CS*

745 Five Patch, *LAC* Building Blocks, *1929*

746  Tin Man
     Oklahoma Boomer,
        *LAC*

747  Indian Hatchet

748  Bells

749  Joseph's Coat
     Scrapbag

750  Amethyst Chain, *NC*

751  Heather Square

752  Star and Cross

753  Indian Tomahawk

754  Quadrille, *NC*

755  Chain of Diamonds

756  Star of Wonder

757  Postage Stamp Block

758  Dutch Puzzle, *AMS*

759  Lehigh Maze, *NC*

760  No Name

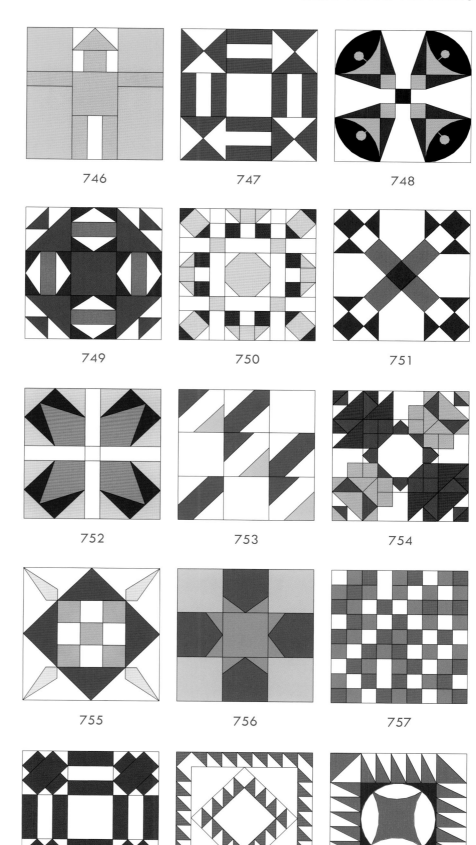

746

747

748

749

750

751

752

753

754

755

756

757

758

759

760

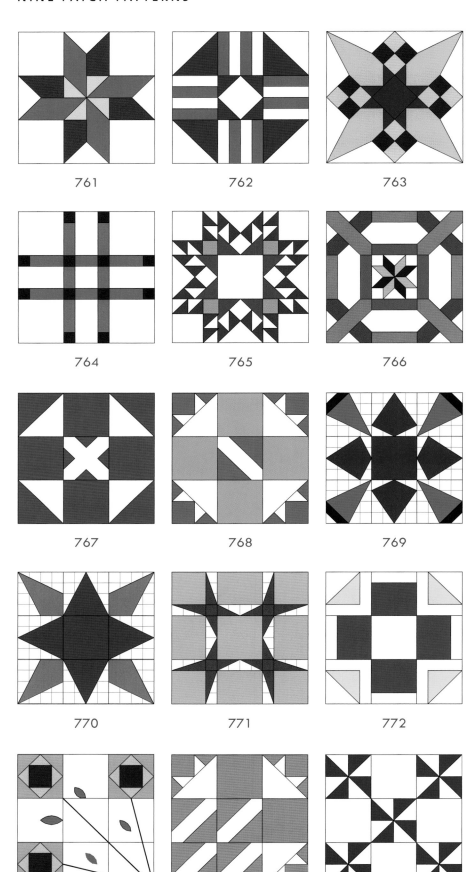

761

762

763

764

765

766

767

768

769

770

771

772

773

774

775

761 Two Colors, *CoM*

762 Crossroads, *NC*

763 Indianapolis

764 Tic Tac Toe

765 Doreen's Dutch Tiles (tulips appliquéd in corners), in memory of Doreen Speckmann, *Nancy Rink, QN, 2000*

766 The Compass and Chain

767 Flying Cross, *HH* Double Cross, *HH*

768 Montgomery

769 California Snowflake, *QN*

770 Starburst

771 Acrobats

772 Water Mill, *GC*

773 Triple Rose, *AMS*

774 Tassel Plant, *LAC*

775 Flutter Wheel, *LAC* Clover Leaf Pin Wheels Windmill

776 Cluster of Stars, *LAC*

777 Star Chain, *QN, 1973*

778 Nevada (9)

779 Nine Patch T, *MD*

780 W.C.T.U., *LAC*

781 Stars and Stripes

782 Old Indian Trail, *KCS*

783 Klondike Star, *HH*

784 Star A, *LAC*
    An A Star, *NC*

785 Little Rock

786 Women's Choice, *QN*

787 Honolulu, *HH*

788 Journey Home
    (appliqués of things
    significant to the
    quilter in the blank
    spaces)

789 Aunt Em's Pattern

790 Spring Is Sprung, *SSQ*

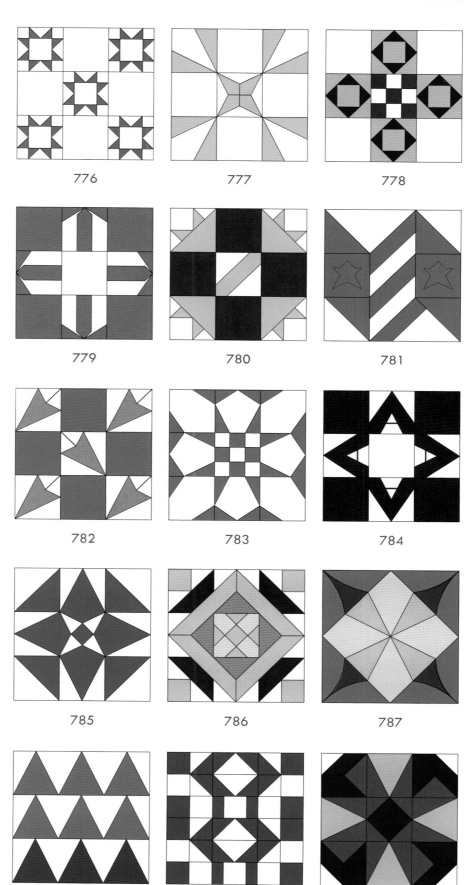

776

777

778

779

780

781

782

783

784

785

786

787

788

789

790

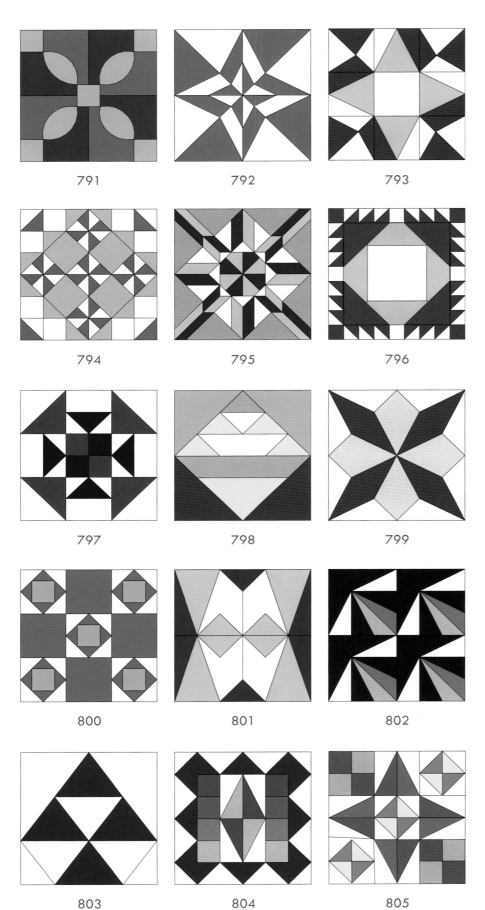

791   State of Idaho

792   Night and Day

793   Carnival, *NC*

794   South Dakota, *HH*

795   Prisms, *RD, LCPQ*

796   Love Entangled, *SSQ*

797   Monkey Wrench
      Variation

798   Ship Block

799   Guiding Star
      Cowboy's Star

800   Nine Patch Square
      Within a Square

801   King's Crown, *LR, QW,*
      *1983*

802   Building the Stars

803   Charm, *LAC*

804   Hoosier Wonder, *QN*

805   Spring Star, *QN, 1994*

791    792    793

794    795    796

797    798    799

800    801    802

803    804    805

806  Holland Magic, *QN*

807  Amish Whirl, *QN*

808  Fort Knox, *QN*

809  Finnigan's Wake, *QN*

810  Star in Space, *QN*

811  Twin Darts

812  Cobra, *QN, 1994*

813  Alice's Favorite

814  The Kite

815  Honolulu Quilt Block,
     *HH*

816  Greek Cross, *LAC*

817  Dutch Mill, *LAC*

818  Magic Circle, *LAC*

819  Garden Maze, *NC*

820  County Fair

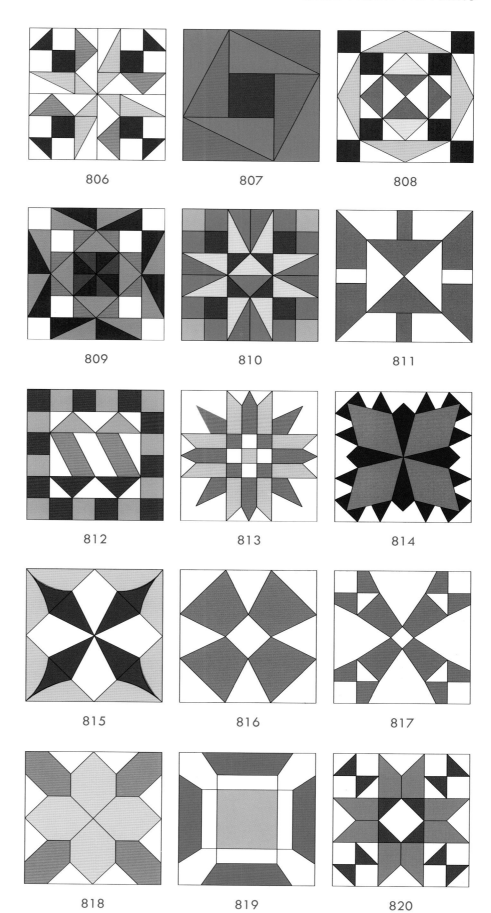

806          807          808

809          810          811

812          813          814

815          816          817

818          819          820

5,500 QUILT BLOCK DESIGNS

821   Star of Erin, *NC*

822   English Ivy, *KCS*
       Autumn Leaves, *NC*
       The Clover Blossom

823   Lone Tree
       English Thistle

824   Tree of Life

825   Amish Shoofly

826   Rolling Squares, *NC*

827   The Bat, *AMS*
       The Bat's Block, *NC*

828   Victorian Maze, *NC*

829   Mrs. Cleveland's
       Choice
       Mrs. Cleveland's
       Favorite

830   Happy New Year

831   Loop the Loop

832   Pieced Pinwheels

833   Texas Fireside

834   Nell's Swinging Star

835   Lost and Found

821   822   823

824   825   826

827   828   829

830   831   832

833   834   835

836 Lattice Star

837 Homeward Star

838 Heart

839 Four Crosses

840 Corn and Beans, *HH*
    Northwind
    Simple Design, *HH*

841 Rebel Patch

842 New Hampshire
    Granite Block, *WB*

843 Boxes and Baskets

844 All in a Spin

845 Smokehouse Block

846 T-Square

847 Domino Net, *NC*

848 Indian Mat, *NC*

849 Crossed Chains, *NC*

850 T Quilt, *LAC*

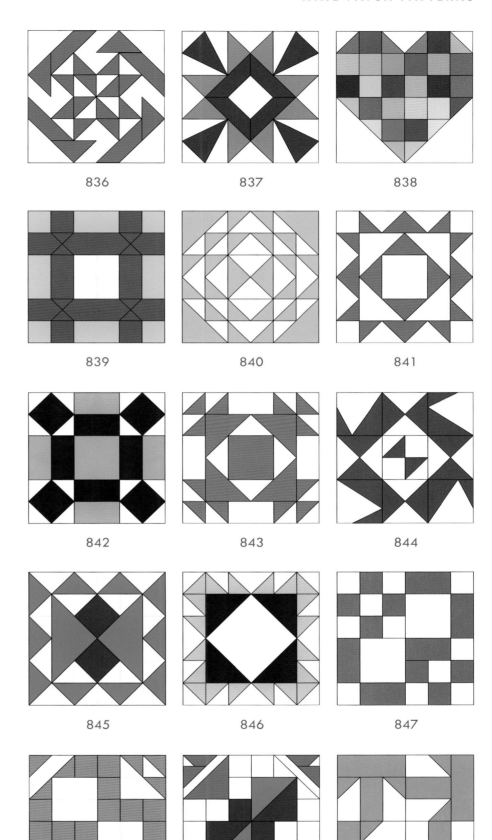

836

837

838

839

840

841

842

843

844

845

846

847

848

849

850

851   852   853

854   855   856

857   858   859

860   861   862

863   864   865

5,500 QUILT BLOCK DESIGNS

851   No Name

852   Alphabet Block L

853   Kitchen Woodbox, *KCS*

854   Hour Glass, *NC*

855   St. Paul

856   Tree Top Twist, *RMS,*
      *SSQ*

857   New York

858   St. Gregory's Cross

859   Star Flower, *GD*

860   Heavenly Bodies

861   Housewife

862   Whirling Star, *NC*

863   Tee

864   Shooting Star, *AG*

865   Arrowhead Star
      Variation

866 Orion's Wheel

867 Night Vision, *QN*

868 Lone Star, *AB, OCS*

869 Magnolia, *LW, OCS*
   Sawtooth

870 Confetti Block, *TQ*

871 Jet Stream, *SSQ*

872 King's Crown

873 Four Triangles, *FJ*

874 V-Block, *QN*

875 Cross and Diamond
   Star

876 Double Irish Chain, *LW*

877 Fred's Spool

878 Shadows
   Sunlight and Shadows
   Rainbow Block
   Roman Stripe

879 Windblown Lily

880 All Those Fish

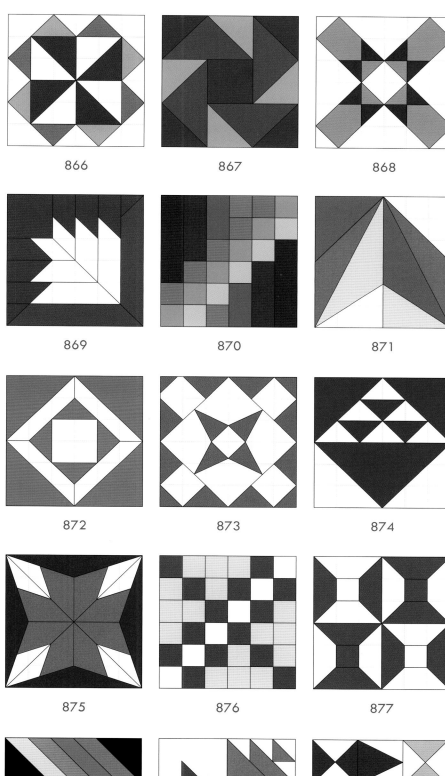

866

867

868

869

870

871

872

873

874

875

876

877

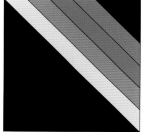

878

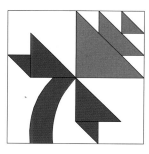

879

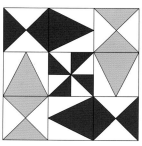

880

5,500 QUILT BLOCK DESIGNS

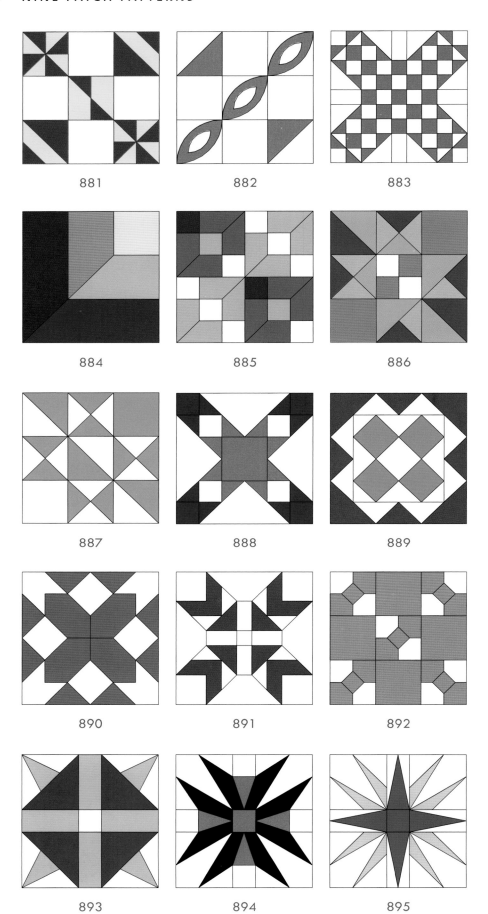

881

882

883

884

885

886

887

888

889

890

891

892

893

894

895

881 Amelia Earhart

882 Lock and Chain, *LAC*

883 Antique Red and White Quilt, *TQ*

884 Double Attic Windows

885 Lover's Locket, *GB, 1990*

886 Strawberry Patch

887 Massachusetts

888 Star Pattern

889 Treasure Box

890 Repeat X, *FJ*

891 Darts and Squares, *FJ*

892 Joseph's Necktie, *LAC*

893 Block of Many Triangles

894 The Crab

895 Night Sky, *MM*

896 Double Cross, *HH*
   Flying Cross, *HH*

897 State of New Jersey,
   *HH*

898 Starshadow, *QN*

899 Crossroads Star, *QN*

900 Paradox, *QN*

901 Modern Flame

902 Missouri Corn Field,
   *QW*

903 Idaho Star, *AK*

904 Cross and Crown

905 Stylized Eagle, *AK*

906 Love Entangled

907 Smith Autograph Quilt,
   *CAM*

908 Swastika Patch, *LAC*

909 Double Star Flower, *AK*

910 Bandstand

896        897        898

899        900        901

902        903        904

905        906        907

908        909        910

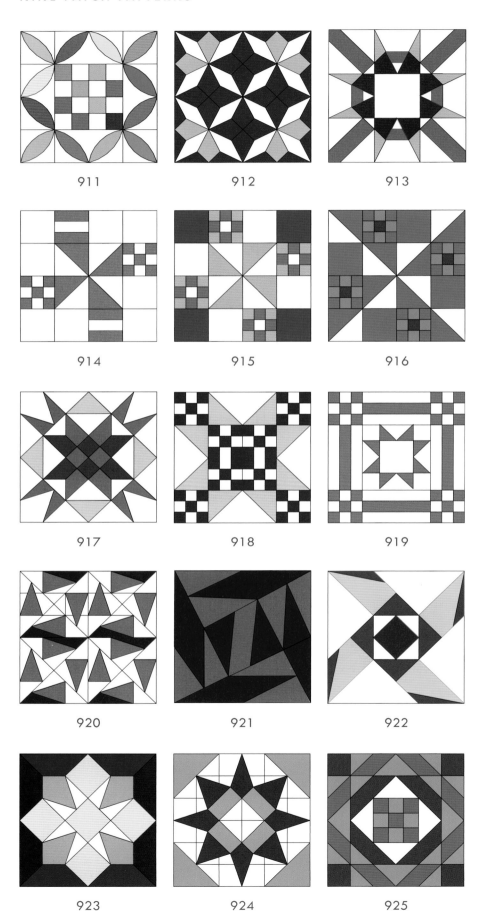

911   Honeybee

912   Four Star Block, *NC*

913   Lover's Knot

914   Lady of the White
        House

915   White House, *NC*
        Lady in the White
        House

916   Unnamed

917   Quiet Love, *SSQ, 1987*

918   Bridle Path, *KCS*

919   Mother's Fancy Star, *IS*
        Evening Star
        Mother's Fancy, *LAC*

920   Entertaining Motions

921   Triangle Puzzle, *LAC*
        Triangle Trails, *NC*

922   Eccentric Star

923   Nine Patch Star
        Grandmother's Choice

924   North Carolina Star

925   Afternoon Shadows,
        *SSQ, 1987*

926 Annapolis Patch

927 Sugar Loaf, *KCS*
Arrowheads
Flat Iron, *NC*

928 Winged Square, *OCS*

929 Arkansas Traveler

930 Radiant Star

931 London Square

932 Pine Burr, *NP*

933 Stars and Stripes

934 House That Jack Built,
*LAC*
Triple Stripe, *GD*

935 Arizona Star

936 Virginia Reel, *QWB*

937 Chuck-A-Luck, *NC*,
*1937*

938 The H Square Quilt,
*KCS*
"4H" Club Quilt, *KCS*

939 Star Mosaic

940 Kankakee Checkers, *NC*

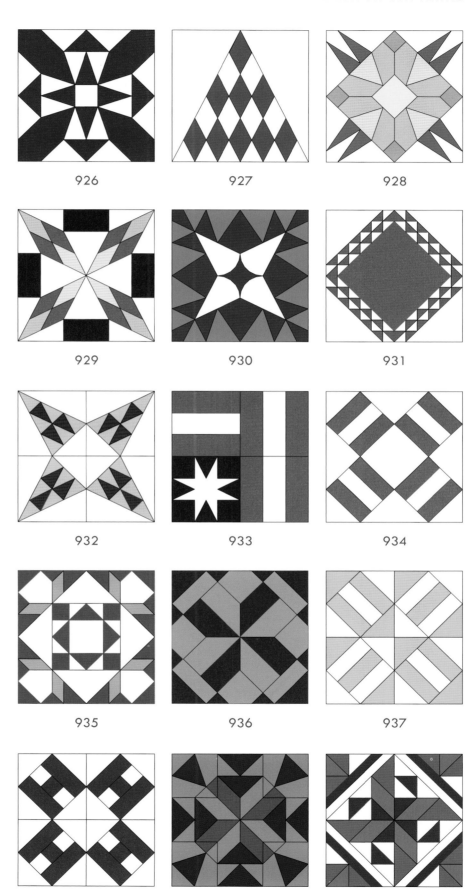

926

927

928

929

930

931

932

933

934

935

936

937

938

939

940

941 Dog Tooth Violet, *NC*

942 Sky Rocket
Starlight, *NP*
Jewel Boxes, *NP*

943 Autumn Night

944 Four Squares, *NC*

945 Chinese Holidays, *NC*

946 Sailboat

947 Thorny Thicket

948 Chuck-A-Luck, *NC*

949 Harlequin Star
Forgotten Star

950 Flying Geese

951 Water Wiggle

952 July's Summer Sky

953 Love's Dream

954 Children of Israel

955 Unnamed, *AMS*

941    942    943

944    945    946

947    948    949

950    951    952

953    954    955

956 Blue Skies

957 Happy Hunting Grounds

958 New Mexico

959 Ocean Wave, *KCS*

960 The Sapphire Quilt Block, *KCS*

961 Danish Star

962 Medallion Square

963 Cross and Crown

964 Holiday Crossing, *RMS, SSQ, 1983*

965 Hopes and Wishes

966 Snowbound, *RMS, SSQ, 1983*

967 Crossroads

968 Exea's Star, *CS* Ella's Star, *HH*

969 State of South Dakota

970 Peach Blow

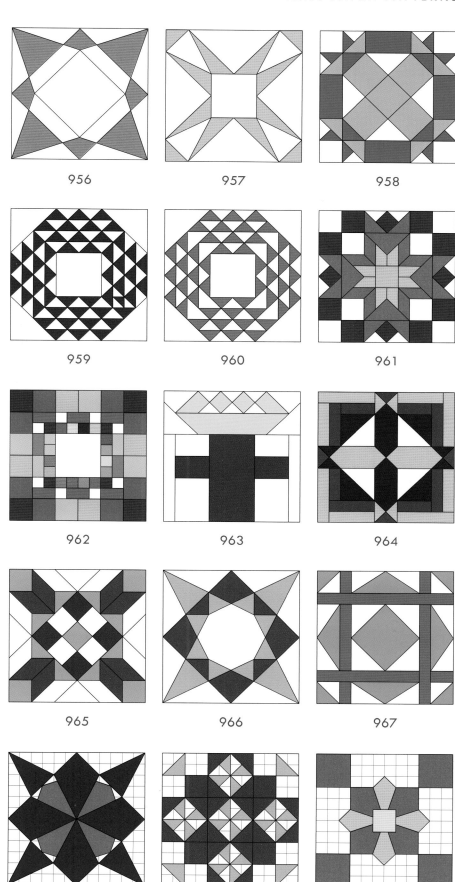

956

957

958

959

960

961

962

963

964

965

966

967

968

969

970

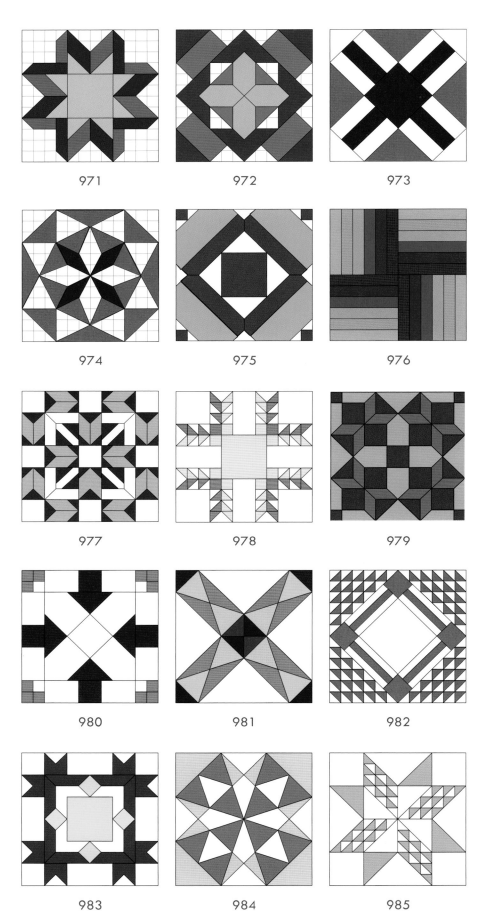

971 · Christmas Star
Bright Star

972 · Three Cheers

973 · At the Depot

974 · Harrisburg Quilt Block

975 · Magic Squares, *NC*

976 · Paddle Wheel

977 · Sailing Darts, *AK, 1965*

978 · Texas Treasure, *NP*

979 · Diamond Cross

980 · Indian Arrow

981 · America's Pride

982 · State of Iowa, *HH*

983 · Easy Ways

984 · Vermont

985 · The Twinkling Star

971

972

973

974

975

976

977

978

979

980

981

982

983

984

985

986 The Twinkling Star, *NC*

987 Aunt Rachel's Star, *1942*

988 Star Trek, *QN, 1974*

989 Quilt Without a Name

990 Crossed Arrows, *Ruby Hinson Duncan*

991 Danger Signals, *NP*

992 Augusta

993 Grandmother's Dream, *LAC*

994 Snowball, *AMS*

995 Illinois Road, *NC*

996 Tangled Arrows

997 Rising Star

998 King's Highway

999 Lone Star

1000 Pharlemina's Favorite, *HH*
Charleston Quilt Block, *HH*
Circle Four, *HH*

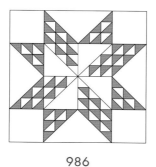

986

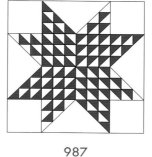

987

988

989

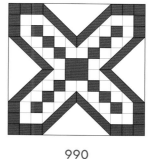

990

991

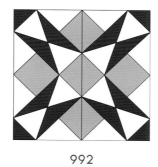

992

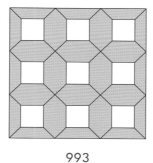

993

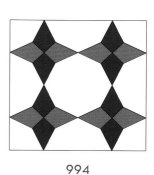

994

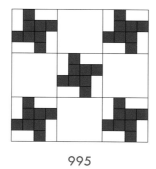

995

996

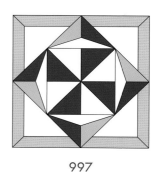

997

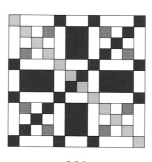

998

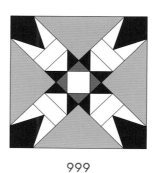

999

1000

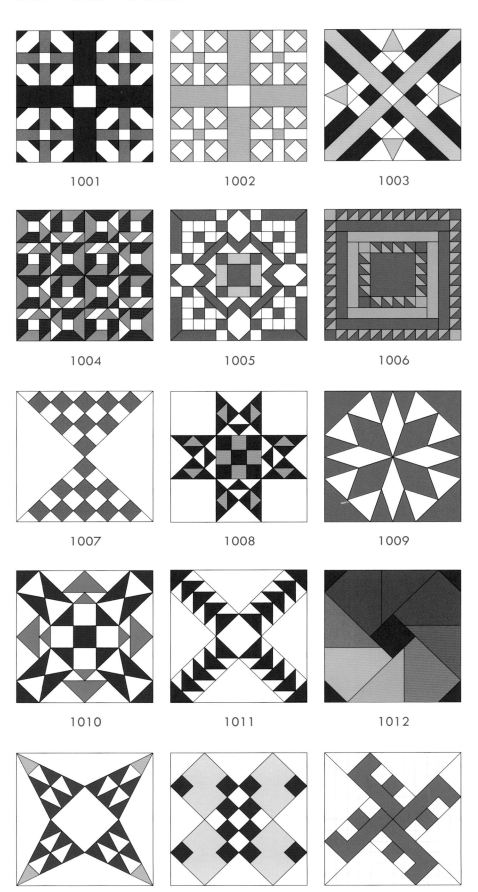

5,500 QUILT BLOCK DESIGNS

1001 A Scrap Patch

1002 Economy

1003 Yuletide, *HaM, SSQ, 1983*

1004 Flower and Fern, *RMS, QW, 1983*

1005 Ancient Castle, *Ruby Hinson Duncan, QW, 1982*

1006 Stony Point Quilt Block, *HH* State of Massachusetts, *HH*

1007 New Hour Glass

1008 Santa Fe Quilt Block President's Block

1009 St. Louis Star

1010 Prairie Belle Quilt Block

1011 Baltimore Belle Wild Goose Chase

1012 Morning Glory, *MM*

1013 Lost Children

1014 Eva's Delight Old Fashioned Pieced Block, *NC*

1015 Flora's Favorite

1016 Philippine Islands Quilt Block, *HH*

1017 Birds on the Tracks

1018 A Walk in the Garden

1019 Bats in the Belfry

1020 Pinwheel

1021 West Virginia

1022 Best Wishes

1023 Kiowa Cross, *SSQ*

1024 Double Square, *GD*

1025 Bright Side

1026 Kaleidoscope

1027 McDougall String Quilt, *SSQ*

1028 Star in the Window, *Betty McMillion, QW, 1984*

1029 Saturn Block

1030 This Way 'n That, *RMS, SSQ, 1986*

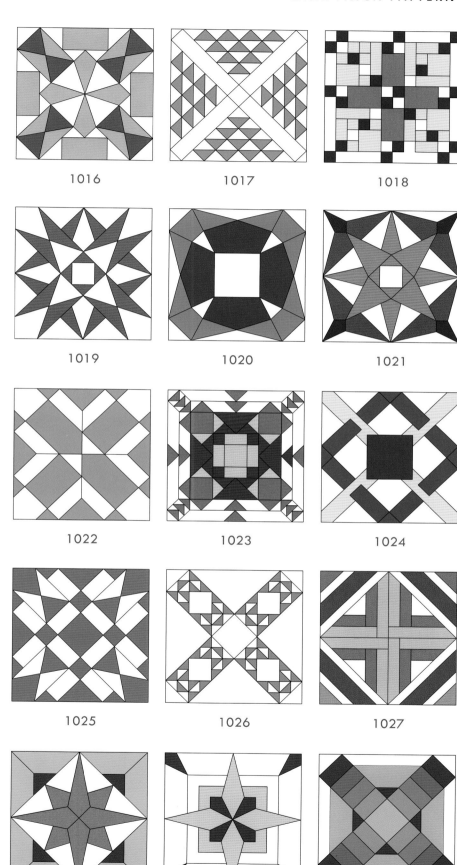

1016          1017          1018

1019          1020          1021

1022          1023          1024

1025          1026          1027

1028          1029          1030

5,500 QUILT BLOCK DESIGNS

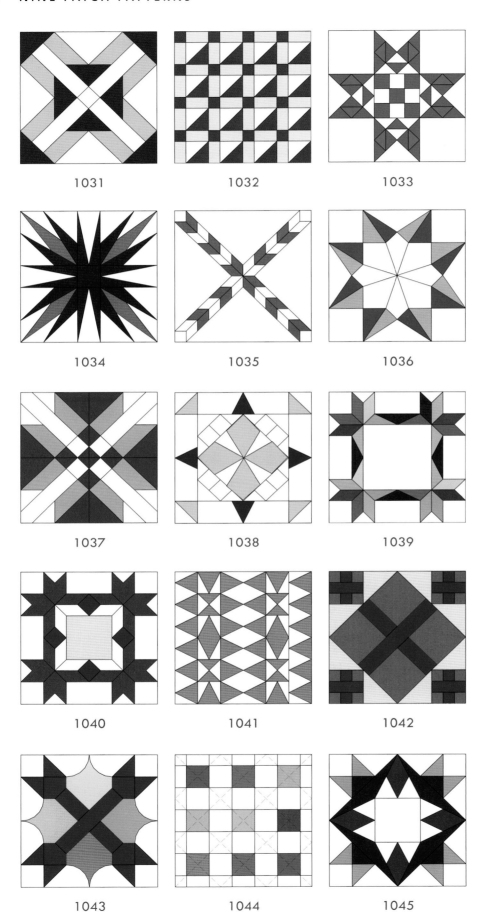

1031

1032

1033

1034

1035

1036

1037

1038

1039

1040

1041

1042

1043

1044

1045

1031 Texas Tears

1032 Windowpane, *PQ*

1033 Economy Star

1034 Fantasy Flower, *MM*

1035 Goose Chase

1036 Custer's Last Stand

1037 Mexican Cross

1038 Strawflower

1039 Chicken Foot

1040 Golgotha

1041 Lost Ship

1042 Cabin Windows

1043 Pathfinder

1044 Church Windows

1045 Starry Sky

1046 Pudding and Pie

1047 Steps to the Garden, *NC*

1048 Kentucky Crossroads
Crossroads to Texas

1049 Joseph's Coat

1050 Desert Blooms, *QM, 1993*

1051 Rose Compass, *TQ*

1052 Rainbow, *AG*

1053 Star of Hope, *SSQ, 1993*

1054 Sunflower

1055 Tangled Stars

1056 No Name

1057 Four Mills, *RF, 1940*

1058 Four Mills Variation, *MM*

1059 Four Mills Variation, *SSQ, 1989*

1060 Fairy Tale

1046    1047    1048

1049    1050    1051

1052    1053    1054

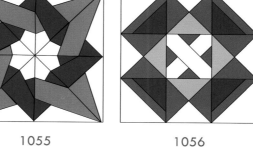

1055    1056    1057

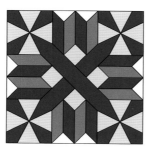

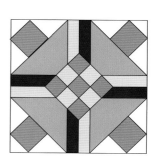

1058    1059    1060

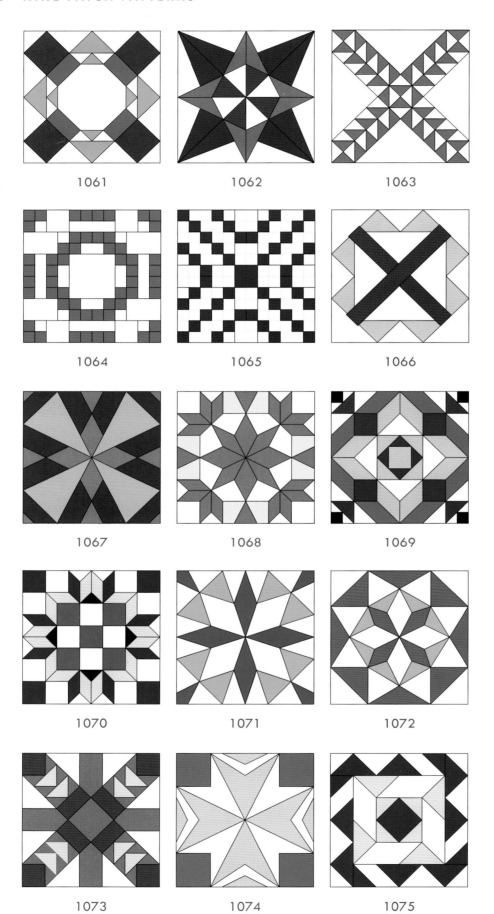

1061       1062       1063

1064       1065       1066

1067       1068       1069

1070       1071       1072

1073       1074       1075

1061  All Kinds, *LAC*
      Beggar's Block
      Cats and Mice
      Turnstile, *NP*

1062  Sarah's Direction

1063  Flock of Birds, *NP*

1064  Summer Garden, *NC*

1065  Steps to the Garden,
      *NC*

1066  Texas Tears, *LAC*
      Cross and Crown
      Crowned Cross
      Double T, *NC*

1067  Diamond
      Kaleidoscope, *MM*

1068  Pinwheel Star

1069  Mosaic Squares, *NC*

1070  Friendship Star, *LW*

1071  Leo's Lion,
      *Sandra Hatch*, *QW*

1072  Harrisburg

1073  Spokane, *NP*

1074  Columbia, *HH*

1075  Spinning Jenny, *NC*

1076  Anchors Aweigh, *LW*

1077  Cubist Rose

1078  Brick Pavement

1079  Irish Chain Patch

1080  Crazy Block, *Sharlene Jorgenson*

1081  Sawtooth

1082  Missionary Baptist, *CoM*

1083  Winged Square, *NC*

1084  Butterfly Bush, *NC*

1085  Diamond Star, *NC*

1086  Poinsettia, *OCS*

1087  Royal Gems, *AK*

1088  Jonathan Livingston Seagull

1089  Amish Scrap Star

1090  Wisconsin Maze

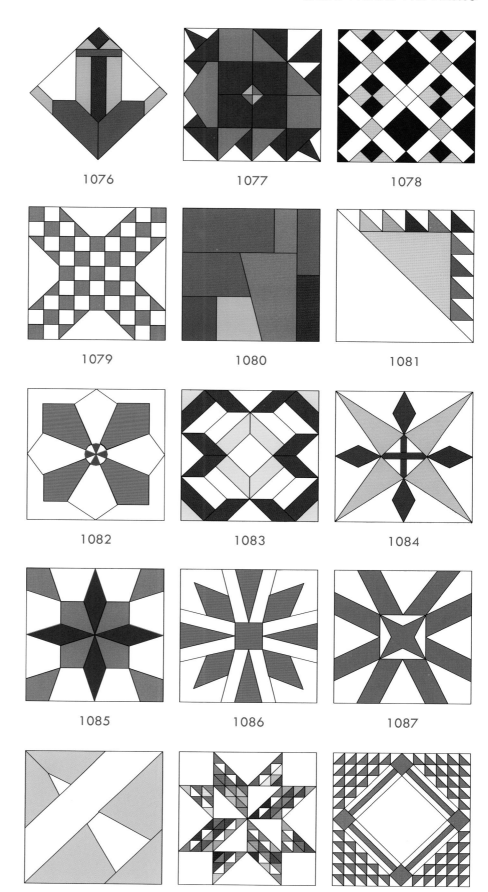

1076

1077

1078

1079

1080

1081

1082

1083

1084

1085

1086

1087

1088

1089

1090

1091 Pretty Kettle of Fish, *QN, 1985*

1092 Railroad Crossing

1093 The String Quilt, *KCS*

1094 Virginia Reel, *CS*
Tangled Lines, *LAC*

1095 Celtic Plaid, *MM*

1096 Thousand Islands, *NC*

1097 Washington, *HH*

1098 Sundance

1099 Autograph Quilt, *KCS*

1100 Endless Squares, *NC*

1101 Autograph Patch

1102 Kentucky Crossroads, *NC*

1103 Picture Frames, *KCS*

1104 Silver Maple, *PP*

1105 Rough Diamond, *SSQ*

1106 Night and Day, *QWO*

1107 Railroad Crossing, *KCS*

1108 Jacob's Ladder, *KCS*

1109 Diamonds in the
Corners, *KCS*

1110 The Red, the White
and the Blue
Red Cross

1111 Timberline, *CR, QN,
1990*

1112 Cut Diamond, *VJ, SSQ,
1984*

1113 Friendship Chain, *KCS*

1114 Flowering Nine Patch,
*KCS*

1115 Southside Star, *KCS*

1116 Whirling Star

1117 Sunbeam Block, *KCS*
Squared Star, *HAS*
Whippoorwill, *NC*

1118 No Name

1119 Heather Square, *NC*

1120 A Beauty Block, *CS*

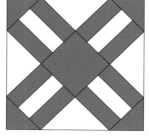

1106

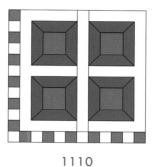

1107

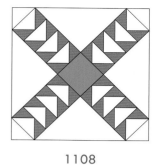

1108

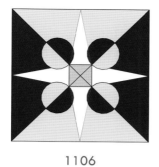

1109

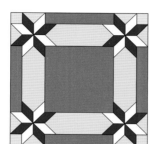

1110

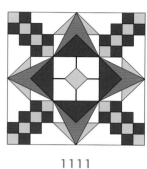

1111

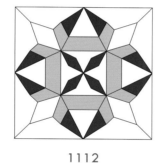

1112

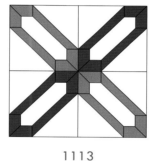

1113

1114

1115

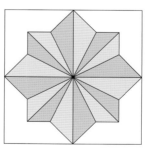

1116

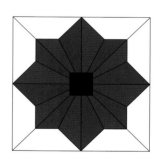

1117

1118

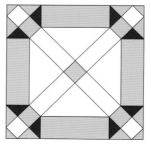

1119

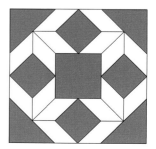

1120

5,500 QUILT BLOCK DESIGNS

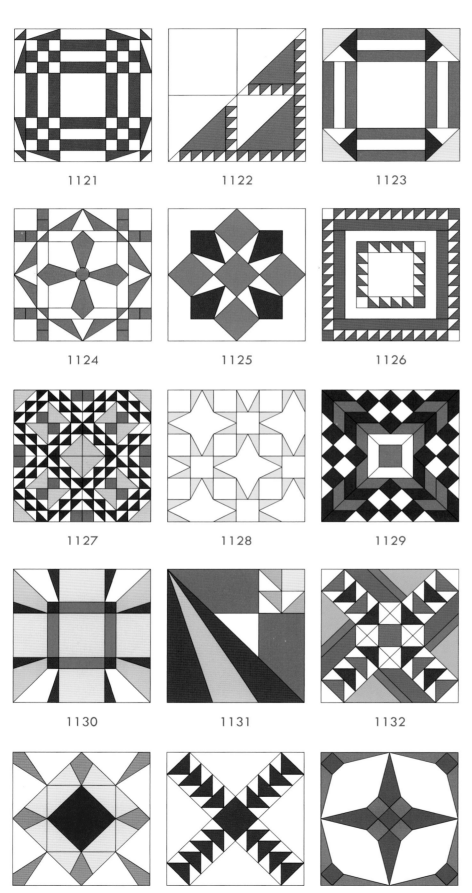

1121
1122
1123
1124
1125
1126
1127
1128
1129
1130
1131
1132
1133
1134
1135

1121 Spider's Den

1122 Maryland Beauty

1123 The Double Arrow, *KCS*

1124 Heart's Desire

1125 Grandmother's Choice

1126 Massachusetts

1127 Avian Waves, *TQr, 1990*

1128 In Narcissus Motif, *KCS*

1129 Sentry's Pastime, *NC*

1130 Star Above the Stable,
   *HMD, SSQ, 1984*

1131 Shepherd's Watch,
   *HMD, SSQ, 1984*

1132 Sunshine Over the
   Rockies, *Mary Lou
   Endres, QN, 1990*

1133 Courtenay Crown

1134 Flying Geese

1135 Blue Heaven, *NC*

1136 Michigan Favorite, *FJ*

1137 Candy Canes, *HaM,
SSQ, 1983*

1138 Stars in Flight, *SSQ,
1985*

1139 Ribbons

1140 Star Explosion

1141 Heavenly Bodies

1142 Moorish Mosaic

1143 Ribbon Square

1144 Pink Dogwood, *QN*

1145 Spring Fancy, *Doris
Sprecher, TQr*

1146 Calico Mosaic, *NC*

1147 Spring Tulips

1148 Four Patch Chain

1149 Chaos Theory, *QN*

1150 Sweet Buds, *RMS, SSQ,
1987*

1136

1137

1138

1139

1140

1141

1142

1143

1144

1145

1146

1147

1148

1149

1150

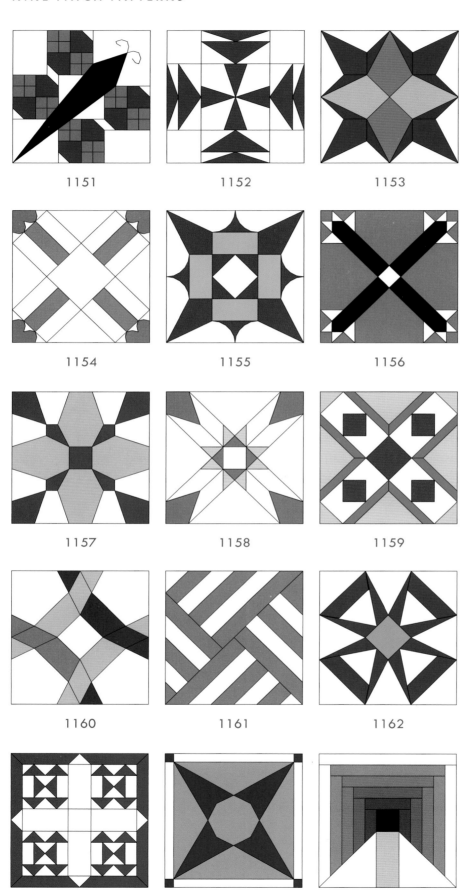

1151   1152   1153

1154   1155   1156

1157   1158   1159

1160   1161   1162

1163   1164   1165

1151   Dragonfly, *Ruby Hinson Duncan, SSQ, 1988*

1152   Falling Leaves

1153   Tulip Bouquet

1154   Cupid's Arrows, *Judy St. John, QW, 1989*

1155   Dawn, *QW, 1986*

1156   Rosemary, *HH*

1157   Sapphire Net, *NC*

1158   Lone Star, *LW, OCS*

1159   Waterwheel

1160   Saracen Chain

1161   Chevrons

1162   Lover's Knot, *AB*

1163   Framed Cross, *QW, 1981*

1164   The Evening Star, *KCS*

1165   Tennessee Mine Shaft

1166 Mexican Siesta, *NC*
Sombrero Appliqué, *NC*

1167 Victory, *CS*

1168 Star Explosion

1169 Walled City, *MM*

1170 Mother's Fancy, *LAC*

1171 Green Cross, *NC*

1172 Shooting Star

1173 The World's Fair

1174 Columbia Quilt Block

1175 Marigold Garden
(diagonal set), *QN*,
*1982*

1176 Indian Paint Brush, *QN*

1177 Chain Links

1178 Pleasant Paths, *FJ*

1179 Spinning Stars, *QN*

1180 Sailboats Variation

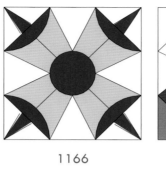
1166

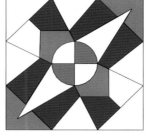
1167

1168

1169

1170

1171

1172

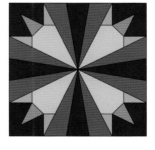
1173

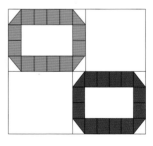
1174

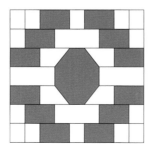
1175

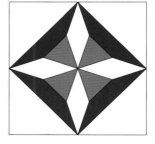
1176

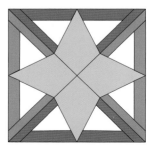
1177

1178

1179

1180

1181

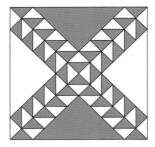

1182

1181 String Quilt
Broken Spider Web, *NC*
Ruby's Star

1182 Old Maid's Ramble,
*WD*

# FOUR PATCH PATTERNS

4 X 4 GRID

8 X 8 GRID

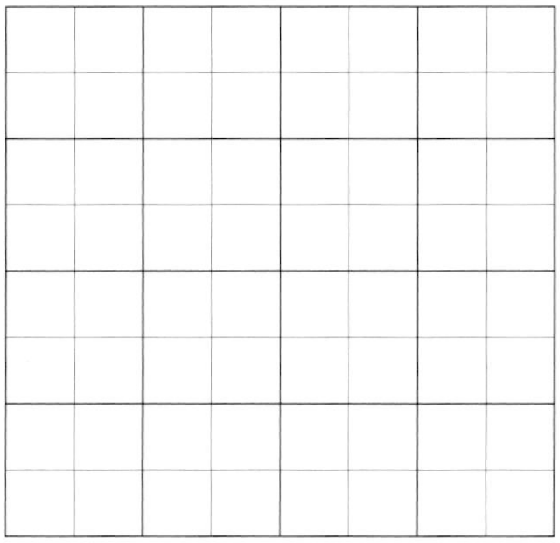

FOUR PATCH PATTERNS ARE MADE ON A GRID OF 4 x 4 SQUARES
THESE PATTERNS ARE EASILY DRAFTED TO ANY BLOCK SIZE DIVISIBLE BY 4

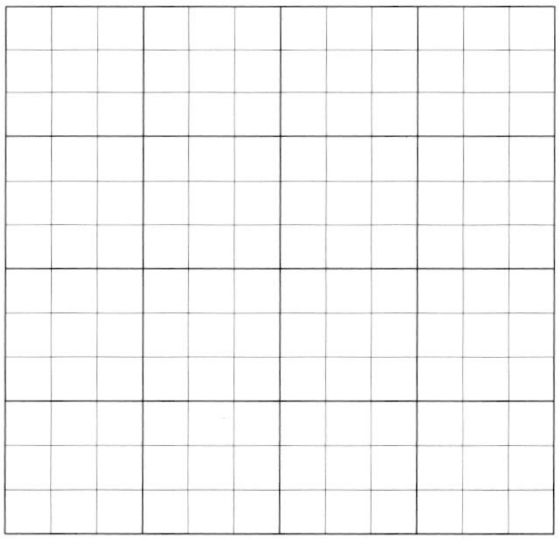

12 X 12 GRID

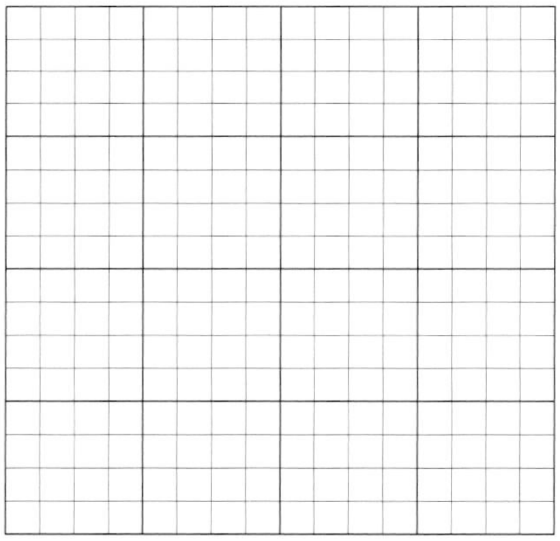

16 X 16 GRID

1183  Four Patch

1184  Mosaic #20, *LAC*
Check
Checkerboard
Four Patch

1185  World's Fair Block, *LAC*

1186  Squares Within
Squares, *NC*

1187  Carmen's Block, *NP*

1188  Autumn Tints

1189  Squares upon Squares,
*FJ*
Rocky Road

1190  Tam's Patch

1191  Cog Wheels, *KCS*

1192  London Stairs, *KCS*
Endless Stairs, *HH*
Endless Stair, *NC*
Winding Stairway

1193  Hit or Miss
Hairpin Catcher

1194  Sheep Fold Quilt, *KCS*
Nine Patch, *LAC*
A Plain Block, *LHJ, 1896*
Irish Chain

1195  Arrowhead Puzzle

1196  Salute to Loyalty, *KCS*

1197  Scot's Plaid
Bonnie Scotsman
Scotch Quilt

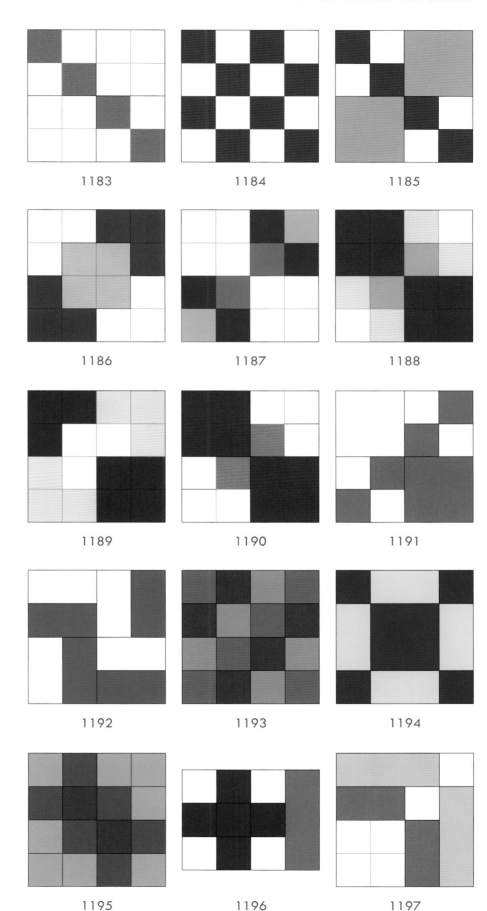

1183

1184

1185

1186

1187

1188

1189

1190

1191

1192

1193

1194

1195

1196

1197

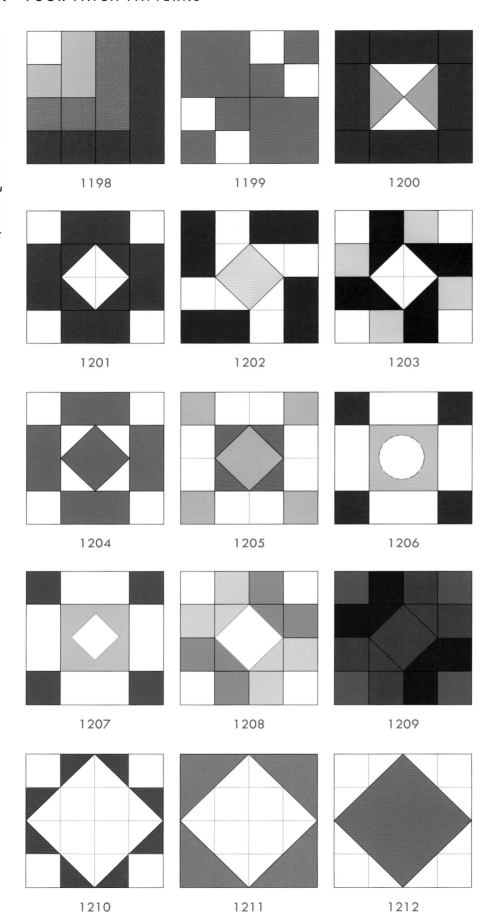

1198  Rainbow Flower

1199  Four Patch

1200  Windows

1201  Oh, Susannah
      Mr. Roosevelt's Necktie
      Susannah, *LAC*

1202  Susannah

1203  Susannah

1204  New Album, *LAC*
      Geometric, *QW*

1205  Fair and Square, *KCS*

1206  Circle in a Frame, *KCS*

1207  The Yellow Square, *KCS*

1208  Mr. Roosevelt's Necktie

1209  Y-Bridge
      Mr. Roosevelt's Necktie

1210  Art Square, *LAC*
      Village Square, *NC*
      Dottie's Choice, *FJ*

1211  Shoofly

1212  Broken Sash, *NC*
      Dutch Tile, *NC*
      Diamond in the Square
      Friendship Album
        Quilt
      Triangle Design

1213 Right and Left, *LAC*

1214 Sugar Bowl Quilt, *NC*

1215 Southern Belle

1216 Electric Fan, *HH*

1217 Shooting Squares, *NP*

1218 Letter L

1219 Windmill

1220 Four Knaves

1221 Economy
Hour Glass, *LAC*
This and That, *KCS*
Thrift Block, *NC*

1222 Twelve Triangles, *KCS*
Shadow Boxes

1223 Album

1224 King's Crown, *KCS*

1225 Square and Points, *KCS*
Eight Point Star

1226 Evening Star
Two Patch Quilt, *OCS*

1227 Evening Star, *LAC*
Cluster of Stars

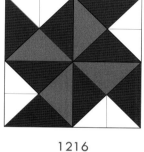
1213

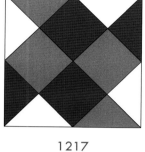
1214

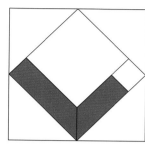
1215

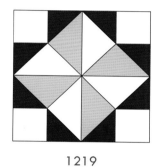
1216

1217

1218

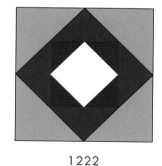
1219

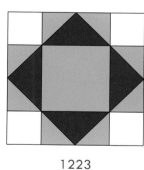
1220

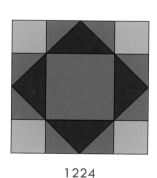
1221

1222

1223

1224

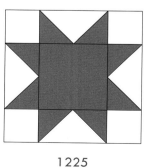
1225

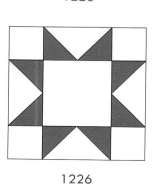
1226

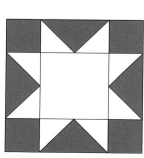
1227

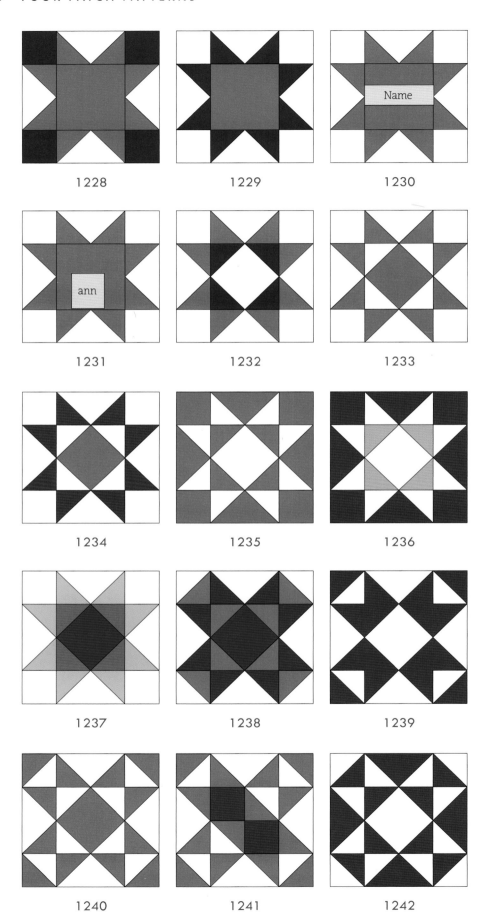

1228 Austin, *HH*
Optical Sawtooth

1229 Sawtooth, *FF, 1884*
Nameless Star, *NC*
Sawtooth

1230 Album Quilt

1231 Coral Court Friendship
Star

1232 Variable Star

1233 Crystal Star, *KCS*

1234 Crystal Star
Joining Star, *NP*
Lone Star
Peaceful Hours
Star of Virginia
Texas Star

1235 Ohio Star
Mosaic #10, *LAC*

1236 The Cog Block, *KCS*

1237 Eight Pointed Star, *FJ*

1238 Tippecanoe and Tyler,
Too

1239 Star

1240 An Envelope Motif, *KCS*

1241 Chisholm Trail, *KCS*

1242 Mosaic #19, *LAC*
Mosaic #7, *NC*

1243 Wheel of Time, *CS*

1244 Four Patch Fox and
Goose, *KCS*

1245 Old Grey Goose, *NP*

1246 Margaret's Choice
Quilt Block

1247 Blazing Arrow Point
Blazing Arrows

1248 Moon and Star

1249 Sarah's Choice, *CS*

1250 Barbara Frietchie Star
Pieced Star
Pierced Star
Star Puzzle, *LAC*
Wind Mill Quilt

1251 Annie's Choice
Anna's Choice

1252 Solitaire

1253 Pigs in a Blanket

1254 Magic Cross Design,
*1931*

1255 Martha Washington
Star
Flying Cloud, *CS*
Solomon's Star, *NC*

1256 Dewey's Victory, *CS*
Annie's Choice, *CS*
Martha Washington
Star, *1926*
Octagonal Star, *1928*
Queen Victoria

1257 Star & Pinwheels, *NC*

1243    1244    1245

1246    1247    1248

1249    1250    1251

1252    1253    1254

1255    1256    1257

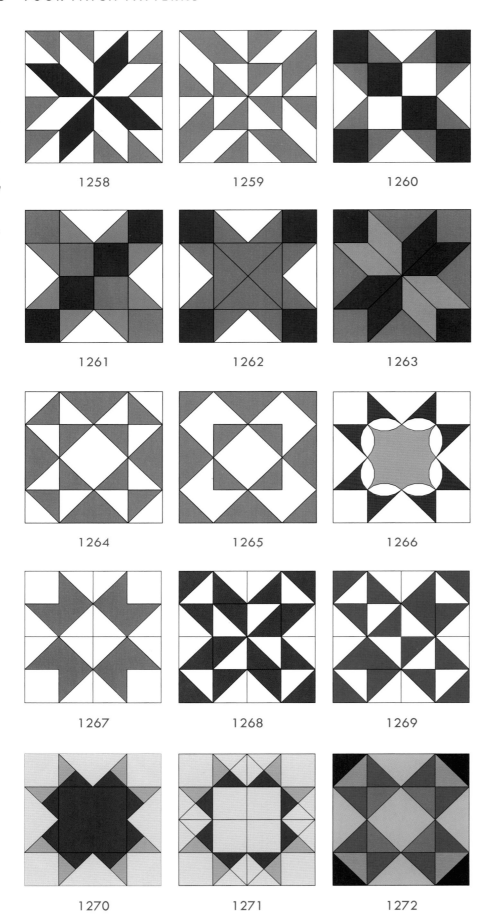

1258  Star of the Milky Way

1259  Squire Smith's Choice

1260  Indian Star, *KCS*

1261  Winged Four Patch,
       *KCS*

1262  Arrow Star

1263  Sunlight and Shadows,
       *KCS*

1264  Star

1265  Star

1266  French Star
       Flaming Sun, *NC*
       Gleaming Sun

1267  Ribbon Star, *LAC*

1268  Mosaic #13, *LAC*

1269  Mosaic #11, *LAC*

1270  Centennial

1271  Aunt Addie's Album,
       *HH*

1272  Rolling Star Quilt

1273 Razz-Ma-Tazz

1274 Constellation

1275 Flying Colors, *KCS*

1276 Pinwheel Star

1277 Mother's Dream

1278 July 4th, *KCS*

1279 Sickle, *KCS*

1280 The Sickle

1281 Old Maid's Puzzle, *NC*

1282 Fox and Geese

1283 Crosses and Losses,
   *LAC*
   Fox and Geese
   Bouncing Betty

1284 Old Maid's Puzzle, *KCS*
   Hourglass
   School Girl's Puzzle

1285 Triangle Weave

1286 Goose and Goslings
   Bow Tie Variation
   Crosses and Losses
   Double X, *LAC*
   Fox and Geese

1287 Double X, *LAC*

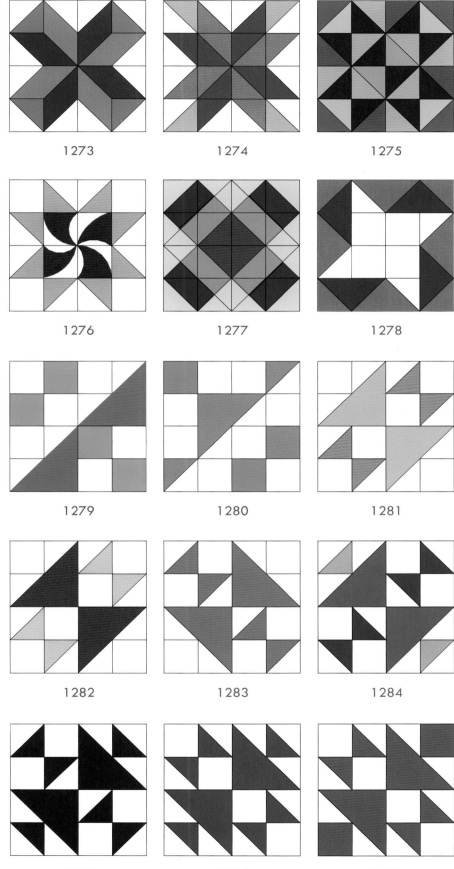

1273

1274

1275

1276

1277

1278

1279

1280

1281

1282

1283

1284

1285

1286

1287

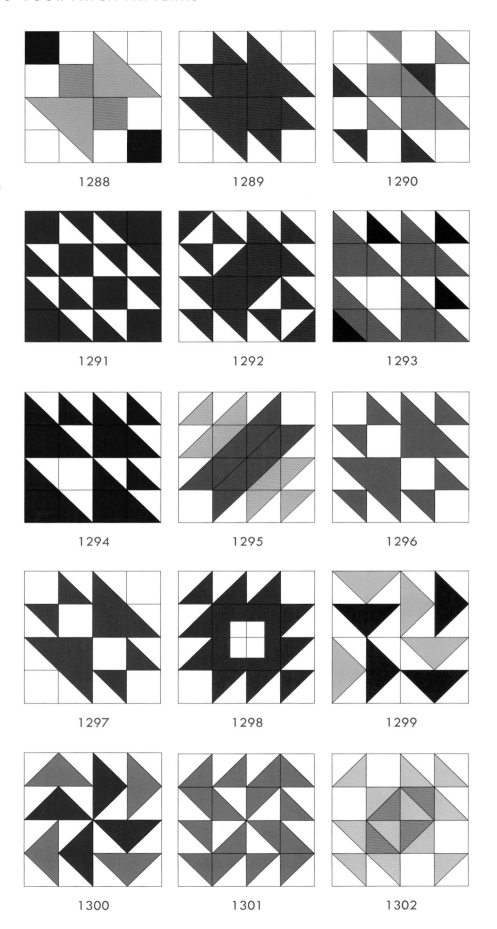

1288
1289
1290
1291
1292
1293
1294
1295
1296
1297
1298
1299
1300
1301
1302

1288 Buckeye Beauty, *KCS*
Double Four Patch
Gay Scrap Quilt, *LW*
Going to Chicago, *NP, 1933*
Jacob's Ladder
New Four Patch, *1884*
Railroad, *NC, 1934*
Railroad Crossing
World's Fair, *1933*

1289 The Anvil

1290 Wild Duck

1291 Hovering Hawks
Hovering Birds
Triple X

1292 Double Cross, *HH*

1293 Airplane

1294 Aircraft, *NC*
Dutchman's Puzzle

1295 Mrs. Taft's Choice

1296 Double X

1297 Double X

1298 Rocky Mountain Puzzle

1299 Return of the Swallows

1300 Dutchman's Puzzle, *LAC*
Dutchman's Wheel, *OF,
1898*
Wheel, *OF, 1894*
Wild Goose Chase

1301 Yankee Puzzle

1302  Flying Dutchman

1303 Bachelor's Puzzle
Building Blocks, *GD*
Kansas Whirligig, *QW,
1989*
The Pinwheel, *KCS*
Road to Jerusalem, *NC*

1304 Swastika, *KCS*
Battle Ax of Thor
Catch Me If You Can
Chinese 10,000 Perfections
Devil's Dark Horse

Devil's Puzzle
Favorite of the Peruvians
Flyfoot
Heart's Seal
Indian Emblem, *KCS*
Mound Builders
Pure Symbol of Right
  Doctrine
Spider
Virginia Reel
Wind Power of the Osages
Winding Blades, *KCS*
Whirligig, *HHJ*
Zig Zag, *CoM*

1305 Little Lost Sailboat

1306 Ladies Wreath, *LAC*

1307 Ship
The Mayflower, *KCS*
Tad Lincoln's Sailboat
Little Ship of Dreams

1308 Flying Fish

1309 Cotton Reel

1310 Big Dipper
Bow Ties, *NC*
Envelope Quilt, *KCS*
Hour Glass, *KCS*
Pork and Beans
The Whirling Blade, *KCS*
Yankee Puzzle

1311 Broken Dishes
Double Square, *KCS*

1312 Double Square

1313 Triangle Combination

1314 Small Triangles, *KCS*

1315 Triangles and Squares,
  *KCS*

1316 Trails
Bright Futures

1317 The Cypress, *KCS*

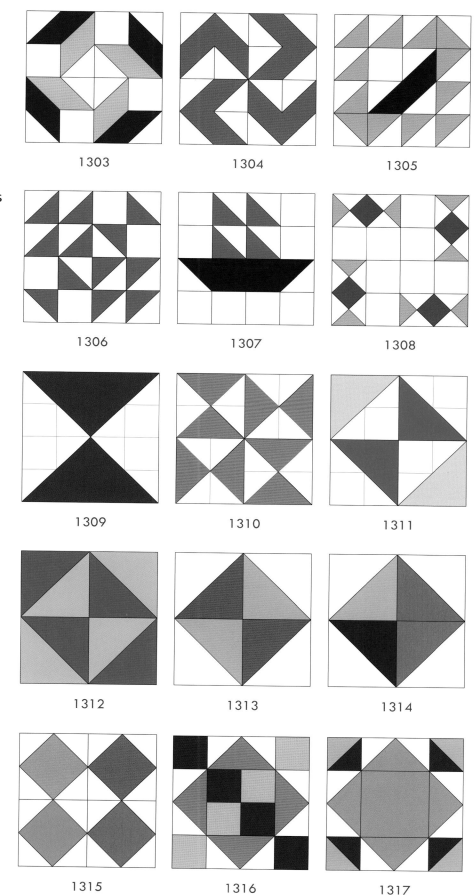

1303  1304  1305

1306  1307  1308

1309  1310  1311

1312  1313  1314

1315  1316  1317

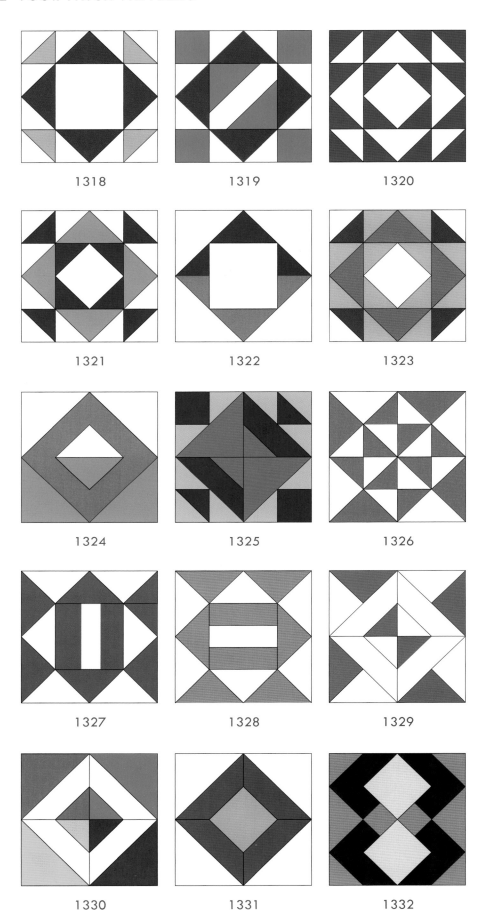

1318 The Cypress

1319 Signature

1320 Mosaic #16, *LAC*
   Connecticut, *NP*

1321 Mosaic #12, *NC*
   Hour Glass, *NP*

1322 Checkerboard Quilt

1323 Canadian Gardens, *NP*

1324 Linking Blocks

1325 Anvil

1326 Peace and Plenty

1327 Broken Path

1328 End of the Road, *KCS*

1329 Blockade, *KCS*

1330 Friendship

1331 Friday the 13th, *KCS*

1332 Rail Fence

1318

1319

1320

1321

1322

1323

1324

1325

1326

1327

1328

1329

1330

1331

1332

1333 Whirlpool

1334 Pinwheel

1335 Ribbons
Grandma's Red &
White
Patience Corners, *LAC*

1336 Maltese Cross, *LAC*
Iron Cross, *NC*
King's Cross, *NC*

1337 Fancy Stripe

1338 Broken Dishes
Mosaic #21, *LAC*
Mosaic #6, *NC*

1339 Windmill

1340 Empire Star

1341 Waste Not

1342 Balkan Puzzle, *NC*
Windblown Square, *NC*

1343 Windblown Square

1344 Flywheel

1345 Whirlygig

1346 Economy, *HH*

1347 Hourglass, *NP*

1333

1334

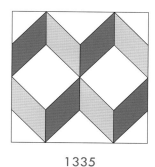
1335

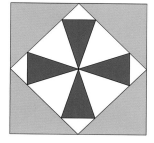
1336

1337

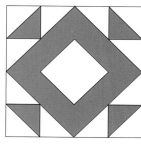
1338

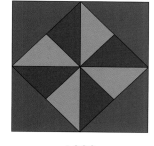
1339

1340

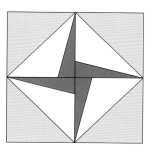
1341

1342

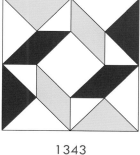
1343

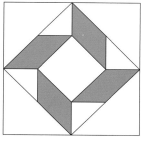
1344

1345

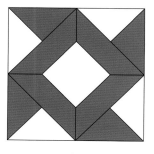
1346

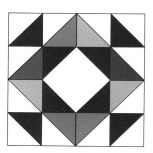
1347

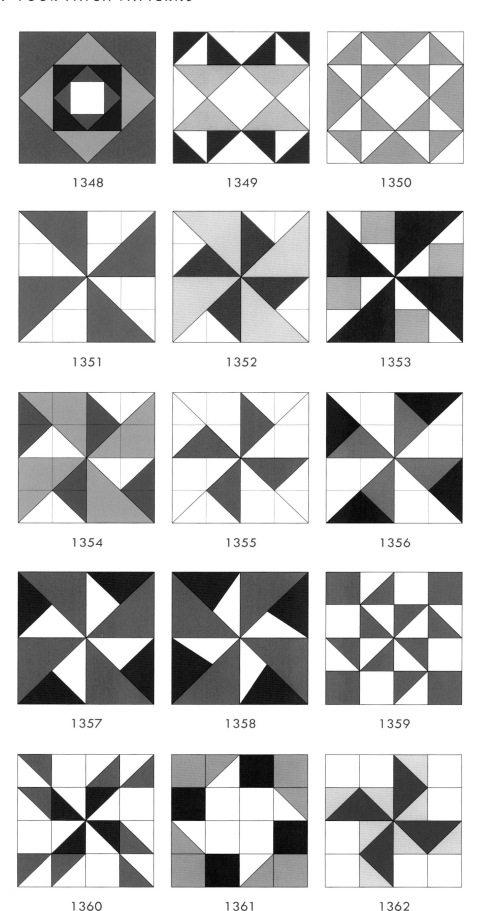

1348    1349    1350

1351    1352    1353

1354    1355    1356

1357    1358    1359

1360    1361    1362

1348   Square on Square, *NP*

1349   Mosaic #15, *LAC*

1350   Mosaic #19, *LAC*

1351   Pinwheel
       Broken Wheel
       Corn Design
       Crow's Foot
       Fan Mill
       Four Leaf Clover
       Fly
       Kathy's Ramble
       Millwheel
       Mosaic #9, *LAC*
       Old Crow
       Sugarbowl
       Watermill
       Water Wheel
       Windmill, *OF, 1898*

1352   Double Pinwheel
       Old Windmill, *NC*
       Windmill

1353   Brave World, *FJ, 1944*
       Brown World, *NC*

1354   Broken Pinwheel

1355   Turnstile, *LAC*

1356   Whirlwind

1357   Whirligig

1358   Double Pinwheel

1359   Flying X, *KCS*
       Double Quartet
       X Quartet, *WW*

1360   Year's Favorite

1361   Pinwheel
       Paper Pinwheels, *NP*

1362   Louisiana, *HH*

1363 Whirlwind
 Modern Envelope, *KCS*
 Pinwheel
 Twin Sisters, *LAC*
 Water Wheel
 Windmill, *GD*

1364 Windmill, *GC*
 Whirligig, *KCS*

1365 Arkansas Crossroads,
 *KCS*

1366 Streak of Lightning

1367 Shadow Box

1368 Jewel

1369 Birds in the Air

1370 Birds in the Air

1371 Flock
 Flock of Geese

1372 Sawtooth

1373 Northern Lights

1374 Double X

1375 Nelson's Victory

1376 Window

1377 Broken Dish

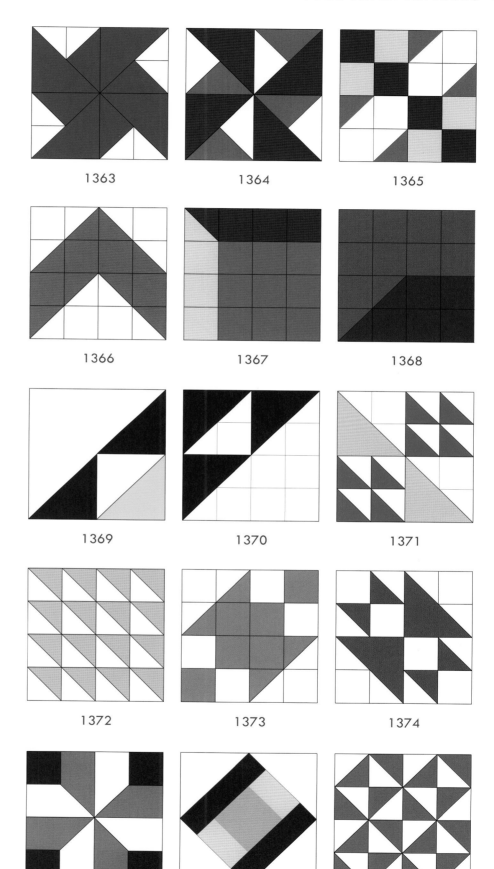

1363

1364

1365

1366

1367

1368

1369

1370

1371

1372

1373

1374

1375

1376

1377

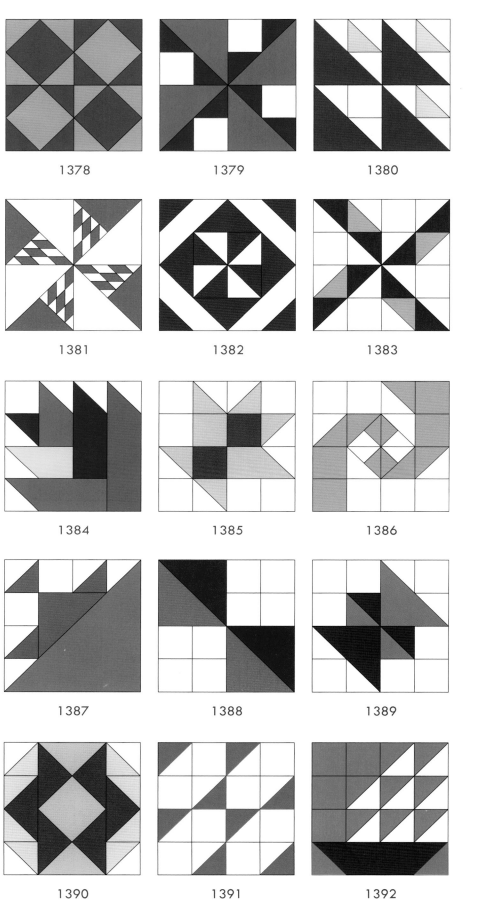

1378    1379    1380
1381    1382    1383
1384    1385    1386
1387    1388    1389
1390    1391    1392

1378   Small Triangle Quilt
1379   Spinner
1380   Aircraft
1381   Dutch Windmill
1382   Mosaic #8, *NC*
1383   Windmill
1384   Pineapple Plant
1385   Baby Bunting
1386   Snail's Trail, *KCS*
1387   Ships at Sea
1388   Cotton Reels
1389   Picket Fence
1390   Butterfly
1391   The X-Quisite, *LAC*
1392   Sailboat

1393 Box, *LAC*

1394 Contrary Husband, *KCS*
    Box, *LAC*
    Box Car Patch, *NC*
    Eccentric Star, *GC*
    Open Book
    The Open Box, *AG*
    Roads to Berlin

1395 Roads to Berlin, *KCS*

1396 Flying Bats, *KCS*
    Around the Chimney
    Diamond Point
    Slashed Album, *LAC*

1397 Mosaic #1
    Hither and Yon
    Spool

1398 Windmill

1399 Churn Dash, *NC*

1400 Cheyenne, *KCS*

1401 Little Cedar Tree

1402 A Signature Quilt, *KCS*

1403 Red Cross

1404 Heart

1405 The Anvil

1406 Connecticut, *HH*
    Shoemaker's Puzzle,
        *HH*

1407 Block Island Puzzle

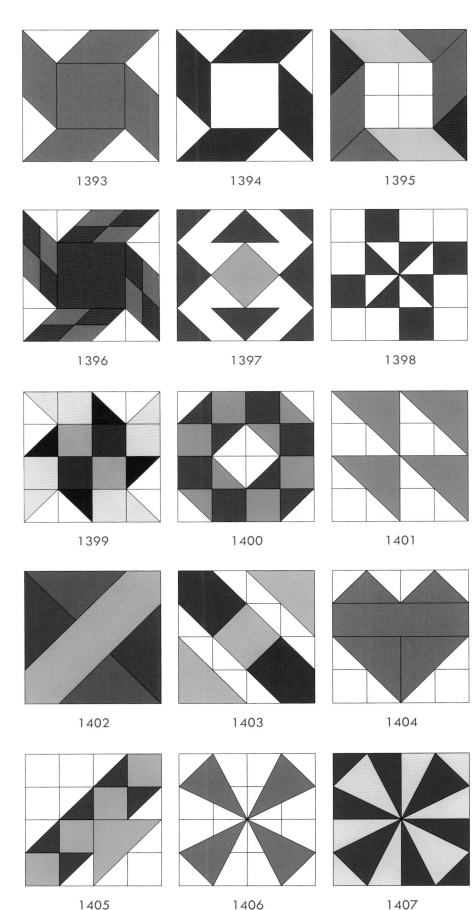

1393

1394

1395

1396

1397

1398

1399

1400

1401

1402

1403

1404

1405

1406

1407

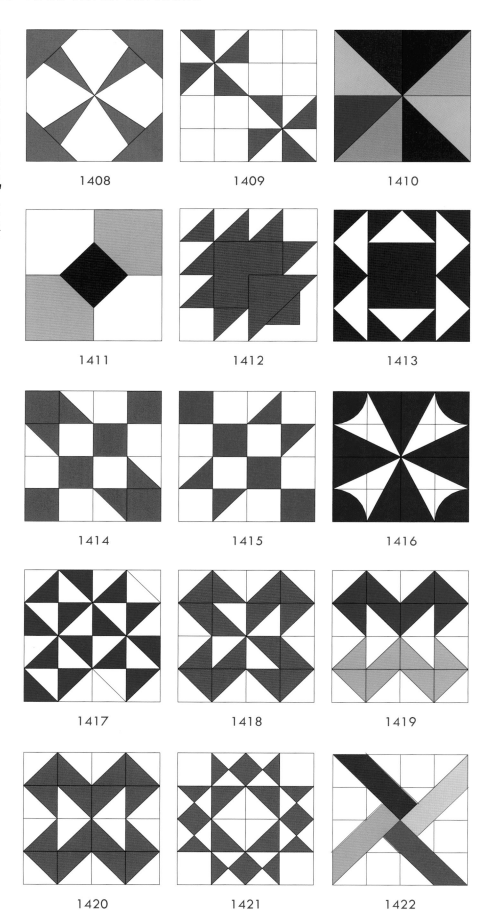

1408 Plain Sailing, *CoM*

1409 Flashing Windmills, *NC*
Pinwheels

1410 The Gay Pinwheel

1411 Bowtie
Colonial Bow Tie, *GC*
Necktie, *LAC*
Peekhole, *WW, 1931*

1412 Swallow

1413 Buzzard's Roost

1414 Road to Oklahoma, *KCS*

1415 Road to Oklahoma
Crockett Cabin Quilt

1416 Spider Web

1417 Broken Dishes
Old Tippecanoe, *LAC*
Broken Promises, *QN*

1418 Colorado Block
Colorado Beauty

1419 Double Z

1420 Hourglass
Double Z

1421 Square & Star

1422 Windmill

1423 Ribbon Block, *KCS*
  Beach and Boots, *NC*
  Ribbon Border, *LAC*
  Watered Ribbon &
    Border, *LAC*

1424 Pinwheel

1425 Old Windmill

1426 Puss in the Corner, *LAC*

1427 Sunshiny Day

1428 Tea Leaf

1429 Crazy Quilt

1430 Crazy Quilt Flower

1431 Tulip

1432 Beacon Lights

1433 Noon & Light

1434 Royal Star

1435 The Seasons, *KCS*
  Maud's Album Block,
    *NP*
  Pointed Tile

1436 Mother's Choice, *KCS*
  Cotton Boll, *KCS*
  Formal Garden
  Mother's Choice, *KCS*
  A Cross Is Mother's
    Choice, *KCS*

1437 Pointed Tile

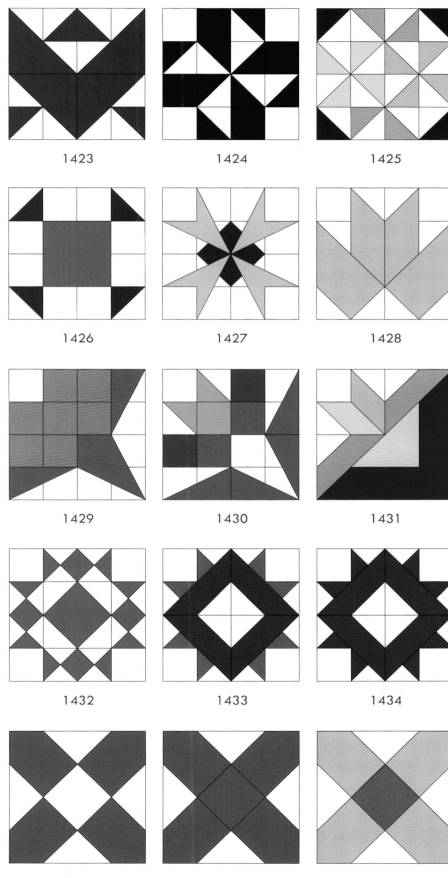

1423    1424    1425

1426    1427    1428

1429    1430    1431

1432    1433    1434

1435    1436    1437

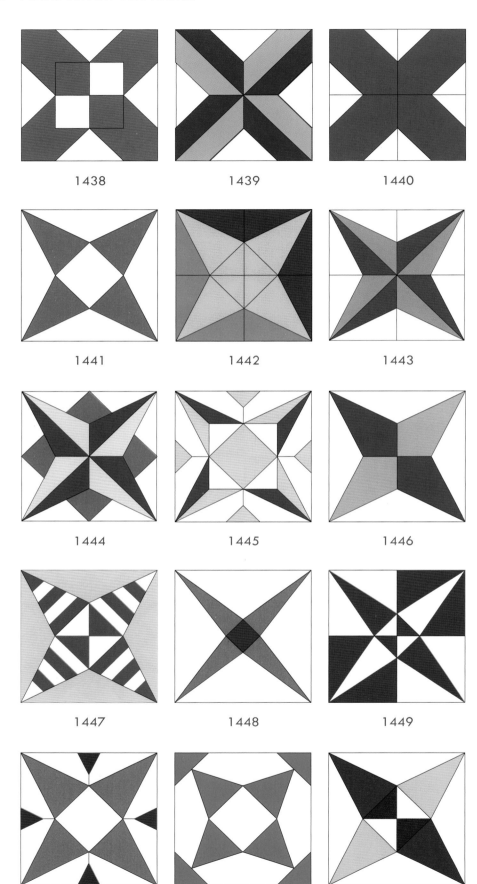

1438

1439

1440

1441

1442

1443

1444

1445

1446

1447

1448

1449

1450

1451

1452

1438 Indian Star, *KCS*

1439 King's X, *FJ*
Hide and Seek, *AK*

1440 Lattice, *NP*
A Quilt of Variety, *KCS*
Cotton Boll, *KCS*
Five Cross, *CS*
Five Crosses, *NC*
Lovely Patchwork, *NC*
The Quint Five Quilt,
*KCS*

1441 World Without End
Amethyst
Diamond Star
Golden Wedding Quilt,
*NP*
The Priscilla, *LAC*
Star and Diamond
Rocky Road to Kansas
(strip pieced scraps),
*LAC*

1442 Kaleidoscope

1443 Job's Troubles

1444 Star

1445 World's Fair, *LW*

1446 World Without End
Black and White, *OCS*
Bamboo Quilt, *OCS*
Diamonds Galore, *OCS*

1447 Kite, *CS*

1448 Massachusetts Priscilla

1449 Crossed Canoes, *LAC*
The Dragon Fly, *KCS*
Indian Canoes, *KCS*
Santa Fe Quilt, *CoM*
Twinkling Star

1450 Forgotten Star

1451 Milkmaid's Star, *KCS*

1452 Sugar Cone

1453  Duck Tracks

1454  Pinwheel

1455  Poinsettia

1456  Arrowhead

1457  Winged Square

1458  Meteor

1459  Pale Star

1460  Trailing Star
   Mosaic, *LAC*
   Mosaic #1, *NC*
   Old Poinsettia, *NC*
   Spinning Stars, *NP*

1461  Clay's Choice
   Beauty Patch
   Clay's Favorite
   Clay's Star
   Harry's Star
   Henry of the West
   Star of the West

1462  Pinwheel Askew

1463  Mosaic #12, *NC*

1464  Mosaic #9, *LAC*

1465  The North Star, *KCS*
   Whirling Star

1466  Shooting Star, *LAC*
   Meteor Quilt, *NP*
   Stardust, *KCS Quilt
      Contest*

1467  Pineapple Quilt, *1862*

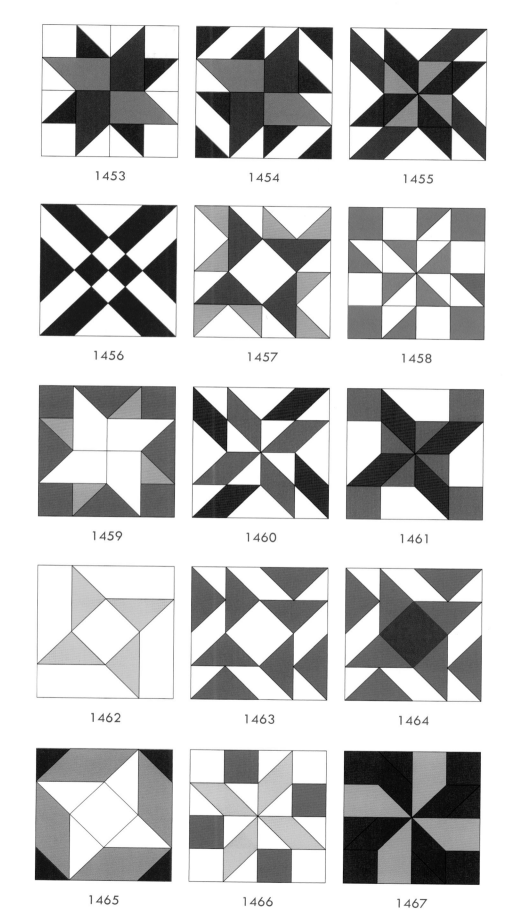

1453

1454

1455

1456

1457

1458

1459

1460

1461

1462

1463

1464

1465

1466

1467

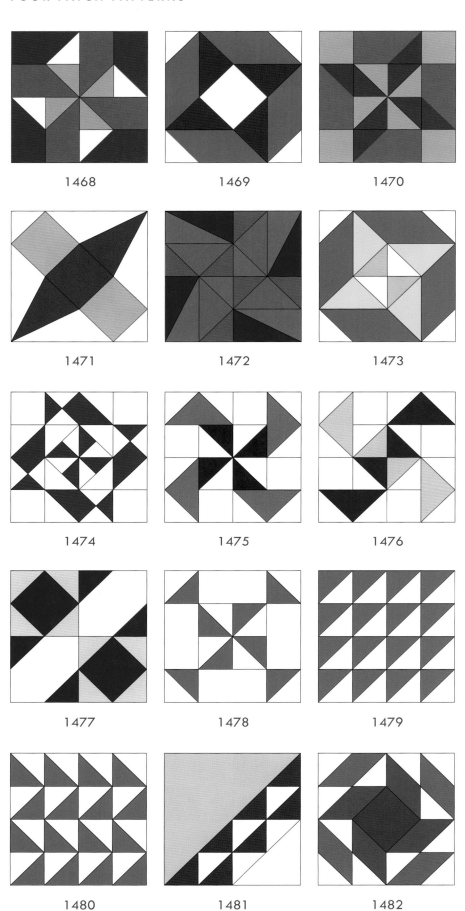

1468   Petronella, *QM, 1992*

1469   Rose Trellis, *NC*

1470   Shooting Star

1471   Blue Heaven

1472   Popcorn

1473   Next Door Neighbor
       Square Up, *HH*

1474   Catch as You Can

1475   Seesaw

1476   Next Door Neighbor

1477   Monastery Windows,
       *NC*

1478   Windmill, *OCS*

1479   Mosaic #10, *NC*
       Mosaic #17, *LAC*
       Ann and Andy
       Triangle Tiles

1480   Hopscotch, *NC*

1481   Path Through the
       Woods, *CaS*

1482   Mosaic #6

1483 Tippecanoe

1484 Sailboat

1485 Octagons and Squares, *KCS*

1486 Twilight

1487 Mosaic #5, *NC*
Winged Arrow, *NP*

1488 End of the Day, *FJ*

1489 Mill Wheel

1490 Spool and Bobbin

1491 Belle's Favorite

1492 Symmetry in Motion

1493 Windy City, *QN*

1494 Tall Ships, *QW, 1986*

1495 Double Pinwheel
Whirl, *QN, 1993*

1496 Mosaic #4, *NC*
Mosaic #6, *LAC*
Zig Zag Tile Quilt

1497 Friendship Chain, *1900*

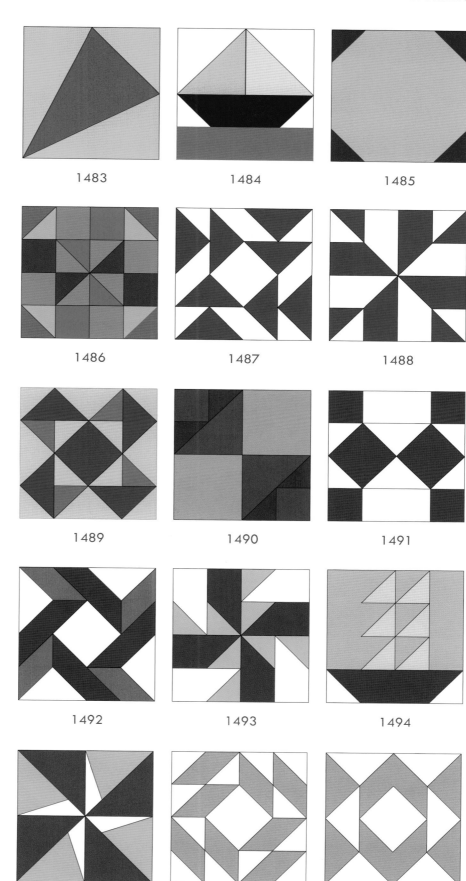

1483

1484

1485

1486

1487

1488

1489

1490

1491

1492

1493

1494

1495

1496

1497

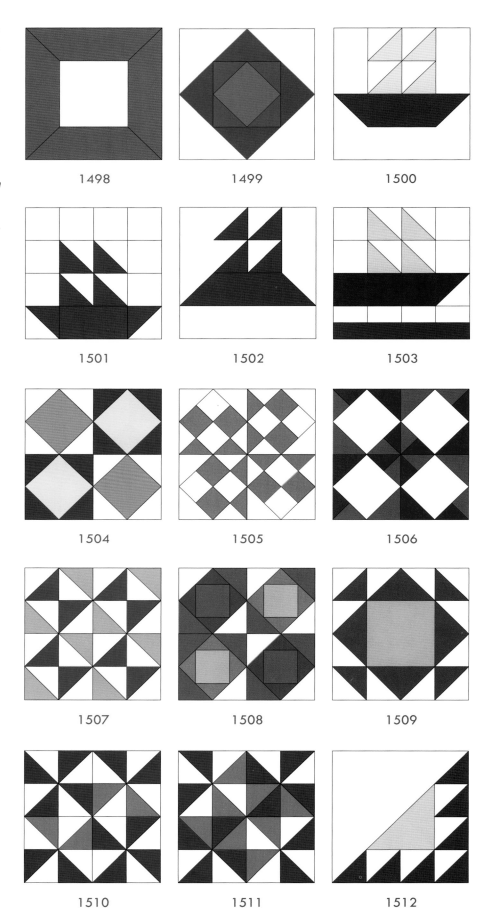

1498

1499

1500

1501

1502

1503

1504

1505

1506

1507

1508

1509

1510

1511

1512

1498 The Diversion Quilt, *KCS*

1499 Economy, *KCS*

1500 The Ship, *MD*

1501 Fishing Boats, *NC*

1502 Sailboat Oklahoma, *KCS*

1503 Sailboat Quilt, *NP*

1504 Alamanizer, *NC*
Eight Point All Over, *QN*
Pavement Pattern
Shoo Fly
Triangles and Squares, *KCS*
Triangle Beauty, *OCS*

1505 Yokohama Banner, *NC*
Whirling Squares, *NP*

1506 Arrowhead Puzzle, *AMS*

1507 Port and Starboard, *NC*

1508 This and That, *KCS*

1509 Magic Triangles, *OCS*

1510 Simplicity, *HH*

1511 Milly's Favorite, *1911*

1512 Lend and Borrow, *KCS*
Geometric
Indian Meadow, *WW*
Little Saw Tooth, *WW*
Rocky Glen, *WW*
Saw Tooth, *WW*

1513 Oklahoma Square
    Dance, *KCS*
    Square Dance, *OCS*
    Starry Night
    All Around the Star, *NC*

1514 Airplane

1515 Signature

1516 Seesaw

1517 Migration

1518 Quilt in Light and Dark

1519 Idle Moments

1520 Counterpane, *NC*

1521 Country Village

1522 Light and Shadows, *NC*

1523 Gold Nuggets, *AK*

1524 Diversion Quilt, *KCS*

1525 Islam, *NC*

1526 Granny's Choice

1527 Our Editor

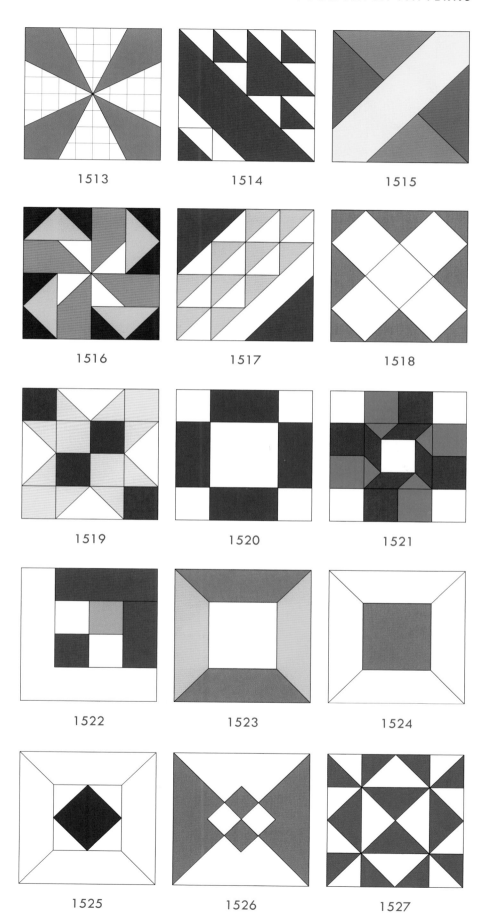

1513     1514     1515

1516     1517     1518

1519     1520     1521

1522     1523     1524

1525     1526     1527

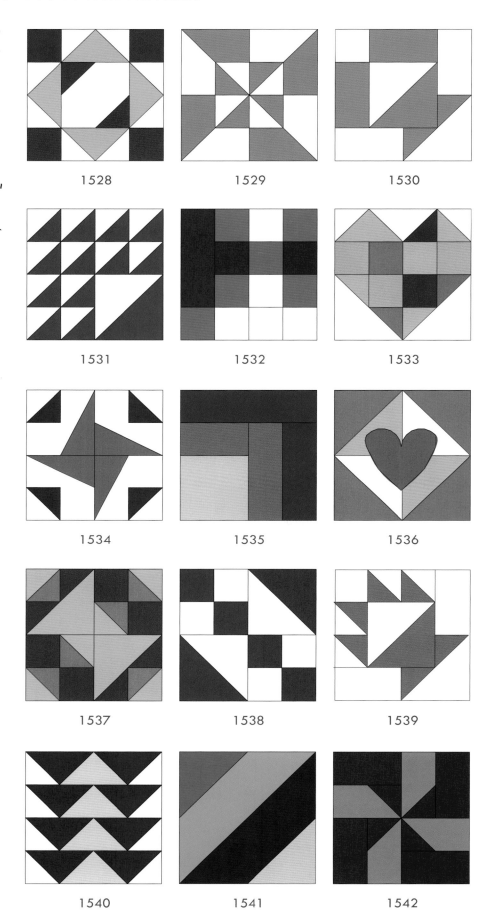

1528   1529   1530

1531   1532   1533

1534   1535   1536

1537   1538   1539

1540   1541   1542

1528 Signature Friendship Quilt, *KCS*

1529 Double Windmill

1530 Fish Basket Block

1531 Friendship Quilt

1532 Diagonal Square, *OCS*

1533 Romance, *TQr*, *1992*

1534 Liberty Star, *QW*, *1988*

1535 Garden Shadows, *QM*, *1994*

1536 Heart Spangled Star

1537 Grandma's Spool

1538 Jewel Box

1539 Cactus Pot Block

1540 Tit for Tat

1541 Lightning, *LS*, *1990*

1542 Maypole Dance, *QM*

1543 Bonny Scotland, *JM*

1544 The Sail Boat, *KCS*

1545 A Victory Quilt, *KCS*
Arrowhead

1546 A Scrap Zigzag, *KCS*

1547 The Maple Leaf, *KCS*

1548 Posy Patch

1549 Simple Block
Flower Bed

1550 Ship of Dreams

1551 Picture Window

1552 Fox Chase
Biloxi

1553 Light and Dark, *KCS*

1554 Electric Fan, *CS*

1555 Star of the East, *FJ*
Midnight Stars, *NC*

1556 Pinwheel, *AG*

1557 Sunshiny Day, *FJ*

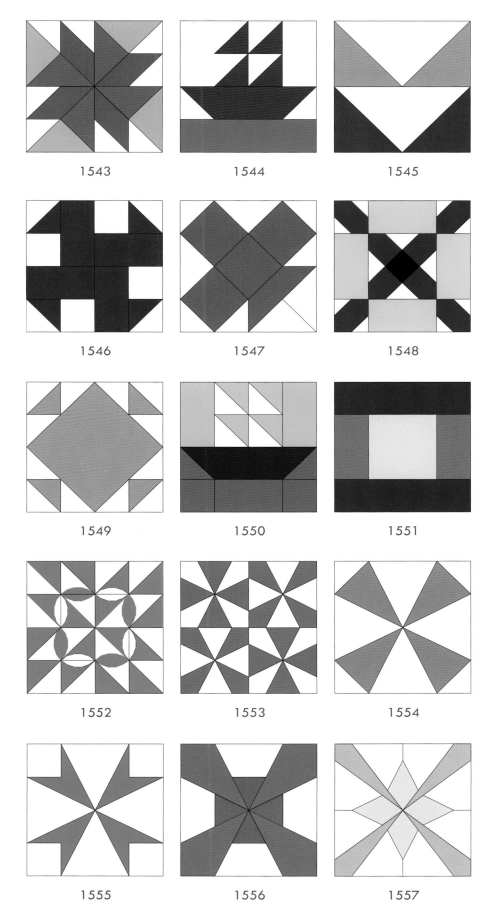

1543

1544

1545

1546

1547

1548

1549

1550

1551

1552

1553

1554

1555

1556

1557

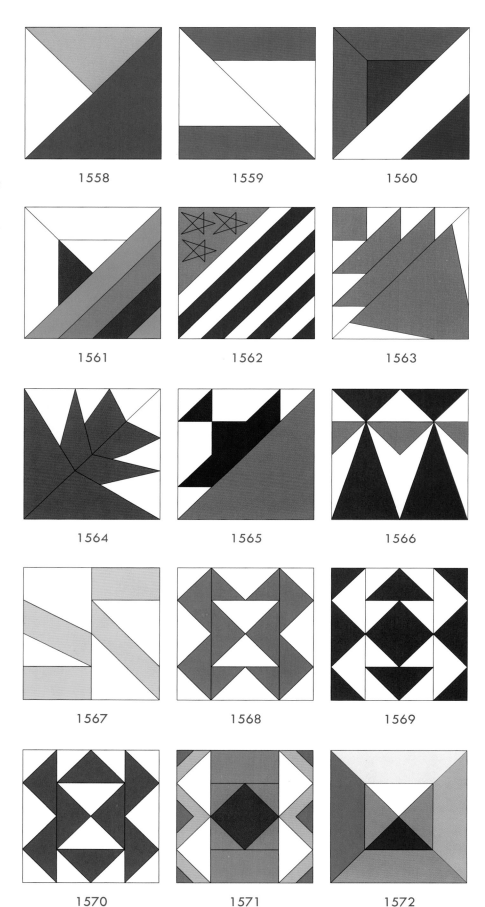

1558

1559

1560

1561

1562

1563

1564

1565

1566

1567

1568

1569

1570

1571

1572

1558 Pigeons in the Coop, *QN*
Rocky Mountain
Shadow Box
Waste Not, Want Not

1559 Good Luck, *FJ*

1560 No Name

1561 Peter's Quilt, *Nancy Crow*

1562 Red, White and Blue, *FJ*

1563 Winter Cactus, *MJ*

1564 Winter Cactus, *MJ*

1565 Ship at Sea, *Dakota Farmer, 1927*

1566 Lilies, *QW, 1980*

1567 College Chain, *1902*

1568 Brown Goose
Devil's Claws
Double Z
Framed X, *FJ*
Gray Goose
Old Gray Goose, *NC*
Old Maid's Puzzle
Mosaic #22, *LAC*

1569 Empire Star, *HH*
Star of the West

1570 Fool's Puzzle, *CoM*

1571 Diamond Stripe

1572 Terrace Floor, *Helen White, QN, 1999*

1573 Twilight

1574 Swing Your Partner, *QN*

1575 Rhapsody in Blue, *QN*

1576 The Diamond Bar, *QN*

1577 Thunderbird (diagonal set), *QN*

1578 Forest Paths

1579 Gold Nuggets, *NC*

1580 Our Editor

1581 Cherokee Spirit

1582 Old Glory Four Patch

1583 Mosaic #3, *LAC*

1584 Double Cross

1585 A Red, White and Blue Criss Cross

1586 Macaroon Patchwork

1587 Indian Arrowhead

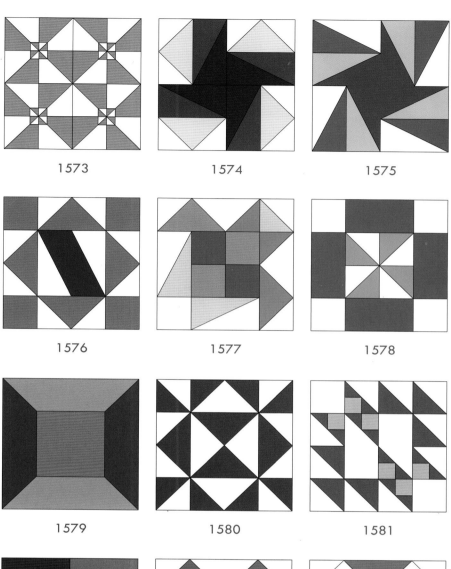

1573  1574  1575

1576  1577  1578

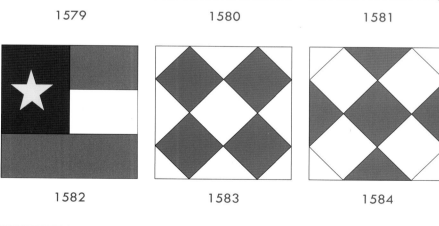

1579  1580  1581

1582  1583  1584

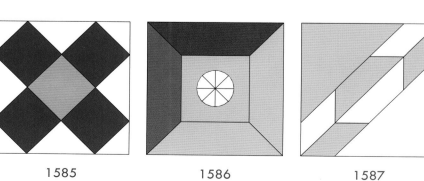

1585  1586  1587

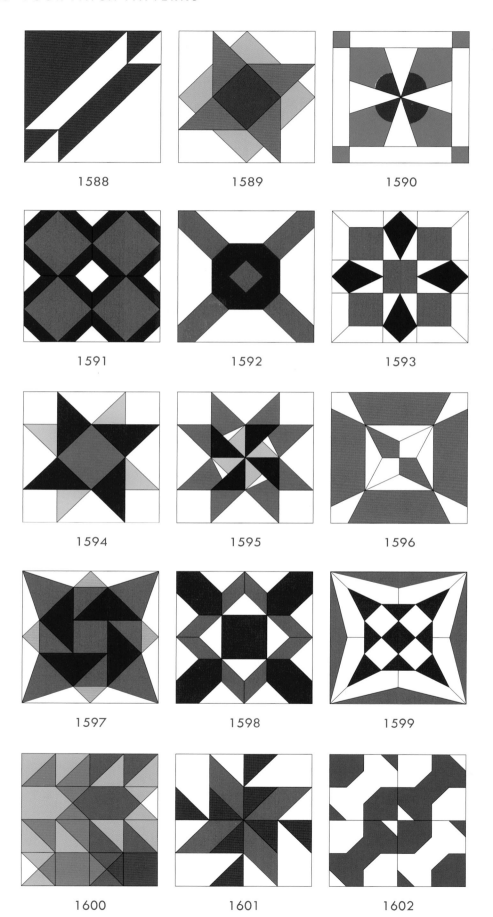

1588   1589   1590

1591   1592   1593

1594   1595   1596

1597   1598   1599

1600   1601   1602

1588  Old Maid's Rambler

1589  All That Jazz, *JM*
      Kitty Corner, *JM*

1590  Four Leaf Clover, *NM*

1591  Flower Bed, *NC*
      A Simple Design, *NC*

1592  Saddlebag

1593  Nine Patch Star

1594  Judy's Star, *JM*

1595  Star Shine

1596  Buck 'n Wing

1597  Merry-Go-Round, *RMS,*
      *SSQ, 1986*

1598  Jim Dandy, *NC*

1599  Prudence's Star, *OCS*

1600  Fish Tales

1601  Land of Lincoln, *JM*

1602  Spools
      Dog Bone

1603 White House Steps

1604 Frame

1605 Swastika

1606 Odds and Ends

1607 Tea Rose

1608 Going Home

1609 Paddle Wheel

1610 Necktie, *KCS*

1611 Bow Tie Wreath
    Magic Circle
    Morning Patch, *LAC*

1612 Irish Chain

1613 Flying Clouds

1614 Steps to Glory

1615 Interlocking O's,
    *Doris Dace*

1616 Fanny's Favorite
    Diamond Ring, *CS*
    Grandma's Choice,
    *1938*
    My Favorite, *NC, 1933*
    Old Favorite, *NC*

1617 No Name, *LCPQ*

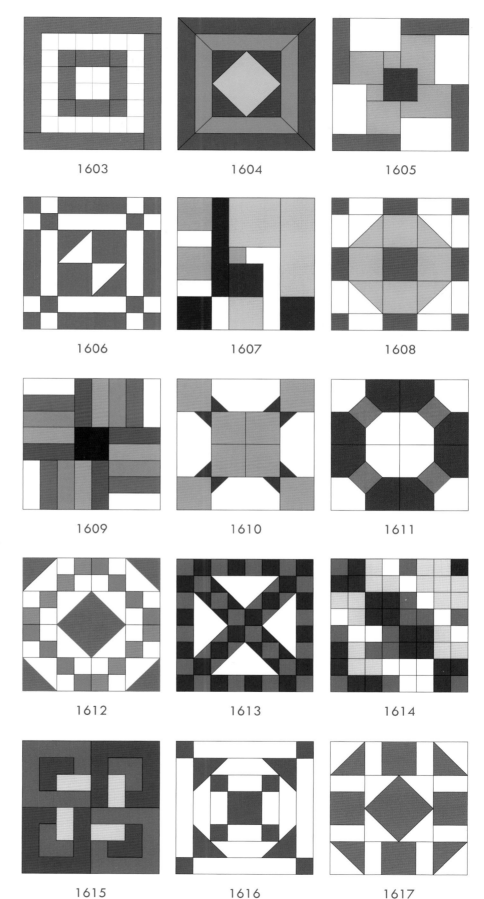

1603

1604

1605

1606

1607

1608

1609

1610

1611

1612

1613

1614

1615

1616

1617

5,500 QUILT BLOCK DESIGNS

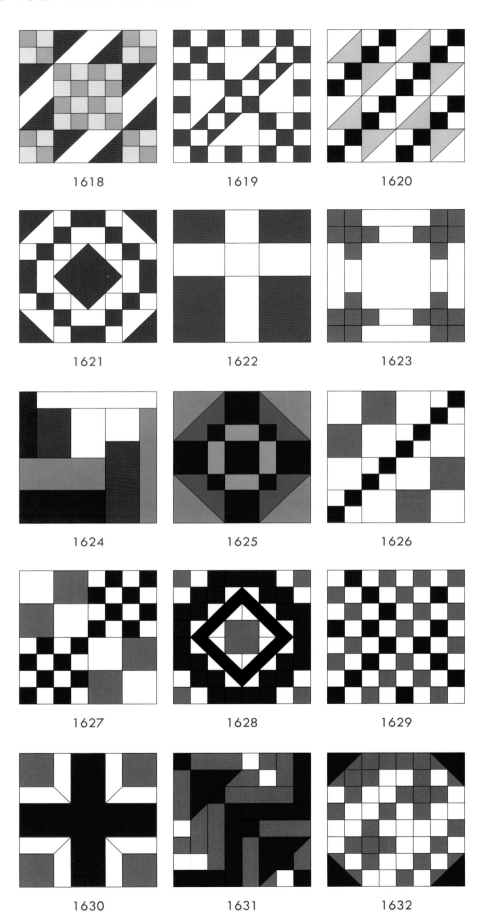

1618

1619

1620

1621

1622

1623

1624

1625

1626

1627

1628

1629

1630

1631

1632

1618  Sunny Lanes, *NP*

1619  Flying Clouds

1620  Buckeye Beautiful

1621  Jewel Box

1622  The White Cross

1623  The Rosebud

1624  Century of Progress

1625  Patio Garden, *MM*

1626  Carrie Nation Quilt, *KCS*

1627  Four Patch

1628  Aunt Em's Pattern

1629  Postage Stamp

1630  The Red Cross Quilt, *KCS*

1631  Geese in Flight, *NC*

1632  Autumn Star, *NC*

1633 Scroll Work, *AMS*

1634 Iowa Star, *LAC*
Texas Ranger

1635 Signal Light, *NP*

1636 Lucky Star, *LW*

1637 Star of Four Points, *KCS*
Twinkling Stars, *CoM*
Time and Tide

1638 Star and Dot, *1910*

1639 Periwinkle
Snowball, *Carrie Hall*

1640 Flaming Star, *NP*
Northern Lights, *NP*
Eight Pointed Star, *LAC*
Mariner's Compass,
*HAS*
Mother's Delight

1641 Blazing Star
Four Pointed Star
Mother's Delight, *CaS*
St. Louis, *CaS*

1642 Blazing Star, *NC*

1643 Blazing Star

1644 Rainbow Star, *MM*

1645 Star Bound, *QN, 1990*

1646 Sparkling Crystals

1647 Rolling Star
Kaleidoscope

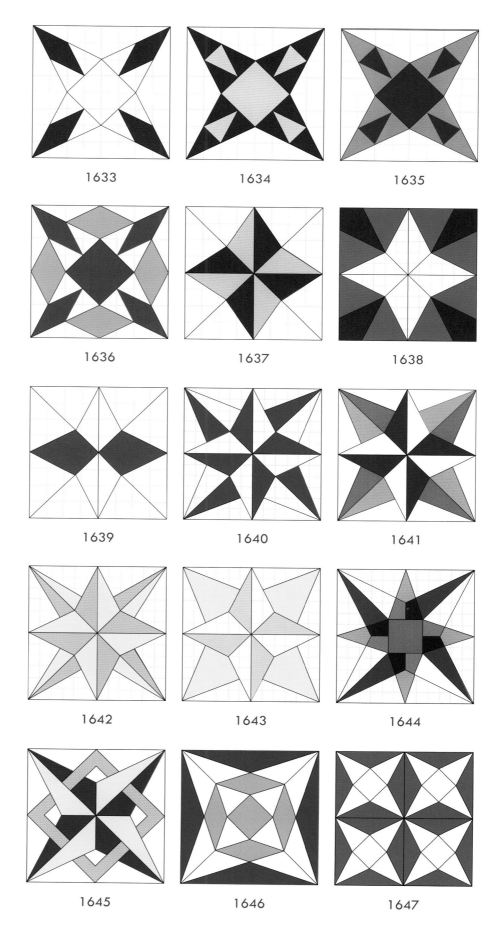

1633 1634 1635

1636 1637 1638

1639 1640 1641

1642 1643 1644

1645 1646 1647

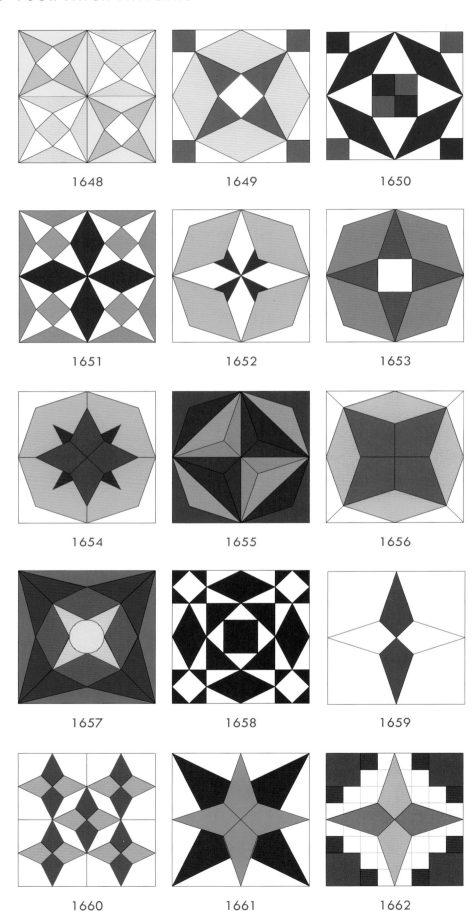

1648    1649    1650

1651    1652    1653

1654    1655    1656

1657    1658    1659

1660    1661    1662

1648  Golden Wedding

1649  Her Sparkling Jewels, *KCS*
      Arrowhead, *WBM*
      The Gem Block, *WBM*
      Idaho, *WBM*
      Sparkling Jewel, *NC*

1650  Jewel, *KCS*

1651  Amethyst
      Crazy Quilt Star, *NC*
      Diamond Star
      North Dakota, *HH*
      The Priscilla, *LAC*
      Quilt Star, *NC*
      Rocky Road to Kansas,
        *LAC*
      Star and Diamond
      The Windmill
      Windmill Star, *GC*
      World Without End

1652  Unnamed,
        *GLB, 1858*

1653  Windmill Star, *KCS*

1654  No Name

1655  Diamond Ring

1656  Marathon

1657  Autumn Moon, *RMS,*
        *SSQ, 1987*

1658  Storm at Sea, *KCS*

1659  The Kite Quilt, *KCS*
      Arkansas Snowflake,
        *KCS*
      Arkansas Star, *KCS*
      Star Kites, *NC*

1660  Pontiac Star, *CS*

1661  Double Star, *HH*

1662  Steps to the Stars

1663 Indian Hatchets, *LAC*

1664 Robbing Peter to Pay
    Paul
    Triangle of Squares, *NC*

1665 Signatures for Golden
    Memories, *KCS*
    Friendship
    Golden Memories
    Paths to Piece, *HM*

1666 Kansas Dugout

1667 Robbing Peter to Pay
    Paul

1668 Friendship Quilt, *KCS*

1669 A Striped Plain Quilt,
    *KCS*

1670 Road to Tennessee

1671 Thirteen Squares

1672 Pennsylvania
    Crossroads

1673 Kentucky Chain

1674 Interwoven Puzzle,
    *1933*

1675 Star and Cross

1676 Night and Day, *NC*
    Geometric Illusion
    Mosaic #4, *LAC*
    White Cross

1677 Pillar to Post

1663      1664      1665

1666      1667      1668

1669      1670      1671

1672      1673      1674

1675      1676      1677

5,500 QUILT BLOCK DESIGNS

1678 · 1679 · 1680 · 1681 · 1682 · 1683 · 1684 · 1685 · 1686 · 1687 · 1688 · 1689 · 1690 · 1691 · 1692

1678  Snowy Morning, *HaM*,
       *SSQ, 1983*

1679  Devil's Puzzle

1680  Flyfoot

1681  Good Fortune, *CS*
       Cross Bars, *NP*

1682  Three Crosses

1683  Gem Block, *WW*
       The Road to Paris

1684  Broken Dishes, *NM*,
       *1918*
       The Dewey, *NP*
       Double Squares, *LAC*
       Jack in the Pulpit, *CS*

1685  Mother's Favorite

1686  The Friendship Quilt

1687  Mosaic #1, *LAC*
       Mosaic #3, *NC*

1688  Jericho

1689  Jaywalker, *NC*

1690  Columbia Pinwheel

1691  Name Unknown

1692  Name Unknown

1693 Diadem

1694 Fort Sumter, *NC*

1695 Mosaic #2, *NC*
Mosaic #5, *LAC*
Jack in the Pulpit
Toad in the Puddle

1696 Scotch Plaid, *CaS*
Scotch Squares, *NC*

1697 Four Corner Puzzle, *KCS*

1698 Ella's Star, *QWO*,
*1987*

1699 Ring Around the Posy

1700 Four Points, *LAC*
Four Point, *HHJ*
Lattice and Square, *NC*

1701 Star and Arrows

1702 Aztec Jewel,
*Virginia Outerbacker*,
*QN*

1703 Rock of Ages

1704 Mountain Peak, *KCS*
Cross Stitch, *NC*
Maud's Album Quilt,
*NP*
Old Italian Design, *FJ*
Snow Block, *NC*
Snowflake, *LAC*

1705 Diamond Ring
My Favorite, *NC*
Old Favorite, *NC*

1706 Home Treasure
Flying X, *NC*

1707 Around the Corner, *NC*

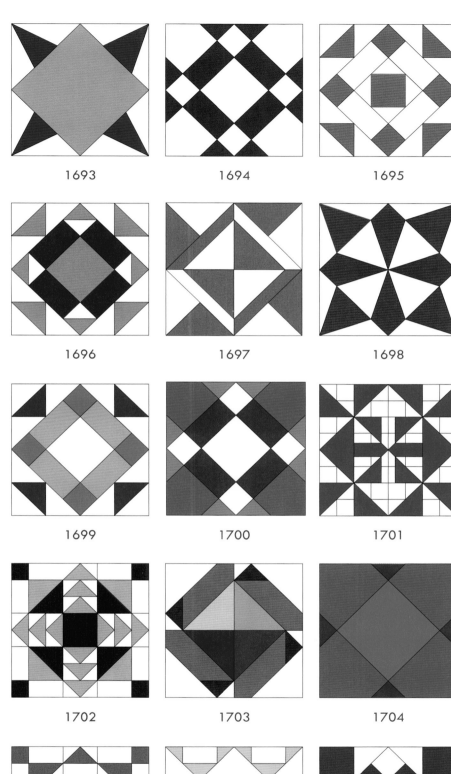

1693

1694

1695

1696

1697

1698

1699

1700

1701

1702

1703

1704

1705

1706

1707

1708

1709

1710

1711

1712

1713

1714

1715

1716

1717

1718

1719

1720

1721

1722

1708 Journey to California, *KCS*

1709 The Album, *KCS*

1710 Grandmother's Favorite, *KCS*

1711 The Gate or H Quilt, *KCS*

1712 Depression, *KCS*

1713 Arrant Redbirds Variation

1714 Arrant Red Birds

1715 Framed Star

1716 Friendship Knot

1717 Coffin Star

1718 Summer's Dream

1719 Temple Court Hull's Victory

1720 Road to California

1721 Pride of Ohio

1722 Star and Chains, *LAC* Rolling Star Ring Around the Star

1723 Coxcomb, *NC*

1724 Country Path

1725 Twisted Ribbons, *QN, 1993*

1726 Crazy Anne Pinwheel, *FJ*

1727 Wings of Eagles

1728 Pennsylvania

1729 Interlocking Squares, *KCS*

1730 Crazy Loons

1731 Navajo

1732 Banded Triangle, *MLM, SSQ, 1983*

1733 Bows and Paper, *HaM, SSQ, 1983*

1734 Spring Has Come

1735 Expanding Universe, *MM*

1736 Porto Rico

1737 Star Premo

1723        1724        1725

1726        1727        1728

1729        1730        1731

1732        1733        1734

1735        1736        1737

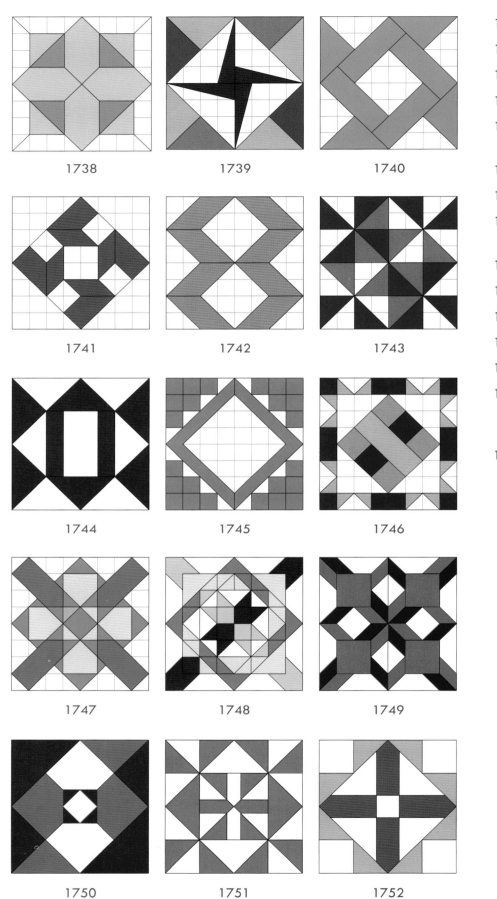

1738    1739    1740

1741    1742    1743

1744    1745    1746

1747    1748    1749

1750    1751    1752

1738  Empire Cross

1739  Waste Not Variation

1740  Water Wheel

1741  Kansas Beauty, *CS*

1742  John's Original Quilt
       Block

1743  Milly's Favorite

1744  Broken Path

1745  Memory Block, *LAC*
       Album, *MD*

1746  Lily

1747  Shaded Crossroad

1748  Nancy's Fancy

1749  West Virginia, *HH*

1750  Square Block, *QW, 1982*

1751  Belle of West Virginia,
       *HH*
       Frankfort, *HH*

1752  Cross Within Cross, *NP*
       Grandmother's Choice
       French Patchwork

1753  Grandmother's Cross

1754  Far Horizons

1755  Good Enough, *HH*

1756  Cats and Mice

1757  Crazy Loons

1758  Our Next President
    Quilt
    President's Choice

1759  Twist Patchwork

1760  Five Patch Star, *OCS*

1761  Star Points, *FJ*

1762  Duck and Ducklings

1763  Garden Patch

1764  Court House Lawn, *NC*

1765  Light and Shadows,
    *KCS*

1766  Casement Window,
    *KCS*

1767  The Red Cross Quilt,
    *KCS*
    Washington Sidewalk

1753      1754      1755

1756      1757      1758

1759      1760      1761

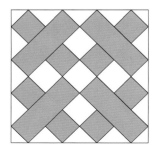

1762      1763      1764

1765      1766      1767

1768

1769

1770

1771

1772

1773

1774

1775

1776

1777

1778

1779

1780

1781

1782

1768 The Album, *KCS*
Chimney Sweep
Cross Patch, *WW, 1931*
Friendship Chain, *NC*

1769 Friendship Quilt, *KCS*
Album, *OF, 1894*
Basket Weave
Friendship Quilt, *KCS*
Five Crosses
Puzzle

1770 The Album, *KCS*

1771 Friendship Quilt, *KCS*

1772 Salute to the Colors,
*KCS*

1773 Tenallytown Square,
*NC*
Washington Pavement

1774 Roman Cross, *LAC*

1775 Chicago Pavements, *CS*

1776 Basement Window
Katie's Favorite, *NC*

1777 Tinted Chains, *NC*

1778 Sarah's Favorite, *LAC*
Sally's Favorite, *NP*

1779 Home Treasure

1780 Fellowship, *RMS, SSQ,*
*1986*

1781 Small Business

1782 Hazy Daisy, *NC*

1783 Spindles and Stripes,
 *KCS*

1784 Beautiful Star, *LAC*
 Arrow Star

1785 Oriental Star, *NC*
 Dervish Star, *GD*
 Star of the Orient, *NC*

1786 Exploding Star

1787 Home Again, *FJ*

1788 Concord

1789 Wandering Flower, *KCS*

1790 Shooting Star, *MM*

1791 Compass Kaleidoscope

1792 Mill and Stars, *NC*

1793 Star, *OCS*
 Star of the East, *OCS*

1794 Four Seasons, *RMS, SSQ*

1795 Seminole Star

1796 Winding Walk

1797 Fox Chase
 Biloxi
 Winding Walk

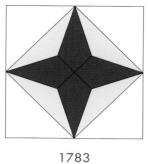

1783

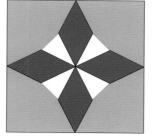

1784

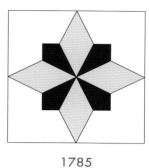

1785

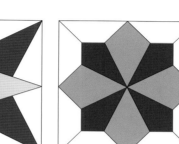

1786

1787

1788

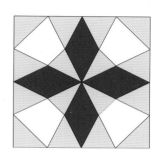

1789

1790

1791

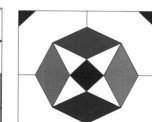

1792

1793

1794

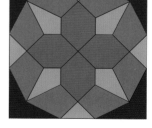

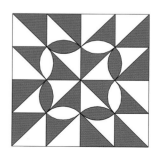

1795

1796

1797

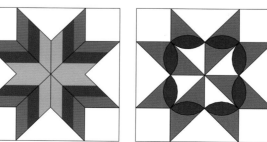

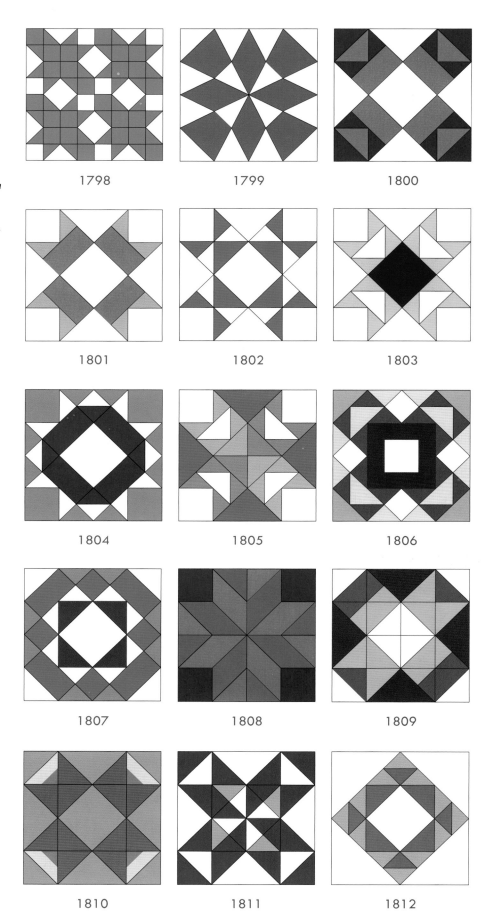

1798      
1799      
1800

1801      
1802      
1803

1804      
1805      
1806

1807      
1808      
1809

1810      
1811      
1812

1798   Cubes and Tile, *NC*
      Cube Lattice, *LAC*
      Idle Moments, *NC*

1799   Concord

1800   Aunt Nancy's Favorite, *CS*

1801   Autograph Quilt Block, *CS*

1802   Missouri Star, *NC*

1803   Northumberland Star
      Eight Pointed Star, *NC*

1804   Memory Blocks, *NC*

1805   Wild Geese

1806   Colonial Garden, *PF*

1807   Tombstone Quilt, *NC*

1808   Pinwheel, *1899*

1809   Open Window

1810   Diamond Stripe

1811   Stars and Pinwheels
      Stars and Squares, *LAC*
      Rising Star

1812   Memory Wreath
      The Wedding Ring

1813 Virginia Reel
     Monkey Wrench
     Indiana Puzzle
     Snail's Trail

1814 Wheel of Fortune

1815 Jig Jog Puzzle

1816 Broken Band, *1920*

1817 Pineapple Variation

1818 Star Light
     Perpetual Motion, *NC,*
     *1936*

1819 Old Poinsettia Block
     Mosaic #18, *LAC*
     Spinning Stars

1820 Pinwheel Star

1821 Eight Hands Around,
     *LAC*

1822 Stockyard's Star for
     Nebraska

1823 Free Trade Block
     Coronation, *NP*
     Free Trade Patch

1824 Odd Fellows Chain, *LAC*
     Odd Fellow's March,
     *1918*
     Old Maid's Ramble
     San Diego, *NP*

1825 White Hemstitch, *GD*

1826 Cross and Square, *NC*
     Home Treasure, *OCS*

1827 Crown of Thorns, *NP*

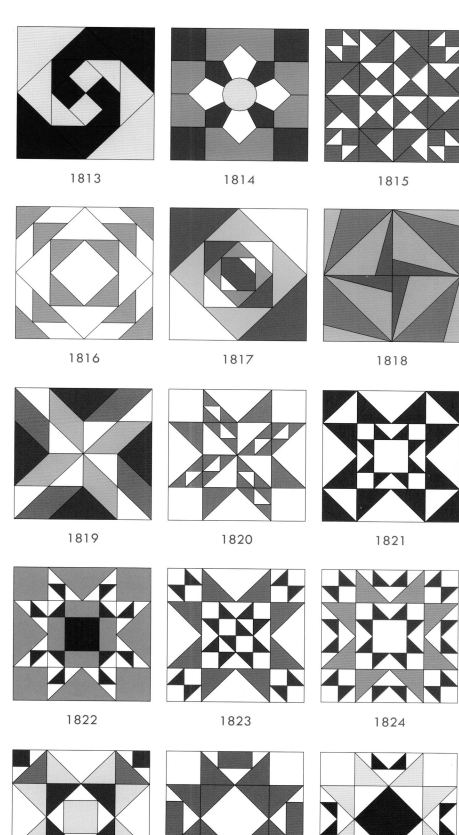

1813   1814   1815

1816   1817   1818

1819   1820   1821

1822   1823   1824

1825   1826   1827

1828
1829
1830

1831
1832
1833

1834
1835
1836

1837
1838
1839

1840
1841
1842

1828 Susannah, *NP*

1829 Star of Bethlehem

1830 No Name, *LCPQ*

1831 Illinois Corn & Beans, *SSQ, 1986*

1832 Cross on Cross

1833 Checkerboard Star, *MM*

1834 Diamond Star

1835 King's Star

1836 White Mountain Star, *Gloria Cosgrove, SSQ*

1837 Lucky Pieces, *NP*

1838 Blueberry Patch

1839 Rambler, *KCS*
Blossom Time
Spring Beauty, *KCS*
I Excel
IXL, *KCS*
Old Maid's Ramble (2 colors), *LAC*

1840 Railroad Crossing

1841 Friendship Quilt

1842 Pyramids, *NC*

1843 Indian Trails, *KCS*
Bear's Paw, *LAC*
Forest
Irish Puzzle
North Wind
Rambling Road
Winding Walk

1844 Kansas Troubles, *LAC*
Delectable Mountains
Grand Right and Left, *FJ*

1845 Barrister's Block, *LAC*
Lawyer's Puzzle
The Saw, *PP*

1846 The Lost Ship
Delectable
Appalachians, *QT*
Rocky Glen

1847 New Barrister's Block,
*NC*

1848 World's Fair Puzzle, *LAC*

1849 Wild Goose Chase

1850 Square Deal, *KCS*

1851 Sunshine, *LAC*

1852 Roll on Columbia

1853 Old Maid's Puzzle, *FJ*

1854 Merry-Go-Round, *KCS*
Eternal Triangle

1855 An Ocean Wave of
Many Prints, *KCS*
Ocean Wave
Octagon, *CoM*
Odd Fellows Quilt
Odds and Ends, *CoM*
Waves of the Ocean,
*HH*

1856 Bright Stars, *NC*

1857 Devil's Claws, *LAC*
Bright Stars, *NC*
Corner Star
Cross Plains, *CS*
The Crowfoot, *MD*
Des Moines, *HH*
Idaho Beauty, *HH*

1843  1844  1845

1846  1847  1848

1849  1850  1851

1852  1853  1854

1855  1856  1857

1858

1859

1860

1861

1862

1863

1864

1865

1866

1867

1868

1869

1870

1871

1872

1858 Cinderella, *TQr, 1991*

1859 Windmill

1860 Jagged Edge

1861 Indian Hatchet

1862 Century
Grandmother's
Pinwheel

1863 Blindman's Fancy, *LAC*

1864 Indian Hatchet

1865 Delectable Mountains

1866 Sawtooth Puzzle

1867 Mineral Wells, *NP*

1868 Sugar Bowl Block

1869 Lily Quilt Pattern, *LAC*
Des Moines, *HH*
Botch Handle

1870 Parasol

1871 Name Unknown

1872 Name Unknown

1873 The Bride's Bouquet

1874 Nosegay

1875 Shooting Star

1876 Single Lily

1877 Four Buds, *PF*

1878 Indian Patch, *FJ*

1879 Starry Path

1880 Utah Star

1881 Breeches Quilt, *WBM, 1939*
  Britches Quilt, *AMS*
  Dutchman's Breeches
  Dutchman's Puzzle, *NC*
  Mississippi
  Mississippi Daisy, *HH*

1882 Little Boy's Breeches, *KCS*
  Little Boy's Britches, *KCS*

1883 Roman Stripe
  Rainbow Block
  Shadow Quilt
  Shadows

1884 Fun Patch
  Houndstooth
  Houndstooth Scrap Patch
  Scrap Bag
  Scrap Patch

1885 Tallahassee Block

1886 Indian Chief

1887 Cowboy Star, *KCS*
  Arkansas Traveler
  Teddy's Choice, *LAC*
  Travel Star

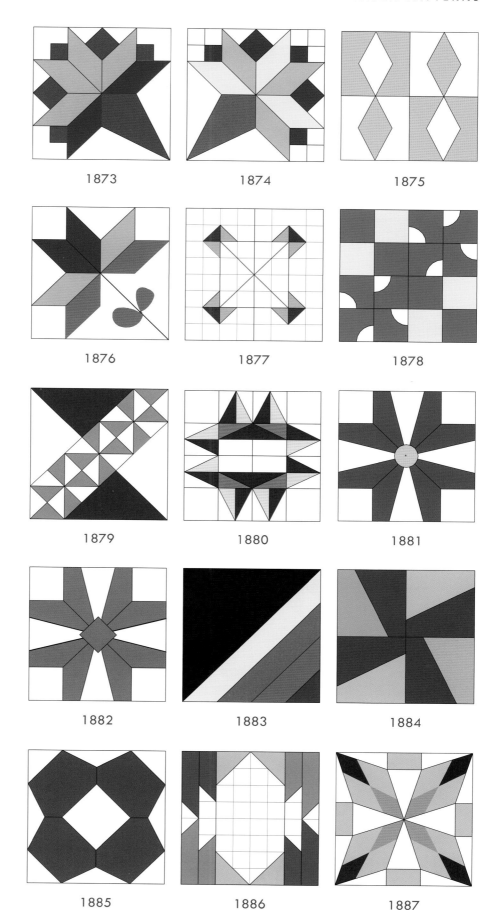

1873      1874      1875

1876      1877      1878

1879      1880      1881

1882      1883      1884

1885      1886      1887

5,500 QUILT BLOCK DESIGNS

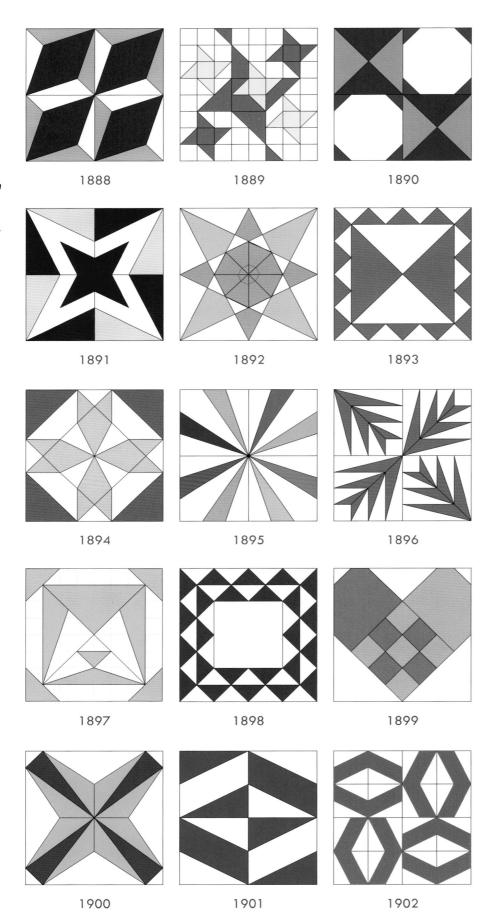

1888

1889

1890

1891

1892

1893

1894

1895

1896

1897

1898

1899

1900

1901

1902

1888 Blue Boutonnieres

1889 Stars Galore, *Clara Buschschulte*, *QN*

1890 Buttons and Bows

1891 Stars and Stripes

1892 Southern Star

1893 Aunt Mary's Double Irish Chain, *CS*

1894 Aimee's Choice

1895 Endless Chain, *LW* Crazy Star, *GD*

1896 Palm Leaf Hosannah

1897 Mystic Emblem

1898 Our Village Green, *1935*

1899 Woven Heart

1900 Wandering Path

1901 Left and Right, *NC, 1935* Chevron

1902 Beg and Borrow, *NC*

1903  Ocean Wave, *OF*

1904  Hummingbird
      Dramatic Patch, *OCS*
      Rock Garden

1905  Fairy Star, *NC*

1906  Double Z, *NC*

1907  Calypso, *Vickie Loh*

1908  Arrowhead
      Laurel Wreath
      Michigan Beauty
      Star of Many Points

1909  Kansas Star

1910  Maltese Cross, *NP*

1911  Black Beauty, *NC*
      Blackford's Beauty, *LAC*
      The Hunt, *FJ*
      Mrs. Smith's Favorite,
       *NCS, 1930*
      Star and Stripe, *NC*
      Stepping Stones, *KCS*

1912  Ruby Roads, *NC*

1913  Evening Star

1914  Jupiter Star

1915  The Spider Web, *KCS*

1916  Morning Star
      Kaleidoscope Quilt

1917  A Spider Web Gone
       Awry
      North Carolina Star

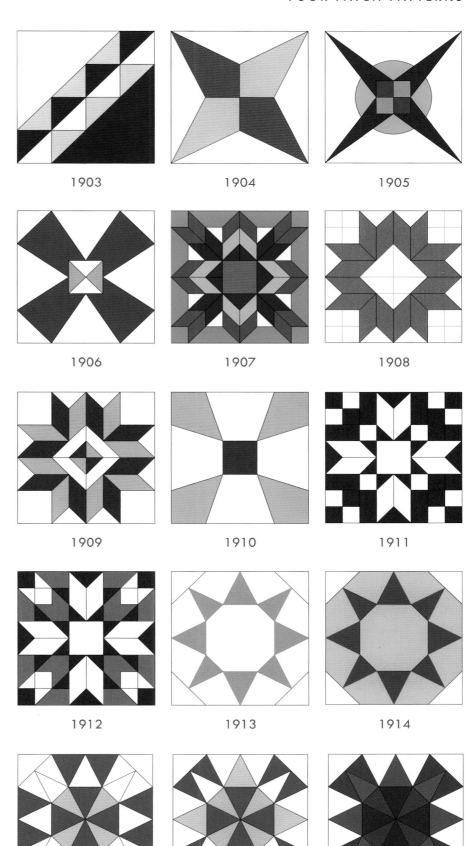

1903      1904      1905

1906      1907      1908

1909      1910      1911

1912      1913      1914

1915      1916      1917

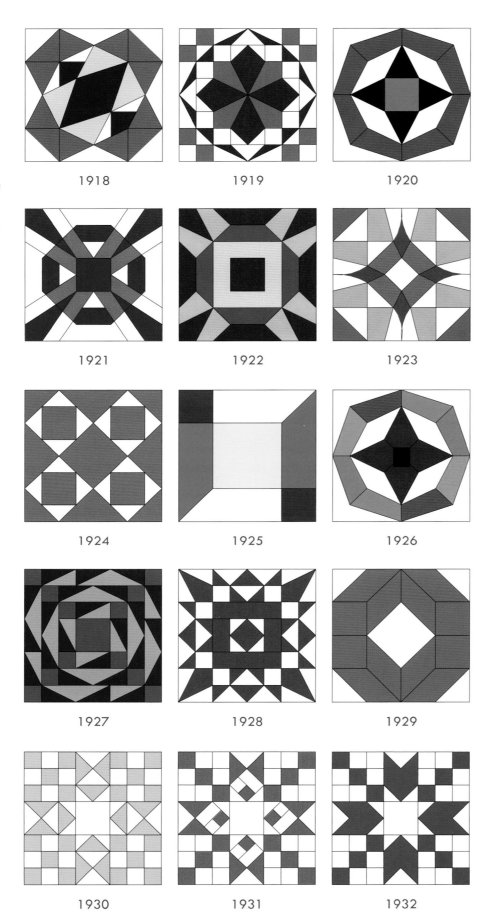

1918    1919    1920

1921    1922    1923

1924    1925    1926

1927    1928    1929

1930    1931    1932

1918   Dove in the Window

1919   Little Giant

1920   A Coverlet in Jewel
       Tones, *KCS*

1921   True Lover's Knot

1922   Satellite

1923   Dogwood, *LW*

1924   Pride of Holland, *FJ*

1925   Unnamed, *OCS*

1926   Star & Crown

1927   Windy City, *QN*

1928   Constellation

1929   Optical Illusion

1930   Winged Nine Patch,
       *KCS*

1931   Arrowhead

1932   Good Cheer
       Stepping Stones

1933 Mountain Meadows

1934 Albany

1935 Black Diamond Quilt Block

1936 Baton Rouge Quilt Block
Good Friends

1937 Summer Star, *KCS*

1938 Arrow Points, *NP*

1939 Arrowhead, *KCS*
The Arrowhead Quilt, *HAS*

1940 Arrowheads

1941 Friendship Star, *OCS*

1942 West Virginia

1943 Sunburst

1944 Springfield, *HH*
Springfield Patch, *LAC*

1945 No Name Star

1946 Peaceful Hours

1947 Diamond Star
Eight Diamonds and a Star, *AMS*
Oriental Star, *NC*

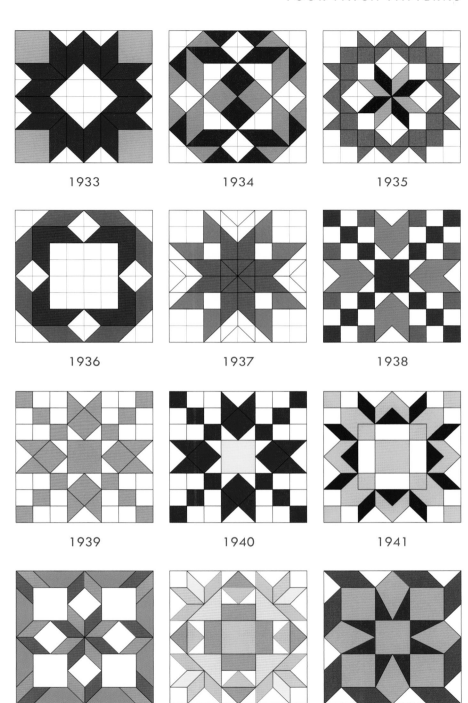

1933     1934     1935

1936     1937     1938

1939     1940     1941

1942     1943     1944

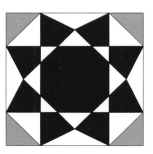
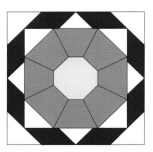

1945     1946     1947

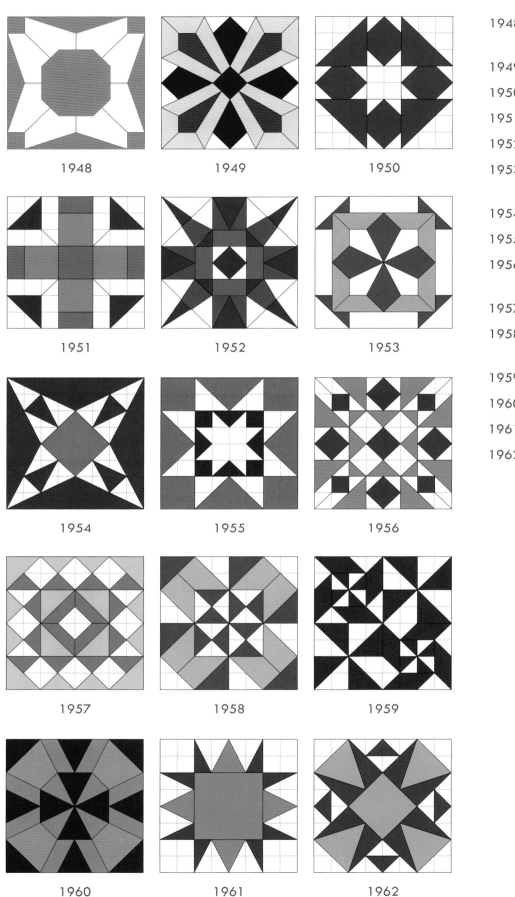

1948   The Name Is Hesper, *KCS*

1949   Album Flower

1950   Goshen Star, *CS*

1951   Watermill

1952   Gem Star, *QM, 1993*

1953   Reminiscences, *HaM,*
          *SSQ, 1983*

1954   Texas Star

1955   Double Star

1956   State of South Carolina
          Cross and Square

1957   Sister Mary's Star

1958   World's Pride Quilt
          Block

1959   Jane's Favorite

1960   Olympia

1961   Dervish Star

1962   1904 Star

1963 Jacob's Ladder
New Double Four
Patch

1964 State House, *NC*
Double Four Patch, *HHJ*
New Four Patch, *1914*

1965 Missouri Windmills,
*QN*

1966 Hither and Yon
Spool

1967 Grandmother's Prize
Puzzle
Housewife

1968 Acorns

1969 Specialty Square, *RMS*,
*SSQ*, *1987*

1970 Memory Chain, *FJ*

1971 Chain Links Quilt, *NC*

1972 Flying Checkers

1973 Good Luck Token

1974 Tulip Twirl, *QM*, *1992*

1975 Salt Lake City

1976 No Name

1977 Old Maid's Ramble,
*LAC*
Double Triangle

1963

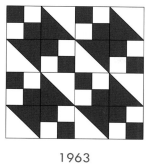
1964

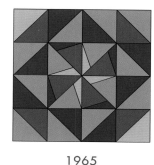
1965

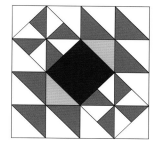
1966

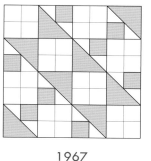
1967

1968

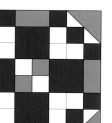
1969

1970

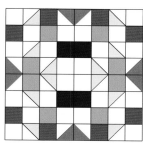
1971

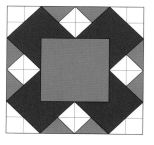
1972

1973

1974

1975

1976

1977

5,500 QUILT BLOCK DESIGNS

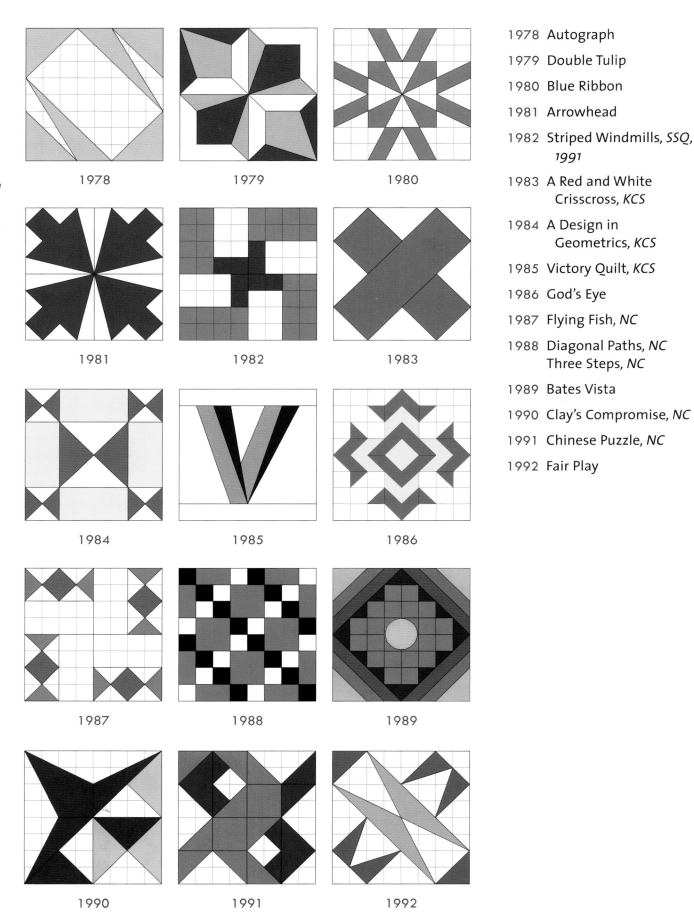

1978 — 1979 — 1980

1981 — 1982 — 1983

1984 — 1985 — 1986

1987 — 1988 — 1989

1990 — 1991 — 1992

1978 Autograph

1979 Double Tulip

1980 Blue Ribbon

1981 Arrowhead

1982 Striped Windmills, *SSQ, 1991*

1983 A Red and White Crisscross, *KCS*

1984 A Design in Geometrics, *KCS*

1985 Victory Quilt, *KCS*

1986 God's Eye

1987 Flying Fish, *NC*

1988 Diagonal Paths, *NC*
Three Steps, *NC*

1989 Bates Vista

1990 Clay's Compromise, *NC*

1991 Chinese Puzzle, *NC*

1992 Fair Play

1993 Whirligig
Farmers' Wife
Double Pinwheel, *NC*

1994 Whirligig

1995 Morning Star

1996 King's Cross
Kaleidoscope
Octagons, *NP*
Semi-Octagon, *HHJ*
Will o the Wisp, *FJ*
Windmill, *KCS*

1997 Double Pinwheel

1998 Starburst, *Arleen Boyd*

1999 Cupid's Arrowpoint

2000 Mary's Squares

2001 Electric Fan

2002 Sister Nan's Cross

2003 Wandering Jew

2004 Spool and Bobbin, *NC,
1936*

2005 Reverse X, *GC*

2006 Missouri Windmills

2007 Harvest Home

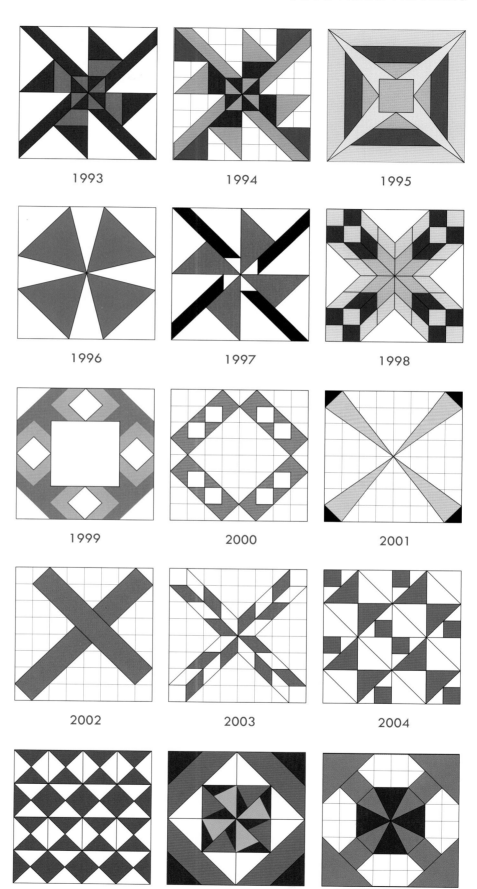

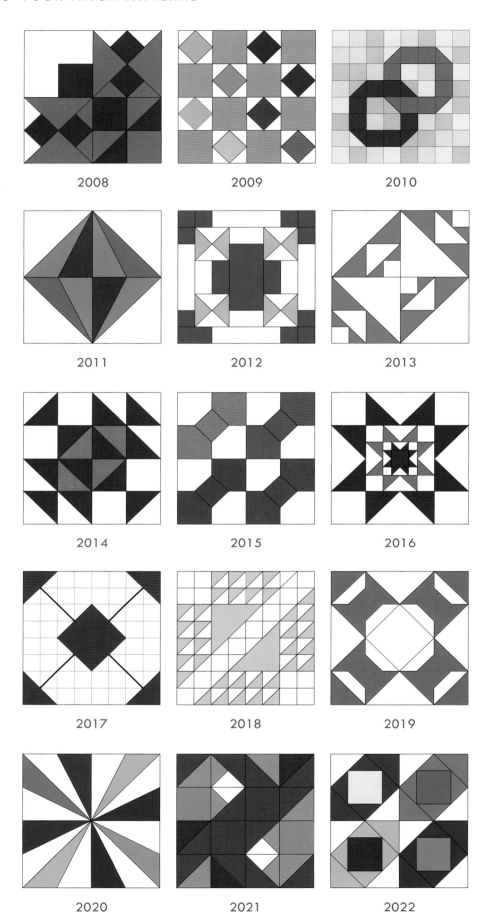

5,500 QUILT BLOCK DESIGNS

2008   2009   2010

2011   2012   2013

2014   2015   2016

2017   2018   2019

2020   2021   2022

2008  Floral Centerpiece

2009  Four Patch Scrap

2010  Wedding Rings

2011  Chinese Lanterns, *NC*

2012  Scottish Cross, *KCS*

2013  Blacks and Whites, *NC*

2014  Flying Dutchman, *NC*

2015  Necktie, *NC*

2016  Stars in a Star

2017  Spider Web

2018  Bismarck
        Primrose Path, *NP*

2019  The Secret Drawer, *KCS*
        Arkansas Traveler
        Spools

2020  Thrifty Wife, *KCS*

2021  Block of Many
        Triangles, *KCS*

2022  This and That, *KCS*

2023 New Star

2024 Army Star

2025 Georgetown Circles

2026 Providence Block

2027 Star

2028 Five Patch
#7222, *OCS*

2029 Wild Geese

2030 Windmill, *FJ*

2031 Arrow Crown

2032 Victorian Butterflies,
*Joyce Timson, SSQ*

2033 The Oak Grove Star
Quilt Block, *KCS*

2034 West Virginia Star

2035 Rising Star

2036 Nicole

2037 The Long Pointed Star,
*KCS*

2023

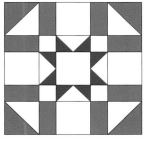

2024

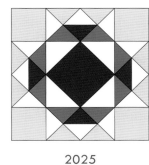

2025

2026

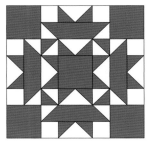

2027

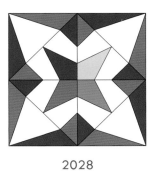

2028

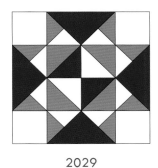

2029

2030

2031

2032

2033

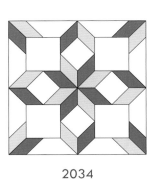

2034

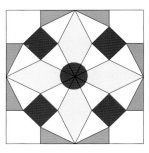

2035

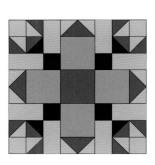

2036

2037

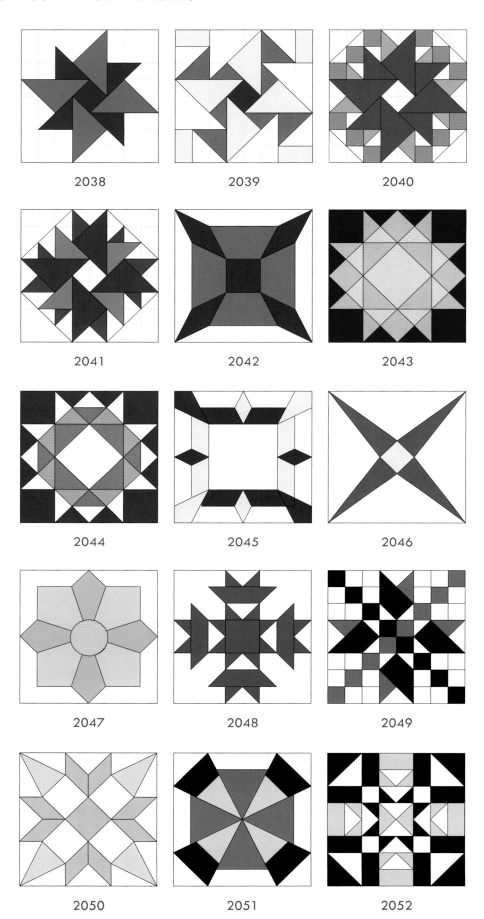

2038

2039

2040

2041

2042

2043

2044

2045

2046

2047

2048

2049

2050

2051

2052

2038 Double Windmill, *NC*

2039 Whirligig, *NC*

2040 Peony and Forget Me Nots, *NC*

2041 Double Aster, *NC*

2042 Square and Diamonds, *KCS*

2043 Square and Triangles, *KCS*

2044 Georgetown Puzzle, *NC*
Memory Fruit, *NC*

2045 A Frame with Diamonds, *KCS*

2046 Hobby Nook, *KCS*

2047 Eight Point Snowflake, *KCS*

2048 Cross and Star

2049 Arrowheads

2050 Prairie Queen

2051 Denver, *HH*
Amazing Windmill, *NC*
Autumn Leaves
Boston Pavement
Farmer's Wife
Merry-Go-Round, *NC*
Mystic Maze, *NC*
Spider Web

2052 Tracks in the Snow, *HaM, SSQ, 1983*

2053 Northern Lights, *NC*

2054 End of Day

2055 Bowtie in Pink and White, *KCS*

2056 Midget Necktie, *KCS*

2057 The World Fair Quilt, *KCS*

2058 A Friendship Block in Diamonds, *KCS*

2059 Thousand Stars Quilt, *KCS*

2060 Parquetry for a Quilt Block, *KCS*

2061 The Windmill

2062 Flying Kite, *KCS*
Pinwheel, *GC*

2063 Kaleidoscope, *NP*

2064 Plaited Block, *NC*

2065 Autumn Stars, *PF*
Golden Chains, *NC*

2066 John's Pinwheel

2067 Path Through the Woods, *CaS*
Linton Pathway

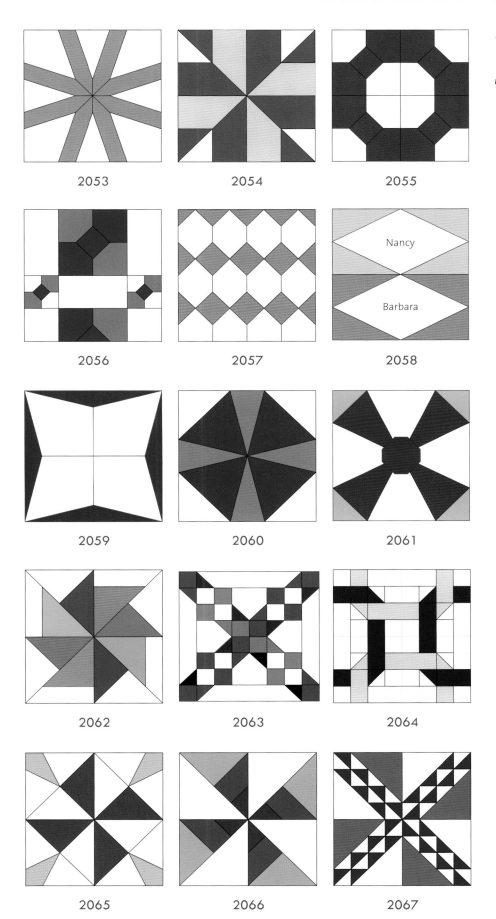

2053    2054    2055

2056    2057    2058

2059    2060    2061

2062    2063    2064

2065    2066    2067

5,500 QUILT BLOCK DESIGNS

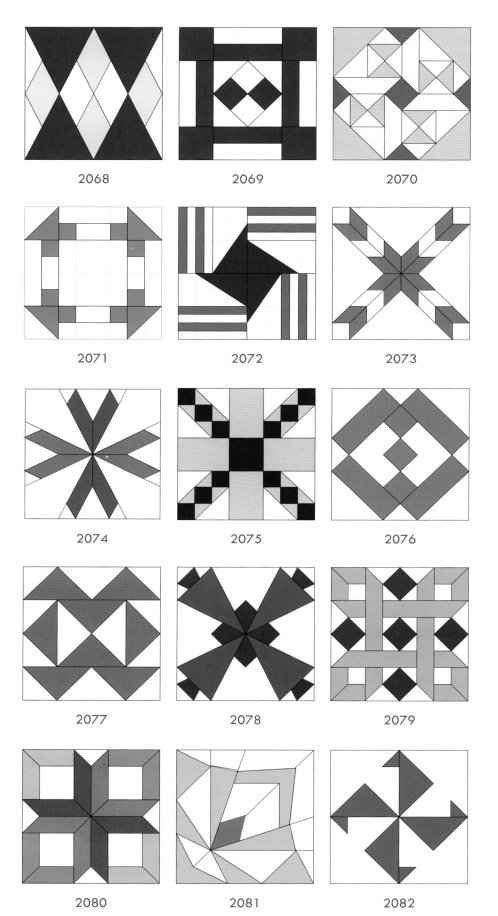

2068
2069
2070

2071
2072
2073

2074
2075
2076

2077
2078
2079

2080
2081
2082

2068  Four Diamonds

2069  Coxey's Camp, *LAC*
       Coxey's Army, *NC*

2070  Spinning Hour Glass, *NC*

2071  Ruins of Jericho, *NC*

2072  The Old Stars and Stripes, *1991*

2073  The Winding Blade

2074  The V Block

2075  Buffalo Ridge, *NC*
       Country Roads, *QW*, *1979*
       Grandmother's Fancy, *CoM*

2076  Board Meeting

2077  No Name Available

2078  Pennsylvania Tree, *HH*

2079  Diamond Knot, *NC*

2080  Box Quilt, *NP*

2081  Queen's Treasure, *OCS*

2082  Lindy's Plane

2083 Stuffed Stockings, *HaM, SSQ, 1983*

2084 Jet Stream

2085 Flying Kites, *MLM, SSQ, 1982*

2086 Tilted Triangles

2087 Nosegay, *NC*
Stepping Stones, *KCS*

2088 Spider Web, *KCS*

2089 Vermont, *NP*

2090 Choices, *MM*

2091 Brickwork

2092 Pineapples

2093 Stepping Stones, *NP*
Road to California, *LAC*
Crossroads, *NCS, 1938*

2094 Odd Fellow's Cross

2095 Railroad

2096 Garden Mosaic

2097 Bowbells, *NC*

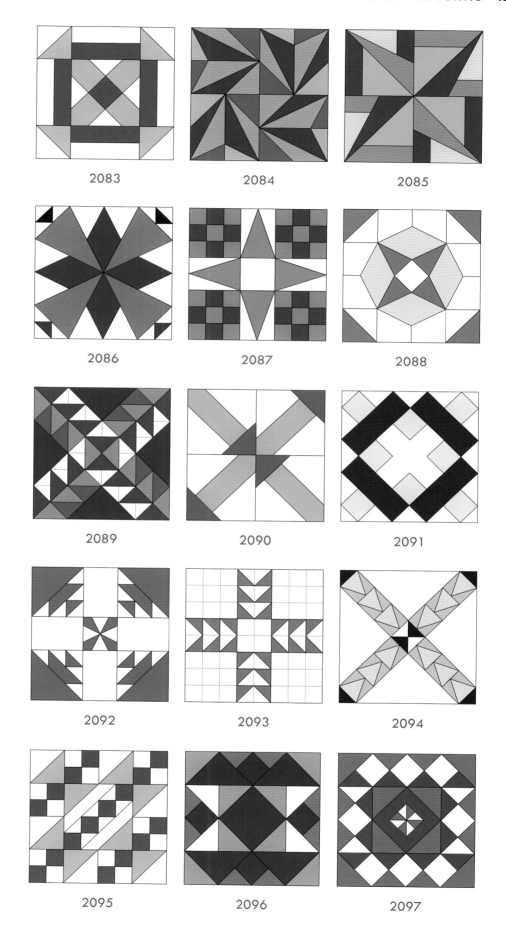

2083  2084  2085

2086  2087  2088

2089  2090  2091

2092  2093  2094

2095  2096  2097

2098 Pine Burr Block

2099 Tulips, *AMS*

2100 Missouri Star

2101 Mississippi Star, *AK*

2102 Blowing in the Wind

2103 Wheel of Fortune

2104 Unnamed, *1880*

2105 Shady Pine

2106 World's Fair

2107 Flyfoot

2108 King's Cross

2109 Arrow Crown

2110 Flowering Cross

2111 Divided Cross

2112 Gothic Pattern

2113 Lena's Choice

2114 Fields and Fences, *QM, 1993*

2115 Flower Bed

2116 Glitter, Glitter

2117 Monterey

2118 Green Mountain Star
Aunt Mary's Star

2119 Crossword Puzzle

2120 Fluffy Patches, *SSQ, 1986*

2121 Fantasy World, *MLM, SSQ, 1986*

2122 Starry Cross

2123 Alpha

2124 Table for Four, *NP*

2125 Watermill, *GC*

2126 Colombian Puzzle

2127 Double Square

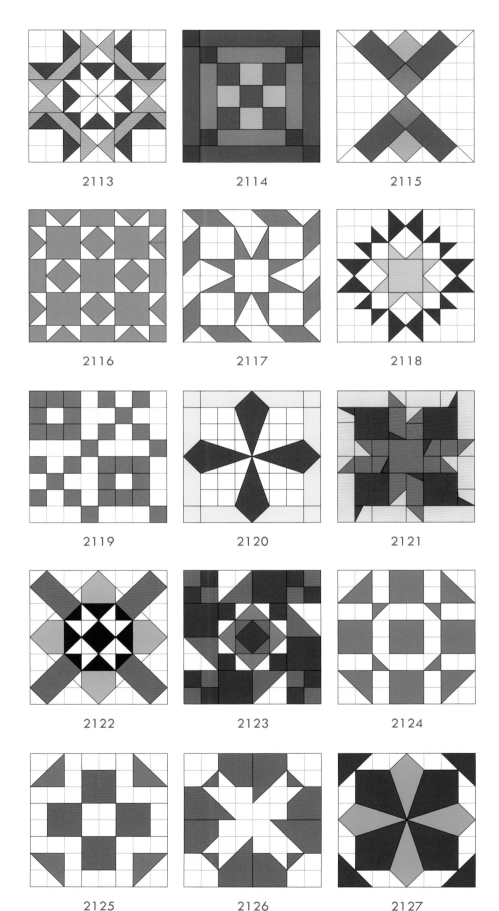

2113

2114

2115

2116

2117

2118

2119

2120

2121

2122

2123

2124

2125

2126

2127

2128 Farmer's Fields

2129 Harbor View

2130 Alaska, *HH*

2131 Crow's Foot, *LAC*
     Arrowheads, *NP*

2132 Signs of Spring, *FJ*

2133 Triple Link Chain, *NC*

2134 Depression, *KCS*

2135 Name Unknown

2136 Mosaic #2, *LAC*

2137 Square on Square, *NP*
     Scrap, *CS*

2138 Broken Crystals

2139 Triangles and Squares

2140 Design for Pariotism,
     *KCS*

2141 Square Diamond

2142 Fox and Geese

2143 Tulip

2144 Double Tulip

2145 Cabbage Rose

2146 Dinah's Choice, *HH*

2147 Baskets (diagonal set)

2148 Lightning

2149 Images

2150 Farmer's Fields

2151 In the Arbor

2152 Chain and Bar

2153 Tumbleweed

2154 Christmas Star

2155 Spider Legs

2156 Nine Patch Variation

2157 Irish Chain

5,500 QUILT BLOCK DESIGNS

2143

2144

2145

2146

2147

2148

2149

2150

2151

2152

2153

2154

2155

2156

2157

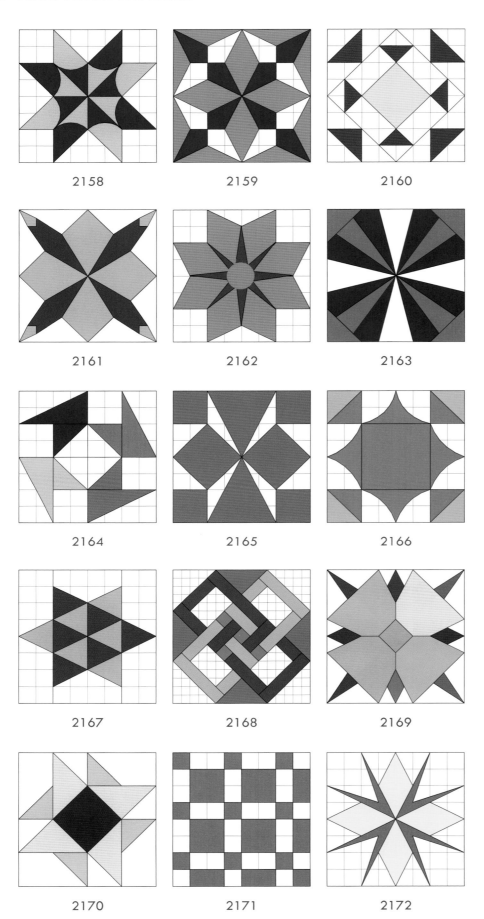

5,500 QUILT BLOCK DESIGNS

2158

2159

2160

2161

2162

2163

2164

2165

2166

2167

2168

2169

2170

2171

2172

2158 Sailor's Joy

2159 Sacramento

2160 Scotch Plaid

2161 Rosepoint

2162 Sunflower

2163 Nova

2164 Fancy Foot

2165 Butterfly in Angles

2166 Cypress

2167 Six Point Star

2168 Lucky Knot, *NC*

2169 Ann's Scrap Quilt,
     *LW, OCS*

2170 Wheat Field, *JM*

2171 Checkers, *NC*

2172 Stars over Texas

2173  Caps for Witches and Dunces, *KCS*

2174  Boise

2175  To Market, to Market

2176  Chalice

2177  Lily of the Field

2178  Rocket Ship

2179  Star and Cross

2180  Beacon Lights

2181  Ohio Star

2182  Midsummer Garden

2183  Chain of Diamonds

2184  Miller's Daughter

2185  Jubilee

2186  Boston Belle

2187  Martha's Choice

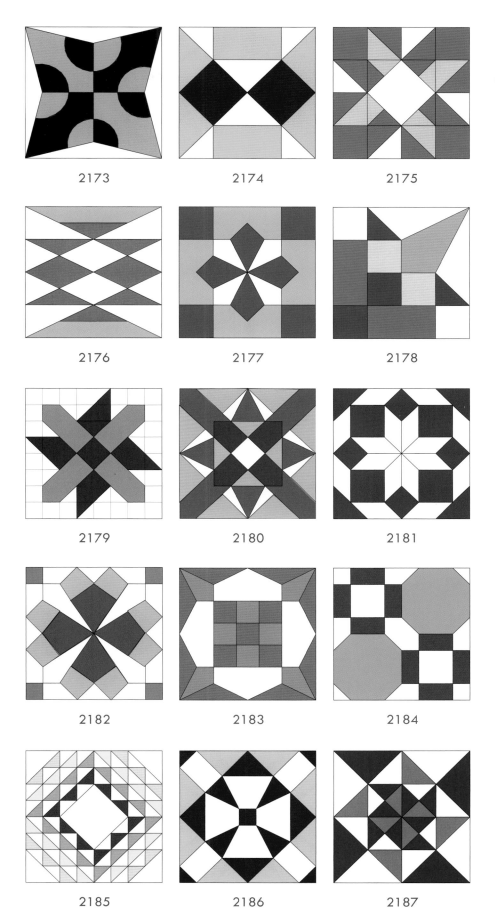

5,500 QUILT BLOCK DESIGNS

2173

2174

2175

2176

2177

2178

2179

2180

2181

2182

2183

2184

2185

2186

2187

5,500 QUILT BLOCK DESIGNS

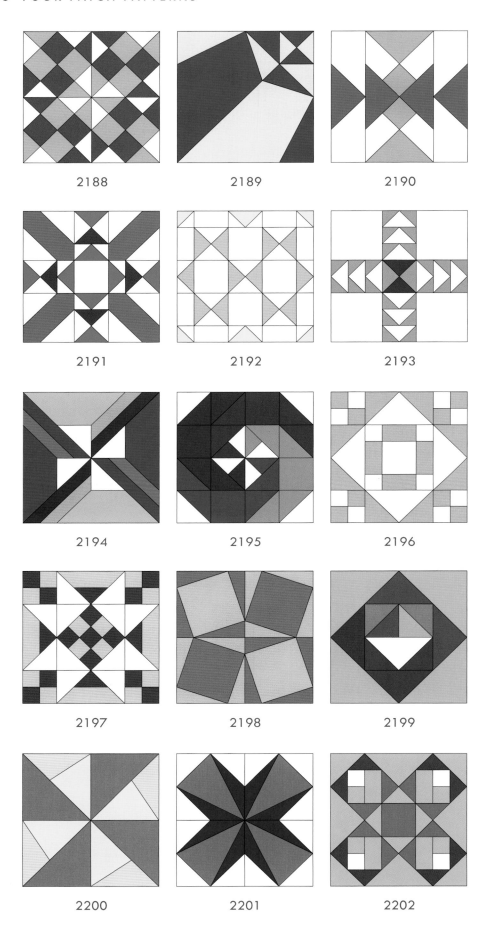

2188

2189

2190

2191

2192

2193

2194

2195

2196

2197

2198

2199

2200

2201

2202

2188 Whirling Squares

2189 Allentown

2190 Road to Damascus, *HH*

2191 Annapolis, *NC*

2192 Washington Star, *AK, 1966*

2193 Jacob's Ladder, *GD*

2194 Moving Fans & Fast Pinwheels, *Dianne Carroll Blue Ribbon Quilts*

2195 Vortex

2196 Valley Falls Square, *SSQ, 1985*

2197 Pieced Star Variation

2198 Square Dance, *QW, 1990*

2199 Anna's Love Quilt, *LCPQ*

2200 Missouri Windmill

2201 Star Fire

2202 Beautiful Crown, *SSQ, 1993*

2203 Cat's Eye, *QW, 1988*

2204 Stars and Squares, *KCS*
      Rising Star

2205 Rising Star Block

2206 Eight Hands Around,
      *LAC*

2207 Lone Star

2208 Primrose Path

2209 Calico Bouquet

2210 Mayflower

2211 Wild Waves

2212 Turkey Giblets, *NC*

2213 Blue Fields Variation,
      *LCPQ*

2214 V-Block, *LAC*
      Victory Quilt
      Churchill Block

2215 Grandmother's Own

2216 Inspiration

2217 Columbia Puzzle

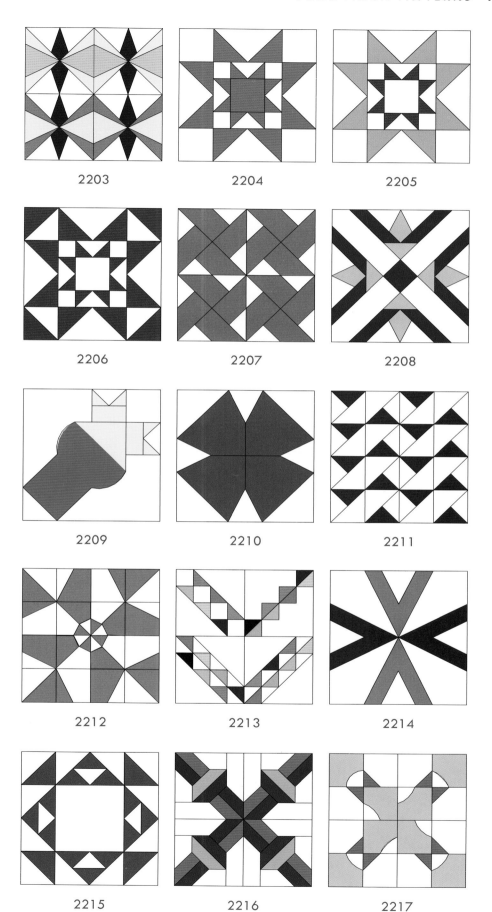

2203     2204     2205

2206     2207     2208

2209     2210     2211

2212     2213     2214

2215     2216     2217

5,500 QUILT BLOCK DESIGNS

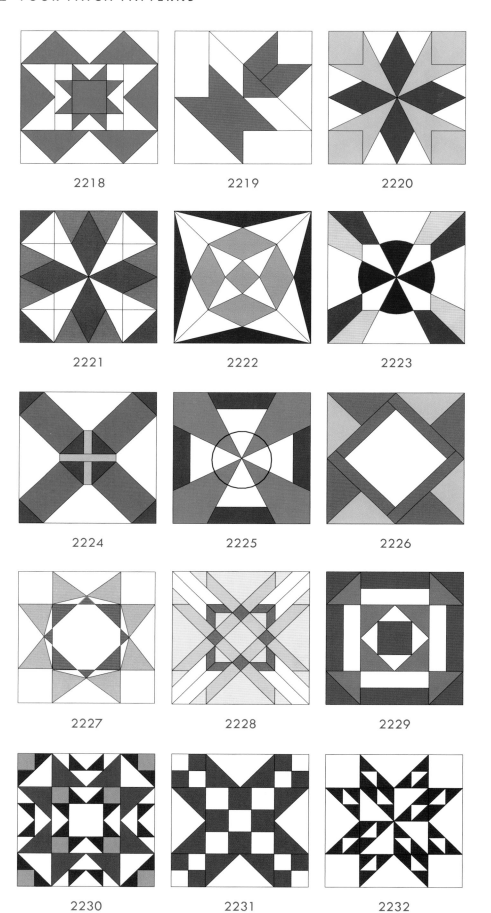

2218

2219

2220

2221

2222

2223

2224

2225

2226

2227

2228

2229

2230

2231

2232

2218 Eight Hands Around

2219 The Disk
Basket of Diamonds, *KCS*
Flower Basket, *KCS*
Flower Pot, *HH*
Jersey Tulip
Rainbow Cactus

2220 Key West

2221 Key West Beauty

2222 Night Before Christmas, *OCS*

2223 Holiday Bells, *OCS*

2224 Double Cross

2225 State of Nevada

2226 Economy Quilt Block

2227 Charm Star, *AMS*

2228 Holiday Crossroads, *HaM, 1983*

2229 Triangles and Stripes, *LAC*

2230 Castle Garden, *NC*

2231 Mrs. Lloyd's Favorite, *CS*

2232 Sparkling Star

2233 Lemon Star

2234 Criss-Cross, *GC*

2235 Locked Star

2236 Pieced Tulips

2237 Sugar Bowl Block

2238 Moynihan's Crusade, *QW, 1985*

2239 Green Cross

2240 Sun and Stars Quilt

2241 Tulips

2242 Squares and Diamonds

2243 Jewel, *GC*

2244 Beacon Lights, *NP*

2245 Colonial Pavement, *OCS*

2246 Shooting Star

2247 Duck Creek Puzzle

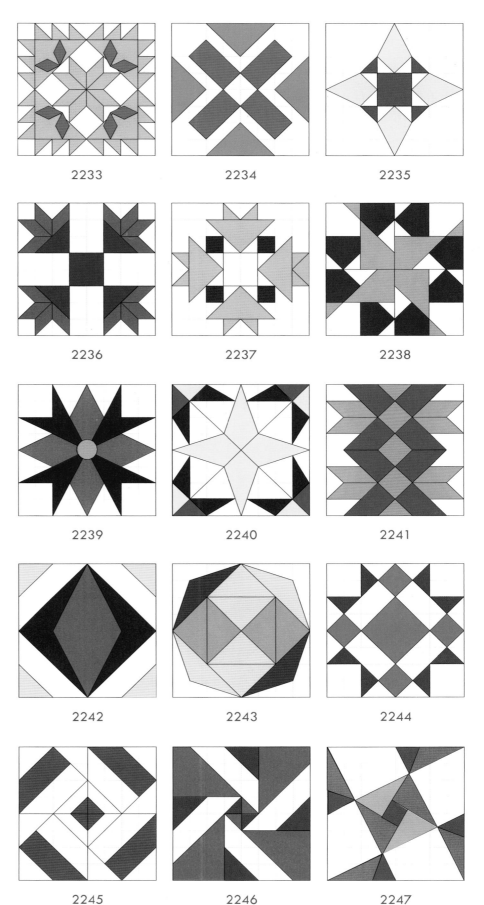

2233     2234     2235

2236     2237     2238

2239     2240     2241

2242     2243     2244

2245     2246     2247

5,500 QUILT BLOCK DESIGNS

2248   2249   2250

2251   2252   2253

2254   2255   2256

2257   2258   2259

2260   2261   2262

2248  Irish Plaid, *NC*

2249  Totem

2250  Irish Puzzle, *LAC*
       Climbing Rose
       Flying Dutchman
       Forest Path
       Indian Trail
       Kansas Troubles
       North Wind
       Old Maid's Ramble
       Prickly Pear
       Rambling Road
       Rambling Rose
       Storm at Sea
       Tangled Tares
       Weather Vane

2251  Land's End, *QN*

2252  Neighborhoods, *MM*

2253  Indian Maize, *NC*

2254  Star of Mystery

2255  Surprise Package, *QEQ,*
       *1991*

2256  Cross of Geneva, *NC*

2257  Geometrical Star Quilt
       Block

2258  Nautilus

2259  Colombian Puzzle, *CS*

2260  April Tulips, *QN*

2261  Girl's Joy, *LAC*
       Maiden's Delight, *NC*

2262  Hobson's Kiss, *NC*

2263  Flower Pot, *GC*

2264  Jewel Star, *AK, 1963*

2265  John F. Kennedy Star, *AK, 1964*

2266  Windmill and Outline

2267  Criss Cross, *FJ*

2268  Full Blown Tulip, *OCS*

2269  Arkansas Diamond, *NC*

2270  Crazy Pieces, *MoM*

2271  Snail's Trail, *LAC*
Journey to California, *KCS*
Ocean Wave
Whirligig Quilt

2272  Four-Four Time, *FJ*

2273  Four Squares, *NC*

2274  Star and Square, *OF, 1894*
Courtyard Square, *AK*

2275  Double Windmill, *NC*

2276  Bacon Patch, *NC*

2277  Manila Quilt Design, *1899*

2263

2264

2265

2266

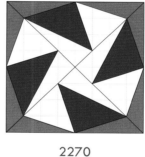

2267

2268

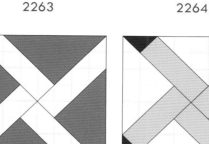

2269

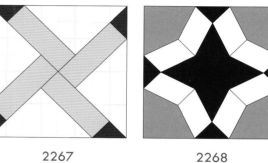

2270

2271

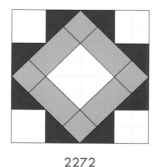

2272

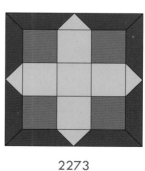

2273

2274

2275

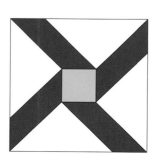

2276

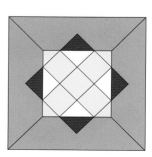

2277

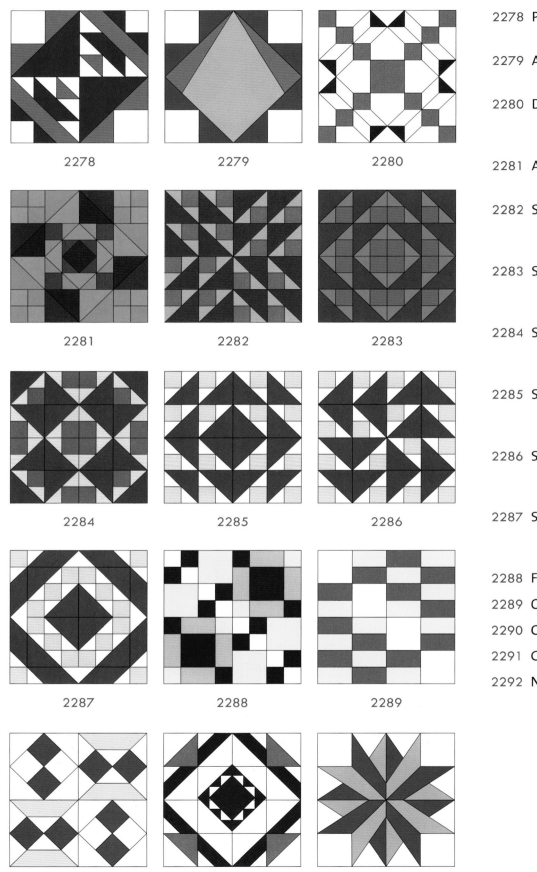

2278

2279

2280

2281

2282

2283

2284

2285

2286

2287

2288

2289

2290

2291

2292

2278 Path to Bethlehem, *HMD, SSQ, 1984*

2279 A Child Is Born, *HMD, SSQ, 1984*

2280 Diamond Cross, *Michelle Clary, SSQ, 1982*

2281 Alpha, *Crea Guarino, SSQ, 1982*

2282 Six Windows of Sunshine, Window #1, *QN*

2283 Six Windows of Sunshine, Window #2, *QN*

2284 Six Windows of Sunshine, Window #3, *QN*

2285 Six Windows of Sunshine, Window #4, *QN*

2286 Six Windows of Sunshine, Window #5, *QN*

2287 Six Windows of Sunshine, Window #6, *QN*

2288 Four Squares, *NC*

2289 Ohio Trail, *NC*

2290 Conventional

2291 Golden Stairs, *LW, OCS*

2292 North Star, *LW, OCS*

2293 Wheels, *PF*

2294 Taking Wing, *QN*

2295 Whirling Star, *LW, OCS*

2296 Star and Crescent, *KCS*
 Alaska Chinook, *NC*
 Compass
 Four Winds, *NP*
 Friendship Medley
  Quilt
 King's Crown
 Lucky Star
 Star Crescent
 Star of the Four Winds
 Star of the West

2297 Four Leaf Clover, *NC*

2298 Florentine Diamond,
 *CS*

2299 Diamond Solitaire, *WB*

2300 Arkansas Traveler
 Travel Star

2301 Diamond Chain, *NC*
 Linked Diamonds

2302 A Rosette of Points,
 *KCS*

2303 Riviera, *NC*

2304 Mountain Star, *QN*
 Stars and Stripes, *LCPQ*

2305 New Star, *AK*

2306 Shooting Stars, *NC*

2307 Ohio, *HH*
 Ohio Star
 State of Ohio, *HM*

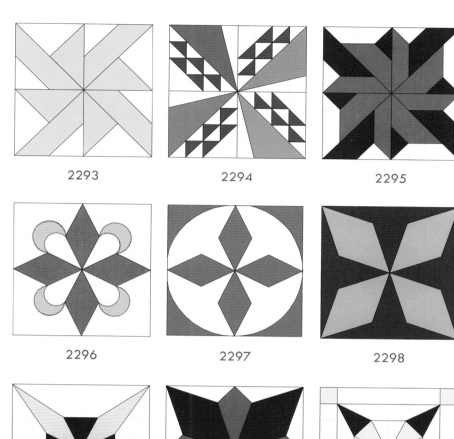

2293

2294

2295

2296

2297

2298

2299

2300

2301

2302

2303

2304

2305

2306

2307

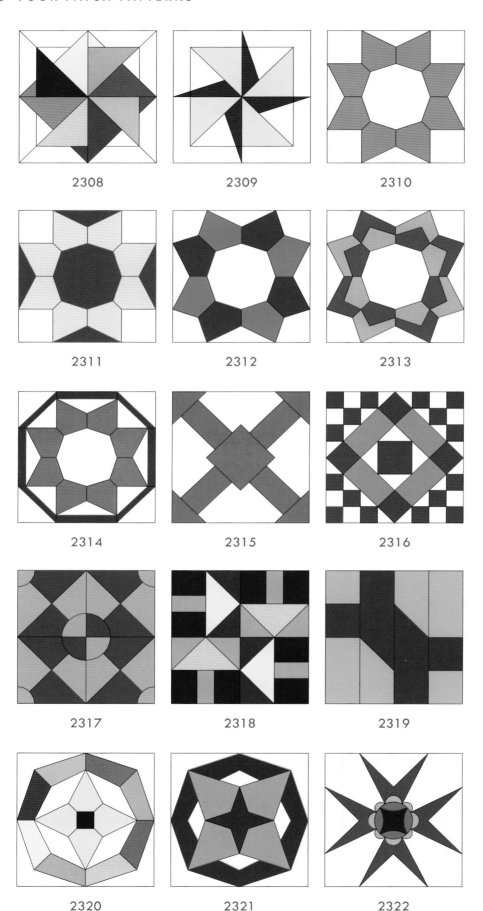

2308 Spinning Color Wheel, *QN*

2309 Pinwheel Parade, *AK, 1966*

2310 Friendship Star, *KCS, 1933*
Alma's Choice, *NC*

2311 Missouri Daisy, *KCS*

2312 Ring Around the Rosy, *HH*

2313 Ring Around the Rosy, *HH*
Mother's Choice, *KCS*

2314 Sunflower Quilt, *1900*

2315 I Do

2316 Unnamed, *GLB, 1858*

2317 Lansing

2318 Campaign Trail, *QN*

2319 Millie's Quilt

2320 Star and Crown

2321 Drucilla's Delight

2322 North Star

2323  3D Nine Patch

2324  Buried Treasure

2325  St. Valentine

2326  Topaz Trail (8x10), *NC*

2327  Hide and Seek

2328  Wild Goose Chase

2329  Rolling Stone

2330  Satellite

2331  Diamonds, *AB, OCS*

2332  MacKenzie's Square,
      *NC*

2333  Alabama Rambler, *NC*

2334  Pieced Flower, *QW*

2335  Colombian Puzzle

2336  Roads to Oklahoma
      Crossed Roads to
      Oklahoma

2337  Cul-de-Sac
      Neighborhood
      Our Neighborhood

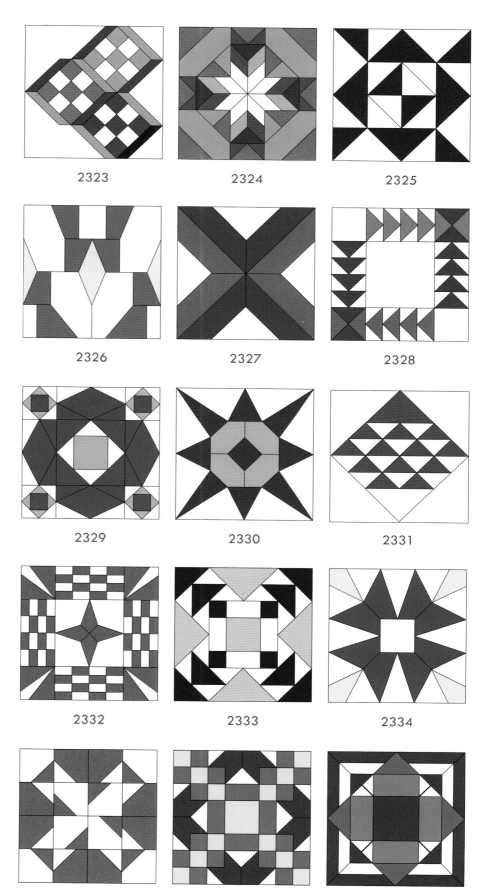

2323          2324          2325

2326          2327          2328

2329          2330          2331

2332          2333          2334

2335          2336          2337

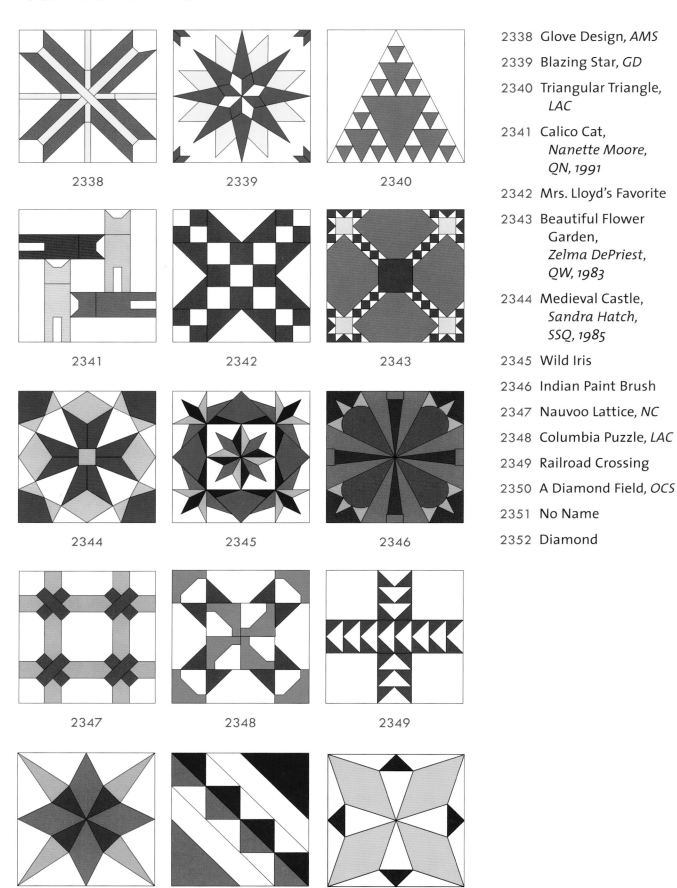

2338

2339

2340

2341

2342

2343

2344

2345

2346

2347

2348

2349

2350

2351

2352

2338 Glove Design, *AMS*

2339 Blazing Star, *GD*

2340 Triangular Triangle, *LAC*

2341 Calico Cat, *Nanette Moore, QN, 1991*

2342 Mrs. Lloyd's Favorite

2343 Beautiful Flower Garden, *Zelma DePriest, QW, 1983*

2344 Medieval Castle, *Sandra Hatch, SSQ, 1985*

2345 Wild Iris

2346 Indian Paint Brush

2347 Nauvoo Lattice, *NC*

2348 Columbia Puzzle, *LAC*

2349 Railroad Crossing

2350 A Diamond Field, *OCS*

2351 No Name

2352 Diamond

2353 Ozark Trail

2354 Annamae's Star

2355 Star and Cone

2356 Laced Star

2357 Shoemaker's Puzzle

2358 Butterfly

2359 Star of the West

2360 Love Doves (reverse second block to face first), *SSQ, 1993*

2361 Flags and Ships (8x6 grid)

2362 Ancient Nine Patch

2363 Arkansas Traveller

2364 Windy City, *JM*

2365 Stars in a Star Variation

2366 Four Patch Chain

2367 Lori's Star, *Wanda Sturrock*

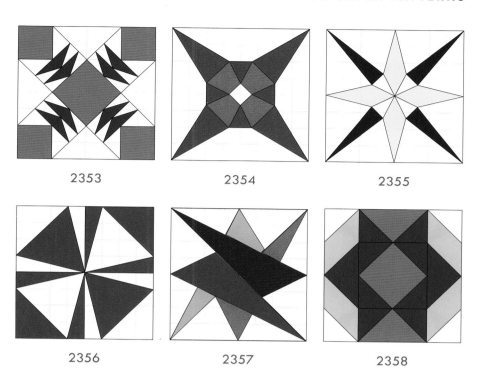

2353
2354
2355

2356

2357

2358

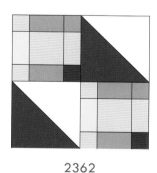
2359

2360
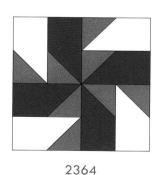
2361

2362
2363
2364

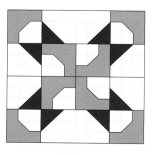
2365

2366

2367

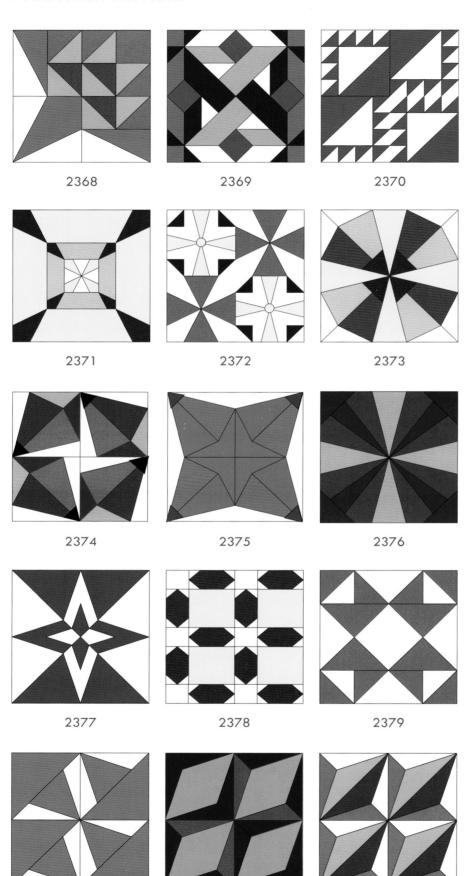

2368

2369

2370

2371

2372

2373

2374

2375

2376

2377

2378

2379

2380

2381

2382

2368 Nosegay, *SSQ, 1987*

2369 Razzle Dazzle, *Judy Rehme, QW, 1986*

2370 Flamingo's Flight, *SSQ*

2371 Prisms, *Caldelina Schumann, QW, 1989*

2372 Pink Dogwood, *Ruby Hinson Duncan, QW, 1987*

2373 Parasol, *MLM, QW*

2374 Parasol Variation, *MLM, QW*

2375 Parasol Variation 2, *MLM, QW*

2376 Nova, *SSQ, 1987*

2377 Natchez Star

2378 Mother's Morning Star, *QW*

2379 Mosaic, *LAC*

2380 Dilemma, *QWO*

2381 Cosmic Cube, *MM*

2382 Art Deco Tulip, *MM*

2383 Helping Hands, *RMS, SSQ, 1987*

2384 Boardwalk, *QN, 1985*

2385 Beacon

2386 Beyond the Stars

2387 Latticework
Kentucky Chain

2388 High Noon

2389 Heavenly Stars, *QN, 1988*

2390 Stars and Arrows

2391 Name Unknown

2392 Garden Square Block

2393 Grandfather's Choice

2394 Vestibule

2395 Cross and Square

2396 Love's Dream (heart appliqué in center square), *SSQ, 1987*

2397 Duck Wheel,
*Carol Bruce*

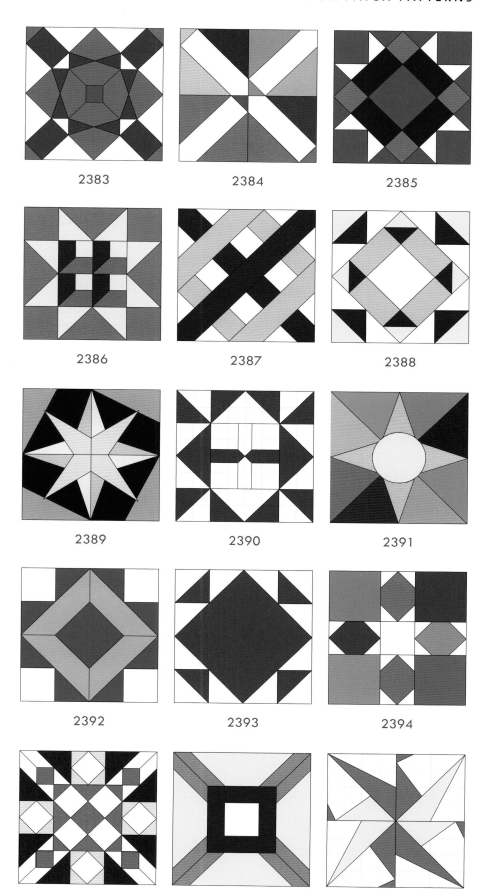

2383

2384

2385

2386

2387

2388

2389

2390

2391

2392

2393

2394

2395

2396

2397

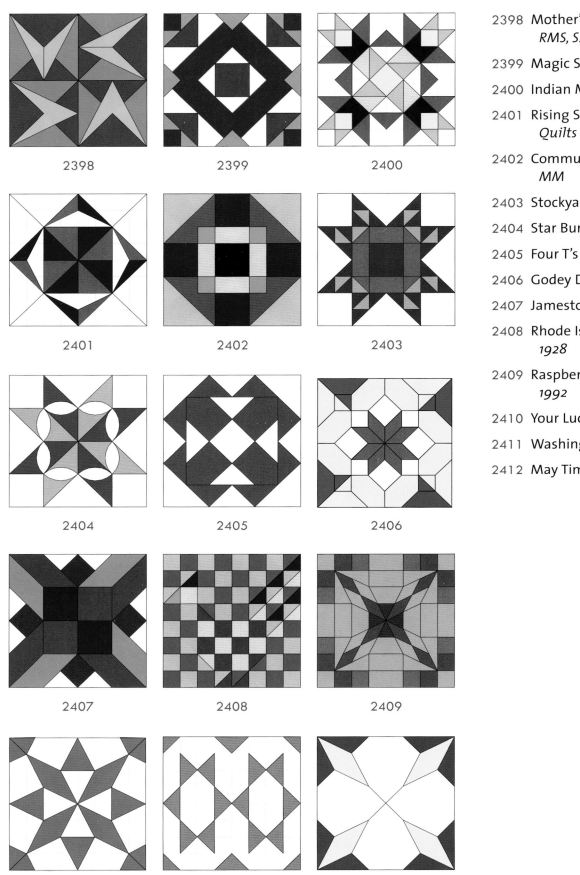

2398
2399
2400

2401
2402
2403

2404
2405
2406

2407
2408
2409

2410
2411
2412

2398 Mother's Dilemma, *RMS, SSQ*

2399 Magic Squares

2400 Indian Maize

2401 Rising Star, *QW Star Quilts*

2402 Community Center, *MM*

2403 Stockyard's Star

2404 Star Burst Quilt

2405 Four T's

2406 Godey Design

2407 Jamestown Square, *NC*

2408 Rhode Island Red, *NM, 1928*

2409 Raspberry Parfait, *QM, 1992*

2410 Your Lucky Star, *OCS*

2411 Washington Star

2412 May Time Quilt, *WB*

2413 Double Twist Star
Block

2414 Cornhusker's Star,
*Jan Stehlik, LCPQ*

2415 Space Station, *Mr.
Leslie Robson, SSQ*

2416 Diamond Solitaire,
*AMS*

2417 Tulip Garden,
*Mrs. Eldon Bauer,
QN, 1970*

2418 Whirligig

2419 Castles in Spain, *NP*

2420 Texas Two Step

2421 Patience Corners, *LAC*

2422 Twist Patchwork

2423 Geometric

2424 T-Square

2425 Improved Nine Patch

2426 Aunt Abbie's Own

2427 Geometric Album

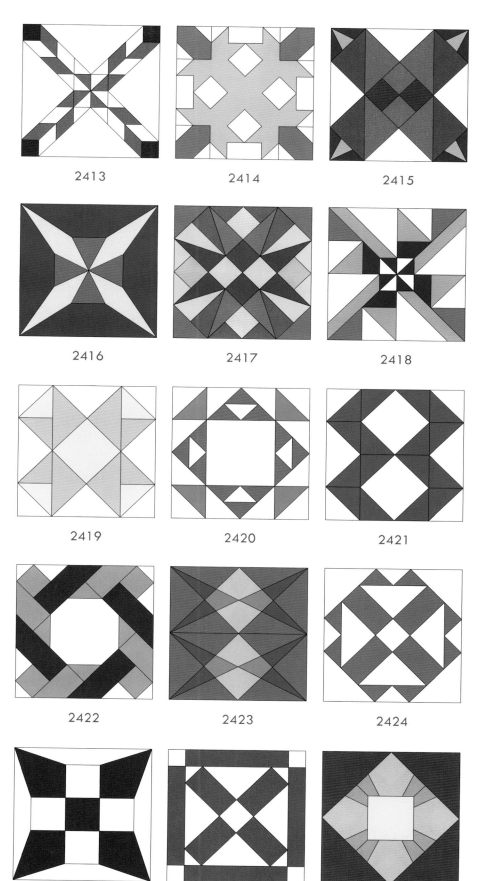

2413

2414

2415

2416

2417

2418

2419

2420

2421

2422

2423

2424

2425

2426

2427

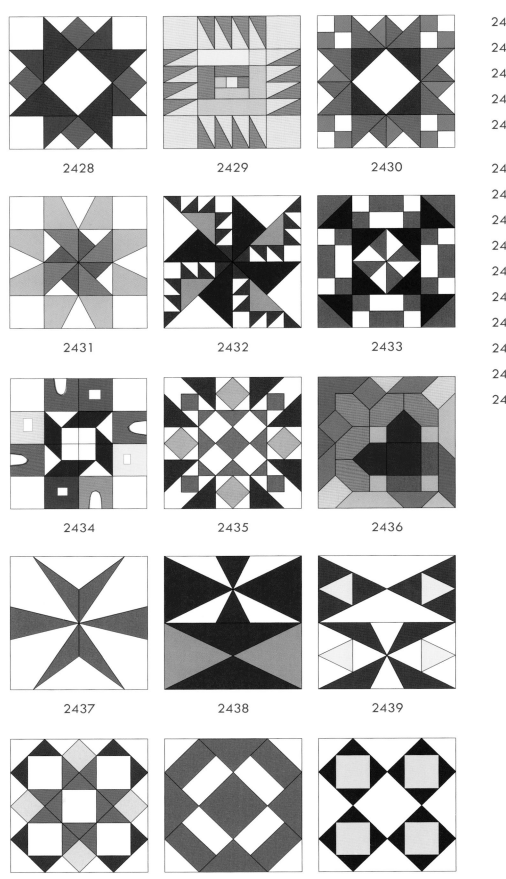

2428 | 2429 | 2430

2431 | 2432 | 2433

2434 | 2435 | 2436

2437 | 2438 | 2439

2440 | 2441 | 2442

2428 Home Grown

2429 Friends & Family, *RMS*

2430 Use It All

2431 Telluride Puzzle, *QN*

2432 Kansas Troubles Variation

2433 Secret Passage

2434 Country Village, *QW*

2435 Cross and Square

2436 Crusader's Heart

2437 The Star Fish (6x8), *NC*

2438 Whirlwind, *WW*

2439 42nd Street

2440 Federal Square, *NC*

2441 Grecian Square

2442 The Star and Block, *LCPQ, 1979*

2443 Godey Design

2444 Saw Toothed Star, *GH*
Single Star, *GH*

2445 Free Trade, *KCS*

2446 Galaxy

2447 Lisa's Choice

2448 Charm Quilt
Dog Bone

2449 Scrap Bag Squares, *QN*

2450 The North Star, *KCS*

2451 The Four Corners, *NC*

2452 Rose Garden, *NC*

2453 Zig-Zag, *WW*

2454 Shepherd's Crossing,
*KCS*
Four Square, *NC*
Grandmother's Own,
*LAC*

2455 Morning Patch, *LAC*

2456 Ray, *NC*

2457 Tete-A-Tete, *NC*

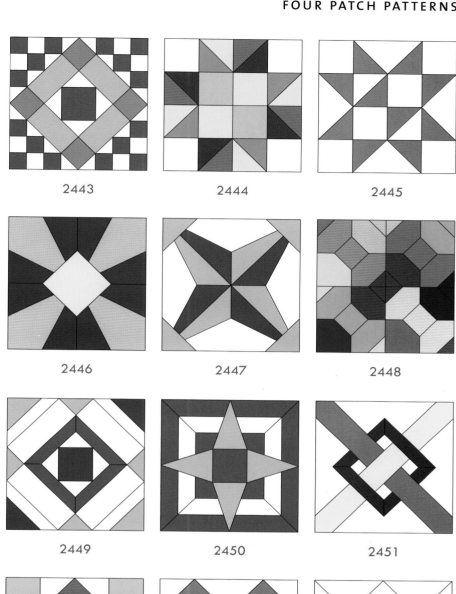

2443  2444  2445

2446  2447  2448

2449  2450  2451

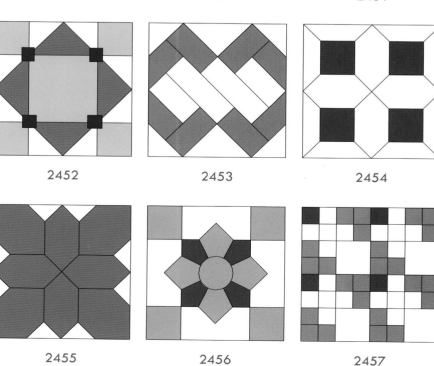

2452  2453  2454

2455  2456  2457

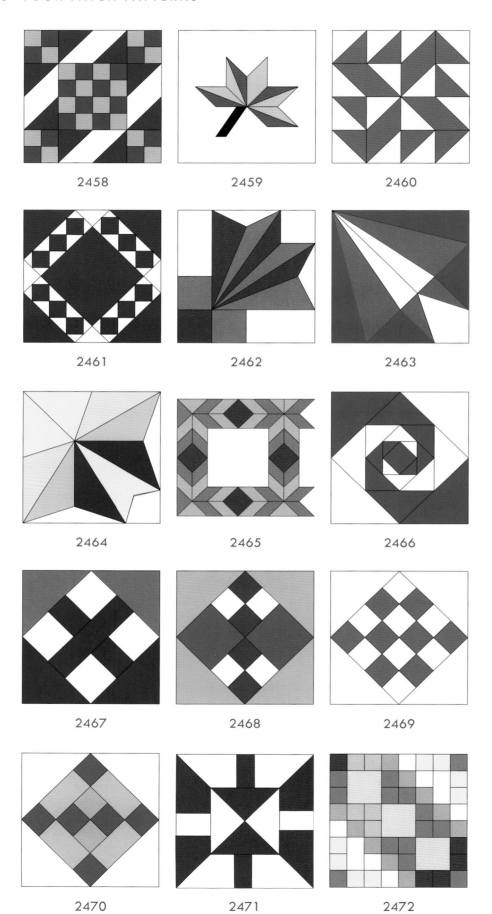

2458  Sunny Lanes, *NP*

2459  Autumn Leaves, *QWB*, *1976*

2460  Rosie's Purina Whirligig

2461  Blue Fields

2462  Victorian Fan, *SSQ*, *1982*

2463  First Morning Rays, *SSQ*, *1982*

2464  Starburst, *SSQ*, *1982*

2465  Cupid's Arrow Point

2466  Virginia Reel, *MoM* Pig's Tail, *MoM*

2467  Pattern Without a Name, *NC*

2468  Improved Four Patch

2469  Kansas Dugout

2470  Lola, *AK*

2471  Twin Darts, *FJ*

2472  Attic Stairs, *NC*

2473 Brickwork, *MM*

2474 Arrowhead Puzzle
(continuous design)

2475 Pieced Heart

2476 Irish Spring

2477 Stacked Stars

2478 Banner Quilt, *OCS*

2479 Hedgework

2480 Ozark Mountains, *NC*

2481 Flying Geese, *NC*

2482 Cross and Crown

2483 Spinning L

2484 Birds and Kites, *NC*

2485 The Chieftain, *NC*

2486 Windmill, *AMS*

2487 Day and Night, *OCS*

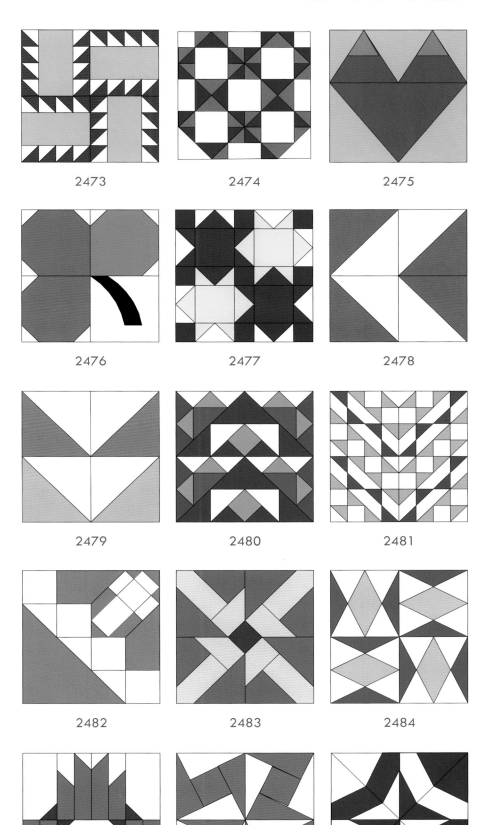

2473     2474     2475

2476     2477     2478

2479     2480     2481

2482     2483     2484

2485     2486     2487

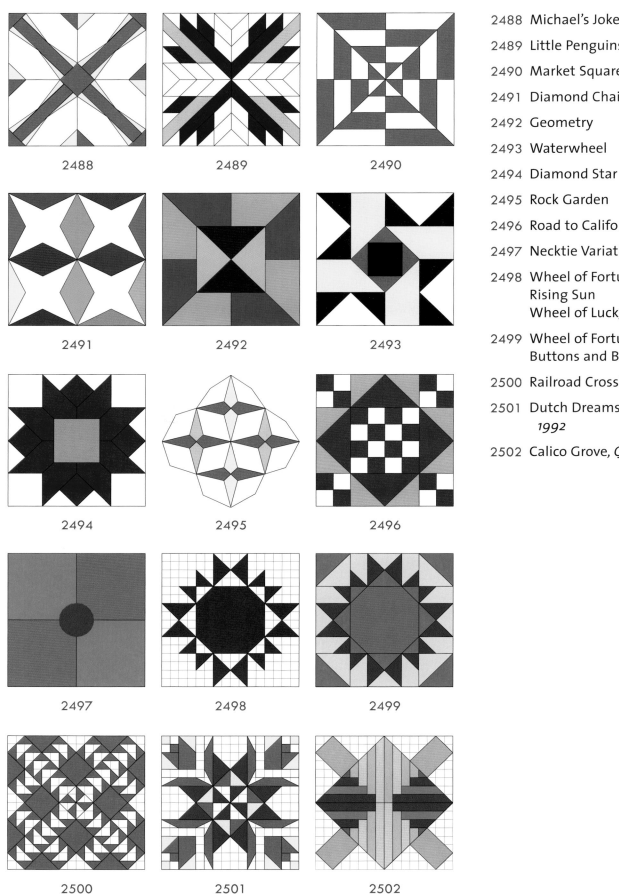

2488

2489

2490

2491

2492

2493

2494

2495

2496

2497

2498

2499

2500

2501

2502

2488 Michael's Joke

2489 Little Penguins, *NC*

2490 Market Square, *NC*

2491 Diamond Chain

2492 Geometry

2493 Waterwheel

2494 Diamond Star

2495 Rock Garden

2496 Road to California

2497 Necktie Variation

2498 Wheel of Fortune, *LAC*
Rising Sun
Wheel of Luck, *NC*

2499 Wheel of Fortune
Buttons and Bows

2500 Railroad Crossing

2501 Dutch Dreams, *QM*,
*1992*

2502 Calico Grove, *QM*, *1992*

2503 Plum Island Compass

2504 Season's Joy, *HaM, SSQ, 1983*

2505 Reindeer on the Roof, *HaM, SSQ, 1983*

2506 Starry Path, *AB, OCS*

2507 Morning Star

2508 Bossburg Wonder

2509 Sitka Quilt Block

2510 Star of the Night

2511 Sixteen Patch

2512 Aunt Lucinda's Double Irish Chain
     Aunt Lucinda's Quilt Block

2513 Sue's Delight

2514 Footbridge

2515 Candles

2516 Sunburst

2517 World's Fair

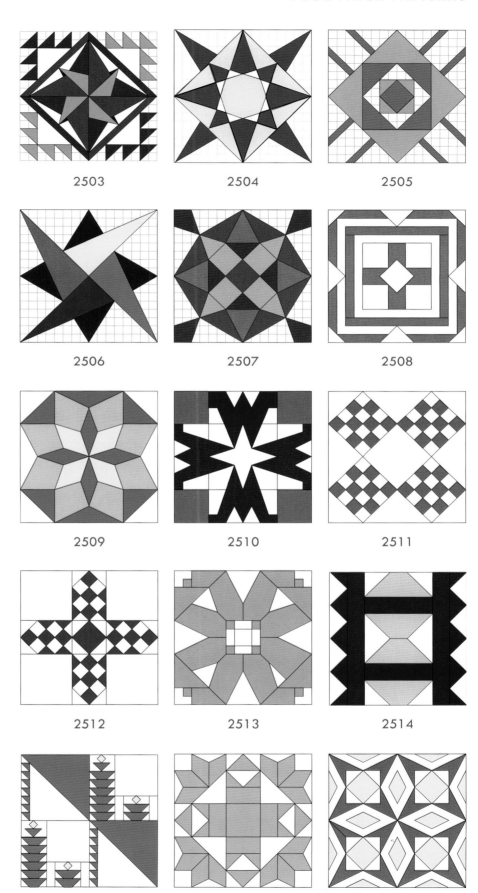

2503　　2504　　2505

2506　　2507　　2508

2509　　2510　　2511

2512　　2513　　2514

2515　　2516　　2517

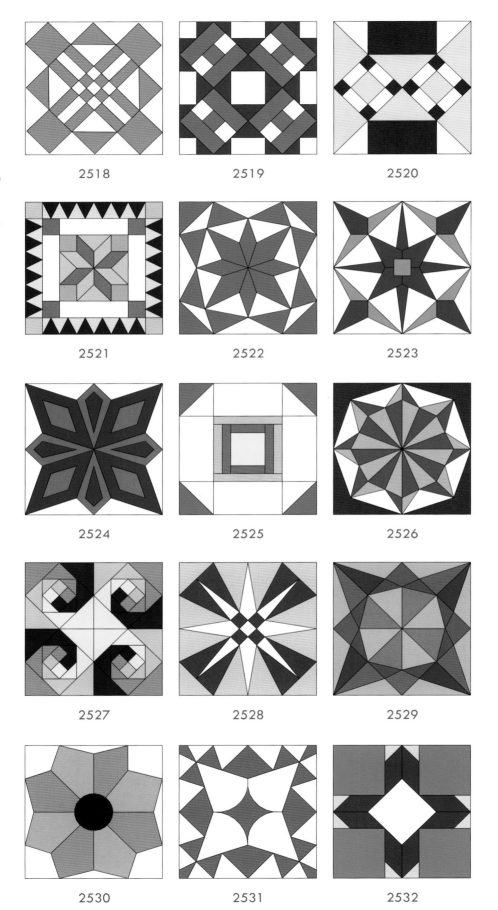

2518

2519

2520

2521

2522

2523

2524

2525

2526

2527

2528

2529

2530

2531

2532

2518 Sonnie's Playhouse

2519 Five Square

2520 Peace and Plenty

2521 Old Spanish Tile

2522 Western Spy

2523 West Virginia

2524 Star of Empire

2525 Yankee Charm

2526 Parasol

2527 Galaxy

2528 Santa's Guiding Star, *AMS, 1931*

2529 Fitz's Phenomena, *Karen Fitzgerald, QW, 1982*

2530 Eight Points in a Square, *KCS*

2531 Radiant Star

2532 Leaves and Flowers, *KCS*

2533  Wild Goose Chase

2534  Chrysanthemum Block

2535  Spinning Star

2536  Mayflower, *QN, 1988*

2537  Broken Crystals

2538  Spider Web

2539  North Star, *HMD* and
       *SSQ, 1984*

2540  South Carolina, *HH*

2541  Railroad Crossing, *QN*

2542  Stellar Reflections, *QW,
       1991*

2543  Glory Vine, *NC*

2544  Wild Iris, *QN, 1992*

2545  Stripes & Stars, *QM,
       1994*

2546  Missouri's Gateway
       Star, *AK*

2547  Enigma, *NC*

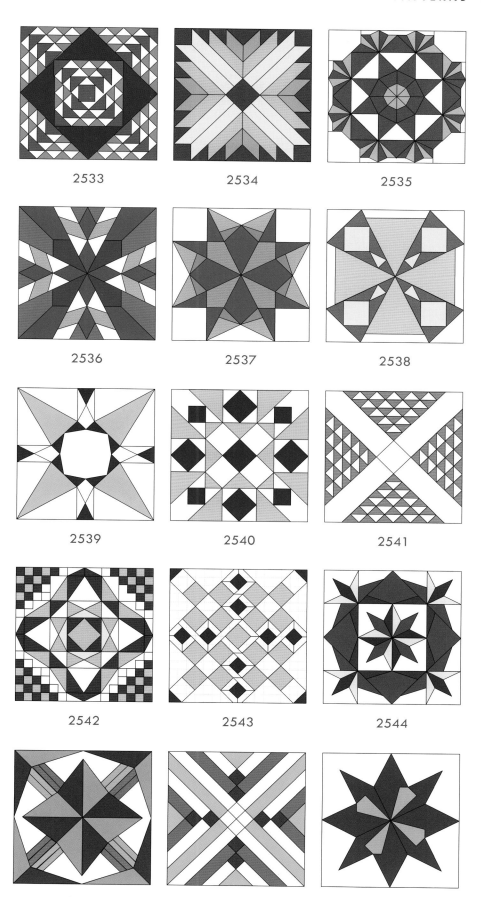

2533  2534  2535

2536  2537  2538

2539  2540  2541

2542  2543  2544

2545  2546  2547

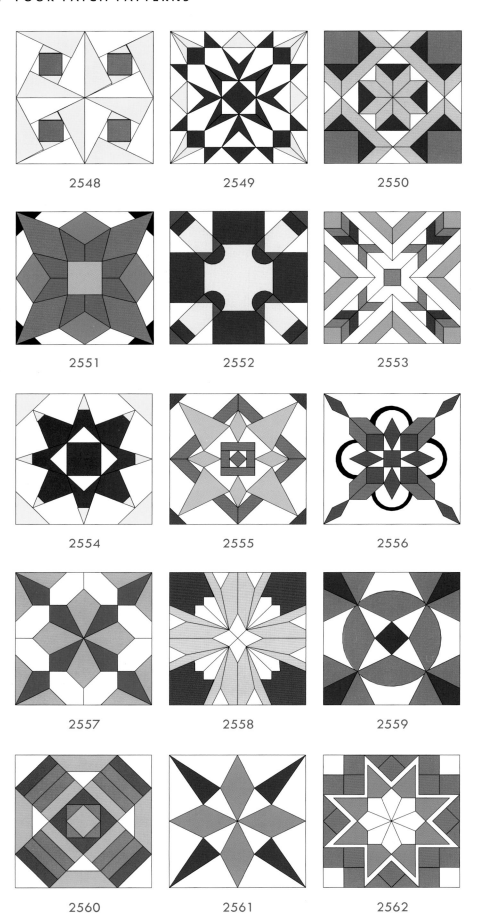

2548

2549

2550

2551

2552

2553

2554

2555

2556

2557

2558

2559

2560

2561

2562

2548 Kaleidoscope, *FJ*

2549 Constellation, *NC*

2550 Magic Carpet

2551 Sea & Shadows

2552 Starry Pavement, *OCS*

2553 Persian Star

2554 Space Ships, *QN*

2555 Stars and Triangles

2556 Bachelor's Puzzle, *GD*

2557 Print and Plain, *FJ*

2558 Star of the Night, *HH*

2559 Rose in Summer, *OCS*

2560 Garden Gazebo,
    *Rhoda Goldberg*

2561 Star and Cone, *PF*

2562 Plaid Star

2563 Twinkling Star, *NC*

2564 Morning Star, *LW, OCS*

2565 Rising Star, *LW, OCS*

2566 Enigma Star

2567 Connecticut Yankee

2568 Dutch Mill

2569 Kitchen Woodbox

2570 Lattice Square
     Interwoven Puzzle
     Lattice Strips

2571 Twisted Thread Box
     Twisted Spool Box
     Twisted Spools
     Twisting Spool

2572 Rock Garden, *AMS*

2573 Scottish Cross

2574 Shooting Star

2575 State Fair Block

2576 Tulip and Star

2577 Desert Rose, *NC*

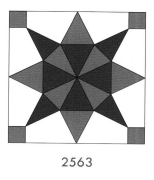

2563

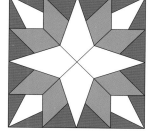

2564

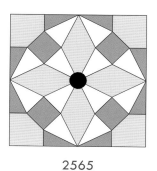

2565

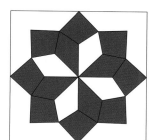

2566

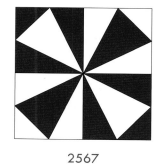

2567

2568

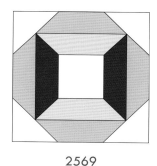

2569

2570

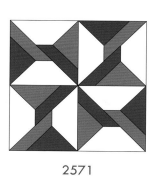

2571

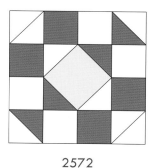

2572

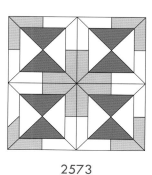

2573

2574

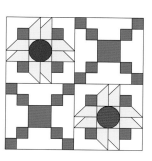

2575

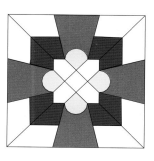

2576

2577

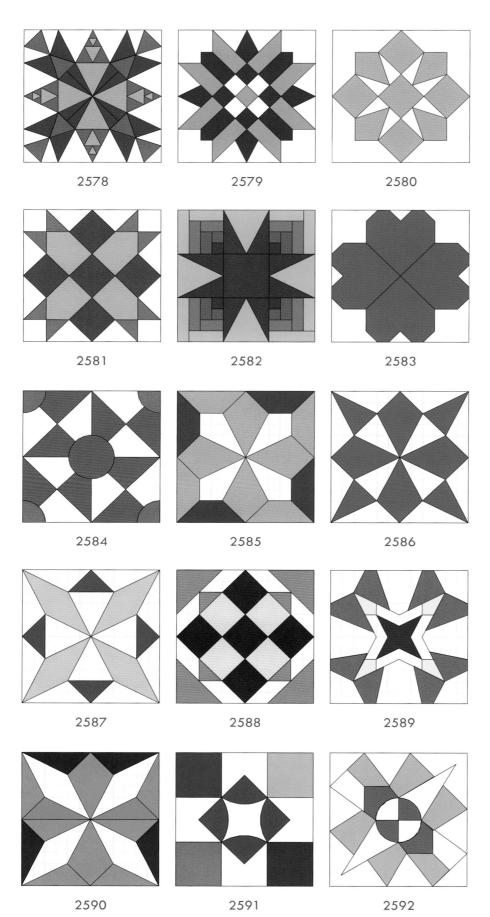

2578 Arrow of Peace

2579 Alice's Favorite

2580 Nine Patch Star, *LW, OCS*

2581 Wild Irish Rose, *JM*

2582 Black Magic (diagonal set), *Elizabeth Stevens, Blue Ribbon Quilts*

2583 Four Leaf Clover

2584 Grecian Square
Greek Square

2585 Unnamed

2586 Whirling Star, *GD*

2587 Diamond

2588 Block & Tackle, *JM, Ultimate Book of Quilt Block Patterns*

2589 Shooting Star, *PP*

2590 Century of Progress, *FJ*
Counter Charm, *HH*

2591 Window Squares, *GC*

2592 Victory, *CS*

2593 Faceted Crystals

2594 Lady of the Lake, *HH*

2595 Goblet Four

2596 Scrap Quilt Bouquet

2597 South Dakota

2598 Star Chain
    Yankee Star
    Yankee Star Chain

2599 Star Ray
    Sun Ray

2600 Blazed Trail, *NC*

2601 Large Star, *LHJ, 1896*
    Crow's Foot, *NP*

2602 Maltese Cross Block,
    *NC*

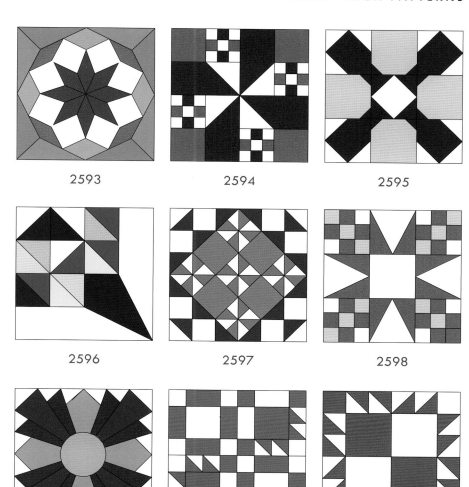

2593    2594    2595

2596    2597    2598

2599    2600    2601

2602

5,500 QUILT BLOCK DESIGNS

# FIVE PATCH PATTERNS

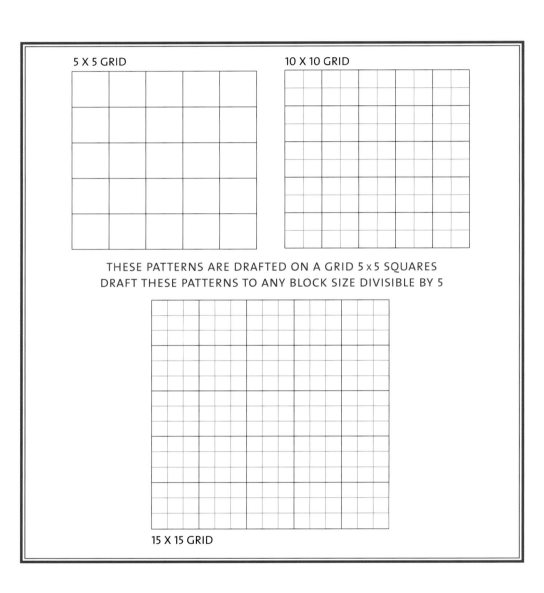

5 X 5 GRID

10 X 10 GRID

THESE PATTERNS ARE DRAFTED ON A GRID 5 x 5 SQUARES
DRAFT THESE PATTERNS TO ANY BLOCK SIZE DIVISIBLE BY 5

15 X 15 GRID

2603 Sunshine and Shadow

2604 Double V, *KCS*

2605 Brock House

2606 Children's Delight, *LAC*

2607 Five Patch

2608 Plaid

2609 Flying Square, *LAC*

2610 Star & Cross

2611 Blocks in a Box

2612 Multiple Square

2613 Unnamed, *QN*

2614 Missouri River Valley

2615 Alaska Homestead

2616 Fool's Square, *KCS*

2617 Butterfly at the
　　Crossroads, *KCS*
　　Algonquin Charm, *NC*
　　Simple Sue

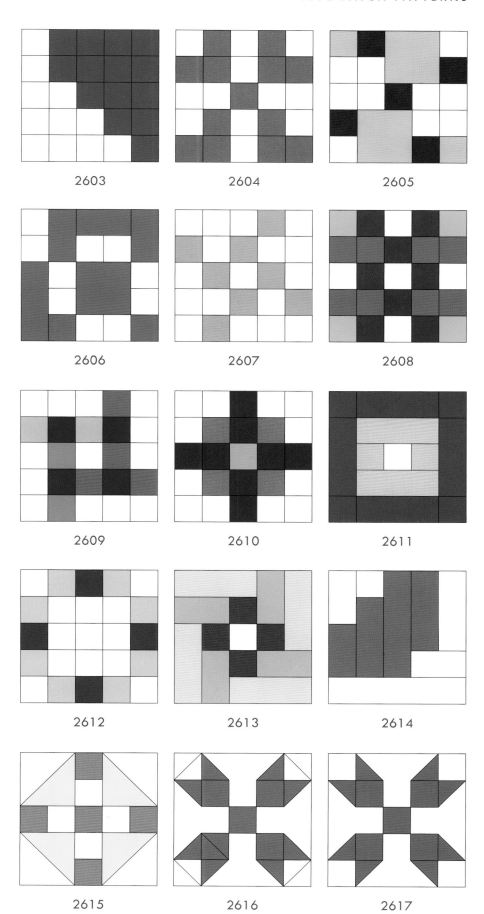

2603　　　　2604　　　　2605

2606　　　　2607　　　　2608

2609　　　　2610　　　　2611

2612　　　　2613　　　　2614

2615　　　　2616　　　　2617

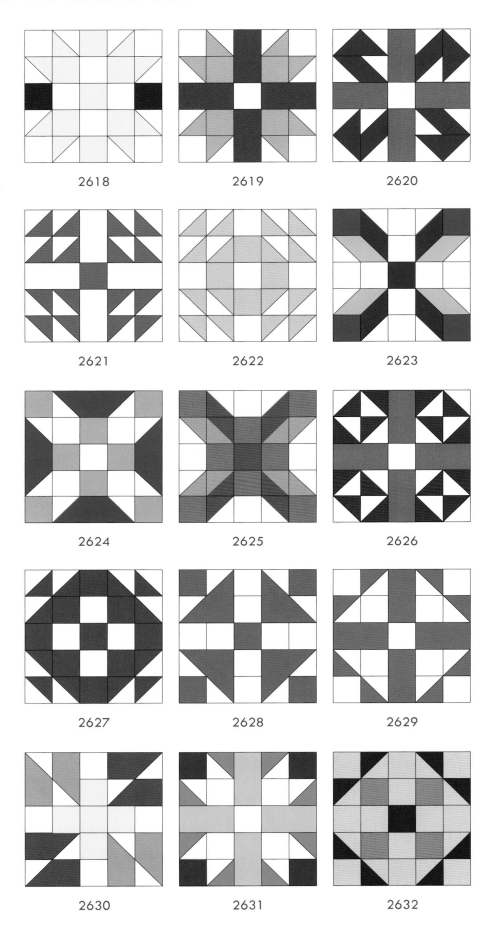

2618    2619    2620

2621    2622    2623

2624    2625    2626

2627    2628    2629

2630    2631    2632

2618  Sister's Choice, *LAC*
      Churn Dasher, *HH*
      Five Patch Star
      Four & Star
      4X Star, *LAC*
      Star and Cross

2619  E-Z Quilt, *KCS*

2620  Jack in the Box, *KCS*
      Whirligig
      Wheel of Fortune, *NC*

2621  Flying Geese
      Handy Andy
      Wheel of Chance, *NC*

2622  Single Wedding Ring,
          *KCS*
      Georgetown Circle
      Memory Wreath
      Nest and Fledgling,
          *KCS*
      Odd Scraps Patchwork,
          *LAC*
      Rolling Stone, *TFW,*
          *1920*
      Wedding Ring, *LAC*

2623  Wild Rose and Square

2624  Rolling Star

2625  Jack's Blocks

2626  Red Cross, *LAC*

2627  Duck and Ducklings

2628  Grandmother's Choice,
          *LAC*
      Duck and Ducklings

2629  Grandmother's Choice
      Cross Within a Cross
      French Patchwork

2630  Z-Cross
      Crazy House, *LAC*

2631  Bright Jewel

2632  Marion's Choice

2633 Rocky Mountain Chain,
    *HH*
    Tumbling Blocks, *CoM*

2634 Georgia, *HH*
    State of Georgia, *WB*,
    *1935*

2635 Bat Wing

2636 Broken Arrows

2637 Domino

2638 Follow the Leader
    Crazy Ann
    Twist and Turn

2639 Captain's Wheel

2640 Farmer's Daughter, *LAC*
    Two Crosses, *NC*

2641 Crazy Ann

2642 Honey's Choice
    Grandma's Choice, *NC*
    Grandma's Favorite, *CS*

2643 Clown, *LAC*

2644 Providence Block, *NC*

2645 Double Sawtooth

2646 Lady of the Lake

2647 Square & Half Square

2633     2634     2635

2636     2637     2638

2639     2640     2641

2642     2643     2644

2645     2646     2647

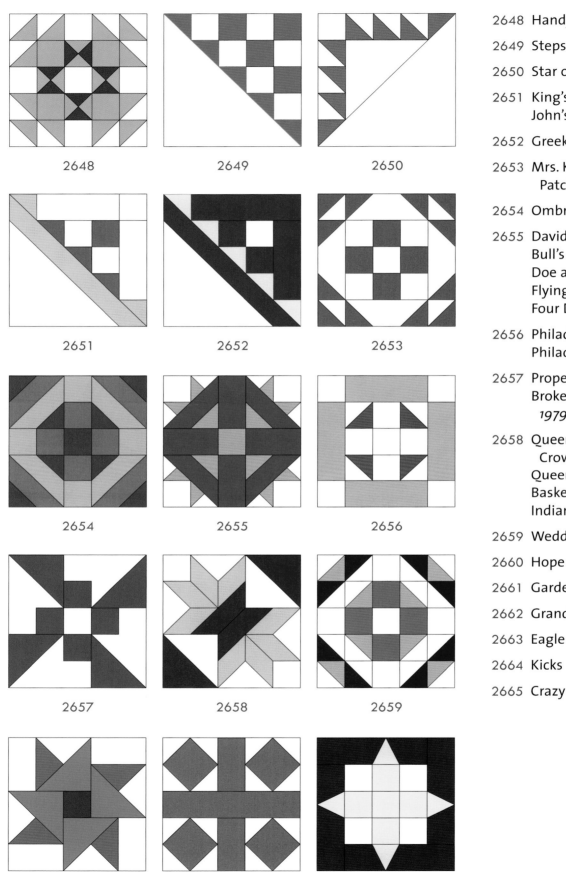

2648
2649
2650
2651
2652
2653
2654
2655
2656
2657
2658
2659
2660
2661
2662

2648 Handy Andy

2649 Steps to the Altar

2650 Star of Hope

2651 King's Crown
     John's Favorite

2652 Greek Cross

2653 Mrs. Keller's Nine
     Patch

2654 Ombre

2655 David & Goliath
     Bull's Eye
     Doe and Darts
     Flying Darts
     Four Darts

2656 Philadelphia Pavement
     Philadelphia Block, *NC*

2657 Propeller, *LAC*
     Broken Arrows, *QW*,
     *1979*

2658 Queen Charlotte's
     Crown, *NC*
     Queen's Crown, *NC*
     Basket Design, *NC*
     Indian Meadow

2659 Wedding Rings

2660 Hope of Hartford

2661 Garden of Eden

2662 Grandmother's Cross

2663 Eagle

2664 Kicks

2665 Crazy House, *LAC*

2666 Churn Dash

2667 Double Wrench, *FF, 1884*
Aeroplane, *WW, 1931*
Airplane, *HHJ*
Alaska Homestead
Bear Paw Design, *CoM*
Bride's Knot, *1913*
The Broad Axe, *1928*
Churn Dash
The Crow's Nest, *KCS*
Dragon's Head, *WW*
French 4's, *NP*
Hens and Chickens
Hole in the Barn Door
Honey Dish
Maltese Cross, *1913*
Monkey Wrench, *OF, 1898*
Pioneer Patch
Square Triangles
T Design
T Quartette
True Lover's Knot
Wrench, *OF, 1896*

2668 Pinwheel Square, *LAC*

2669 Wishing Ring, *MD*

2670 Tents of Armageddon
Ocean Waves, *LAC*
Thousands of Triangles

2671 Square Dance

2672 Souvenir

2673 Hills of Vermont

2674 Pinwheel

2675 Spinning Star

2676 Grandmother Percy's Puzzle, *HH*

2677 Home Circle
Mrs. Anderson's Quilt, *MD*
Rolling Square, *MD*
Garden of Eden, *MD*

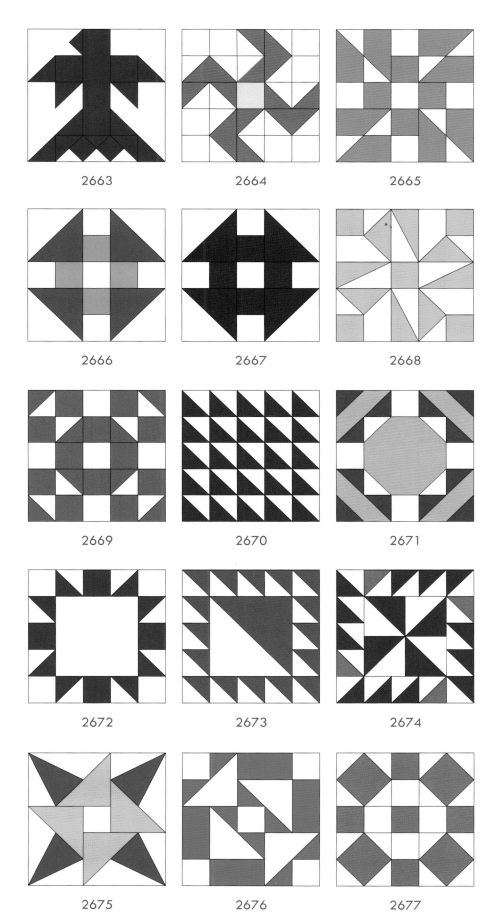

2663

2664

2665

2666

2667

2668

2669

2670

2671

2672

2673

2674

2675

2676

2677

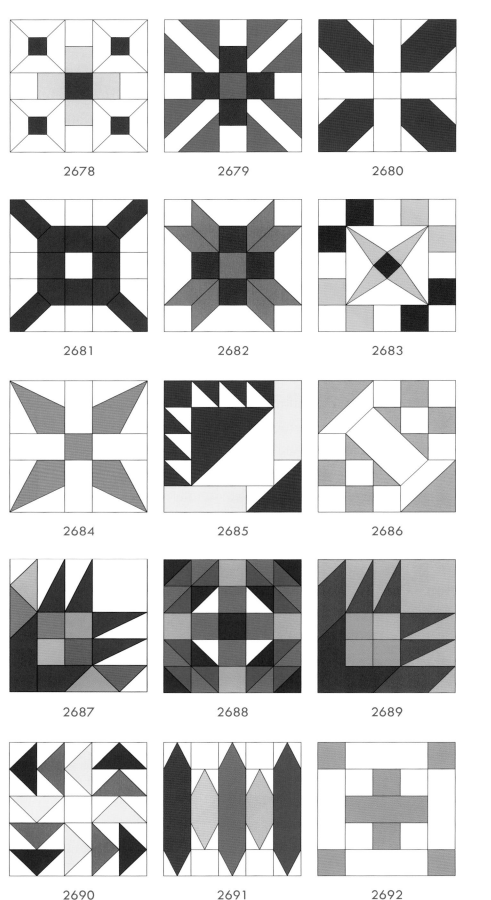

2678 2679 2680

2681 2682 2683

2684 2685 2686

2687 2688 2689

2690 2691 2692

2678 Tete A Tete, *NC*, *1937*
Tote a Tote

2679 No Name, *OCS*

2680 Spool Block, *NC*

2681 Sunbeam, *WW*

2682 Miller's Daughter, *NC*, *1937*

2683 Young Man's Fancy, *LW*

2684 King David's Crown

2685 Altar Candle

2686 Spool

2687 Fish

2688 Odd Scraps Patchwork

2689 Southern Pine

2690 Flying Geese

2691 Picket and Posts, *AK*, *1966*

2692 Red Cross, *NP*

2693 Candle in the Window, *Mrs. Elmer Wicklund, SSQ*

2694 Clown's Choice

2695 Crown of Thorns
Georgetown Circle
Memory Wreath

2696 Star and Octagon, *1930s*

2697 English Wedding Ring, *NP*
Mill Wheel, *NP*
Odd Scraps Patchwork, *LAC*
Old-Fashioned Wedding Ring
Vice President's Block, *NC*

2698 Wedding Ring, *KCS*
Old English Wedding Ring, *KCS*

2699 Dewey Dream Quilt, *1899*

2700 Round the Corner, *NP*
Johnny Round the Corner, *NP*

2701 New England Block, *1930*
Greek Cross, *KCS*

2702 Father's Choice

2703 Christmas Star
Red Cross, *HH*

2704 Baton Rouge Block, *NC*

2705 King's Crown

2706 Strength in Union

2707 Strength in Union, *NC*

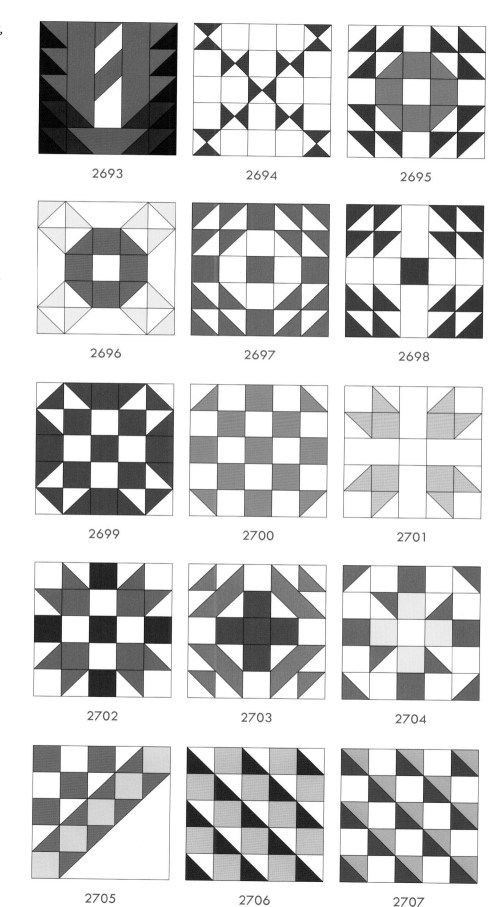

2693

2694

2695

2696

2697

2698

2699

2700

2701

2702

2703

2704

2705

2706

2707

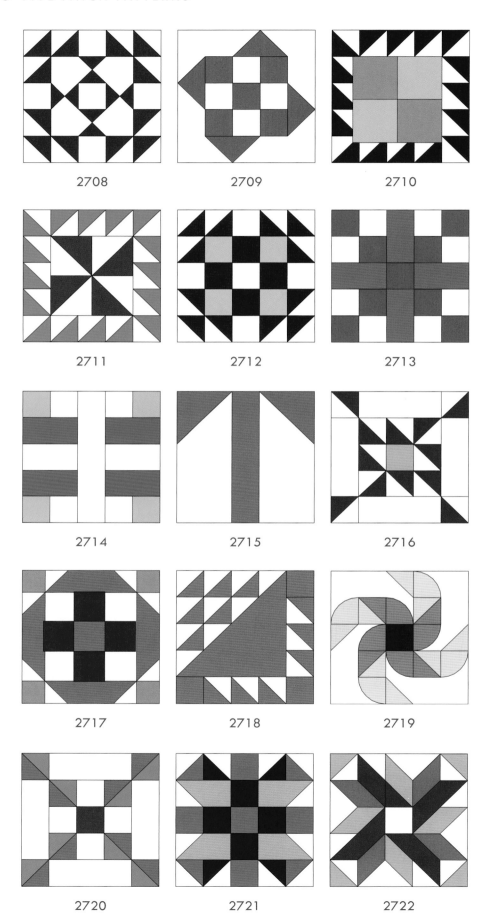

2708     2709     2710

2711     2712     2713

2714     2715     2716

2717     2718     2719

2720     2721     2722

2708 Handy Andy, *LAC*
Foot Stool, *NC*
Mrs. Jones Favorite

2709 Rolling Nine Patch, *AK*

2710 Gay Two Patch Quilt,
*OCS*

2711 Beginner's Delight,
*OCS*

2712 English Wedding Ring

2713 Country Roads

2714 Double R

2715 Skinny T Quilt

2716 Twister

2717 Santa Fe Trail,
*JM*

2718 Lady of the Lake

2719 Amish Pin Wheel

2720 Whirling Square, *NC*

2721 Sister's Choice

2722 Flying Stars

2723 Times Remembered, *LCPQ, 1865*

2724 Star and Cross Block for Hearth & Home Quilt

2725 Duck's Foot

2726 Churn Dasher, *HH*

2727 Guam Quilt Block, *HH*

2728 Banded Cross Block, *HH*

2729 Sacramento Quilt Block, *HH* Sacramento City, *NC*

2730 Nine Patch Star, *HH*

2731 Souvenir of Friendship

2732 Tumbling Ties, *QN*

2733 Indian Design

2734 Bricks and Blocks, *SSQ, 1985*

2735 Pieced Heart Block

2736 Red Cross, *1887*

2737 Job's Tears

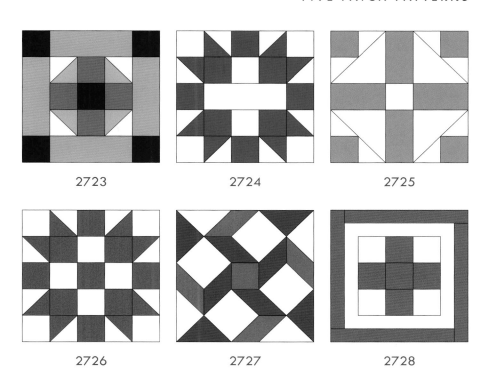

2723

2724

2725

2726

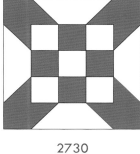

2727

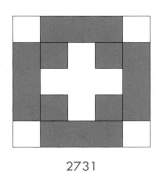

2728

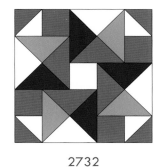

2729

2730

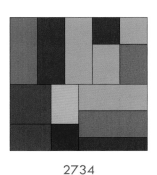

2731

2732

2733

2734

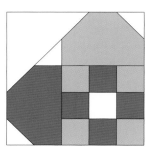

2735

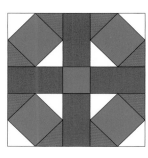

2736

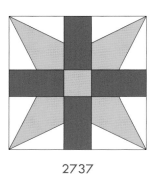

2737

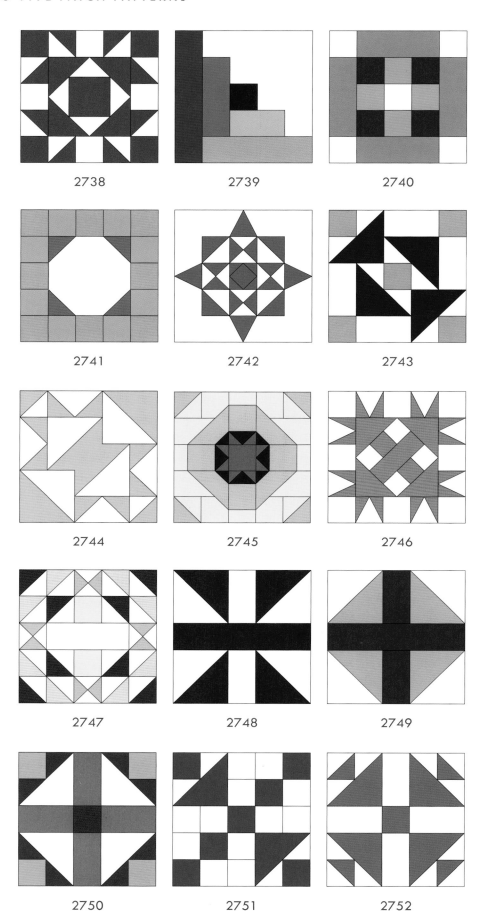

2738
2739
2740

2741
2742
2743

2744
2745
2746

2747
2748
2749

2750
2751
2752

2738  Snowflake

2739  Formal Garden

2740  Cross Patch

2741  Friendly Pleasures

2742  Prairie Sunrise, *HH*

2743  Grandmother's Puzzle

2744  Double Basket, *HHJ*

2745  Wheels, *QW*, *1988*

2746  Corner Star

2747  Memory Block

2748  Diamond Panes, *NC*

2749  Texas Puzzle, *AK*, *1965*

2750  Duck's Foot, *HH*

2751  Spinning Tops, *NC*

2752  Duck and Ducklings
Corn and Beans
Ducklings
Fox and Geese, *NC*
Hen and Chickens
Handy Andy
Shoo Fly
Wild Goose Chase, *CaS*

2753 Wild Goose Chase, *LW*

2754 Whirling Five Patch, *KCS*

2755 Duck and Ducklings, *LAC*
　　 Aunt Kate's Choice

2756 Monkey Wrench, *NC*

2757 Red Cross, *CS*

2758 Wedding Ring

2759 Jack in the Box

2760 Alpine Cross, *NC*

2761 Building Blocks, *NC*

2762 Japanese Friendship Block, *SSQ, 1990*

2763 Does Double Duty, *NC*

2764 Lily Pond, *NC*

2765 Pattern Without a Name, *NC*

2766 Autumn Leaf

2767 Old Indian Trail

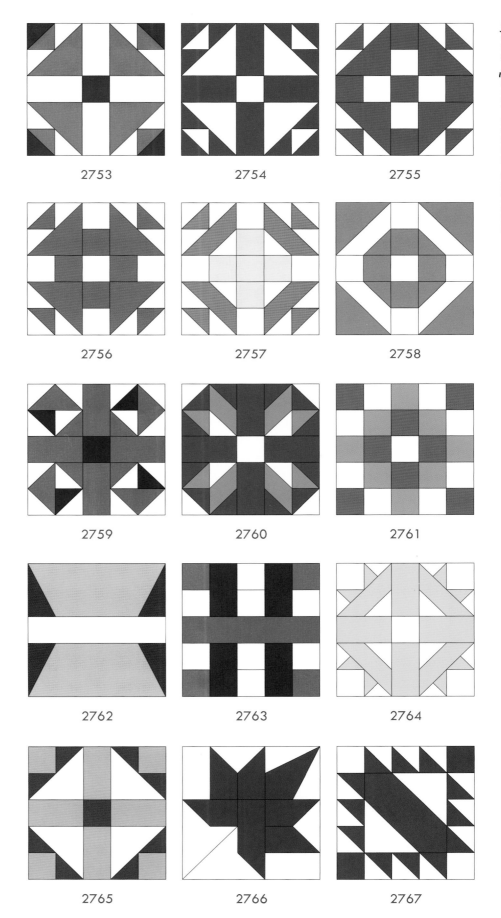

2753　　　　2754　　　　2755

2756　　　　2757　　　　2758

2759　　　　2760　　　　2761

2762　　　　2763　　　　2764

2765　　　　2766　　　　2767

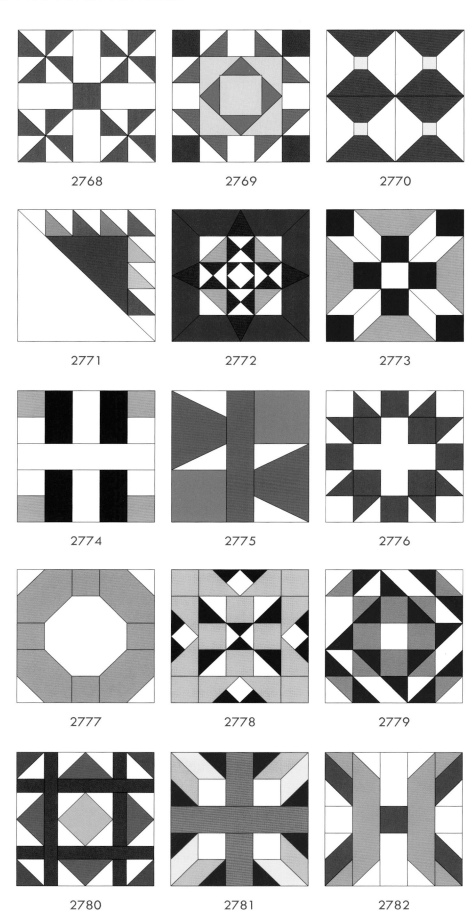

2768 Grandma's Choice
     Simple Design, *LAC*

2769 Tea Party

2770 Grandmother's Own

2771 Sawtooth

2772 Prairie Sunrise

2773 Farmer's Daughter, *CS*
     Corner Posts, *KCS*
     Flying Birds, *NC*
     Jack's Blocks, *GC*
     Rolling Stone

2774 Does Double Duty, *NC*

2775 Twist Around, *MM*

2776 Friendship Block
     A Name on Each
       Friendship Block
     Hearth & Home Quilt,
       *HH*
     Star and Cross, OCS

2777 Wedding Ring

2778 Alaska Territory

2779 Comet
     Halley's Comet

2780 Crossroads
     Crossed Roads

2781 Dakota Gold
     Gold Brick

2782 Domino

2768    2769    2770

2771    2772    2773

2774    2775    2776

2777    2778    2779

2780    2781    2782

2783 Double Irish Chain
    Grandmother's Irish
      Chain, *CS*
    Irish Chain
    Cube Lattice
    Mary Moore's Double
      Irish Chain (with
      four-leaf clover
      appliqué in plain
      blocks)
    Double Irish Cross
      (with four-leaf clover
      appliqué in plain
      blocks)
    Double Irish Chain
      (with four hearts
      appliqué in plain
      blocks)
    Tiger Lily (with tiger
      lily appliqué in plain
      blocks)

2784 Triple Irish Chain
    Single Irish Chain
    Three Irish Chains,
      *MoM*

2785 Nine Patch Irish Chain

2786 Forty Niner Quilt

2787 Irish Chain

2788 Single Irish Chain

2789 Double Irish Chain

2790 Steps to the Light
      House, *NP*
    Steps to the White
      House, *NC*

2791 Irish Chain, *CoM*

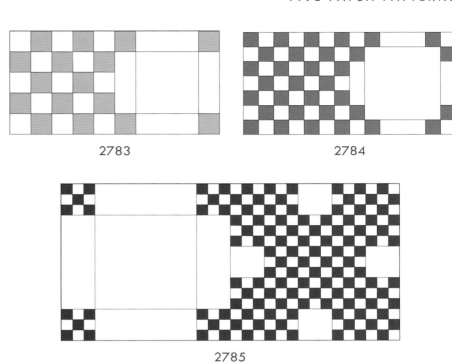

2783　　　　　　　　2784

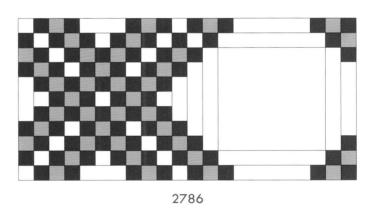

2785

2786

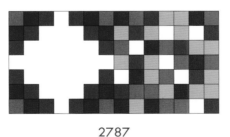

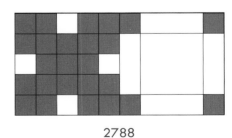

2787　　　　　　　　2788

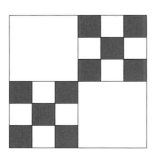

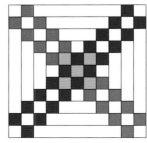

2789　　　　　2790　　　　　2791

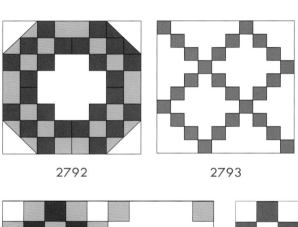

2792

2793

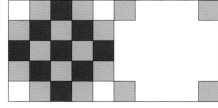

2794

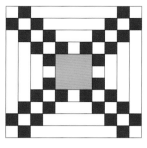

2795

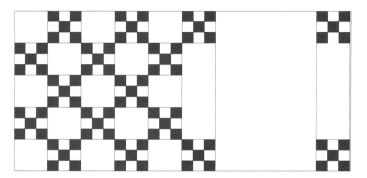

2796

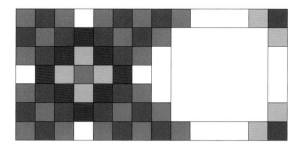

2797

2798

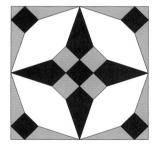

2799

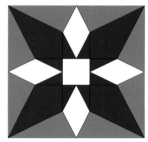

2800

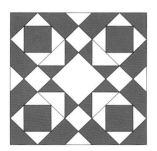

2801

2792 An Irish Chain Hint

2793 Chained Five Patch
Double Irish Chain
Mrs. Hoover's Colonial
  Quilt
Nellie's Choice

2794 Domino Chain

2795 Dogwood Blossoms

2796 Double Irish Chain

2797 Jewel Box

2798 Double Irish Chain

2799 Blue Heaven, *NC*

2800 Lasting Blossom, *RMS,*
  *SSQ,*

2801 Joseph's Coat, *LAC*
Polly's Favorite

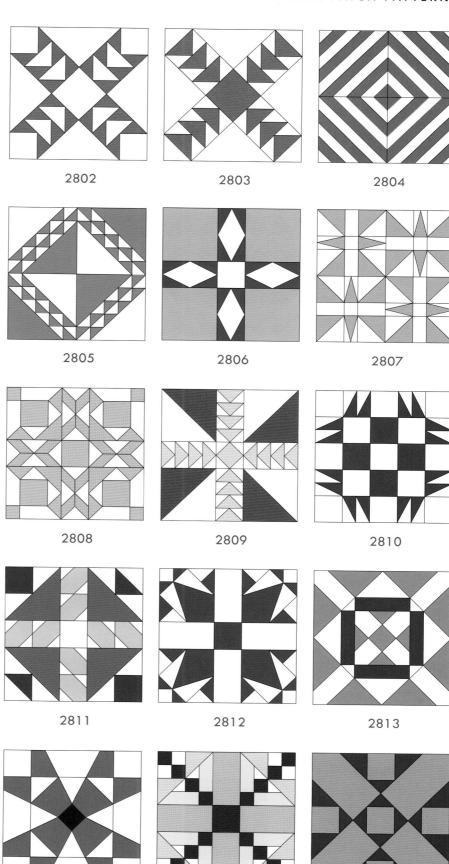

5,500 QUILT BLOCK DESIGNS

2802 Odd Fellows, *LAC*
Baltimore Belle, *CS*
An Effective Square,
*HH*
Flying Geese
Odd Fellows Cross, *NC*
Odd Fellows Patch

2803 Windmill, *1930*

2804 New Jersey, *NP*

2805 Linton, *LAC*
Sun and Shade, *NP*

2806 Darting Minnows

2807 Sewing Circle, *HH*,
*1900*

2808 Cathedral Window, *NC*,
*1933*

2809 Woodland Path, *NC*,
*1934*

2810 Pigeon Toes

2811 Mare's Nest

2812 Ladies' Delight, *LAC*

2813 Century of Progress

2814 Dutch Mill, *LAC*
Holland Mill, *NC*

2815 Easy Do

2816 Handy Andy

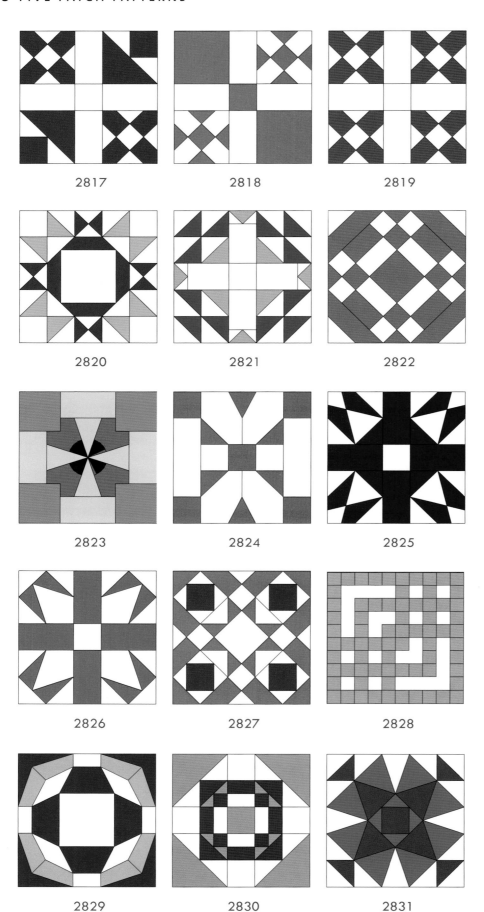

2817
2818
2819
2820
2821
2822
2823
2824
2825
2826
2827
2828
2829
2830
2831

2817 Leap Frog, *LAC*

2818 Widower's Choice

2819 Bachelor's Puzzle, *LAC*
The Seasons, *NC*
Joy's Delight, *NCS*
Mrs. Anderson's
Favorite, *NCS*

2820 King David's Crown

2821 Album

2822 Domino Square

2823 Four Leaf Clover

2824 Oregon

2825 New Star, *LAC*
Heavenly Problem, *NP*
Heavenly Puzzle, *NC*

2826 Cross and Star, *LAC*
Star and Cross, *NC*

2827 Devil's Claws

2828 Carpenter's Square

2829 Rustic Wheel

2830 Harmony Square, *NC*

2831 Wisconsin

2832 Uncle Sam's Favorite

2833 Castor and Pollux

2834 Broken Heart

2835 Uncle Sam's Hourglass,
*NC*

2836 Mona and Monette,
*NP*

2837 Gamecocks, *NC*

2838 Squares

2839 California

2840 Starry Lane
Patch Quilt Design, *NC*
Star Lane

2841 Ozark Trail, *KCS*

2842 Domino and Star

2843 Lewis and Clark

2844 Old Fashioned Daisy

2845 Hedgerow

2846 King's Crown

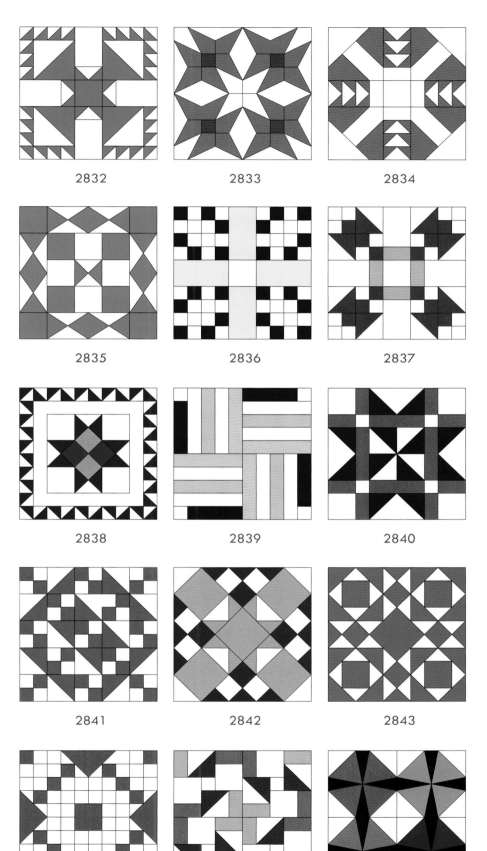

2832  2833  2834

2835  2836  2837

2838  2839  2840

2841  2842  2843

2844  2845  2846

5,500 QUILT BLOCK DESIGNS

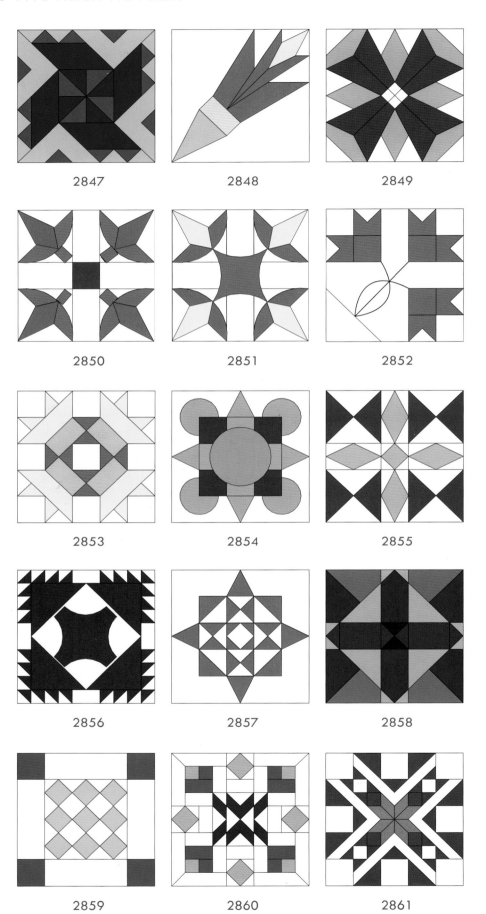

2847    2848    2849

2850    2851    2852

2853    2854    2855

2856    2857    2858

2859    2860    2861

2847 Dutch Waterways

2848 Shooting Star

2849 Japanese Poppy

2850 Swallows

2851 Turkey Tracks

2852 Cluster of Stars

2853 Golden Royalty

2854 Disney Fantasy

2855 Minnesota

2856 Old Maid's Puzzle

2857 King of the Mountain

2858 Beacon

2859 Nine Patch Design

2860 Posy Plot

2861 Leavenworth Star

2862 Fish in the Dish

2863 Pine Burr

2864 Granny's Favorite

2865 Broken Branch

2866 Jericho Walls

2867 Fair and Square

2868 Album

2869 Friendship

2870 Domino and Square,
 *LAC*
 Domino and Squares,
 *NC*

2871 Triangle Puzzle, *GD*

2872 Airplane

2873 Carrie's Choice

2874 Japanese Gardens

2875 Maine Woods

2876 Cross and Crown
 Goose Tracks
 Signal

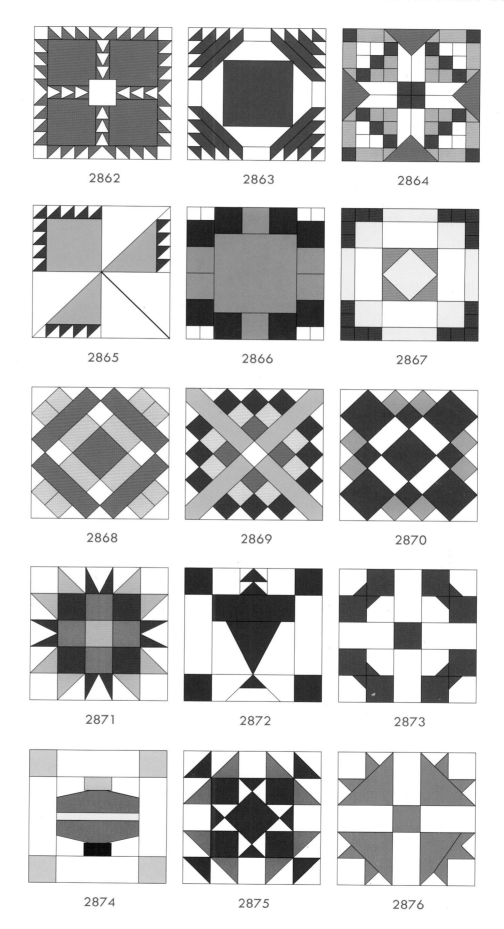

2862  2863  2864

2865  2866  2867

2868  2869  2870

2871  2872  2873

2874  2875  2876

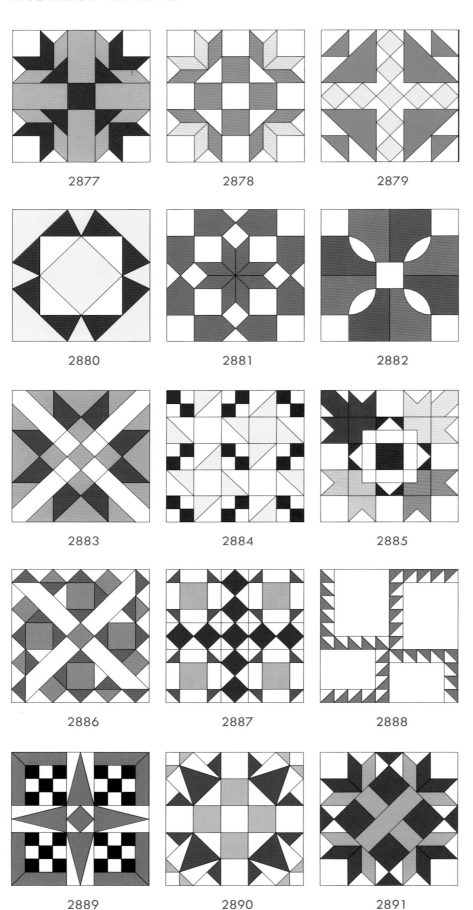

2877 Doe and Darts

2878 Bull's Eye

2879 Bird's Nest

2880 Cousteau's Calypso

2881 St. Louis Block
St. Louis Star, *LAC*
Star of St. Louis, *NC*
Variable Star, *NC*

2882 Idaho

2883 Mexican Cross

2884 Milky Way

2885 Autumn Leaves

2886 Grape Vine

2887 Indian Squares, *NC*
Through the Years, *NC*

2888 Grandmother's
Pinwheel

2889 Waverly Star (strip
pieced center points)

2890 Quilter's Delight, *NC*

2891 Washington Quilt
Block

2892 The Wind Wheel Quilt Block

2893 Hartford Quilt Block, *HH*

2894 Church Windows, *NC*

2895 Evening Quiet, *RMS, SSQ, 1983*

2896 Expectations, *HaM, SSQ, 1983*

2897 French Garden, *QM, 1992*

2898 Mystic Maze

2899 No Name

2900 Solomon's Temple, *KCS* King Solomon's Temple, *CS*

2901 Zig-Zag

2902 Aunt Mary's Squares, *GC*

2903 Double Star, *HH*

2904 Mexican Rose, *Marguerite Ickis* Mexican Star North Star Panama Block, *NC* Shining Hour, *FJ* Star and Cross, *LAC*

2905 Rain or Shine, *NC*

2906 Sunbeam Crossroad, *NC*

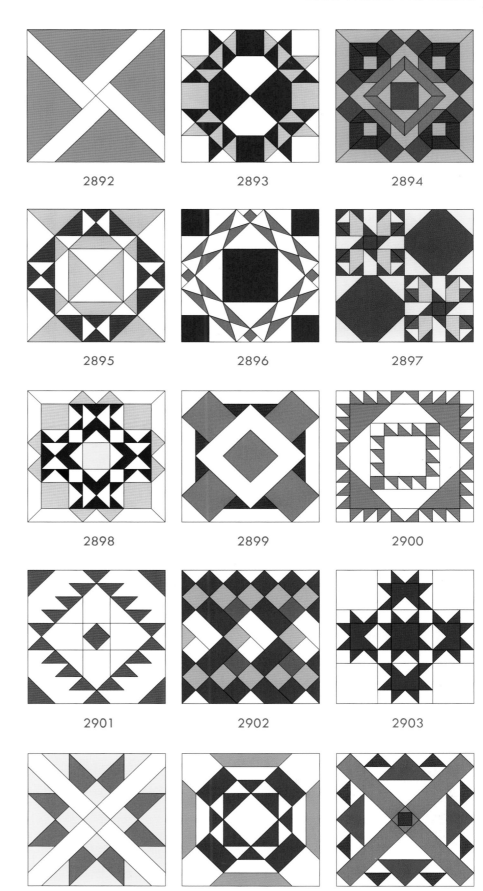

2892  2893  2894

2895  2896  2897

2898  2899  2900

2901  2902  2903

2904  2905  2906

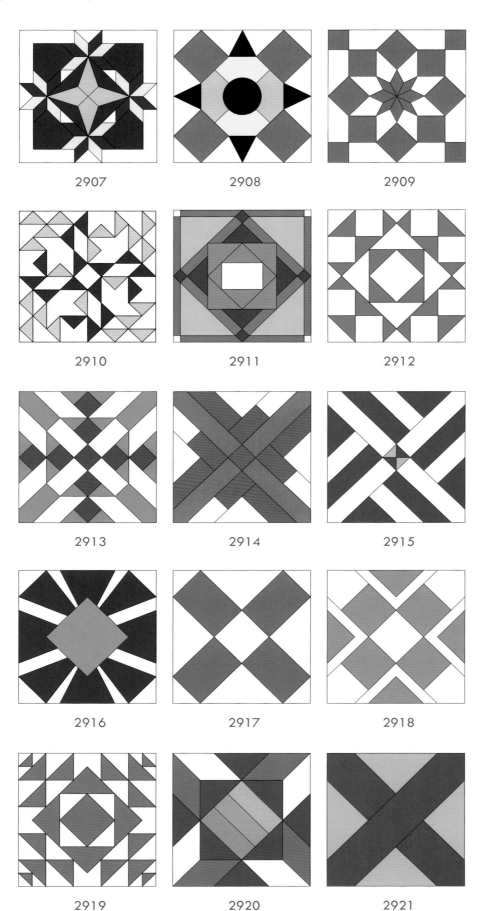

2907
2908
2909
2910
2911
2912
2913
2914
2915
2916
2917
2918
2919
2920
2921

2907 Victorian Star,
  *Alice Vail*, SSQ

2908 Chained Star, *LW*

2909 Starlight, *LAC*

2910 Yellow Clover, *NC*

2911 Aunt Anna's Album
  Block, *CS*

2912 Hill and Crag, *NC*

2913 Garden Paths, *NC*

2914 Whirling L, *QN*

2915 Mary Tenny Gray Travel
  Club Patch

2916 Drive a Crooked Mile,
  *MM*

2917 Crossroads

2918 Crisscross, *GC*

2919 Lighthouse, *NC*

2920 No Name, *OCS*

2921 Old Italian Block, *NC*

2922  Broken Irish Chain, *NC*

2923  Prairie Sunrise

2924  Star and Corona, *NC*

2925  Scrapbag, *NC*

2926  Hartford

2927  Prized Possession

2928  Blue Bell Block, *NC*

2929  Polly's Favorite

2930  The Texas Star Quilt Block

2931  Ice Cream Cone

2932  Single Chain and Knot, *NC*

2933  Cross and Crown, *LAC*
      Bouquet's Quilt, *NP*
      Tulip Wreath

2934  Cross and Crown

2935  Flying Geese, *LW*

2936  Square and a Half, *LAC*

2922

2923

2924

2925

2926

2927

2928

2929

2930

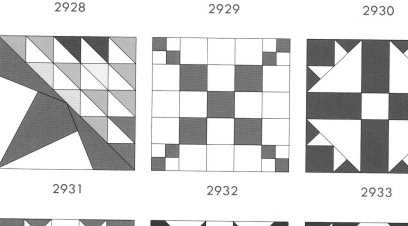

2931

2932

2933

2934

2935

2936

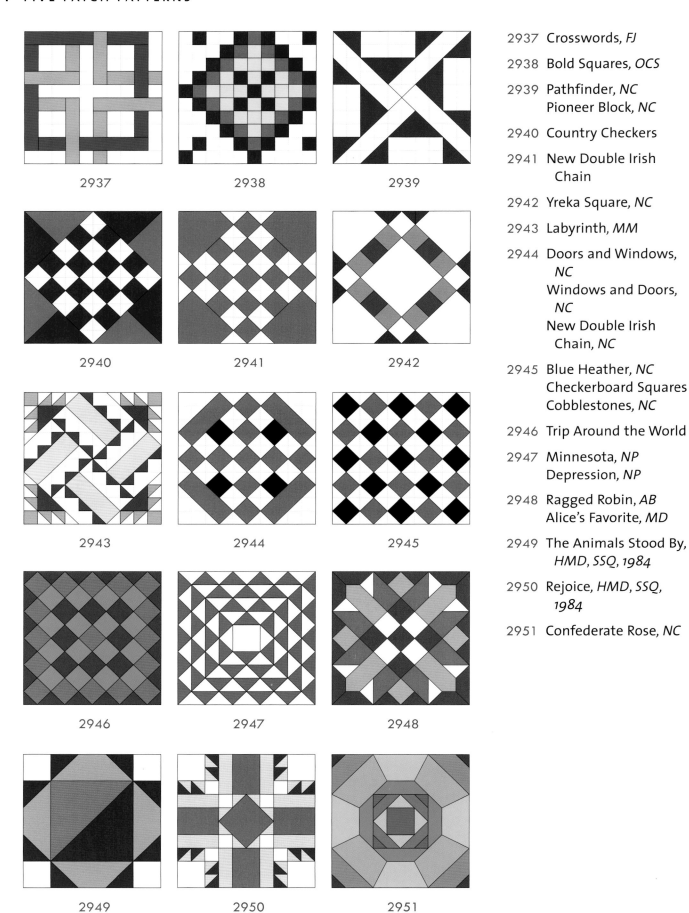

2937

2938

2939

2940

2941

2942

2943

2944

2945

2946

2947

2948

2949

2950

2951

2937  Crosswords, *FJ*

2938  Bold Squares, *OCS*

2939  Pathfinder, *NC*
      Pioneer Block, *NC*

2940  Country Checkers

2941  New Double Irish
      Chain

2942  Yreka Square, *NC*

2943  Labyrinth, *MM*

2944  Doors and Windows,
      *NC*
      Windows and Doors,
      *NC*
      New Double Irish
      Chain, *NC*

2945  Blue Heather, *NC*
      Checkerboard Squares
      Cobblestones, *NC*

2946  Trip Around the World

2947  Minnesota, *NP*
      Depression, *NP*

2948  Ragged Robin, *AB*
      Alice's Favorite, *MD*

2949  The Animals Stood By,
      *HMD, SSQ, 1984*

2950  Rejoice, *HMD, SSQ,
      1984*

2951  Confederate Rose, *NC*

2952 Roman Roads, *NC*
Odd Star, *NC*

2953 Puritan Maiden, *NC*

2954 Federal Chain

2955 Atlanta, *HH*
Love Chain

2956 Patch Quilt Design, *NC*

2957 Rosemary

2958 State of Oregon, *HH*

2959 Railroad Crossing

2960 Diamonds in the
Corners, *KCS*

2961 Butterfly Wings, *QM,
1992*

2962 Memory Block

2963 Heart

2964 Star and Cross
Mexican Cross
Mexican Rose
Mexican Star

2965 Going Home, *Nancy
Johnson-Srebro,
TQ #26*

2966 Diamonds Are Forever,
*MM*

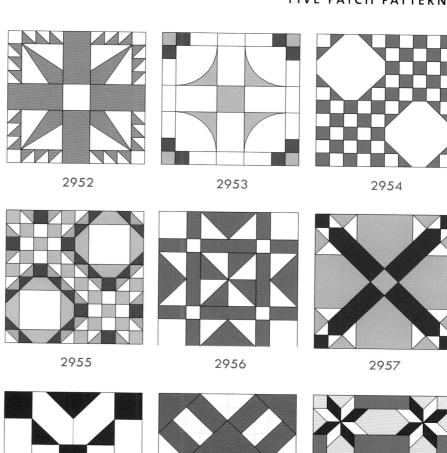

2952

2953

2954

2955

2956

2957

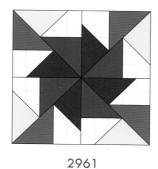

2958

2959

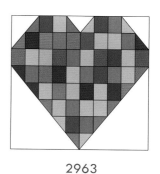

2960

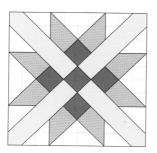

2961

2962

2963

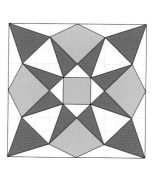

2964

2965

2966

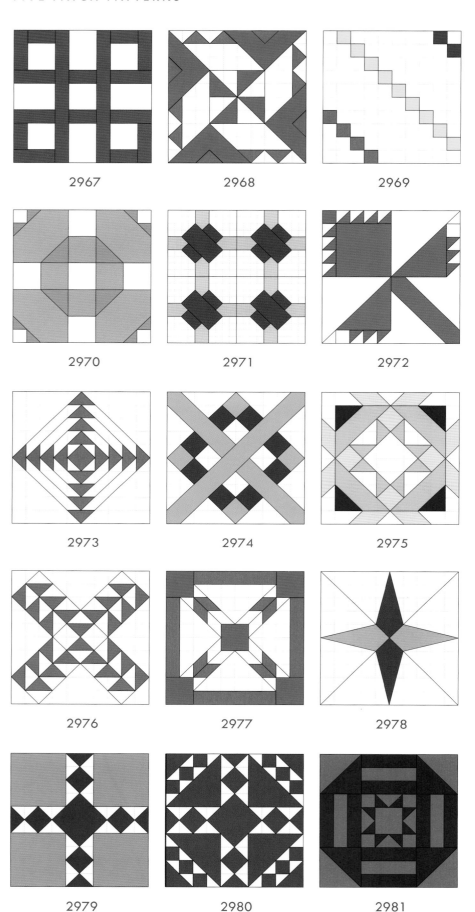

2967

2968

2969

2970

2971

2972

2973

2974

2975

2976

2977

2978

2979

2980

2981

2967 Stripes and Squares

2968 Dutch Waterways

2969 Kite's Tail

2970 Whirling Snow, *RMS, 1982*

2971 Nauvoo Lattice

2972 Lily of the Field

2973 Church Steps

2974 Across the Square, *RMS*

2975 Diamonds of Hope, *Joyce Mueller, QN 2000*

2976 Old Maid's Puzzle

2977 The Air Port, *KCS*

2978 Danish Stars, *KCS*

2979 A Four Square Block with Diamonds

2980 Coronation Block

2981 Star in the Window

2982 Pieced Heart Block

2983 Gentleman's Fancy

2984 Double Link, *AMS*
Friendship Links, *NC*
Friendship Quilt

2985 Hit or Miss

2986 Viola's Scrap Quilt

2987 Modern Blocks, *OCS*

2988 Country Charm, *OCS*

2989 Hill and Hollow, *NC*

2990 Grandmother's Choice

2991 Lincoln Quilt Block, *HH*

2992 California Snowflake

2993 Morning Star, *SSQ*

2994 Stars and Squares, *SSQ*,
*1986*

2995 Joshua's Turn, *SSQ*,
*1987*

2996 Rainbow Square, *AG*

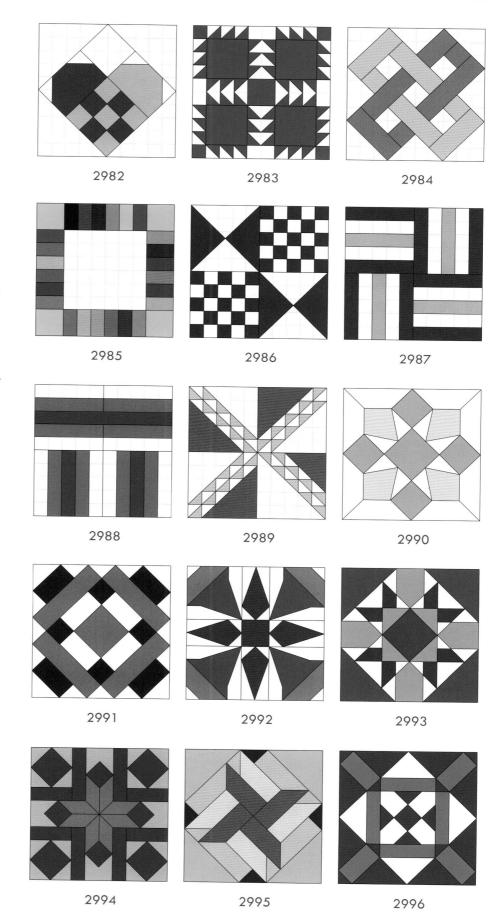

2982

2983

2984

2985

2986

2987

2988

2989

2990

2991

2992

2993

2994

2995

2996

2997   2998   2999

3000   3001   3002

3003   3004   3005

3006   3007   3008

3009   3010   3011

2997 Flying Geese

2998 Starry Nine Patch

2999 Tumbling Star, *SSQ*

3000 Star for Lahoma, *SSQ*

3001 Kaleidoscope,
   *Quilts and Co.*

3002 Bell's Star

3003 Sunbeam, *WW, 1928*

3004 Constellation, *QM,
   1992*

3005 The Farmer's Wife

3006 Pine Burr

3007 A Simple Design, *LAC*

3008 Broken Heart, *1931*

3009 Criss Cross, *HH*

3010 Railroad Crossing

3011 Idle Hours, *FJ*

3012 Confederate Rose, *NC*
    Conventional Rose, *FJ*

3013 The Flashing Star, *AK,
    1965*

3014 Farmer's Wife

3015 Starflower Wreath,
    *LW, OCS*

3016 Marigold Garden, *QN*

3017 Marigold Garden, *QN*

3018 Nine Patch Nose Gay,
    *MoM*

3019 Rays of Sunlight

3020 Road to Home, *RMS,
    SSQ, 1985*

3021 Cowboy's Star

3022 The Rainbow Square,
    *Gammell*

3023 Magnolia Block, *NC*

3024 Star of Manhattan, *AK*

3025 Star and Corona, *NC*

3026 Flying Star, *NC*

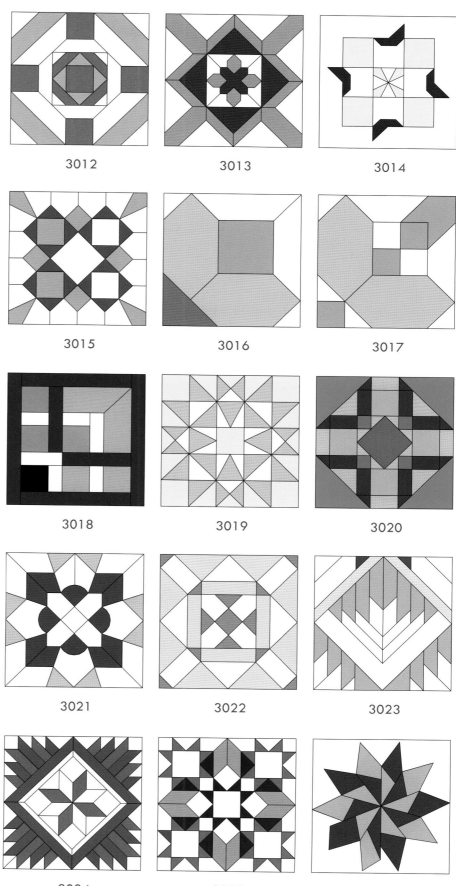

3012

3013

3014

3015

3016

3017

3018

3019

3020

3021

3022

3023

3024

3025

3026

5,500 QUILT BLOCK DESIGNS

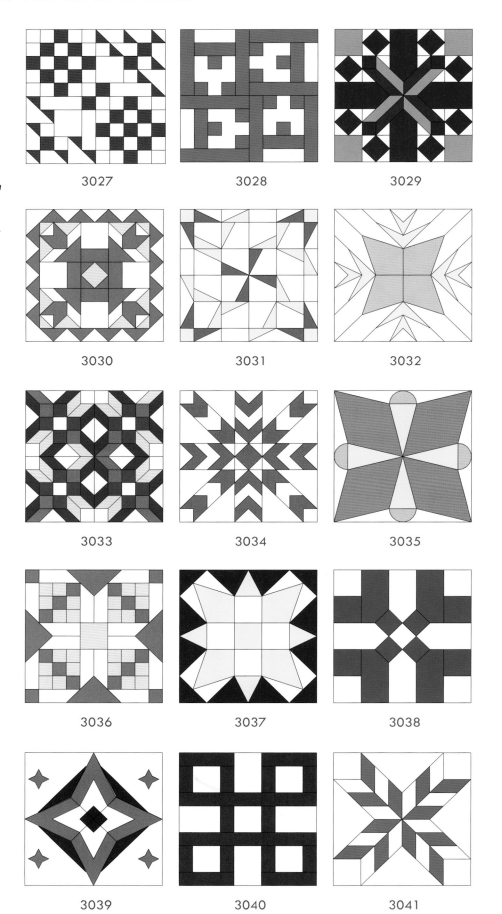

3027

3028

3029

3030

3031

3032

3033

3034

3035

3036

3037

3038

3039

3040

3041

3027 Spanish Squares, *NC*

3028 Four E Block, *LAC*

3029 City Blocks, *QN*

3030 Constellation

3031 Star and Mill Block, *NC*

3032 Double Star, *OCS*

3033 Climbing Roses, *NC*

3034 Indian Patch

3035 Star of the West
Compass
Four Birds
Four Winds
King's Star

3036 Granny's Favorite, *NC*

3037 New Star of North
Carolina, *NC*

3038 Mother's Own, *CS*
Forks

3039 Nativity Star, *QN*

3040 Strip Squares, *LAC*
Stripes and Squares,
*NC*

3041 Crossroads, *OF, 1898*

3042 Baker's Dozen, *JM*

3043 Ellis Island Block, *JM*

3044 Mrs. Keller's Nine Patch

3045 Hero's Welcome, *JM*

3046 November Nights, *JM*

3047 China Doll, *JM*

3048 Sunday Best, *JM*

3049 The Commons, *MM*

3050 Triple Square and Double Circle, *Kei Kobayashi*

3051 Pinwheel Skew

3052 White House Rose

3053 Old Star, *LAC*
Roman Roads, *NC*
Cross and Star, *CS*

3054 Premium Star, *LAC*

3055 Squares and Square, *NP*

3056 Squares and Oblongs Geometric Block

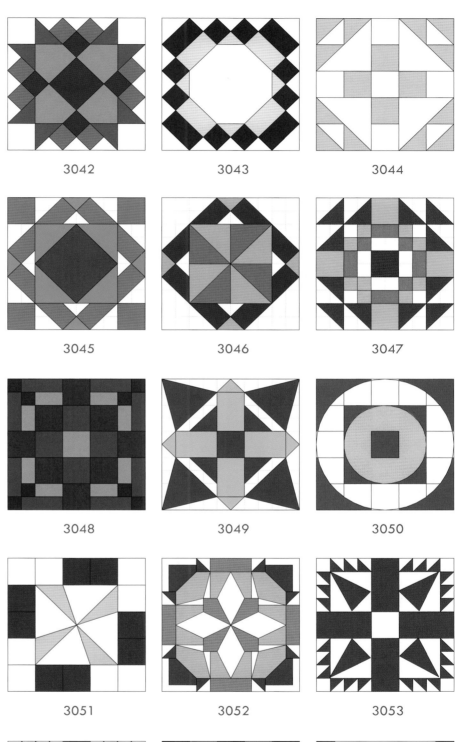

3042    3043    3044

3045    3046    3047

3048    3049    3050

3051    3052    3053

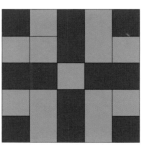
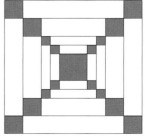

3054    3055    3056

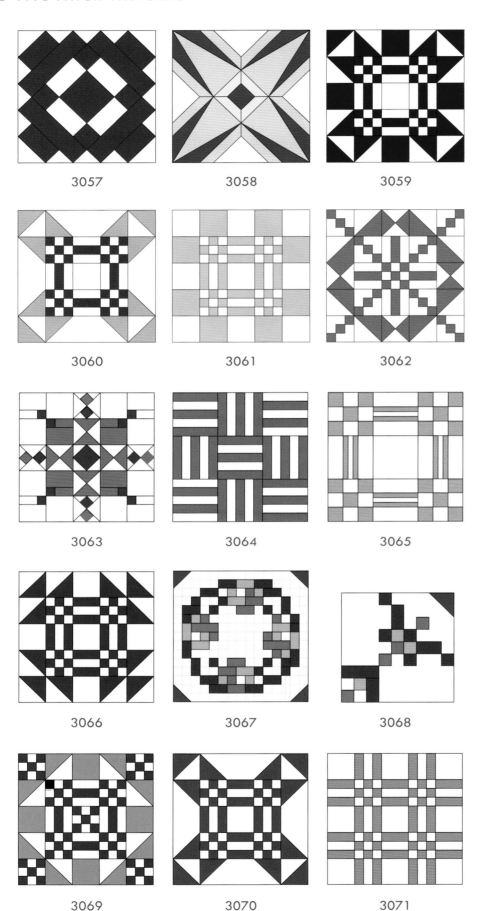

3057
3058
3059

3060
3061
3062

3063
3064
3065

3066
3067
3068

3069
3070
3071

3057 Lincoln, *HH*
Album, *LAC*

3058 Framed Star

3059 New Mexico
Mexican Block
Missouri Puzzle

3060 The New Mexican Star

3061 Album Quilt, *LAC*
Album Patch

3062 Walled City, *MM*,
*2001*

3063 Maryland, *HH*

3064 Five Stripes, *LAC*
Colt's Corral, *PP*

3065 Mountain Homespun,
*NC*

3066 Goose in the Pond, *LAC*
Gentleman's Fancy,
*Modern Priscilla*
Geometric Garden, *MD*
Mrs. Wolf's Red
Beauty, *MD*
Patchwork Fantasy,
*HM*
Scrap Bag, *KCS*
Spider's Den
Unique Nine Patch
Young Man's Fancy

3067 Early American Wreath,
*Ann Orr*

3068 Early American Wreath
(corner block)

3069 Missouri Puzzle
Queen's Crown, *NC*
Young Man's Fancy

3070 New Mexico, *HH*

3071 Squares and Stripes
Album Quilt
South Carolina Album
Block

3072 Father's Fancy, *JM, QN*

3073 An Odd Patchwork

3074 Burgoyne Surrounded
Beauregard's
 Surroundings
Burgoyne's Puzzle, *HAS*
Homespun, *MoM*
An Odd Patchwork, *LAC*
Road to California
Wheel of Fortune

3075 Balance

3076 Checkered Square

3077 Bachelor's Puzzle

3078 Unnamed, *CoM, 1923*

3079 All My Family, *RMS,
SSQ, 1987*

3080 Railroad Crossing, *NC*

3081 State of West Virginia

3082 Old Blue
Tulip Variation

3083 Country Lanes

3084 The Kite

3085 Dragonfly, *Ruby
Hinson Duncan*

3086 Blue Blades Flying

3072

3073

3074

3075

3076

3077

3078

3079

3080

3081

3082

3083

3084

3085

3086

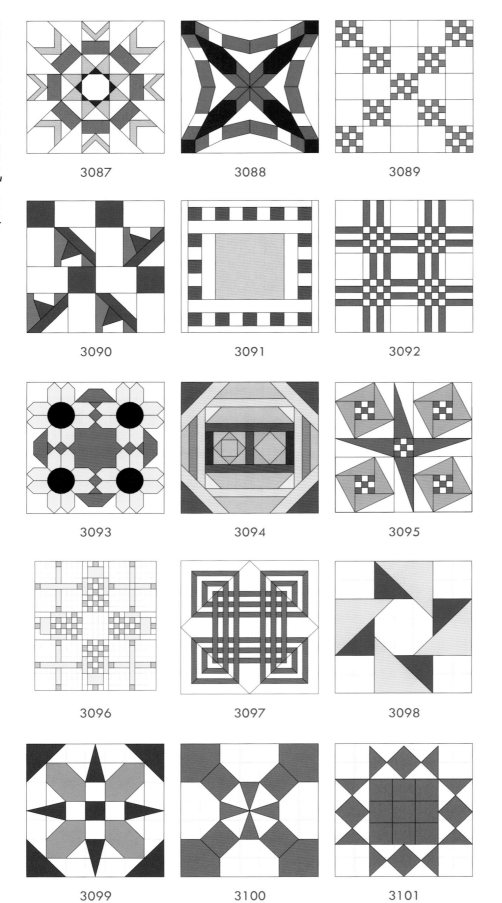

3087 Name of block caption: 3087

3088

3089

3090

3091

3092

3093

3094

3095

3096

3097

3098

3099

3100

3101

3087 President Truman,
*Zelma DePriest,
Aunt Kate's Quilting
Bee, 1973*

3088 Peggy Anne's Special,
*KCS*

3089 Country Lanes,
*MoM*
Cross in the Square

3090 Over the Waves,
*Zelma DePriest, QW,
1983*

3091 Dewey Block, *CS*

3092 Unnamed Four Patch

3093 Modern Daisy, *NC*

3094 Amy's Inspiration
(22 grid)

3095 Blue for Julie (21 grid),
*Jan Magee, QN*

3096 Pineapple Squares
(23 grid), *NC*

3097 All Tangled Up
(26 grid)

3098 Broken Saw Blades, *NC*

3099 Name Unknown

3100 Housewife's Dream

3101 Uncle Sam's Hourglass

3102 Diamond Cross
   Ratchet Wheel

3103 Walls of Jericho

3104 Red Cross

3105 Dove

3106 Rosebud, *AMS*
   Tea Rose

3107 Country Roads

3108 Bear's Paw
   Cat's Paw
   Chinese Block Pattern
   Duck's Foot in the
     Mud, *NC*

3109 Bear's Tracks
   Bear's Foot, *LAC*
   Bear's Paw
   The Best Friend
   Cat's Paw, *NP*
   Duck's Foot in the Mud
   Hand of Friendship
   Illinois Turkey Track,
     *MD*
   Tea Leaf Design

3110 Nine Patch

3111 Hemstitch

3112 Stonemason's Puzzle,
     *LAC*
   City Streets, *NP*

3113 Lincoln's Platform, *LAC*
   Three in a Corner

3114 Prickly Pear, *KCS*

3115 Hens & Chickens, *LAC*

3116 Autumn Leaf

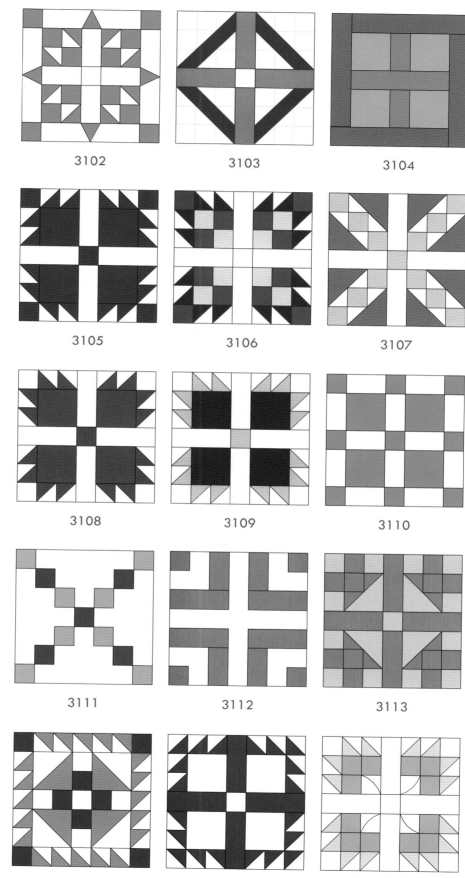

3102   3103   3104

3105   3106   3107

3108   3109   3110

3111   3112   3113

3114   3115   3116

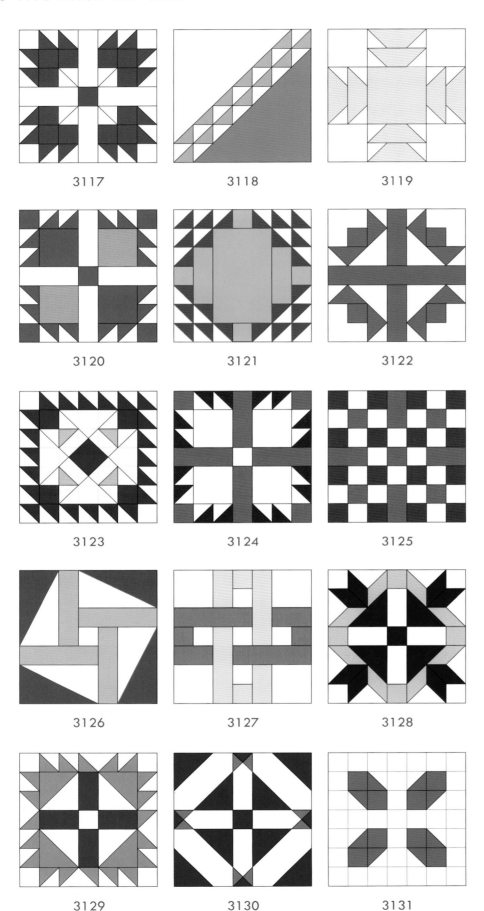

3117

3118

3119

3120

3121

3122

3123

3124

3125

3126

3127

3128

3129

3130

3131

3117  Peony

3118  City Square

3119  Easter Lily

3120  Doves in the Window, *NC*
      Four Birds, *NC, 1935*

3121  Old Maid's Puzzle

3122  Cross and Crown

3123  Queen Victoria's Crown

3124  Path of Thorns

3125  Shadow Cross

3126  Lacy Latticework

3127  Chain Link

3128  David & Goliath
      Four Darts
      Bull's Eye
      Flying Darts
      Doe and Darts

3129  No Name, *QW, 1979*

3130  My Country for Loyalty, *KCS*

3131  Lone X, *PP*

3132  Our Country, *KCS*

3133  Schoenrock Cross, *NC*

3134  Party Platform, *QN*

3135  Fancy Flowers

3136  Road to California

3137  Star of the Night, *NC*

3138  Seminole Square, *NC*

3139  The Stanley

3140  Four Queens

3141  Duck's Foot in the Mud

3142  Indian Design

3143  Courthouse Steps

3144  Whatchamacallit

3145  Log Cabin

3146  Four Queens

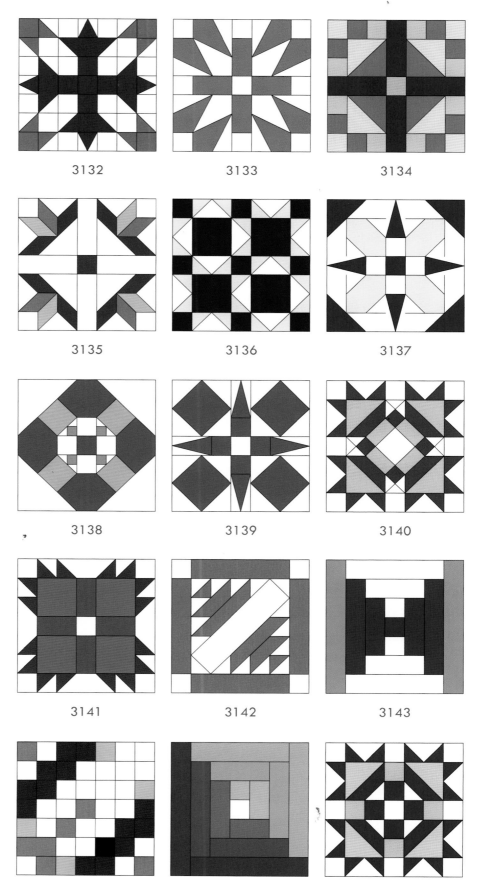

3132      3133      3134

3135      3136      3137

3138      3139      3140

3141      3142      3143

3144      3145      3146

5,500 QUILT BLOCK DESIGNS

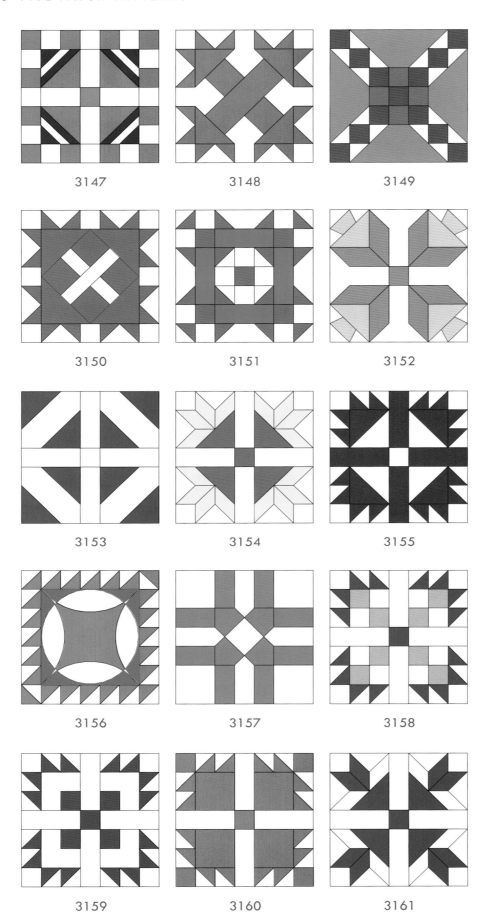

3147

3148

3149

3150

3151

3152

3153

3154

3155

3156

3157

3158

3159

3160

3161

3147 Abe Lincoln's Platform

3148 Corner Star

3149 Fox and Geese, *1898*

3150 Cluster of Lilies, *KCS*
Pond Lily

3151 Greek Cross, *KCS*

3152 Candleglow

3153 The White Square
Quilt, *KCS*

3154 Pieced Tulips

3155 Cross and Crown

3156 Christmas Spirit, *SSQ*

3157 Mother's Own

3158 Bear's Paw, *GC*
The Best Friend, *GC*

3159 Autumn Tints, *NC*

3160 Dove in the Window,
*LAC*

3161 Goose Tracks, *LAC*
Blue Birds Flying, *HM*
Italian Beauty
Pride of Italy

3162 Dove at the
       Crossroads, *CS*
       Lily Pond, *NC*
       Sage Bud

3163 Cross and Crown

3164 Fanny's Fan, *LAC*
       Modern Tulip, *GC*

3165 Old Fashioned Quilt

3166 Crossed Square,
       *HHJ*

3167 Old Maid's Puzzle, *CoM*

3168 Bouquet, *LW*

3169 Stars Over Tennessee,
       *AK, 1966*

3170 Boxed Squares, *MM*

3171 Scrap Basket, *MM*

3172 Lily Quilt Pattern, *LAC*
       Botch Handle
       Des Moines, *HH*

3173 Chimney Sweep,
       *Coats and Clark*
       Maltese Cross

3174 Queen Victoria's
       Crown, *PP*

3175 Acanthus, *NC*

3176 Mosaic Rose, *AK*

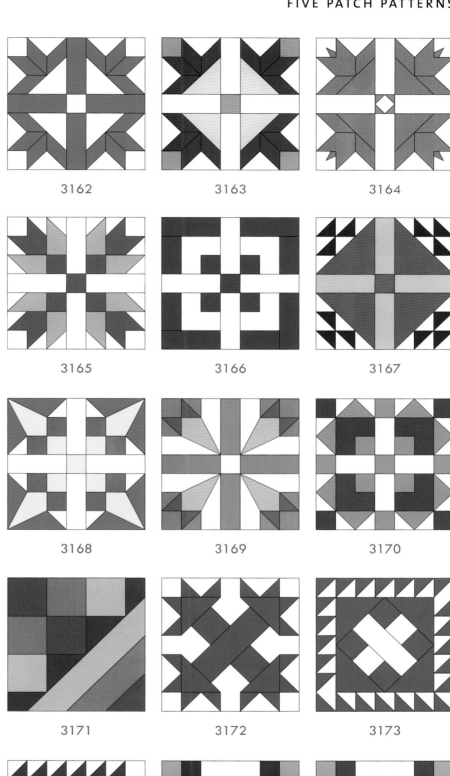

3162

3163

3164

3165

3166

3167

3168

3169

3170

3171

3172

3173

3174

3175

3176

5,500 QUILT BLOCK DESIGNS

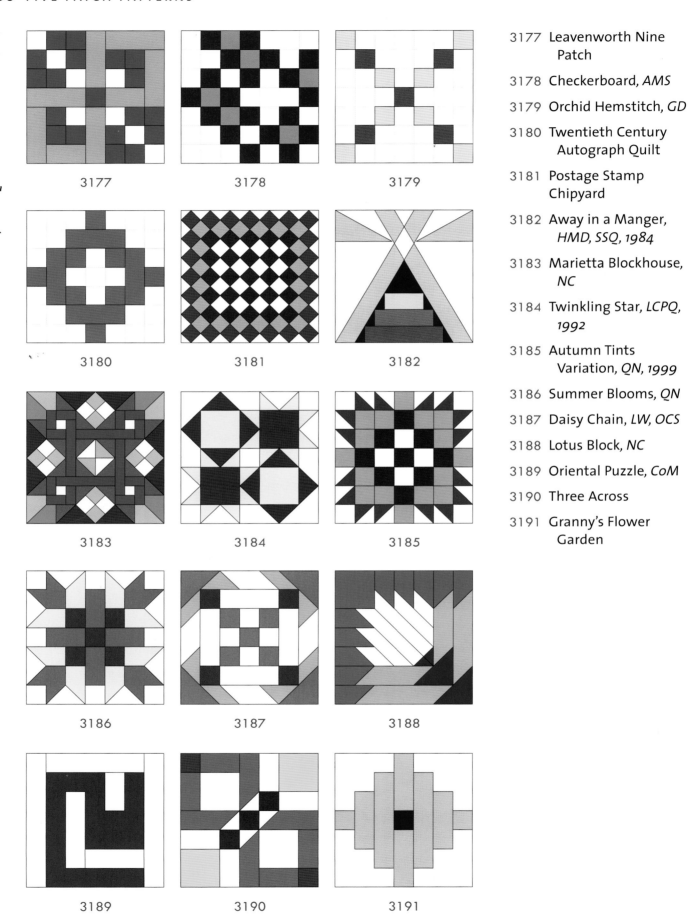

3177    3178    3179

3180    3181    3182

3183    3184    3185

3186    3187    3188

3189    3190    3191

3177 Leavenworth Nine Patch

3178 Checkerboard, *AMS*

3179 Orchid Hemstitch, *GD*

3180 Twentieth Century Autograph Quilt

3181 Postage Stamp Chipyard

3182 Away in a Manger, *HMD, SSQ, 1984*

3183 Marietta Blockhouse, *NC*

3184 Twinkling Star, *LCPQ, 1992*

3185 Autumn Tints Variation, *QN, 1999*

3186 Summer Blooms, *QN*

3187 Daisy Chain, *LW, OCS*

3188 Lotus Block, *NC*

3189 Oriental Puzzle, *CoM*

3190 Three Across

3191 Granny's Flower Garden

3192  Chevrons, *AK*

3193  Gold Brick, *AMS*

3194  Twisted Ribbon

3195  Calgary Stampede, *JM*

3196  Hollywood Star, *JM*

3197  Taos Treasure, *JM*

3198  Blazing Star

3199  Four Square, *HH*

3200  Rail Fence

3201  The Airport, *KCS*

3202  State of Arkansas

3203  Solomon's Temple

3204  Crowned Star, *SSQ*

3205  Old Maid's Puzzle

3206  Maltese Cross
      Easter Lily

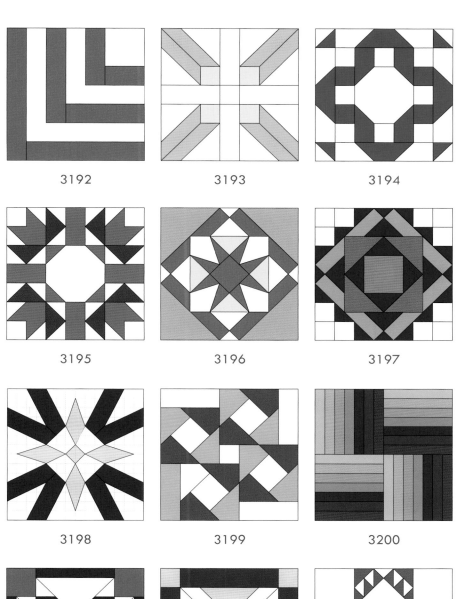

3192   3193   3194

3195   3196   3197

3198   3199   3200

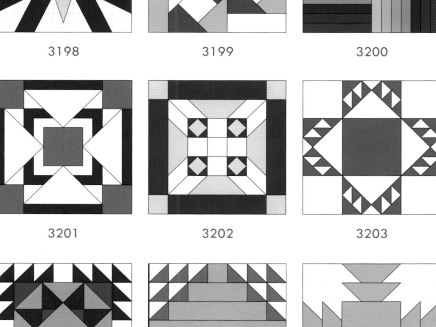

3201   3202   3203

3204   3205   3206

5,500 QUILT BLOCK DESIGNS

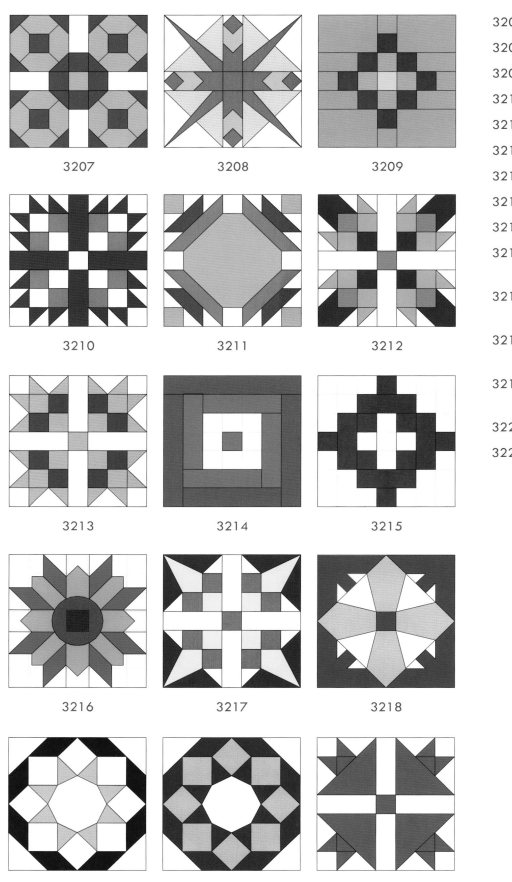

3207      3208      3209

3210      3211      3212

3213      3214      3215

3216      3217      3218

3219      3220      3221

3207   Mrs. Wilson's Favorite

3208   Horizon Star, *QWO*

3209   Southwest Cross

3210   Best Friends

3211   Altar Steps, *PP*

3212   Name Unknown

3213   Pink Magnolia

3214   Amish Squares

3215   Autograph Quilt

3216   The Gardener's Prize, *AMS*

3217   Saint Nicholas' Adventures, *OCS*

3218   Swords and Plowshares, *KCS*

3219   The Kansas Dust Storm, *KCS*

3220   Grandma's Brooch, *KCS*

3221   Goose Tracks
The Crossroads, *TFW*
Crow's Foot
Dove in the Window, *KCS*
Duck Paddle, *HHJ*
Fancy Flowers, *GC*
Lily Corners

3222 Circling Swallows

3223 Crystal Star

3224 St. Louis Star

3225 St. Louis Star Variation

3226 Swirls

3227 Pineapple

3228 No Name, *QW, 1984*

3229 Spring Tulips,
    *Big Block Quilts, 1994*

3230 Bluebirds Flying, *QN,*
    *1985*

3231 Cross and Crown
    Variation

3232 Birds in the Air

3233 Bachelor's Puzzle

3234 No Name (hearts
    appliquéd in light
    squares), *SSQ, 1985*

3235 Petit Park, *QN*

3236 Montana Maze, *NC*
    Mountain Maze

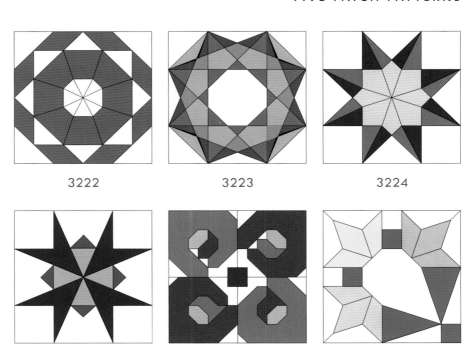

3222      3223      3224

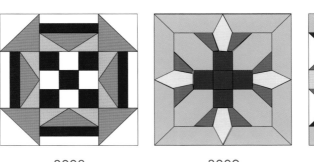
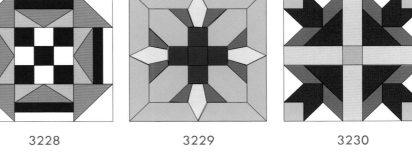

3225      3226      3227

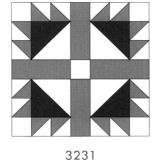

3228      3229      3230

3231      3232      3233

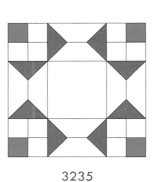

3234      3235      3236

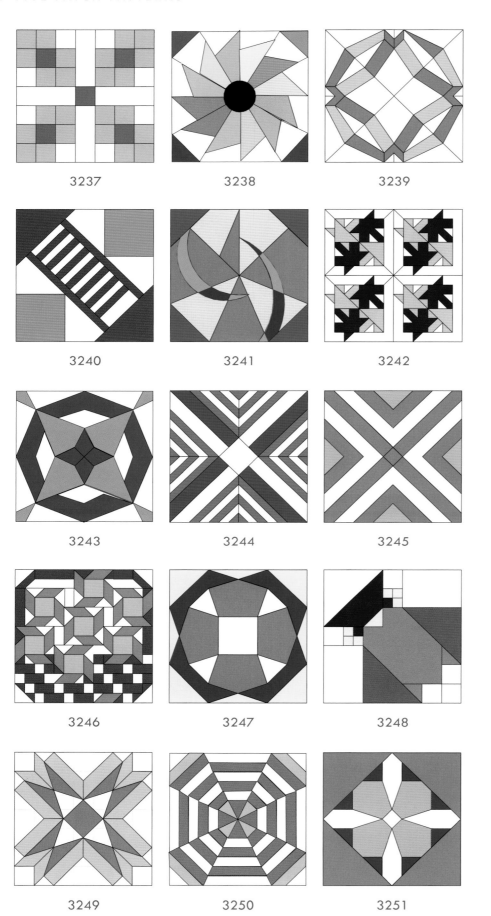

3237 Tonganoxie Nine Patch

3238 Appalachian Sunburst

3239 Double Friendship Knot, *LW*

3240 Ladders and Building Blocks

3241 Code Star

3242 Falling Leaves

3243 Drucilla's Delight, *QN*

3244 State of Michigan, *HH*

3245 Ribbons, *MLM, QW, 1984*

3246 Pinwheel Rose Basket

3247 Pinwheel, *LW, OCS*

3248 Owliver, *Carla Schoenthal, SSQ, 1985*

3249 Bright Star, *RMS, SSQ, 1986*

3250 Spider Web

3251 The Airplanes, *AG, Book of American Patchwork Quilts*

3252 Pieced Pineapple, *OCS*

3253 Wishing Star

3254 Friendship Square

3255 Stained Glass Star,
      *Jane LaRocca, SSQ*

3256 Nebraskaland

3257 Persian, *LAC*

3258 Guthrie, *HH*

3259 Yellow Lilies, *NC*

3260 Dogwood, *PP*

3261 Migration South,
      *Donna Meese, SSQ,*
      *1986*

3262 Jan's Bicentennial Star,
      *QW, 1987*

3263 Tudor Rose, *NC*

3264 St. Paul, *HH*
      Lady of the Lake,
      *Prairie Farmer*

3265 Vice President's Quilt,
      *LAC*

3266 Star in Stripes

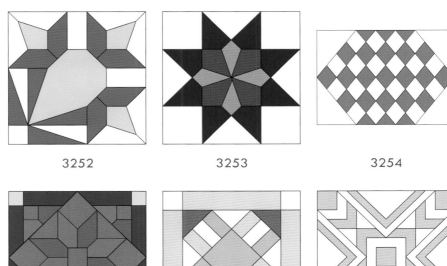

3252

3253

3254

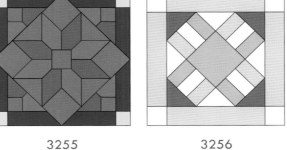

3255

3256

3257

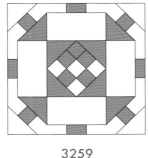
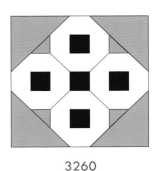

3258

3259

3260

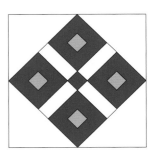

3261

3262

3263

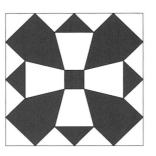
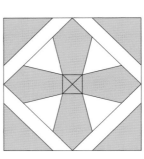

3264

3265

3266

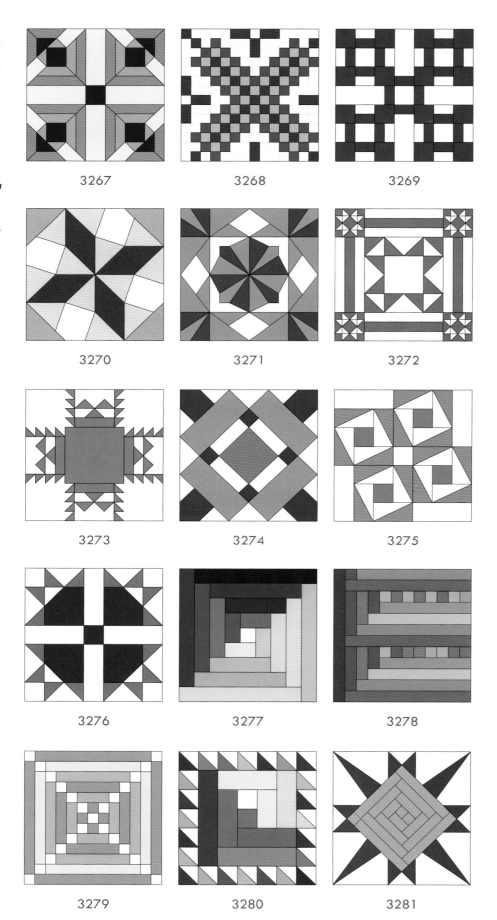

3267

3268

3269

3270

3271

3272

3273

3274

3275

3276

3277

3278

3279

3280

3281

3267 Rhode Island Maple Leaf Star, *AK*

3268 Madame X

3269 True Lover's Knot
Hand
California Oakleaf
Sassafras Leaf

3270 State of Nebraska, *HH*

3271 Wild Iris, *PP*

3272 Ribbon Square, *LAC*

3273 Dove in the Window

3274 Cross

3275 Whirling Square, *NC*

3276 Texas Two Step, *JM*

3277 Log Cabin

3278 Chimneys and Cornerstones

3279 Log Cabin Sherbet

3280 Log Cabin Star

3281 Feathered Log Cabin, *JM, QN, 1993*

3282 Four Patch Log Cabin

3283 Streak of Lightning

3284 Pineapple Log Cabin Variation, *SSQ, 1989*

3285 Three and Five Pineapple Variation, *SSQ, 1989*

3286 Six and Two Pineapple Variation, *SSQ, 1989*

3287 Maltese Cross Pineapple Variation, *SSQ, 1989*

3288 Streak of Lightning Pineapple Variation, *SSQ, 1989*

3289 Melissa's Pinwheel Log Cabin, *Melissa Bernier, SSQ, Log Cabin Collection*

3290 Log Cabin Heart

3291 Courthouse Steps

3292 Stars and Stripes

3293 Spiral Log Cabin

3294 Colorado Log Cabin

3295 Log Cabin Hexagon

3296 Milky Way, *AB, HHA*

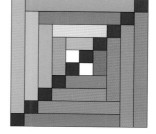

3282

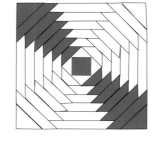

3283

3284

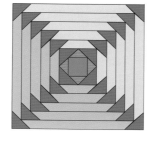

3285

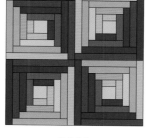

3286

3287

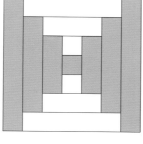

3288

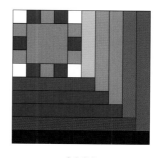

3289

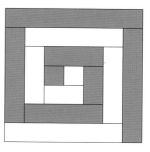

3290

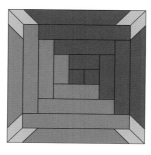

3291

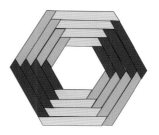

3292

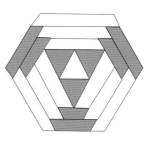

3293

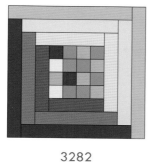

3294

3295

3296

ELEVEN PATCH PATTERNS

11 X 11 GRID

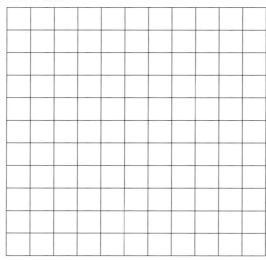

DRAFT TO AN 11" OR 22" BLOCK

3297  Fields and Fences, *NC*

3298  Easter Tide

3299  New Star

3300  Lily Pool

3301  Courthouse Steps

3302  Miss Jackson

3303  White House Steps

3304  Carpenter's Square, *LAC*

3305  Gordian Knot

3306  Interlaced Blocks, *LAC* True Lover's Knot

3307  Persian, *LAC*

3308  Mountain Paths, *QM, 1992*

3309  Chinese Square, *FJ*

3310  Cross of Temperance Cross of Tennessee

3311  Broken Windmills, *NC*

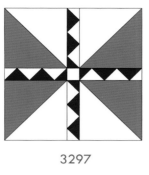

3297

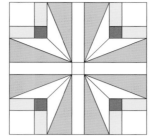

3298

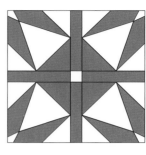

3299

3300

3301

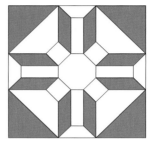

3302

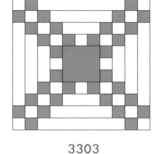

3303

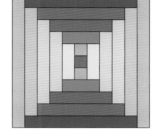

3304

3305

3306

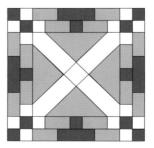

3307

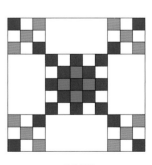

3308

3309

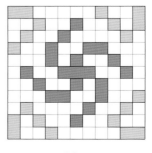

3310

3311

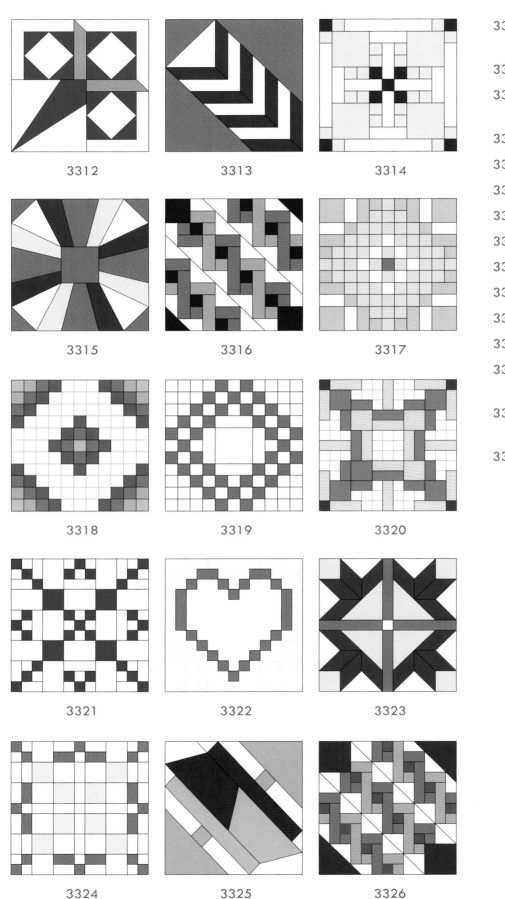

3312

3313

3314

3315

3316

3317

3318

3319

3320

3321

3322

3323

3324

3325

3326

3312 Friendship Bouquet, *AB, OCS*

3313 Sergeant's Chevron, *FJ*

3314 Tahitian Postage Stamp, *QW*

3315 Fanfare

3316 Weaving Paths, *NC*

3317 Golden Glow

3318 Hanging Diamond

3319 Irish Chain, *PP*

3320 Homespun Block, *NC*

3321 Beautiful Mosaic, *FJ*

3322 Pieced Heart

3323 Pieced Tulip Block

3324 Chariot Wheel, *NC* Quilter's Delight, *NC*

3325 Tree and Truth Block, *Mary Walker, 1932*

3326 Weaving Paths, *NC*

3327 Crossword Puzzle

3328 King's Highway

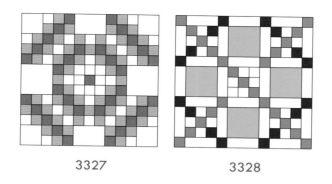

3327          3328

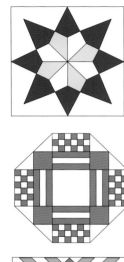

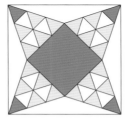

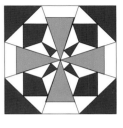
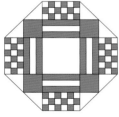
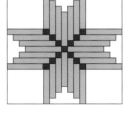
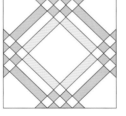
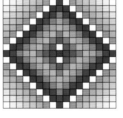

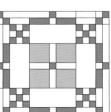

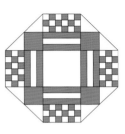

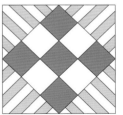

# EIGHTEEN
## PATCH
## PATTERNS

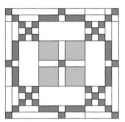
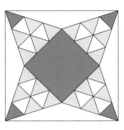

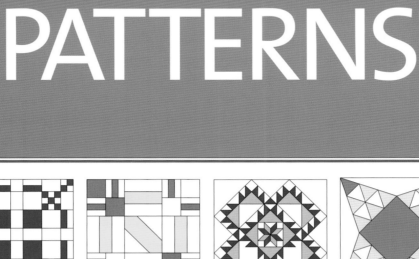

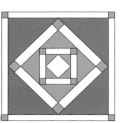
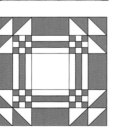

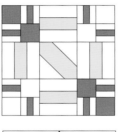

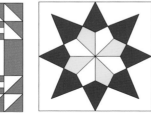

18 X 18 GRID

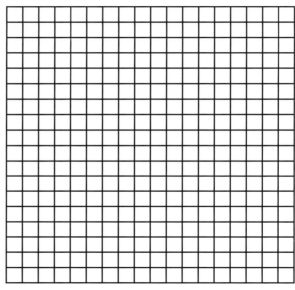

THESE PATTERNS ARE MADE ON A GRID 18 X 18 SQUARES

3329 Miss Nancy

3330 North Star

3331 In Red and White

3332 Bride's Puzzle

3333 Harlequin Star

3334 Enigma

3335 Patchwork Cushion
Top, *KCS*

3336 Lattice Weave, *AK*

3337 Carpenter's Star
(19 patch)

3338 Golden Gates, *LAC*

3339 Missouri Puzzle

3340 Odd Patchwork

3341 Road to California
(17 patch)

3342 Oriental Puzzle, *NC*

3343 Mosaic Block (17 grid)
Grandma's Square
Trip Around the World
(as a continuous
design):
A Trip Around the
World
Grandma's Dream
Postage Stamp
Squares Around the
World
Sun and Shadow
Sunshine and Shadow

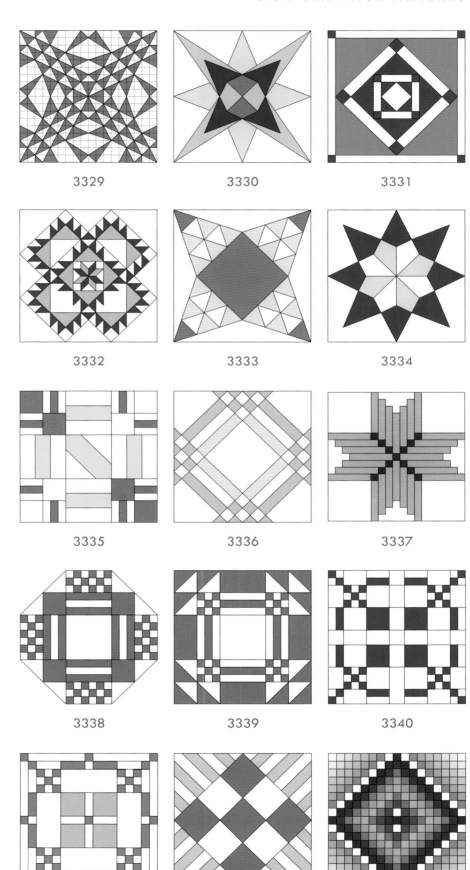

3329  3330  3331

3332  3333  3334

3335  3336  3337

3338  3339  3340

3341  3342  3343

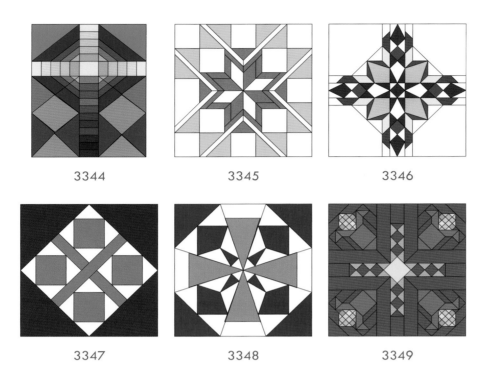

3344

3345

3346

3347

3348

3349

3350

3344 Cross

3345 New Star, *LAC*

3346 Old Rugged Cross

3347 The Savior's Cross

3348 Spider Web

3349 Indian Corn

3350 Summer Rose, *QM*

# TWENTY-FOUR
# PATCH
# PATTERNS

24 X 24 GRID

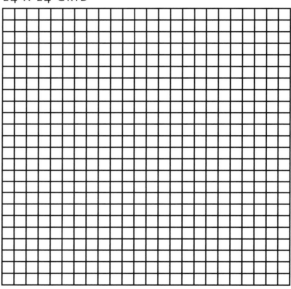

THESE PATTERNS ARE MADE ON A GRID 24 X 24 SQUARES
THEY ARE EASILY DRAFTED TO ANY BLOCK SIZE DIVISIBLE BY 4

3351 State of Nebraska, *HH*
Nebraska, *NC*
Iowa

3352 Shadow Star, *AMS*
Shepherd's Light

3353 Sawtooth Diamond

3354 Unnamed

3355 Kaleidoscope

3356 Nebraska, *HH*

3357 New York Beauty

3358 Bouquet Star
Galactica Star
Star Bouquet

3359 Mountain Homespun,
*NC*

3360 Cubes and Bars, *AMS*,
*1933*

3361 Nebraska, *NC*

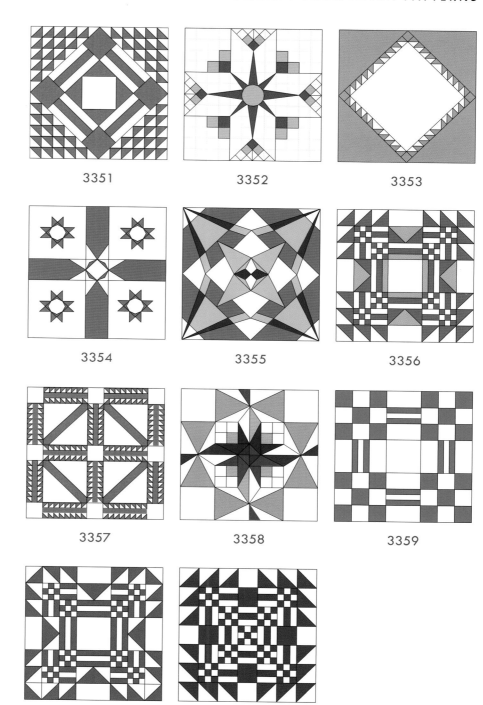

3351  3352  3353

3354  3355  3356

3357  3358  3359

3360  3361

TWELVE
PATCH
PATTERNS

12 X 12 GRID

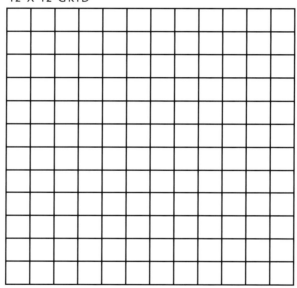

THESE PATTERNS ARE MADE ON A GRID 12 X 12 SQUARES
THEY ARE EASILY DRAFTED TO ANY BLOCK SIZE DIVISIBLE BY 4

3362 Cross and Crown

3363 Sage Bud of Wyoming

3364 The Presidential Armchair

3365 Eastertide Quilt

3366 Wind Star for New Hampshire

3367 Birds in a Square

3368 Rhode Island Maple Leaf Star

3369 Golden Gate

3370 Autumn Leaf

3371 Arizona's Cactus Flower

3372 Pennsylvania Pineapple, *WB*

3373 Lincoln's Hat

3374 Quebec, *NC*

3375 Nebraska Windmill, *QN*

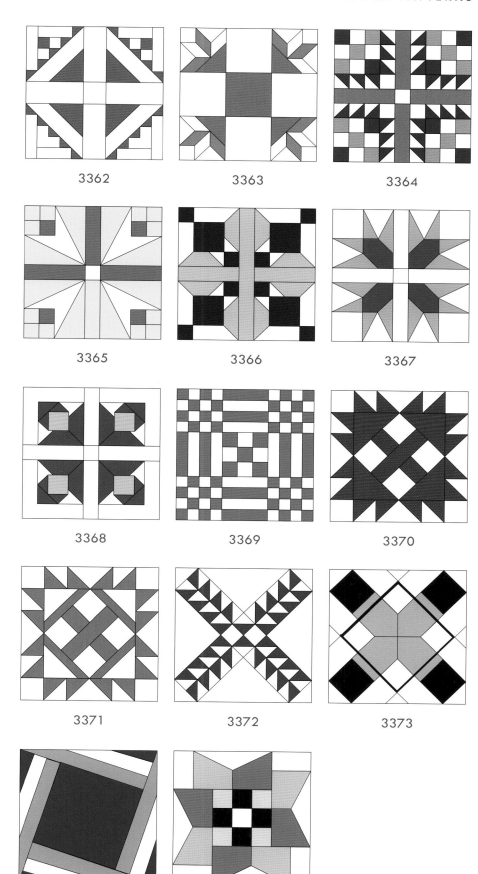

3362

3363

3364

3365

3366

3367

3368

3369

3370

3371

3372

3373

3374

3375

TEN
PATCH
PATTERNS

10 X 10 GRID

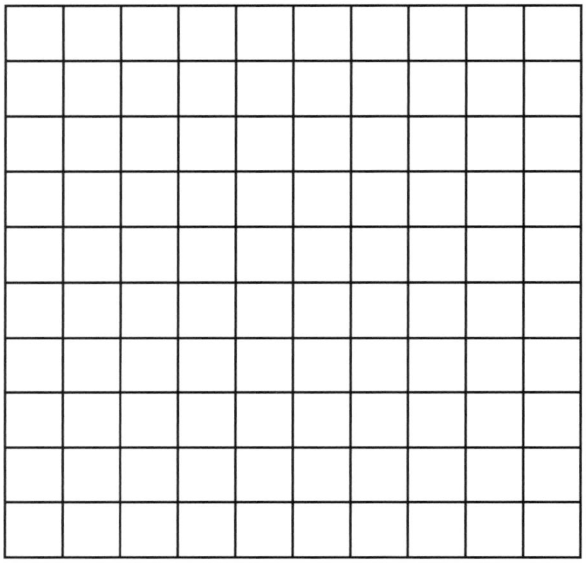

THESE PATTERNS ARE MADE ON A GRID 10 X 10 SQUARES
DRAFT THESE PATTERNS TO ANY BLOCK SIZE DIVISIBLE BY 5

3376 Christmas Cactus

3377 Crossed Squares, *NC*

3376          3377

# EIGHT PATCH PATTERNS

8 X 8 GRID

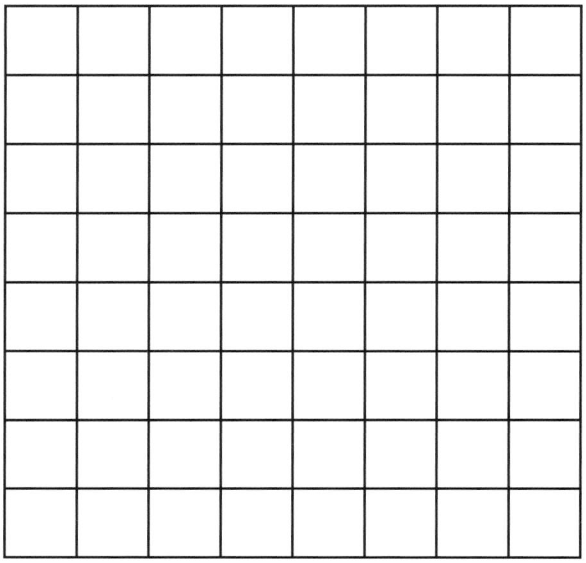

THESE PATTERNS ARE MADE ON A GRID 8 X 8 SQUARES
THEY ARE EASILY DRAFTED TO ANY BLOCK SIZE DIVISIBLE BY 4

3378 North Pole, *QM, 1997*

3379 Priscilla's Dream

3380 Tulip Tile, *AK*

3381 Tracy's Puzzle, *AK*

3382 Broken Star, *NC*

3383 Completed Square, *HH*
     Odd Fellow's Cross

3384 Illinois Star, *NC*

3385 Ships A-Sailing, *WB*

3386 Unnamed

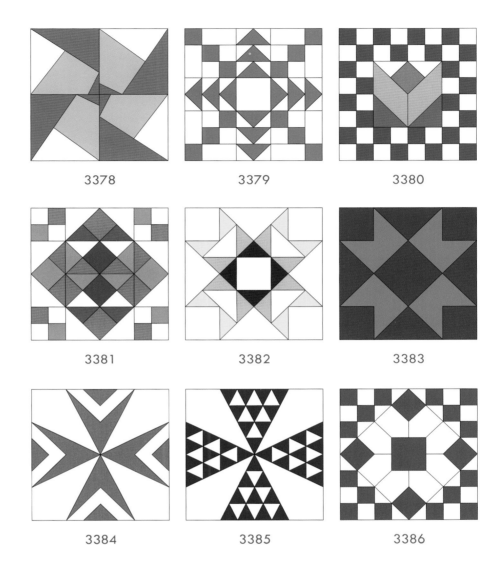

3378  3379  3380

3381  3382  3383

3384  3385  3386

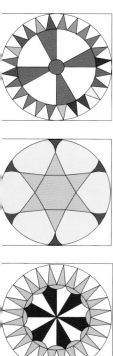
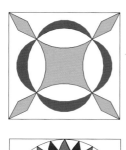
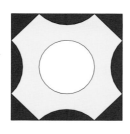
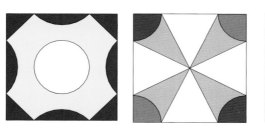
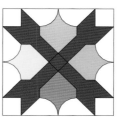
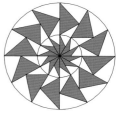

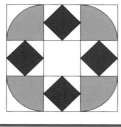
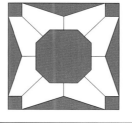
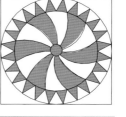
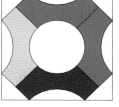

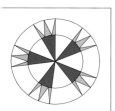
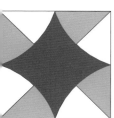
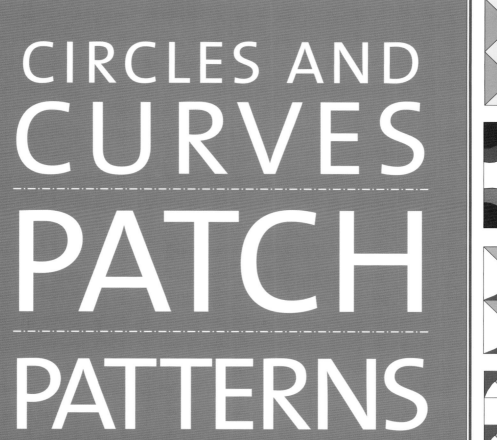

# CIRCLES AND CURVES PATCH PATTERNS

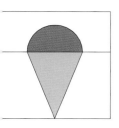

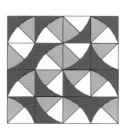
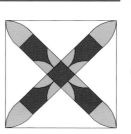
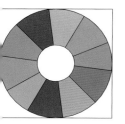

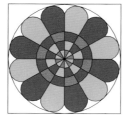
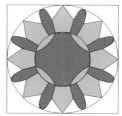
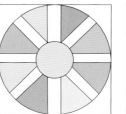

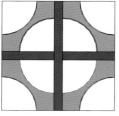

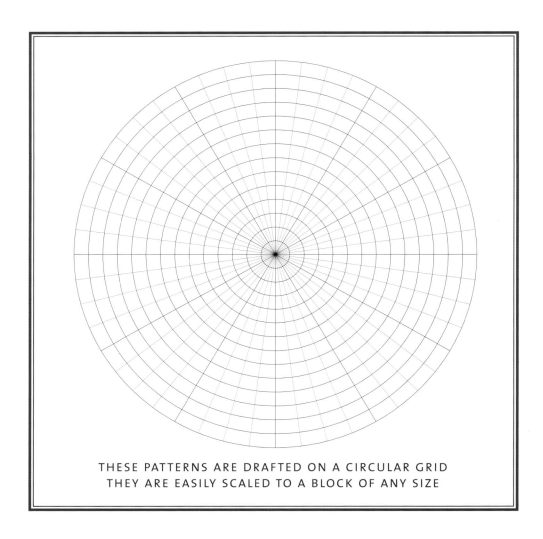

THESE PATTERNS ARE DRAFTED ON A CIRCULAR GRID
THEY ARE EASILY SCALED TO A BLOCK OF ANY SIZE

3387 Grecian Star

3388 Mohawk Trail
Baby Bunting
Chinese Fan
Fan
Path of Fans, *NC*

3389 Dresden Plate
Chrysanthemum, *LAC*
Aster
Friendship Ring
Friendship Wreath
Grandmother's
Sunbonnet
Grandmother's
Sunburst

3390 Baby Bunting, *LAC*
Broken Saw, *CoM*
Chinese Fan, *NC*
The Wanderer, *CoM*

3391 Rainbow Block, *NC*
Indian Raid
Summer Fancy, *LW*,
*OCS*

3392 Trenton

3393 Blue Blazes

3394 Pig Pen, *KCS*
Fair Play, *LAC*
Quarter Turn
Wedding Ring

3395 Nocturne

3396 Josephine Knot

3397 Hidden Flower

3398 Queen's Crown

3399 Queen's Crown

3400 Pullman Puzzle
Baseball
Roman Pavements, *NC*
Snowball

3401 Compass
Robbing Peter to Pay
Paul

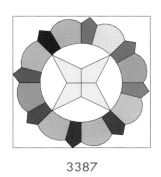
3387

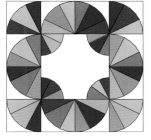
3388

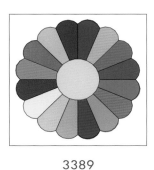
3389

3390

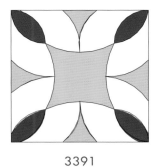
3391

3392

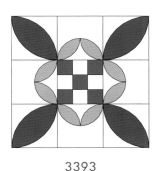
3393

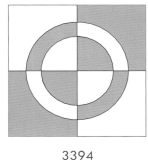
3394

3395

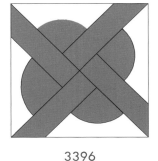
3396

3397

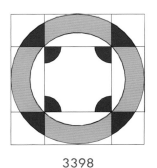
3398

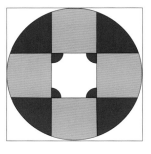
3399

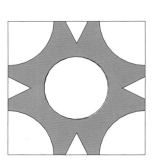
3400

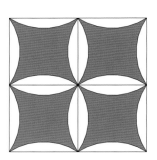
3401

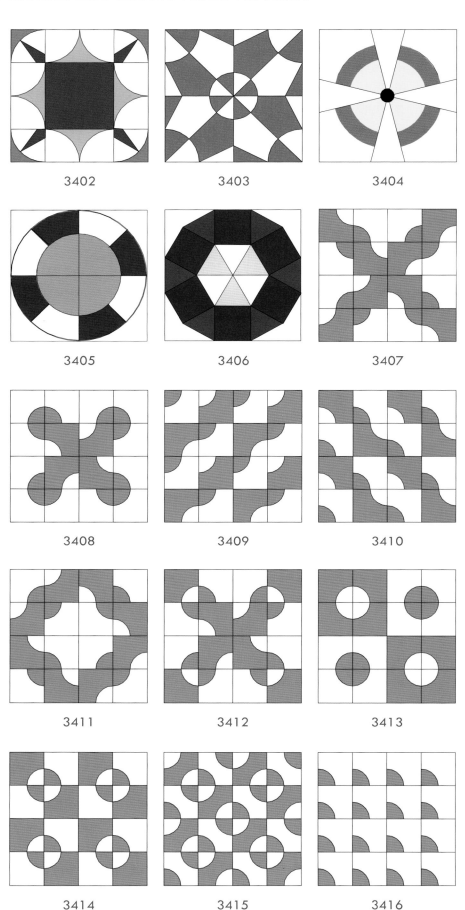

3402

3403

3404

3405

3406

3407

3408

3409

3410

3411

3412

3413

3414

3415

3416

3402 Queen's Pride

3403 Old Maid Combination

3404 Air Ship Propeller
Texas Tulip

3405 Circle Within Circle

3406 Four O'Clock

3407 Drunkard's Path
Boston Trail
Crazy Quilt
Crooked Path, *NP*
Country Cousin, *NC*
Drunkard's Trail
Endless Trail, *NP*
Old Maid's Puzzle
Pumpkin Vine
Robbing Peter to Pay Paul
Solomon's Puzzle
Wanderer's Path in the
Wilderness
Wandering Path of the
Wilderness
Wonder of the World, *LAC*
World's Wonder, *NC*
(with alternate plain
squares):
Oregon Trail, *CaS*
Solomon's Puzzle, *CaS*

3408 Wonder of the World
Wish U Well

3409 Falling Timbers

3410 Vine of Friendship
Diagonal Stripes
Dove
Falling Timbers
Snake Trail

3411 Dove, *KCS*

3412 Fool's Puzzle

3413 Polka Dots, *AMS*

3414 Snowball

3415 Steeplechase
Indiana Puzzle, *CaS*
Rob Peter to Pay Paul
Snowball

3416 Dirty Windows, *NC*
Snowy Windows, *QN*

3417 Around the World

3418 Drunkard's Path
Variation
Falling Timbers, *AMS*

3419 Drunkard's Trail, *GC*
Rocky Road to Dublin,
*GC*

3420 Country Husband
Oregon Trail, *CaS*
Road to California, *WB*
Rocky Road to Dublin

3421 Millwheel
Bow and Arrows
Maltese Cross
Marble, *KCS*
Pullman's Puzzle
The Silk Patch
Snowball, *NC*
Steeplechase

3422 Snowball, *LAC*

3423 Chain Quilt, *KCS*

3424 Ghost Walk, *NC*

3425 Old Maid's Puzzle
Sunshine and Shadow,
*QN*

3426 Cleopatra's Puzzle, *NC*
King Tut's Crown

3427 Fool's Puzzle
Canadian Puzzle
Happy Thought

3428 Fool's Puzzle, *LAC*
Arkansas Troubles

3429 Wonder of the World
I Wish You Well
Tumbleweed

3430 Turtle on a Quilt, *KCS*
The Terrapin, *KCS*

3431 Boston Puzzle
The Winding Blade,
*KCS*

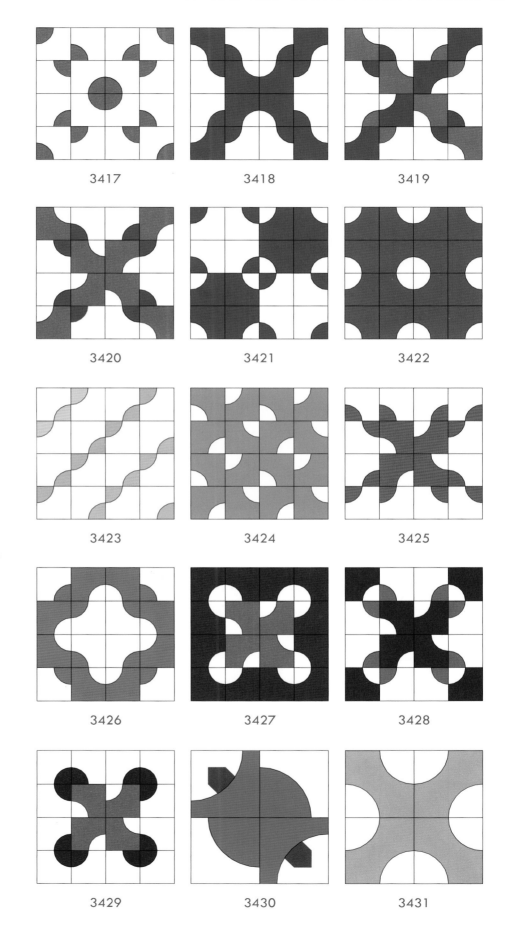

3417     3418     3419

3420     3421     3422

3423     3424     3425

3426     3427     3428

3429     3430     3431

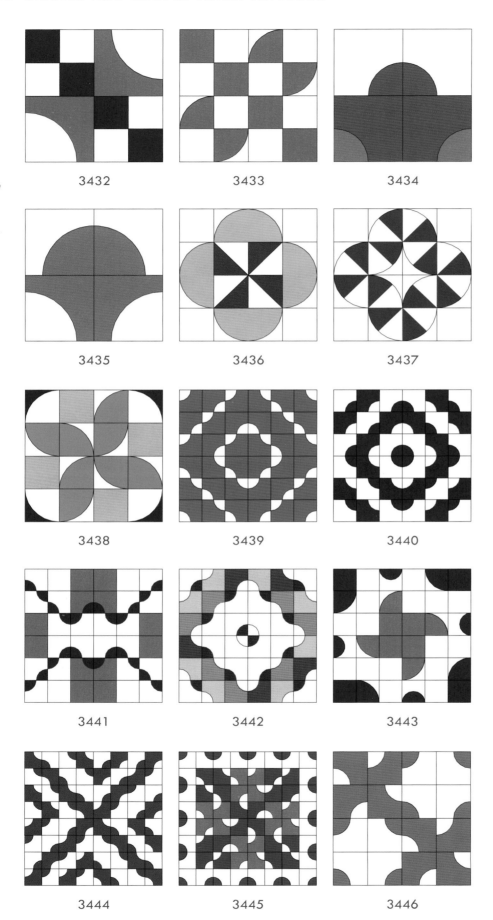

5,500 QUILT BLOCK DESIGNS

3432

3433

3434

3435

3436

3437

3438

3439

3440

3441

3442

3443

3444

3445

3446

3432 Pictures in the Stairwell

3433 Oklahoma Dogwood

3434 Mushrooms, *FJ*

3435 Seashells, *OCS*

3436 Time and Energy, *QN*

3437 The Winding Trail

3438 Windflower, *LW*

3439 Chain Links, *AMS, 1958*

3440 Nonesuch, *AMS*
Love Ring
Jigsaw Puzzle, *KCS*
Ozark Puzzle, *LCPG*

3441 The Road Home, *NC*

3442 Around the World

3443 Unnamed, *LW, OCS*

3444 Rob Peter to Pay Paul

3445 Quilter's Delight, *NC*

3446 Wonder of the World

3447 Indian Patch

3448 Twinkling Star
Star and Crescent

3449 Grecian Square
Greek Square

3450 Scrap Happy, *OCS*

3451 Electric Fan, *KCS*

3452 Alabama Beauty

3453 Homemaker

3454 Indiana

3455 Country Crossroads

3456 Crossroads
Crossroads to
Bachelor's Hall, *HH*
Crossed Roads to Texas

3457 Caesar's Crown

3458 Millwheel, *OCS*
Wagon Wheel

3459 Compass, *KCS*

3460 Utah

3461 Ohio Beauty

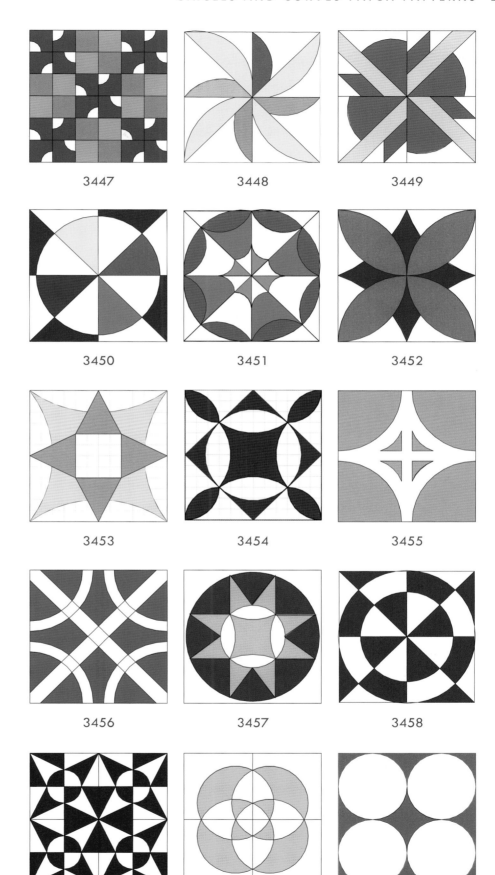

3447     3448     3449

3450     3451     3452

3453     3454     3455

3456     3457     3458

3459     3460     3461

5,500 QUILT BLOCK DESIGNS

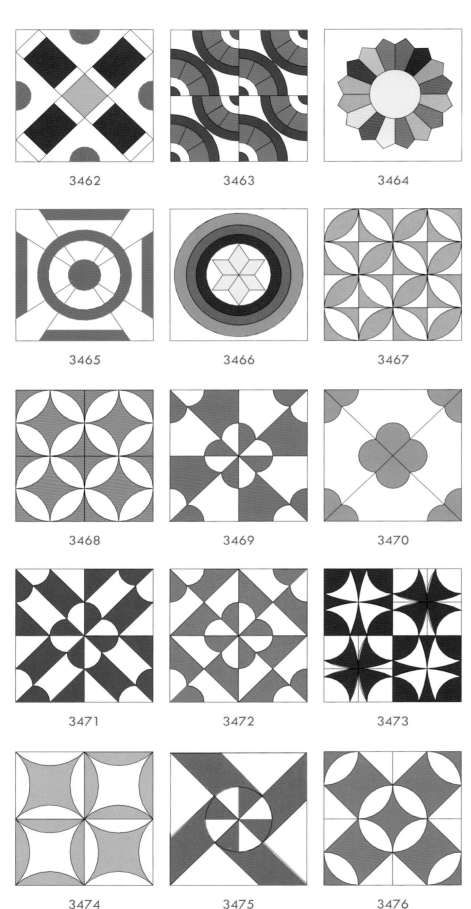

3462    3463    3464

3465    3466    3467

3468    3469    3470

3471    3472    3473

3474    3475    3476

3462   Old Missouri

3463   Snake in the Hollow

3464   Dresden Plate

3465   Nevada

3466   Rainbow Star

3467   Orange Peel
      Flower Petals
      Melon Patch

3468   Bay Leaf

3469   Hearts and Gizzards
      Borrow and Return
      Dutch Rose, *NC*
      Dutch Windmill, *OCS*
      Hearts and Flowers
      Lazy Daisy
      Lover's Knot, *NP*
      Morning Glory, *AMS*
      Petal Quilt
      Pierrot's Pom Pom
      Primrose, *TFW*
      Snowball
      Springtime Blossoms, *MD*
      Tennessee Snowball, *WW*
      Wheel of Fortune
      Windmill, *OCS*

3470   Hearts and Gizzards, *LAC*
      Friendship Quilt, *QN*
      Hearts
      Pierrot's Pom Pom
      Aunt Jerusha, *NC*

3471   Martha's Choice, *NC*
      Virginia's Choice, *NC*

3472   Springtime Blossoms

3473   Winding Ways, *LAC*
      Four Leaf Clover, *NC*
      Nashville, *HH*
      Robbing Peter to Pay Paul
      Wheel of Mystery, *KCS*

3474   Robbing Peter to Pay Paul
      Dolly Madison's Workbox
      Love Ring, *KCS*
      Mary's Choice

Orange Peel
Sugar Bowl, *NP*
Turn About Quilt, *LW*

3475 Boston Puzzle

3476 Name Unknown

3477 Baseball, *LAC*
Circle Design, *GC*

3478 Odds and Ends

3479 Circle Cross

3480 Robbing Peter to Pay
Paul

3481 Baseball, *LAC*
Snowball (strip
piece assorted
fabrics to form
the segments, center
strips white),
*QW, 1979*
Fireball (strip pieced
with center strips
red), *QW, 1979*

3482 New Moon

3483 Yuletide, *AK*

3484 Tobacco Leaf

3485 Merry Go Round, *OCS*

3486 The Formal Flower
Bed, *KCS*

3487 Square and Compass
Fore and Aft

3488 Four Patch, *OCS*
Southern Moon, *OCS*

3489 Pride of the Prairie,
*LW, OCS*
Spinning Whirligigs

3490 Evelyne's Whirling
Dust Storm, *KCS*

3491 Sun, Moon & Stars

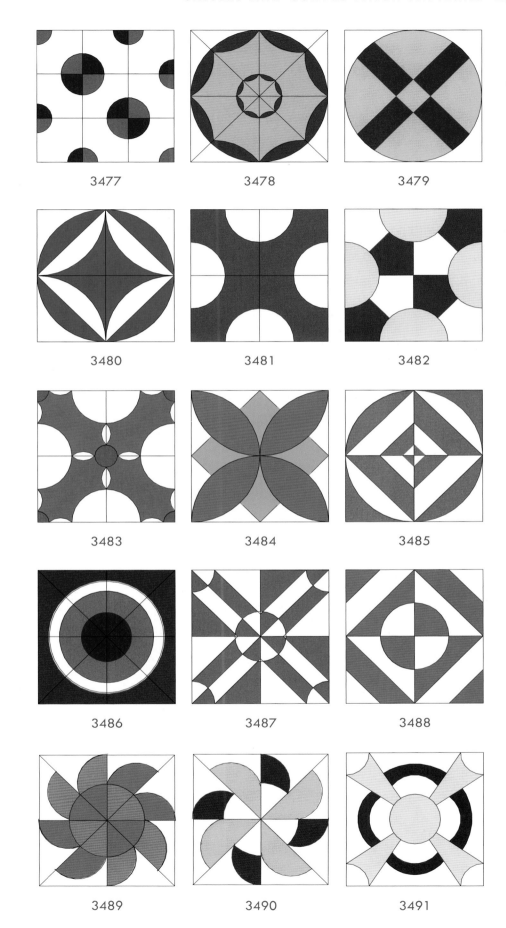

3477  3478  3479

3480  3481  3482

3483  3484  3485

3486  3487  3488

3489  3490  3491

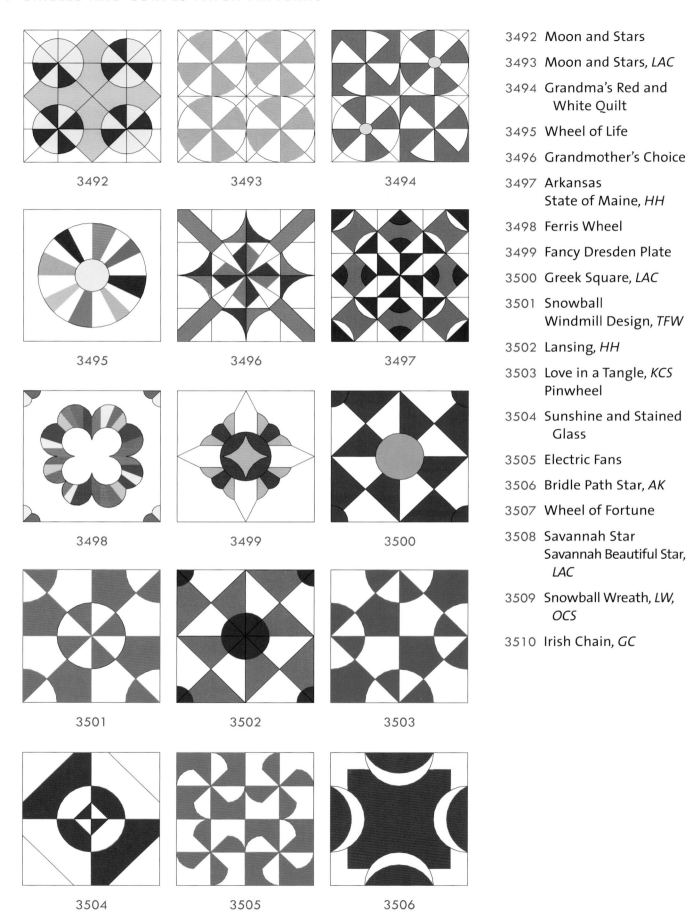

3492
3493
3494

3495
3496
3497

3498
3499
3500

3501
3502
3503

3504
3505
3506

3492 Moon and Stars

3493 Moon and Stars, *LAC*

3494 Grandma's Red and White Quilt

3495 Wheel of Life

3496 Grandmother's Choice

3497 Arkansas
State of Maine, *HH*

3498 Ferris Wheel

3499 Fancy Dresden Plate

3500 Greek Square, *LAC*

3501 Snowball
Windmill Design, *TFW*

3502 Lansing, *HH*

3503 Love in a Tangle, *KCS*
Pinwheel

3504 Sunshine and Stained Glass

3505 Electric Fans

3506 Bridle Path Star, *AK*

3507 Wheel of Fortune

3508 Savannah Star
Savannah Beautiful Star, *LAC*

3509 Snowball Wreath, *LW, OCS*

3510 Irish Chain, *GC*

3511 The Kansas Beauty

3512 Job's Tears
Endless Chain
Kansas Troubles
Rocky Road to Kansas
Slave Chain
Texas Tears

3513 Friendship Ring, *KCS*

3514 Sunburst

3515 Lillian's Favorite, *CS*
Monkey Puzzle, *AMS*

3516 Reminiscent of the
Wedding Ring, *KCS*
Remnant Ovals (curved
segments strip pieced
with scrap fabrics), *KCS*

3517 Four Leaf Clover, *KCS*

3518 Pin Cushion, *LAC*
Cushion Design
Orange Peel
Rob Peter and Pay Paul
Pincushion and Cucumbers

3519 Compass, *LAC*
Corn and Beans, *NC*

3520 Dolly Madison's Workbox,
*CaS*
Butter and Eggs, *NC*
Mutual Benefit, *CS*
Peter and Paul
Robbing Peter to Pay Paul
Steeplechase

3521 Tea Leaf, *LAC*
Bay Leaf, *GD*
Circle upon Circle, *MD*
Compass
Lafayette Orange Peel, *HAS*
Lover's Knot, *GC*
Pincushion
True Lover's Knot, *NC*

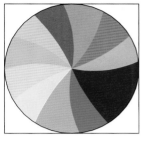

3507

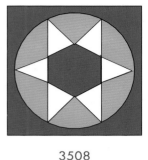

3508

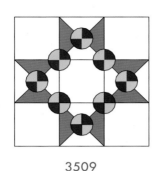

3509

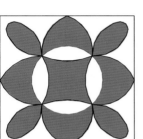

3510

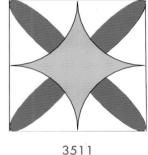

3511

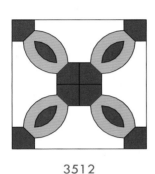

3512

3513

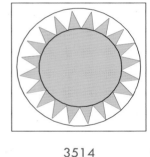

3514

3515

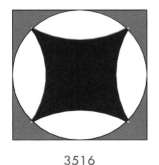

3516

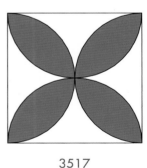

3517

3518

3519

3520

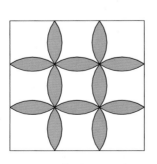

3521

3522

3523

3524

3525

3526

3527

3528

3529

3530

3531

3532

3533

3534

3535

3536

3522  Winner's Circle

3523  Chinese Gongs, *NC*

3524  Estelle's Choice, *HH*
       Jockey Cap
       Millwheel

3525  Elsie's Favorite

3526  New State Quilt Block

3527  Rose Dream, *KCS*
       Broken Square, *KCS*
       Endless Chain, *NC*
       Lover's Bowtie
       Lover's Knot
       Martha
       True Lover's Knot, *HAS*

3528  Whale Block, *LAC*

3529  Light and Dark, *AK*

3530  London Bridge, *AK*

3531  Orange Peel, *LAC*
       Lafayette Orange Peel
       Save a Piece

3532  Melon Patch
       Flower Petals

3533  Joseph's Coat, *OCS*

3534  Melon Patch, *WW*
       Magic Circle

3535  Grist Mill, *NC*
       Melon Patch Quilt, *LW*

3536  Nine Patch

3537 Improved Nine Patch
Bailey Nine Patch, *MD*
Circle upon Circle, *KCS*
Dinner Plate
Four Leaf Clover, *KCS*
Nine Patch Variation
Bridge Quilt (with card
suits appliquéd), *KCS*

3538 Black Beauty, *CS*
Red Buds, *NC*

3539 Washington Snowball,
*CS*

3540 Virginia Snowball, *NC*
Washington Snowball,
*HH*

3541 Snowball, *LAC*
Baseball
Pullman Puzzle

3542 Jupiter's Moons

3543 Hearts and Diamonds,
*HAS*

3544 Ladies Beautiful Star

3545 The Star Sapphire, *KCS*

3546 Circle and Star, *HH*

3547 Compass Point

3548 Twist and Turn, *AB, OCS*
Summer and Winter,
*OCS*

3549 The Car Wheel Quilt,
*KCS*

3550 Carolina Favorite, *LW,
OCS*

3551 Ladies' Fancy, *LAC*

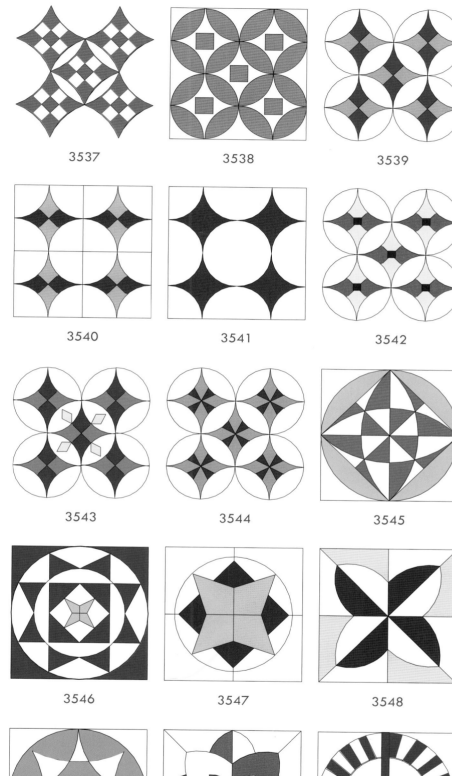

3537  3538  3539

3540  3541  3542

3543  3544  3545

3546  3547  3548

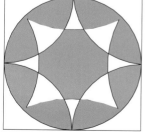

3549  3550  3551

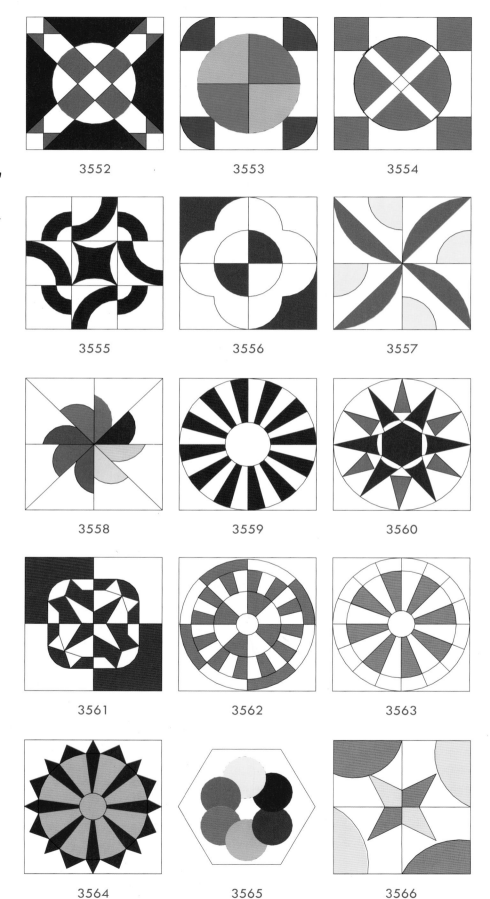

3552

3553

3554

3555

3556

3557

3558

3559

3560

3561

3562

3563

3564

3565

3566

3552 Hazel Valley Crossroads, *KCS*

3553 Pilot Wheel, *GC*

3554 Cart Wheel, *GC*

3555 Broken Circle, *KCS*

3556 Snowball Flower, *OCS*

3557 Waving Plumes, *LW, OCS*

3558 The Pinwheel

3559 True Lovers' Buggy Wheel, *KCS* Wheel of Chance

3560 Rolling Pin Wheel

3561 Oklahoma, *HH*

3562 Wheel of Fortune

3563 Wheel of Fortune

3564 Oriental Star

3565 Roses of Picardy

3566 Twist and Turn, *LW, OCS*

3567 The Lover's Chain
Lover's Links

3568 Springtime, *QW, 1983*

3569 Mississippi Oakleaf
Cactus Blossom Patch,
*LAC*
Cactus Bloom, *NC*

3570 The Royal, *LAC*
Grecian Cross
Royal Cross

3571 Snail's Trail

3572 Wings, *LAC*

3573 Bird's Eye View

3574 Boston

3575 East and West
The Broken Stone, *KCS*
Lover's Quarrel, *AMS*
New Wedding Ring

3576 Give and Take

3577 Illinois Snowball

3578 Tangled Trails, *PF, 1854*

3579 Bush's Points of Light,
*SSQ, 1992*

3580 Sun Over
Transmountain,
*Sheila Rodriguez,
PQ, 1986*

3581 Moon Over the
Mountain

3567

3568

3569

3570

3571

3572

3573

3574

3575

3576

3577

3578

3579

3580

3581

5,500 QUILT BLOCK DESIGNS

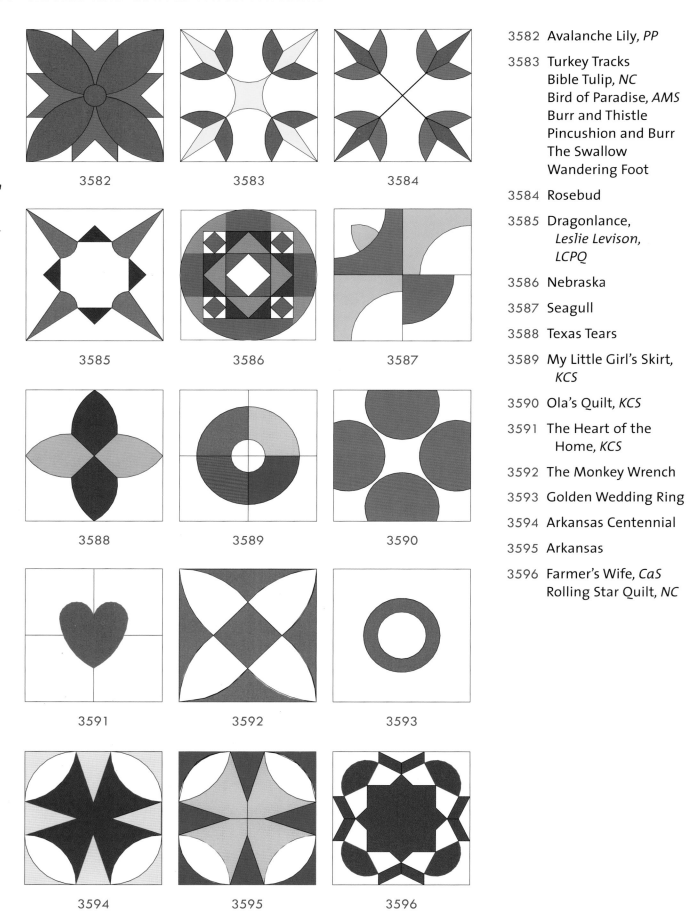

3582     3583     3584

3585     3586     3587

3588     3589     3590

3591     3592     3593

3594     3595     3596

3582   Avalanche Lily, *PP*

3583   Turkey Tracks
Bible Tulip, *NC*
Bird of Paradise, *AMS*
Burr and Thistle
Pincushion and Burr
The Swallow
Wandering Foot

3584   Rosebud

3585   Dragonlance,
*Leslie Levison,*
*LCPQ*

3586   Nebraska

3587   Seagull

3588   Texas Tears

3589   My Little Girl's Skirt,
*KCS*

3590   Ola's Quilt, *KCS*

3591   The Heart of the
Home, *KCS*

3592   The Monkey Wrench

3593   Golden Wedding Ring

3594   Arkansas Centennial

3595   Arkansas

3596   Farmer's Wife, *CaS*
Rolling Star Quilt, *NC*

3597 Wagon Wheels, *KCS*
Old Fashioned Wagon
Wheels

3598 Fan and Ring,
*Margaret Dewey, KCS*

3599 Pointed Ovals, *KCS*
Love's Chain, *NC*

3600 The Quilter's Fan, *KCS*

3601 Around the World, *KCS*

3602 Lost Paradise, *KCS*

3603 The Full Moon, *KCS*

3604 The Broken Stone, *KCS*

3605 Friendship Knot, *KCS*

3606 Hands All Around, *KCS*

3607 Drunkard's Trail, *KCS*
Rainbow Quilt

3608 The Four Winds, *KCS*

3609 Orange Peel Variation,
*PQ*

3610 Hearts and Flowers

3611 Arab Tent
Chimney Swallow

3597    3598    3599

3600    3601    3602

3603    3604    3605

3606    3607    3608

3609    3610    3611

5,500 QUILT BLOCK DESIGNS

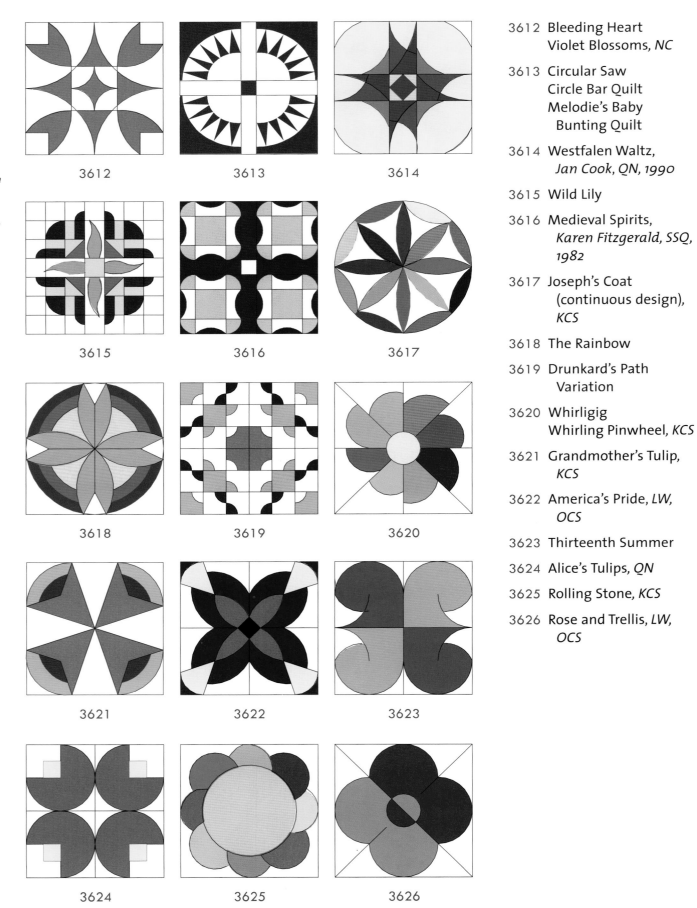

3612

3613

3614

3615

3616

3617

3618

3619

3620

3621

3622

3623

3624

3625

3626

3612 Bleeding Heart
Violet Blossoms, *NC*

3613 Circular Saw
Circle Bar Quilt
Melodie's Baby
Bunting Quilt

3614 Westfalen Waltz,
*Jan Cook, QN, 1990*

3615 Wild Lily

3616 Medieval Spirits,
*Karen Fitzgerald, SSQ,
1982*

3617 Joseph's Coat
(continuous design),
*KCS*

3618 The Rainbow

3619 Drunkard's Path
Variation

3620 Whirligig
Whirling Pinwheel, *KCS*

3621 Grandmother's Tulip,
*KCS*

3622 America's Pride, *LW,
OCS*

3623 Thirteenth Summer

3624 Alice's Tulips, *QN*

3625 Rolling Stone, *KCS*

3626 Rose and Trellis, *LW,
OCS*

3627 Pieced Sunflower
Single Sunflower
Sunflower

3628 Aster

3629 Sunburst

3630 Mariner's Compass

3631 Mariner's Compass

3632 Mariner's Compass
Sunburst
Sunrise, *GD*

3633 Starry Compass,
*Paula Libby, LCPQ*

3634 Mariner's Compass

3635 Compass

3636 Sunrise

3637 Georgetown Circle

3638 Sylvia's Choice

3639 Sundials,
*Gayle Ropp, QT*

3640 Sunburst

3641 Without Constraint,
*PAG*

3627

3628

3629

3630

3631

3632

3633

3634

3635

3636

3637

3638

3639

3640

3641

3642   The Wishing Star, *HaM*, *SSQ*, *1986*

3643   Sunburst Star

3644   Farmer's Delight Triple Sunflower

3645   Devil's Puzzle

3646   Suspension Bridge

3647   The Wheel of Fortune, *HH*

3648   Car Wheels Harvest Sun (two colors)

3649   Rolling Pinwheel

3650   Irish Chain

3651   Fortune's Wheel

3652   Star of the West, *LAC*

3653   Rainbow, *LAC*

3654   Slashed Star, *LAC* Mariner's Compass Sunrise Pattern

3655   Sunset Star New York (full circle)

3656   Tic-Tac-Toe, *QN*, *1975*

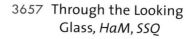

5,500 QUILT BLOCK DESIGNS

3657 Through the Looking
    Glass, *HaM*, *SSQ*

3658 Rosebud Quilt, *KCS*

3659 Tulip Pattern, *KCS*

3660 The Tulip Quilt, *KCS*

3661 Sunset Quilt Block,
    *QW*, *1985*

3662 Joseph's Coat

3663 Cog Wheels

3664 Oil Fields of Oklahoma,
    *KCS*

3665 Honey Bee, *KCS*

3666 Jinx Star, *KCS*

3667 Missouri Morning Star,
    *KCS*

3668 Rising Sun, *KCS*

3669 Friendship Quilt, *KCS*
    Block and Ring

3670 Strawberry
    Friendship Ring
    Full Blown Tulip
    Oriental Star
    Pilot's Wheel

3671 Mace Head, *NC*

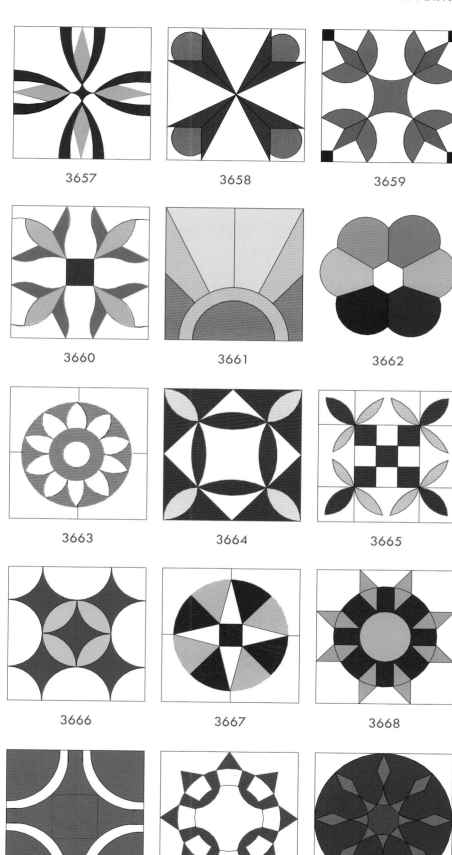

3657     3658     3659

3660     3661     3662

3663     3664     3665

3666     3667     3668

3669     3670     3671

5,500 QUILT BLOCK DESIGNS

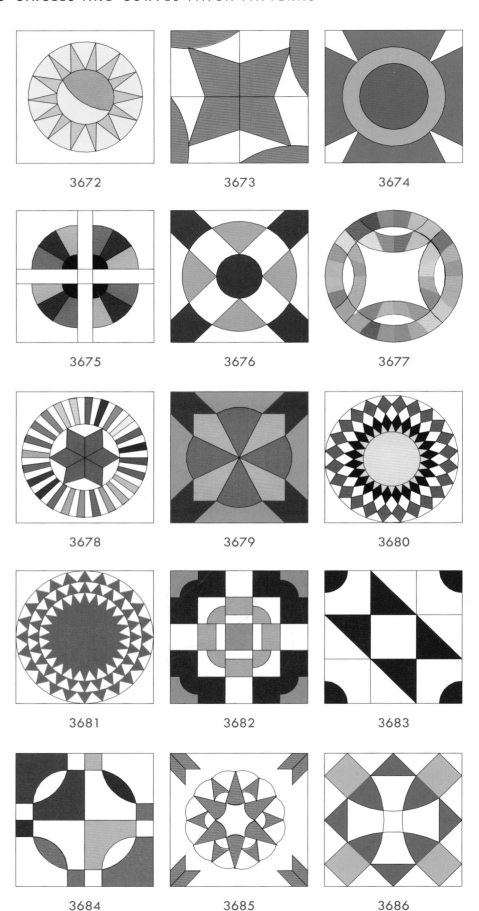

3672   Moon in Eclipse, *1800s*

3673   Twist and Turn, *LW, OCS*

3674   Name Unknown, *QW, 1987*

3675   Color Wheels

3676   Wagon Wheels

3677   Double Wedding Ring

3678   Lincoln Quilt, *1865*

3679   Whirling Stars

3680   Sunburst

3681   Sawtooth Circle

3682   Savannah Squares

3683   Wishing Well

3684   Cactus Rose

3685   Album Quilt

3686   Lady of the Lake

3672     3673     3674

3675     3676     3677

3678     3679     3680

3681     3682     3683

3684     3685     3686

3687 The Name Is Hesper, *KCS*

3688 The Moon Is New, *KCS*

3689 Quilter's Fan, *KCS*

3690 Ice Cream Cone, *KCS*

3691 Ice Cream Cone, *KCS*

3692 Lost Paradise, *KCS*

3693 Circular Flying Geese, *Judy Mathieson*

3694 Circular Flying Geese Variation

3695 Pathfinder

3696 Yellow Point

3697 Flywheel
Circle Saw, *KCS*
Oklahoma Star
Rising Sun, *LAC*
Wagon Wheel, *HH*
Wheel of Life, *HAS*

3698 Cogwheel

3699 Star and Planets

3700 Southern Pride

3701 Bride's Prize

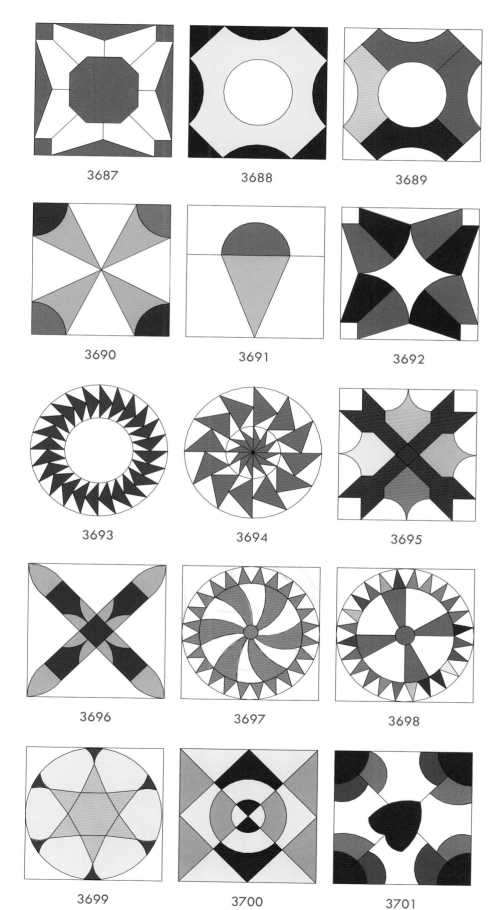

3687

3688

3689

3690

3691

3692

3693

3694

3695

3696

3697

3698

3699

3700

3701

5,500 QUILT BLOCK DESIGNS

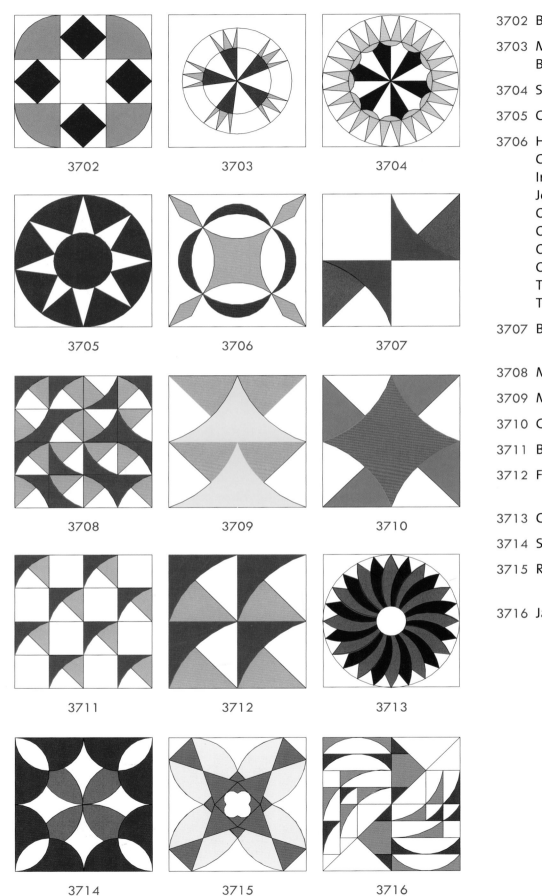

3702

3703

3704

3705

3706

3707

3708

3709

3710

3711

3712

3713

3714

3715

3716

3702 Broken Squares

3703 Mountain Pink, *NC*
Broken Crown, *KCS*

3704 Sunburst

3705 Charity Wheel

3706 Hickory Leaf, *LAC*
Compass, *CaS*
Irish Chain, *HH*
Job's Patience
Oak Leaf
Orange Peel, *CaS*
Orange Slices
Order #11
The Reel
Texas Pointer, *KCS*

3707 Butterfly Migration,
*QW, 1989*

3708 Mixed Emotions

3709 Mountain Peaks

3710 Garden Paths

3711 Bows and Arrows

3712 Four and Twenty
Blackbirds

3713 Circular Saw, *HH*

3714 Springtime, *LW, OCS*

3715 Rose Windows, *LW,
OCS*

3716 Jacques in the Boat,
*QN*

3717 Pride of the Bride,
     *AB, OCS*

3718 Borrow and Return,
     *Coats & Clark*

3719 A Winding Trail, *NC*

3720 Round Table, *CS*

3721 Four Buds, *KCS*

3722 Wedding Ring
     Bouquet
     Formal Elegance

3723 Indian Summer
     Broken Circle
     Sunflower

3724 Wheel of Fortune
     Buggy Wheel
     Sunflower

3725 Fanny's Favorite

3726 White Rose

3727 Flo's Fan
     Rainbow Quilt Design,
     *NP*

3728 Imperial Fan

3729 Sunrise, Sunset

3730 Grandmother's Fan

3731 Fan Quadrille,
     *MoM*

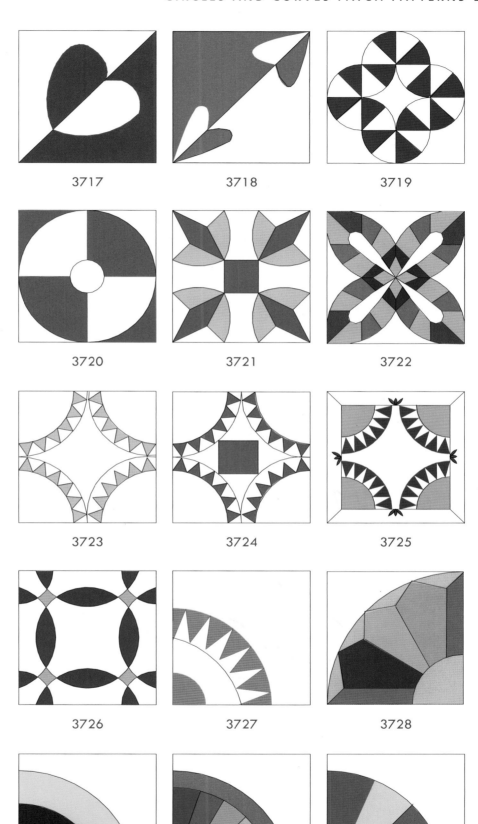

3717         3718         3719

3720         3721         3722

3723         3724         3725

3726         3727         3728

3729         3730         3731

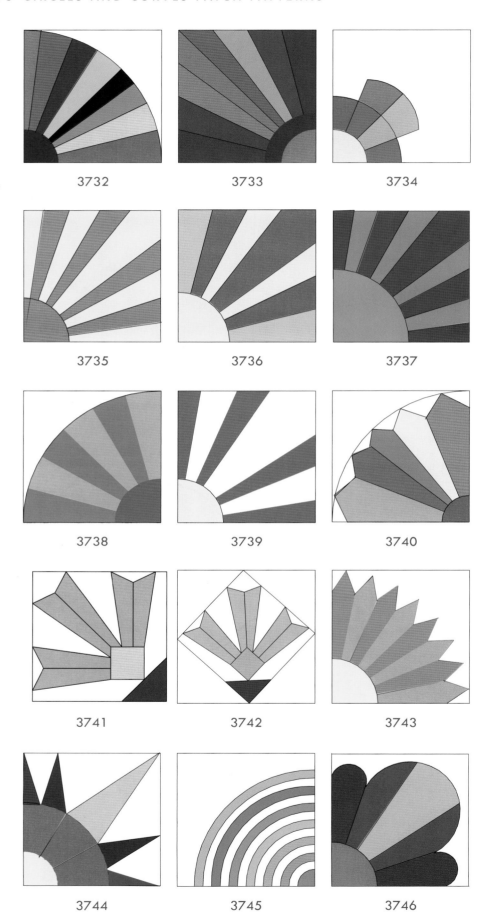

3732 Grandmother's Fan
Fan Quilt, *KCS*
Formosa Fan, *NC*

3733 Friendship Fan, *NC*

3734 Unnamed

3735 Kansas Sunshine, *CS,*
*1910*
Sunshine
Friendship Fan, *CS*

3736 Rebecca's Fan, *KCS*

3737 Friendship Fan, *NM*

3738 Grandmother's Fan

3739 Harvest Sun

3740 Mary's Fan

3741 Floral Bouquet

3742 Floral Bouquet

3743 Eight Point Fan

3744 Rising Sun, *AB*

3745 Caroline's Fan

3746 Grandmother's Scrap
Quilt, *AB*

3747 Fan Patchwork, *LAC*
A Fan of Many Colors, *KCS*
Grandmother's Fan
Mary's Fan, *HAS*

3748 Japanese Fan, *LW*

3749 Unnamed Fan

3750 Lattice Fan

3751 Fannie's Fan

3752 Japanese Fan
Grandmother's Fan

3753 Fanny's Fan
Grandmother's Fan
Mother's Fan

3754 Flower of Autumn, *KCS*

3755 Fan

3756 Fan, *LAC*

3757 Art Deco Fans

3758 The Pride of East
Kingston, *Nancy
Kiman, SSQ, 1989*

3759 Milady's Fan, *AMS*
Chinese Fan

3760 Victorian Fan

3761 Milady's Fan

3747

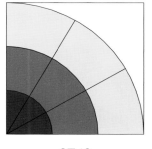

3748

3749

3750

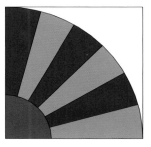

3751

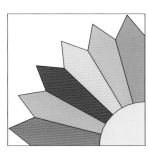

3752

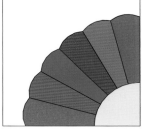

3753

3754

3755

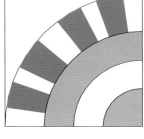

3756

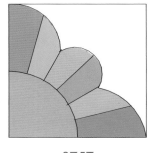

3757

3758

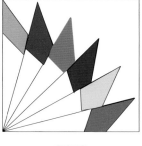

3759

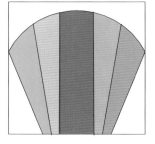

3760

3761

5,500 QUILT BLOCK DESIGNS

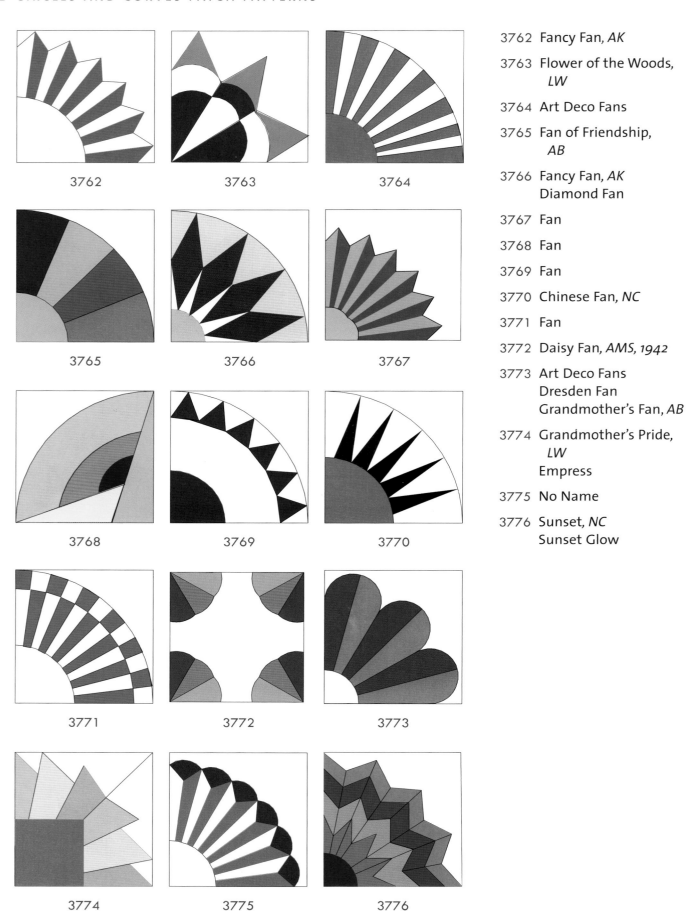

3762

3763

3764

3765

3766

3767

3768

3769

3770

3771

3772

3773

3774

3775

3776

3762 Fancy Fan, *AK*

3763 Flower of the Woods, *LW*

3764 Art Deco Fans

3765 Fan of Friendship, *AB*

3766 Fancy Fan, *AK* Diamond Fan

3767 Fan

3768 Fan

3769 Fan

3770 Chinese Fan, *NC*

3771 Fan

3772 Daisy Fan, *AMS, 1942*

3773 Art Deco Fans Dresden Fan Grandmother's Fan, *AB*

3774 Grandmother's Pride, *LW* Empress

3775 No Name

3776 Sunset, *NC* Sunset Glow

3777 Fringed Aster, *1943*

3778 Wedding Ring

3779 Circle of Fans,
 *TQr, 1992*

3780 Broken Circle
 Sunflower

3781 King David's Crown

3782 Kansas Sunflower

3783 Ferris Wheel

3784 Grandma's Favorite,
 *1971*

3785 Daisy Wheel, *MM*

3786 Carnival, *MM*

3787 Oriole Window, *KCS*
 Circular Saw, *KCS*
 Four Little Fans, *KCS*

3788 Red, White and Blue,
 *CoM*

3789 Squared Circle, *HM*

3790 Friendship Ring, *LW*

3791 Spinning Wheel

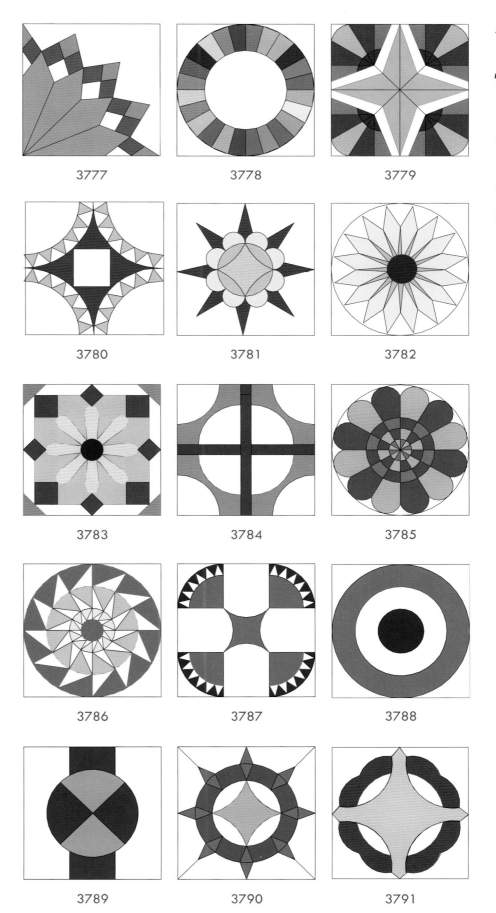

3777

3778

3779

3780

3781

3782

3783

3784

3785

3786

3787

3788

3789

3790

3791

5,500 QUILT BLOCK DESIGNS

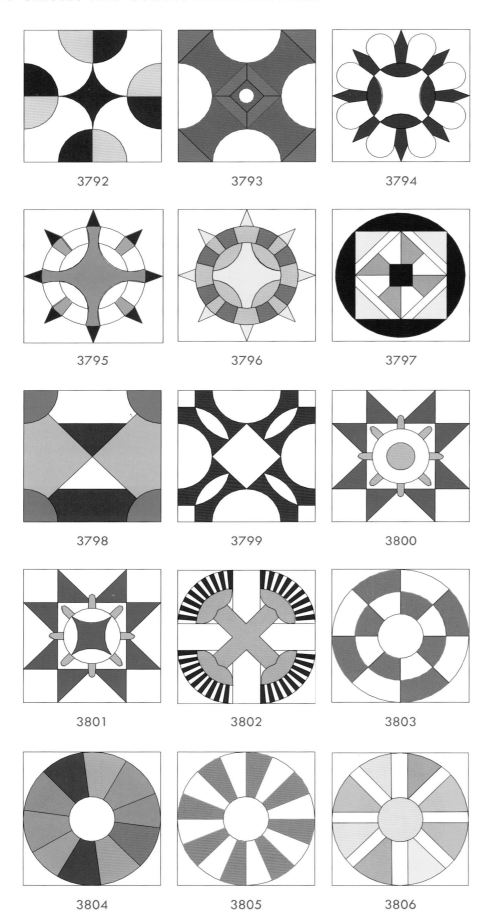

3792 Half Moon Block, *NC*
      Moon Block, *NC*

3793 Babe Ruth Diamond, *QN*

3794 The Sunflower, *LAC*

3795 The Pilot's Wheel

3796 Whirling Wheel, *HM*

3797 Old Mill Wheel, *AK*

3798 Hour Glass, *NC*

3799 The Stockade, *CS*

3800 Rose Album, *LAC*

3801 Rose Album

3802 Claws, *NC*

3803 Wheel of Fortune

3804 Baby Aster

3805 Wheel of Fortune

3806 Double Rainbow, *LW*
      Ozark Sunflower, *KCS*
      Pieced Sunflower, *KCS*

3807 Wheel of Fortune

3808 Chariot Wheel

3809 Windblown Daisy, *NC*

3810 Wheel of Time

3811 Parasol Block, *NC*

3812 Pinwheel Quilt

3813 Feathered Star, *LW*

3814 Southern Star, *HH*

3815 Rhododendron Star, *QN*

3816 Spinning Ball

3817 Whirl Wind, *PP*

3818 Spinning Ball Spiral

3819 Noonday
A Brave Sunflower
Kansas Sunflower
Oklahoma Sunburst, *KCS*
Rising Sun
Russian Sunflower
Sunburst

3820 Noxall Quilt Block
Narcissus

3821 Peeled Orange, *NC*

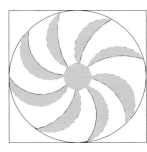

3807

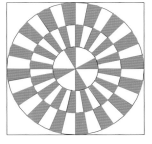

3808

3809

3810

3811

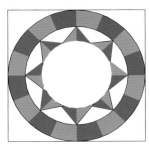

3812

3813

3814

3815

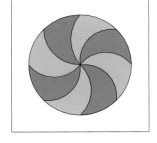

3816

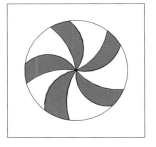

3817

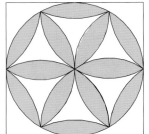

3818

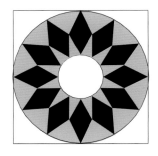

3819

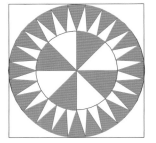

3820

3821

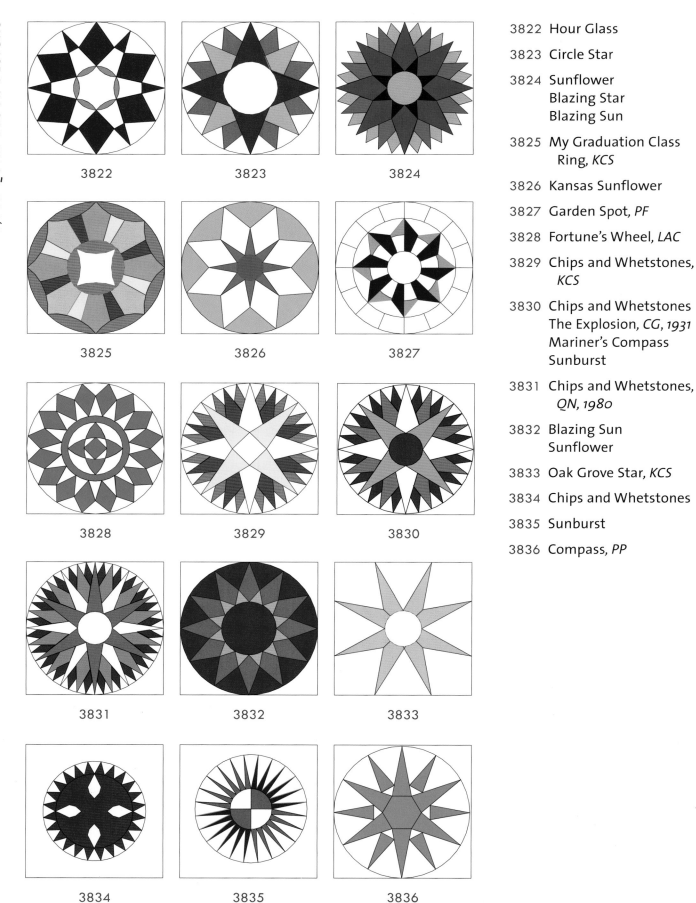

3822

3823

3824

3825

3826

3827

3828

3829

3830

3831

3832

3833

3834

3835

3836

3822 Hour Glass

3823 Circle Star

3824 Sunflower
Blazing Star
Blazing Sun

3825 My Graduation Class
Ring, *KCS*

3826 Kansas Sunflower

3827 Garden Spot, *PF*

3828 Fortune's Wheel, *LAC*

3829 Chips and Whetstones,
*KCS*

3830 Chips and Whetstones
The Explosion, *CG, 1931*
Mariner's Compass
Sunburst

3831 Chips and Whetstones,
*QN, 1980*

3832 Blazing Sun
Sunflower

3833 Oak Grove Star, *KCS*

3834 Chips and Whetstones

3835 Sunburst

3836 Compass, *PP*

3837 Sunflower

3838 The Buzz Saw, *KCS*

3839 Indian Paintbrush, *PP*

3840 Car Wheel, *KCS*

3841 Mariner's Compass

3842 Compass Star Quilt

3843 Mariner's Compass

3844 French Star

3845 Cog Wheels, *LAC*
      Harvest Sun
      Pennsylvania Wheel
        Quilt, *HH*
      Topeka, *HH*

3846 Signature

3847 Sunburst, *GC, 1931*

3848 The Sunburst,
        *Modern Priscilla*

3849 Pyrotechnics, *LAC*

3850 Petal Circle in a
        Square, *KCS*

3851 Pyrotechnics, *LAC*
      Wheel, *FJ*
      Wheel of Fortune

3837

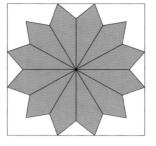
3838

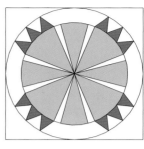
3839

3840

3841

3842

3843

3844

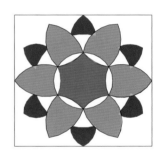
3845

3846

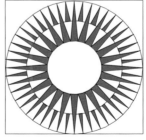
3847

3848

3849

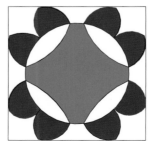
3850

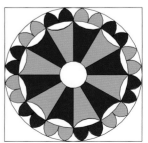
3851

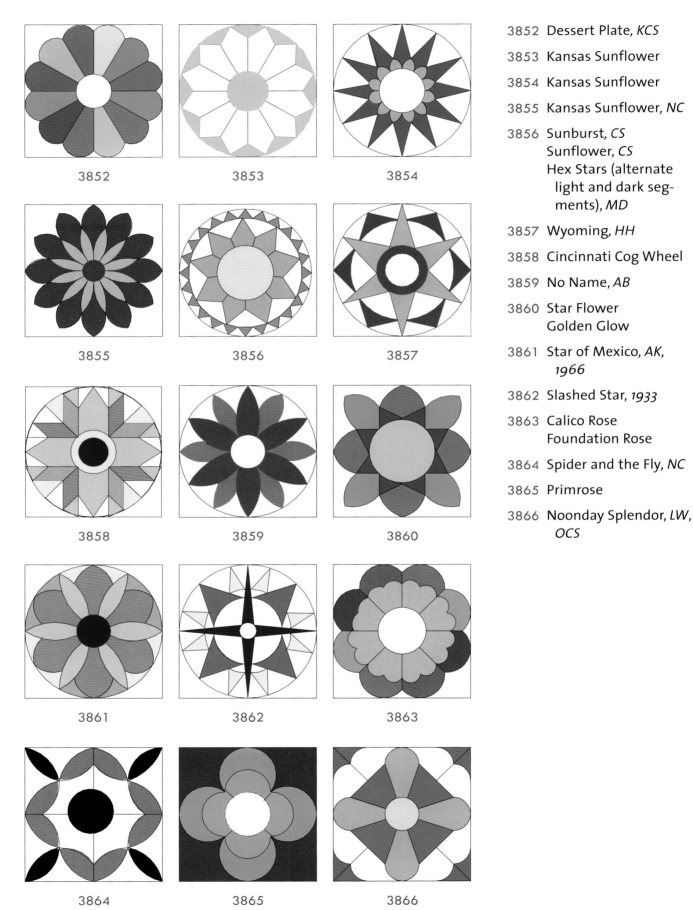

3852

3853

3854

3855

3856

3857

3858

3859

3860

3861

3862

3863

3864

3865

3866

3852 Dessert Plate, *KCS*

3853 Kansas Sunflower

3854 Kansas Sunflower

3855 Kansas Sunflower, *NC*

3856 Sunburst, *CS*
Sunflower, *CS*
Hex Stars (alternate light and dark segments), *MD*

3857 Wyoming, *HH*

3858 Cincinnati Cog Wheel

3859 No Name, *AB*

3860 Star Flower
Golden Glow

3861 Star of Mexico, *AK, 1966*

3862 Slashed Star, *1933*

3863 Calico Rose
Foundation Rose

3864 Spider and the Fly, *NC*

3865 Primrose

3866 Noonday Splendor, *LW, OCS*

3867 Full Blown Rose, *NC*

3868 Airship, *CoM*

3869 Magnolia Blossom

3870 Star of West Virginia, *HH*

3871 Pilot Wheel, *GC*

3872 Orange Peel, *GD*

3873 Noonday Lily, *HAS*

3874 Painted Snowball, *NC*

3875 Wyoming Patch, *LAC*
     Texas Sunflower, *CoM*

3876 The Jewel, *AMS*
     Hummingbirds, *NC*

3877 No Name

3878 Spool of 1966, *AK*

3879 Dogwood Bloom, *CS*

3880 Fox and Geese, *LAC*

3881 Tulip Wheel

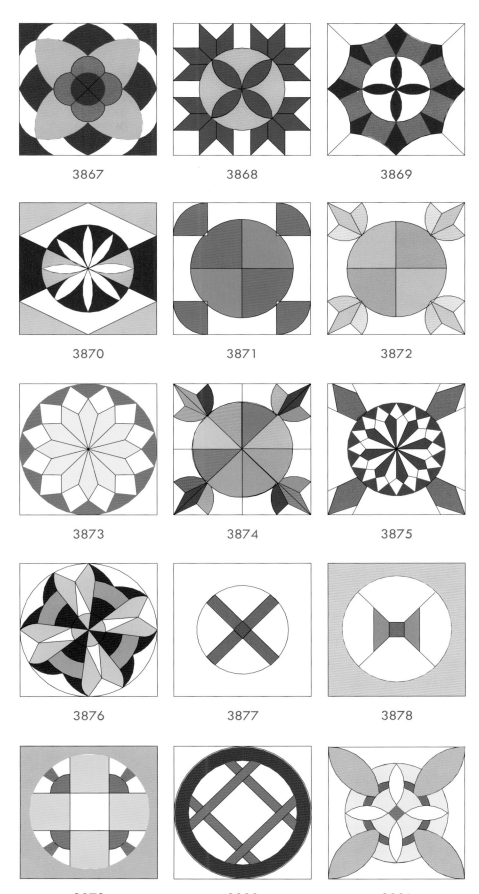

3867    3868    3869

3870    3871    3872

3873    3874    3875

3876    3877    3878

3879    3880    3881

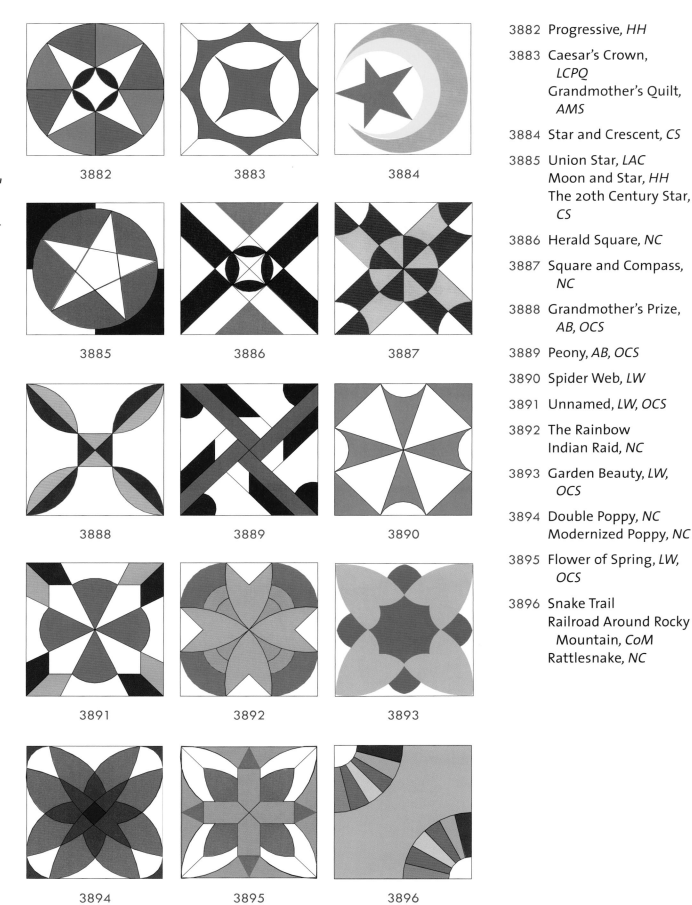

3882

3883

3884

3885

3886

3887

3888

3889

3890

3891

3892

3893

3894

3895

3896

3882 Progressive, *HH*

3883 Caesar's Crown, *LCPQ*
Grandmother's Quilt, *AMS*

3884 Star and Crescent, *CS*

3885 Union Star, *LAC*
Moon and Star, *HH*
The 20th Century Star, *CS*

3886 Herald Square, *NC*

3887 Square and Compass, *NC*

3888 Grandmother's Prize, *AB, OCS*

3889 Peony, *AB, OCS*

3890 Spider Web, *LW*

3891 Unnamed, *LW, OCS*

3892 The Rainbow
Indian Raid, *NC*

3893 Garden Beauty, *LW, OCS*

3894 Double Poppy, *NC*
Modernized Poppy, *NC*

3895 Flower of Spring, *LW, OCS*

3896 Snake Trail
Railroad Around Rocky Mountain, *CoM*
Rattlesnake, *NC*

3897 Whirling Fans, *AB, OCS*
Double Fans

3898 Rainbow, *AMS*

3899 Snake in the Hollow,
*QN*
Gypsy Trail

3900 The Sea Shell Quilt,
*KCS*

3901 The Bleeding Heart,
*1898*

3902 Mariner's Compass
Mary Strickler's Quilt

3903 Black Eyed Susan

3904 Golden Corn

3905 Alcazar, *NC*
A Young Man's
Invention, *KCS*

3906 Double L

3907 Wheels

3908 Wedding Ring
Bouquet, *AMS*

3909 Corsage Bouquet, *AMS*

3910 Tennessee Circle

3911 King's Crown, *PF*

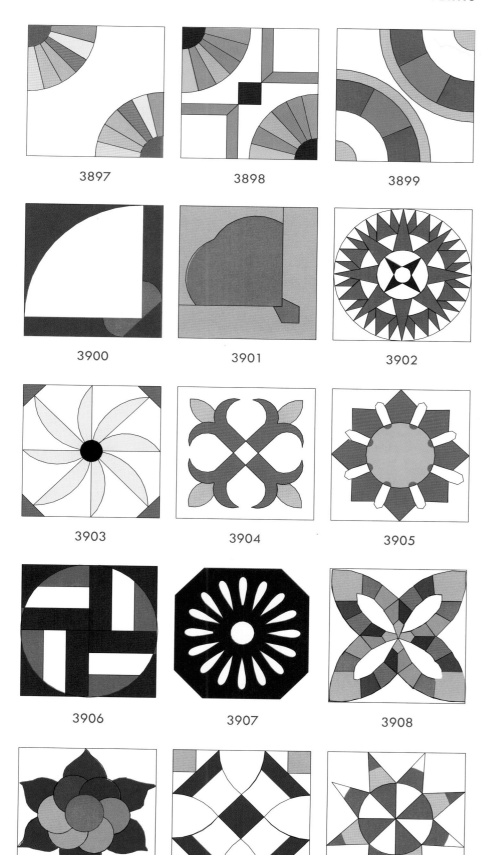

3897

3898

3899

3900

3901

3902

3903

3904

3905

3906

3907

3908

3909

3910

3911

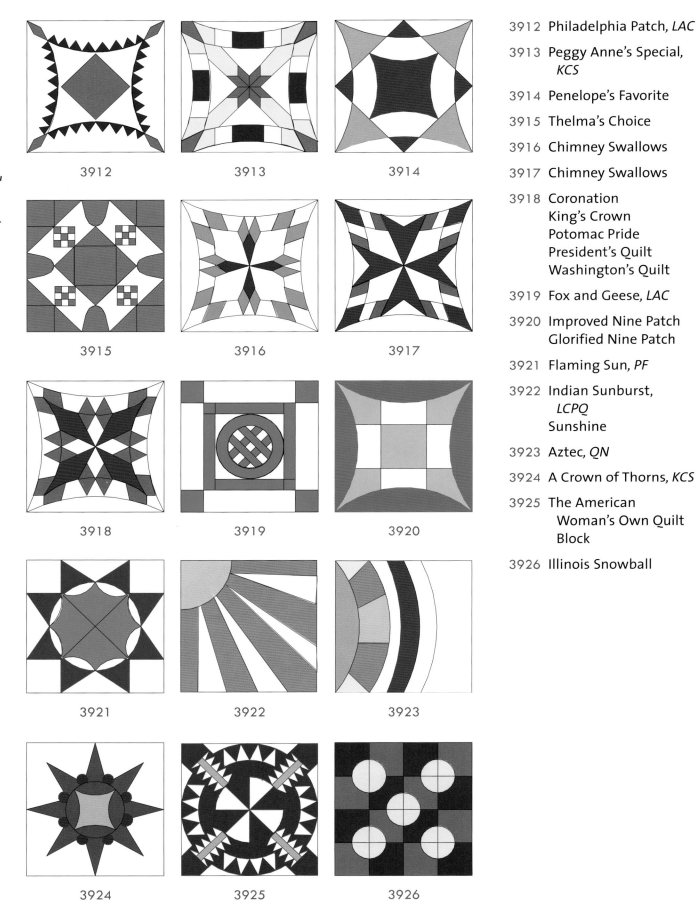

3912 Philadelphia Patch, *LAC*

3913 Peggy Anne's Special, *KCS*

3914 Penelope's Favorite

3915 Thelma's Choice

3916 Chimney Swallows

3917 Chimney Swallows

3918 Coronation
King's Crown
Potomac Pride
President's Quilt
Washington's Quilt

3919 Fox and Geese, *LAC*

3920 Improved Nine Patch
Glorified Nine Patch

3921 Flaming Sun, *PF*

3922 Indian Sunburst,
*LCPQ*
Sunshine

3923 Aztec, *QN*

3924 A Crown of Thorns, *KCS*

3925 The American
Woman's Own Quilt
Block

3926 Illinois Snowball

3927  Arkansas Star

3928  Kaleidoscope, *MM*

3929  Butterfly Quadrille

3930  Noonday Sun

3931  Sylvia's Choice

3932  Broken Circle, *CS*
      Sunburst
      Sunflower, *KCS*
      Suspension Bridge, *LAC*

3933  Wheel of Fortune
      Buggy Wheel

3934  Setting Sun
      Indian Summer

3935  A Red, White and Blue
      Quilt, *MD*

3936  Lady Finger, *LHJ*
      Lady Finger and
         Sunflower
      Grandmother's
         Engagement Ring,
         *MoM*

3937  Sunflower

3938  Jupiter's Moons, *NC*

3939  Saturn's Rings
      Grist Mill

3940  Duke's Dilemma

3941  Bleeding Heart, *PP*

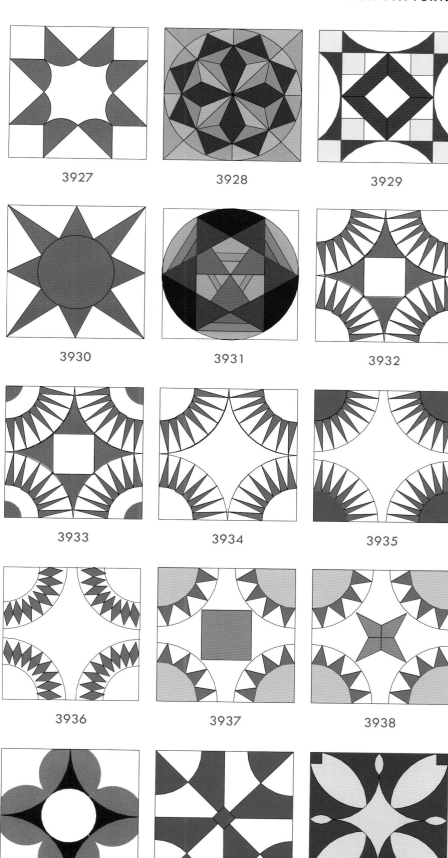

3927     3928     3929

3930     3931     3932

3933     3934     3935

3936     3937     3938

3939     3940     3941

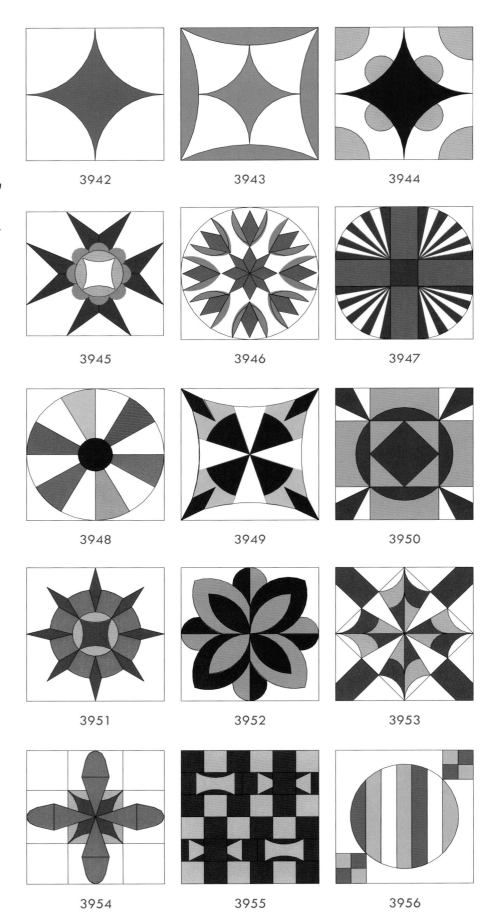

3942

3943

3944

3945

3946

3947

3948

3949

3950

3951

3952

3953

3954

3955

3956

3942 Doors and Windows

3943 Elsie's Favorite, *CS*

3944 The Rosebud, *KCS*

3945 North Star

3946 Cottage Tulips

3947 Color Wheel

3948 Color Wheel

3949 Christmas Day, *QW, 1987*

3950 Center Ring, *MLM, SSQ, 1983*

3951 Caesar's Crown

3952 Carolina Favorite

3953 Grandmother's Choice

3954 Paducah Peony

3955 Chain Bridge, *Sharyn Durham, SSQ, 1983*

3956 Candy Drops, *Ursula Michael, SSQ, 1989*

3957 Cameo Quilt (continuous scrap design)

3958 Behold...a Star, *QWO*

3959 Circle Petal in a Square, *KCS*

3960 Bay Leaf

3961 Autumn Kaleidoscope, *Norma Robson, SSQ, 1985*

3962 Apple Cores, *Dorothy Herbston, QWO, 1988*

3963 Autumn Spinning Star, *Dorothy Herbston, QWO, 1988*

3964 Rattlesnake

3965 Kansas Sunrise

3966 Sunflower Sunburst

3967 Sunflower

3968 Swallow's Nest

3969 Paragon Quilt Block

3970 Palm Leaf

3971 Papa's Delight, *CS*

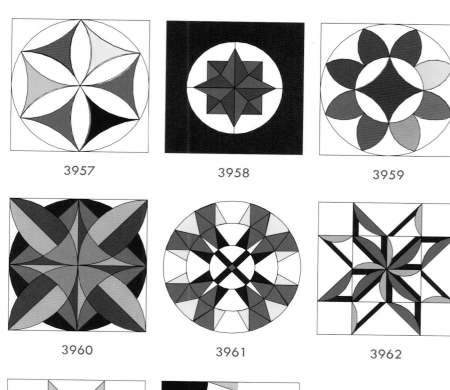

3957

3958

3959

3960

3961

3962

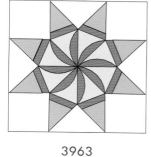

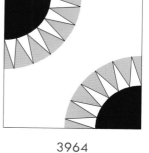

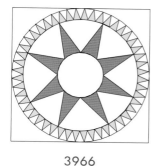

3963

3964

3965

3966

3967

3968

3969

3970

3971

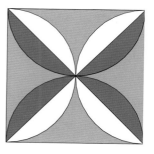

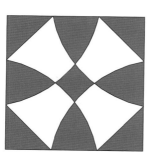

3972

3973

3974

3975

3976

3977

3978

3979

3980

3981

3982

3983

3984

3985

3986

3972 Raleigh Quilt Block, *HH* Tennessee Circles

3973 Queen of the May

3974 Queen's Delight

3975 Roast Rods

3976 Round Table

3977 Samoa

3978 Rosette Quilt Pattern

3979 Soul Knot

3980 Scuppernong Hull Quilt Block

3981 Square and Circle

3982 The Stockade

3983 Southern Star

3984 Around the World

3985 Drunkard's Path

3986 Baby Bunting

3987  Country Fields

3988  China Plate
      Fancy Dresden Plate

3989  Dresden Plate

3990  Dresden Plate
      Baby Aster

3991  Swirl Dresden Plate

3992  Dresden Plate

3993  Dresden Plate

3994  Dresden Plate

3995  Dresden Plate

3996  Dresden Plate

3997  Dresden Flower

3998  Pilot Wheel

3999  Cartwheel

4000  Broken Squares

4001  Daniel's Device, *MLM,
      QWO, 1985*

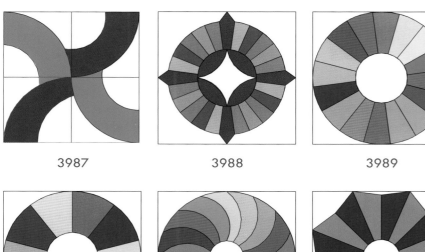

3987   3988   3989

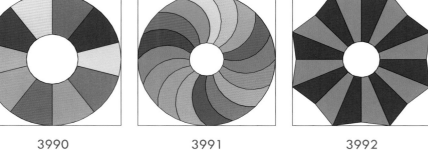

3990   3991   3992

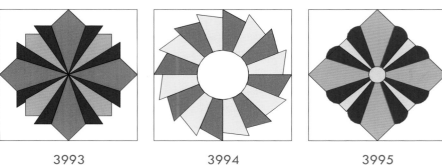

3993   3994   3995

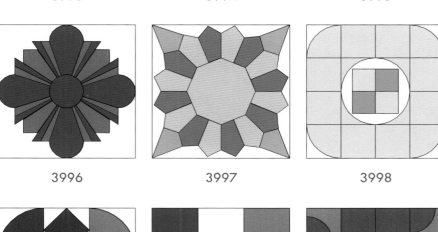

3996   3997   3998

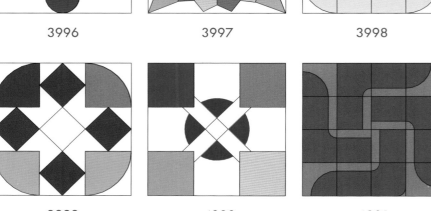

3999   4000   4001

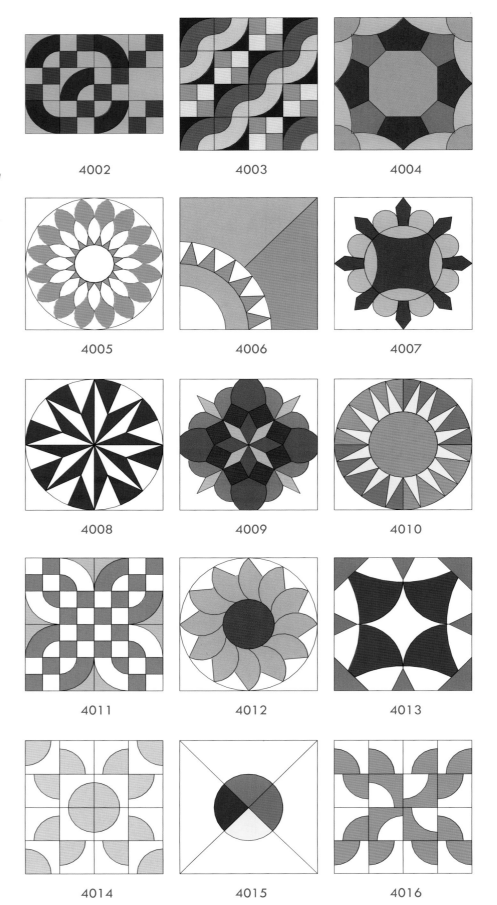

4002

4003

4004

4005

4006

4007

4008

4009

4010

4011

4012

4013

4014

4015

4016

4002 Mountain Trail

4003 Mountain View

4004 Friendship Garden

4005 Crown of Thorns

4006 Giant Dahlia

4007 Crown of Thorns

4008 Mariner's Compass, *Compuquilt.com*

4009 Kite Variation, *PQ*

4010 Prairie Flowers

4011 Dogwood Blossom, *KCS*

4012 Sunflower

4013 Morning Glory

4014 Harvest Moon, *Judy Rehmel, QW*

4015 Baby's Ball Friendship Quilt, *QW*

4016 Sunshine and Shadow

4017 Wishing Well

4018 Baseball

4019 Greek Cross, *LAC*
Cross Patch
Maltese Cross, *NC*
Work-basket, *HH*

4020 An Heirloom Quilt, *OCS*

4021 No Name

4022 Grandmother's Brooch
of Love

4023 Cross Roads, *HAS*

4024 The Great Circle Quilt,
*AMS*

4025 Lost Paradise, *KCS*

4026 Evergreen, *HAS*

4027 Twist, *NC*

4028 Double Pinwheel, *LW*,
*OCS*

4029 Hunter's Horns, *AG*

4030 Friendship Circle, *LW*,
*OCS*

4031 Round Robin, *CS*

5,500 QUILT BLOCK DESIGNS

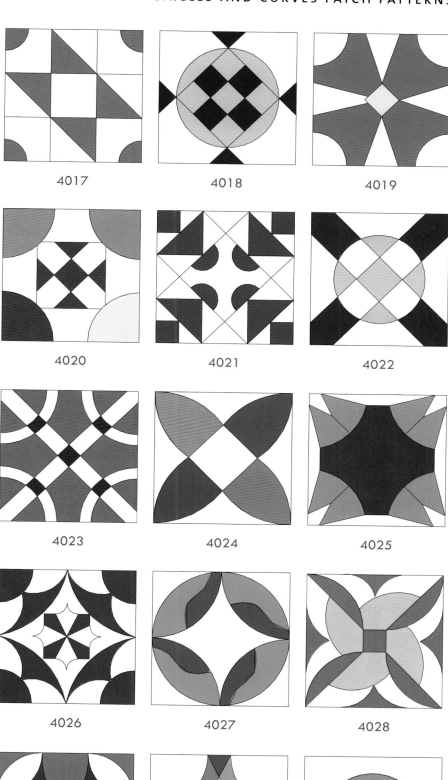

4017

4018

4019

4020

4021

4022

4023

4024

4025

4026

4027

4028

4029

4030

4031

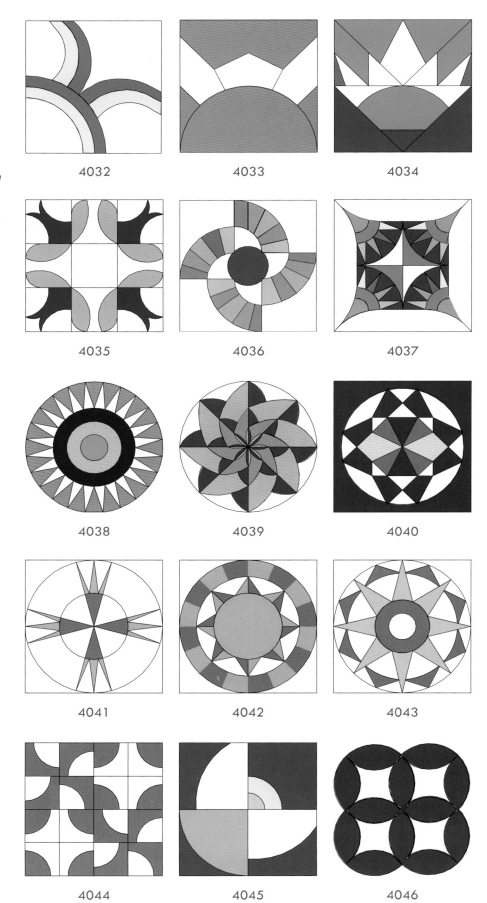

4032

4033

4034

4035

4036

4037

4038

4039

4040

4041

4042

4043

4044

4045

4046

4032 Grandma's Fan, *PF*

4033 Queen's Crown

4034 Sunrise, *PF*, *1977*

4035 Bluebell, *KCS*, *1940*

4036 Letha's Electric Fan, *KCS*

4037 Friendship, *1871*

4038 Rocky Mountain Variation
Rocky Mountain Fan (1/4 of Rocky Mountain Variation)

4039 Rocky Mountain Star, *Gail Garber*, *SSQ*, *1991*

4040 Gemstones

4041 Mountain Pink

4042 Rhododendron Star

4043 Wyoming Quilt Block, *HH*

4044 Wandering Path of the Wilderness, *HH*

4045 Amish Angel, *PQ*

4046 Tea Leaves

4047 Cockleburr, *LAC*

4048 Washington Merry-Go-Round

4049 Violet Blossoms

4050 Butterfly in the Garden

4051 The Snowball, *KCS*

4052 Byrd at the South Pole, *NC*

4053 Perry's Expedition, *NC*

4054 Gothic Windows

4055 Pieced Sunflower, *KCS*

4056 Spring Beauty

4057 Everglades, *NC*

4058 Bay Leaf, *AMS*

4059 Illinois Star

4060 Bride's Quilt, *OCS*
Heart Quilt, *OCS*

4061 Foundation Rose

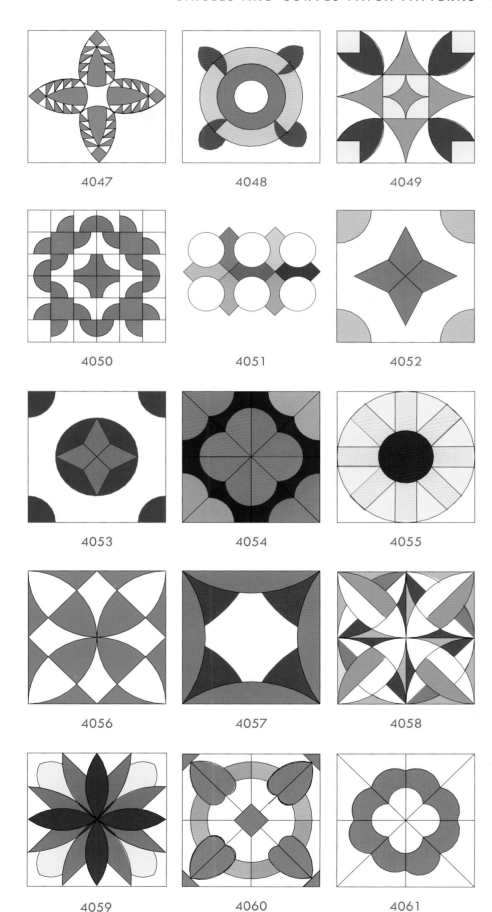

4047

4048

4049

4050

4051

4052

4053

4054

4055

4056

4057

4058

4059

4060

4061

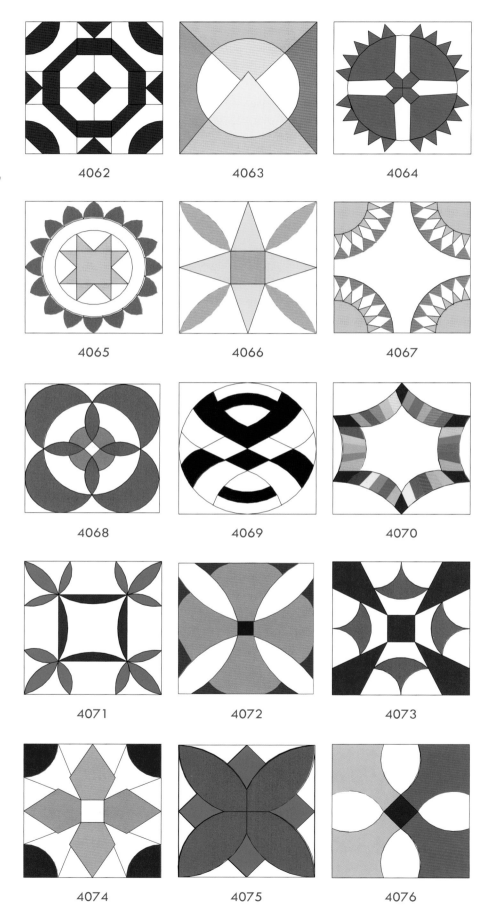

4062

4063

4064

4065

4066

4067

4068

4069

4070

4071

4072

4073

4074

4075

4076

4062 Wedgewood Tiles, *NC*

4063 Equivalents,
  *Rebecca Rohrkaste,*
  *QN*

4064 Chips and Whetstones

4065 Flower Star

4066 Morning Star

4067 Missouri Beauty

4068 Lena's Magic Circles

4069 Good Fortune

4070 Triple Wedding Ring

4071 Shamrock

4072 Airplanes

4073 Priscilla's Prize, *LW, OCS*

4074 Sunset Star, *LW, OCS*

4075 Flower Bed

4076 Flowering Snowball,
  *AK*

4077 Garden Bloom, *LW, OCS*

4078 Spirit of 1849, *NC*

4079 Sunshine and Shadow

4080 Rolling Stars

4081 Wheel of Fate, *CS*

4082 Circle in a Circle

4083 Delaware

4084 Utah, *HH*

4085 Missouri Trouble, *NC*

4086 Arms to Heaven, *NC*

4087 Star of the Decathlon, *QN*

4088 Quilter's Pride, *AB, OCS*

4089 Anna's Pride, *KCS*

4090 Paducah Peony, *NC*

4091 Sweet Clover

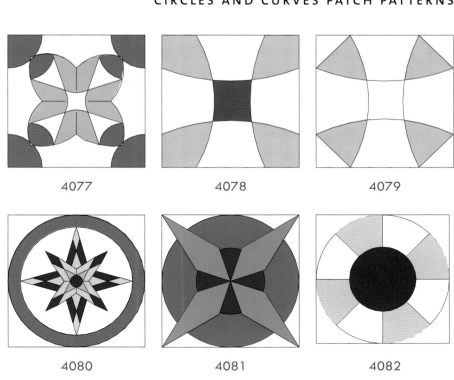

4077    4078    4079

4080    4081    4082

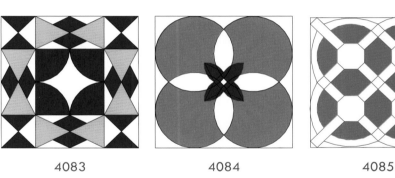

4083    4084    4085

4086    4087    4088

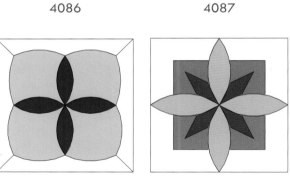

4089    4090    4091

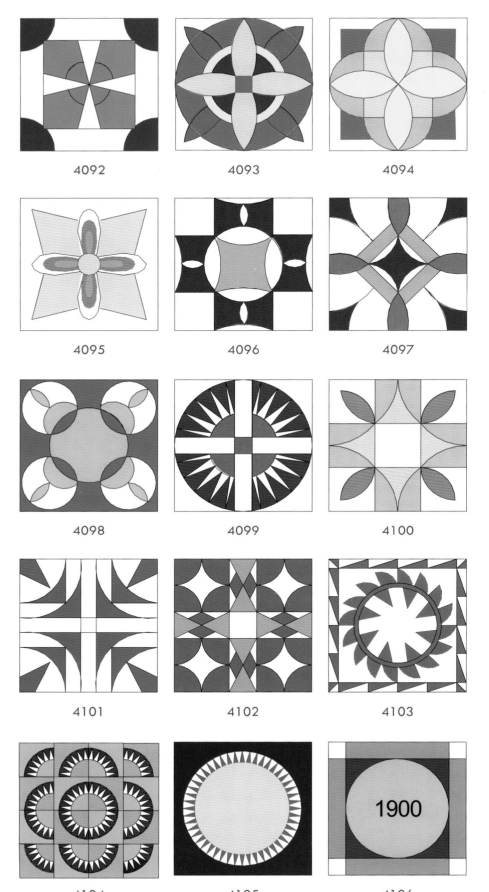

4092 Four Leaf Clover, *NC*

4093 Tulip Wheel, *GD*

4094 Day Lily Garden, *AK*

4095 Points and Petals, *KCS*

4096 Unnamed, *AMS*

4097 Linked Squares, *LW, OCS*

4098 Hero's Crown

4099 Fredonia Cross, *MD*

4100 Morning Star, *NC*

4101 Mayflower, *LW, OCS*

4102 Delaware, *HH*

4103 Circular Saw

4104 Full and Change of the Moon, *late 1800s*

4105 New York Beauty

4106 End of the Century Patchwork, *1899*

4107 Road to California, *CaS*

4108 Pinwheel

4109 Unnamed

4110 Peony, *LW, OCS*

4111 Hearts and Darts, *AK*

4112 Birds in the Air

4113 Moon and Swastika, *NC*

4114 Honolulu, *HH*

4115 Quatrefoils

4116 Crisscross, *LW, OCS*

4117 Penelope's Favorite, *NC*
Penn's Puzzle, *NC*

4118 Posies Round the
Square, *NM*
Dandelion Quilt, *QN*
The Posey Quilt, *KCS*
Spice Pinks (with ruf-
fled flowers in the
corners), *MD*
Sweetheart Garden
(with rosebuds in the
corners), *NC*

4119 Squares and Crosses,
*NC*

4120 Dahlia, *AMS*

4121 Sunburst
Sunrise

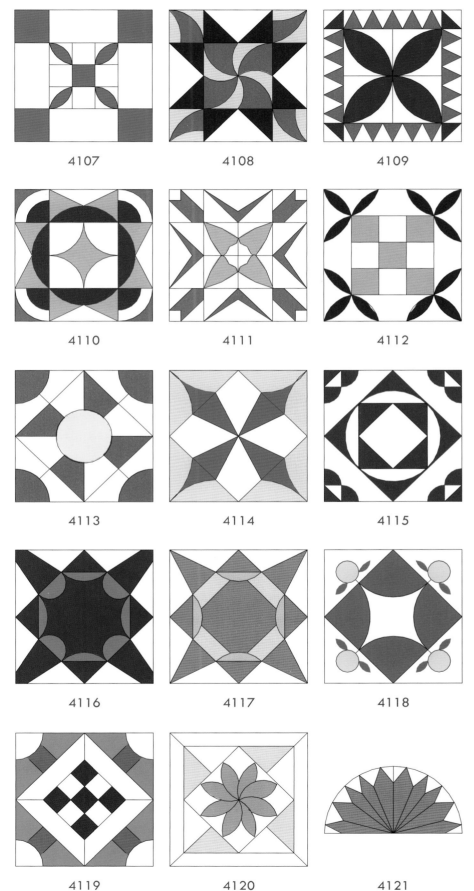

4107  4108  4109

4110  4111  4112

4113  4114  4115

4116  4117  4118

4119  4120  4121

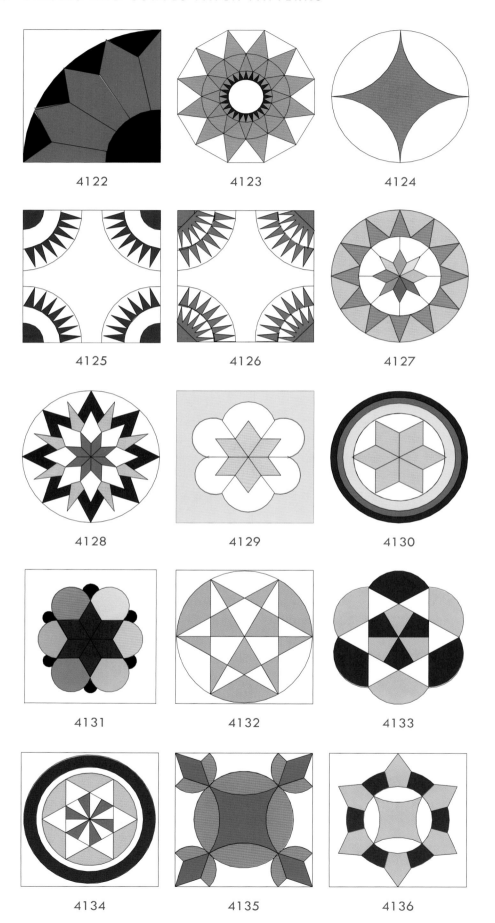

4122

4123

4124

4125

4126

4127

4128

4129

4130

4131

4132

4133

4134

4135

4136

4122 Imperial Fan, *KCS*

4123 Man in the Moon, *AMS*

4124 Cathedral Window

4125 Crown of Thorns
New York Beauty, *MoM*
Rocky Mountain, *PP*
Rocky Mountain Road
Split Rail

4126 Spice Pink, *QN*

4127 Party Plate Quilt, *WB*,
*1943*

4128 Texas Star

4129 Buttercup, *PP*

4130 Rainbow Star Quilt,
*HAS*

4131 Star and Planets

4132 Savannah Beautiful
Star, *LAC*
Southern Plantation,
*NC*
Sylvia's Choice, *CS*

4133 Savannah Beautiful
Star

4134 Ohio Star, *AK*

4135 Devil's Footprints, *NC*
Milwaukee's Own, *LAC*
Mississippi Oak Leaves,
*NC*

4136 Caesar's Crown
Grecian Star
Whirling Wheel

4137 Indian Wedding Ring
　　　Pickle Dish
　　　Sweetwater Quilt

4138 Double Wedding Ring
　　　Around the World, *CaS*
　　　Double Wedding
　　　　Bands, *MoM*
　　　Endless Chain
　　　King Tut, *CaS*
　　　The Rainbow
　　　Rainbow Wedding Ring
　　　Wedding Ring
　　　Wedding Ring Chain, *GD*

4139 A New Wedding Ring,
　　　*NM*, *1930*

4140 Whig's Defeat
　　　Democrat's Fancy
　　　Fanny's Favorite
　　　Grandmother's
　　　　Engagement Ring,
　　　　*MoM*
　　　The Lady Finger, *LHJ*,
　　　　*1912*
　　　The Lotus, *LHJ*
　　　Lotus Blossom
　　　Missouri Beauty
　　　Richmond Beauty

4141 Flight of the Wild
　　　Goose

4142 Star of Diamonds
　　　The Star, *HH*

4143 Dahlia
　　　Sunburst

4144 Star Chain, *KCS*

4145 The Sunflower, *LAC*
　　　Chinese Star, *GC*
　　　Queen of the May, *CS*

4146 A Quilt Pattern

4147 Grandmother's
　　　Favorite

4148 Hands All Around, *PF*
　　　Caesar's Crown
　　　Friendship Ring
　　　Grecian Star

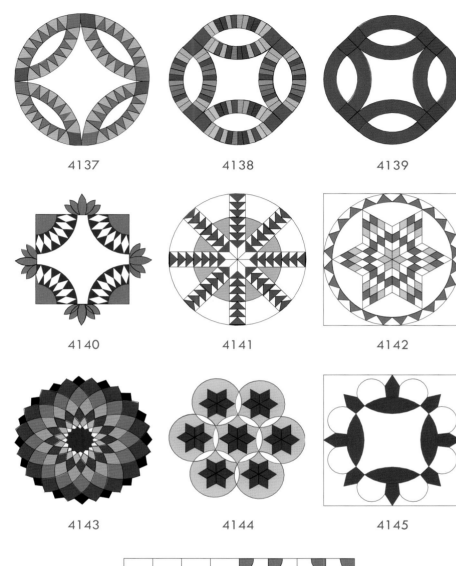

4137　　　　4138　　　　4139

4140　　　　4141　　　　4142

4143　　　　4144　　　　4145

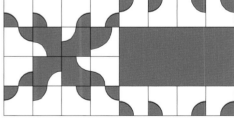

4146

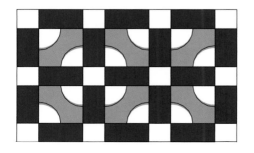

4147

4148

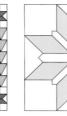
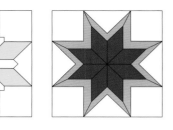

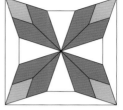
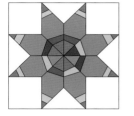

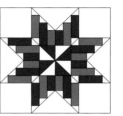

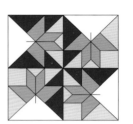

# OCTAGONS, DIAMONDS, AND EIGHT POINT STARS

# PATCH

# PATTERNS

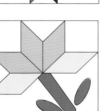

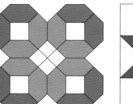
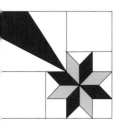

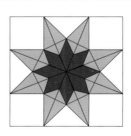

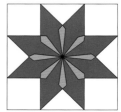

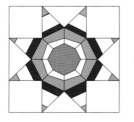

THESE PATTERNS ARE DRAFTED ON AN OCTAGONAL GRID
THEY ARE EASILY SCALED TO A BLOCK OF ANY SIZE

4149 Meadow Flower

4150 Old Staffordshire

4151 Lucky Star, *NC*

4152 Flying Saucer
     Carnival Time

4153 Target

4154 Mystic Maze

4155 Missouri Wonder, *KCS*

4156 Octagon Tile

4157 Grandmother's Dream,
     *LAC*

4158 Mosaic, *GC*

4159 Venetian Design, *LAC*

4160 Jewel

4161 Missouri Daisy

4162 Oriental Star, *NC*
     Eight Diamonds and a
     Star, *AMS*

4163 Hawaii

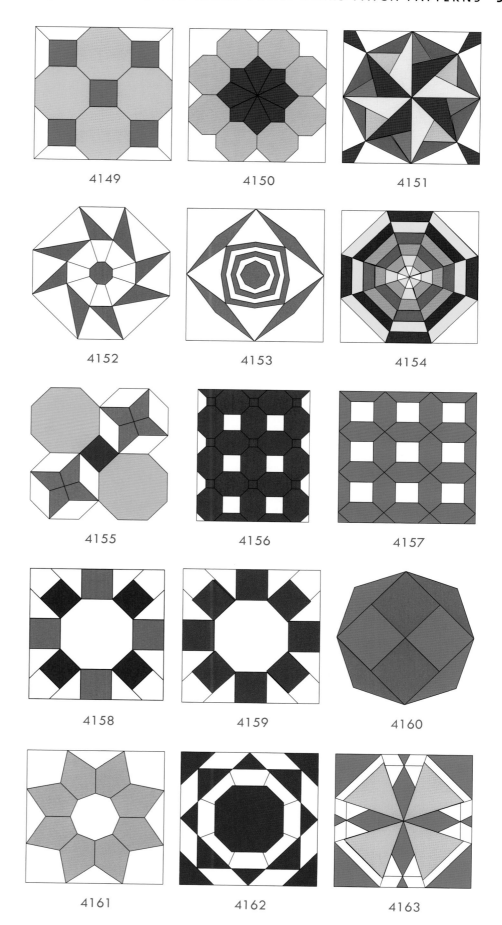

4149  4150  4151

4152  4153  4154

4155  4156  4157

4158  4159  4160

4161  4162  4163

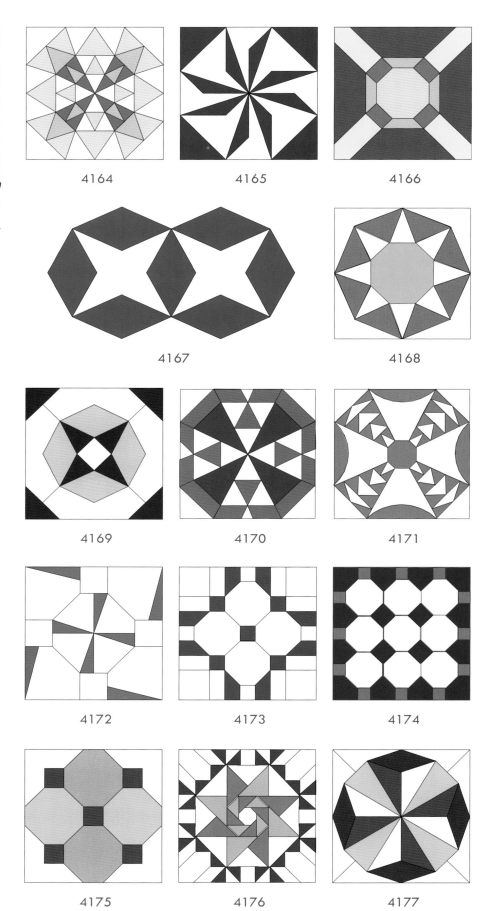

4164

4165

4166

4167

4168

4169

4170

4171

4172

4173

4174

4175

4176

4177

4164  Precious Gems

4165  Star of the East

4166  Imari Plate, *PQ*

4167  Diamond & Star

4168  Rising Sun

4169  Spider Web

4170  Aerial Beacon, *SSQ,*
      *1989*

4171  Dusty Miller

4172  Waterwheels, *NC*

4173  Catalpa Flower, *NC*

4174  Nine Snowballs, *NC*

4175  Meadow Flower, *LW,*
      *OCS*

4176  Unfolding Star

4177  Skyscrapers, *QN*

4178  The Sunflower

4179  Chained Star, *LW, OCS*

4180  Rising Star, *LW, OCS*

4181  Ozark Cobblestones

4182  Five Cross, *CS*
      Church Windows
      Lattice Block, *NC*
      Ogden Corners, *WB,*
      *1935*

4183  Old-Fashioned Quilt
      Ozark Tile Pattern, *KCS*

4184  Puzzle Tile, *LAC*
      Endless Chain
      Mosaic Patchwork #4

4185  Red Cross, *KCS*
      A Red, White & Blue
      Color Scheme, *KCS*

4186  Chinese Puzzle, *KCS*
      Mosaic Patchwork #3
      Tile Patchwork, *LAC*

4187  Octagon, *LAC*
      An All Over Pattern of
      Octagons, *KCS*
      Job's Trouble, *CS*
      Mechanical Blocks
      Octagonal, *NC*
      Octagons
      Ozark Cobblestones
      Snowballs, *NC*

4188  Octagon Block, *NC*
      Patriot's Quilt
      White Mountains, *NC*

4189  Dove in the Window

4190  Wedding Ring Tile, *WB,*
      *1941*

4191  Bluet Quilt, *NP*
      Hummingbird
      Periwinkle

4192  Periwinkle

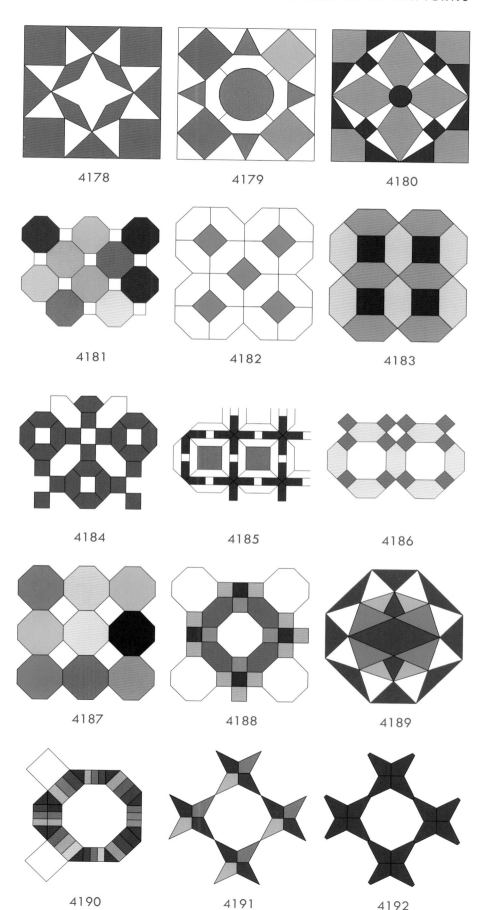

4178   4179   4180

4181   4182   4183

4184   4185   4186

4187   4188   4189

4190   4191   4192

5,500 QUILT BLOCK DESIGNS

4193

4194

4195

4196

4197

4198

4199

4200

4201

4202

4203

4204

4205

4206

4207

4193 Crystal Star

4194 The Peaceful Valley Quilt

4195 Parquetry Design for Patchwork

4196 Memory Chain

4197 Rock Garden

4198 Patriotic Star Block

4199 Rolling Star, *MM*

4200 Island Creek Hustler, *HH*

4201 Rolling Star

4202 Name Unknown

4203 Name Unknown

4204 Twist

4205 Kaleidoscope

4206 Patchwork Sofa Quilt

4207 Twist Patchwork, *GLB, 1851*
Plaited Block
Ribbon Twist
Twisted Rope, *LAC*

4208 Rolling Stone
    Job's Trouble Quilt
      Block
    Snowball

4209 Honeycomb Variation

4210 Garden Path

4211 Saw Blades, *QW*
    Windmills

4212 Star Dancer,
    *Tristan Audrey Mor*,
    *TQ*

4213 Kite String Quilt

4214 Whirling Hexagons

4215 Periwinkle Variation

4216 Periwinkle
    Hummingbird

4217 Hexagon Beauty

4218 Puss in the Corner

4219 Morning Star, *OCS*

4220 Clydescape
    Wheel of Fortune

4221 Rock Garden

4222 Memory Chain

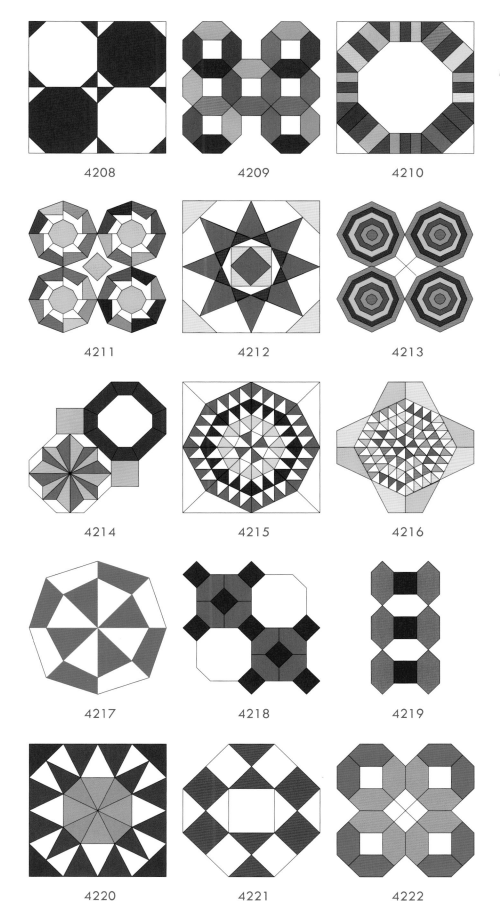

4208      4209      4210

4211      4212      4213

4214      4215      4216

4217      4218      4219

4220      4221      4222

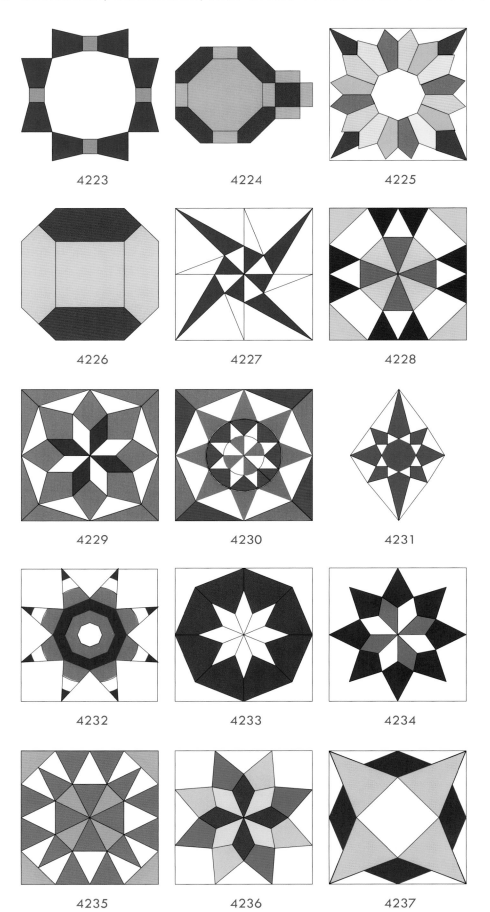

4223

4224

4225

4226

4227

4228

4229

4230

4231

4232

4233

4234

4235

4236

4237

4223 True Lover's Knot, *AMS*

4224 White Mountains, *NC*

4225 Dresden Flower Quilt

4226 Kansas Dugout, *AMS*
     Lattice Block, *NC*
     Ogden Corners, *WB*

4227 Rolling Star

4228 Octagon Wheel

4229 Pole Star

4230 State of Oklahoma, *HH*

4231 Comet Star

4232 Helena

4233 Tennessee Mountain
     Laurel

4234 Enigma, *LAC*
     North Star, *NP*
     St. Louis Block, *NP*

4235 Grandma's Surprise

4236 Wishing Star, *WB*
     New Star
     Star of St. Louis, *NC*

4237 Geometrical Star

4238  Godey Design

4239  Wheel of Fortune, *KCS*
      Road to Fortune, *OCS*
      Pinwheel Quilt,
        *McCall's*

4240  Target, *MoM*

4241  String Quilt

4242  Topsy Turvy

4243  Diamond Head, *NC*

4244  Emerald Block, *NC*

4245  Bull's Eye

4246  Midsummer Night, *NC*

4247  Ladies' Chain, *CS*

4248  Spinning Star

4249  Morning Star

4250  Joseph's Coat

4251  Carousel, *EH, LCPQ*

4252  Spring Blooms

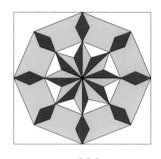
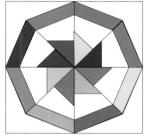

4238 4239 4240

4241 4242 4243

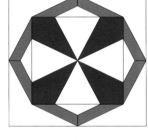

4244 4245 4246

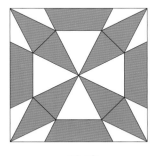

4247 4248 4249

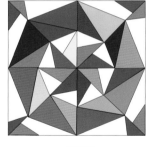
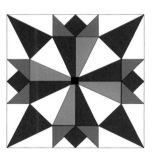

4250 4251 4252

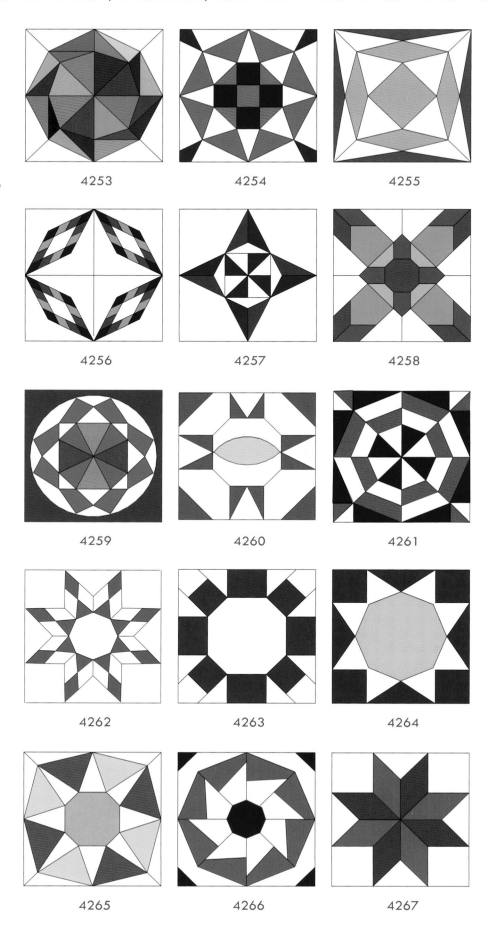

4253    Diamond Circle, *KCS*

4254    Kaleidoscope

4255    Morning Star (6), *SSQ*

4256    No Name, *LW, OCS*

4257    No Name Octagon

4258    Rising Star, *QW, 1991*

4259    Heavenly Bodies,
         *Star Quilts*

4260    Gemstones

4261    Homecoming, *QN*

4262    LeMoyne Star
         Lemon Star

4263    Mosaic, *GC*
         Venetian Design, *LAC*

4264    Star of Sweden

4265    Rising Sun, *LW*

4266    Friendship Circle, *LW*

4267    Eight Point Star
         Diamond
         Diamond Design, *WW*
         Eastern Star, *McCall's*
         Hanging Diamonds
         Idaho Star, *NC*
         Lemon Star
         Puritan Star
         Star of LeMoyne
         The Star, *KCS*

4268    Star
         Eight Point Star
         Eight Pointed Star, *LAC*
         Shasta Daisy, *LW*
         Simple Star, *CaS*
         The Southern Star, *KCS*
         Star Bed Quilt, *HH*
         Twinkle, Twinkle Little
            Star, *KCS*
         Variable Star

4269    Arrow Star, *KCS*

4270    LeMoyne Star &
            Windmill
         Pin Wheel
         Star of the Milky Way
         Twinkle Star

4271 LeMoyne Star
Lemon Star
The Divided Star
Louisiana Star, *AK, 1965*
North Star, *HAS*
Star of the East

4272 Silver and Gold, *KCS*
Gold and Silver, *NC*
Winter Stars, *NC*

4273 Liberty Star, *KCS*
Star of Bethlehem
Stars of Stripes
Tennessee, *HH*

4274 Patriotic Star, *KCS*
Blazing Star
Blazing Star of Minnesota
Bright Morning Star
Combination Feathered
 Star
Eastern Star
Little Star, *NC*
Morning Star, *KCS*
Quilt of the Century, *CW*
Rising Star, *NP*
Star of the Bluegrass,
 *MoM*
Star of the East, *CaS*
Sunburst Star

4275 Starry Heavens, *KCS*

4276 Flying Bat, *LAC*
Dove in the Window
Doves, *HAS*
Flying Star, *HAS*
Polaris Star
Witches Star, *NC*

4277 The Spider Web, *KCS*

4278 Wandering Jew, *CS*
The Winding Blades, *KCS*

4279 Olympiad

4280 Christmas Star, *KCS*

4281 Friendship Knot, *KCS*
Starry Crown

4282 Friendship Knot, *LW*
Friendship Wreath

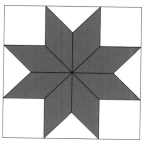

4268

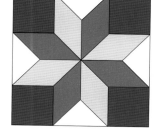

4269

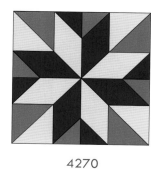

4270

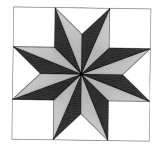

4271

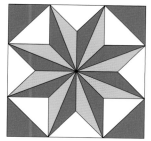

4272

4273

4274

4275

4276

4277

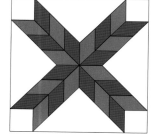

4278

4279

4280

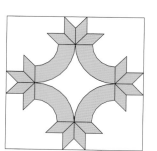

4281

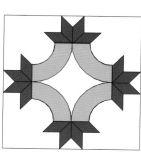

4282

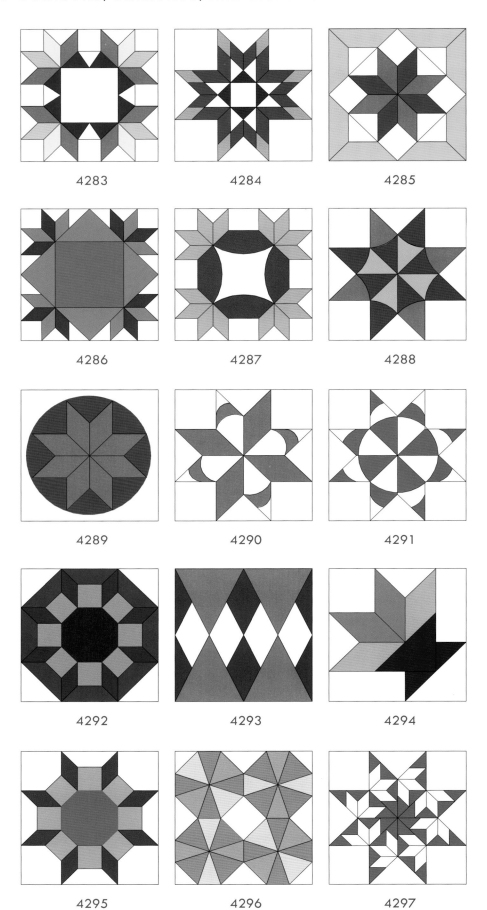

4283  Lotus Star, *VS*

4284  Northumberland Star, *CS*

4285  Brunswick Star, *LW*, *OCS*

4286  Swallows in the Window, *KCS*

4287  Hands All Around, *LAC*
All Hands Round, *CaS*
Center Table Quilt, *CoM*
Old Fashioned Star Quilt
Wreath of Lilies

4288  Sailor's Joy, *CS*

4289  Log Cabin Star

4290  The King's Crown, *LAC*

4291  King's Star, *NC*

4292  The Castle Wall

4293  Four Diamonds

4294  Texas Cactus

4295  Dogwood, *LBC*

4296  Kaleidoscope

4297  Whirling Star, *KCS*
Circling Swallows
Falling Star
Flying Barn Swallows, *NC*
Flying Swallow, *LAC*
Flying Swallows, *AMS*
Flying Star
The Wreath, *LW*

4283    4284    4285

4286    4287    4288

4289    4290    4291

4292    4293    4294

4295    4296    4297

4298 Diamond Star, *HH*
Diamond Star #2, *CS*

4299 Dove in the Window
Airplanes, *FJ*
Bluebirds for
Happiness, *MoM*
The Bluebirds
The Dove
Four Birds, *WW*
Four Doves
Four Swallows

4300 Formosa Tea Leaf, *KCS*

4301 Missouri Star, *KCS*
Shining Star
Star and Arrow, *NC*

4302 Love in a Mist, *FJ*

4303 Chips and Whetstones,
*KCS*

4304 Royal Diamonds, *KCS*

4305 Star of Hope, *KCS*
Celestial Sphere, *NC*
Twinkling Stars, *LAC*

4306 Connecticut Star, *FJ*

4307 Goldfish, *KCS*
An Airplane Motif, *KCS*
Bass and Trout, *QW*
Dove in the Window
Fish, *CS*
Fish Block
Fish Circle, *LCPQ*
Flying Fish, *KCS*
Starfish, *LCPQ*
Trout and Bass Block, *NC*
Whirligig, *CS*

4308 Pole Star, *HH*

4309 Bouquet in a Fan

4310 Diamond Cluster in a
Frame

4311 Rolling Star

4312 Hunter's Star
Indian Arrowhead,
*AMS*

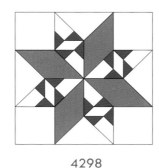
4298

4299

4300

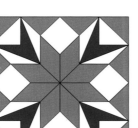
4301

4302

4303

4304

4305

4306

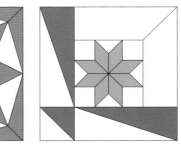
4307

4308

4309

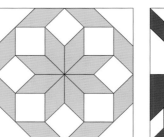
4310

4311

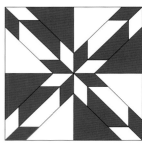
4312

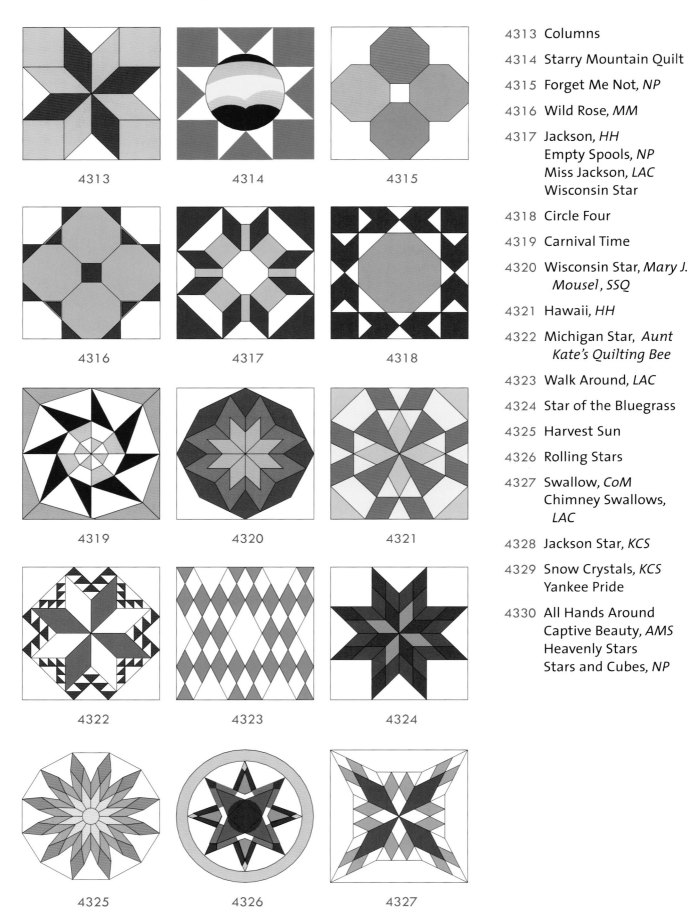

4313

4314

4315

4316

4317

4318

4319

4320

4321

4322

4323

4324

4325

4326

4327

4313 Columns

4314 Starry Mountain Quilt

4315 Forget Me Not, *NP*

4316 Wild Rose, *MM*

4317 Jackson, *HH*
Empty Spools, *NP*
Miss Jackson, *LAC*
Wisconsin Star

4318 Circle Four

4319 Carnival Time

4320 Wisconsin Star, *Mary J. Mousel*, *SSQ*

4321 Hawaii, *HH*

4322 Michigan Star, *Aunt Kate's Quilting Bee*

4323 Walk Around, *LAC*

4324 Star of the Bluegrass

4325 Harvest Sun

4326 Rolling Stars

4327 Swallow, *CoM*
Chimney Swallows, *LAC*

4328 Jackson Star, *KCS*

4329 Snow Crystals, *KCS*
Yankee Pride

4330 All Hands Around
Captive Beauty, *AMS*
Heavenly Stars
Stars and Cubes, *NP*

4331 The Double Star Quilt
Circle Saw, *KCS*
Dutch Rose, *LAC*
Eccentric Star, *GC*
Morning Star
Octagonal Star, *HH*
Orphan Star, *HAS*
Star and Diamond
Star of the East, *MD*
Triple Star, *HHJ*

4332 Lone Star of Paradise, *KCS*

4333 Dutch Rose
Octagon Star

4334 Carpenter's Wheel
Black Diamond, *CS*
Diadem Star, *HH*
Double Star, *HH*
Knickerbocker Star, *WB*
Lone Star of Paradise
Star of Bethlehem, *CS*
Star Quilt Block
Star Within a Star
Sunflower, *NP*
Twinkling Star, *NP*

4335 Bethlehem Star
Christmas Memory Quilt,
*QN*
Jewels in a Frame
Star of Bethlehem, *KCS*
Star of the Magi, *NC*
Winged Star, *KCS*

4336 Rolling Star

4337 Eight Pointed Broken Star

4338 Broken Star

4339 Carpenter's Wheel

4340 Dutch Rose, *CS*
Mother's Choice, *NM, 1918*

4341 Black Diamond, *NM*

4342 The Starbright Quilt
Circle Saw
Star of the East

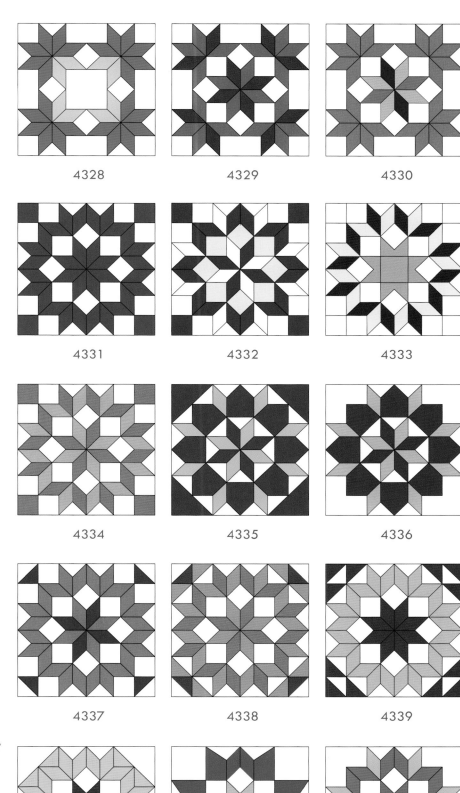

4328    4329    4330

4331    4332    4333

4334    4335    4336

4337    4338    4339

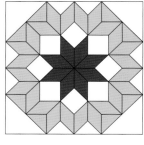
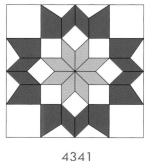
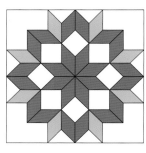

4340    4341    4342

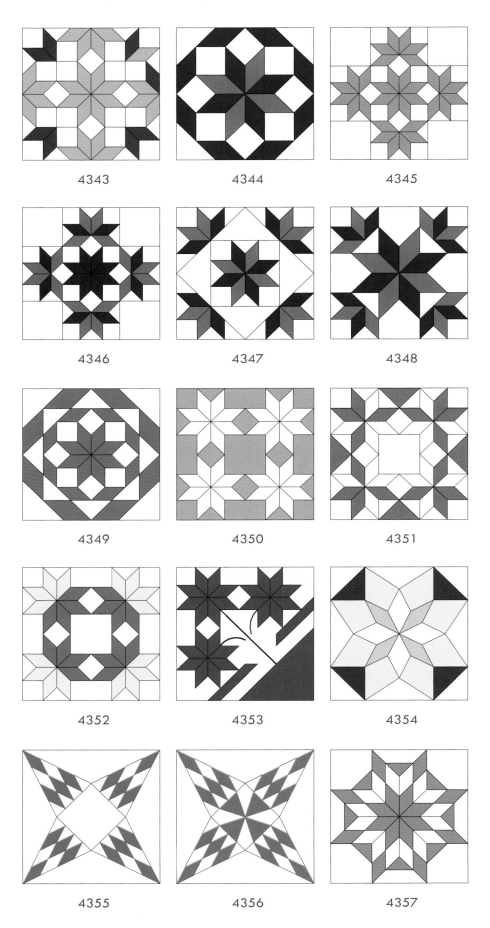

4343

4344

4345

4346

4347

4348

4349

4350

4351

4352

4353

4354

4355

4356

4357

4343 Poinsettias, *QN, 1975*

4344 Rolling Star, *LAC*
Brunswick Star
Chained Star
Cross and Crown
Rolling Stone
Virginia Reel

4345 Victory Star, *CS*

4346 Cubes and Tiles, *NC*
Double Star, *HH*
Star, *OF*
Stars and Cubes, *LAC*
Yankee Pride

4347 A Flash of Diamonds,
*KCS*

4348 Blazing Star
LeMoyne Star

4349 Star and Chains

4350 Four Stars Patchwork,
*LAC*
The Four Stars
Old Maid's Patience,
*NC*

4351 Diamond Wedding
Block, *NC*

4352 The Maple Leaf, *1931*

4353 President's Quilt

4354 Sitka Star

4355 Buckeye Beauty, *NC*
Rockingham's Beauty,
*LAC*

4356 Star of Many Points,
*NC*

4357 Blazing Star, *LAC*
Carpenter's Wheel
Variation
Virginia Star
Harvest Star

4358 Columbus Quilt Block

4359 Four Block Star, *AK*

4360 Cleveland Tulip
Carolina Lily
Pineys, *NM*
Tree Quilt Pattern

4361 Missouri Quilt Block,
*HH*

4362 State of California, *HH*

4363 Virginia's Star

4364 Tennessee Star

4365 Pinwheel Star, *WW*
Modern Star

4366 Aurora Borealis

4367 Missouri

4368 Peony

4369 Tennessee Star

4370 Octagon Star

4371 Octagonal Star

4372 Kaleidoscope Star

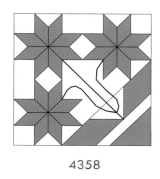

4358

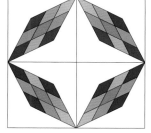

4359

4360

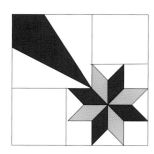

4361

4362

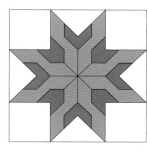

4363

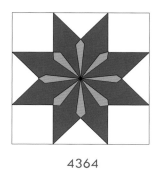

4364

4365

4366

4367

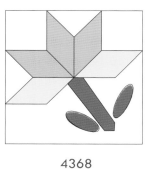

4368

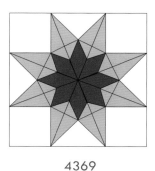

4369

4370

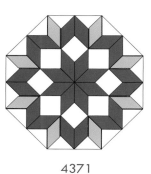

4371

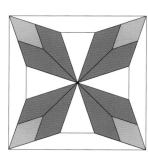

4372

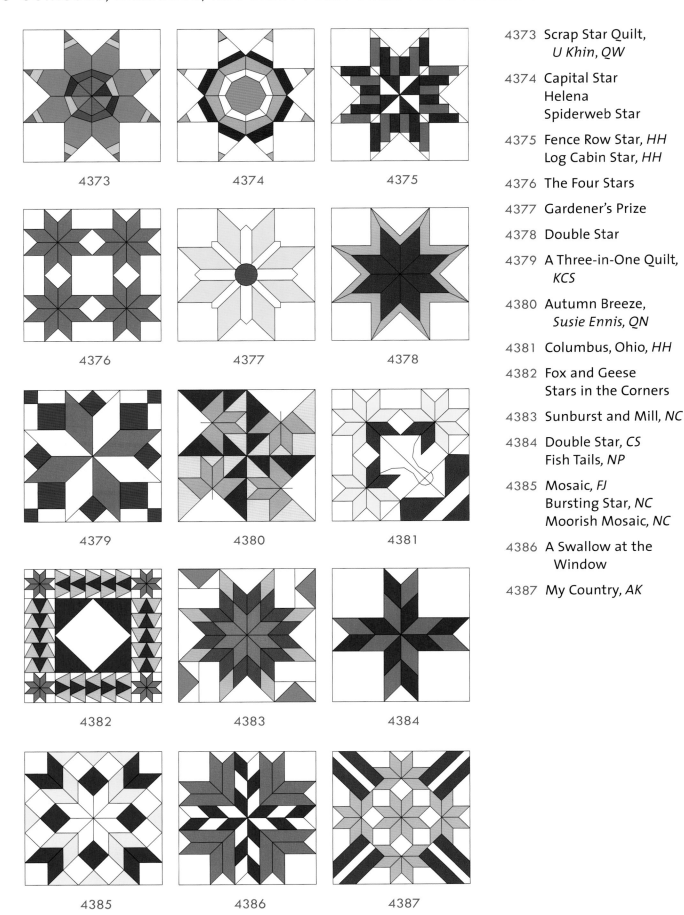

4373 Scrap Star Quilt,
*U Khin, QW*

4374 Capital Star
Helena
Spiderweb Star

4375 Fence Row Star, *HH*
Log Cabin Star, *HH*

4376 The Four Stars

4377 Gardener's Prize

4378 Double Star

4379 A Three-in-One Quilt,
*KCS*

4380 Autumn Breeze,
*Susie Ennis, QN*

4381 Columbus, Ohio, *HH*

4382 Fox and Geese
Stars in the Corners

4383 Sunburst and Mill, *NC*

4384 Double Star, *CS*
Fish Tails, *NP*

4385 Mosaic, *FJ*
Bursting Star, *NC*
Moorish Mosaic, *NC*

4386 A Swallow at the
Window

4387 My Country, *AK*

4388 My Mother's Star

4389 Parallelogram, *KCS*
Design for Light and
Dark, *CoM*

4390 Calico Stars

4391 Star Shower, *NC*

4392 The Triple Star Quilt

4393 Star Net, *NC*

4394 Westward Ho, *NC*

4395 Turtle

4396 Compass, *AMS*
Calico Compass, *NC*

4397 Octagon Star, *CoM*

4398 Octagon Star, *FJ*

4399 Ring Around the Star,
*WB*

4400 National Star, *PF*
Patty's Star

4401 Kentucky's Twinkling
Star

4402 Little Star

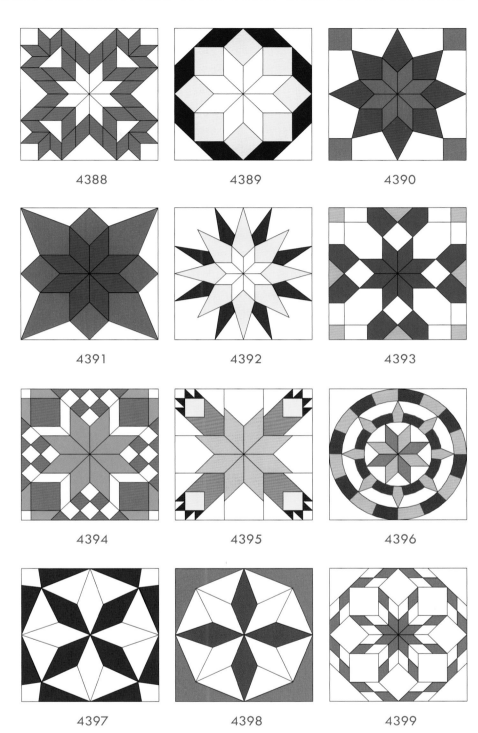

4388

4389

4390

4391

4392

4393

4394

4395

4396

4397

4398

4399

4400

4401

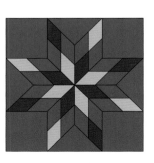

4402

4403  Star Fish, *HAS*

4404  Tangled Cobwebs

4405  Star Chain

4406  County Fair, *NC*
        County Farm, *NC*

4407  Flaming Star, *NC*

4408  Helena

4409  Plaid Star

4410  Carrie Bird Star

4411  Double Star, *HAS*

4412  Cockcomb, *HAS*

4413  Maple Leaf and Rose

4414  State of California, *HH*

4415  Diamond Jubilee, *JM*

4416  Aloha, *JM*

4417  September Star, *JM*

4418 Writer's Block, *JM*

4419 Eyes of Blue, *JM*

4420 March Winds, *JM*

4421 Motown Sounds, *JM*

4422 Cornucopia

4423 Stained Glass Window

4424 All American Star

4425 Christmas Star, *Ursula Michael, QW, 1988*

4426 Whirling Tulip

4427 Summer Star Flower

4428 Old Maid's Patience

4429 Pinwheel Star

4430 Starburst

4431 Peony

4432 Wandering Diamond

4418    4419    4420

4421    4422    4423

4424    4425    4426

4427    4428    4429

4430    4431    4432

5,500 QUILT BLOCK DESIGNS

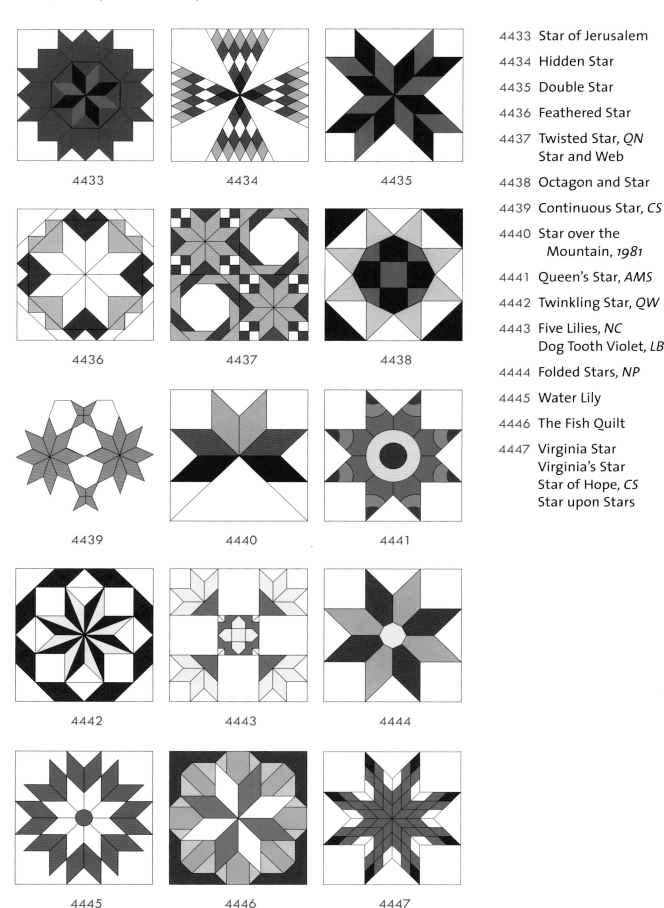

4433

4434

4435

4436

4437

4438

4439

4440

4441

4442

4443

4444

4445

4446

4447

4433 Star of Jerusalem

4434 Hidden Star

4435 Double Star

4436 Feathered Star

4437 Twisted Star, *QN*
Star and Web

4438 Octagon and Star

4439 Continuous Star, *CS*

4440 Star over the
Mountain, *1981*

4441 Queen's Star, *AMS*

4442 Twinkling Star, *QW*

4443 Five Lilies, *NC*
Dog Tooth Violet, *LBC*

4444 Folded Stars, *NP*

4445 Water Lily

4446 The Fish Quilt

4447 Virginia Star
Virginia's Star
Star of Hope, *CS*
Star upon Stars

4448 Star of Alabama,
 *MoM*

4449 Star Bouquet

4450 Virginia Star

4451 National Star, *PF*
 Patty's Star

4452 Grandmother's Choice

4453 Blazing Star of
 Kentucky

4454 Rising Sun

4455 Aunt Dinah's Star, *HAS*

4456 Star Flowers, *NC*

4457 Star of Bethlehem
 Star of Alabama

4458 Triple Star Flower

4459 Walk Around, *LAC*
 Boston Corners, *NC*
 Country Crossroads
 Double X's, *NC*
 Guide Post, *MoM*
 Web of Diamonds, *NC*

4460 Modern Tulip, *AK*

4461 Diamonds, *LAC*
 Boston Corners, *NC*
 Heritage Quilt

4462 Shadow Trail, *MoM*

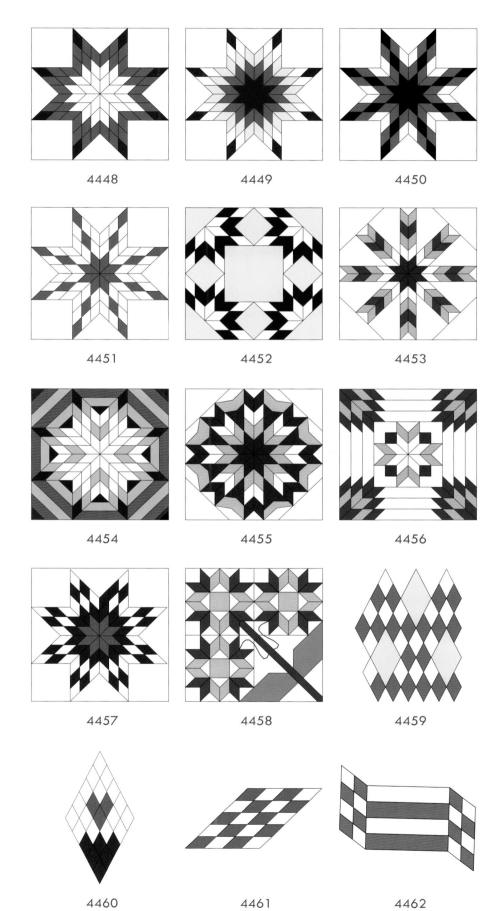

4448  4449  4450

4451  4452  4453

4454  4455  4456

4457  4458  4459

4460  4461  4462

5,500 QUILT BLOCK DESIGNS

4463

4464

4466

4467

4465

4468

4469

4470

4471

4472

4473

4463 Diamonds, *LAC*

4464 Diamond Design

4465 Springtime in the Ozarks

4466 Diamonds, *NP*
Guide Post
Boson Corners, *NC*
Walk Around

4467 Nine Patch Diamond

4468 Log Cabin Diamond

4469 Evening Star

4470 Star Flower

4471 Lazy Daisy

4472 Stars and Stripes

4473 Tulip Ring, *AK*

4474 Lone Star, *LAC*
　　　An Aesthetic Quilt, *HH*
　　　Blazing Star
　　　Glitter Star
　　　Morning Star, *CaS*
　　　Overall Star Pattern
　　　Pride of Texas, *HAS*
　　　Rainbow Star
　　　Rising Star
　　　Rising Sun
　　　Star of Bethlehem
　　　Star of the East
　　　Star of Stars, *HAS*
　　　Stars upon Star, *LAC*
　　　Sunburst Star, *LW*
　　　(size can be increased
　　　　by adding rows of
　　　　diamonds; the largest
　　　　I saw had 11 inner
　　　　rows before branch-
　　　　ing into star points
　　　　containing 10 rows
　　　　each)

4475 Prairie Star
　　　Harvest Star
　　　Harvest Sun
　　　Ship's Wheel

4476 The Lincoln Quilt
　　　(from a quilt pieced
　　　by Abraham Lincoln's
　　　mother), *LBC*

4477 Kaleidoscope Star
　　　(continuous design)

4478 Star and Wreath, *NC*
　　　Pinwheel Star, *LAC*

4474

4475

4476

4477

4478

4479

4480

4479 Shooting Star

4480 Candles of Heaven,
*Pat Flynn Kyser,*
*QW, 1989*

4481 LeMoyne Star, *QN*

4482 Diamond Star, *NC*

4483 No Name, *AMS*

4484 Prairie Star
Harvest Sun
Ship's Wheel
Stars upon Stars

4481

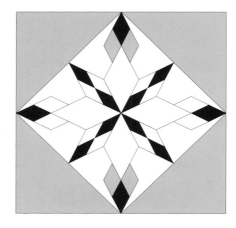

4482

4483

4484

4485 Thunderbird and Sioux Star

4486 Prairie Crocus

4487 Broken Star
Blazing Star
Diadem Star
Star of Bethlehem

4488 Pineapple Cactus

4489 Michigan Star,
*Aunt Kate's Quilting Bee*

4490 Pine Burr

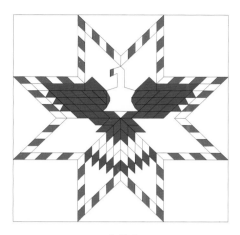

4485

4486

4487

4488

4489

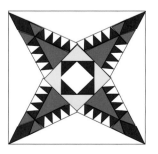

4490

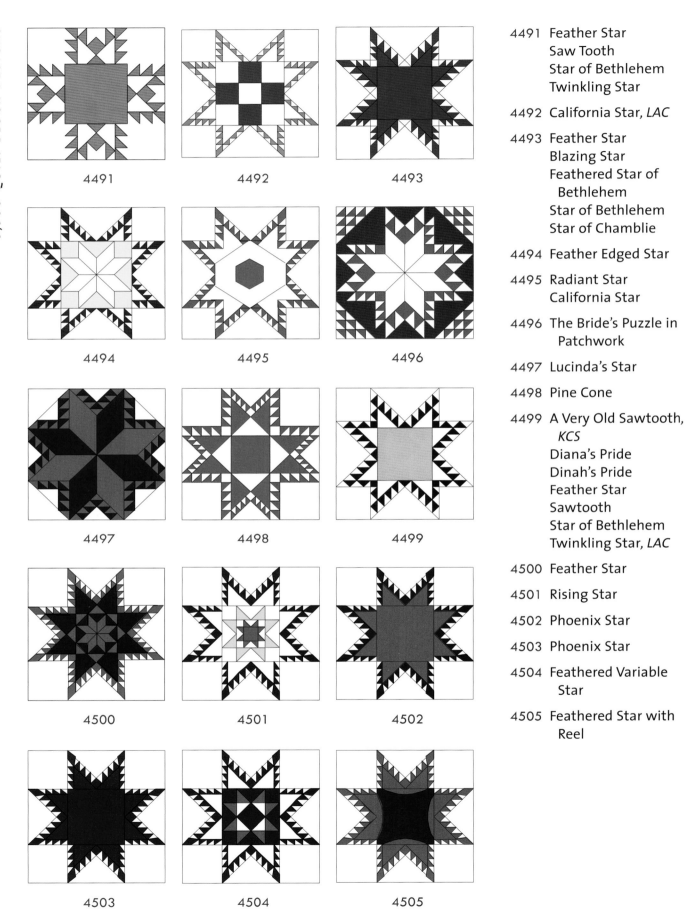

4491    4492    4493

4494    4495    4496

4497    4498    4499

4500    4501    4502

4503    4504    4505

4491 Feather Star
      Saw Tooth
      Star of Bethlehem
      Twinkling Star

4492 California Star, *LAC*

4493 Feather Star
      Blazing Star
      Feathered Star of
        Bethlehem
      Star of Bethlehem
      Star of Chamblie

4494 Feather Edged Star

4495 Radiant Star
      California Star

4496 The Bride's Puzzle in
      Patchwork

4497 Lucinda's Star

4498 Pine Cone

4499 A Very Old Sawtooth,
      *KCS*
      Diana's Pride
      Dinah's Pride
      Feather Star
      Sawtooth
      Star of Bethlehem
      Twinkling Star, *LAC*

4500 Feather Star

4501 Rising Star

4502 Phoenix Star

4503 Phoenix Star

4504 Feathered Variable
      Star

4505 Feathered Star with
      Reel

4506 Feathered Star

4507 Pierre, *HH*

4508 Radiant Star, *AMS*
Star of Bethlehem
Chestnut Burr, *AMS*

4509 Feathered LeMoyne
Star
Feather Edged Star
Feathered Star

4510 Twinkling Star

4511 Star Diamond, *LHJ*
Triangle Star, *HHJ*

4512 Feathered Star

4513 Feather Star

4514 Sawtooth Star

4515 Feather Star

4516 The Hour Glass, *HHJ*

4517 Joining Star, *LAC*

4518 Morning Star, *NC*

4519 Summer Sun, *NC*

4520 California Star, *AK*

4506
4507
4508
4509
4510
4511
4512
4513
4514
4515
4516
4517
4518
4519
4520

4521

4522

4523

4524

4525

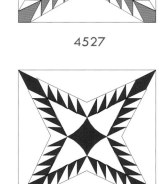

4526

4527

4528

4529

4530

| 4521 | Feathered Star |
| 4522 | Octagonal Star |
| 4523 | Halley's Comet, *NC* |
| 4524 | California Star |
| 4525 | Pike's Peak, *CS* <br> Bride's Fancy, *CS* |
| 4526 | Star Spangled Banner |
| 4527 | The Mayflower Quilt, *MD* |
| 4528 | Philippines, *LAC* |
| 4529 | The Double Pineapple |
| 4530 | Philadelphia Patch |

4531  Philadelphia Patch, *LAC*

4532  Five Pointed Star, *LAC*
      Star in a Square
      Union Star

4533  Union Star
      State of Texas

4534  Star of the West, *LAC*
      Texas (starting at the
        top T-E-X-A-S is
        embroidered in each
        point), *HH*

4535  The American Way,
        *RMS, SSQ*

4536  New York

4537  Red, White and Blue

4538  Stars and Stripes

4539  Twentieth Century
        Star

4540  Texas Ranger's Badge

4531

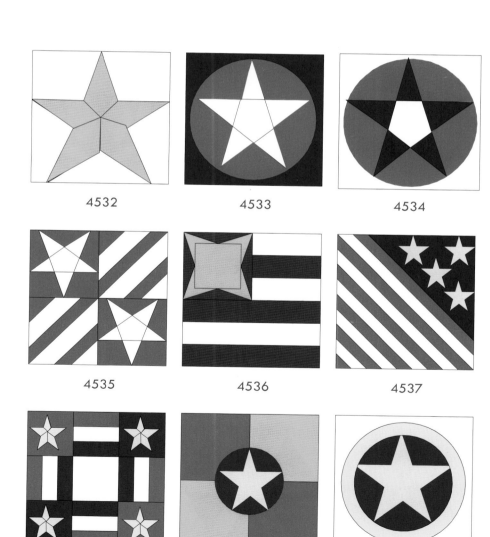

4532          4533          4534

4535          4536          4537

4538          4539          4540

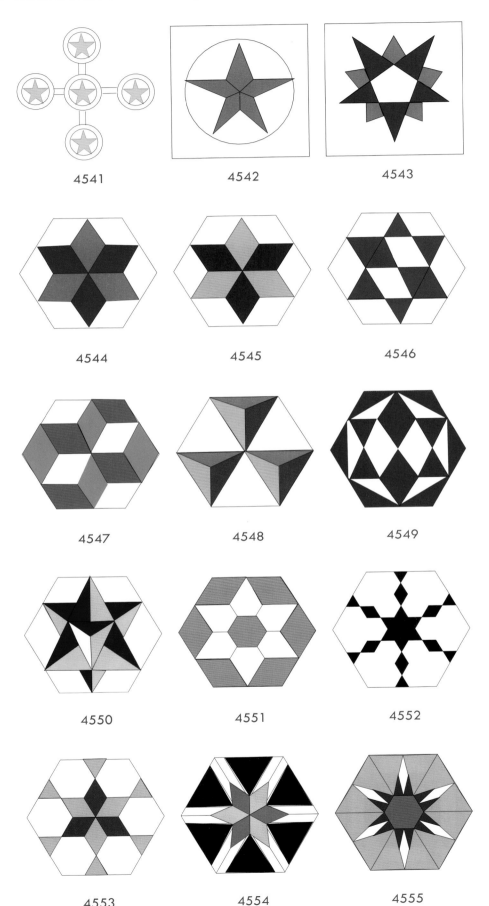

4541

4542

4543

4544

4545

4546

4547

4548

4549

4550

4551

4552

4553

4554

4555

4541 Star of the City of Indianapolis, *KCS*

4542 Star and Ring

4543 Star upon Star

4544 Eisenhower Star
Jacob's Ladder
Stair Step Quilt

4545 Little Girls' Star, *KCS*
Pennsylvania Hex, *WD*
(set with plain hexagons):
Star Bouquet Quilt, *HAS*
Morning Star

4546 Kentucky

4547 Block Puzzle

4548 Wonder of Egypt

4549 Madison Block

4550 Bezelled Star

4551 Dolly Madison's Star, *HAS*
Dolly Madison Pattern, *KCS*
Desert Flower
Desert Rose
Friendship Hexagon, *NP*
Hexagon Stars, *NP*
Hexagonal Star, *HH*
Solomon's Garden
Star Garden, *KCS*
Texas Star, *LAC*

4552 Trail of Diamonds, *MM*

4553 The Hexagon Star, *KCS*
Brilliant Star, *NP*
Pointing Star, *KCS*

4554 Mother's Prayers, *KCS*

4555 Star of the West

4556 Florida Star

4557 Diamonds and Arrow
 Points
 Favorite, *OF, 1894*

4558 Oklahoma Star
 The Mountain Star

4559 Ozark Diamond
 Ozark Star, *KCS*

4560 Ozark Diamond, *KCS*
 Ma Perkin's Flower
 Garden

4561 Hexagon, *LAC*
 Hexagon Beauty
 An Old Fashioned
 Wheel Quilt
 Spider Web

4562 Crazy Tile
 (continuous design),
 *KCS*

4563 Boutonniere

4564 Stop Sign

4565 Star Center in French
 Bouquet, *KCS*
 Snow Crystals, *KCS*

4566 Wagon Wheel, *AK*

4567 Twinkling Star,
 *MoM*

4568 Morning Star, *LW*

4569 Morning Star, *KCS*

4570 Dolly Madison Pattern

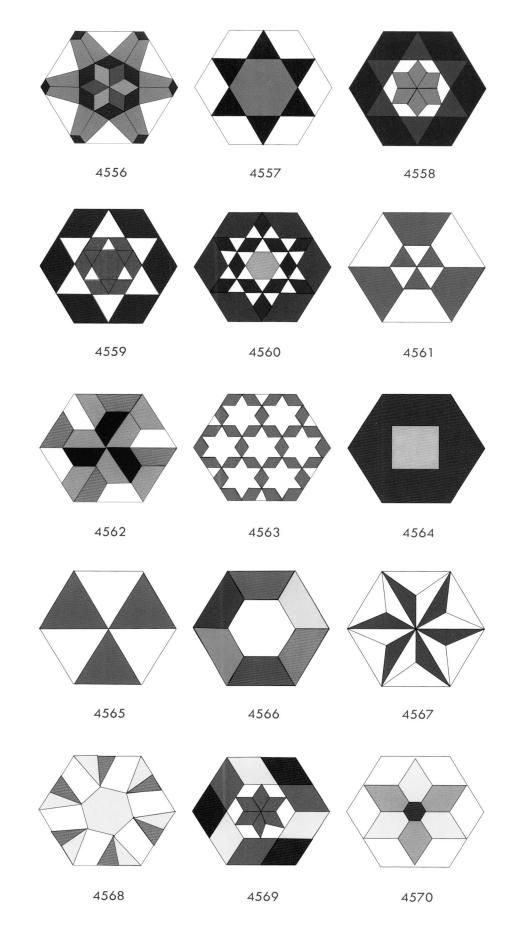

4556

4557

4558

4559

4560

4561

4562

4563

4564

4565

4566

4567

4568

4569

4570

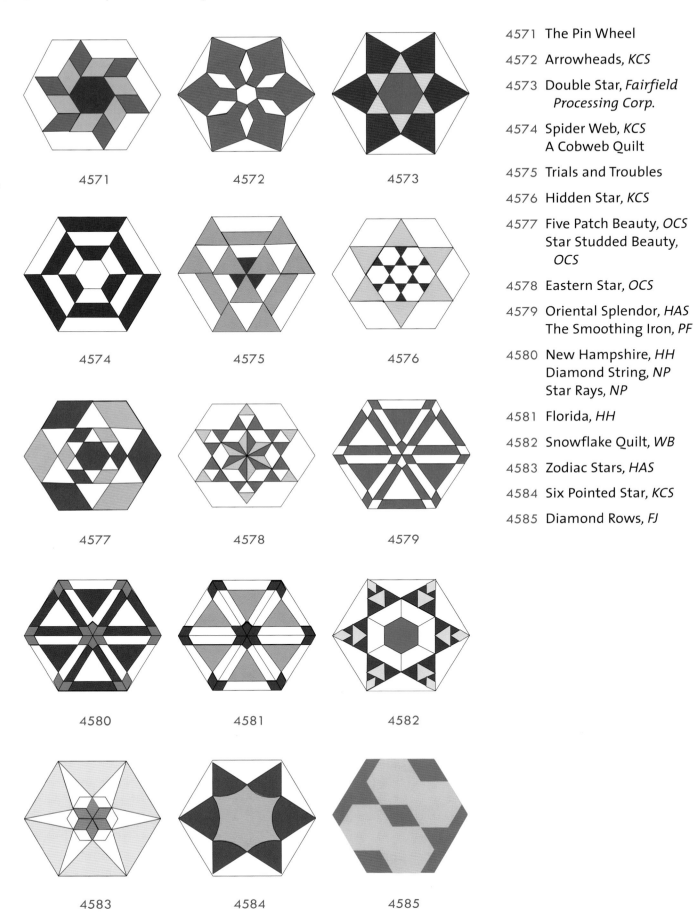

4571    The Pin Wheel

4572    Arrowheads, *KCS*

4573    Double Star, *Fairfield Processing Corp.*

4574    Spider Web, *KCS*
A Cobweb Quilt

4575    Trials and Troubles

4576    Hidden Star, *KCS*

4577    Five Patch Beauty, *OCS*
Star Studded Beauty, *OCS*

4578    Eastern Star, *OCS*

4579    Oriental Splendor, *HAS*
The Smoothing Iron, *PF*

4580    New Hampshire, *HH*
Diamond String, *NP*
Star Rays, *NP*

4581    Florida, *HH*

4582    Snowflake Quilt, *WB*

4583    Zodiac Stars, *HAS*

4584    Six Pointed Star, *KCS*

4585    Diamond Rows, *FJ*

4586 Hexagons and Flowers, *OCS*

4587 Endless Chain, *OCS*

4588 Pinwheel, *OCS*

4589 Rock Wall, *LCPQ*

4590 Dutch Tile

4591 Grandmother's Flower Basket, *QN, 1980*

4592 Cosmos, *HAS*
Gay Cosmos Quilt, *HAS*

4593 Kansas Sunflower, *QW*

4594 Flower Star
Star and Crescent
Twinkling Star

4595 Sparkling Dew, *NC*

4596 Morning Star, *NC*

4597 Collinsville Rose Star, *QN*

4598 Montana Star, *HH*
Star of Montana, *HH*

4599 Modernistic Star, *AMS*

4600 Unnamed, *OCS*

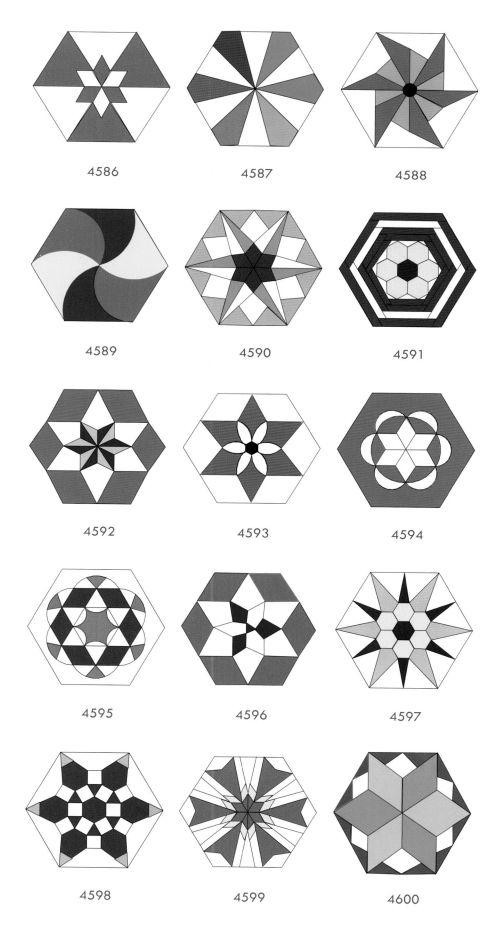

4586

4587

4588

4589

4590

4591

4592

4593

4594

4595

4596

4597

4598

4599

4600

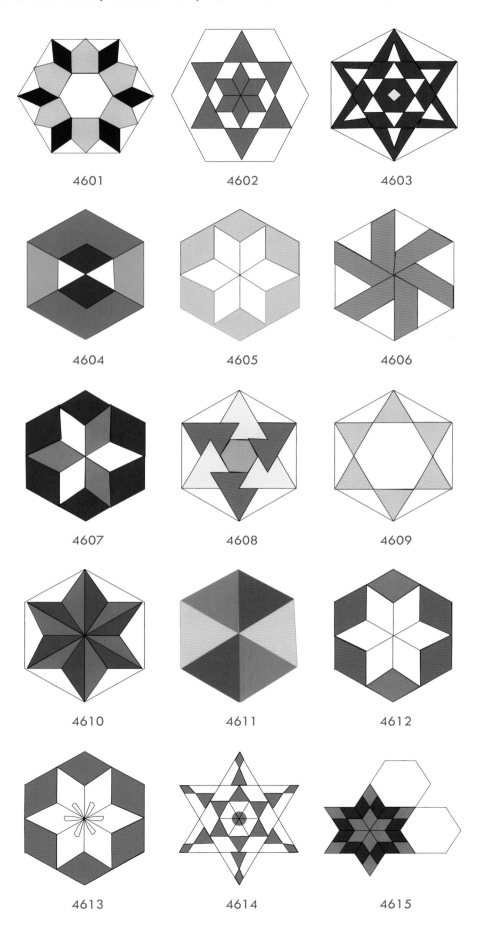

4601 Aunt Martha's Rose

4602 Oklahoma Star

4603 Double Star

4604 Spider Web

4605 Tea Box
Star Quilt

4606 Texas Trellis
Maple Leaf
Whirligig
Whirling Hexagons
Whirling Triangles

4607 Hexagonal, *HHJ*
Hexagonal Star, *CW*
Rising Star, *CW*

4608 Interlocked Star

4609 Star of Bethlehem
Diamonds and Arrow
Points, *KCS*
A Pattern of Chinese
Origin, *KCS*
(set with plain
hexagons):
Aunt Etta's Diamond
Quilt
Pointing Star

4610 Hexagon Star

4611 Kaleidoscope

4612 Builder's Blocks, *KCS*
Star and Box Quilt, *KCS*

4613 Dutch Tile, *KCS*
Arabian Star

4614 Colorado Star

4615 Morning Star

4616  Three Patch, *LW*

4617  Pinwheel Star

4618  Double Link, *NC*

4619  A Six Point Flower
        Garden

4620  Ozark Star, *KCS*

4621  The Diamond, *OF, 1896*
        Flower Garden Block,
        *KCS*

4622  Dutch Tile, *KCS*
        Arabian Star
        Star of Bethlehem

4623  Dutch Tile, *KCS*

4624  Jacob's Coat, *AMS*

4625  Unnamed, *OCS*

4626  Hexagon Snowflake,
        *QN*

4627  Stars and Stripes
        Forever, *SSQ, 1992*

4628  Blue Flower Garden

4629  Hexagonal

4630  Star and Blocks
        The Columbia, *LAC*
        Columbia Star

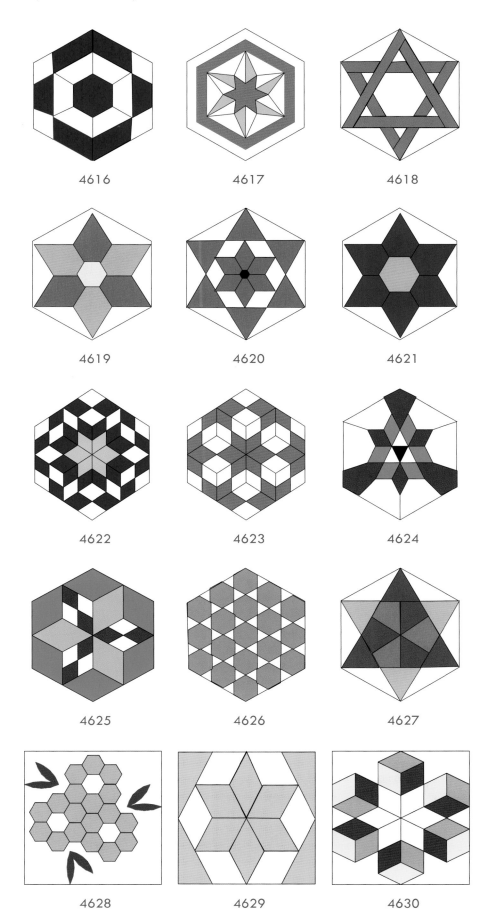

4616

4617

4618

4619

4620

4621

4622

4623

4624

4625

4626

4627

4628

4629

4630

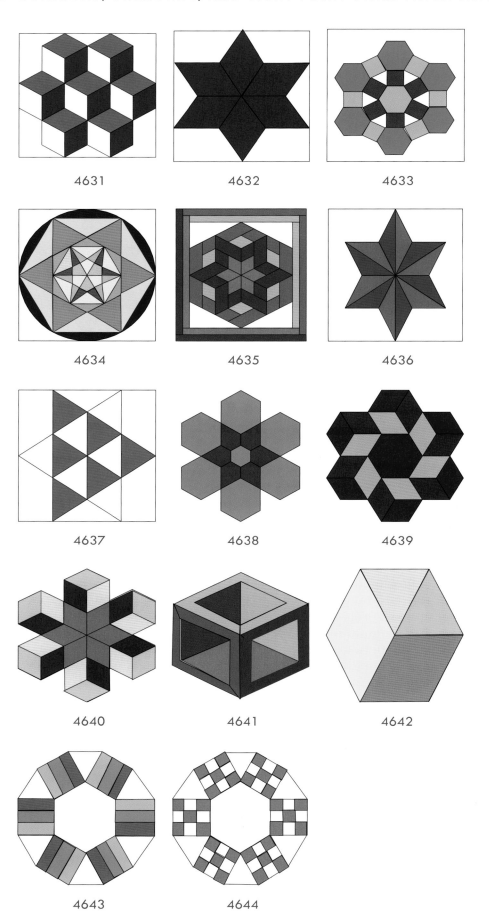

4631

4632

4633

4634

4635

4636

4637

4638

4639

4640

4641

4642

4643

4644

4631 Diamond Cube

4632 Morning Star
Star of Bethlehem

4633 Joseph's Coat, *LW*
Rolling Stone

4634 Roulette Wheel Star,
*Aunt Kate's Quilting
Bee*

4635 Twinkling Diamond
Log Cabin, *QW, 1993*

4636 Star of the East

4637 Saw Tooth Pattern

4638 On a Clear Night

4639 Spinning Blocks

4640 Star and Blocks

4641 See Through Block

4642 Open Top Box

4643 Wedding Tile
Faithful Circle, *AMS*

4644 Jack's Chain
Rosalia's Flower
Garden, *KCS*

4645 Ferris Wheel
Block Patchwork, *LAC*
Merry-Go-Round
(continuous design)
Morning Glory
Venetian Quilt
Wandering Paths

4646 Flower Garden
Aunt Jemima's Flower
Garden
Bride's Bouquet, *TFW*
Country Tile
French Bouquet
French Rose Garden
Grandmother's Flower
Garden
Grandmother's Rose
Garden
The Hexagon
Honeycomb

Martha Washington's
  Rose Garden
Mosaic
Old Fashioned Flower
  Garden
Rainbow Tile
(with dark joining
  rows):
Flower Garden
Garden Walk
Job's Troubles
Martha Washington's
  Flower Garden
Wheel of Life

4647 Mosaic

4648 Hexagon-Scrap Pattern
Century
Friendship Quilt
Hit or Miss
Honeycomb
Mosaic
Poor Boy

4649 Merry-Go-Round
Morning Glory

4650 Snow Crystal

4651 Tumbling Hexagons
Colonial Garden, *GC*
Rose Star One Patch,
  *OCS*

4652 Texas Star
Lemon Star

4653 Sunburst Star

4654 Cube Work, *LAC*
Diamond Cube, *LAC*
Tea Box, *FJ*

4655 Seven Sisters
Seven Stars, *LAC*
Seven Stars in a
  Cluster

4656 Skyscraper

4657 Orange Peel

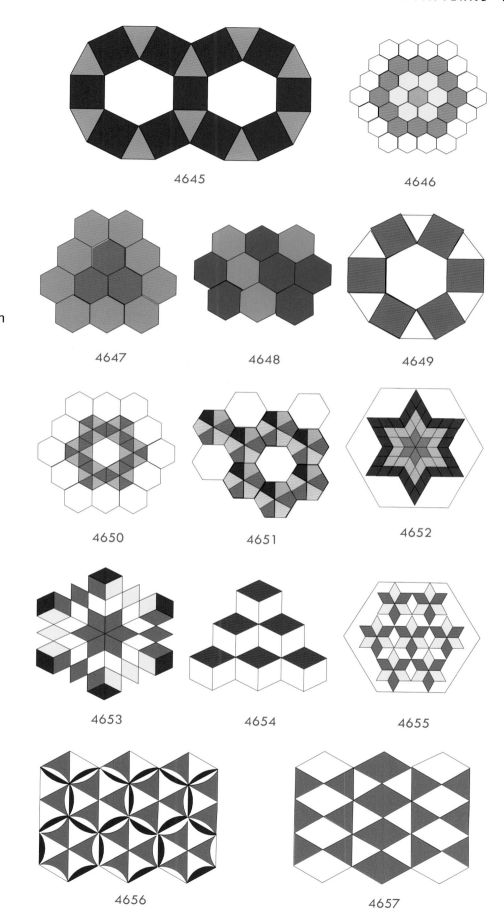

4645

4646

4647

4648

4649

4650

4651

4652

4653

4654

4655

4656

4657

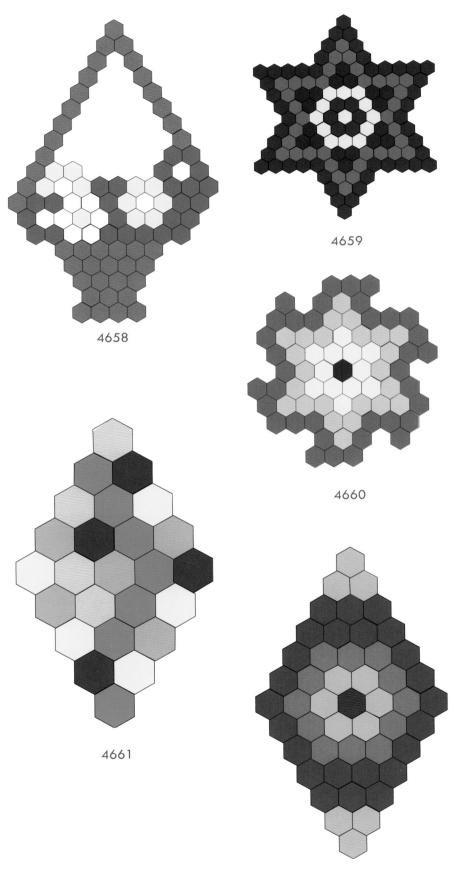

4658 Hexagon Flower
    Basket

4659 Grandmother's Flower
    Garden
    Grandmother's Star
    Garden
    Hexagon Star

4660 Star Hexagon

4661 Rainbow Tile
    Diamond Field

4662 Martha Washington's
    Flower Garden

4659

4658

4660

4661

4662

4663 Whirling Diamonds,
     *KCS*

4664 Variegated Diamonds,
     *LAC*

4665 Baby's Blocks
     Block Pattern
     Box Patchwork
     Box Pattern
     Box upon Box, *NP*
     Building Blocks
     Cubework
     Dancing Cubes, *PF*
     Disappearing Blocks,
      *MoM*
     English T Box
     Godey's 1851
     Golden Cubes, *NC*
     Grandma's Red and
      White
     The Heavenly Steps
     Jacob's Ladder, *WD*,
      *1940*
     Patience Corners, *LAC*
     Shifting Cubes, *HH*
     Stairs of Illusion
     Stairstep Quilt, *WD*
     Steps to the Altar
     Tumbling Blocks
     Variegated Diamonds

4666 Baby Block
     Box Quilt
     Cube Work
     Pandora's Block
     Pandora's Box
     Tea Box
     Tumbling Blocks

4667 Glory Block, *KCS*
     Glory Design, *WW*
     Old Glory, *NC*

4668 Blazing Star, *NP*
     Lone Star, *NP*
     Lone Star of Texas, *NP*
     The Sunburst, *NP*

4669 Baby Blocks

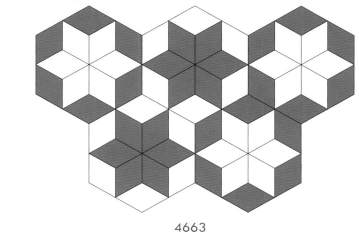

4663

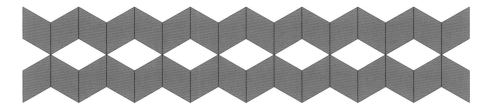

4664

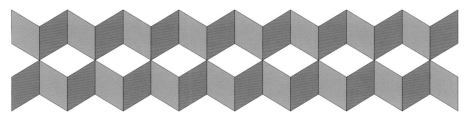

4665

4666

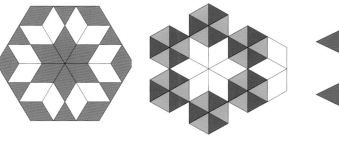

4667           4668           4669

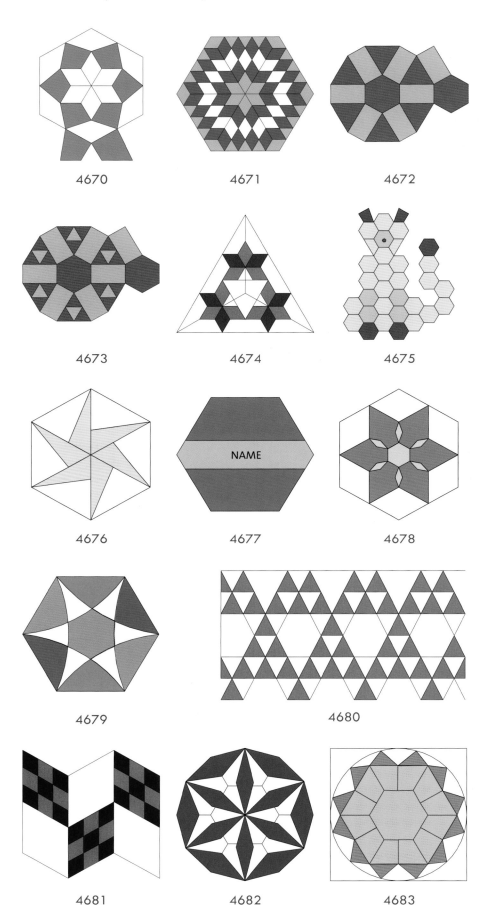

4670  A Pretty Patchwork,
         *HH*

4671  Columbia Star

4672  Joseph's Coat

4673  Wagon Wheel

4674  Star Flower, *1870*

4675  Hexacat,
         *Madeline Hawley, QC*

4676  Pinwheel

4677  Friendship Patch

4678  Arrowheads

4679  Star of the Mountains

4680  Tumbling Hexagons

4681  Diamond Nine Patch

4682  Chained Star

4683  Queen of the May

4670

4671

4672

4673

4674

4675

4676

4677

4678

4679

4680

4681

4682

4683

4684 Basket of Berries

4685 North Star

4686 Turning Triangles
Whirling Hexagons

4687 Trials and Troubles

4688 Hexagon and
Diamonds

4689 Basket of Flowers,
*Betty Boyink*

4690 Grandmother's Star,
*1944*

4691 The Pyramids, *PF*

4692 Spider Web

4693 A Pretty Patchwork

4694 Windblown Star

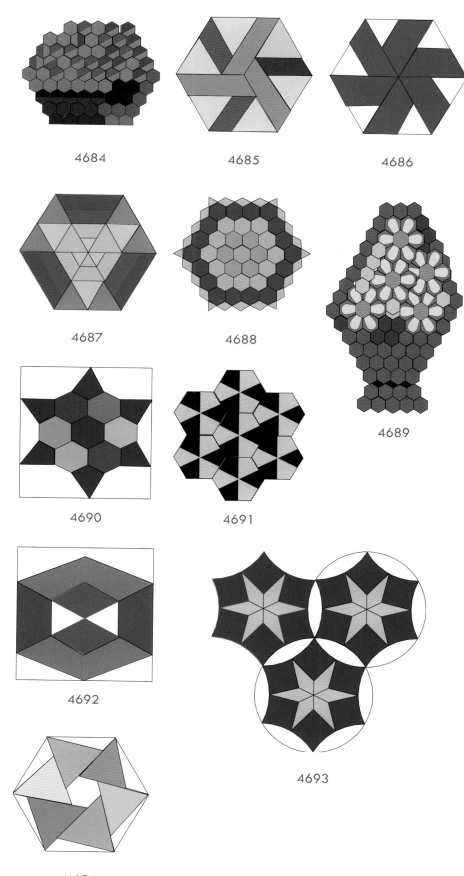

4684

4685

4686

4687

4688

4689

4690

4691

4692

4693

4694

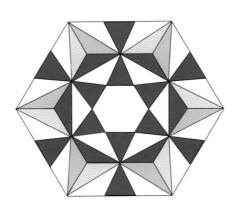

4695

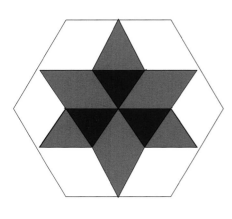

4696

4697

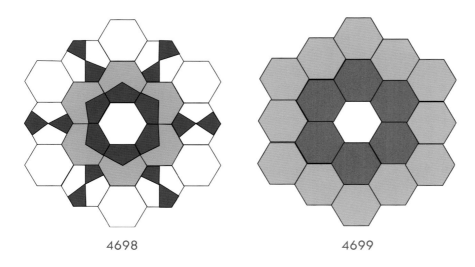

4698                    4699

4695 Mosaic,
    *Linda Halpin, 1984*

4696 Snowflake

4697 A Trip to Egypt
    (a continuous design
    building from the
    center out), *HAS*
    Triangle Mosaic

4698 Rose Star One Patch,
    *LW*
    Canadian
      Conventional Star
    Colonial Flower
      Garden
    Hexagons

4699 Hexagon Patchwork,
    *GLB, 1835*
    Honeycomb
    Colonial Bouquet
    Six-Sided Patchwork

4700 Charm
Endless Chain
Honeycomb Patch
Simplicity's Delight

4701 Ocean Wave

4702 Chevron, *OCS*

4703 Crazy Kite
Charm Packet Odyssey,
*Pat Moore, QN*

4704 Old Colony Star

4705 Brunswick Star, *LAC*

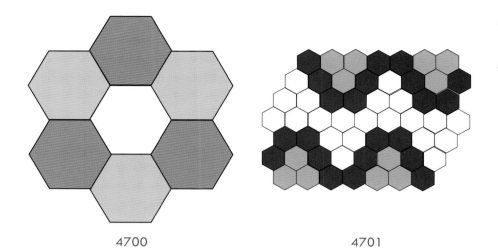

4700

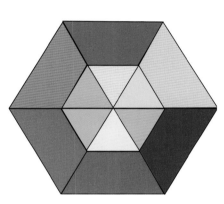

4701

4702

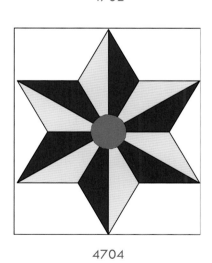

4703

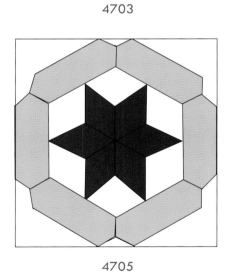

4704

4705

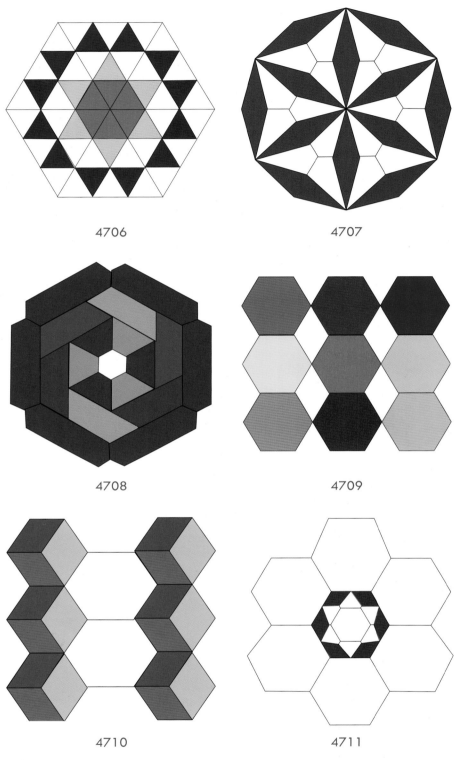

4706

4707

4708

4709

4710

4711

4706 One Thousand Pyramids

4707 Chained Star
Diamond Beauty Quilt
Poinsettia Quilt, *HAS*

4708 Granddaughter's
Flower Garden,
*SSQ, 1987*

4709 Hexagons and
Diamonds

4710 Diamond Hexagon, *NP*

4711 Pepper and Salt
Shakers

4712  Variable Triangles

4713  Octagon, *FJ*

4714  Flower Basket

4715  Windy City

4716  Star of David

4717  Trapezoid

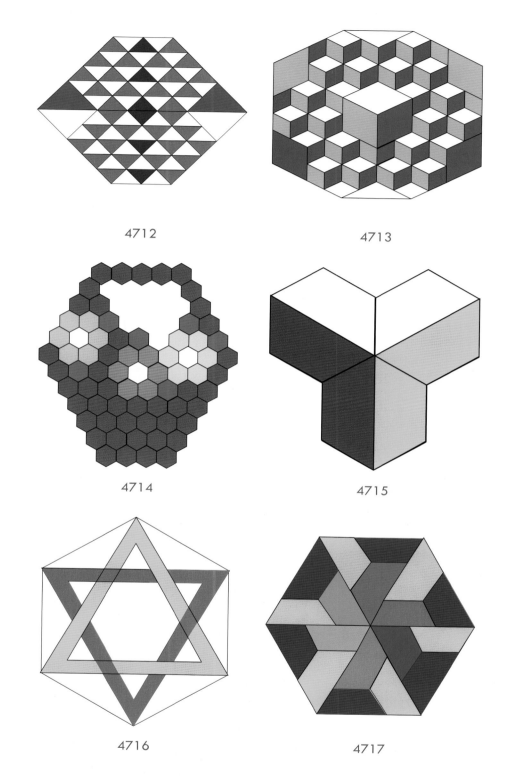

4712

4713

4714

4715

4716

4717

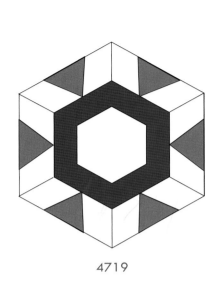

4718

4719

4718 Hexagon Star

4719 Floating Clouds

4720 Pointing Star

4721 Ducks in a Pond

4722 Star Bouquet

4723 Sam's Quilt

4724 Snowflake

4725 Snowflake

4726 Flower Trail

4727 Ocean Wave

4728 Diamond Field

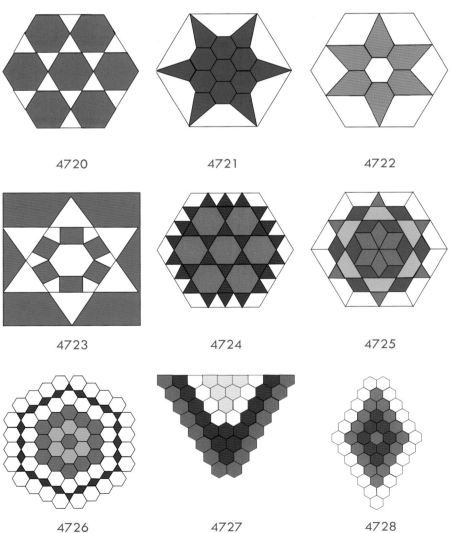

4720

4721

4722

4723

4724

4725

4726

4727

4728

4729 Hexagon Flower Block

4730 Star and Crescent

4731 Star and Planets

4732 Orange Peel Variation

4733 Inspiration

4734 Hexagon and
    Triangles,
    *Jenny Beyer*

4735 Starfish Block

4736 Starfish Block

4737 Sam's Quilt, *CS*

4738 Thunderbird

4739 Compass in a Hexagon

4740 Inner City

4741 Flower

4742 Grandmother's
    Cartwheel

4743 Tile Pattern

4729    4730    4731

4732    4733    4734

4735    4736    4737

4738    4739    4740

4741    4742    4743

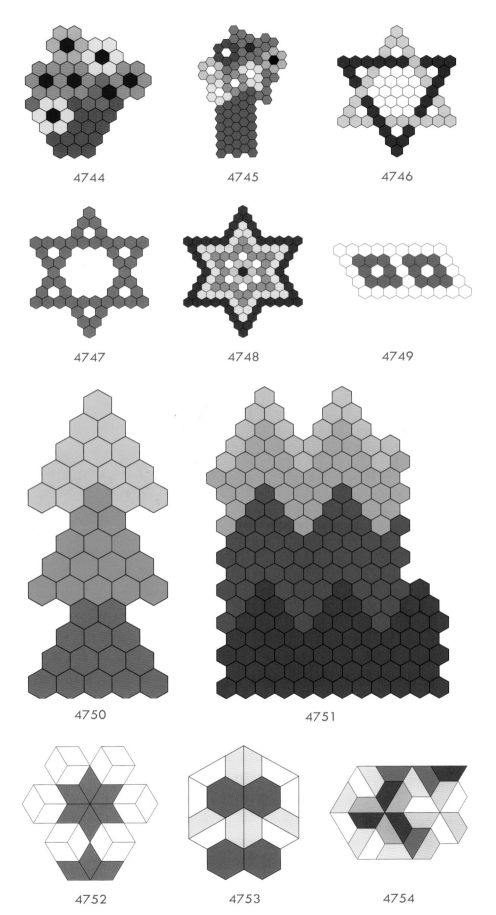

5,500 QUILT BLOCK DESIGNS

4744

4745

4746

4747

4748

4749

4744 Flowerpot

4745 Vase of Flowers

4746 Interlocked Star

4747 Star of David

4748 Hexagon Star

4749 Diamond Chain

4750 Arrowheads

4751 Hexagon Waves

4752 Tiny Star
Aunt Stella's Pattern
Star and Blocks

4753 Monk's Puzzle, *NC*

4754 Crazy Tile, *KCS*
Ecclesiastical, *LAC*
Right Angle Patchwork

4750

4751

4752

4753

4754

4755 Ecclesiastical

4756 Star and Diamonds, *NC*

4757 The Sirius Star Quilt, *HAS*

4758 Red and White Quilt
Sawtooth
Sawtooth Diamond

4759 Who'd a Thought It
(scrap quilt, continue
adding rows to
desired size)

4760 Chrysanthemum Quilt
Top

4761 Save-All, *AMS*
Save All Chain
Happy Memories

4762 Cow

4755

4756

4757

4758

4759

4760

4761

4762

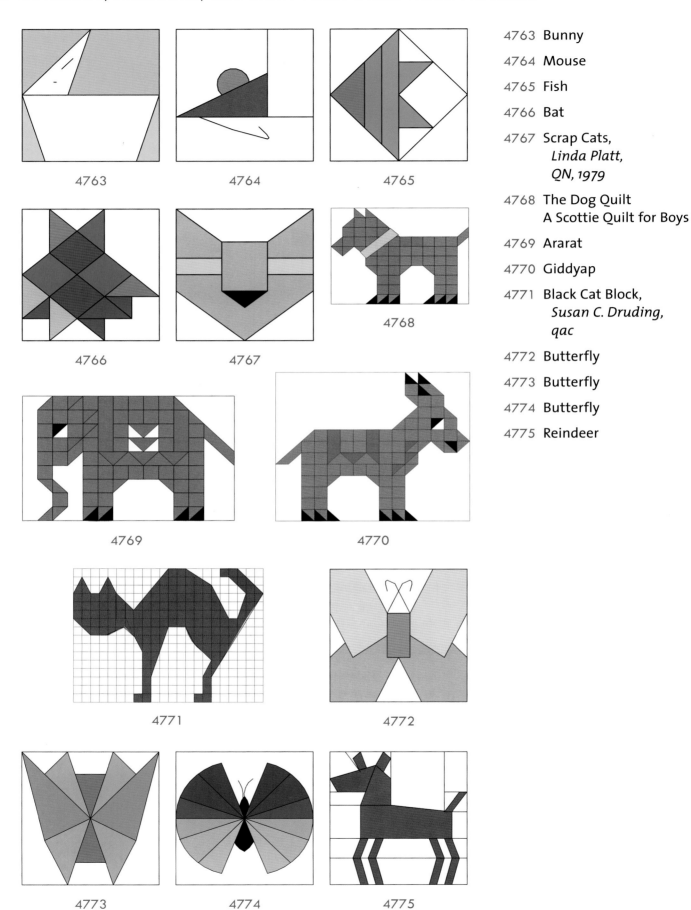

4763   Bunny

4764   Mouse

4765   Fish

4766   Bat

4767   Scrap Cats,
         *Linda Platt,*
         *QN, 1979*

4768   The Dog Quilt
         A Scottie Quilt for Boys

4769   Ararat

4770   Giddyap

4771   Black Cat Block,
         *Susan C. Druding,*
         *qac*

4772   Butterfly

4773   Butterfly

4774   Butterfly

4775   Reindeer

4776 Swallow's Flight, *AMS*

4777 Little Turtle in a Box, *SSQ, 1988*

4778 Calico Cat

4779 Three Little Kittens, *AMS*

4780 Fish

4781 Flying Fish, *QC*

4782 Fish

4783 Scottie Dog

4784 Cats in the Attic, *QM, 1989*

4785 Cat

4786 Winner's Circle, *QM, 1992*

4787 Ducks in a Row, *QN, 1987*

4788 Pieced Duck

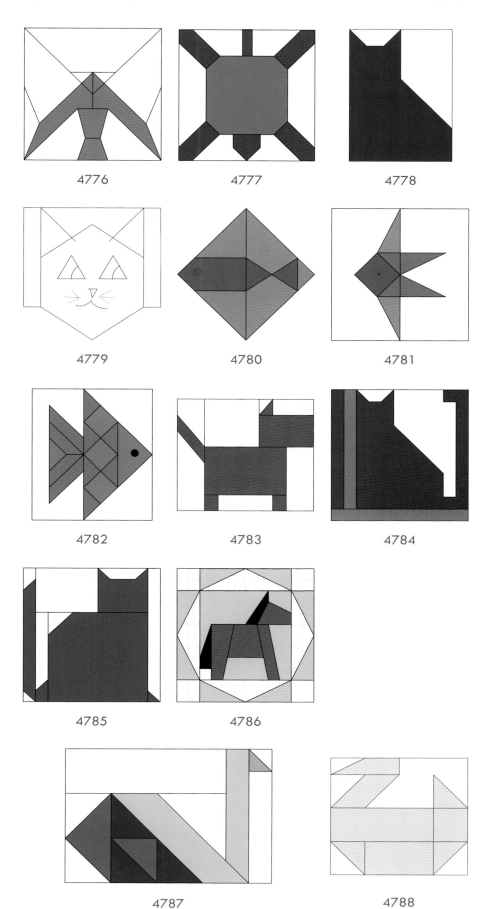

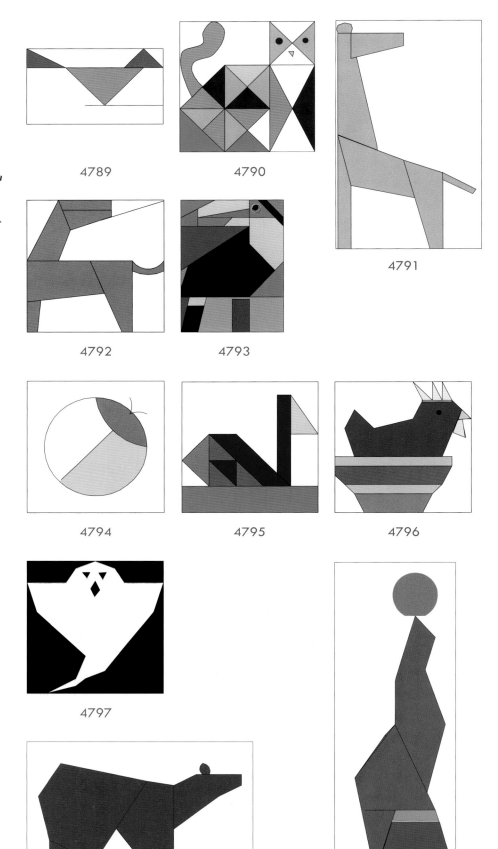

4789

4790

4791

4792

4793

4794

4795

4796

4797

4798

4799

4789 Bird Feeder,
*Doreen Burbank,
SSQ, 1990*

4790 Cat, *QN*

4791 Giraffe,
*Margit Echols, QC*

4792 Zebra,
*Margit Echols, QC*

4793 Toucan,
*Margaret Rolfe*

4794 Lady Bug,
*Aunt Kate's Quilting
Bee*

4795 Duck

4796 Miss Henrietta,
*piecebynumber.com*

4797 Ghost,
*piecebynumber.com*

4798 Bear

4799 Seal,
*Margit Echols, TQ*

4800 Fish

4801 Turkey, *geocities.com/ Heartland/Acres*

4802 Frog

4803 Elephant, *Woman's Home Companion*

4804 Butterfly

4805 Butterfly

4806 Nighttime Butterflies, *RM*

4807 Pieced Butterfly #1408, *CoM*

4808 Duck

4809 Bug

4810 Fowl Weather, *Alice L. Vail, SSQ*

4811 Hippopotamus, *PP*

4812 Reindeer, *PP*

4813 Seal, *PP*

4814 Ostrich, *PP*

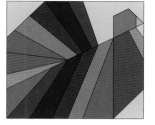

4800

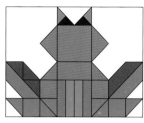

4801

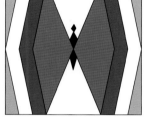

4802

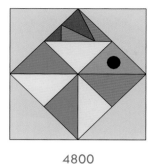

4803

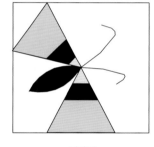

4804

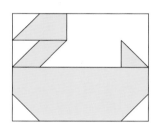

4805

4806

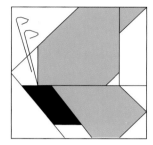

4807

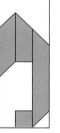

4808

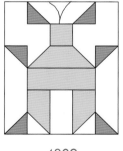

4809

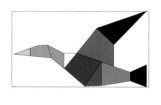

4810

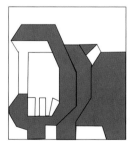

4811

4812

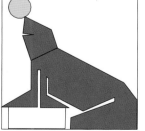

4813

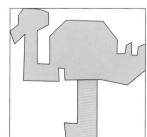

4814

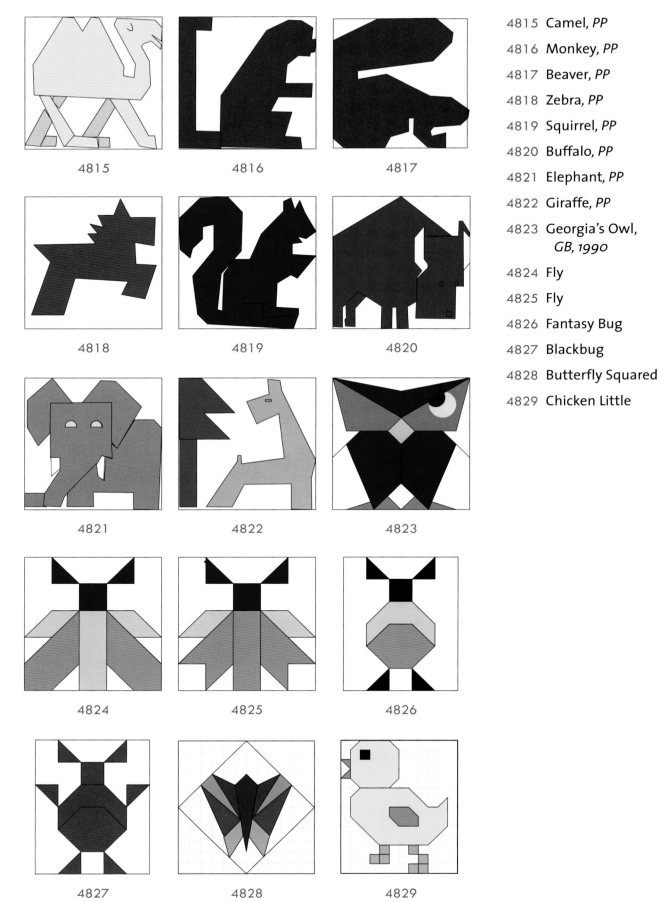

4815

4816

4817

4818

4819

4820

4821

4822

4823

4824

4825

4826

4827

4828

4829

4815 Camel, *PP*

4816 Monkey, *PP*

4817 Beaver, *PP*

4818 Zebra, *PP*

4819 Squirrel, *PP*

4820 Buffalo, *PP*

4821 Elephant, *PP*

4822 Giraffe, *PP*

4823 Georgia's Owl, *GB, 1990*

4824 Fly

4825 Fly

4826 Fantasy Bug

4827 Blackbug

4828 Butterfly Squared

4829 Chicken Little

4830 Elephant

4831 Cowboy Boot,
    *Susan C. Druding*

4832 Perky Pumpkin,
    *Marilyn Busch,*
    *SSQ, 1985*

4833 Ice Cream Bowl

4834 Ice Cream Bowl, *LAC*

4835 Pumpkin

4836 Chinese Lantern, *CW*

4837 A Japanese Garden,
    *KCS*

4838 The Bell, *KCS*

4839 Coffee Cups, *KCS*
    The Cup and the
    Saucer, *KCS*

4840 The Ice Cream Cone

4841 Four Vases, *KCS*

4842 The Goblet Quilt, *KCS*
    The Old Fashioned
    Goblet
    Tumbler
    Water Glass

4843 The Soldier Boy, *KCS*
    Soldier at the Window

4844 The Ice Cream Cone

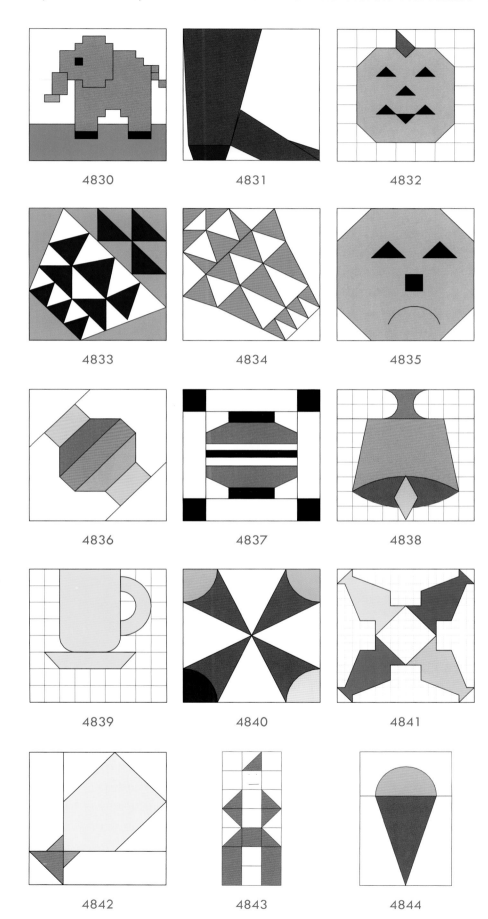

4830    4831    4832

4833    4834    4835

4836    4837    4838

4839    4840    4841

4842    4843    4844

5,500 QUILT BLOCK DESIGNS

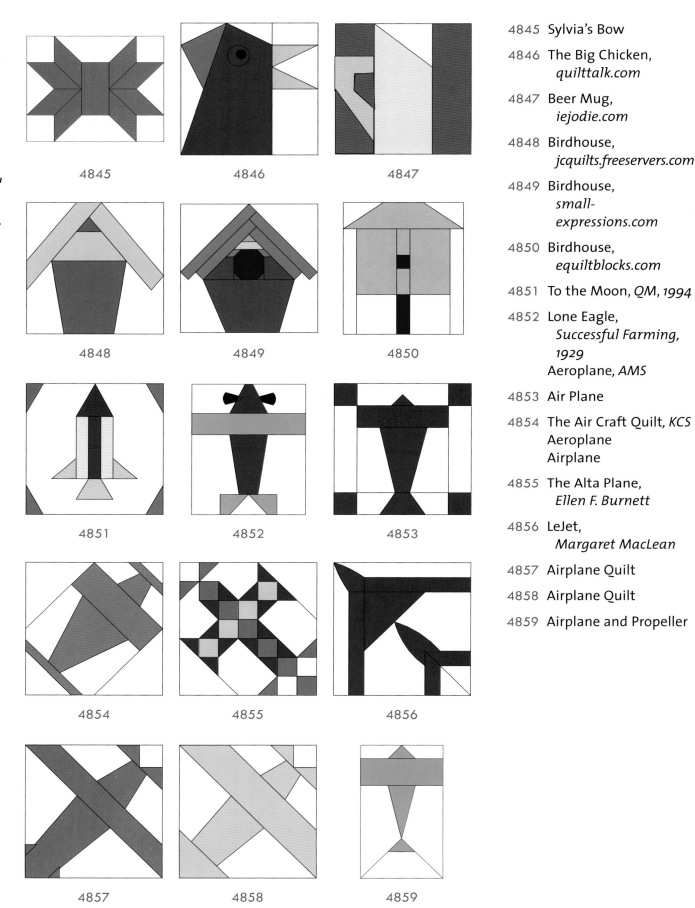

4845

4846

4847

4848

4849

4850

4851

4852

4853

4854

4855

4856

4857

4858

4859

4845 Sylvia's Bow

4846 The Big Chicken,
 *quilttalk.com*

4847 Beer Mug,
 *iejodie.com*

4848 Birdhouse,
 *jcquilts.freeservers.com*

4849 Birdhouse,
 *small-expressions.com*

4850 Birdhouse,
 *equiltblocks.com*

4851 To the Moon, *QM, 1994*

4852 Lone Eagle,
 *Successful Farming,
 1929*
 Aeroplane, *AMS*

4853 Air Plane

4854 The Air Craft Quilt, *KCS*
 Aeroplane
 Airplane

4855 The Alta Plane,
 *Ellen F. Burnett*

4856 LeJet,
 *Margaret MacLean*

4857 Airplane Quilt

4858 Airplane Quilt

4859 Airplane and Propeller

4860 Lone Eagle Airplane

4861 Aeroplanes

4862 Truck

4863 Truck

4864 Airplane, *NC*

4865 Air Ways

4866 Lindbergh's Night
Flight

4867 Truck Patch

4868 Boat in a Bottle,
*Lyn Peare Sandberg,
QN, 1991*

4869 Baby Food Jar (3"x3"),
*winnowing.com*

4870 Wine Bottle (3"x6"),
*geocities.com*

4871 Bottle, *qac*

4872 Wine Glass, *qac*

4873 Perfume Block,
*quiltaholics.com*

4874 Mason Jar,
*geocities.com*

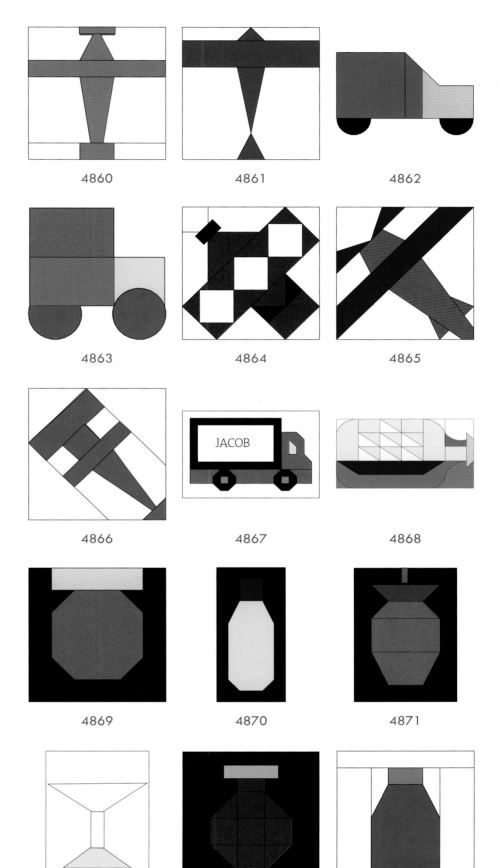

4860   4861   4862

4863   4864   4865

4866   4867   4868

4869   4870   4871

4872   4873   4874

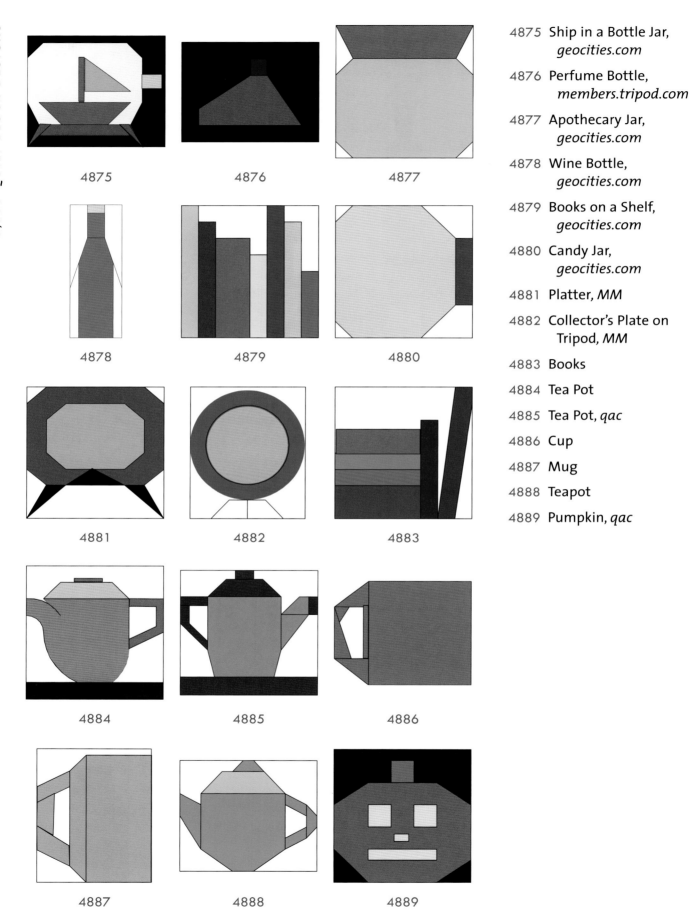

5,500 QUILT BLOCK DESIGNS

4875

4876

4877

4878

4879

4880

4881

4882

4883

4884

4885

4886

4887

4888

4889

4875 Ship in a Bottle Jar, *geocities.com*

4876 Perfume Bottle, *members.tripod.com*

4877 Apothecary Jar, *geocities.com*

4878 Wine Bottle, *geocities.com*

4879 Books on a Shelf, *geocities.com*

4880 Candy Jar, *geocities.com*

4881 Platter, *MM*

4882 Collector's Plate on Tripod, *MM*

4883 Books

4884 Tea Pot

4885 Tea Pot, *qac*

4886 Cup

4887 Mug

4888 Teapot

4889 Pumpkin, *qac*

4890 Pumpkin, *qac*

4891 Pumpkin, *qac*

4892 Pumpkin, *qac*

4893 Pumpkin, *MM*

4894 Baby Shoe, *qac*

4895 Auntie's Kitties,
     *auntie.com/qzine*

4896 Candlestick

4897 Telephone,
     *Aunt Kate's Quilting
     Bee*

4898 Harvest Grapes

4899 Japanese Lantern, *KCS*

4900 Crocodile, *PP*

4901 Cup

4902 Workbox
     Kitchen Woodbox

4903 Angel

4904 Lamp, *qac*

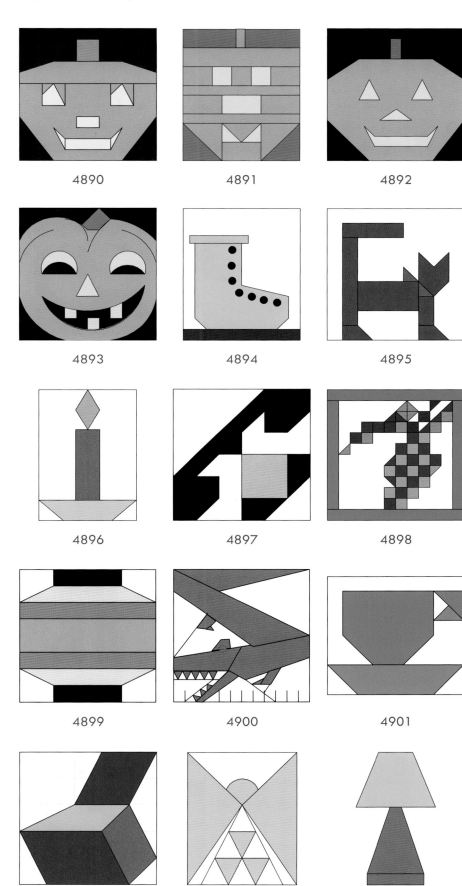

4890
4891
4892
4893
4894
4895
4896
4897
4898
4899
4900
4901
4902
4903
4904

5,500 QUILT BLOCK DESIGNS

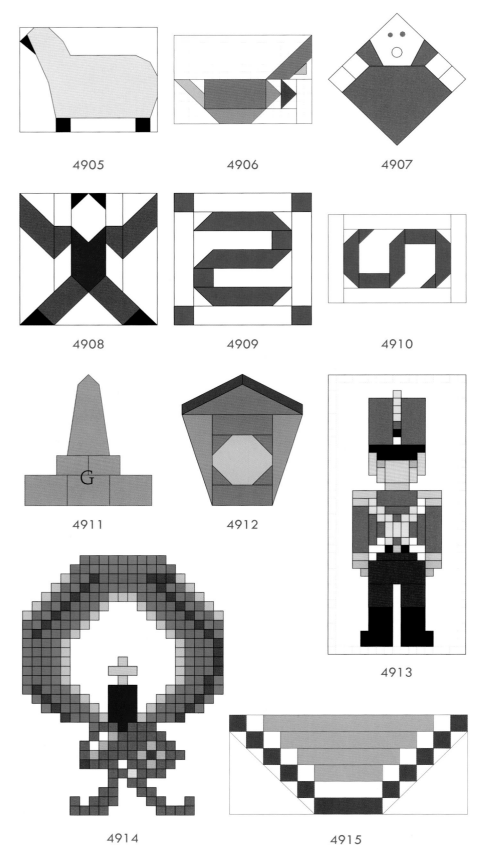

4905

4906

4907

4908

4909

4910

4911

4912

4913

4914

4915

4905  Sheep

4906  Teapot

4907  Baby Dolls

4908  Acrobat

4909  The Mountain Road,
       *KCS*

4910  The Flowing Ribbon,
       *KCS*

4911  Garfield's Monument,
       *LAC*

4912  Birdhouse

4913  Toy Soldier

4914  Christmas Wreath

4915  Watermelon

4916 The Bell, *KCS*

4917 Sunbonnet Sue

4918 Diaper Pins,
   *Rhoda Ochser*
   *Goldberg,*
   *Quilting & Patchwork*
   *Dictionary*

4919 Hobby Horse

4920 Teapot

4921 Blouses, *MM*

4922 Let's Get Pinned, *GB*

4923 Panda Patch

4924 Hobby Horse
   Rocking Horse

4925 Hobby Horse

4926 Bow
   Pieced Ribbon
   Ribbon
   Ribbon Bow

4927 Television Quilt, *QW,*
   *1977*

4928 Bow Knots, *NC*

4929 Thunderbird

4916

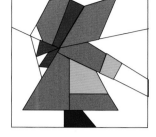
4917

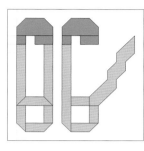
4918

4919

4920

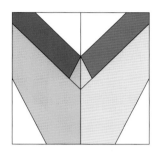
4921

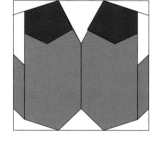
4922

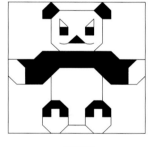
4923

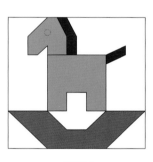
4924

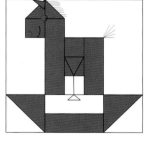
4925

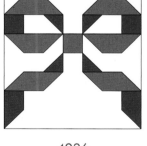
4926

4927

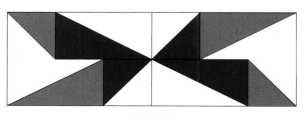
4928

4929

5,500 QUILT BLOCK DESIGNS

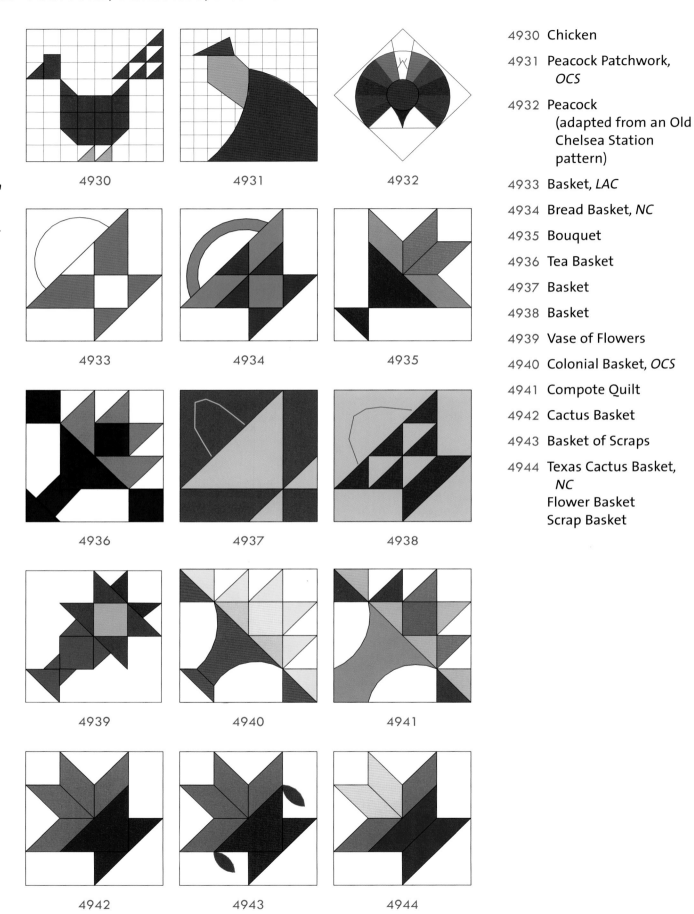

4930

4931

4932

4933

4934

4935

4936

4937

4938

4939

4940

4941

4942

4943

4944

4930 Chicken

4931 Peacock Patchwork, *OCS*

4932 Peacock (adapted from an Old Chelsea Station pattern)

4933 Basket, *LAC*

4934 Bread Basket, *NC*

4935 Bouquet

4936 Tea Basket

4937 Basket

4938 Basket

4939 Vase of Flowers

4940 Colonial Basket, *OCS*

4941 Compote Quilt

4942 Cactus Basket

4943 Basket of Scraps

4944 Texas Cactus Basket, *NC*
Flower Basket
Scrap Basket

4945 Cactus Pot

4946 Sugar Bowl, *NC*

4947 Basket, *NP*

4948 Flower Basket, *LAC*
Betty's Basket, *NP*
Basket Quilt

4949 Simple Flower Basket,
*NC*

4950 Baby Bunting

4951 Strawberry Basket

4952 Basket
Hanging Basket

4953 Flower Basket
Basket of Diamonds
Cactus Basket
Desert Rose
The Disk, *LAC*
Flower Pot
Jersey Tulip
Rainbow Cactus

4954 Grandmother's Basket

4955 A Basket Patch, *HH*

4956 Basket, *1850*

4957 Grandmother's Basket,
*KCS*

4958 Basket

4959 Flower Basket

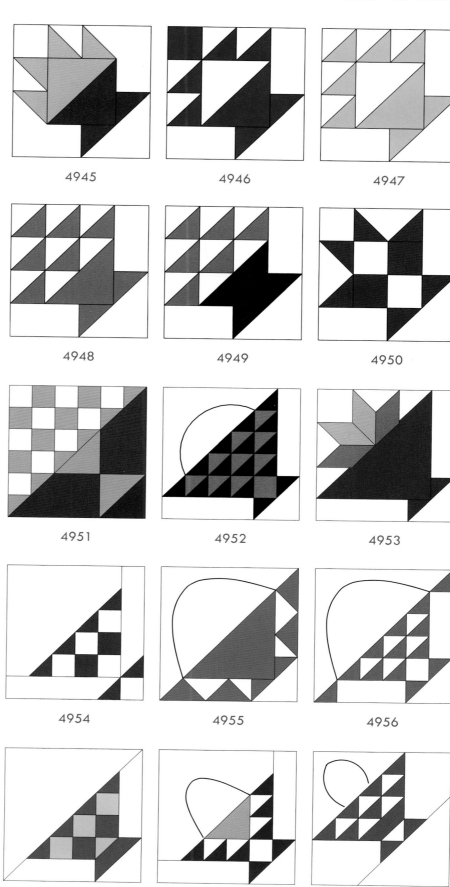

4945    4946    4947

4948    4949    4950

4951    4952    4953

4954    4955    4956

4957    4958    4959

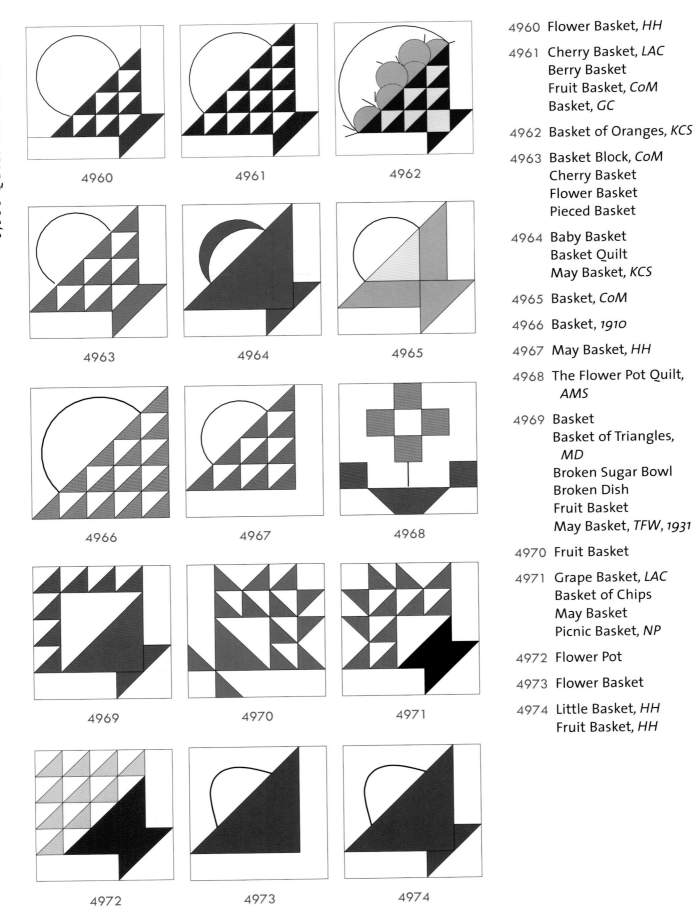

5,500 QUILT BLOCK DESIGNS

4960

4961

4962

4963

4964

4965

4966

4967

4968

4969

4970

4971

4972

4973

4974

4960 Flower Basket, *HH*

4961 Cherry Basket, *LAC*
Berry Basket
Fruit Basket, *CoM*
Basket, *GC*

4962 Basket of Oranges, *KCS*

4963 Basket Block, *CoM*
Cherry Basket
Flower Basket
Pieced Basket

4964 Baby Basket
Basket Quilt
May Basket, *KCS*

4965 Basket, *CoM*

4966 Basket, *1910*

4967 May Basket, *HH*

4968 The Flower Pot Quilt,
*AMS*

4969 Basket
Basket of Triangles,
*MD*
Broken Sugar Bowl
Broken Dish
Fruit Basket
May Basket, *TFW, 1931*

4970 Fruit Basket

4971 Grape Basket, *LAC*
Basket of Chips
May Basket
Picnic Basket, *NP*

4972 Flower Pot

4973 Flower Basket

4974 Little Basket, *HH*
Fruit Basket, *HH*

4975 Basket

4976 Dresden Basket, *GD*
Red Basket

4977 Basket

4978 Basket Quilt, *1899*
The Basket
Cherry Basket
Colonial Basket, *1861*
Flower Basket

4979 Leafy Basket, *LW*

4980 Cake Stand, *LAC*
Basket, *HH*
Fruit Basket

4981 Basket, *1898*

4982 Fruit Basket

4983 Flower Pot, *KCS*

4984 Flower Basket, *CS*
Peach Basket, *NP*

4985 Cake Stand, *NC*
May Basket (colors
reversed), *KCS*

4986 Basket of Chips, *CoM*
Basket of Flowers
Chip Basket, *TFW*
Flower Pot
Anna's Basket

4987 Bea's Basket

4988 Basket, *HH*

4989 Wedding Basket,
*QM, 1993*

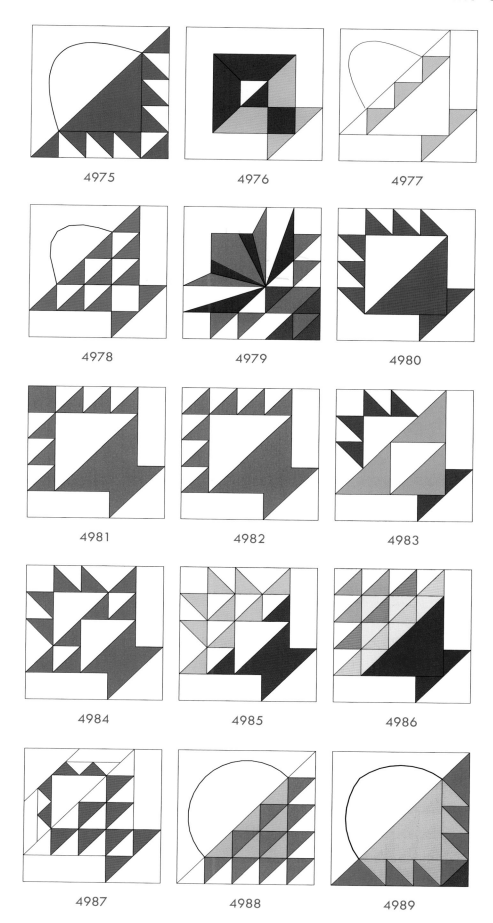

4975

4976

4977

4978

4979

4980

4981

4982

4983

4984

4985

4986

4987

4988

4989

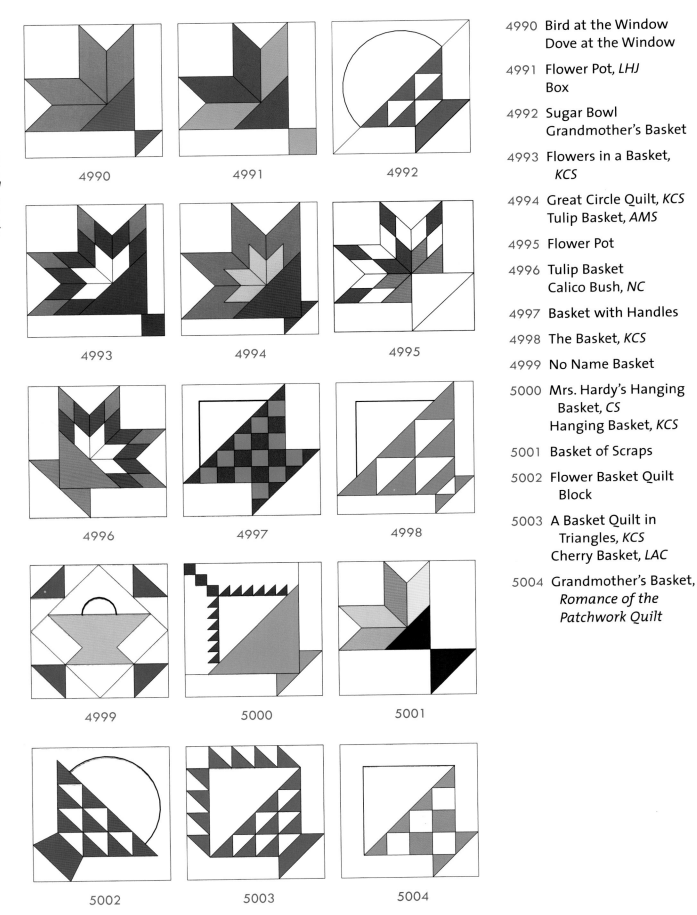

| | | |
|---|---|---|
| 4990 | 4991 | 4992 |
| 4993 | 4994 | 4995 |
| 4996 | 4997 | 4998 |
| 4999 | 5000 | 5001 |
| 5002 | 5003 | 5004 |

4990 Bird at the Window
Dove at the Window

4991 Flower Pot, *LHJ*
Box

4992 Sugar Bowl
Grandmother's Basket

4993 Flowers in a Basket,
*KCS*

4994 Great Circle Quilt, *KCS*
Tulip Basket, *AMS*

4995 Flower Pot

4996 Tulip Basket
Calico Bush, *NC*

4997 Basket with Handles

4998 The Basket, *KCS*

4999 No Name Basket

5000 Mrs. Hardy's Hanging
Basket, *CS*
Hanging Basket, *KCS*

5001 Basket of Scraps

5002 Flower Basket Quilt
Block

5003 A Basket Quilt in
Triangles, *KCS*
Cherry Basket, *LAC*

5004 Grandmother's Basket,
*Romance of the
Patchwork Quilt*

5005 May Basket

5006 Fruit Basket, *NP*

5007 Fruit Basket, *HH*

5008 Nine Patch Basket,
     *Connie Litfin, QN*

5009 Aunt Em's Basket,
     *LCPQ*

5010 Cherry Basket, *KCS*

5011 Colonial Basket,
     *Romance of the
     Patchwork Quilt*

5012 Flower Basket, *KCS*
     Basket of Diamonds
     The Disk, *LAC*
     Flower Pot
     Jersey Tulip
     Rainbow Cactus

5013 Flower Pot, *KCS*
     May Basket, *NC*

5014 Cactus Basket Block

5015 Hicks Flower Basket,
     *KCS*

5016 Basket of Diamonds,
     *KCS*

5017 Christmas Basket, *QW*,
     *1991*

5018 Basket of Bright
     Flowers, *KCS*

5019 Tulips in a Vase, *CaS*

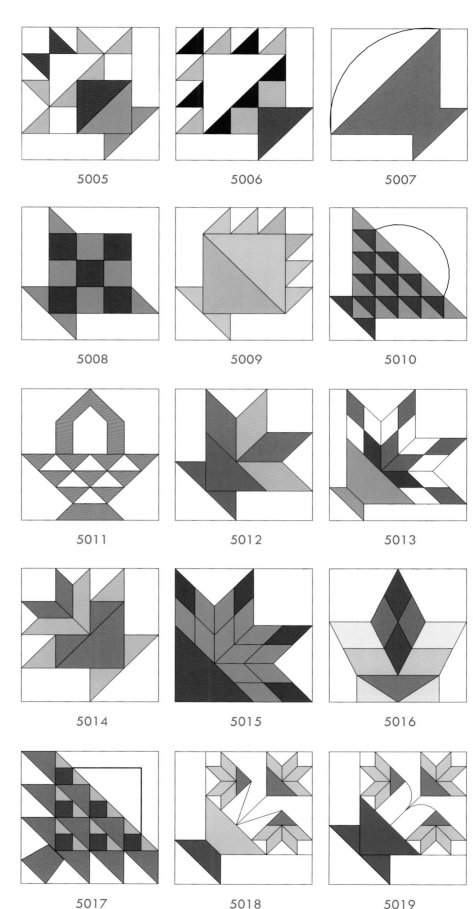

5005     5006     5007

5008     5009     5010

5011     5012     5013

5014     5015     5016

5017     5018     5019

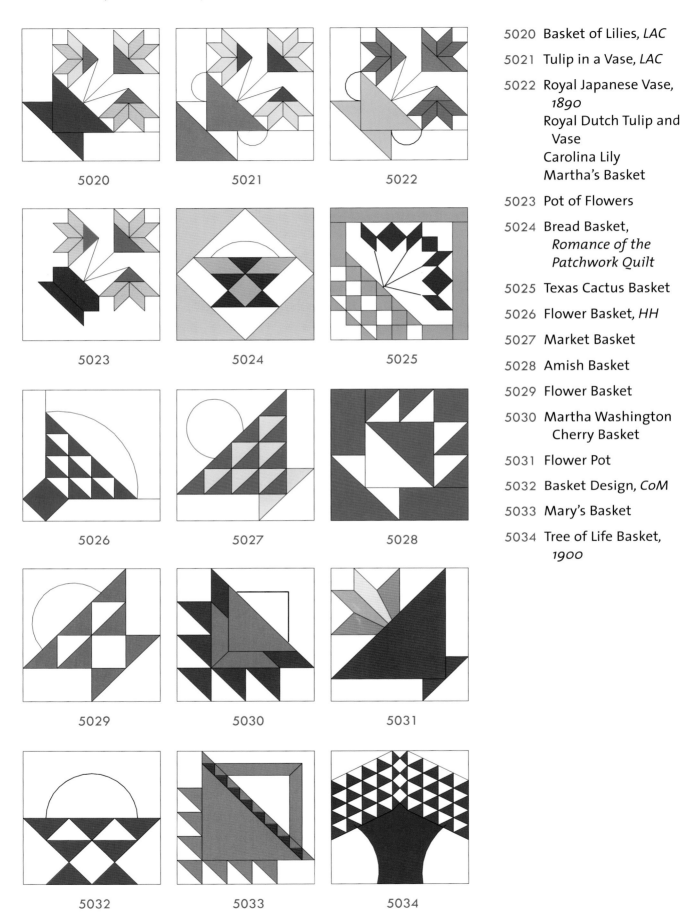

5020    Basket of Lilies, *LAC*

5021    Tulip in a Vase, *LAC*

5022    Royal Japanese Vase,
          *1890*
          Royal Dutch Tulip and
          Vase
          Carolina Lily
          Martha's Basket

5023    Pot of Flowers

5024    Bread Basket,
          *Romance of the
          Patchwork Quilt*

5025    Texas Cactus Basket

5026    Flower Basket, *HH*

5027    Market Basket

5028    Amish Basket

5029    Flower Basket

5030    Martha Washington
          Cherry Basket

5031    Flower Pot

5032    Basket Design, *CoM*

5033    Mary's Basket

5034    Tree of Life Basket,
          *1900*

5035 Basket of Lilies

5036 Four Little Baskets, *LAC*
     Four Baskets, *NC*

5037 Postage Stamp Basket

5038 Basket

5039 Japanese Basket

5040 Cherry Basket

5041 Old Fashioned Fruit
     Basket

5042 Basket of Flowers

5043 Flower Pot

5044 Flower Basket, *CaS*

5045 Tulip Basket
     (4 tulips, 2 leaves), *NC*

5046 Basket

5047 Basket of Tulips

5048 Victorian Basket, *QM*,
     *1992*

5049 Missouri Memories

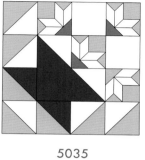

5035

5036

5037

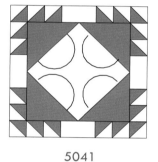

5038

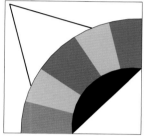

5039

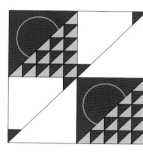

5040

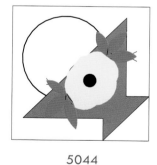

5041

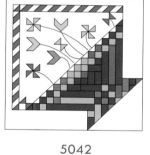

5042

5043

5044

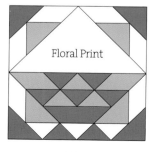

5045

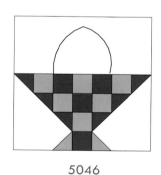

5046

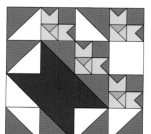

5047

Floral Print

5048

5049

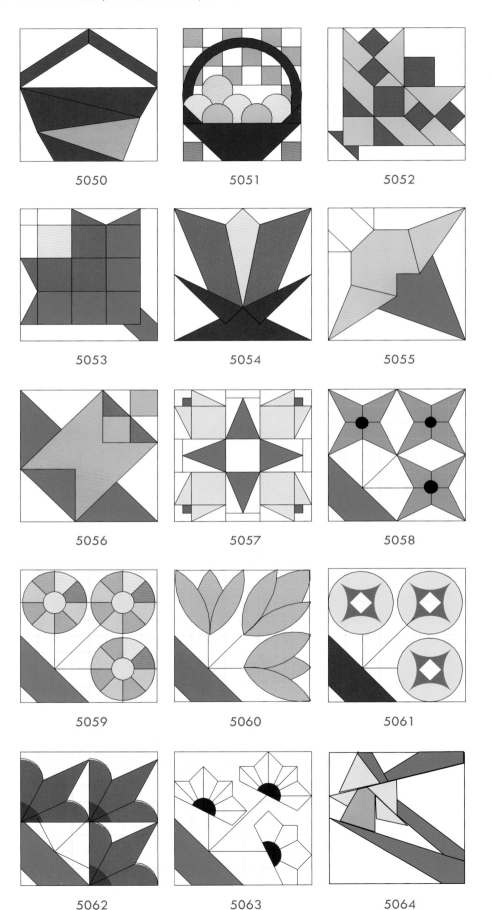

5050

5051

5052

5053

5054

5055

5056

5057

5058

5059

5060

5061

5062

5063

5064

5050 Basket, *his.com/~ queenbee/frugal*

5051 Egg Basket

5052 Flower Basket

5053 Crocus

5054 Tulip Time

5055 Trumpet Flower

5056 Trumpet Flower

5057 Magnolia Bud, *NC* Pink Magnolias, *NC*

5058 Snowdrop (Bowl of Flowers Series), *OCS*

5059 Aster (Bowl of Flowers Series), *OCS*

5060 Tulip (Bowl of Flowers Series), *OCS*

5061 Rose (Bowl of Flowers Series), *OCS*

5062 Lily (Bowl of Flowers Series), *OCS*

5063 Poppy (Bowl of Flowers Series), *OCS*

5064 Daffodils

5065 Tulip, *OCS*

5066 Old Fashioned Garden, *OCS*

5067 Friendship Flowers, *OCS*

5068 Oriental Poppy
  Modernistic California
  Poppy

5069 Tennessee Tulip

5070 Crocus, *OCS*

5071 Tulip Garden, *OCS*

5072 Egyptian Lotus Flower

5073 Brown-Eyed Susan

5074 Tulips, *AMS*

5075 Fantasy Flower (8)

5076 Pansy (8)

5077 Stylized Flower

5078 Pieced Tulip

5079 Bud,
  *his.com*

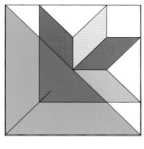
5065

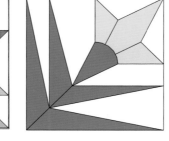
5066

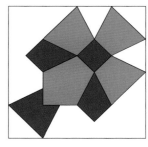
5067

5068

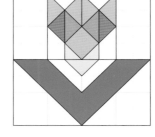
5069

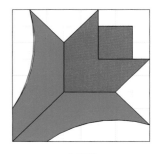
5070

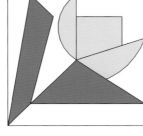
5071

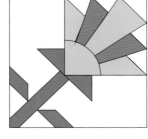
5072

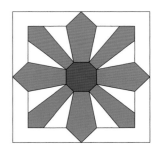
5073

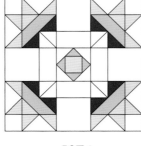
5074

5075

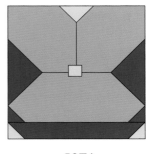
5076

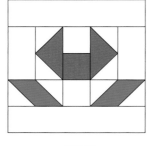
5077

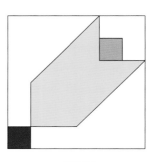
5078

5079

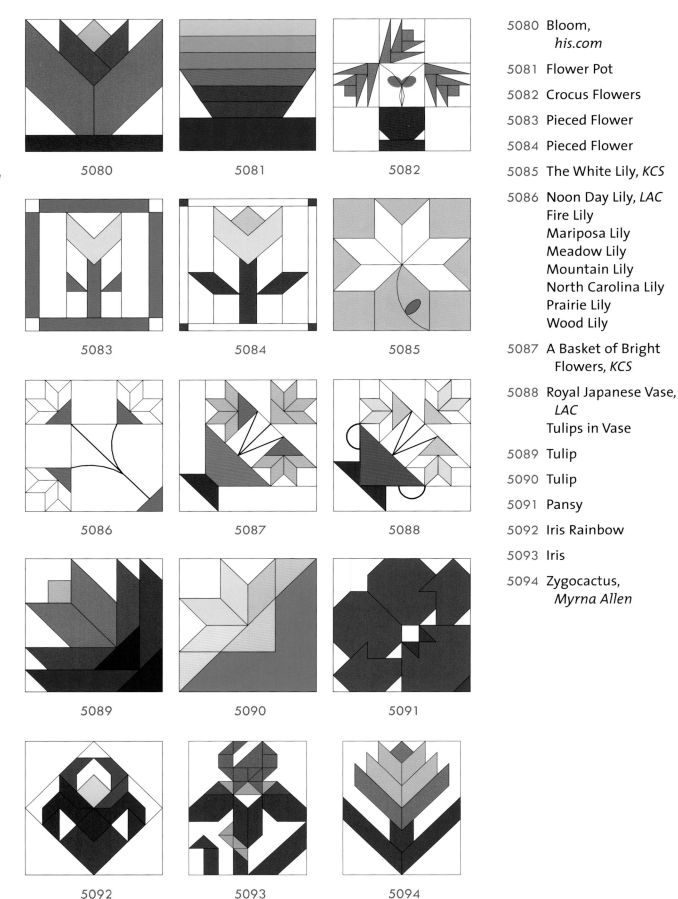

5080

5081

5082

5083

5084

5085

5086

5087

5088

5089

5090

5091

5092

5093

5094

5080 Bloom,
   *his.com*

5081 Flower Pot

5082 Crocus Flowers

5083 Pieced Flower

5084 Pieced Flower

5085 The White Lily, *KCS*

5086 Noon Day Lily, *LAC*
   Fire Lily
   Mariposa Lily
   Meadow Lily
   Mountain Lily
   North Carolina Lily
   Prairie Lily
   Wood Lily

5087 A Basket of Bright
   Flowers, *KCS*

5088 Royal Japanese Vase,
   *LAC*
   Tulips in Vase

5089 Tulip

5090 Tulip

5091 Pansy

5092 Iris Rainbow

5093 Iris

5094 Zygocactus,
   *Myrna Allen*

5095 Art Deco Tulip

5096 Modernistic Pansy, *NC*
Pansy

5097 Pieced Pansy

5098 Modernistic Pansy

5099 Modernistic California
Poppy

5100 Primrose Patch

5101 Modernistic Trumpet
Vine (9)
Trumpet Vine

5102 Modernistic Rose

5103 Palm Flower

5104 Triple Sunflower

5105 Daisy Block

5106 Star Bouquet

5107 Aunt Martha's Tulips

5108 Lily of the Valley, *QW*,
*1989*

5109 Evening Flower, *OCS*

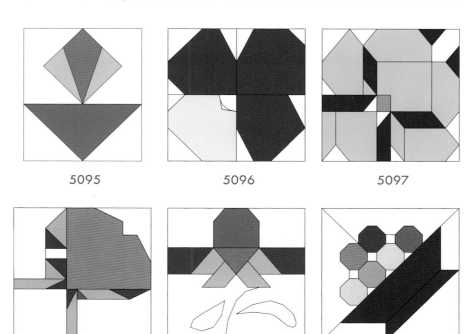

5095

5096

5097

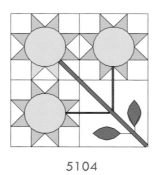

5098

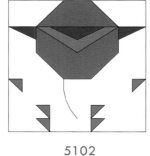

5099

5100

5101

5102

5103

5104

5105

5106

5107

5108

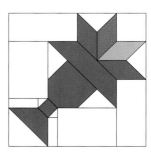

5109

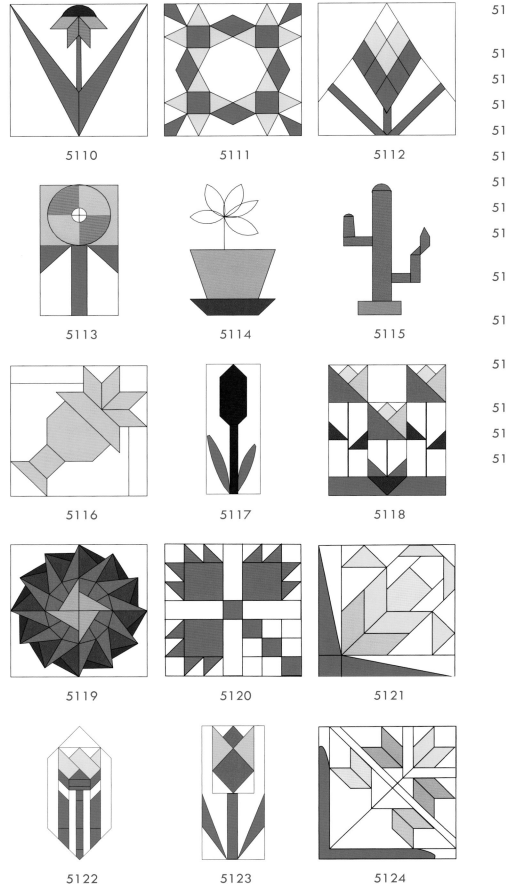

5110    5111    5112

5113    5114    5115

5116    5117    5118

5119    5120    5121

5122    5123    5124

5110 Nouveau Lily Quilt, *Helen Rose, SSQ, 1990*

5111 Star Flower Wreath

5112 Texas Bluebonnet, *QN*

5113 Zinnias

5114 Flower in a Pot

5115 Cactus

5116 Star Bouquet

5117 Cattail

5118 Tulip Garden (12x4), *QM, 1992*

5119 Poinsettia Star, *piecebynumber.com*

5120 Thistles in the Mist, *SSQ*

5121 Jack in the Pulpit Indian Turnip

5122 Oriental Tulip, *NC*

5123 Tulips

5124 Bellflower, *OCS*

5125  Camellia, *QM, 1993*

5126  Baby Rose

5127  Tulip

5128  Tiger Lilies

5129  Peonys

5130  Lily Pool

5131  Tulips

5132  Chrysanthemum

5133  Just Enough Tulips

5134  Diamond Rose,
       *Sandra Pierson, QW,
       1983*

5135  North Carolina Lily
       The Double Tulip, *MD*

5136  Rose Trellis

5137  Iris Rainbow, *QW, 1980*

5138  Double Tulip

5139  Tulip

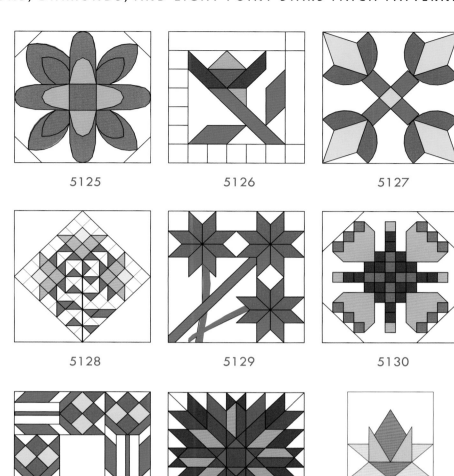

5125

5126

5127

5128

5129

5130

5131

5132

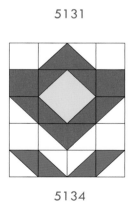

5133

5134

5135

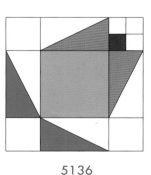

5136

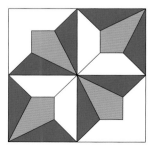

5137

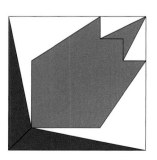

5138

5139

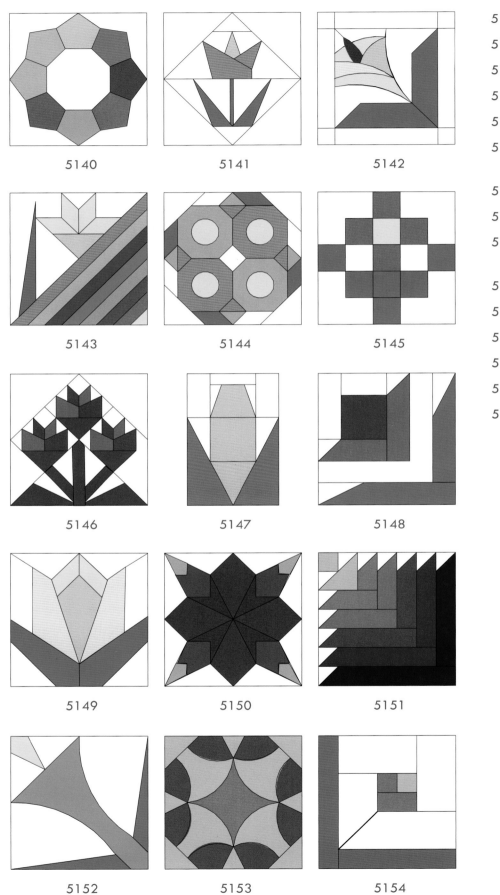

5,500 QUILT BLOCK DESIGNS

5140 Cornflower

5141 Spring Tulip

5142 Calla Lily, *OCS*

5143 Tulips

5144 Wild Rose Wreath, *TQ*

5145 Meadow Flowers, *QN, 1990*

5146 Autumn Lily, *TQ*

5147 Corn

5148 Log Cabin Rosebud, *TQr*

5149 Crocus

5150 Rosebuds

5151 Desert Blooms

5152 Trumpet Flower

5153 Morning Glory, *OCS*

5154 Rosebud Patchwork

5140    5141    5142

5143    5144    5145

5146    5147    5148

5149    5150    5151

5152    5153    5154

5155 Lily of the Valley

5156 Nosegay, *OCS*

5157 Iris, *OCS*

5158 Acorn

5159 Rose Garden

5160 Oriental Rose, *NC*

5161 Pond Lily, *OCS*

5162 A Lily Quilt
   The Fire Lily
   The Mariposa Lily
   The Mountain Lily
   The Meadow Lily
   The Prairie Lily
   The Tiger Lily
   The Wood Lily

5163 Tulip, *OCS*

5164 My Tulip Garden, *RMS, SSQ, 1989*

5165 Conventional Tulip

5166 Pansy Quilt, *HAS*

5167 Shasta Daisy, *LW*

5168 Wild Iris, *PP*

5169 Orange Bud, *AMS*

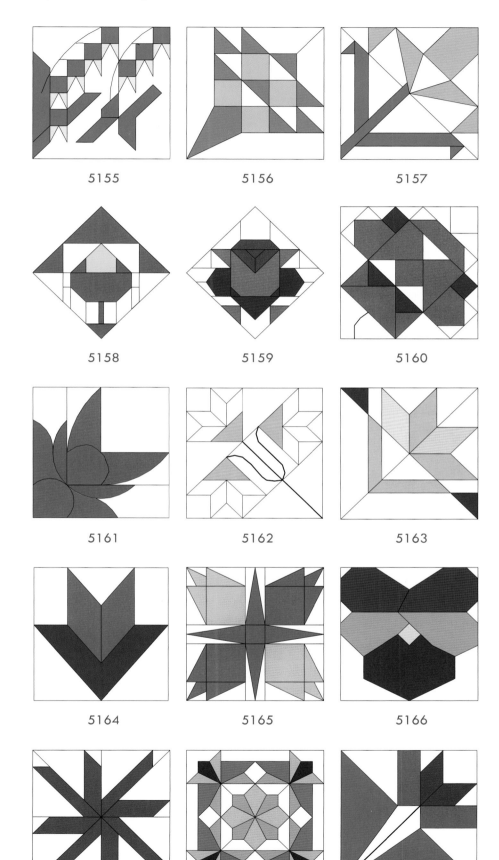

5155  5156  5157  5158  5159  5160  5161  5162  5163  5164  5165  5166  5167  5168  5169

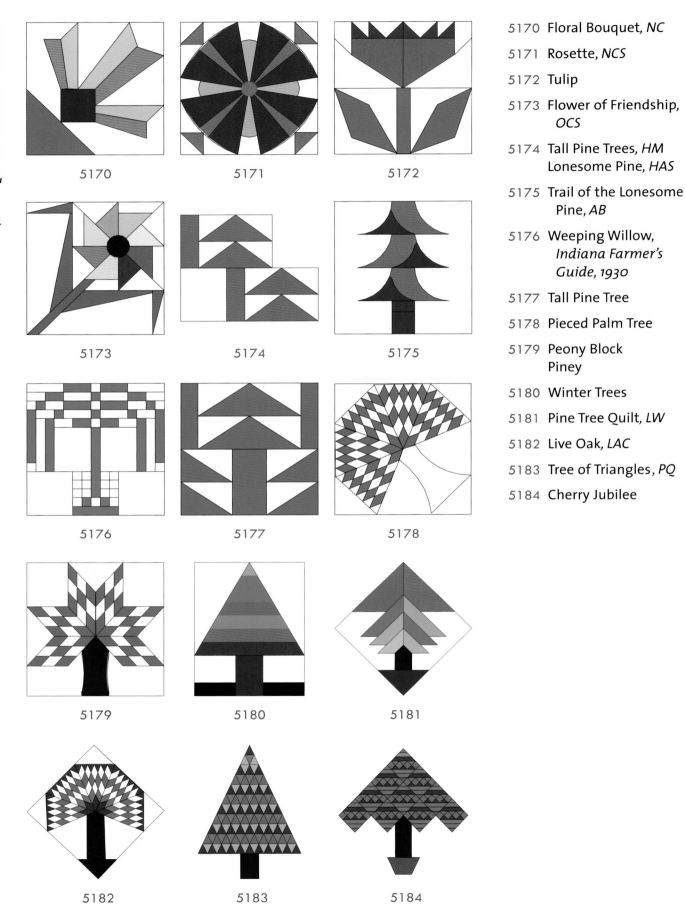

5,500 QUILT BLOCK DESIGNS

5170

5171

5172

5173

5174

5175

5176

5177

5178

5179

5180

5181

5182

5183

5184

5170 Floral Bouquet, *NC*

5171 Rosette, *NCS*

5172 Tulip

5173 Flower of Friendship, *OCS*

5174 Tall Pine Trees, *HM* Lonesome Pine, *HAS*

5175 Trail of the Lonesome Pine, *AB*

5176 Weeping Willow, *Indiana Farmer's Guide, 1930*

5177 Tall Pine Tree

5178 Pieced Palm Tree

5179 Peony Block Piney

5180 Winter Trees

5181 Pine Tree Quilt, *LW*

5182 Live Oak, *LAC*

5183 Tree of Triangles, *PQ*

5184 Cherry Jubilee

5185 Pines in the Snow, *QT, 1988*
Pine Forest

5186 Pine Tree

5187 Pine Tree

5188 Winter Pines

5189 Pine Tree

5190 Pine Tree
Temperance Tree

5191 Norway Pine
Pine Tree, *OCS*

5192 Pine Tree Quilt Design

5193 Patch Blossom

5194 Christmas Trees

5195 Christmas Tree

5196 Evergreen

5197 North Woods

5198 Pine Tree

5199 Southern Pine

5,500 QUILT BLOCK DESIGNS

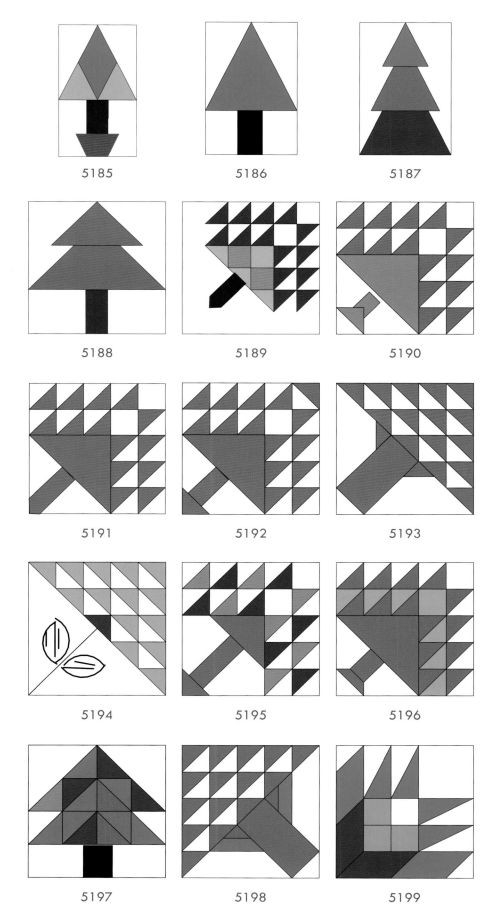

5185 5186 5187
5188 5189 5190
5191 5192 5193
5194 5195 5196
5197 5198 5199

5,500 QUILT BLOCK DESIGNS

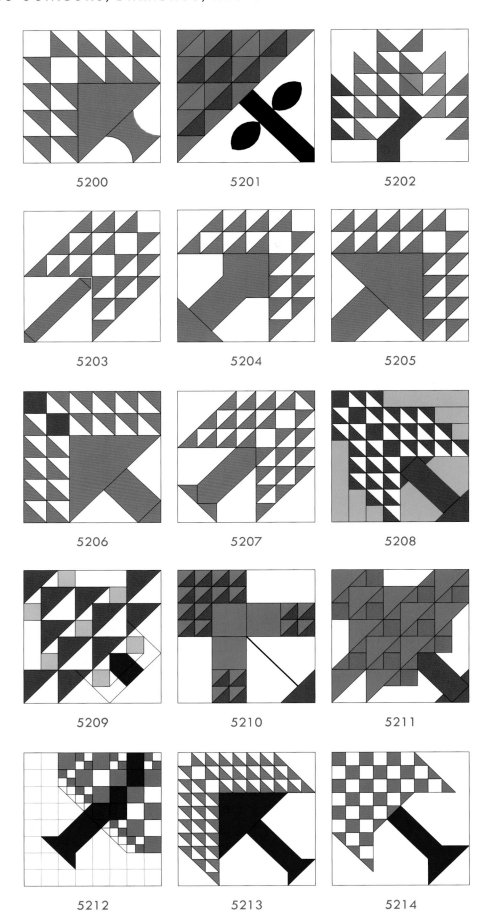

5200
5201
5202

5203
5204
5205

5206
5207
5208

5209
5210
5211

5212
5213
5214

5200 Pine Tree

5201 Christmas Tree

5202 Delaware Sea Pines, *QN*

5203 Christmas Tree, *KCS* Pine Tree

5204 Centennial Tree, *HH*

5205 Evergreen Tree Pine Tree

5206 Temperance Tree

5207 Tree of Paradise

5208 Tree of Life

5209 Apple Tree

5210 Tree of Life

5211 Apple Tree

5212 Tree of Temptation

5213 Pine Tree

5214 Little Beech Tree

5215 Tree of Paradise

5216 Christmas Tree

5217 Patchwork Pines

5218 The Forest for the Trees

5219 Tree of Life

5220 Scrappy Tree Block #1, *QEQ, 1993*

5221 Scrappy Tree Block #2, *QEQ, 1993*

5222 Scrappy Tree Block #3, *QEQ, 1993*

5223 Arching Tree

5224 Cascade Pride, *QW, 1981*

5225 Pine Tree

5226 Pine Tree Quilt, *OCS*

5227 Temperance Tree, *OF, 1894*
Tree of Paradise

5228 Tree of Paradise

5229 Tree of Paradise

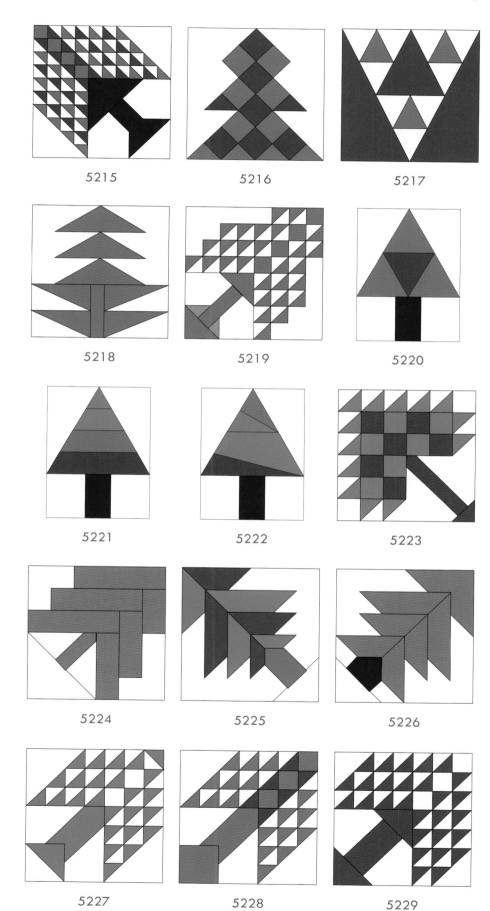

5215

5216

5217

5218

5219

5220

5221

5222

5223

5224

5225

5226

5227

5228

5229

5,500 QUILT BLOCK DESIGNS

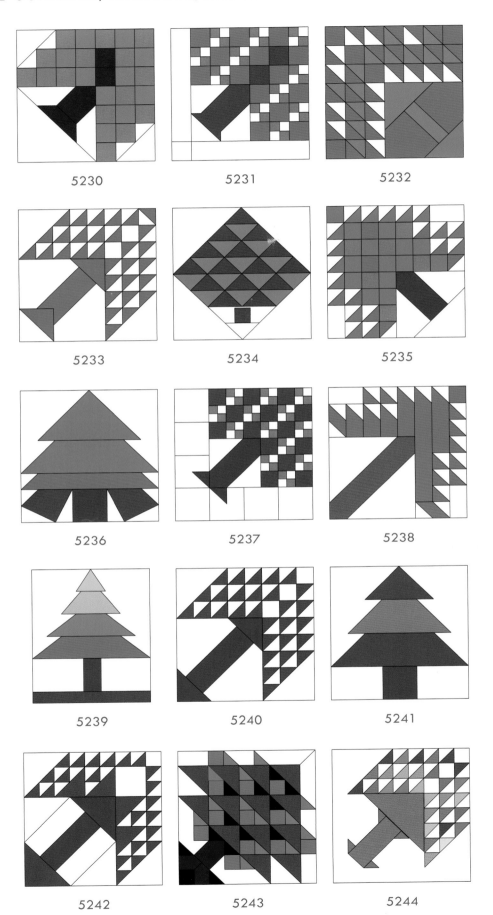

5230
5231
5232

5233
5234
5235

5236
5237
5238

5239
5240
5241

5242
5243
5244

5230  Tree of Temptation

5231  Tree of Temptation
      Enchanted Forest

5232  Everlasting Tree Block

5233  Tree of Paradise
      Centennial Tree
      Temperance Tree
      Washington's Elm
      Washington Tree

5234  Christmas Tree

5235  Apple Tree

5236  Christmas Tree

5237  Tree of Temptation

5238  Proud Tree

5239  Fir Tree

5240  Evergreen Tree, *HH*

5241  Pine Tree Block

5242  Evergreen Tree

5243  Family Tree

5244  Evergreen Tree

5245  Cone Tree

5246  Christmas Tree

5247  Weeping Willow

5248  Temperance Tree

5249  Cherry Tree

5250  Tennessee Pine

5251  Pine Tree

5252  South Jersey Pines

5253  Indiana Redbud

5254  Pine Tree

5255  Pine Tree

5256  Tree of Paradise, *FJ*

5257  Tree of Paradise, *LAC*
Tree
Christmas Tree Patch,
  *CoM*
The Pine Tree

5258  Tree of Paradise
Tree of Life

5259  Pine Tree
Tree of Paradise

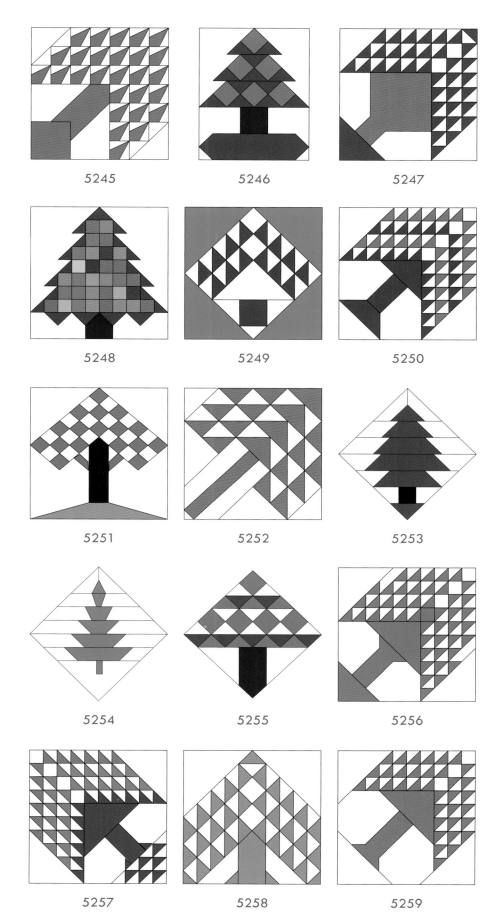

5245

5246

5247

5248

5249

5250

5251

5252

5253

5254

5255

5256

5257

5258

5259

5,500 QUILT BLOCK DESIGNS

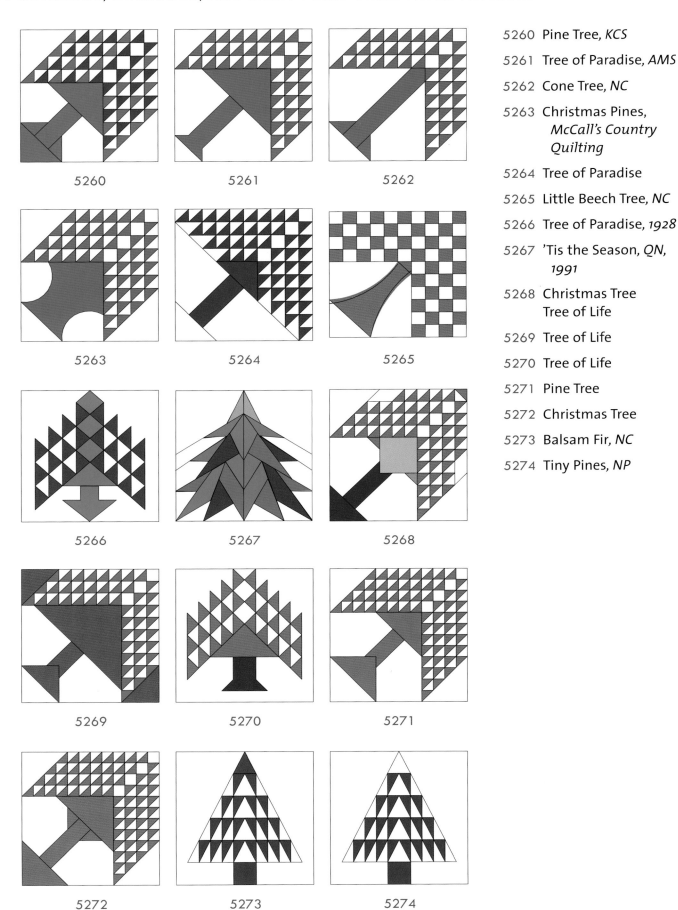

5260

5261

5262

5263

5264

5265

5266

5267

5268

5269

5270

5271

5272

5273

5274

5260  Pine Tree, *KCS*

5261  Tree of Paradise, *AMS*

5262  Cone Tree, *NC*

5263  Christmas Pines,
      *McCall's Country
      Quilting*

5264  Tree of Paradise

5265  Little Beech Tree, *NC*

5266  Tree of Paradise, *1928*

5267  'Tis the Season, *QN,
      1991*

5268  Christmas Tree
      Tree of Life

5269  Tree of Life

5270  Tree of Life

5271  Pine Tree

5272  Christmas Tree

5273  Balsam Fir, *NC*

5274  Tiny Pines, *NP*

5275 Christmas Tree, *KCS*
     The Pine Forest
     Pine Tree, *LAC*

5276 Temperance Tree
     Tree of Paradise, *MoM*

5277 Pine Tree

5278 Tree of Life

5279 Trail of the Lonesome
     Pine

5280 Florida Forest

5281 The Red Schoolhouse

5282 Log Cabin

5283 Calendar House Quilt

5284 House

5285 House

5286 House

5287 Lighthouse

5288 The Star's Exhibition
     Home Quilt Block
     Pattern, *KCS*

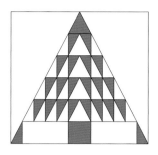
5275

5276

5277

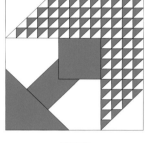
5278

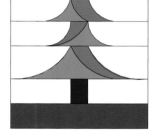
5279

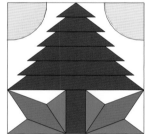
5280

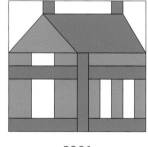
5281

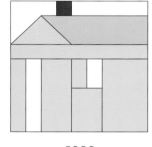
5282

5283

5284

5285

5286

5287

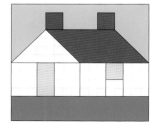
5288

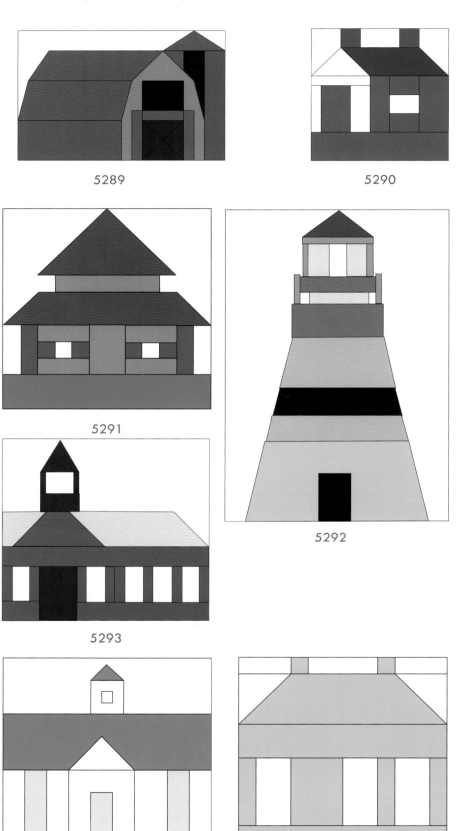

5289

5290

5291

5292

5293

5294

5295

5289 Barn

5290 House Contest Block

5291 The Lighthouse,
   *his.com/~ queenb*

5292 The Train Station,
   *Debby Kratovil,*
   *his.com/!queenb*

5293 Church

5294 Country Church

5295 Pieced Schoolhouse
   Block

5296 Village Church, *LAC*

5297 The Old Homestead, *LAC*

5298 Little Red House, *LAC*
House
Lincoln's Cabin Home, *HH*
Log Cabin
Old Home
Old Kentucky Home
Tippecanoe, *HH*

5299 Log Cabin Quilt

5300 Jack's House, *LAC*

5301 Iowa Barns

5302 Honeymoon Cottage (12x16)

5303 House
Back to School

5304 Pioneer Cottage Block

5305 Honeymoon Cottage (13)

5306 Village Schoolhouse, *RM*

5307 Red Barn

5308 Courthouse Square

5309 House on a Hill

5310 Schoolhouse

5,500 QUILT BLOCK DESIGNS

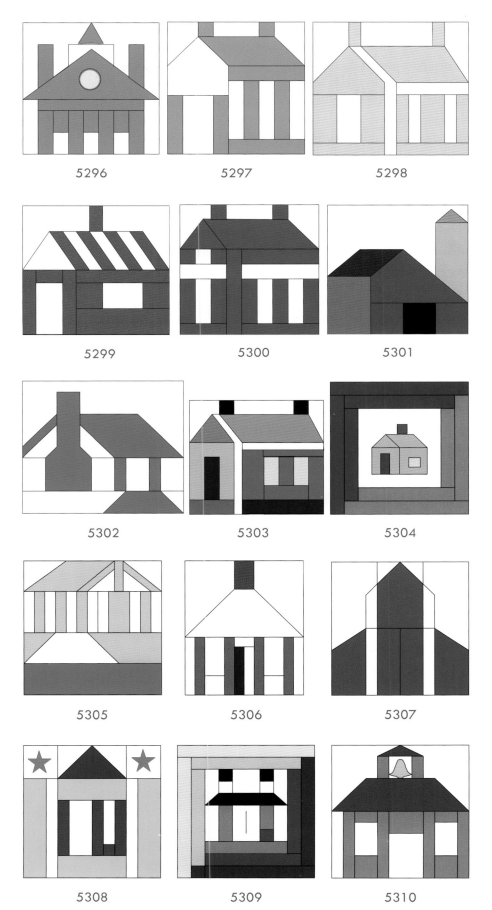

5296   5297   5298

5299   5300   5301

5302   5303   5304

5305   5306   5307

5308   5309   5310

5,500 QUILT BLOCK DESIGNS

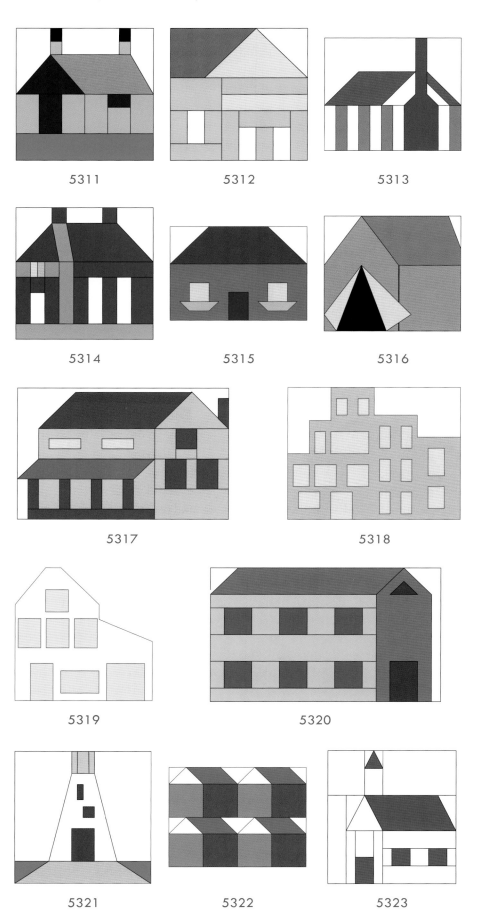

5311
5312
5313
5314
5315
5316
5317
5318
5319
5320
5321
5322
5323

5311  House on a Hill

5312  Home Sweet Home

5313  House with a Chimney

5314  Schoolhouse

5315  House

5316  Home Is Where the House Is, *TQr, 1991*

5317  Home Is Where the Quilt Is , *TQr, 1991*

5318  Apartment

5319  Big House

5320  House

5321  Lighthouse, *quiltmag.com*

5322  Houses

5323  Country Church

5324 Castle

5325 Hallelujah Hall, *GB*

5326 Amazing Grace, *GB*

5327 Hillside Village, *GB*

5328 Barn

5329 Barn with Silo

5330 Big Barn

5331 Church
     Country Church

5332 Country Meeting
     House

5333 House with Fence

5334 Cabin

5335 Suburban House

5336 Ohio Schoolhouse

5337 Town Hall

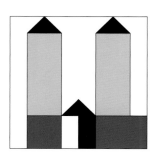

5324

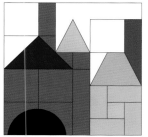

5325

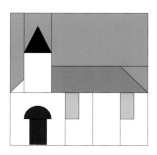

5326

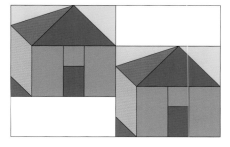

5327

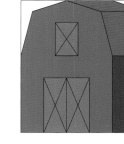

5328

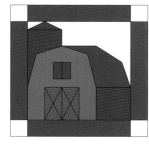

5329

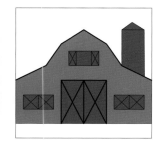

5330

5331

5332

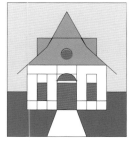

5333

5334

5335

5336

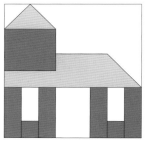

5337

5,500 QUILT BLOCK DESIGNS

5338    Kites in the Air

5339    Flight of Geese

5340    Flying Geese

5341    Desert Storm

5342    Arabesque, *QM, 1994*

5343    Lattice for Maypole
           Dance

5344    Trumpet Vine

5345    No Name Strippie

5346    Tit for Tat, *AK*

5347    Arrowheads
           Herringbone
           Prickly Path
           The Path of Thorns
           Saw Blades
           Tree Everlasting

5348    Flags

5349    Roman Stripes and
           Squares

5350 Herringbone

5351 Chevron

5352 Border 1

5353 Border 2

5354 Border 3

5355 Border 4

5356 Border 5

5357 Border 6

5358 Border 7

5359 Tiffany, *QW, 1986*

5360 Coarse Woven
     Fine Woven

5350
5351
5352
5353
5354
5355
5356
5357
5358
5359
5360

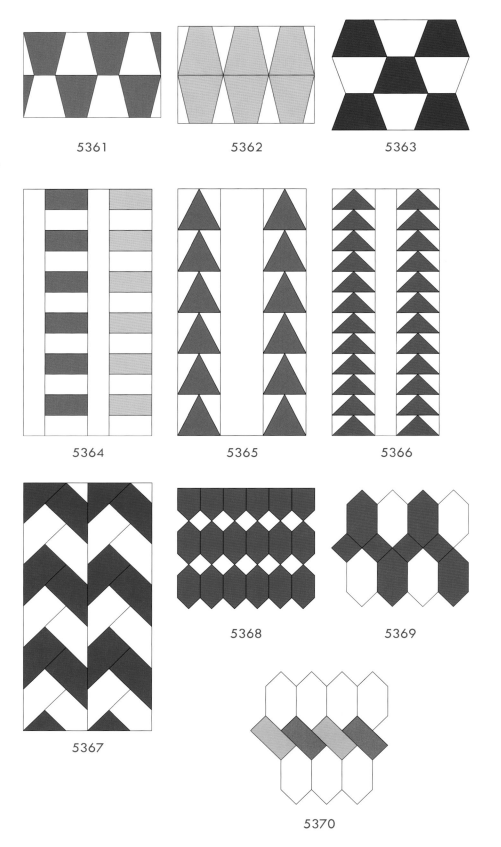

5361

5362

5363

5364

5365

5366

5367

5368

5369

5370

5361 The Tumbler, *LAC*

5362 Tumbler
Flower Pot, *GD*

5363 Tumbler, *LAC*
Out of This World, *OCS*

5364 Chinese Coins
Bars

5365 Wild Goose Chase, *LAC*
Birds in Flight
Geese in Flight
Wild Geese Flying

5366 Wild Goose Chase

5367 Twist and Turn, *LAC*
Braid
Pioneer Braid

5368 Fantastic Patchwork,
*LAC*
Quintettes, *NP*
Stained Glass

5369 Rail Fence, *NC*

5370 Rope, *WW*

5371 Godey's Lady's Book,
     *1863*

5372 Rope Strands, *KCS*

5373 Fenceworm, *PQ*

5374 Rail Fence Quilt, *KCS*

5375 The Mowing Machine,
     *KCS*

5376 Bamboo Spread, *OCS*
     Spindles

5377 Triangular Triangles,
     *LAC*
     Triangle Quilt, *QW*
     Triangular Trees

5378 Flat Iron Patchwork

5379 Sugar Loaf
     The Pyramid

5380 Picket Fence, *KCS*
     Fine Woven Patchwork,
       *LAC*
     Featheredge Stripe
     Fence Rail
     Streak of Lightning

5381 Picket Fence, *KCS*

5382 Trellis

5371          5372

5373

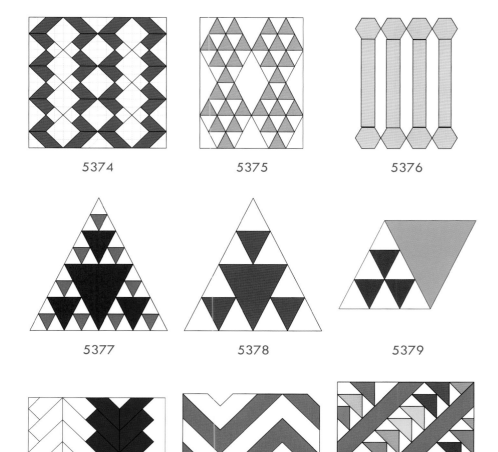

5374          5375          5376

5377          5378          5379

5380          5381          5382

5383

5384

5385

5386

5387      5388      5389      5390

5383 Building Blocks

5384 Wave, *OCS*
     Rail Fence, *OCS*

5385 Butterfly Quilt

5386 Wild Goose Chase, *KCS*

5387 Migrating Geese

5388 Kite's Tail

5389 Nothing Wasted, *FJ,*
     *1937*

5390 Stacked Bricks
     Brick Walk

5391 Streak of Lightning

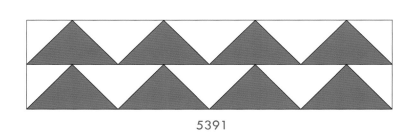

5391

5392  Mountain Memories

5393  Delectable Mountains
       Variation
       Sawtooth

5394  Summer Trees

5395  Border 8

5396  Ribbons 'n Pinwheels,
       *QN, 1987*

5397  Four Windmills, *NC*

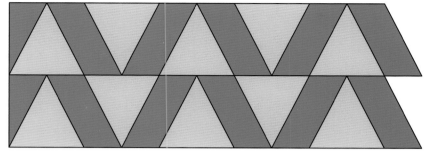

5392

5393

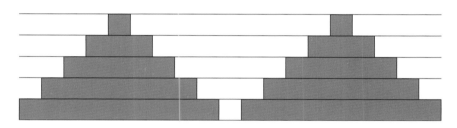

5394

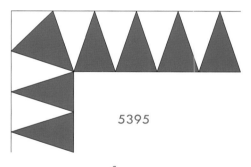

5395

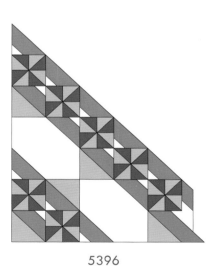

5396

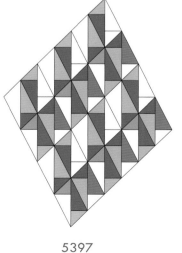

5397

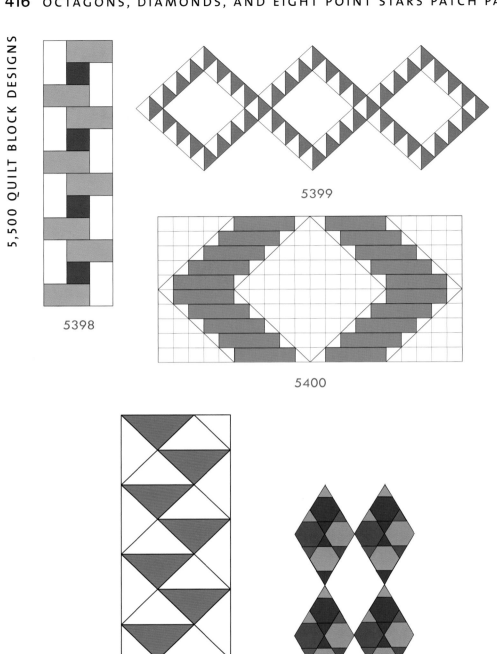

5398

5399

5400

5401

5402

5403

5398 Patience Corners
Border

5399 Sawtooth Triangles
Streak of Lightning

5400 Bridal Stairway
Patchwork Block, *KCS*

5401 Migration

5402 Double Diamonds

5403 Double Braid

5404 Fence Rail

5405 Lover's Knot

5406 Floral Frame, *QN, 1993*

5407 Streak of Lightning

5408 Zig Zag

5409 Pyramids
Thousand Pyramids
Joseph's Coat
Red Shields, *NC*
Triangles

5410 Pyramids

5411 Pyramids

5412 Pyramids

5413 Fence Row Quilt, *KCS*
Dog's Tooth
The Lace Edge Quilt,
   *KCS*
Lightning Streak
Mountains and Valleys
Snake Fence
Zig Zag

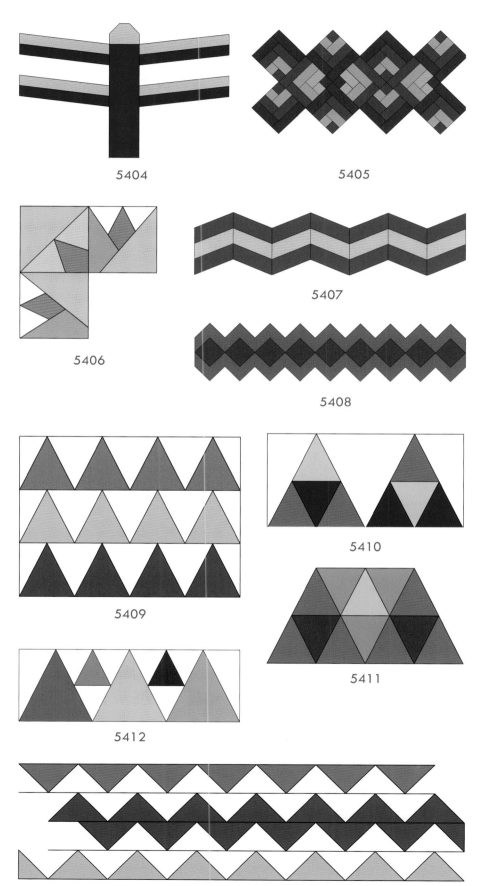

5404

5405

5406

5407

5408

5409

5410

5411

5412

5413

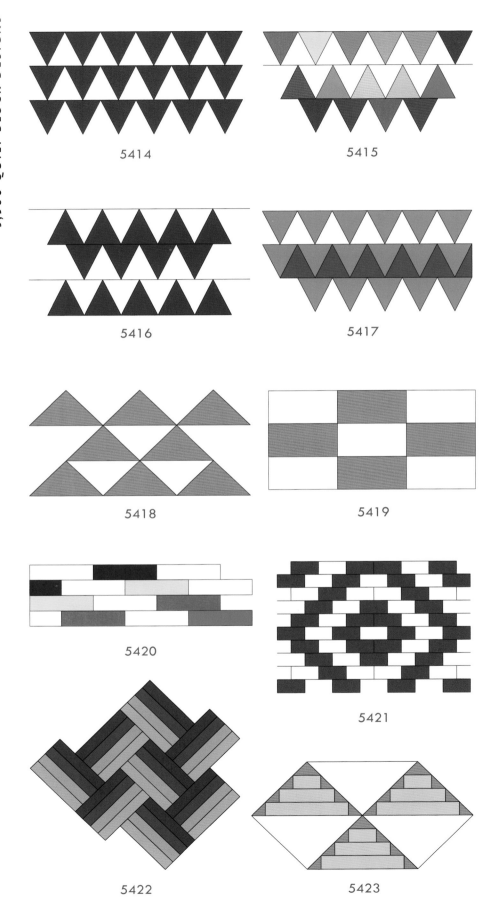

5414

5415

5416

5417

5418

5419

5420

5421

5422

5423

5414 Lightning, *NC*
Dog's Tooth

5415 Lace Edge Quilt
Lightning Strips

5416 Dog's Tooth
Rail Fence
Snake Fence
Streak o' Lightning
Zig Zag

5417 Chained Lightning
Land of the Pharaoh,
*NC*
A Thousand Pyramids,
*NC*

5418 Ocean Waves, *LAC*
Tents of Armageddon
Thousands of Triangles

5419 Hairpin Catcher
Brickwall

5420 Depression, *KCS*
Brickwall
Brickwork
General Sherman's
Quilt
Old Garden Wall
Streak of Lightning
Zig Zag

5421 Brickwork Quilt, *LAC*

5422 Orange Pekoe, *NC*

5423 Pyramids, *LAC*
Pieced Pyramids

5424 Box upon Box, *NP*

5425 Diamond Rainbow

5426 Quilter's Rainbow
Charm Quilt

5427 Hawks in Flight, *NC*

5428 Spring and Fall, *NC*

5429 Wavy Navy

5430 Spider Legs

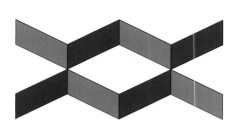

5424

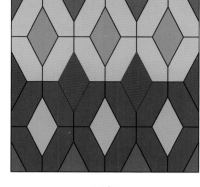

5425

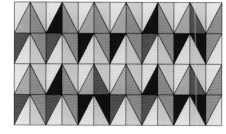

5426

5427

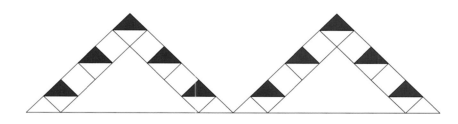

5428

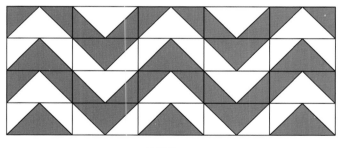

5429

5430

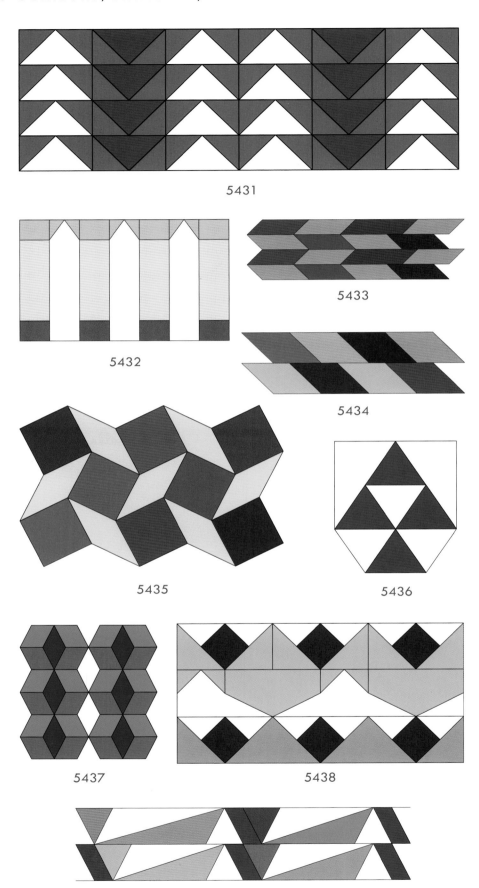

5431

5432

5433

5434

5435

5436

5437

5438

5439

5431 Wild Goose Chase

5432 Picket Fence, *AMS*

5433 Parallelogram Charm Quilt

5434 Diamond Charm Quilt

5435 Magic Squares

5436 Charm, *LAC*

5437 Variegated Diamonds

5438 Hills and Valley

5439 Cumberland Gap, *NC*

5440 Zig Zag Blocks, *GC*

5441 Sawtooth Triangles

5442 Migration

5443 No Name

5444 Clam Shells
Fishscale
Mushroom Shell
Over the Waves
Sea Shell
Sea Shells on the
Beach, *KCS*
Shell
Shell Chain
Sugar Scoop

5445 Charmed Path, *QM,*
*1992*

5446 Goin' Home, *QM, 1992*

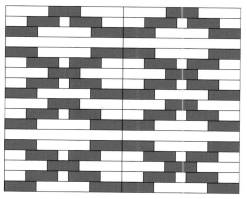

5440

5441

5442

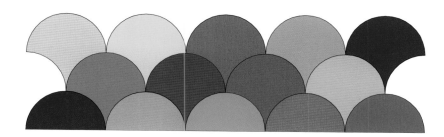

5443

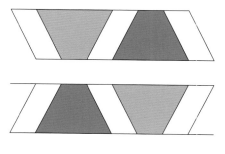

5444

5445                5446

5,500 QUILT BLOCK DESIGNS

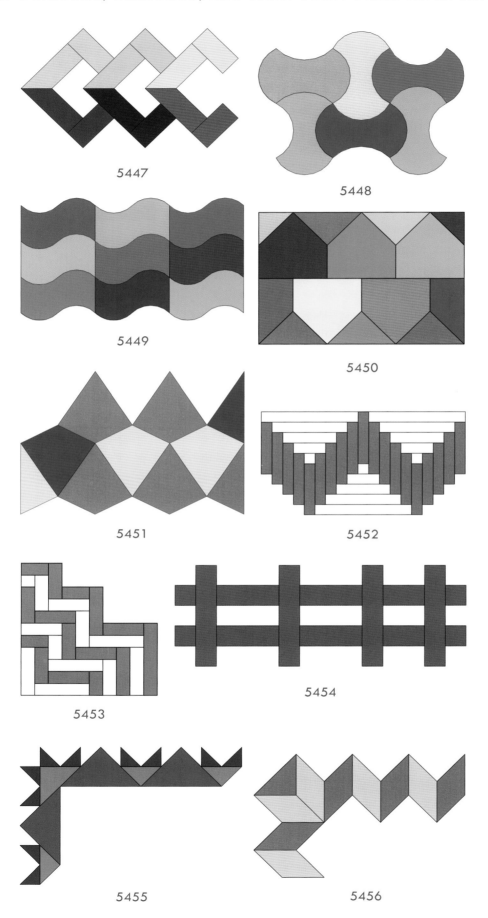

5447

5448

5449

5450

5451

5452

5453

5454

5455

5456

5447 Harvest Chain, *QM, 1992*

5448 Spool
Always Friends
Axe Blade
Apple Core
Badge of Friendship
Charm
Double Ax
Double Ax Head, *OCS*
Double Bit Axe
Friendship Chain
Friendship Quilt, *KCS*
Jigsaw
Mother's Oddity

5449 Cracker

5450 House

5451 Kite

5452 Coarse Woven Patchwork, *LAC*

5453 Five Woven Patchwork, *LAC*

5454 Rail Fence Border

5455 Border 9

5456 Border 10

5457 Border 11

5458 Border 12

5459 Border 13

5460 Delectable Mountains Variation

5461 Delectable Mountains Variation

5462 Building Blocks

5463 Delectable Mountains

5464 Rail Fence Wave

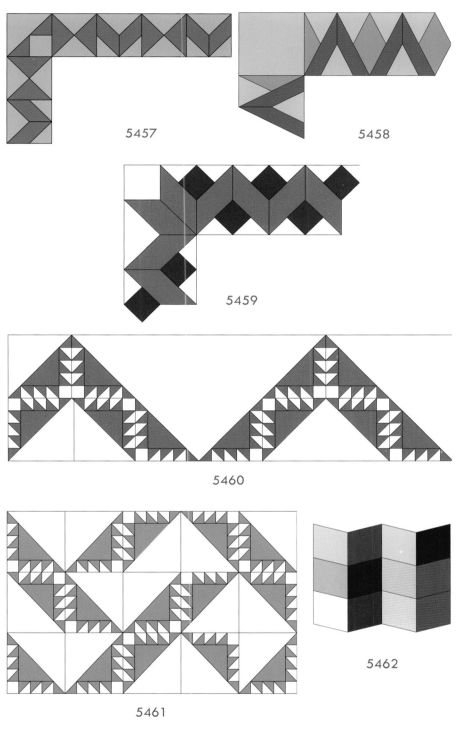

5457

5458

5459

5460

5461

5462

5463

5464

5,500 QUILT BLOCK DESIGNS

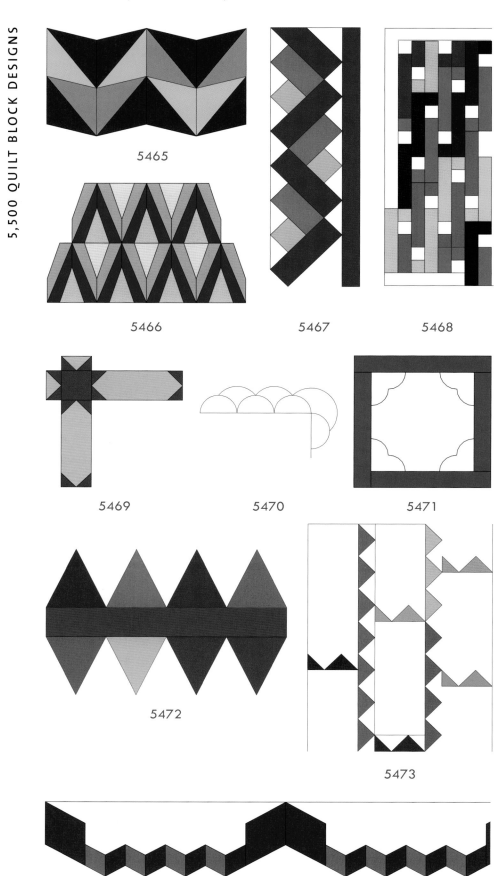

5465

5466

5467

5468

5469

5470

5471

5472

5473

5474

5465 Concertina

5466 Scrap Pyramid

5467 Woven Fences, *QM*, *1994*

5468 Chain Reaction, *QEQ*

5469 Sashing Strip or Border

5470 Scallop Border

5471 Photo Bracket Corners with Sashing

5472 Triangles

5473 Grandma's Zig Zag

5474 Hexagon Border

5475 Cupid's Darts, *NC*

5476 Fields and Furrows

5477 Diamond Jubilee

5478 Yo-Yo, *GC, 1932*
    Bed of Roses
    Bon-Bon, *QN*
    Heirloom Pillow
    Pinwheel
    Powder Puff
    Puff
    Puffball
    Rosette
    Suffolk Puffs
    Yorkshire Daisy

5479 Biscuit Quilt, *OF*
    Bun Quilt
    Puffed Squares
    Raised Patchwork
    Swiss Patchwork

5480 Ice Cream Cone

5481 Segmented Diamonds

5482 Honeycomb Quilt

5483 Teepee Town
    Sugar Cone

5484 Crystal Honeycomb

5485 Tea Leaf Strippie

5486 A Floral Strippie

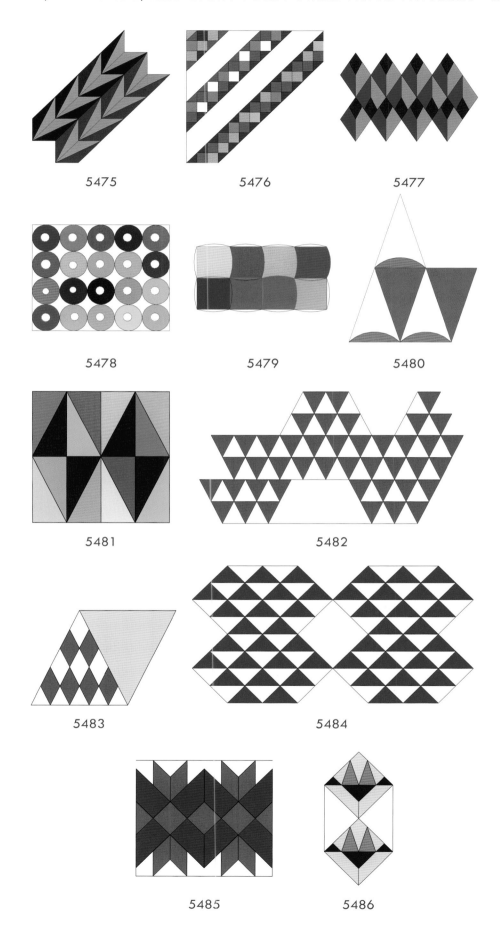

5475

5476

5477

5478

5479

5480

5481

5482

5483

5484

5485

5486

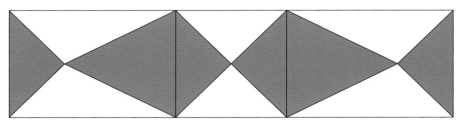

5487

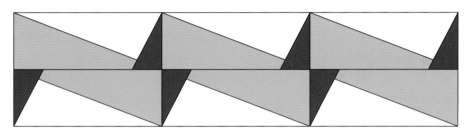

5488

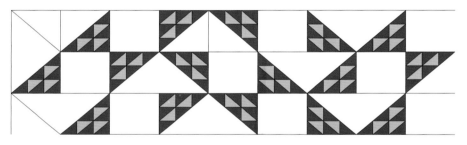

5489

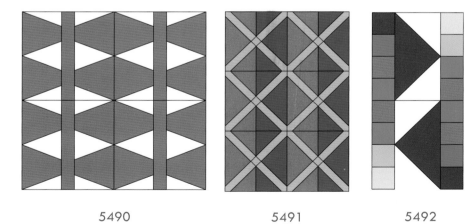

5490                5491                5492

5487 Fish Border

5488 Chaos, *AK, 1973*

5489 Over the Waves

5490 Sylvia's Beige and Brown

5491 Unnamed

5492 Marquee

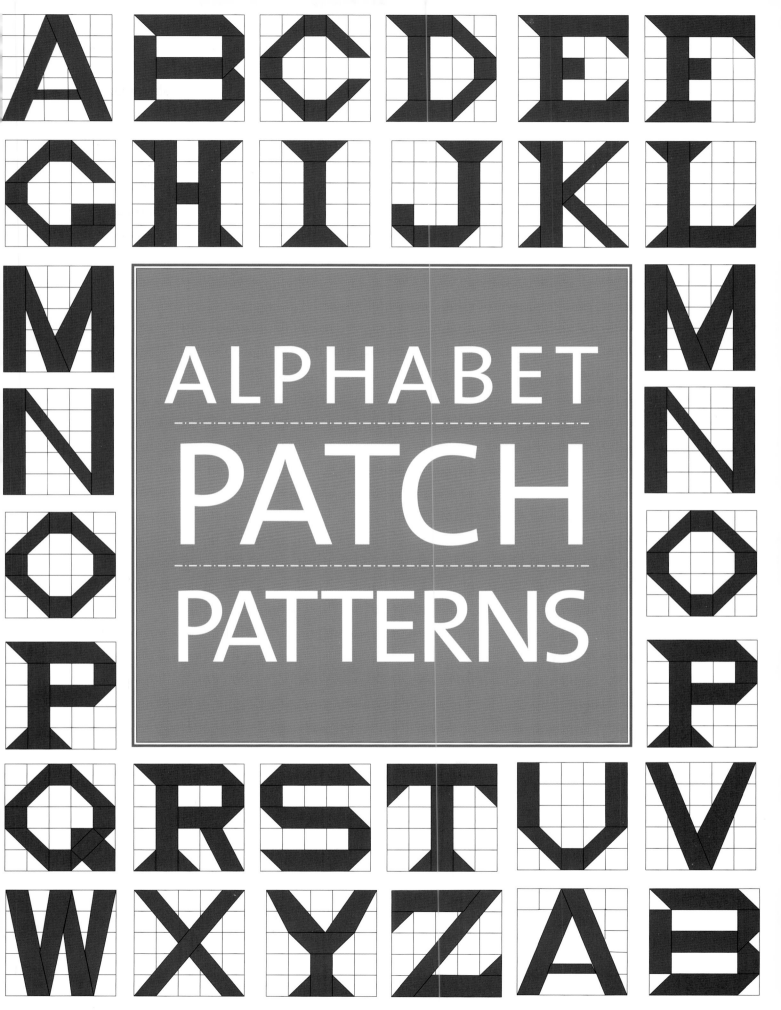

# ALPHABET PATCH PATTERNS

5 X 5 GRID

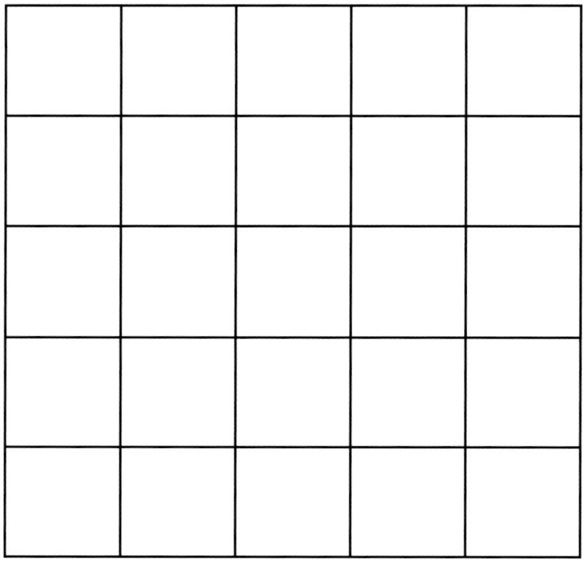

THESE PATTERNS ARE DRAFTED ON A GRID 5 X 5 SQUARES
SCALE THESE PATTERNS TO A BLOCK OF ANY SIZE

5493 A—initial

5494 B—initial

5495 C—initial

5496 D—initial

5497 E—initial

5498 F—initial

5499 G—initial

5500 H—initial

5501 I—initial

5502 J—initial

5503 K—initial

5504 L—initial

5505 M—initial

5506 N—initial

5507 O—initial

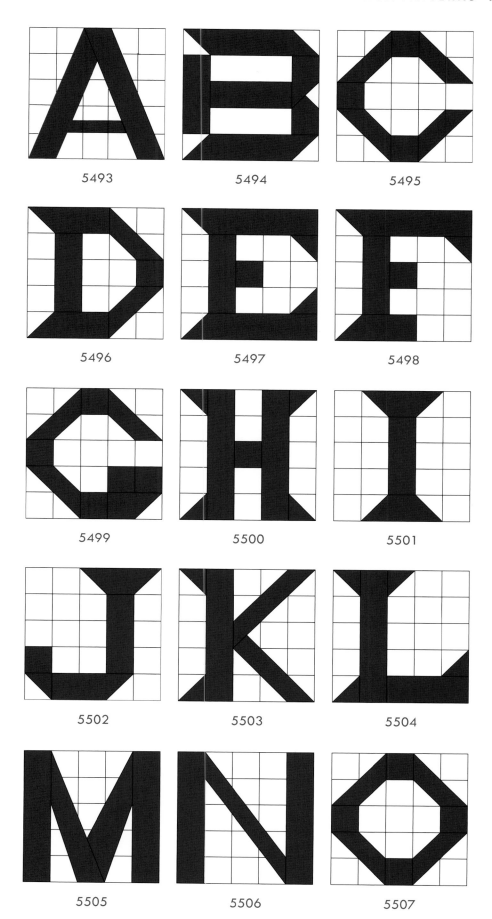

5493

5494

5495

5496

5497

5498

5499

5500

5501

5502

5503

5504

5505

5506

5507

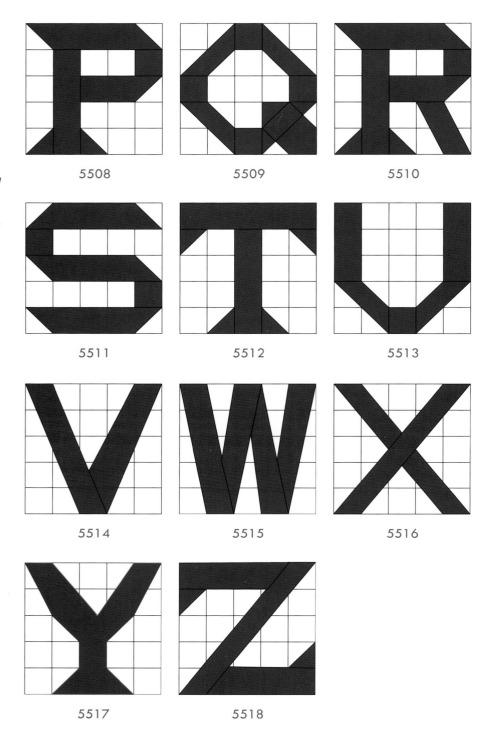

5508

5509

5510

5511

5512

5513

5514

5515

5516

5517

5518

5508 P—initial
5509 Q—initial
5510 R—initial
5511 S—initial
5512 T—initial
5513 U—initial
5514 V—initial
5515 W—initial
5516 X—initial
5517 Y—initial
5518 Z—initial

# INTERNATIONAL SIGNAL FLAGS
## PATCH
## PATTERNS

SEMAPHORE QUILTS USE A VARIETY OF PATCH PATTERN GRIDS. COUNT THE NUMBER OF SQUARES ACROSS OR DOWN TO DETERMINE WHICH GRID A DESIGN USES AND SCALE THAT NUMBER TO A BLOCK OF THE DESIRED SIZE.

5519 A—semaphore
5520 B—semaphore
5521 C—semaphore
5522 D—semaphore
5523 E—semaphore
5524 F—semaphore
5525 G—semaphore
5526 H—semaphore
5527 I—semaphore
5528 J—semaphore
5529 K—semaphore
5530 L—semaphore
5531 M—semaphore
5532 N—semaphore
5533 O—semaphore

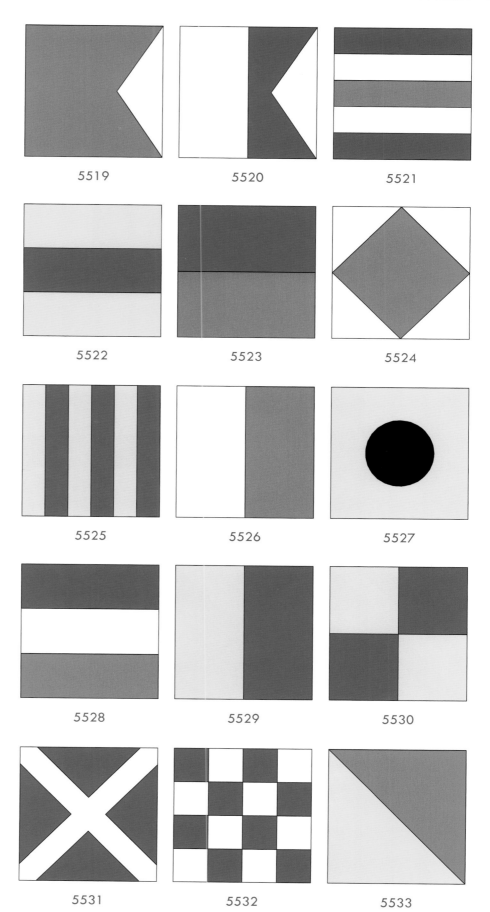

5519 5520 5521
5522 5523 5524
5525 5526 5527
5528 5529 5530
5531 5532 5533

5,500 QUILT BLOCK DESIGNS

5534

5535

5536

5537

5538

5539

5540

5541

5542

5543

5544

5534 P—semaphore

5535 Q—semaphore

5536 R—semaphore

5537 S—semaphore

5538 T—semaphore

5539 U—semaphore

5540 V—semaphore

5541 W—semaphore

5542 X—semaphore

5543 Y—semaphore

5544 Z—semaphore

# Index

An A Star, 63
Abe Lincoln's Platform, 227
Acanthus, 229
Acorn(s), 145, 397
Acrobat(s), 62, 380
Across the Square, 216
Adam's Refuge, 58
Aerial Beacon, 322
Aeroplane(s), 195, 376, 377
Aesthetic Quilt, 343
Afternoon Shadows, 72
Aimee's Choice, 140
Air Castle, 26
Air Craft Quilt, 376
Air Ship Propeller, 268
Air Ways, 377
Aircraft, 100, 106
Airplane and Propeller, 376
Airplane Motif, 331
Airplane Quilt, 376
Airplane(s), 100, 115, 195, 209, 234, 312, 331, 376, 377
Airport (Air Port), 216, 231
Airship, 299
Alabama, 54
Alabama Beauty, 271
Alabama Rambler, 169
Alamanizer, 114
Alaska, 156
Alaska Chinook, 167
Alaska Homestead, 191, 195
Alaska Territory, 202
Albany, 143
Album, 14, 20, 46, 95, 128, 130, 132, 206, 209, 222
Album Flower, 144
Album Patch, 222
Album Quilt, 96, 222, 286
Album Star, 27
Alcazar, 301
Algonquin Charm, 191
*Alice Brooks*; Diamonds, 169; Fan of Friendship, 292; Friendship Bouquet, 242; Grandmother's Fan, 292; Grandmother's Prize, 300; Grandmother's Scrap Quilt, 290; Lone Star, 69; Lover's Knot, 88; Milky Way, 237; No Name curved pattern, 298; Peony, 300; Pride of the Bride, 289; Quilter's Pride, 313; Ragged Robin, 214; Rising Sun, 290; Starry Path, 181; Trail of the Lonesome, 398; Twist and Turn, 277; Whirling Fans, 301
Alice's Favorite, 65, 186, 214
Alice's Tulips, 282
All American Star, 339
All Around the Star, 115
All Hallows, 24
All Hands Around, 332
All Hands Round, 330
All in a Spin, 67
All Kinds, 82
All My Family, 223
All Over Pattern of Octagons, 323
All Points, 56
All Tangled Up, 224
All That Jazz, 120
All Those Fish, 69
Allen, Myrna, 392
Allentown, 160
Alma's Choice, 168
Aloha, 338
Alpha, 155, 166
Alphabet Block L, 68
Alphabet patterns, 429–430
Alpine Cross, 201
Alta Plane, 376
Altar Candle, 196
Altar Steps, 232
Always Friends, 422
Amazing Grace, 409
Amazing Windmill, 150
Amelia Earhart, 70
American Chain, 50

American Homes, 48
American Way, 349
American Woman's Own Quilt Block, 302
America's Pride, 76, 282
Amethyst, 110, 124
Amethyst Chain, 61
Amish Angel, 310
Amish Basket, 388
Amish Pin Wheel, 198
Amish Scrap Star, 83
Amish Shoofly, 66
Amish Squares, 232
Amish Star, 30, 41
Amish Whirl, 65
Amy's Inspiration, 224
Anchors Aweigh, 83
Ancient Castle, 78
Ancient Nine Patch, 171
Angel, 379
Animals Stood By, 214
Ann and Andy, 112
Annamae's Star, 171
Annapolis, 160
Annapolis Patch, 73
Anna's Basket, 385
Anna's Choice, 97
Anna's Love Quilt, 160
Anna's Pride, 313
Annie's Choice, 97
Ann's Scrap Quilt, 158
Antique Red and White Quilt, 70
Antique Tile Block, 17
Anvil, 100, 102, 107
Apartment, 408
Apothecary Jar, 378
Appalachian Sunburst, 234
Apple Core(s), 305, 422
Apple Leaf, 16
Apple Tree, 400, 402
April Tulips, 164
Arab Tent, 281
Arabesque, 410
Arabian Star, 354, 355
Arabic Lattice, 51
Arabic Latticework, 46
Ararat, 370
Arbor Window, 19, 20
Arching Tree, 401
Arizona, 21
Arizona Star, 73
Arizona's Cactus Flower, 255
Arkansas, 26, 274, 280
Arkansas Centennial, 280
Arkansas Crossroads, 105
Arkansas Diamond, 165
Arkansas Snowflake, 41, 124
Arkansas Star, 30, 41, 42, 124, 303
Arkansas Traveler, 73, 139, 148, 167
Arkansas Traveller, 44, 171
Arkansas Troubles, 269
Arms to Heaven, 313
Army Star, 149
Around the Chimney, 107
Around the Corner, 127
Around the World, 269, 270, 281, 306, 317
Arrangement of Small Pieces, 38
Arrant Redbirds, 128
Arrant Redbirds Variation, 128
Arrow, 54
Arrow Crown, 149, 154
Arrow of Peace, 186
Arrow Points, 143
Arrow Star, 98, 133, 328, 329
Arrowhead Puzzle, 93, 114, 179
Arrowhead Quilt, 143
Arrowhead Star, 24
Arrowhead Star Variation, 68
Arrowhead(s), 73, 111, 117, 124, 141, 142, 143, 146, 150, 156, 352, 360, 368, 410
Art Deco Fans, 291, 292
Art Deco Tulip, 172, 393
Art Square, 94

Aster, 267, 283, 390
At the Depot, 76
At the Square, 12, 54
Atlanta, 215
Attic Stairs, 178
Attic Window, 15
Augusta, 46, 77
Aunt Abbie's Own, 175
Aunt Addie's Album, 98
Aunt Anna's Album Block, 212
Aunt Dinah, 27, 39
Aunt Dinah's Star, 341
Aunt Eliza's Star, 25, 26
Aunt Em's Basket, 387
Aunt Em's Pattern, 63, 122
Aunt Etta's Diamond Quilt, 354
Aunt Jemima's Flower Garden, 356, 357
Aunt Jerusha, 272
*Aunt Kate*; Bridle Path Star, 274; Chaos, 426; Chevrons, 231; Courtyard Square, 165; Cross Patch, 55; Day Lily Garden, 314; Double Star Flower, 71; Fancy Fan, 291; Flashing Star, 219; Flowering Snowball, 312; Four Block Star, 335; Gold Nuggets, 115; Hearts and Darts, 315; Hide and Seek, 110; Idaho Star, 71; Jewel Star, 165; John F. Kennedy Star, 247; Leaf Star, 236; Light and Dark, 276; Lola, 178; London Bridge, 276; Louisiana Star, 329; Mississippi Star, 154; Missouri's Gateway Star, 183; Modern Tulip, 341; Mosaic Rose, 229; My Country, 336; New Star, 167; Ohio Star, 316; Oklahoma Twister, 43; Old Mill Wheel, 294; Picket and Posts, 196; Pinwheel Parade, 168; Rhode Island Maple, 236; Rolling Nine Patch, 198; Royal Gems, 83; Sailing Darts, 76; Spool of 1966, 299; Star of Manhattan, 219; Star of Mexico, 298; Stars over Tennessee, 200; Stylized Eagle, 71; Texas Puzzle, 200; Tit for Tat, 410; Tracy's Puzzle, 263; Tulip Ring, 342; Tulip Tile, 263; Wagon Wheel, 351; Washington Star, 150; Yuletide, 273
Aunt Kate's Quilting Bee; Lady Bug, 372; Michigan Star, 332, 345; Roulette Wheel Star, 356; Telephone, 379
Aunt Katie's Choice, 201
Aunt Lottie's Star, 26
Aunt Lucinda's Double Irish Chain, 181
Aunt Lucinda's Quilt Block, 181
Aunt Malvina's Chain, 15
Aunt Malvina's Quilt, 60
Aunt Martha Studios; Aeroplane, 376; Arrow, 54; Arrowhead Puzzle, 114; Bat, 66; Bay Leaf, 311; Bird of Paradise, 280; Britches Quilt, 139; Captive Beauty, 270; Charm Star, 162; Checkerboard, 230; Chestnut Burr, 347; Chinese Coin, 40; Compass, 337; Corsage Bouquet, 301; Cubes and Bars, 251; Dahlia, 315; Daisy Fan, 292; Diamond Solitaire, 175; Diamond Star, 24; Double Link, 217; Dutch Puzzle, 167; Eight Diamonds and a Star, 143, 321; Faithful Circle, 356; Falling Timbers, 269; Flower Pot Quilt, 384; Flying Swallows, 330; Gardener's Prize, 232; Glove Design, 170; Gold Brick, 231; Grandmother's Quilt, 300; Great Circle Quilt, 309; Improved Nine Patch, 18; Indian Arrowhead, 331; Indian Puzzle, 40; Jacob's Coat, 355; Jewel, 299; Kansas Dugout,

326; Lover's Quarrel, 279; Lucky Clover, 43; Man in the Moon, 316; Milady's Fan, 291; Modernistic Star, 353; Monkey Puzzle, 275; Monkey Wrench, 40; Morning Glory, 272; Mystery Flower Garden, 25; Nonesuch, 270; Orange Bud, 397; Patch as Patch Can, 47; Picket Fence, 420; Polka Dots, 268; Queen's Star, 340; Radiant Star, 347; Rainbow, 301; Rock Garden, 185; Rosebud, 225; Santa's Guiding Star, 182; Save-All, 369; Scroll Work, 123; Shadow Star, 251; Snowball, 77; Sprite, 49; Swallow's Flight, 371; Three Little Kittens, 371; Tree of Paradise, 404; Triple Rose, 62; True Lover's Knot, 326; Tulip Basket, 386; Tulip(s), 154, 391; Unnamed curved pattern, 314; Unnamed nine patch, 74; Wedding Ring Bouquet, 301; Windmill, 179
Aunt Martha's Rose, 354
Aunt Martha's Tulips, 393
Aunt Mary's Double Irish Chain, 140
Aunt Mary's Squares, 211
Aunt Mary's Star, 155
Aunt Nancy's Favorite, 134
Aunt Patsy's Pet, 18
Aunt Patty's Favorite, 18
Aunt Rachel's Star, 77
Aunt Stella's Pattern, 368
Aunt Sukey's Choice, 23
Aunt Tryphosa's Favorite, 53
Aunt Vina's Favorite, 21
Auntie.com/qzine, 379
Auntie's Kitties, 379
Aurora Borealis, 335
Austin, 96
Autograph, 51, 146
Autograph Patch, 84
Autograph Quilt, 84, 232
Autograph Quilt Block, 134
Autumn Breeze, 36
Autumn Kaleidoscope, 305
Autumn Leaf (Leaves), 14, 66, 150, 178, 201, 210, 225, 255
Autumn Lily, 396
Autumn Maze, 24
Autumn Moon, 124
Autumn Night, 74
Autumn Spinning Star, 305
Autumn Star(s), 122, 151
Autumn Tints, 93, 228
Autumn Tints Variation, 230
Autumn Trails, 15
Avalanche Lily, 280
Avian Waves, 86
Away in a Manger, 230
Axe Blade, 422
Aztec, 302
Aztec Jewel, 127
Babe Ruth Diamond, 294
Baby Aster, 294, 307
Baby Basket, 384
Baby Bunting, 106, 267, 306, 383
Baby Dolls, 380
Baby Food Jar, 377
Baby Rose, 395
Baby Shoe, 379
Baby('s) Block(s), 359
Baby's Fall Friendship Quilt, 308
Bachelor's Puzzle, 60, 100, 184, 206, 223, 233
Back to School, 407
Bacon Patch, 165
Badge of Friendship, 422
Bailey Nine Patch, 277
Baker's Dozen, 221
Balance, 223
Balkan Puzzle, 103
Ballot Box, 49
Balsam Fir, 404
Baltimore Belle, 78, 205

Bamboo Quilt, 110
Bamboo Spread, 413
Banded Cross Block, 199
Banded Triangle, 129
Bandstand, 71
Banner Quilt, 179
Barbara Bannister Star, 42
Barbara Frietchie Star, 97
Barn, 406, 409
Barn with Silo, 409
Barrister's Block, 137
Bars, 412
Baseball, 267, 273, 277, 309
Basement Window, 132
Basket Block, 384
Basket Design, 194, 388
Basket of Berries, 361
Basket of Bright Flowers, 387, 392
Basket of Chips, 384, 385
Basket of Diamonds, 162, 383, 387
Basket of Flowers, 361, 385, 389
Basket of Lilies, 388, 389
Basket of Oranges, 384
Basket of Scraps, 382, 386
Basket of Triangles, 384
Basket of Tulips, 389
Basket Patch, 383
Basket Quilt, 383, 384, 385
Basket Quilt in Triangles, 386
Basket Weave, 17
Basket Weave Friendship Quilt, 132
Basket with Handles, 386
Basket(s), 157, 382, 383, 384, 385, 386, 389, 390
Bass and Trout, 331
Bat, 66, 370
Bat Wing, 193
Bates Vista, 146
Baton Rouge Block, 197
Baton Rouge Quilt Block, 143
Bat's Block, 66
Bats in the Belfry, 79
Battle Ax of Thor, 53, 100
Battle of the Alamo, 37
Battlegrounds, 45
Bauer, Mrs. Eldon, 175
Bay Leaf, 272, 275, 305, 311
Beach and Boots, 109
Beacon, 173, 208
Beacon Light(s), 22, 109, 159, 163
Bear, 372
Bear Paw Design, 195
Bear Tracks, 14
Bear's Den, 54
Bear's Foot, 225
Bear('s) Paw, 14, 136, 225, 228
Bear's Tracks, 225
Bea's Basket, 385
Beauregard's Surroundings, 223
Beautiful Crown, 160
Beautiful Flower Garden, 170
Beautiful Mosaic, 242
Beautiful Star, 133
Beauty Block, 85
Beauty Patch, 111
Beaver, 374
Becky's Nine Patch, 18
Bed of Roses, 425
Beer Mug, 376
Beg and Borrow, 140
Beggar('s) Block(s), 20, 55, 56, 59, 82
Beginner's Choice, 16, 43
Beginner's Delight, 198
Behold...a Star, 305
Belle of West Virginia, 130
Belle's Favorite, 113
Bellflower, 394
Bell(s), 49, 61, 375, 381
Bell's Star, 218
Bernier, Melissa, 237
Berry Basket, 384
Best Friend(s), 225, 228, 232
Best of All, 23
Best Wishes, 79
Bethlehem Star, 333

Betty's Basket, 383
Betty's Choice, 54
Betty's Delight, 43
Beyer, Jenny, 367
Beyond the Stars, 173
Bezelled Star, 350
Bible Tulip, 280
Big Barn, 409
Big Block Quilts, 233
Big Chicken, 376
Big Dipper, 101
Big House, 408
Big O, 11
Big T, 29
Biloxi, 117, 133
Bird at the Window, 386
Bird Feeder, 372
Bird of Paradise, 28, 280
Birdhouse, 376, 380
Birds and Kites, 179
Bird's Eye View, 279
Birds in a Square, 255
Birds in Flight, 412
Birds in the Air, 13, 15, 38, 105, 233, 315
Bird's Nest, 210
Birds of the Air, 13
Birds on the Tracks, 79
Birthday Cake, 32
Biscuit Quilt, 425
Bishop Hill, 55
Bismarck, 148
Black and White, 110
Black Beauty, 141, 277
Black Cat Block, 370
Black Diamond, 333
Black Diamond Quilt Block, 143
Black Eyed Susan, 301
Black Magic, 186
Blackbug, 374
Blackford's Beauty, 141
Blacks and Whites, 148
Blazed Trail, 187
Blazing Arrow Point, 97
Blazing Arrows, 97
Blazing Star, 123, 170, 231, 296, 329, 334, 343, 345, 346, 359
Blazing Star of Kentucky, 341
Blazing Star of Minnesota, 329
Blazing Sun, 296
Bleeding Heart, 282, 301, 303
Blindman's Fancy, 138
Block & Tackle, 186
Block and Ring, 285
Block Circle, 39
Block Island Puzzle, 107
Block of Many Triangles, 70, 148
Block Patchwork, 356, 357
Block Pattern, 359
Block Puzzle, 350
Blockade, 102
Blockhouse, 58
Blocks and Stars, 27
Blocks in a Box, 11, 191
Bloom, 392
Blossom Time, 136
Blossoming Cactus, 23
Blouses, 381
Blowing in the Wind, 154
Blue Bell Block, 213
Blue Birds (Bluebirds) Flying, 233
Blue Birds Flying, 228
Blue Blades Flying, 223
Blue Blazes, 267
Blue Boutonnieres, 140
Blue Chains, 37
Blue Fields, 178
Blue Fields Variation, 161
Blue Flower Garden, 355
Blue for Julie, 224
Blue Heather, 214
Blue Heaven, 86, 112, 204
Blue Ribbon, 146
Blue Ribbon Quilts; Black Magic, 186; Moving Fans & Fast Pinwheels, 160
Blue Skies, 75
Bluebell, 310
Blueberry Patch, 136
Bluebirds, 331
Bluebirds for Happiness, 331
Bluet Quilt, 323
Board Meeting, 152
Boardwalk, 173
Boat in a Bottle, 377
Bobbin, 50
Boise, 159
Bold Squares, 214
Bon-Bon, 425
Bonesteel, Georgia; Amazing Grace, 409; Georgia's Owl, 374; Hallelujah Hall, 409; Hillside Village, 409; Let's Get Pinned, 381; Lover's Locket, 70
Bonnie Scotsman, 93
Bonny Scotland, 117
*Book of American Patchwork Quilts*, 234
Books, 378
Books on a Shelf, 378
Borders, 411, 415, 416, 421, 422–423, 424–426
Borrow and Return, 272, 289
Bossburg Wonder, 181
Boston, 279
Boston Belle, 159
Boston Corners, 341, 342
Boston Pavement, 150
Boston Puzzle, 269, 272, 273
Boston Trail, 268
Botch Handle, 138, 229
Bottle, 377
Bouncing Betty, 99
Bouquet, 229
Bouquet in a Fan, 331
Bouquet Star, 251
Bouquet's Quilt, 213
Boutonniere, 351
Bow, 50, 381
Bow Knots, 381
Bow Tie Variation, 99
Bow Tie Wreath, 121
Bow Ties, 101
Bowbells, 153
Bowknot, 60
Bow(s) and Arrows, 269, 288
Bows and Paper, 129
Bowtie, 108
Bowtie in Pink and White, 151
Box Car Patch, 107
Box Patchwork, 359
Box Pattern, 359
Box Quilt, 152, 359
Box upon Box, 359, 419
Boxed Squares, 229
Boxed T, 14, 45
Box(es), 13, 19, 30, 107, 386
Boxes and Baskets, 67
Boyd, Arleen, 147
Boyink, Betty, 361
Boy's Fancy, 27
Boy's Nonsense, 27
Boy's Playmate, 27
Braced Star, 25, 26
Bradford Nine Patch, 53
Braid, 412
Brave Sunflower, 295
Brave World, 104
Bread Basket, 382, 388
Breeches Quilt, 139
Brick Pavement, 83
Brick Walk, 414
Bricks and Blocks, 199
Brickwall, 418
Brickwork, 153, 179, 418
Bridal Stairway Patchwork Block, 416
Bride's Bouquet, 139, 356, 357
Bride's Fancy, 348
Bride's Knot, 195
Bride's Prize, 287
Bride's Puzzle, 34, 247
Bride's Puzzle in Patchwork, 346
Bride's Quilt, 311
Bridge Quilt, 277
Bridle Path, 72
Bridle Path Star, 274
Bright Futures, 101
Bright Hopes Twist, 11
Bright Jewel, 192
Bright Morning Star, 329
Bright Side, 79
Bright Star(s), 45, 76, 137, 234
Brilliant Star, 350
Britches Quilt, 139
Broad Arrow(s), 46
Broad Axe, 195
Brock House, 191
Broke Sugar Bowl, 384
Broken Arrows, 193, 194
Broken Band, 135
Broken Branch, 209
Broken Circle, 278, 289, 303
Broken Circle Sunflower, 293
Broken Crown, 288
Broken Crystals, 156, 183
Broken Dish(es), 39, 101, 103, 105, 108, 126, 384
Broken Heart, 207, 218
Broken Irish Chain, 213
Broken Path(s), 53, 102, 130
Broken Pinwheel, 104
Broken Plate, 19
Broken Promises, 108
Broken Rainbows, 48
Broken Sash, 94
Broken Saw, 267
Broken Saw Blades, 224
Broken Spider Web, 90
Broken Square(s), 276, 288, 307
Broken Star, 263, 333, 345
Broken Stone, 279, 281
Broken Sugar Bowl, 36
Broken Wheel, 39, 40, 104
Broken Windmills, 241
Broken Window, 33
Brown Goose, 118
Brown World, 104
Brown-Eyed Susan, 391
Bruce, Carol, 173
Brunswick Star, 330, 334
Buck 'n Wing, 120
Buckeye Beautiful, 122
Buckeye Beauty, 100, 334
Buckwheat, 44
Bud, 391
Buffalo, 374
Buffalo Ridge, 152
Bug, 373
Buggy Wheel, 289, 303
Builder's Blocks, 45, 354
Building Blocks, 54, 60, 100, 201, 359, 414, 423
Building the Stars, 64
Bull's Eye, 194, 210, 226, 327
Bun Quilt, 425
Bunny, 370
Burbank, Doreen, 372
Burgoyne Surrounded, 223
Burgoyne's Puzzle, 223
Buried Treasure, 169
Burnett, Ellen F., 376
Burnham Square, 59
Burr and Thistle, 280
Bursting Star, 30, 336
Busch, Marilyn, 375
Buschschulte, Clara, 140
Bush's Points of Light, 279
Butter and Eggs, 275
Buttercup, 316
Butterfly, 47, 106, 171, 370, 373
Butterfly at the Crossroads, 191
Butterfly Block, 42
Butterfly Bush, 83
Butterfly in Angles, 158
Butterfly in the Garden, 311
Butterfly Migration, 288
Butterfly Quadrille, 303
Butterfly Quilt, 414
Butterfly Quilt Block, 21
Butterfly Squared, 374
Butterfly Wings, 215
Buttons and Bows, 140, 180
Buzz Saw, 297
Buzz Saw Charm, 34
Buzzard's Roost, 108
Byrd at the South Pole, 311
Cabbage Rose, 157
Cabin, 409
Cabin Windows, 80
*Cabot, Nancy*, 72; An A Star, 63; Acanthus, 229; Aircraft, 100; Alabama Rambler, 169; Alamanizer, 114; Alaska Chinook, 167; Alcazar, 301; Algonquin Charm, 191; All Around the Star, 115; Alma's Choice, 168; Alpine Cross, 201; Amazing Windmill, 150; Amethyst Chain, 61; Annapolis, 160; Antique Tile Block, 17; Arkansas Diamond, 165; Arms to Heaven, 313; Around the Corner, 127; Attic Stairs, 178; Aunt Jerusha, 272; Aunt Lottie's Star, 26; Aunt Malvina's Chain, 15; Aunt Patsy's Pet, 18; Autumn Leaves, 66; Autumn Star, 122; Autumn Tints, 228; Bacon Patch, 165; Balkan Puzzle, 103; Balsam Fir, 404; Basket Design, 194; Baton Rouge Block, 197; Bat's Block, 66; Beach and Boots, 109; Beacon Light, 22; Bear Tracks, 14; Beg and Borrow, 140; Bible Tulip, 280; Birds and Kites, 179; Bishop Hill, 55; Black Beauty, 141; Blacks and Whites, 148; Blazed Trail, 187; Blazing Star, 123; Blockhouse, 58; Blossoming Cactus, 23; Blue Bell Block, 213; Blue Chains, 37; Blue Heather, 214; Blue Heaven, 86, 204; Boston Corners, 341; Bow Knots, 381; Bow Ties, 101; Bowbells, 153; Box Car Patch, 107; Boy's Playmate, 27; Bread Basket, 382; Bright Star(s), 45, 137; Broad Arrows, 46; Broken Irish Chain, 213; Broken Plate, 19; Broken Rainbows, 48; Broken Sash, 94; Broken Saw Blades, 224; Broken Spider Web, 90; Broken Star, 263; Broken Windmills, 241; Brown World, 104; Buckeye Beauty, 334; Buffalo Ridge, 152; Building Blocks, 201; Bursting Star, 336; Butterfly Bush, 83; Butterfly Quilt Block, 21; Byrd at the South Pole, 311; Cactus Bloom, 279; Cake Stand, 385; Calico Bush, 386; Calico Compass, 337; Calico Mosaic, 87; Carnival, 41, 64; Castle Garden, 162; Catalpa Flower, 322; Cathedral Window, 205; Celestial Sphere, 331; Chain Links Quilt, 145; Chariot Wheel, 242; Checkers, 158; Chieftain, 179; Chinese Fan, 267, 292; Chinese Gongs, 276; Chinese Holidays, 74; Chinese Lanterns, 148; Chinese Puzzle, 146; Chuck-A-Luck, 73, 74; Church Windows, 211; Churn Dash, 107; City Streets, 53; Claws, 294; Clay's Compromise, 146; Cleopatra's Puzzle, 269; Climbing Roses, 220; Cobblestones, 214; Cone Tree, 404; Confederate Rose, 214, 219; Constellation, 184; Corn and Beans, 275; Counterpane, 115; Country Cousin, 268; County Fair, 338; County Farm, 338; Court House Lawn, 131; Coxcomb, 129; Coxey's Army, 152; Crazy Quilt Star, 124; Creole Puzzle, 21; Cross and Square, 135; Cross of Geneva, 164; Cross Stitch, 127; Crossed Chains, 67; Crossed Square, 259; Crossroads, 62; Cubes and Tile(s), 134, 334; Cumberland Gap, 420; Cupid's Darts, 425; Dancing Pinwheels, 41; Delaware Crosspatch, 51; Desert Rose, 185; Devil's Footprints, 316; Diagonal Paths, 146; Diamond Chain, 167; Diamond Head, 327; Diamond Knot, 152; Diamond Panes, 200; Diamond Plaid Block, 57; Diamond Star, 83, 344; Diamond Wedding Block, 334; Dirty Windows, 268, 269; Does Double Duty, 201, 202; Dog Tooth Violet, 74; Domino and Squares, 209; Domino Net, 67; Doors and Windows, 214; Double Aster, 150; Double Hour Glass, 14; Double Irish Chain, 203; Double Link, 355; Double Pinwheel, 147; Double Poppy, 300; Double T, 82; Double Windmill, 150, 165; Double X's, 341; Double Z, 141; Doves in the Window, 226; Duck's Foot in the Mud, 14, 225; Dutch Rose, 272; Dutch Tile, 94; Dutchman's Puzzle, 139; Eccentric Star, 13; Eight Pointed Star, 134; Emerald Block, 327; Empty Spool, 15; Endless Chain, 276; Endless Squares, 84; Endless Stair, 17, 93; Enigma, 183; Everglades, 311; Fairy Star, 141; Far West, 58, 59; Federal Chain, 18; Federal Square, 176; Fields and Fences, 241; Fifty Four Forty or Fight, 12; Fishing Boats, 114; Five Crosses, 110; Five Lilies, 340; Five Spot, 20; Flaming Sun, 98; Flashing Windmills, 108; Flat Iron, 73; Flight of Swallows, 38; Floral Bouquet, 398; Flower Bed, 120; Flying Barn Swallows, 330; Flying Birds, 202; Flying Dutchman, 148; Flying Fish, 146; Flying Geese, 179; Flying Leaves, 46; Flying Shuttles, 37; Flying Star, 219; Flying X, 127; Foot Stool, 198; Formosa Fan, 290; Fort Sumter, 127; Four and Nine Patch, 18; Four Baskets, 389; Four Birds, 226; Four Clowns, 55; Four Corners, 177; Four Leaf Clover, 167, 272, 314; Four Square(s), 74, 165, 166, 177; Four Star Block, 72; Four Windmills, 415; Four Winds, 35; Fox and Geese, 200; Friendship Chain, 132; Friendship Fan, 290; Friendship Links, 217; Fringed Square, 23; Full Blown Rose, 299; Gamecocks, 207; Garden Maze, 56, 65; Garden Paths, 212; Garret Window, 15; Geese in Flight, 122; Georgetown Puzzle, 150; Ghost Walk, 269; Glory Vine, 183; Gold and Silver, 329; Gold Nuggets, 119; Golden Chains, 151; Golden Cubes, 359; Golden Stairs, 36; Good Luck Block, 18; Grandma's Choice, 193; Granny's Favorite, 220; Greek Square, 19; Green Cross, 89; Grist Mill, 276; Hail Storm, 22; Half Moon Block, 294; Halley's Comet, 348; Handcraft, 53; Hard Times Block, 47; Harmony Square, 206; Hawks in Flight, 419; Hazy Daisy, 132; Heather Square, 85; Heavenly Puzzle, 206; Herald Square, 300; Hill and Craig, 212; Hill and Hollow, 217; Hobson's Kiss, 164; Holland Mill, 205; Hopscotch, 112; Hour Glass, 68, 294; Hummingbirds, 299; Idaho Star, 328; Idle Moments, 134; Illinois Road, 77; Illinois Star, 263; Indian Maize, 164; Indian Mat(s), 32, 45, 48, 67; Indian Raid, 300; Indian Squares, 210; Irish Plaid, 164; Iron Cross, 103; Islam, 115; Jamestown Square, 174; Jaywalker, 126; Jim Dandy, 120; Jupiter's Moons, 303; Kankakee Checkers, 73; Kansas Sunflower, 298; Katie's Favorite, 132; Kentucky Crossroads, 84; King's Cross, 103; King's Star, 330; Ladies' Delight, 58; Lady of the Lake, 32; Land of the Pharaoh, 418; Lattice and Square, 127; Lattice Block, 323, 326; Left and Right, 140; Lehigh Maze, 61; Light and Shadows, 115; Lighthouse, 212; Lightning, 418; Lightning in the Hills, 35; Lily Pond, 201, 229; Little Beech Tree, 404; Little Penguins, 180; Little Star, 329; London Square, 32; Lotus Block, 230; Lovely Patchwork, 110; Love's Chain, 281; Lucky Knot, 158; Lucky Star, 321; Mace Head, 285; MacKenzie's Square, 169; Magic Squares, 76; Magnolia Block, 219; Magnolia Bud, 390; Maiden's Delight, 164; Maltese Cross, 309; Maltese Cross Block, 187; Many Pointed Star, 24; Maple Leaf, 45; Marietta Blockhouse, 230; Market Square, 180; Martha's Choice, 272; Mary's Block, 30; May Basket, 387; Mayor's Garden, 20; Medieval Mosaic, 60; Medieval Walls, 60; Meeting House Square, 57; Memory Blocks, 134; Memory Fruit, 150; Merry-Go-Round, 150; Mexican Siesta, 89; Midnight Stars, 117; Midsummer Night, 327; Mill and Stars, 133; Miller's Daughter, 196; Mississippi Oak Leaves, 316; Missouri Star, 134; Missouri Trouble, 313; Modern Daisy, 224; Modernistic Pansy, 393; Modernized Poppy, 300; Monastery Windows, 112; Monkey Wrench, 201; Monk's Puzzle, 368; Montana Maze, 233; Moon and Swastika, 315; Moon Block, 294; Moorish Mosaic, 336; Morning Star, 314, 347, 353; Mosaic #8, 106; Mosaic #5, 113; Mosaic #4, 113; Mosaic #1, 111; Mosaic #7, 96; Mosaic #6, 103; Mosaic #10, 112; Mosaic #3, 126; Mosaic #12, 102, 111; Mosaic #2, 127; Mosaic Squares, 82; Mountain Homespun, 222, 251; Mountain Pink, 288; My Favorite, 121, 127; Mystic Maze, 150; Nameless Star, 96; Nauvoo Lattice, 170; Nebraska, 251; Necktie, 148; New Barrister's Block, 137; New Double Irish Chain, 214; New Star of North Carolina, 220; Night and Day, 125; Nine Snowballs, 322; Northern Lights, 151; Nosegay, 153; Octagon Block, 323; Octagonal, 323; Odd Star, 215; Ohio Trail, 166; Old Favorite, 121, 127; Old Glory, 359; Old Gray Goose, 118; Old Italian Block, 212; Old Maid's Patience, 334; Old Maid's Puzzle, 99; Old Poinsettia, 111; Old Snowflake, 26; Old Windmill, 104; Orange Pekoe, 418; Oriental Puzzle, 247; Oriental Rose, 397; Oriental Star, 133, 143, 321; Oriental Tulip, 394; Original, 33; Ozark Mountains, 179; Pacific Rail Road, 37; Paducah Peony, 313; Painted Snowball, 299; Panama Block, 211; Parasol Block, 295; Patch Quilt Design, 207, 215; Path and Stiles, 59; Pathfinder, 214; Pattern Without a Name, 178, 201; Peeled Orange, 295; Penelope's Favorite, 315; Penn's Puzzle, 315; Peony and Forget Me Nots, 150; Perpetual Motion, 135; Perry's Expedition, 311; Philadelphia Block, 194; Pineapple Squares, 224; Pink Magnolias, 390; Pinwheels, 40;

Pioneer Block, 214; Plaited Block, 151; Port and Starboard, 114; Practical Orchard, 12; Prairie Flower, 42; Prosperity Block, 57; Providence Block, 193; Puritan Maiden, 215; Puss in the Corner, 16, 18; Pyramids, 32, 136; Quadrille, 61; Quarterfoils, 18; Quebec, 255; Queen Charlotte's Crown, 194; Queen's Crown, 194, 222; Quilt Star, 124; Quilter's Delight, 242, 270; Rail Fence, 412; Railroad, 100; Railroad Crossing, 223; Rain or Shine, 211; Rainbow Block, 267; Rattlesnake, 300; Ray, 177; Red Buds, 277; Red Shields, 417; Riviera, 167; Road Home, 270; Road to Jerusalem, 100; Rocky Road to Dublin, 37; Rolling Pinwheel, 41; Rolling Squares, 66; Rolling Star Quilt, 280; Roman Pavement, 267; Roman Roads, 215, 221; Rose Garden, 177; Rose Trellis, 112; Rosebud, 31; Ruby Roads, 141; Ruins of Jericho, 152; Sacramento City, 199; Santa Fe Trail, 57; Sapphire Net, 88; Schoenrock Cross, 227; Scotch Heather, 58; Scotch Squares, 127; Scrapbag, 213; Sea Star, 42; Seasons, 206; Seminole Square, 227; Sentry's Pastime, 86; Shoo Fly, 19; Shooting Star(s), 167; Simple Design, 120; Simple Flower Basket, 383; Single Chain and Knot, 213; Single Irish Chain, 16; Slanted Diamonds, 15; Snow Block, 127; Snowball(s), 11, 269, 323; Solomon's Star, 97; Sombrero Appliqué, 89; Southern Plantation, 316; Spanish Squares, 220; Sparkling Dew, 353; Sparkling Jewel, 124; Spider, 13; Spider and the Fly, 298; Spinning Arrows, 35; Spinning Hour Glass, 152; Spinning Jenny, 82; Spinning Tops, 200; Spirit of 1849, 313; Spirit of St. Louis, 17; Spool and Bobbin, 56, 147; Spool Block, 196; Spring and Fall, 419; Square and Compass, 300; Squares and Crosses, 315; Squares Within Squares, 93; St. Elmo's Fire, 38; Star & Pinwheels, 97; Star and Arrow, 331; Star and Corona, 213, 219; Star and Diamonds, 369; Star and Mill Block, 220; Star and Stripe, 141; Star and Wreath, 343; Star Fish, 176; Star Flowers, 341; Star Kite, 41; Star Kites, 124; Star Net, 337; Star of Erin, 66; Star of Many Points, 334; Star of St. Louis, 210, 326; Star of the Magi, 333; Star of the Night, 227; Star of the Orient, 133; Star of the Sea, 42; Star Shower, 337; Star X, 25; Stars and Stripes, 50; State Fair, 48; State House, 145; Steps to the Garden, 81, 82; Steps to the White House, 203; Storm Signal, 22; Strength in Union, 197; Stripes and Squares, 220; Sugar Bowl, 383; Sugar Bowl Quilt, 95; Summer Garden, 82; Summer Sun, 347; Sun Dial, 56; Sunbeam Crossroad, 211; Sunburst and Mill, 336; Sunset, 292; Swamp Angel, 25; Sweetheart Garden, 315; Swing(ing) in the Center, 20; Tenallytown Square, 132; Tete-a-Tete, 177, 196; Texas Cactus Basket, 382; Thousand Islands, 84; Thousand Pyramids, 418; Three and Six, 13; Three Steps, 146; Thrift Block, 95; Through the Years, 210; Thunder and Lightning, 33; Tinted Chains, 132; Tombstone Quilt, 134; Topaz Trail, 169; Towers of Camelot, 26; Triangle of Squares, 125; Triangle Trails, 72; Tricolor Block, 17; Triple Link Chain, 156; Trout and Bass Block, 331; True Lover's Knot, 275; Tulip Basket, 389; Turkey Giblets, 161; Turkey in the Straw, 20; Twinkling Star, 77, 185; Twist, 309; Two Crosses, 193; Uncle Sam's Hourglass, 207; Union Block, 34; Union Square, 22; Vice President's Block, 197; Village Square, 94; Vines at the Window, 23; Violet Blossoms, 282; Virginia Snowball, 277; Virginia's Choice, 272; Wampum, 46; Waterwheel, 322; Weathervane, 39; Weathervane and Steeple, 47; Weaving Paths, 242; Web of Diamonds, 341; Wedgewood Tiles, 312; Westward Ho, 337; Wheel of Chance, 192; Wheel of Fortune, 192; Wheel of Luck, 180; Whippoorwill, 85; Whirligig, 150; Whirling Square, 198, 236; Whirling Star, 68; White Mountains, 323, 326; Windblown Daisy, 295; Windblown Square, 103; Winding Trail, 289; Windows and Doors, 214; Winged Square, 83; Winter Stars, 329; Witches Star, 329; Woodland Path, 205; World's Wonder, 268; Yankee Charm, 18; Yellow Clover, 212; Yellow Lilies, 235; Yokohama Banner, 114; Yreka Square, 214

Cactus, 394
Cactus Basket, 382, 383
Cactus Basket Block, 387
Cactus Bloom, 279
Cactus Blossom Patch, 279
Cactus Bud, 14
Cactus Pot, 383
Cactus Pot Block, 116
Cactus Rose, 286
Caesar's Crown, 271, 300, 304, 316, 317
Cake Stand, 14, 385
Calendar House Quilt, 405
Calgary Stampede, 231
Calico Bouquet, 161
Calico Bush, 386
Calico Cat, 170, 371
Calico Compass, 337
Calico Grove, 180
Calico Mosaic, 87
Calico Puzzle, 11
Calico Rose, 298
Calico Snowball, 11
Calico Spools, 15
Calico Stars, 337
California, 43, 207
California Oakleaf, 236
California Snowflake, 62, 217
California Star, 346, 347, 348
Calla Lily, 396
Calypso, 141
Camel, 374
Camellia, 395
Cameo Quilt, 305
Campaign Trail, 168
Canadian Conventional Star, 362
Canadian Gardens, 102
Canadian Puzzle, 269
Candle in the Window, 197
Candleglow, 228
Candles, 181
Candles of Heaven, 344
Candlestick, 379
Candy Canes, 87
Candy Drops, 304
Candy Jar, 378
Capital Star, 336
Capital T, 29
*Capper's Weekly*; Chinese Lantern, 375; Eccentric Star, 13; Hexagonal Star, 354; Laurel Wreath, 23; Queen's Favorite, 20; Quilt of the Century, 329; Rising Star, 354; Sherman's March, 19; Union Square, 34
Caps for Witches and Dunces, 158
Captain's Wheel, 193
Captive Beauty, 332
Car Wheel Quilt, 277
Car Wheel(s), 284, 297
Card Basket, 26, 27
Card Trick, 19
Carmen's Block, 93
Carnival, 41, 64, 293
Carnival Time, 321, 332
Carolina Favorite, 277, 304
Carolina Lily, 335, 388
Caroline's Fan, 290
Carol's Scrap Time Quilt, 22
Carousel, 327
Carpenter's Square, 206, 241
Carpenter's Star, 247
Carpenter's Wheel, 333
Carpenter's Wheel Variation, 334
Carrie Bird Star, 338
Carrie Nation Quilt, 122
Carrie's Choice, 209
Carroll, Dianne, 160
Carson City, 27
Cart Wheel, 278
Cartwheel, 307
Cascade Pride, 18, 401
Casement Window, 131
Castle, 409
Castle Garden, 162
Castle Tower, 24
Castle Wall, 330
Castles in Spain, 175
Castor and Pollux, 207
Cat, 371, 372
Catalpa Flower, 322
Catch as You Can, 112
Catch Me if You Can, 53, 100
Cathedral Window, 205, 316
Cats and Mice, 38, 45, 56, 59, 82, 131
Cat's Cradle, 13, 38
Cat's Eye, 161
Cats in the Attic, 371
Cat's Paw, 225
Cattail, 394
Cedars of Lebanon, 45, 46, 48
Celestial Sphere, 331
Celtic Plaid, 84
Centennial, 98
Centennial Tree, 400, 402
Center Ring, 304
Center Table Quilt, 330
Century, 138, 357
Century of Progress, 42, 122, 186, 205
Chain and Bar, 157
Chain and Hourglass, 46, 55
Chain Bridge, 304
Chain Link(s), 89, 226, 270
Chain Links Quilt, 145
Chain of Diamonds, 61, 159
Chain Quilt, 269
Chain Reaction, 424
Chained Dominos, 16
Chained Five Patch, 204
Chained Lightning, 418
Chained Nine Patch, 19
Chained Star, 26, 212, 323, 334, 360, 364
Chalice, 159
Chaos, 426
Chaos Theory, 87
Chariot Wheel, 242, 295
Charity Wheel, 288
Charleston Quilt Block, 77
Charm, 64, 363, 420, 422
Charm Packet Odyssey, 363
Charm Quilt, 177
Charm Star, 162
Charmed Path, 421
Check, 93
Checkerboard, 20, 93, 230
Checkerboard Design, 11
Checkerboard Quilt, 102
Checkerboard Squares, 214
Checkerboard Star, 136
Checkered Square, 223
Checkers, 158
Cheesebox Quilt, 58
Cherokee Spirit, 119
Cherry Basket, 384, 385, 386, 387, 389
Cherry Jubilee, 398
Cherry Tree, 403
Chestnut Burr, 347
Chevron(s), 88, 140, 231, 363, 411
Cheyenne, 107
Chicago Geese, 48
Chicago Pavements, 132
Chicago Star, 56
Chicken, 382
Chicken Foot, 80
Chicken Little, 374
Chief, 49
Chieftain, 179
Child is Born, 166
Children of Israel, 74
Children's Delight, 191
Chimney, 43
Chimney Swallow(s), 281, 302, 332
Chimney Sweep, 132, 229
Chimneys and Cornerstones, 236
China Doll, 221
China Plate, 307
Chinese 10,000 Perfections, 53, 100
Chinese Block Pattern, 225
Chinese Coin(s), 40, 412
Chinese Fan, 267, 291, 292
Chinese Gongs, 276
Chinese Holidays, 74
Chinese Lantern(s), 148, 375
Chinese Puzzle, 146, 323
Chinese Quilt Block, 39
Chinese Square, 241
Chinese Star, 317
Chip Basket, 385
Chips and Whetstones, 296, 312, 331
Chipyard, 230
Chisholm Trail, 96
Choices, 153
Christmas Basket, 387
Christmas Cactus, 259
Christmas Cheer, 46
Christmas Day, 304
Christmas Memory Quilt, 333
Christmas Pines, 404
Christmas Spirit, 228
Christmas Star, 23, 76, 157, 197, 329, 339
Christmas Tree(s), 399, 400, 401, 402, 403, 404, 405
Christmas Wreath, 380
Chrysanthemum, 267, 395
Chrysanthemum Block, 183
Chrysanthemum Quilt Top, 369
Chuck-A-Luck, 73, 74
Church, 406, 409
Church Steps, 216
Church Windows, 80, 211, 323
Churchill Block, 161
Churn Dash, 19, 107, 195
Churn Dasher, 192, 199
Cincinnati Art Museum, 71
Cincinnati Cog Wheel, 298
Cinderella, 138
Circle and Star, 277
Circle Bar Quilt, 282
Circle Cross, 273
Circle Design, 273
Circle Four, 77, 332
Circle in a Circle, 313
Circle in a Frame, 94
Circle of Fans, 293
Circle Petal in a Square, 305
Circle Star, 296
Circle Upon Circle, 275, 277
Circle Within Circle, 268
Circling Swallows, 33, 233, 330
Circular (Circle) Saw, 282, 287, 288, 293, 314, 333
Circular Flying Geese, 287
Circular Flying Geese Variation, 287
Circular grid, 266
City Blocks, 220
City Park, 32
City Square, 32, 226
City Streets, 53, 54, 225
Clam Shells, 421
Clary, Michelle, 166
Claws, 29, 294
Clay's Choice, 111
Clay's Compromise, 146
Clay's Favorite, 111
Clay's Star, 111
Cleopatra's Puzzle, 269
Cleveland Tulip, 335
Climbing Rose(s), 164, 220
Clover Blossom, 66
Clover Leaf, 44, 62
Clown, 193
Clown's Choice, 12, 197
Cluster of Lilies, 228
Cluster of Stars, 63, 95, 208
Clydescape, 325
Coarse Woven, 411
Coarse Woven Patchwork, 422
Coats and Clark; Borrow and Return, 289; Chimney Sweep, 229
Cobblestones, 214
Cobra, 65
Cobweb Quilt, 352
Cobwebs, 15
Cockcomb, 338
Cockleburr, 311
Code Star, 234
Coffee Cups, 375
Coffin Star, 128
Cog Block, 96
Cog Wheels, 93, 285, 297
Cogwheel, 18, 287
Collector's Plate on Tripod, 378
College Chain, 118
Collinsville Rose Star, 353
Colombian Puzzle, 155, 164, 169
Colonial Basket, 382, 385, 387
Colonial Bouquet, 362
Colonial Bow Tie, 108
Colonial Flower Garden, 362
Colonial Garden, 134, 357
Colonial Pavement, 163
Colonial Rose, 45
Color Ways, 17
Color Wheel(s), 286, 304
Colorado Beauty, 108
Colorado Block, 108
Colorado Log Cabin, 237
Colorado Star, 354
Colorado's Arrowhead, 54
Colt's Corral, 222
Columbia, 82, 355
Columbia Pinwheel, 126
Columbia Puzzle, 161, 170
Columbia Quilt Block, 89
Columbia Star, 355, 360
Columbian Star, 57
Columbus, Ohio, 336
Columbus Quilt Block, 335
Columns, 332
Combination Feathered Star, 329
Combination Star, 25, 27
Comet, 202
Comet Star, 326
*Comfort Magazine*, 300, 373, 384; Airship, 299; Basket Block, 384; Basket Design, 388; Basket of Chips, 385; Bear Paw Design, 195; Broken Saw, 267; Center Table Quilt, 330; Christmas Tree Patch, 403; Design for Light and Dark, 337; Dove at the Window, 38; Fool's Puzzle, 118; Friendly Hand, 40; Grandmother's Fancy, 152; Hummingbird, 45; Irish Chain, 203; Missionary Baptist, 83; Octagon, 137; Octagon Star, 337; Odds and Ends, 137; Old Maid's Puzzle, 229; Plain Sailing, 108; Red, White and Blue, 293; Santa Fe Quilt, 110; Swallow, 332; Texas Sunflower, 299; Tumbling Blocks, 193; Twinkling Stars, 42, 123; Two Colors, 62; Unnamed five patch, 223; Wanderer, 267; Wedding March, 56; Zig Zag, 101
Comfort Quilt, 60
Commons, 221
Community Center, 174
Compass, 167, 220, 267, 271, 275, 283, 288, 296, 337
Compass and Chain, 62
Compass in a Hexagon, 367
Compass Kaleidoscope, 133
Compass Point, 277
Compass Star Quilt, 297
Completed Square, 263
Compote Quilt, 382
Compuquilt.com, 308
Concertina, 424
Concord, 133, 134
Cone Tree, 403, 404
Confederate Rose, 214, 219
Confetti, 17
Confetti Block, 69
Connecticut, 102, 107
Connecticut Star, 331
Connecticut Yankee, 185
Constellation, 99, 142, 184, 218, 220
Continental, 55
Continuous Star, 340
Contrary Husband, 107
Contrary Wife, 14, 33, 45
Conventional, 166
Conventional Rose, 219
Conventional Tulip, 397
Cook, Jan, 282
Cookies and Milk, 47
Copeland, Sandra, 60
Coral Court Friendship Star, 96
Corn, 396
Corn and Beans, 13, 41, 67, 200, 275
Corn Design, 104
Corner Posts, 202
Corner Star, 137, 200, 228
Cornerstone, 22
Cornflower, 396
Cornhusker's Star, 175
Cornucopia, 339
Coronation, 135, 302
Coronation Block, 216
Corsage Bouquet, 301
Cosgrove, Gloria, 136
Cosmic Cube, 172
Cosmos, 353
Cottage Tulips, 304
Cotton Boll, 109, 110
Cotton Reel, 101
Cotton Reels, 106
Counter Charm, 186
Counterpane, 115
Country Charm, 217
Country Checkers, 214
Country Church, 406, 408, 409
Country Cousin, 268
Country Crossroads, 271, 341
Country Farm, 25, 30
Country Fields, 307
*Country Gentleman*; Cheesebox Quilt, 58; Explosion, 296; Three by Three, 17
Country Husband, 269
Country Lanes, 223, 224
Country Meeting House, 409
Country Path, 129
Country Roads, 152, 198, 225
Country Tile, 356, 357
Country Village, 115, 176
County Fair, 65, 338
County Farm, 338
Court House Lawn, 131

Courtenay Crown, 86
Courthouse Square, 20, 407
Courthouse Steps, 227, 237, 241
Courtyard Square, 165
Cousteau's Calypso, 210
Coverlet in Jewel Tones, 142
Cow, 369
Cowboy Boot, 375
Cowboy('s) Star, 64, 139, 219
Coxcomb, 129
Coxey's Army, 152
Coxey's Camp, 152
Crab, 70
Crab Claws, 48
Cracker, 21, 422
Crazy Ann, 193
Crazy Anne, 129
Crazy Block, 83
Crazy House, 192, 194
Crazy Kite, 363
Crazy Loons, 129, 131
Crazy Pieces, 165
Crazy Quilt, 109, 268
Crazy Quilt Flower, 109
Crazy Quilt Star, 124
Crazy Star, 140
Crazy Tile, 351, 368
Creole Puzzle, 21
Criss Cross (Crisscross), 163, 165,
    212, 218, 315
Criss Cross Quilt, 16
Crockett Cabin Quilt, 108
Crocodile, 379
Crocus, 390, 391, 396
Crocus Flowers, 392
Crooked Path, 268
Cross, 50, 236, 248
Cross and Chains, 21
Cross and Crown, 71, 75, 82, 179,
    209, 213, 226, 228, 229, 255, 334
Cross and Crown Variation, 233
Cross and Diamond Star, 69
Cross and Square, 135, 144, 173, 176
Cross and Star, 150, 206, 221
Cross Bars, 126
Cross Bars and Squares, 51
Cross in the Square, 224
Cross is Mother's Choice, 109
Cross of Geneva, 164
Cross of Temperance, 241
Cross of Tennessee, 241
Cross on Cross, 136
Cross Patch, 20, 55, 132, 200, 309
Cross Plains, 137
Cross Roads, 309
Cross Stitch, 127
Cross Upon Cross, 38
Cross Within Cross, 130, 192
Crossed Arrows, 77
Crossed Canoes, 110
Crossed Chains, 67
Crossed Roads, 202
Crossed Roads to Oklahoma, 169
Crossed Roads to Texas, 271
Crossed Square(s), 229, 259
Crosses and Losses, 40, 99
Crosspatch, 46, 54
Crossroads, 56, 62, 75, 153, 202, 212,
    220, 232, 271
Crossroads America, 32
Crossroads Star, 71
Crossroads to Bachelor's Hall, 271
Crossroads to Jericho, 21
Crossroads to Texas, 81
Crossword Puzzle, 155, 243
Crosswords, 214
Crow, Nancy, 118
Crowfoot, 137
Crown of Thorns, 35, 135, 197, 302,
    308, 316
Crowned Cross, 82
Crowned Star, 231
Crowning Glory, 31
Crow's Foot, 45, 104, 156, 187, 232
Crow's Nest, 59, 195
Crusader's Heart, 176
Crystal Honeycomb, 425
Crystal Star, 31, 96, 233, 324
Cube Lattice, 134, 203
Cube Work (Cubework), 357, 359
Cubes and Bars, 251
Cubes and Tile(s), 134, 334
Cubist Rose, 83
Cul-de-Sac, 169
Cumberland Gap, 420
Cup, 378, 379
Cup and Saucer, 375
Cupid's Arrow Point, 178
Cupid's Arrowpoint, 147
Cupid's Arrows, 88
Cupid's Darts, 425
Cups and Saucers, 19, 24

Cushion Design, 275
Custer's Last Stand, 80
Cut Diamond, 85
Cut Glass Dish, 38
Cut the Corners, 29
Cypress, 101, 102, 158
Dace, Doris, 121
Daffodils, 390
Dague, Susan, 15
Dahlia, 315, 317
Daisy Block, 393
Daisy Chain, 230
Daisy Fan, 292
Daisy Wheel, 293
Dakota Farmer; Letter O, 40; Ship at
    Sea, 118
Dakota Gold, 202
Dallas Star, 56
Dancing Cubes, 359
Dancing Pinwheels, 41
Dandelion Quilt, 315
A Dandy, 30
Dandy Quilt Block, 30
Danger Signals, 77
Daniel, Roy, 64
Daniel's Device, 307
Danish Star(s), 75, 216
Darting Birds, 14
Darting Minnows, 205
Darts and Squares, 70
David & Goliath, 194, 226
Dawn, 88
Day and Night, 179
Day Lily Garden, 314
Delaware, 313, 314
Delaware Crosspatch, 51
Delaware Sea Pines, 400
Delaware's Flagstones, 18
Delectable Appalachians, 137
Delectable Mountains, 136, 138, 423
Delectable Mountains Variation, 415,
    423
Democrat's Fancy, 317
Denver, 150
Depression, 128, 156, 214, 418
DePriest, Zelma; Beautiful Flower
    Garden, 170; Over the Waves, 224;
    President Truman, 224
Dervish Star, 133, 144
Des Moines, 137, 138, 229
Desert Blooms, 81, 396
Desert Flower, 350
Desert Rose, 185, 350, 383
Desert Sea Pines, 400
Desert Storm, 410
Design in Geometrics, 146
Dessert Plate, 298
Devil's Claw(s), 118, 137, 206
Devil's Dark Horse, 100
Devil's Footprints, 316
Devil's Puzzle, 101, 126, 284
Dewey, 126
Dewey Block, 59, 224
Dewey Dream Quilt, 197
Dewey, Margaret, 281
Dewey's Victory, 97
Diadem, 127
Diadem Star, 333, 345
Diagonal Paths, 146
Diagonal Square, 116
Diagonal Stripes, 268
Diamond & Star, 322
Diamond Bar, 119
Diamond Beauty Quilt, 364
Diamond Chain, 167, 180, 368
Diamond Charm Quilt, 420
Diamond Circle, 328
Diamond Cluster in a Frame, 331
Diamond Cross, 76, 166, 225
Diamond Cube, 356, 357
Diamond Design, 328, 342
Diamond Fan, 292
Diamond Field, 170, 358, 366
Diamond Head, 327
Diamond Hexagon, 364
Diamond in the Square, 94
Diamond Jubilee, 338, 425
Diamond Kaleidoscope, 82
Diamond Knot, 152
Diamond Nine Patch, 360
Diamond Panes, 200
Diamond Plaid Block, 57
Diamond Point, 107
Diamond Rainbow, 419
Diamond Ring, 121, 124, 127
Diamond Rose, 395
Diamond Rows, 352
Diamond Solitaire, 167, 175
Diamond Star, 23, 24, 83, 110, 124,
    136, 143, 180, 331, 344
Diamond String, 352
Diamond Stripe, 118, 134
Diamond Wedding Block, 334

Diamond(s), 169, 170, 186, 328, 341,
    342, 355
Diamonds and Arrow Points, 351, 354
Diamonds Are Forever, 215
Diamonds Galore, 110
Diamonds in the Corners, 85, 215
Diamonds of Hope, 216
Diana's Pride, 346
Diaper Pins, 381
Dilemma, 172
Dinah's Choice, 157
Dinah's Pride, 346
Dinner Plate, 277
Dirty Windows, 268, 269
Disappearing Blocks, 359
Disco, 372, 373
Dish of Fruit, 43
Disk, 162, 383, 387
Disney Fantasy, 208
Diversion Quilt, 114, 115
Divided Cross, 154
Divided Star, 329
Doe and Darts, 194, 210, 226
Does Double Duty, 201, 202
Dog Bone, 120, 177
Dog Quilt, 370
Dog Tooth Violet, 74, 340
Dog's Tooth, 417, 418
Dogwood, 142, 235, 330
Dogwood Bloom, 299
Dogwood Blossom(s), 204, 308
Dolly Madison Pattern, 350, 351
Dolly Madison's Star, 28, 55, 350
Dolly Madison's Workbox, 272, 275
Domino, 16, 193, 202
Domino and Square(s), 209
Domino and Star, 207
Domino Chain, 204
Domino Net, 67
Domino Square, 206
Doors and Windows, 214, 304
Doreen's Dutch Tiles, 62
Doris' Delight, 28
Dottie's Choice, 94
Double Anchor, 21
Double Arrow, 86
Double Aster, 150
Double Attic Windows, 70
Double Ax, 422
Double Ax Head, 422
Double Basket, 200
Double Bit Axe, 422
Double Braid, 416
Double Cross, 62, 71, 100, 119, 162
Double Diamonds, 416
Double Fans, 301
Double Four Patch, 100, 145
Double Friendship Knot, 234
Double Hour Glass, 14, 36
Double Irish Chain, 69, 203, 204
Double Irish Cross, 203
Double L, 49, 51, 301
Double Link, 217, 355
Double Monkey Wrench, 19
Double Necktie, 43, 53
Double Nine Patch, 11, 53
Double Pineapple, 348
Double Pinwheel, 47, 104, 147, 309
Double Pinwheel Whirl, 113
Double Poppy, 300
Double Pyramid(s), 13, 38, 55
Double Quartet, 104
Double R, 198
Double Rainbow, 294
Double Sawtooth, 193
Double Square(s), 79, 101, 126, 155
Double Star, 124, 144, 211, 220, 333,
    334, 336, 338, 340, 352, 354
Double Star Flower, 71
Double Star Quilt, 333
Double T, 16, 19, 29, 82
Double Triangle, 145
Double Tulip, 47, 146, 157, 395
Double Twist Star Block, 175
Double V, 191
Double Wedding Bands, 317
Double Wedding Ring, 286, 317
Double Windmill, 116, 150, 165
Double Wrench, 195
Double X('s), 13, 35, 99, 100, 105, 341
Double Z, 29, 108, 118, 141
Dove at the Crossroads, 229
Dove at the Window(s), 23, 38, 386
Dove of Peace, 35
Dover, 47
Dover Quilt Block, 47
Dove(s), 225, 268, 329, 331
Dove(s) in the Window, 39, 142, 226,
    228, 232, 236, 323, 329, 331
Dragon Fly, 110
Dragonfly, 88, 223
Dragonlance, 280
Dragon's Head, 19, 195

Dramatic Patch, 141
Dresden Basket, 385
Dresden Fan, 292
Dresden Flower, 307
Dresden Flower Quilt, 326
Dresden Plate, 267, 272, 307
Drive a Crooked Mile, 212
Drucilla's Delight, 168, 234
Druding, Susan C.; Black Cat Block,
    370; Cowboy Boot, 375
Drunkard's Path, 268, 306
Drunkard's Path Variation, 269, 282
Drunkard's Trail, 268, 269, 281
Dublin Chain, 54
Dublin Steps, 37
Duck, 372, 373
Duck and Ducklings, 131, 192, 200,
    201
Duck Creek Puzzle, 163
Duck Paddle, 232
Duck Tracks, 111
Duck Wheel, 173
Ducklings, 200
Duck's Foot, 199, 200
Duck's Foot in the Mud, 14, 59, 225,
    227
Ducks in a Pond, 366
Ducks in a Row, 371
Duke's Dilemma, 303
Dumbbell Block, 20
Duncan, Ruby Hinson; Ancient Castle,
    78; Crossed Arrows, 77; Dragonfly,
    88, 223; Pink Dogwood, 172
Durham, Sharyn, 304
Dusty Miller, 322
Dutch Dreams, 180
Dutch Mill, 18, 65, 185, 205
Dutch Nine Patch, 53
Dutch Puzzle, 61
Dutch Rose, 272, 333
Dutch Tile, 94, 353, 354, 355
Dutch Waterways, 208, 216
Dutch Windmill, 106, 272
Dutchman's Breeches, 139
Dutchman's Puzzle, 100, 139
Dutchman's Puzzle Variation, 52
Dutchman's Wheel, 100
Eagle, 194
Early American Wreath, 222
East and West, 279
Easter Lily, 226, 231
Easter Tide, 165
Eastern Star, 24, 328, 329, 352
Eastertide Quilt, 255
Easy Do, 205
Easy Quilt, 11
Easy Ways. 46, 76
Eccentric Star, 13, 72, 107, 333
Ecclesiastical, 368, 369
Economy, 78, 95, 103, 114
Economy Quilt Block, 162
Economy Star, 80
Eddystone Light, 19
Edna's Choice, 17
Effective Square, 205
Egg Basket, 390
Egyptian Lotus Flower, 391
Eight Cornered Box, 12
Eight Diamonds and a Star, 143, 321
Eight Hands Around, 20, 135, 161, 162
Eight patch grids, 92, 262
Eight Point All Over, 114
Eight Point Design, 24
Eight Point Fan, 290
Eight Point Snowflake, 150
Eight Pointed Broken Star, 333
Eight Point(ed) Star, 24, 28, 29, 30, 95,
    96, 123, 134, 328
Eight Points in a Square, 182
Eighteen patch grid, 246
Eisenhower Star, 350
Electric Fan(s), 95, 117, 147, 271, 274
Elephant, 373, 374, 375
Eleven patch grid, 240
Eliza's Star, 26
Ella's Star, 75, 127
Ellis Island Block, 221
Elsie's Favorite, 276, 304
Emerald & Topaz, 52
Emerald Block, 327
Emma C, 56
Empire Cross, 130
Empire Star, 103, 118
Empress, 292
Empty Spool(s), 15, 332
Enchanted Forest, 402
End of Day, 151
End of the Century Patchwork, 314
End of the Day, 113
End of the Road, 102

Endless Chain, 140, 275, 276, 317, 323,
    353, 363
Endless Ribbon, 42
Endless Squares, 84
Endless Stair(s), 17, 93
Endless Trail, 268
Endres, Mary Lou, 86
English Ivy, 44, 66
English T Box, 359
English Thistle, 66
English Wedding Ring, 197, 198
Enigma, 183, 247, 326
Enigma Star, 185
Ennis, Susie, 336
Entertaining Motions, 72
Envelope Motif, 96
Envelope Quilt, 101
Equiltblocks.com, 376
Equivalents, 312
Estelle's Choice, 276
Eternal Triangle, 137
Eva's Delight, 78
Eva's Garden, 35
Evelyne's Whirling Dust Storm, 273
Evening Flower, 393
Evening Quiet, 211
Evening Star, 72, 88, 95, 141, 342
Evening's Last, 47
Everglades, 311
Evergreen, 309, 399
Evergreen Tree, 400, 402
Everlasting Tree Block, 402
Everybody's Favorite, 58
Exea's Star, 75
Expanding Universe, 129
Expectations, 211
Exploding Star, 133
Explosion, 296
Eyes of Blue, 339
E-Z Quilt, 192
F Patchwork, 32
Faceted Crystals, 187
Fair and Square, 19, 94, 209
Fair Play, 50, 146, 267
Fairfield Processing Corp., 352
Fairy Star, 141
Fairy Tale, 81
Faithful Circle, 356
Falling Leaves, 88, 234
Falling Star, 330
Falling Timbers, 268, 269
Family Tree, 402
Fan, 267, 291, 292
Fan and Ring, 281
Fan Mill, 104
Fan of Friendship, 292
Fan of Many Colors, 290
Fan Patchwork, 290
Fan Quadrille, 289
Fan Quilt, 290
Fancy Dresden Plate, 274, 307
Fancy Fan, 292
Fancy Flowers, 227, 232
Fancy Foot, 158
Fancy Stripe, 103
Fanfare, 242
Fanny's Favorite, 121, 289, 317
Fanny's(ie's) Fan, 229, 291
Fantastic Patchwork, 412
Fantasy Bug, 374
Fantasy Flower, 80, 391
Fantasy World, 155
Far Horizons, 131
Far West, 58, 59
Farm and Fireside; Double Wrench, 195;
    Optical Sawtooth, 96
Farm Journal; Airplanes, 331; Aunt
    Patty's Favorite, 18; Beautiful
    Mosaic, 242; Brave World, 104;
    Broad Arrow, 46; Century of
    Progress, 186; Chinese Square, 241;
    Connecticut Star, 331; Conven-
    tional Rose, 219; Criss Cross, 165;
    Crosswords, 214; Darts and
    Squares, 70; Diamond Rows, 352;
    Doris' Delight, 28; Dove's Choice,
    94; Eight Pointed Star, 96; End of
    the Day, 113; Flying Crow, 24; Four-
    Four Time, 165; Framed X, 118;
    Good Luck, 118; Grand Right and
    Left, 136; Home Again, 52, 133;
    Hunt, 141; Idle Hours, 218; Indian
    Patch, 139; Kaleidoscope, 184;
    King's X, 118; Love in a Mist, 331;
    Memory Chain, 145; Michigan
    Favorite, 87; Mosaic, 336; Mush-
    rooms, 270; Nothing Wasted, 414;
    Octagon, 365; Octagon Star, 337;
    Old Italian Design, 127; Old Maid's
    Puzzle, 137; Pinwheel, 129; Pleasant
    Paths, 89; Pride of Holland, 142;
    Print and Plain, 184; Red, White and

Blue, 118; Repeat X, 70; Road to the White House, 36; Sergeant's Chevron, 242; Shining Hour, 211; Signs of Spring, 156; Squares upon Squares, 93; Star of the East, 117; Star Points, 131; Sunshiny Day, 117; Tea Box, 357; Tree of Paradise, 403; Turkey in the Straw, 58; Twelve Crowns, 34; Twenty-four Triangles, 30; Twin Darts, 178; Wheel, 297; Wheel of Destiny, 50; Will o the Wisp, 147; Windmill, 149
Farmer's Daughter, 193, 202
Farmer's Delight, 284
Farmer's Fields, 156, 157
Farmer's Puzzle, 53
Farmer's Wife, 147, 150, 218, 219, 280
The Farmer's Wife; Bride's Bouquet, 356, 357; Chip Basket, 385; May Basket, 384; Old Mill Design, 19; Primrose, 272; Rolling Stone, 192; Windmill design, 274
Father's Choice, 197
Father's Fancy, 223
Favorite, 351
Favorite of the Peruvians, 53, 101
Feather Star, 346, 347
Feather(ed) Edge(d )Star, 346, 347
Feathered LeMoyne Star, 347
Feathered Log Cabin, 236
Feathered Star, 295, 340, 348
Feathered Star of Bethlehem, 346
Feathered Star with Reel, 346
Feathered Variable Star, 346
Featheredge Stripe, 413
Federal Chain, 18, 215
Federal Square, 176
Fellowship, 132
Fence Posts, 17
Fence Rail, 413, 417
Fence Row Quilt, 12, 417
Fence Row Star, 336
Fenceworm, 413
Fernberry, 48
Ferris Wheel, 274, 293, 356, 357
Fields and Fences, 155, 241
Fields and Furrows, 425
Fifty Four Forty or Fight, 12, 28
Fig Leaf, 46
Fine Woven, 411
Fine Woven Patchwork, 413
Finnigan's Wake, 65
Fir Tree, 402
Fire Lily, 392, 397
Fireball, 273
Firecrackers and Skyrockets, 43
Fireside Visitor, 54
First Morning Rays, 178
Fish, 196, 331, 370, 371, 373
Fish Basket Block, 116
Fish Block, 331
Fish Border, 426
Fish Circle, 331
Fish in the Dish, 209
Fish Quilt, 340
Fish Tails (Tales), 120, 336
Fisherman's Reel, 19
Fishing Boats, 114
Fishscale, 421
Fitzgerald, Karen; Fitz's Phenomena, 182; Medieval Spirits, 282
5 X 5 Grid, 426
Five Cross(es), 110, 132, 323
Five Diamonds, 20
Five Lilies, 340
Five Patch, 54, 60, 149, 191
Five Patch Beauty, 352
Five patch grids, 190
Five Patch Star, 131, 192
Five Pointed Star, 349
Five Spot, 20
Five Square, 182
Five Stripes, 222
Five Woven Patchwork, 422
Flag In, Flag Out, 53
Flags, 410
Flags and Ships, 171
Flags (international signal), 433–434
Flagstones, 18, 59
Flaming Star, 123, 338
Flaming Sun, 98, 302
Flamingo's Flight, 172
Flash of Diamonds, 334
Flashing Star, 219
Flashing Windmills, 108
Flat Iron, 73
Flat Iron Patchwork, 413
Flatiron Patch, 43
Flight of Geese, 410
Flight of Swallows, 38
Flight of the Wild Goose, 317
Floating Clouds, 366

Flock, 105
Flock of Birds, 82
Flock of Geese, 13, 38, 105
Floral Bouquet, 290, 398
Floral Centerpiece, 148
Floral Frame, 417
Floral Strippie, 425
Flora's Favorite, 78
Florentine Diamond, 167
Florida, 352
Florida Forest, 405
Florida Star, 351
Flo's Fan, 289
Flower, 367
Flower and Fern, 78
Flower Basket, 162, 365, 382, 384, 385, 387, 388, 389, 390
Flower Basket Quilt Block, 386
Flower Bed, 117, 120, 155, 312
Flower Fields, 32
Flower Garden, 356, 357
Flower Garden Block, 355
Flower Garden Path, 38
Flower in a Pot, 394
Flower of Autumn, 291
Flower of Friendship, 398
Flower of Spring, 300
Flower of the Woods, 292
Flower Petals, 272, 276
Flower Pot (Flowerpot), 162, 165, 383, 384, 385, 386, 387, 388, 389, 392, 412
Flower Pot Quilt, 384
Flower Star, 312, 353
Flower Trail, 366
Flowering Cross, 154
Flowering Nine Patch, 85
Flowering Ribbon, 380
Flowering Snowball, 312
Flowers in a Basket, 386
Fluffy Patches, 155
Flutter Wheel, 44, 62
Flutterbye, 50
Fly, 104, 374
Fly Foot, 154
Flyaway Feathers, 60
Flyfoot, 101, 126
Flying Barn Swallows, 330
Flying Bat(s), 107, 329
Flying Birds, 13, 38, 202
Flying Checkers, 145
Flying Cloud(s), 97, 121, 122
Flying Cross, 62, 71
Flying Crow, 24
Flying Darts, 194, 226
Flying Dutchman, 44, 100, 148, 164
Flying Fish, 101, 146, 331, 371
Flying Geese, 13, 74, 86, 179, 192, 196, 205, 213, 218, 410
Flying Kite(s), 151, 153
Flying Leaves, 46
Flying Saucer, 321
Flying Shuttles, 37
Flying Square, 191
Flying Star(s), 198, 219, 329, 330
Flying Swallow(s), 330
Flying X, 44, 57, 104, 127
Flywheel, 103, 287
Folded Stars, 340
Follow the Leader, 39, 193
Fool's Puzzle, 118, 268, 269
Fool's Square, 191
Foot Prints in the Sands of Time, 37
Foot Stool, 198
Footbridge, 181
Fore and Aft, 273
Forest, 136
Forest for the Trees, 401
Forest Path(s), 119, 164
Forget Me Not, 332
Forgotten Star, 74, 110
Formal Elegance, 289
Formal Flower Bed, 273
Formal Garden, 13, 109, 200
Formosa Fan, 290
Formosa Tea Leaf, 331
Fort Knox, 65
Fort Sumter, 127
Fortune's Wheel, 284, 296
Forty Niner Quilt, 203
42nd Street, 176
Foundation Rose, 298, 311
Four & Star, 192
Four and Nine Patch, 18
Four and Twenty Blackbirds, 288
Four Baskets, 389
Four Birds, 220, 226, 331
Four Block Star, 335
Four Buds, 139, 289
4 X 4 grid, 92
Four Clowns, 55

Four Corner Puzzle, 127
Four Corners, 26, 27, 177
Four Crosses, 67
Four Crowns, 32, 33, 34
Four Darts, 194, 226
Four Diamonds, 152, 330
Four Doves, 331
Four E Block, 220
Four H, 17
Four Knaves, 95
Four Leaf Clover, 18, 104, 120, 167, 186, 206, 272, 275, 277, 314
Four Little Baskets, 389
Four Little Fans, 293
Four Mills, 81
Four Mills Variation, 81
Four O'Clock, 268
Four Part Striped Block, 17
Four Patch, 93, 94, 122, 273
Four Patch Chain, 87, 171
Four Patch Fox and Goose, 97
Four patch grids, 92
Four Patch Log Cabin, 237
Four Patch Scrap, 148
Four Point, 127
Four Pointed Star, 42, 123
Four Points, 127
Four Queens, 227
Four Seasons, 133
Four Ships Sailing, 22
Four Square Block with Diamonds, 216
Four Square(s), 38, 74, 165, 166, 177, 231
Four Star Block, 72
Four Stars, 334
Four Stars Patchwork, 334
Four Swallows, 331
Four T Square, 29
Four Triangles, 69
Four T's, 174
Four Vases, 375
Four Windmills, 415
Four Winds, 35, 167, 220, 281
Four X Quilt, 25
Four X's, 25
Four-Four Time, 165
"4H" Club Quilts, 73
4X Star, 192
Fowl Weather, 373
Fox and Geese, 99, 156, 200, 228, 299, 302, 336
Fox Chase, 117, 133
Frame, 34, 121
Frame with Diamonds, 150
Framed Cross, 88
Framed Squares, 34
Framed Star, 128, 222
Framed X, 118
Frank, Robert, 81
Frankfort, 130
Fredonia Cross, 314
Fred's Spool, 69
Free Trade Block, 135
Free Trade Patch, 135
French 4's, 195
French Bouquet, 356, 357
French Garden, 211
French Patchwork, 130, 192
French Rose Garden, 356, 357
French Star, 98, 297
Fresh Start, 97
Friday the 13th, 102
Friendly Hand, 40
Friendly Pleasures, 200
Friends & Family, 176
Friendship, 102, 125, 209, 310
Friendship Album Quilt, 94
Friendship Block, 34, 39, 202
Friendship Block in Diamonds, 151
Friendship Bouquet, 242
Friendship Chain, 85, 113, 132, 422
Friendship Circle, 309, 328
Friendship Fan, 290
Friendship Flowers, 391
Friendship Garden, 308
Friendship Hexagon, 350
Friendship Knot, 128, 281, 329
Friendship Links, 217
Friendship Medley Quilt, 167
Friendship Name Chain, 15
Friendship Patch, 360
Friendship Quilt, 39, 40, 60, 125, 126, 132, 136, 217, 272, 285, 357, 422
Friendship Ring, 267, 275, 285, 293, 317
Friendship Square, 235
Friendship Star, 12, 26, 27, 82, 143, 168
Friendship Wreath, 267, 329
Fringed Aster, 293

Fringed Square, 23
Frog, 373
Fruit Basket, 384, 385, 387
Full and Change of the Moon, 314
Full Blown Rose, 299
Full Blown Tulip, 165, 285
Full Moon, 281
Fun Patch, 139
Fundamental Nine Patch, 53
Galactica Star, 251
Galahad's Shield, 32
Galaxy, 32, 177, 182
Galaxy Star, 43
Gamecocks, 207
Gammell, Alice; Airplanes, 234; Hunter's Horns, 309; Open Box, 107; Pinwheel, 117; Rainbow, 81; Rainbow Square, 217, 219; Shooting Star, 68
Garber, Gail, 310
Garden Beauty, 300
Garden Bloom, 313
Garden Gazebo, 184
Garden Maze, 56, 65
Garden Mosaic, 153
Garden of Eden, 194, 195
Garden Patch, 28, 131
Garden Path(s), 24, 38, 54, 212, 288, 325
Garden Shadows, 116
Garden Spot, 296
Garden Square, 29
Garden Square Block, 173
Garden Walk, 28, 357
Gardener's Prize, 47, 232, 336
Garfield's Monument, 380
Garret Window, 15
Gate or H Quilt, 128
Gay Cosmos Quilt, 353
Gay Pinwheel, 108
Gay Scrap Quilt, 100
Gay Two Patch Quilt, 198
Geese in Flight, 122, 412
Gem Block, 124, 126
Gem Star, 144
Gemstones, 310, 328
General Sherman's Quilt, 418
Gentleman's Fancy, 30, 217, 222
Geocities.com; Apothecary Jar, 378; Books on a Shelf, 378; Candy Jar, 378; Mason Jar, 377; Ship in a Bottle Jar, 378; Turkey, 373; Wine Bottle, 377, 378
Geometric, 94, 114, 175
Geometric Album, 175
Geometric Block, 221
Geometric Garden, 222
Geometric Illusion, 125
Geometrical Star, 326
Geometrical Star Quilt Block, 164
Geometry, 180
Georgetown Circle(s), 149, 192, 197, 283
Georgetown Puzzle, 150
Georgia, 193
Georgia's Owl, 374
Ghost, 372
Ghost Walk, 269
Giant Dahlia, 308
Giddyap, 370
Gier, Arlene, 57
Giraffe, 372, 374
Girl's Joy, 164
Give and Take, 279
Gleaming Sun, 98
Glitter, Glitter, 155
Glitter Star, 343
Glory Be, 59
Glory Block, 359
Glory Design, 359
Glory Vine, 183
Glove Design, 170
Godey Design, 174, 177, 327
Godey's Lady's Book; Hexagon Patchwork, 362; Twist Patchwork, 324; Unnamed four patch, 124, 168
Godey's 1851, 359
God's Eye, 146
Goin' Home, 421
Going Home, 121, 215
Going to Chicago, 36, 100
Gold and Silver, 329
Gold Brick, 202, 231
Gold Nuggets, 115, 119
Golda, Gem Star, 55
Goldberg, Rhoda; Diaper Pins, 381; Garden Gazebo, 184
Golden Chains, 151

Golden Corn, 301
Golden Cubes, 359
Golden Gate(s), 38, 54, 247, 255
Golden Glow, 242, 298
Golden Hands; Saw Toothed Star, 177; Single Star, 177
Golden Memories, 125
Golden Royalty, 208
Golden Stairs, 16, 36, 166
Golden Steps, 53
Golden Wedding, 124
Golden Wedding Quilt, 110
Golden Wedding Ring, 280
Goldfish, 331
Golgotha, 38, 80
Good Cheer, 142
Good Enough, 131
Good Fortune, 49, 126, 312
Good Friends, 143
Good Luck, 44, 118
Good Luck Block, 18
Good Luck Token, 145
Goose and Goslings, 99
Goose Chase, 80
Goose Creek, 18
Goose in the Pond, 222
Goose Tracks, 56, 209, 228, 232
Gordian Knot, 241
Goshen Star, 144
Gothic Pattern, 154
Gothic Windows, 311
Grand Right and Left, 136
Granddaughter's Flower Garden, 364
Grandfather's Choice, 173
Grandma Dexter; Bachelor's Puzzle, 184; Bay Leaf, 275; Blazing Star, 170; Building Blocks, 100; Crazy Star, 140; Dervish Star, 133; Double Square, 79; Dresden Basket, 385; Flower Pot, 412; Jacob's Ladder, 160; Orange Peel, 299; Orchid Hemstitch, 230; Star Flower, 68; Sunrise, 283; Triangle Puzzle, 209; Triple Stripe, 73; Tulip Wheel, 314; Wedding Ring Chain, 317; Whirling Star, 186; White Hemstitch, 135; Windmill, 105
Grandma's Brooch, 232
Grandma's Choice, 121, 193, 202
Grandma's Dream, 247
Grandma's Fan, 310
Grandma's Favorite, 193, 293
Grandma's Hopscotch, 44
Grandma's Red and White, 103, 274, 359
Grandma's Spool, 116
Grandma's Square, 247
Grandma's Star, 28
Grandma's Surprise, 326
Grandma's Zig Zag, 424
Grandmother Clark; Arbor Window, 20; Aunt Mary's Squares, 211; Basket, 384; Bear's Paw, 228; Best Friend, 228; Cart Wheel, 278; Chinese Star, 317; Circle Design, 273; Colonial Bow Tie, 108; Colonial Garden, 357; Criss Cross (Crisscross), 163, 212; Double Hour Glass, 36; Drunkard's Trail, 269; Eccentric Star, 107, 333; Fancy Flowers, 232; Flower Pot, 165; Irish Chain, 274; Jack's Blocks, 202; Jewel, 163; Laurel Wreath, 24; Lover's Knot, 275; Modern Star, 24; Modern Tulip, 229; Mosaic, 321, 328; Pilot Wheel, 278, 299; Pinwheel, 151; Pussy in the Corner, 16; Rocky Road to Dublin, 269; Sunburst, 297; Water Mill (Watermill), 62, 155; Water Wheel, 105; Windmill Star, 124; Window Squares, 186; Yo-Yo, 425
Grandmother Percy's Puzzle, 195
Grandmother Short's Quilt, 18
Grandmother's Basket, 383, 386
Grandmother's Brooch of Love, 309
Grandmother's Cartwheel, 367
Grandmother's Choice, 72, 86, 130, 192, 217, 274, 304, 341
Grandmother's Cross, 131, 194
Grandmother's Dream, 58, 77, 321
Grandmother's Engagement Ring, 303, 317
Grandmother's Fan, 289, 290, 291, 292
Grandmother's Fancy, 152
Grandmother's Favorite, 128, 317
Grandmother's Flower Basket, 353
Grandmother's Flower Garden, 356, 357, 358
Grandmother's Own, 42, 161, 177, 202
Grandmother's Pinwheel, 138, 210
Grandmother's Pride, 20, 292
Grandmother's Prize, 300

Grandmother's Prize Puzzle, 145
Grandmother's Quilt, 300
Grandmother's Rose Garden, 356, 357
Grandmother's Scrap Quilt, 290
Grandmother's Star, 361
Grandmother's Star Garden, 358
Grandmother's Sunbonnet, 267
Grandmother's Sunburst, 267
Grandmother's Tulip, 282
Granny's Choice, 115
Granny's Favorite, 209, 220
Granny's Flower Garden, 230
Grape Basket, 384
Grape Vine, 210
Gray Goose, 118
Great Circle Quilt, 309, 386
Grecian, 19
Grecian Cross, 279
Grecian Design, 19
Grecian Square, 19, 176, 186, 271
Grecian Star, 267, 316, 317
Greek Cross, 19, 65, 194, 197, 228, 309
Greek Square, 19, 186, 271, 274
Green Cross, 89, 163
Green Mountain Star, 155
Green River, 15
Gretchen, 49
Grist Mill, 276, 303
Guam Quilt Block, 199
Guarino, Crea, 166
Guide Post, 341, 342
Guiding Star, 42, 64
Guthrie, 235
Gypsy Trail, 301
H Quilt, 21
H Square Quilt, 73
Haight, Ernie; Carousel, 327; Patio Tiles, 18
Hail Storm, 22
Hairpin Catcher, 93, 418
Half Moon Block, 294
Hall, Carrie, 123
Hallelujah Hall, 409
Halley's Comet, 202, 348
Halpin, Linda, 362
Hand, 236
Hand of Friendship, 225
Hand Weave, 52, 53
Handcraft, 53
Hands All Around, 281, 317, 330
Handwoven, 53
Handy Andy, 30, 192, 194, 198, 200, 205
Hanging Basket, 383, 386
Hanging Diamond(s), 242, 328
Happy Home, 24
Happy Hunting Grounds, 75
Happy Memories, 369
Happy New Year, 66
Happy Thought, 269
Harbor View, 156
Hard Times Block, 47
Harlequin Star, 74, 247
Harmony Square, 206
Harrisburg, 82
Harrisburg Quilt Block, 76
Harrison, 38
Harrison Quilt, 38
Harrison Rose, 38
Harry's Star, 111
Hartford, 213
Hartford Quilt Block, 211
Harvest Chain, 422
Harvest Grapes, 379
Harvest Home, 147
Harvest Moon, 308
Harvest Star, 334, 343
Harvest Sun, 284, 290, 297, 332, 343, 344
Hatch, Sandra; Leo's Lion, 82; Medieval Castle, 170
Hawaii, 321, 332
Hawks in Flight, 419
Hawley, Madeline, 360
Hay's Corner, 44
Hazel Valley Crossroads, 278
Hazy Daisy, 132
Heart of the Home, 280
Heart Quilt, 311
Heart Spangled Star, 116
*Hearth & Home*; Aesthetic Quilt, 343; Alabama, 54; Alaska, 156; Atlanta, 215; Augusta, 46; Aunt Addie's Album, 98; Aunt Eliza's Star, 25; Austin, 96; Banded Cross Block, 199; Basket, 385; Basket Patch, 383; Belle of West Virginia, 130; Cedars of Lebanon, 46; Centennial Tree, 400; Charleston Quilt block, 77; Churn Dasher, 192, 199; Circle and Star, 277; Circle Four, 77; Circular Saw, 288; Columbia, 82; Columbus, Ohio, 336; Completed Square, 263; Connecticut, 107; Corn and Beans, 67; Counter Charm, 186; Criss Cross, 218; Crossroads to Bachelor's Hall, 271; Crossroads to Jericho, 21; Delaware, 314; Denver, 150; Des Moines, 137, 138, 229; Diadem Star, 333; Diamond Star, 331; Dinah's Choice, 157; Double Cross, 62, 71, 100; Double Star, 124, 211, 333, 334; Double T, 19; Dover, 47; Duck's Foot, 200; Economy, 103; Effective Square, 205; Electric Fan, 95; Ella's Star, 75; Empire Star, 118; Endless Stairs, 17, 93; Estelle's Choice, 276; Everybody's Favorite, 58; Fair Play, 50; Fence Row Star, 336; Florida, 352; Flower Basket, 384, 388; Flower Pot, 162; Flying Cross, 62, 71; Four Square, 231; Frankfort, 130; Friendship Quilt, 40; Friendship Star, 26; Fruit Basket, 384, 387; Georgia, 193; Good Enough, 131; Grandmother Percy's Puzzle, 195; Guam Quilt Block, 199; Guthrie, 235; Happy Home, 24; Hartford Quilt Block, 211; Hawaii, 332; Hearth & Home Quilt, 202; Hexagonal Stars, 350; Honolulu, 63, 315; Honolulu Quilt Block, 65; Idaho Beauty, 137; Illinois, 19; Irish Chain, 288; Island Creek Hustler, 324; Jackson, 332; Jefferson City, 21; Kansas, 32; Klondike Star, 63; Lady of the Lake, 187; Lansing, 274; Lincoln, 222; Lincoln Quilt Block, 217; Lincoln's Cabin Home, 407; Little Basket, 384; Log Cabin Star, 336; Louisiana, 104; Maryland, 222; Mississippi, 40; Mississippi Daisy, 139; Missouri Quilt Block, 335; Montana Star, 353; Moon and Star, 300; Mrs. Dewey's Choice, 56; Mrs. Fay's Favorite Friendship Block, 38; Nashville, 272; Nebraska, 251; New Hampshire, 352; New Snowball, 18, 59; Nine Patch Star, 199; North Dakota, 124; Octagonal Star, 333; Ohio, 167; Oklahoma, 278; Pennsylvania, 49; Pennsylvania Tree, 152; Pennsylvania Wheel Quilt, 297; Pharlemina's Favorite, 77; Philippine Islands Quilt Block, 79; Pierre, 347; Pole Star, 331; Prairie Sunrise, 200; Pretty Patchwork, 360; Progressive, 300; Queen of May, 56; Rail Fence, 231; Raleigh Quilt Block, 306; Red Cross, 197; Rhode Island, 60; Right Hand of Fellowship, 26; Ring Around the Rosy, 168; Road to Damascus, 160; Rocky Mountain Chain, 193; Rosemary, 88; Sacramento Quilt Block, 199; Salem, 27; Sewing Circle, 205; Shifting Cubes, 359; Shoemaker's Puzzle, 107; Simple Design, 67; Simplex Star, 11, 12; Simplicity, 114; South Carolina, 183; South Dakota, 64; Southern Star, 295; Springfield, 143; On the Square, 54; Square Up, 112; St. Paul, 235; Star, 317; Star Bed Quilt, 328, 329; Star of Montana, 353; Star of the Night, 184; Star of West Virginia, 299; State of California, 335, 338; State of Iowa, 76; State of Maine, 274; State of Massachusetts, 78; State of Michigan, 234; State of Nebraska, 236, 251; State of New Jersey, 71; State of Oklahoma, 326; State of Oregon, 225; State of Virginia, 31; Stony Point Quilt Block, 78; Tennessee, 329; Tippecanoe, 407; Topeka, 297; True Blue, 19; Utah, 313; Virginia, 31; Wagon Wheel, 287; Wandering Lover, 38; Wandering Path of the Wilderness, 310; Washington, 84; Washington Snowball, 277; Waves of the Ocean, 137; West Virginia, 130; Wheel of Fortune, 284; Workbasket, 309; Wyoming, 298; Wyoming Quilt Block, 310
Hearth & Home Quilt, 199, 202
Heart(s), 51, 67, 107, 215, 272
Hearts and Darts, 315
Hearts and Diamonds, 277
Hearts and Flowers, 272, 281
Hearts and Gizzards, 272
Heart's Desire, 86
Heart's Seal, 53, 101
Heather Square, 61, 85
Heavenly Bodies, 68, 87, 328
Heavenly Problem, 206
Heavenly Puzzle, 206
Heavenly Stars, 173, 332
Heavenly Steps, 359
Hedgerow, 207
Hedgework, 179
Heirloom Pillow, 425
Heirloom Quilt, 309
Helena, 326, 336, 338
Helping Hands, 173
Hemstitch, 225
Hen and Her Chicks, 53
Henry of the West, 24, 111
Hen(s) and Chickens, 19, 195, 200, 225
Her Sparkling Jewels, 124
Herald Square, 300
Herbston, Dorothy; Apple Cores, 305; Autumn Spinning Star, 305
Heritage Quilt, 341
Hero's Crown, 314
Hero's Welcome, 221
Herringbone, 410, 411
Hex Stars, 298
Hexacat, 360
Hexagon and Diamonds, 361
Hexagon and Triangles, 367
Hexagon Beauty, 325, 351
Hexagon Border, 424
Hexagon Flower Basket, 358
Hexagon Flower Block, 367
Hexagon Patchwork, 362
Hexagon Snowflake, 355
Hexagon Waves, 368
Hexagon(al), 351, 354, 355, 356, 357, 362
Hexagon(al) Star(s), 350, 354, 358, 366, 368
Hexagons and Diamonds, 364
Hexagons and Flowers, 353
Hexagon-Scrap Pattern, 357
Hickory Leaf, 288
Hicks Flower Basket, 387
Hidden Flower, 267
Hidden Star, 19, 340, 352
Hide and Seek, 110, 169
High Noon, 173
Hill and Craig, 212
Hill and Hollow, 217
Hill(s) and Valley, 47, 420
Hills of Vermont, 195
Hillside Village, 409
Hippopotamus, 373
His.com; Basket, 390; Bloom, 392; Bud, 391; Lighthouse, 406; Train Station, 406
Historic Oak Leaf, 44
Hit or Miss, 93, 217, 357
Hither and Yon, 107, 145
H.M. Designs; Animals Stood By, 214; Away in a Manger, 230; Child is Born, 166; No Room at the Inn, 18; North Star, 183; Path to Bethlehem, 166; Rejoice, 214; Shepherd's Watch, 86; Star Above the Stable, 86; Three Kings' Journey, 51
Hobby Horse, 381
Hobby Nook, 150
Hobson's Kiss, 164
Hole in the Barn Door, 12, 19, 59, 195
Holiday Bells, 162
Holiday Crossing, 75
Holiday Crossroads, 162
Holland Magic, 65
Holland Mill, 205
Hollywood Star, 231
Home Again, 52, 133
Home Art Studios; Arrowhead Quilt, 143; Aunt Dinah's Star, 341; Burgoyne's Puzzle, 223; Bursting Star, 30; Cockcomb, 338; Cosmos, 353; Cross Roads, 309; Dolly Madison's Star, 350; Double Star, 338; Doves, 329; Evergreen, 309; Flying Star(s), 329; Gay Cosmos Quilt, 353; Grandmother's Pride, 20; Hearts and Diamonds, 277; Lafayette Orange Peel, 275; Lonesome Pine, 398; Mariner's Compass, 123; Mary's Fan, 290; Noonday Lily, 299; North Star, 329; Oriental Splendor, 352; Orphan Star, 333; Pansy Quilt, 397; Poinsettia Quilt, 364; Pride of Texas, 343; Rainbow Star Quilt, 316; Sirius Star Quilt, 369; Squared Star, 85; Star Bouquet Quilt, 350; Star Fish, 338; Star of Stars, 343; True Lover's Knot, 276; Wheel of Life, 287; Zodiac Stars, 352
Home Circle, 195
Home Crown, 176
Home Is Where the House Is, 408
Home Is Where the Quilt Is, 408
Home Sweet Home, 408
Home Treasure, 127, 132, 135
Homecoming, 328
Homemaker, 271
Homespun, 56, 223
Homespun Block, 242
Homeward Bound, 16
Homeward Star, 67
Honey Bee, 285
Honey Dish, 195
Honeybee, 72
Honeycomb, 356, 357, 362
Honeycomb Patch, 363
Honeycomb Quilt, 425
Honeycomb Variation, 325
Honeymoon, 26
Honeymoon Cottage, 407
Honey's Choice, 193
Honolulu, 63, 315
Honolulu Quilt Block, 65
Hoosier Wonder, 64
Hope of Hartford, 194
Hopes and Wishes, 75
Hopscotch, 23, 112
Horizon Star, 232
Hosannah, 140
Houndstooth, 139
Houndstooth Scrap Patch, 139
Hour Glass(s) (Hourglass), 11, 12, 37, 38, 68, 95, 99, 101, 102, 103, 294, 296, 347
House Contest Block, 406
House on Hill, 407, 408
House that Jack Built, 73
House with Chimney, 408
House with Fence, 409
*Household Arts*, 237
*Household Journal*; Airplane, 195; Crossed Square, 229; Double Basket, 200; Double Four Patch, 145; Duck Paddle, 232; Four Point, 127; Hexagonal, 354; Hour Glass, 347; Semi-Octagon, 147; Whirligig, 101
*Household Magazine*; Blue Birds Flying, 228; Capital T, 29; Patchwork Fantasy, 222; Paths to Piece, 125; Squared Circle, 293; Tall Pine Trees, 398; Whirling Wheel, 294
House(s), 405, 407, 408, 422
Housewife, 68, 145
Housewife Quilt Block, 23
Housewife's Dream, 57, 224
Hovering Birds, 100
Hovering Hawks, 37, 100
H-Square, 11
Hull's Victory, 128
Hummingbird(s), 45, 141, 299, 323, 325
Hunt, 141
Hunter's Horns, 309
Hunter's Star, 331
I Do, 168
I Excel, 136
I Wish You Well, 269
Ice Cream Bowl, 375
Ice Cream Cone, 213, 287, 375, 425
Ickis, Marguerite, 211
Idaho, 124, 210
Idaho Beauty, 137
Idaho Star, 71, 328
Idle Hours, 218
Idle Moments, 115, 134
Iejodie.com, 376
Illinois, 19
Illinois Corn & Beans, 136
Illinois Road, 77
Illinois Snowball, 279, 302
Illinois Star, 263, 311
Illinois Turkey Track, 225
Images, 157
Imari Plate, 322
Imperial Fan, 289, 316
Imperial T, 29, 30
Improved Four Patch, 178
Improved Nine Patch, 18, 175, 277, 302
In Narcissus Motif, 86
In Red and White, 247
In the Arbor, 157
Independence Square, 55
Indian Arrow, 76
Indian Arrowhead, 119, 331
Indian Canoes, 110
Indian Chief, 139
Indian Corn, 248
Indian Design, 199, 227
Indian Emblem, 101
Indian Hammer, 19
Indian Hatchet(s), 61, 125, 138
Indian Head, 38
Indian Maize, 164, 174
Indian Mat(s), 32, 45, 48, 67
Indian Meadow, 114, 194
Indian Paint Brush, 89, 170, 297
Indian Patch, 139, 220, 271
Indian Plume, 35
Indian Puzzle, 23, 40
Indian Raid, 267, 300
Indian Squares, 210
Indian Star, 98, 110
Indian Summer, 289, 303
Indian Sunburst, 302
Indian Tomahawk, 61
Indian Trail, Old, 201
Indian Trail(s), 136, 164
Indian Turnip, 394
Indian Wedding Ring, 317
Indiana, 271
*Indiana Farmer's Guide*, 398
Indiana Puzzle, 13, 40, 135, 268
Indiana Redbud, 403
Indianapolis, 62
*Indianapolis Star*, 72
Indianapolis, Star of, 350
Inner City, 367
Inspiration, 161, 367
Interlaced Blocks, 241
Interlocked Squares, 17
Interlocked Star, 354, 368
Interlocking O's, 121
Interlocking Squares, 129
International signal flag patterns, 433–434
Interwoven, 53
Interwoven Puzzle, 125, 185
Iowa, 251
Iowa Barns, 407
Iowa Star, 123
Iris, 392, 397
Iris Rainbow, 392, 395
Irish Chain, 93, 121, 157, 203, 242, 274, 284, 288
Irish Chain Hint, 204
Irish Chain Patch, 83
Irish Plaid, 164
Irish Puzzle, 136, 164
Irish Spring, 179
Iron Cross, 103
Islam, 115
Island Creek Hustler, 324
Italian Beauty, 228
IXL, 136
Jack and Six, 13
Jack in the Box, 192, 201
Jack in the Pulpit, 126, 127, 394
Jackknife, 26
Jack's Blocks, 192, 202
Jack's Chain, 356
Jack's Delight, 27
Jack's House, 407
Jacks on Six, 13
Jackson, 332
Jackson Quilt Block, 59
Jackson Star, 332
Jacob's Coat, 355
Jacob's Ladder, 35, 36, 85, 100, 145, 160, 350, 359
Jacques in the Boat, 288
Jagged Edge, 138
James, Michael, 118
Jamestown Square, 174
Jane's Favorite, 144
Jan's Bicentennial Star, 235
January Thaw, 27
Japanese Basket, 389
Japanese Fan, 290
Japanese Friendship Block, 201
Japanese Garden(s), 209, 375
Japanese Lantern, 47, 379
Japanese Poppy, 208
Japanese Scrap Quilt, 42
Jaywalker, 126
Jcquilts.freeservers.com, 376
Jefferson City, 21
Jericho, 126
Jericho, Ruins of, 152
Jericho Walls, 209
Jersey Tulip, 162, 383, 387
Jet Stream, 69, 153
Jewel, 21, 105, 124, 163, 299, 321
Jewel Box, 116, 122, 204
Jewel Boxes, 74
Jewel Star, 165
Jewels in a Frame, 333
Jig Jog Puzzle, 135
Jigsaw, 422
Jigsaw Puzzle, 270
Jim Dandy, 120

Jinx Star, 285
Joan's Doll Quilt, 19
Job's Patience, 288
Job's Tears, 199, 275
Job's Trouble Quilt Block, 325
Job's Trouble(s), 110, 323
Job's Troubles, 357
Jockey Cap, 276
John F. Kennedy Star, 165
Johnny(ie) Round the Corner, 39, 197
John's Favorite, 194
John's Original Quilt Block, 130
John's Pinwheel, 151
Johnson, Victoria, 85
Johnson-Srebro, Nancy, 215
Joining Star, 96, 347
Jonathan Livingston Seagull, 83
Jorgenson, Sharlene, 83
Josephine Knot, 267
Joseph's Coat, 54, 61, 81, 204, 276, 282, 285, 327, 356, 360, 417
Joseph's Necktie, 70
Joshua's Turn, 217
Journey Home, 63
Journey to California, 128, 165
Joy Bells, 20
Joyce's Mystery Block, 34
Joy's Delight, 206
Jubilee, 159
Judy in Arabia, 28
Judy's Star, 120
July 4th, 99
July's Summer Sky, 74
Jupiter Star, 141
Jupiter's Moons, 277, 303
Just Enough Tulips, 395
Kaleidoscope, 79, 110, 123, 147, 151, 184, 218, 251, 303, 324, 328, 330, 354
Kaleidoscope Quilt, 141
Kaleidoscope Star, 335, 343
Kankakee Checkers, 73
Kansas, 32
Kansas Beauty, 130, 275
*Kansas City Star*; Air Craft Quilt, 376; Air Port, 216; Airplane Motif, 331; Airport, 231; Album, 20, 128, 132; All Over Pattern of Octagons, 323; Anna's Pride, 313; Apple Leaf, 16; Arkansas Crossroads, 105; Arkansas Snowflake, 41, 124; Arkansas Star, 30, 41, 124; Around the World, 281; Arrangement of Small Pieces, 38; Arrow Star, 328, 329; Arrowhead Star, 24; Arrowhead(s), 143, 352; Autograph Quilt, 84; Basket, 386; Basket of Bright Flowers, 387, 392; Basket of Diamonds, 162, 387; Basket of Oranges, 384; Basket Quilt in Triangles, 386; Basket Weave Friendship Quilt, 132; Bell, 375, 381; Block of Many Triangles, 148; Blockade, 102; Bluebell, 310; Bowtie in Pink and White, 151; Bridal Stairway Patchwork Block, 416; Bridge Quilt, 277; Bridle Path, 72; Broken Circle, 278; Broken Crown, 288; Broken Square, 276; Broken Stone, 279, 281; Broken Sugar Bowl, 36; Broken Window (2), 33; Buckeye Beauty, 100; Builder's Blocks, 45, 354; Butterfly at the Crossroads, 191; Buzz Saw, 297; Calico Puzzle, 11; Caps for Witches and Dunces, 159; Car Wheel, 297; Car Wheel Quilt, 277; Carrie Nation Quilt, 122; Casement Window, 131; Cedars of Lebanon, 48; Century of Progress, 42; Chain Quilt, 269; Cherry Basket, 387; Cheyenne, 107; Chinese Puzzle, 323; Chinese Quilt Block, 39; Chips and Whetstones, 331; Chisholm Trail, 96; Christmas Star, 23, 329; Christmas Tree, 400, 405; Circle in a Frame, 94; Circle Petal in a Square, 305; Circle Saw, 287, 333; Circle Upon Circle, 277; Circular Saw, 293; Cluster of Lilies, 228; Coffee Cups, 375; Cog Block, 96; Cog Wheels, 93; Comfort Quilt, 60; Compass, 271; Contrary Husband, 107; Contrary Wife, 14; Corner Posts, 202; Cornerstone, 22; Cotton Boll, 109, 110; Coverlet in Jewel Tones, 142; Cowboy Star, 139; Crazy Tile, 351, 368; Cross and Chains, 21; Cross is Mother's Choice, 109; Crown of Thorns, 302; Crow's Nest, 195; Crystal Star, 31, 96; Cup and Saucer, 375; Cups and Saucers, 19, 24; Cypress, 101; Danish Stars, 216; Depression, 128, 156, 418; Design for Patriotism, 156; Design in Geometrics, 146; Dessert Plate, 298; Dewey, Margaret, 281; Diamond Circle, 328; Diamonds and Arrow Points, 354; Diamonds in the Corners, 85, 215; Diversion Quilt, 114, 115; Dogwood Blossoms, 308; Dolly Madison Pattern, 350; Double Anchor, 21; Double Arrow, 86; Double Square, 101; Double V, 191; Dove in the Window, 232; Dragon Fly, 110; Drunkard's Trail, 281; Dutch Tile, 354, 3554444; Economy, 114; Eight Point Snowflake, 150; Eight Points in a Square, 182; Electric Fan, 271; End of the Road, 102; English Ivy, 66; Envelope Motif, 96; Envelope Quilt, 101; Evelyne's Whirling Dust Storm, 273; Evening Star, 88; E-Z Quilt, 192; Fair and Square, 19, 94; Fan of Many Colors, 290; Fan Quilt, 290; Fence Row Quilt, 12, 417; Fifty-Four Forty or Fight, 28; Flag In, Flag Out, 53; Flash of Diamonds, 334; Flower Basket, 162, 387; Flower Garden Block, 355; Flower of Autumn, 291; Flower Pot, 385, 387; Flowering Nine Patch, 85; Flowering Ribbon, 380; Flowers in a Basket, 386; Flying Bats, 107; Flying Colors, 99; Flying Fish, 331; Flying Kite, 151; Flying X, 104; Fool's Square, 191; Formal Flower Bed, 273; Formosa Tea Leaf, 331; Four Buds, 289; Four Corner Puzzle, 127; Four Crowns, 34; Four H, 17; Four Leaf Clover, 275, 277; Four Little Fans, 293; Four Part Striped Block, 17; Four Patch Fox and Goose, 97; Four Pointed Star, 42; Four Vases, 375; Four Winds, 281; "4H" Club Quilts, 73; Frame with Diamonds, 150; Free Trade, 177; Friday the 13th, 102; Friendship Block in Diamonds, 151; Friendship Chain, 85; Friendship Knot, 281, 329; Friendship Name Chain, 15; Friendship Quilt, 39, 125, 132, 285, 422; Friendship Ring, 275; Friendship Star, 168; Full Moon, 281; Garden Walk, 28; Gate or H Quilt, 128; Glory Block, 359; Goblet Quilt, 375; Goldfish, 331; Grandma's Brooch, 232; Grandma's Hopscotch, 44; Grandmother's Basket, 383; Grandmother's Favorite, 128; Grandmother's Tulip, 282; Great Circle Quilt, 386; Greek Cross, 197, 228; Guiding Star, 42; H Square Quilt, 73; Hands All Around, 281; Hazel Valley Crossroads, 278; Heart of the Home, 280; Her Sparkling Jewels, 124; Hexagon Star, 350; Hicks Flower Basket, 387; Hidden Star, 352; Hobby Nook, 150; Honey Bee, 285; Hopscotch, 23; Hour Glass, 101; Ice Cream Cone, 287; Imperial Fan, 316; Imperial T, 30; Indian Canoes, 110; Indian Emblem, 101; Indian Head, 38; Indian Puzzle, 23; Indian Star, 98, 110; Indian Trails, 136; Indiana Puzzle, 40; Indianapolis Star, 350; Interlocked Squares, 17; Interlocking Squares, 129; IXL, 136; Jack in the Box, 192; Jackson Star, 332; Jacob's Ladder, 85; Japanese Garden, 375; Japanese Lantern, 379; Jewel, 124; Jigsaw Puzzle, 270; Jinx Star, 285; Joseph's Coat, 282; Journey to California, 128, 165; July 4th, 99; Kansas Dust Storm, 232; Kansas Star, 31; King's Crown, 95; Kitchen Woodbox, 68; Kite Quilt, 41, 124; Lace Edge Quilt, 417; Leaves and Flowers, 182; Lend and Borrow, 114; Letha's Electric Fan, 310; Liberty Star, 329; Light and Dark, 117; Light and Shadows, 131; Little Boy's Breeches (Britches), 139; Little Girls' Star, 350; London Stairs, 17, 93; Lone Star of Paradise, 333; Long Pointed Star, 149; Lost Goslin', 12; Lost Paradise, 281, 287, 309; Love in a Tangle, 274; Love Ring, 272; Maple Leaf, 117; Marble, 269; Marble Floor, 11; May Basket, 384, 385; Mayflowers, 101; Merry-Go-Round, 137; Midget Necktie, 151; Milkmaid's Star, 110; Missouri Daisy, 168; Missouri Morning Star, 285; Missouri Star, 331; Missouri Wonder, 321; Modern Broken Dish, 20; Modern Envelope, 105; Mona's Choice, 57; Moon is New, 287; Morning Star, 329, 351; Morning Sun, 30; Mother's Choice, 109, 168; Mother's Prayers, 350; Mountain Peak, 127; Mountain Road, 380; Mowing Machine, 413; My Country for Loyalty, 226; My Graduation Class Ring, 296; My Little Girl's Skirt, 280; Name is Hesper, 144, 287; In Narcissus Motif, 86; Necktie, 121; Nest and Fledgling, 192; New Album, 46; New Four Pointer, 53; North Star, 111, 177; Nosegay, 43; Oak Grove Star, 296; Oak Grove Star Quilt Block, 149; Ocean Wave, 75; Ocean Wave of Many Prints, 137; Octagon, 11; Octagons and Squares, 113; Oil Fields of Oklahoma, 285; Oklahoma Square Dance, 115; Oklahoma Sunburst, 295; Ola's Quilt, 280; Old English Wedding Ring, 197; Old Indian Trail, 63; Old Maid's Puzzle, 99; Oriole Window, 293; Our Country, 227; Owl, 39; Ozark Diamond, 351; Ozark Star, 355; Ozark Sunflower, 294; Ozark Tile Pattern, 323; Ozark Trail, 207; Parallelogram, 337; Parquetry for a Quilt, 151; Patchwork Cushion Top, 247; Patriotic Star, 329; Pattern of Chinese Origin, 354; Peggy Anne's Special, 224, 302; Petal Circle in a Square, 297; Picket Fence, 413; Picture Frames, 84; Pieced Sunflower, 294, 311; Pig Pen, 267; Pine Tree, 404; Pinwheel, 12, 100; Pinwheel Quilt, 20; Pointed Ovals, 281; Pointing Star, 350; Points and Petals, 314; Posey Quilt, 315; Prickly Pear, 225; Quilt Mosaic, 23; Quilt of Variety, 110; Quilter's Fan, 281, 287; Quint Five Quilt, 110; Radio Windmill, 51; Rail Fence Quilt, 413; Railroad Crossing, 85; Rambler, 136; Red and White Crisscross, 146; Red Cross, 323; Red Cross Quilt, 122, 131; Red, White and Blue, 323; Reminiscent of the Wedding Ring, 275; Remnant Ovals, 275; Ribbon Block, 109; Rising Sun, 285; Road to Oklahoma, 108; Roads to Berlin, 107; Rolling Stone, 282; Rope and Anchor, 54; Rope Strands, 413; Rosalia's Flower Garden, 356; Rose Dream, 276; Rosebud, 304; Rosebud Quilt, 285; Rosette of Points, 167; Royal Diamonds, 331; Sage Bud, 60; Sail Boat, 117; Sailboat Block, 15; Sailboat Oklahoma, 114; Salute to Colors, 132; Salute to Loyalty, 93; Sandhills Star, 23; Sapphire Quilt Block, 75; Scottish Cross, 148; Scrap Bag, 222; Scrap Zigzag, 117; Sea Shells on Beach, 421; Seasons, 109; Secret Drawer, 148; Shaded Trail, 24; Sheep Fold Quilt, 93; Shepherd's Crossing, 177; Sickle, 99; Signature Friendship Quilt, 116; Signature Quilt, 107; Signatures for Golden Memories, 125; Silent Star, 25; Silver and Gold, 329; Single Wedding Ring, 192; Six Pointed Star, 352; Small Triangles, 101; Snail's Trail, 106; Snow Crystals, 332, 351; Snowball, 311; Soldier Boy, 375; Solomon's Temple, 211; Southern Star, 328, 329; Southside Star, 85; Spider Web, 141, 153, 329, 352; Spindles and Stripes, 133; Spring Beauty, 136; Square and Half Square, 40; Square and Points, 95; Square and Triangles, 150; Square(s) and Diamond(s), 25, 150; Star, 328; Star and Box Quilt, 354; Star and Crescent, 167; Star Center in French Bouquet, 351; Star Chain, 317; Star Garden, 350; Star of Alamo, 42; Star of Bethlehem, 333; Star of Four Points, 123; Star of Hope, 331; Star Sapphire, 277; Stardust, 111; Starry Heavens, 329; Stars and Squares, 161; Star's Exhibition Home Quilt Block Pattern, 405; Stepping Stones, 141, 153; Storm at Sea, 124; String Quilt, 84; Striped Plain Quilt, 48, 125; Sugar Loaf, 73; Summer Star, 143; Sun Rays Quilt, 28; Sunbeam Block, 85; Sunflower, 303; Sunlight and Shadows, 98; Swallows in the Window, 330; Swastika, 100; Swords and Plowshares, 232; Terrapin, 269; Texas Pointer, 288; This and That, 95, 114, 148; Thousand Stars Quilt, 151; Three-in-One Quilt, 336; Thrifty, 16; Thrifty Wife, 148; Triangles and Squares, 101, 114; Triplet, 12; True Lover's Buggy Wheel, 278; Tulip Pattern, 285; Tulip Quilt, 285; Turtle on a Quilt, 269; Twelve Triangles, 95; Twinkle, Twinkle Little Star, 328, 329; Very Old Sawtooth, 346; Victory Quilt, 117, 146; Wagon Wheels, 281; Wandering Flower, 133; Wedding Ring, 197; Wheel of Fortune, 327; Wheel of Mystery, 272; Whirlaround, 47; Whirligig, 105; Whirling Blade, 101; Whirling Diamonds, 359; Whirling Five Patch, 201; Whirling Pinwheel, 41, 282; Whirling Star, 52, 330; White Lily, 392; White Square Quilt, 228; Wild Goose Chase, 414; Winding Blade(s), 101, 269, 329; Windmill, 147; Windmill Star, 124; Winged Four Patch, 98; Winged Nine Patch, 142; Winged Star, 333; Wings in a Whirl, 12; Wishing Ring, 50; Wood Lily, 38; World Fair Quilt, 151; Yellow Square, 94; A Young Man's Invention, 301
Kansas Dugout, 125, 178, 326
Kansas Dust Storm, 232
Kansas Star, 31, 141
Kansas Sunflower, 293, 295, 296, 298, 353
Kansas Sunrise, 305
Kansas Sunshine, 290
Kansas Troubles, 31, 136, 164, 275
Kansas Troubles Variation, 176
Kansas Whirligig, 100
Kathy's Ramble, 104
Katie's Favorite, 132
Kelly's Block, 37
Kentucky, 350
Kentucky Chain, 125, 173
Kentucky Crossroads, 81, 84
Kentucky Patch, 58
Kentucky's Twinkling Star, 337
Key West, 162
Key West Beauty, 162
Khin, U, 336
Kicks, 194
Kiman, Nancy, 291
Kindergarten Block, 13
King David's Crown, 196, 206, 293
King of the Mountain, 208
King Solomon's Temple, 211
King Tut, 317
King Tut's Crown, 269
King's Choice, 34
King's Cross, 103, 147, 154
King's Crown, 64, 69, 95, 167, 194, 197, 207, 301, 302, 330
King's Highway, 77, 243
King's Star, 136, 220, 330
King's X, 110
Kiowa Cross, 79
Kitchen Woodbox, 50, 68, 185, 379
Kite, 49, 65, 110, 223, 422
Kite Quilt, 41, 124
Kite String Quilt, 325
Kite Variation, 308
Kites in Air, 410
Kite's Tail, 216, 414
Kitty Corner, 58, 120
Klondike Star, 63
Knickerbocker Star, 333
Kobayashi, Kei, 221
Kratovil, Debby, 406
Kyser, Pat Flynn, 344
L Quilt, 33
Labyrinth, 214
Lace Edge Quilt, 417, 418
Laced Star, 171
Lacy Latticework, 226
Ladders and Building Blocks, 234
Ladies' Aid, 22
Ladies Aid Album, 46
Ladies Art Company; Air Castle, 26; Album, 222; Album Quilt, 222; All Kinds, 82; Arabic Lattice, 51; Arkansas Traveller, 44; Art Square, 94; At the Square, 12; Aunt Eliza's Star, 26; Aunt Sukey's Choice, 23; Baby Bunting, 267; Bachelor's Puzzle, 206; Barrister's Block, 137; Baseball, 273; Basket, 382; Basket of Lilies, 388; Bear's Foot, 225; Bear's Paw, 136; Beautiful Star, 133; Beggar Block, 55; Blackford's Beauty, 141; Blazing Star, 334; Blindman's Fancy, 138; Block Patchwork, 356, 357; Box, 13, 107; Boxed T, 14, 45; Boy's Nonsense, 27; Braced Star, 26; Brickwork Quilt, 418; Burnham Square, 59; Cactus Blossom Patch, 279; Cake Stand, 385; California Star, 346; Capital T, 29; Carpenter's Square, 241; Cats and Mice, 38, 45; Charm, 64, 420; Cherry Basket, 384, 386; Chicago Star, 56; Children's Delight, 191; Chimney Swallows, 332; Chrysanthemum, 267; Clown, 193; Cluster of Stars, 63; Coarse Woven Patchwork, 422; Cockleburr, 311; Cog Wheels, 297; Columbia, 355; Columbia Puzzle, 170; Columbian Star, 57; Combination Star, 25; Compass, 275; Corn and Beans, 41; Coxey's Camp, 152; Crazy House, 192, 194; Cross and Crown, 213; Cross and Star, 206; Crossed Canoes, 110; Crosses and Losses, 99; Crow's Foot, 156; Cube Lattice, 134; Cube Work, 357; Cut Glass Dish, 38; Devil's Claws, 137; Diamond Cube, 357; Diamond Star, 23; Diamond(s), 341, 342; Disk, 383, 387; Domino and Square, 209; Double Necktie, 43; Double Squares, 126; Double X, 13, 35, 99; Dove in the Window, 228; Dover Quilt Block, 47; Duck and Ducklings, 201; Dutch Mill, 65, 205; Dutch Rose, 333; Dutchman's Puzzle, 100; Ecclesiastical, 368; Eight Hands Around, 135, 161; Eight Point Design, 24; Eight Pointed Star, 123, 328, 329; Enigma, 326; Evening Star, 95; Fair Play, 267; Fan, 291; Fan Patchwork, 290; Fanny's Fan, 229; Fantastic Patchwork, 412; Farmer's Daughter, 193; Fine Woven Patchwork, 413; Five Patch, 54, 60; Five Pointed Star, 349; Five Stripes, 222; Five Woven Patchwork, 422; Flagstones, 18, 59; Flower Basket, 383; Flutter Wheel, 44, 62; Flying Bat, 329; Flying Dutchman, 44; Flying Square, 191; Flying Swallow, 330; Fool's Puzzle, 269; Fortune's Wheel, 296; Four E Block, 220; Four Little Baskets, 389; Four Points, 127; Four Stars Patchwork, 334; 4X Star, 192; Fox and Geese, 299, 302; Garfield's Monument, 380; Gentleman's Fancy, 30; Girl's Joy, 164; Golden Gates, 247; Goose in the Pond, 222; Goose Tracks, 228; Grandmother's Choice, 192; Grandmother's Dream, 77, 321; Grandmother's Own, 177; Grape Basket, 384; Grecian Design, 19; Greek Cross, 65, 309; Greek Square, 274; Hand Weave, 52; Hands All Around, 330; Handy Andy, 198; Hearts and Gizzards, 272; Hens and Chickens, 225; Hexagon, 351; Hickory Leaf, 288; Hour Glass, 95; House that Jack Built, 73; Ice Cream Bowl, 375; Imperial T, 29; Indian Hatchets, 125; Interlaced Blocks, 241; Iowa Star, 123; Irish Puzzle, 164; Jack's House, 407; Joining Star, 347; Joseph's Coat, 204; Joseph's Necktie, 70; Kansas Troubles, 136; King's Crown, 330; Ladies' Aid, 22; Ladies Aid Album, 46; Ladies' Delight, 205; Ladies' Fancy, 277; Ladies Wreath, 101; Leap Frog, 206; Letter X, 12; Lily Quilt Pattern, 138, 229; Lincoln's Platform, 225; Linton, 205; Little Red House, 407; Live Oak, 398; Lock and Chain, 70; Lone Star, 343; Lost Ship, 15; Magic Circle, 65; Maltese Cross, 103; Malvina's Chain, 15; Mayflower, 47; Memory Block, 130; Merry Kite, 38; Milky Way, 40; Milwaukee's Own, 316; Miss Jackson, 332; Moon and Stars, 274; Morning Patch, 121, 177; Morning Star, 31; Mosaic, 111, 172; Mosaic #5, 127; Mosaic #18, 135; Mosaic #11, 98; Mosaic #15, 102, 104; Mosaic #4, 125; Mosaic #9, 104, 111; Mosaic #19, 96, 104; Mosaic #1, 126; Mosaic #17, 112; Mosaic #6, 113; Mosaic #10, 96; Mosaic #13, 98; Mosaic #3, 119;

Mosaic #20, 93; Mosaic #21, 103; Mosaic #22, 118; Mosaic #2, 156; Mother's Fancy, 72, 89; Mrs. Morgan's Choice, 41; Navajo, 32; Necktie, 108; New Album, 94; New Star, 206, 248; Nine Patch, 93; Nonsense, 27; Nonsuch, 53; Noon Day Lily, 392; Ocean Waves, 195, 418; Octagon, 323; Odd Fellows, 205; Odd Fellows Chain, 135; Odd Patchwork, 223; Odd Scraps Patchwork, 192, 197; Odds and Ends, 18; Oklahoma Boomer, 61; Old Colony Star, 363; Old Homestead, 407; Old Maid's Ramble, 136, 145; Old Star, 221; Old Tippecanoe, 108; Orange Peel, 276; Patience Corners, 103, 175, 359; Persian, 235, 241; Philadelphia Patch, 302, 349; Philippines, 348; Pin Cushion, 275; Pine Tree, 405; Pinwheel Square, 195; Pinwheel Star, 343; Practical Orchard, 12; Premium Star, 221; Priscilla, 110, 124; Propeller, 194; Puss in the Corner, 109; Puzzle Tile, 323; Pyrotechnics, 297; Rainbow, 284; Red Cross, 192; Ribbon Border, 109; Ribbon Square, 236; Ribbon Star, 98; Right and Left, 95; Rising Sun, 287; Road to California, 153; Rockingham's Beauty, 334; Rocky Road to California, 37; Rocky Road to Kansas, 110, 124; Rolling Star, 334; Rolling Stone, 40; Roman Cross, 132; Rose Album, 294; Rosebud, 45; Royal, 279; Royal Japanese Vase, 392; Sarah's Favorite, 132; Savannah Beautiful Star, 274, 316; Sawtooth Patchwork, 20; Seven Stars, 357; Shoo Fly, 59; Shoofly, 12; Shooting Star, 111; Simple Design, 202, 218; Sister's Choice, 192; Slashed Album, 107; Slashed Star, 284; Snail's Trail, 165; Snowball(s), 269, 277; Snowflake, 127; Spools, 43; Springfield Patch, 143; St. Louis Star, 210; Star A, 63; Star and Chains, 128; Star and Cross, 211; Star of Many Points, 24; Star of the West, 284, 349; Star Puzzle, 97; Starlight, 212; Stars and Cubes, 334; Stars and Squares, 134; Stars upon Star, 343; Steps to the Altar, 43; Stonemason's Puzzle, 225; Stripe Squares, 220; Sunflower, 294, 317; Sunshine, 137; Susannah, 94; Suspension Bridge, 303; Swastika Patch, 53, 71; Sweet Gum Leaf, 45; Swing in the Center, 20; T Quilt, 41, 67; Tangled Garters, 56; Tangled Lines, 84; Tassel Plant, 62; Tea Leaf, 275; Teddy's Choice, 139; Texas Flower, 16; Texas Star, 350; Texas Tears, 82; Tile Patchwork, 323; T-Quartette, 45; Tree of Paradise, 403; Triangle Puzzle, 72; Triangles and Stripes, 162; Triangular Triangle(s), 170, 413; Tulip Lady Fingers, 43; Tulip(s) in a Vase, 388; Tumbler, 412; Turnstile, 104; Twin Sisters, 105; Twinkling Star(s), 331, 346; Twist and Turn, 412; Twisted Rope, 324; Union, 34; Union Star, 300; Variegated Diamonds, 359; V-Block, 161; Venetian Design, 321, 328; Vice President's Quilt, 235; Walk Around, 332, 341; Washington Puzzle, 51; Watered Ribbon & Border, 109; W.C.T.U., 63; Wedding Ring, 192; Whale Block, 276; Wheel of Fortune, 180; Wild Goose Chase, 412; Winding Ways, 272; Wings, 279; Wonder of the World, 268; World's Fair, 110; World's Fair Block, 93; World's Fair Puzzle, 137; Wyoming Patch, 299; X-Quisite, 106
Ladies Beautiful Star, 277
Ladies' Chain, 327
*Ladies' Circle Patchwork Quilts*; Aunt Em's Basket, 387; Blue Fields Variation, 161; Caesar's Crown, 300; Carousel, 327; Cornhusker's Star, 175; Dragonlance, 280; Fish Circle, 331; Four Ships Sailing, 22; Indian Sunburst, 302; No Name four patch, 121, 136; Ozark Puzzle, 270; Patio Tiles, 18; Prisms, 64; Rock Wall, 353; Star and Block, 176; Starfish, 331; Starry Compass, 283; Stars and Stripes, 167; Times Remembered, 199; Twinkling Star, 230; Voiliers, 52
Ladies' Delight, 58, 205
Ladies' Fancy, 277
*Ladies' Home Journal*; Flower Pot, 386; Lady Finger, 303, 317; Large Star, 187; Lotus, 317; Maple Leaf Design, 46; Plain Block, 93; Star Diamond, 347; Triangle Star, 347; Windmill, 44
Ladies Wreath, 101
Lady Bug, 372
Lady Finger, 303, 317
Lady Finger and Sunflower, 303
Lady in the White House, 72
Lady of the Lake, 32, 187, 193, 198, 235, 286
Lady of the White House, 72
Lafayette Orange Peel, 275, 276
Lamp, 379
Land of Lincoln, 120
Land's End, 164
Lansing, 168, 274
Large Star, 187
Large Star Pattern, 34
LaRocca, Jane, 235
Lasting Blossoms, 204
Lattice, 110
Lattice and Square, 127
Lattice Block, 323, 326
Lattice Fan, 291
Lattice for Maypole Dance, 410
Lattice Square, 185
Lattice Star, 67
Lattice Strips, 185
Lattice Weave, 247
Latticework, 173
Laurel Wreath, 23, 24, 141
Lawyer's Puzzle, 137
Lazy Daisy, 272, 342
Leaf Star, 236
Leafy Basket, 385
Leap Frog, 206
Leavenworth Nine Patch, 230
Leavenworth Star, 208
Leaves and Flowers, 182
Left and Right, 140
Lehigh Maze, 61
LeJet, 376
Lemon Star, 163, 328, 329, 357
LeMoyne Star, 328, 329, 334, 344
LeMoyne Star & Windmill, 328, 329
Lena's Choice, 155
Lena's Magic Circles, 312
Lend and Borrow, 114
Leo's Lion, 82
Letha's Electric Fan, 310
Let's Get Pinned, 381
Letter L, 95
Letter O, 40
Letter patterns, 429–430
Letter X, 12
Levison, Leslie, 280
Lewis and Clark, 207
Libby, Paula, 283
Liberty Star, 116, 329
Light and Dark, 117, 276
Light and Dark design, 337
Light and Shadows, 115, 131
Lighthouse, 212, 405, 406, 408
Lightning, 116, 157, 418
Lightning in the Hills, 35
Lightning Streak, 417. *See also* Streak of Lightning
Lightning Strips, 418
Lilies, 118
Lillian's Favorite, 275
Lily, 130, 390
Lily Corners, 232
Lily of the Field, 159, 216
Lily of the Valley, 393, 397
Lily Palm, 28
Lily Pond, 201, 229
Lily Pool, 241, 395
Lily Quilt Pattern, 138, 229, 397
Lincoln, 222
Lincoln Quilt, 286, 343
Lincoln Quilt Block, 217
Lincoln's Cabin Home, 407
Lincoln's Hat, 255
Lincoln's Platform, 19, 225
Lindbergh's Night Flight, 377
Lindy's Plane, 32, 152
Linked Diamonds, 167
Linked Squares, 314
Linking Blocks, 102
Linoleum, 38
Linton, 205
Linton Pathway, 151
Lisa's Choice, 177
Litfin, Connie, 387
Little Basket, 384
Little Beech Tree, 400, 404
Little Boy's Breeches (Britches), 139
Little Cedar Tree, 107
Little Giant, 142
Little Girls' Star, 350
Little Lost Sailboat, 101
Little Penguins, 180
Little Red House, 407
Little Rock, 63
Little Rock Block, 42
Little Saw Tooth, 114
Little Ship of Dreams, 101
Little Star, 329, 337
Little Turtle in a Box, 371
Live Oak, 398
Lock and Chain, 70
Locked Star, 163
Lockport Batting Company; Chief, 49; Dog Tooth Violet, 340; Dogwood, 330; Lincoln Quilt, 343
Log Cabin, 227, 236, 405, 407
Log Cabin Diamond, 342
Log Cabin Heart, 237
Log Cabin Hexagon, 237
Log Cabin Rosebud, 396
Log Cabin Sherbet, 236
Log Cabin Star, 236, 330, 336
Loh, Vickie, 141
Lola, 178
London Bridge, 276
London Roads, 54, 55
London Square, 32, 73
London Stairs, 17, 93
Lone Eagle, 376
Lone Eagle Airplane, 377
Lone Star, 24, 69, 77, 88, 96, 161, 343, 359
Lone Star of Paradise, 333
Lone Star of Texas, 359
Lone Tree, 66
Lone X, 226
Lonesome Pine, 398
Long Pointed Star, 149
Loop the Loop, 66
Lori's Star, 171
Lost and Found, 66
Lost Children, 78
Lost Goslin', 12
Lost Paradise, 281, 287, 309
Lost Ship(s), 15, 31, 80, 137
Lotus, 317
Lotus Block, 230
Lotus Blossom, 317
Lotus Star, 330
Louisiana, 104
Louisiana Star, 329
Love and Kisses, 43
Love Chain, 215
Love Doves, 171
Love Entangled, 64, 71
Love in a Mist, 23, 331
Love in a Tangle, 57, 274
Love Knot, 15, 19, 45
Love Ring, 270, 272
Lovely Patchwork, 110
Lover's Bowtie, 276
Lover's Chain, 279
Lover's Knot, 72, 88, 272, 275, 276, 417
Lover's Lane, 31
Lover's Links, 279
Lover's Locket, 70
Lover's Quarrel, 279
Love's Chain, 281
Love's Dream, 74, 173
Lucinda's Star, 346
Lucky Block, 18
Lucky Clover, 43
Lucky Knot, 158
Lucky Pieces, 136
Lucky Quilt, 18
Lucky Star, 123, 167, 321
Lucy's Four and Nine, 21
Ludlow's Favorite, 19
Ma Perkin's Flower Garden, 351
Macaroon Patchwork, 119
Mace Head, 285
MacKenzie's Square, 169
MacLean, Margaret, 376
Madame X, 236
Madison Block, 350
Magee, Jan, 224
Maggie's Double Pinwheel, 45
Magic Carpet, 184
Magic Circle, 65, 121, 276
Magic Cross Design, 97
Magic Squares, 76, 174, 420
Magic Triangles, 114
Magnolia, 69
Magnolia Block, 219
Magnolia Blossom, 299
Magnolia Bud, 390
Magnolia Leaf, 14
Maiden's Delight, 164
Main Street, 57
Maine Woods, 209
Malone, Maggie; Art Deco Tulip, 172; Autumn Trails, 15; Blouses, 381; Boxed Squares, 229; Carnival, 293; Celtic Plaid, 84; Checkerboard Star, 136; Choices, 153; Collector's Plate on Tripod, 378; Commons, 221; Community Center, 174; Cosmic Cube, 172; Daisy Wheel, 293; Diamond Kaleidoscope, 82; Diamonds Are Forever, 215; Drive a Crooked Mile, 212; Expanding Universe, 129; Fantasy Flower, 80; Four Mills Variation, 81; Kaleidoscope, 303; Labyrinth, 214; Morning Glory, 78; My Mistake, 48; Neighborhoods, 164; Night Sky, 70; Patio Garden, 122; Platter, 378; Pumpkin, 379; Rainbow Star, 123; Rhode Island Red, 174; Rolling Star, 324; Scrap Basket, 229; Shooting Star, 133; Trail of Diamonds, 350; Twist Around, 202; Walled City, 222; Wild Rose, 332
Maltese Cross, 31, 103, 141, 195, 229, 231, 269, 309
Maltese Cross Block, 187
Maltese Cross Pineapple Variation, 237
Maltese Star, 29
Malvina's Chain, 15
Man in the Moon, 316
Manila Quilt Design, 165
Many Pointed Star, 24
Maple Leaf, 14, 16, 34, 43, 45, 117, 334, 354
Maple Leaf and Rose, 338
Maple Leaf Design, 46
Marathon, 124
Marble, 269
Marble Floor, 11
March Winds, 339
Mare's Nest, 205
Margaret's Choice Quilt Block, 97
Marietta Blockhouse, 230
Marigold Garden, 89, 219
Mariner's Compass, 123, 283, 284, 296, 297, 301, 308
Marion's Choice, 192
Mariposa Lily, 392, 397
Market Basket, 388
Market Square, 180
Marquee, 426
Martha, 276
Martha Washington Cherry Basket, 388
Martha Washington Star, 97
Martha Washington's Flower Garden, 358
Martha Washington's Rose Garden, 357
Martha's Basket, 388
Martha's Choice, 159, 272
Martin, Judy; All That Jazz, 120; Aloha, 338; Baker's Dozen, 221; Block & Tackle, 186; Bonny Scotland, 117; Calgary Stampede, 231; China Doll, 221; Diamond Jubilee, 338; Ellis Island Block, 221; Eyes of Blue, 339; Father's Fancy, 223; Feathered Log Cabin, 236; Hero's Welcome, 221; Hollywood Star, 231; Judy's Star, 120; Kitty Corner, 120; Land of Lincoln, 120; March Winds, 339; Motown Sounds, 339; November Nights, 221; Santa Fe Trail, 198; September Star, 338; Sunday Best, 221; Taos Treasure, 231; Texas Two Step, 236; Wheat Field, 158; Wild Irish Rose, 186; Windy City, 171; Writer's Block, 339
Mary Moore's Double Irish Chain, 203
Mary Strickler's Quilt, 301
Mary Tenny Gray Travel Club Patch, 212
Maryland, 222
Maryland Beauty, 86
Mary's Basket, 388
Mary's Block, 30
Mary's Choice, 272
Mary's Fan, 290
Mary's Squares, 147
Mason Jar, 377
Massachusetts, 70
Massachusetts Priscilla, 110
Mathieson, Judy, 287
Maud's Album Block, 109
Maud's Album Quilt, 127
May Basket, 384, 385, 387
May Time Quilt, 174
Mayflower Quilt, 348
Mayflower(s), 29, 47, 101, 161, 183, 314
Mayor's Garden, 20
Maypole Dance, 116
*McCall's*; Eastern Star, 328; Pinwheel Quilt, 327
*McCall's Country Quilting*, 404
McDougall String Quilt, 79
McKim, Ruby, 19, 373, 407
McMillion, Betty, 79
Meadow Flower(s), 321, 322, 396
Meadow Lily, 392, 397
Mechanical Blocks, 323
Medallion Square, 75
Medieval Castle, 170
Medieval Mosaic, 60
Medieval Spirits, 282
Medieval Walls, 60
Meese, Donna, 235
Meeting House Square, 57
Melissa's Pinwheel Log Cabin, 237
Melodie's Baby Bunting Quilt, 282
Melon Patch, 272, 276
Melon Patch Quilt, 276
Members.tripod.com, 378
Memory, 33
Memory Block(s), 130, 134, 200, 215
Memory Chain, 145, 324, 325
Memory Fruit, 150
Memory Wreath, 134, 192, 197
Merry Kite, 38
Merry-Go-Round, 22, 120, 137, 150, 273, 356, 357
Meteor, 111
Meteor Quilt, 111
Mexican Block, 222
Mexican Cross, 80, 210, 215
Mexican Rose, 211, 215
Mexican Siesta, 89
Mexican Star, 60, 211, 215
Michael, Ursula; Candy Drops, 304; Christmas Star, 339
Michael's Joke, 180
Michigan Beauty, 24, 141
Michigan Favorite, 87
Michigan Star, 332, 345
Midget Necktie, 151
Midnight Star Block, 25
Midnight Stars, 117
Midsummer Garden, 159
Midsummer Night, 327
Migrating Geese, 414
Migration, 115, 416, 421
Migration South, 235
Milady's Fan, 291
Milkmaid's Star, 110
Milky Way, 40, 210, 237
Mill and Stars, 41, 133
Mill Wheel (Millwheel), 104, 113, 197, 269, 271, 276
Miller's Daughter, 159, 196
Millie's Quilt, 168
Milly's Favorite, 114, 130
Milwaukee's Own, 316
Mineral Wells, 138
Minnesota, 208, 214
Miss Henrietta, 372
Miss Jackson, 59, 241, 332
Miss Nancy, 247
Missionary Baptist, 83
Mississippi, 40, 139
Mississippi Daisy, 139
Mississippi Oak Leaves, 316
Mississippi Oakleaf, 279
Mississippi Star, 154
Missouri, 335
Missouri Beauty, 312, 317
Missouri Corn Field, 71
Missouri Daisy, 168, 321
Missouri Memories, 389
Missouri Morning Star, 285
Missouri Puzzle, 59, 222, 247
Missouri Quilt Block, 335
Missouri River Valley, 191
Missouri Star, 134, 154, 331
Missouri Trouble, 313
Missouri Windmill(s), 145, 147, 160
Missouri Wonder, 321
Missouri's Gateway Star, 183
Mixed Emotions, 288
Mixed T, 16, 54
Modern Blocks, 217
Modern Broken Dish, 20
Modern Daisy, 224
Modern Envelope, 105
Modern Flame, 71
*Modern Priscilla*; Gentleman's Fancy, 222; Sunburst, 297
Modern Star, 24, 335
Modern Tulip, 229, 341
Modernistic California Poppy, 391, 393

Modernistic Pansy, 393
Modernistic Rose, 393
Modernistic Star, 353
Modernistic Trumpet Vine, 393
Modernized Poppy, 300
Mohawk Trail, 267
Mollies Choice, 54
Mona and Monette, 207
Mona's Choice, 57
Monastery Windows, 112
Monkey, 374
Monkey Puzzle, 275
Monkey Wrench, 40, 135, 195, 201, 280
Monkey Wrench Variation, 64
Monk's Puzzle, 368
Montana, 55
Montana Maze, 233
Montana Star, 353
Monterey, 155
Montgomery, 62
Montpelier Quilt Block, 20
Moon and Star(s), 97, 274, 300
Moon and Swastika, 315
Moon Block, 294
Moon in Eclipse, 286
Moon is New, 287
Moon Over the Mountain, 279
Moore, Harriet; Bows and Paper, 129; Candy Canes, 87; Cookies and Milk, 47; Expectations, 211; Holiday Crossroads, 162; Reindeer on the Roof, 181; Reminiscences, 144; Season's Joy, 181; Snowy Morning, 126; Stuffed Stockings, 153; Through the Looking Glass, 285; Tracks in the Snow, 150; Wishing Star, 284; Yuletide, 78
Moore, Nanette, 170
Moore, Pat, 363
Moorish Mosaic, 87, 336
Mor, Tristan Audrey, 325
Morning, 39
Morning Glory, 78, 272, 308, 356, 357, 396
Morning Patch, 121, 177
Morning Star, 26, 27, 31, 141, 147, 181, 185, 217, 312, 314, 325, 327, 328, 329, 333, 343, 347, 350, 351, 353, 354, 356
Morning Sun, 30
Mosaic, 24, 25, 44, 45, 111, 172, 321, 328, 336, 357, 362
Mosaic #8, 106
Mosaic #18, 135
Mosaic #11, 98
Mosaic #15, 104
Mosaic #5, 113, 127
Mosaic #4, 113, 125
Mosaic #9, 104, 111
Mosaic #19, 96, 104
Mosaic #1, 107, 111, 126
Mosaic #7, 96
Mosaic #17, 112
Mosaic #6, 103, 112, 113
Mosaic #16, 102
Mosaic #10, 96, 112
Mosaic #13, 98
Mosaic #3, 119, 126
Mosaic #12, 102, 111
Mosaic #20, 93
Mosaic #21, 103
Mosaic #22, 118
Mosaic #2, 127, 156
Mosaic Block (17 grid), 247
Mosaic Patchwork #4, 323
Mosaic Patchwork #3, 323
Mosaic Rose, 229
Mosaic Squares, 82
Mother's Choice, 23, 32, 109, 168, 333
Mother's Delight, 123
Mother's Dilemma, 174
Mother's Dream, 58, 99
Mother's Fan, 291
Mother's Fancy, 72, 89
Mother's Fancy Star, 72
Mother's Favorite, 126
Mother's Morning, 172
Mother's Oddity, 422
Mother's Own, 220, 228
Mother's Prayers, 350
Motown Sounds, 339
Mound Builders, 53, 101
Mountain Homespun, 222, 251
Mountain Lily, 392, 397
Mountain Maze, 233
Mountain Meadows, 143
Mountain Memories, 415
Mountain Mist; Bluebirds for Happiness, 331; Country Lanes, 224; Crazy Pieces, 165; Disappearing Blocks, 359; Double Wedding Bands, 317; Fan Quadrille, 289; Grandmother's Engagement Ring, 303, 317; Guide Post, 341; Homespun, 223; New York Beauty, 316; Nine Patch Nose Gay, 219; Pig's Tail, 178; Shadow Trail, 341; Star of Alabama, 341; Star of the Bluegrass, 329; Target, 327; Three Irish Chains, 203; Tree of Paradise, 405; Twinkling Star, 351; Virginia Reel, 178
Mountain Paths, 241
Mountain Peak(s), 127, 288
Mountain Pink, 288, 310
Mountain Road, 380
Mountain Star, 167, 351
Mountain Trail, 308
Mountain View, 308
Mountains and Valleys, 417
Mouse, 370
Mousel, Mary J., 332
Moving Fans & Fast Pinwheels, 160
Mowing Machine, 413
Moynihan, Mary Lee; Banded Triangle, 129; Center Ring, 304; Daniel's Device, 307; Fantasy World, 155; Flying Kites, 153; Parasol, 172; Parasol Variations, 172; Ribbons, 234; Victorian Square, 43
Moynihan's Crusade, 163
Mr. Roosevelt's Necktie, 94
Mrs. Anderson's Favorite, 206
Mrs. Anderson's Quilt, 195
Mrs. Brown's Choice, 20
Mrs. Bryan's Choice, 21
Mrs. Cleveland's Choice, 66
Mrs. Cleveland's Favorite, 66
*Mrs. Danner*; Album, 130; Alice's Favorite, 214; Bailey Nine Patch, 277; Circle Upon Circle, 275; Crowfoot, 137; Double Pyramids, 38; Double Tulip, 395; Dove at the Windows, 23; Fredonia Cross, 314; Geometric Garden, 222; Hex Stars, 298; Illinois Turkey Track, 225; Mayflower Quilt, 348; Mrs. Anderson's Quilt, 195; Mrs. Wolf's Red Beauty, 222; Nine Patch T, 63; Red, White and Blue, 303; Rolling Square, 195; Ship, 114; Spice Pinks, 315; Springtime Blossoms, 272; Star of the East, 333; Wishing Ring, 195
Mrs. Dewey's Choice, 56
Mrs. Fay's Favorite Friendship Block, 38
Mrs. Hardy's Hanging Basket, 386
Mrs. Hoover's Colonial Quilt, 204
Mrs. Jones Favorite, 198
Mrs. Keller's Nine Patch, 194, 221
Mrs. Lloyd's Favorite, 162, 170
Mrs. Miller's Favorite, 40
Mrs. Morgan's Choice, 41
Mrs. Roosevelt's Favorite, 20
Mrs. Smith's Favorite, 141
Mrs. Taft's Choice, 100
Mrs. Wilson's Favorite, 232
Mrs. Wolf's Red Beauty, 222
Mueller, Joyce, 216
Mug, 378
Multiple Square, 191
Mushroom Shell, 421
Mushrooms, 270
Mutual Benefit, 275
My Country, 336
My Country for Loyalty, 226
My Favorite, 121, 127
My Graduation Class Ring, 296
My Little Girl's Skirt, 280
My Mistake, 48
My Mother's Star, 337
My Tulip Garden, 397
Mystery Block, 39
Mystery Flower Garden, 25
Mystic Emblem, 140
Mystic Maze, 150, 211, 321
Name is Hesper, 144, 287
Name on Each Friendship Block, 202
Name Unknown. *See also* No Name; Unnamed; curve pattern, 272, 273, 286; five patch, 224, 232; four patch, 126, 138, 156, 173; nine patch, 54, 58; octagons, 324
Nameless Star, 96
Nancy's Fancy, 130
Narcissus, 295
Nashville, 272
Natchez Star, 172
National Star, 337, 341
Nativity Star, 220
Nautilus, 164
Nauvoo Lattice, 170, 216
Navajo, 32, 129
Nebraska, 251, 280
Nebraska Windmill, 255
Nebraskaland, 235
Necktie, 108, 121, 148
Necktie Variation, 180
Needle Craft Supply; Crossroads, 153; Joy's Delight, 206; Mrs. Anderson's Favorite, 206; Mrs. Smith's Favorite, 141; Rosette, 398
*Needlecraft Magazine*; Black Diamond, 333; Broken Dishes, 39, 126; Four Leaf Clover, 120; Friendship Fan, 290; Mother's Choice, 333; New Wedding Ring, 317; Pineys, 335; Posies Round the Square, 315; Walled City, 89
Neighborhood(s), 164, 169
Nellie's Choice, 204
Nell's Swinging Star, 66
Nelson's Victory, 105
Nest and Fledgling, 192
Nevada, 63, 272
New Album, 46, 94
New Barrister's Block, 137
New Cross and Crown, 58
New Double Four Patch, 145
New Double Irish Chain, 214
New England Block, 197
New Four Patch, 100
New Four Pointer, 53
New Hampshire, 352
New Hampshire Granite Block, 40, 67
New Home, 12
New Hour Glass, 78
New Irish Chain, 54
New Jersey, 205
New Mexican Star, 222
New Mexico, 75, 222
New Moon, 273
New Nine Patch, 18, 53
New Snowball, 18, 59
New Star, 149, 167, 206, 241, 248, 326
New Star of North Carolina, 220
New State Quilt Block, 276
New Waterwheel, 60
New Wedding Ring, 279, 317
New York, 68, 284, 349
New York Beauty, 251, 314, 316
Next Door Neighbor, 112
Nicole, 149
Night and Day, 42, 64, 85, 125
Night and Noon, 26
Night Before Christmas, 162
Night Sky, 70
Night Vision, 69
Night Watch, 32
Nighttime Butterflies, 373
Nine and Four Patch, 18
Nine Patch, 11, 17, 20, 93, 225, 276
Nine Patch Basket, 387
Nine Patch Checkerboard, 20
Nine Patch Design, 208
Nine Patch Diamond, 342
Nine Patch Frame, 22, 23
Nine patch grids, 10
Nine Patch Irish Chain, 203
Nine Patch Nose Gay, 219
Nine Patch Plaid, 16
Nine Patch Square Within a Square, 64
Nine Patch Star, 12, 72, 120, 186, 199
Nine Patch Star Quilt, 28
Nine Patch T, 63
Nine Patch Variation, 12, 57, 157, 277
Nine Snowballs, 322
1941 9-Patch, 29
1904 Star, 144
No Name. *See also* Name Unknown; Unnamed; basket, 386; border, 421; curved pattern, 292, 298, 299, 309; five patch, 196, 211, 212, 226, 233; four patch, 118, 121, 124, 136, 145, 152, 170; nine patch, 41, 61, 68, 81, 85; octagons, 328; patch, 19, 21; stars, 143, 344; strippie, 410
No Room at the Inn, 18
Nocturne, 267
Nonesuch, 270
Nonsense, 27
Nonsuch, 53
Noon & Light, 109
Noon Day Lily, 392
Noonday, 295
Noonday Lily, 299
Noonday Splendor, 298
Noonday Sun, 303
North Carolina Lily, 392, 395
North Carolina Star, 72, 141
North Dakota, 124
North Pole, 263
North Star, 111, 166, 168, 177, 183, 211, 247, 304, 326, 329, 361
North Wind, 136, 164
North Woods, 399
Northern Lights, 51, 105, 123, 151
Northumberland Star, 134, 330
Northwind, 15, 67
Norway Pine, 399
Nosegay, 43, 139, 153, 172, 397
Nothing Wasted, 414
Nouveau Lily Quilt, 394
Nova, 158, 172
November Nights, 221
Noxall Quilt Block, 295
#7222, 149
Oak Grove Star, 296
Oak Grove Star Quilt Block, 149
Oak Leaf, 288
Ocean Wave of Many Prints, 137
Ocean Wave(s), 75, 137, 141, 165, 195, 363, 366, 418
Octagon and Star, 340
Octagon Block, 323
Octagon grid, 320
Octagon Tile, 321
Octagon Wheel, 326
Octagon(al) Star, 97, 333, 335, 337, 348
Octagon(s), 11, 137, 147, 323, 365
Octagons and Squares, 113
Odd Fellows, 205
Odd Fellows Chain, 135
Odd Fellow('s) Cross, 153, 205, 263
Odd Fellow's March, 135
Odd Fellows Patch, 205
Odd Fellow('s) Quilt, 20, 137
Odd Patchwork, 223, 247
Odd Scraps Patchwork, 192, 196, 197
Odd Star, 215
Odds and Ends, 18, 121, 137, 273
Off to San Francisco, 36
Ogden Corners, 323, 326
Oh, Susannah, 94
Ohio, 167
Ohio Beauty, 271
*Ohio Farmer*; Album, 132; Biscuit Quilt, 425; Crossroads, 220; Diamond, 355; Dutchman's Wheel, 100; Favorite, 351; Jacks on Six, 13; Monkey Wrench, 195; Nine Patch, 11; Ocean Wave, 141; Star, 334; Star and Square, 165; Temperance Tree, 401; Unnamed nine patch, 30; Utility Block, 32; Wheel, 100; Windmill, 104; Wrench, 195
Ohio Schoolhouse, 409
Ohio Star, 24, 25, 96, 159, 167, 316
Ohio Trail, 166
Oil Fields of Oklahoma, 285
Oklahoma, 278
Oklahoma Boomer, 61
Oklahoma Dogwood, 270
Oklahoma Square Dance, 115
Oklahoma Star, 287, 351, 354
Oklahoma Sunburst, 295
Oklahoma Trails and Fields, 18
Oklahoma Twister, 43
Ola's Quilt, 280
Old Bear's Paw, 14
Old Blue, 223
Old Chelsea Station, 328; America's Pride, 282; Ann's Scrap Quilt, 158; Aster, 390; Bamboo Quilt, 110; Bamboo Spread, 413; Banner Quilt, 179; Beginner's Delight, 198; Bellflower, 394; Black and White, 110; Bold Squares, 214; Bowl of Flowers Series, 390; Bride's Quilt, 311; Brunswick Star, 330; Calla Lily, 396; Carolina Favorite, 277; Chained Star, 323; Chevron, 363; Colonial Basket, 382; Colonial Pavement, 163; Country Charm, 217; Crisscross, 315; Crocus, 391; Daisy Chain, 230; Day and Night, 179; Diagonal Square, 116; Diamond Field, 170; Diamonds, 169; Diamonds Galore, 110; Double Ax Head, 422; Double Pinwheel, 309; Double Star, 220; Dramatic Patch, 141; Dutch Windmill, 272; Eastern Star, 352; Endless Chain, 353; Evening Flower, 393; Five Patch Beauty, 352; Five Patch Star, 131; Flower of Friendship, 398; Flower of Spring, 300; Four Patch, 273; Friendship Bouquet, 242; Friendship Circle, 309; Friendship Flowers, 391; Friendship Star, 143; Full Blown Tulip, 165; Garden Beauty, 300; Garden Bloom, 313; Gay Two Patch Quilt, 198; Golden Stairs, 166; Golden Steps, 53; Grandmother's Prize, 300; Heart Quilt, 311; Heirloom Quilt, 309; Hexagons and Flowers, 353; Holiday Bells, 162; Home Treasure, 135; Iris, 397; Joseph's Coat, 276; Lily, 390; Linked Squares, 314; Lone Star, 69, 88; Magic Triangles, 114; Magnolia, 69; Mayflower, 314; Meadow Flower, 322; Merry-Go-Round, 273; Millwheel, 271; Modern Blocks, 217; Morning Glory, 396; Morning Star, 185, 325; Night Before Christmas, 162; Nine Patch Star, 186; No Name five patch, 196, 212; Noonday Splendor, 298; North Star, 166; Nosegay, 397; #7222, 149; Old Fashioned Garden, 391; Out of This World, 412; Peacock Patchwork, 382; Peony, 300, 315; Pieced Pineapple, 235; Pine Tree, 399; Pine Tree Quilt, 401; Pinwheel, 234, 353; Poinsettia, 83; Pond Lily, 397; Poppy, 390; Pride of the Bride, 289; Pride of the Prairie, 273; Priscilla's Prize, 312; Prudence's Star, 120; Queen's Treasure, 152; Quilter's Pride, 313; Rail Fence, 414; Rising Star, 185, 323; Road to Fortune, 327; Rose, 390; Rose and Trellis, 282; Rose in Summer, 184; Rose Star One Patch, 357; Rose Windows, 288; Saint Nicholas' Adventures, 232; Scrap Happy, 271; Seashells, 270; Simplicity, 12; Snowball Flower, 278; Snowball Wreath, 274; Snowdrop, 390; Southern Moon, 273; Springtime, 288; Square Dance, 115; Star, 133; Star and Cross, 202; Star of the East, 133; Star Studded Beauty, 352; Starflower Wreath, 219; Starry Path, 181; Starry Pavement, 184; Summer and Winter, 277; Summer Fancy, 267; Sunset Star, 312; Treasure Chest, 26; Triangle Beauty, 114; Tulip, 390; Tulip Garden, 391; Twist and Turn, 277, 278, 286; Two Patch Quilt, 95; Unnamed curved pattern, 270, 300; Unnamed four patch, 142; Unnamed star, 353, 355; Wave, 414; Waving Plumes, 278; Whirling Fans, 301; Whirling Star, 167; Windmill, 112, 272; Winged Square, 73; Your Lucky Star, 174
Old Colony Star, 363
Old Crow, 104
Old English Wedding Ring, 197
Old Fashioned, Daisy, 207
Old Fashioned Flower Garden, 357
Old Fashioned Fruit Basket, 389
Old Fashioned Garden, 391
Old Fashioned Goblet, 375
Old Fashioned Pieced Block, 78
Old Fashioned Pinwheel, 28
Old Fashioned Quilt, 229, 323
Old Fashioned Star Quilt, 330
Old Fashioned Wagon Wheels, 281
Old Fashioned Wheel Quilt, 351
Old Favorite, 121, 127
Old Garden Wall, 418
Old Glory, 359
Old Glory Four Patch, 119
Old Gray (Grey) Goose, 97, 118
Old Home, 407
Old Homestead, 407
Old Indian Trail, 63, 201
Old Italian Block, 212
Old Italian Design, 127
Old Kentucky Home, 407
Old Maid Combination, 268
Old Maid's Patience, 334, 339
Old Maid's Puzzle, 13, 99, 118, 137, 208, 216, 226, 229, 231, 268, 269
Old Maid's Ramble, 90, 135, 136, 145, 164
Old Maid's Rambler, 120
Old Mail, 20
Old Mill Design, 19
Old Mill Wheel, 294
Old Missouri, 272
Old Poinsettia, 111
Old Poinsettia Block, 135
Old Rugged Cross, 248
Old Snowflake, 26
Old Spanish Tile, 182
Old Staffordshire, 321
Old Star, 221
Old Stars and Stripes, 152
Old Tippecanoe, 25, 108
Old Windmill, 104, 109
Old-Fashioned Wedding Ring, 197
Olympia, 144
Olympiad, 329
Ombre, 194
On a Clear Night, 356

On the Square, 54
One Thousand Pyramids, 364
One Way, 13
Open Book, 107
Open Box, 107
Open Top Box, 356
Open Window, 134
Optical Illusion, 41, 142
Optical Sawtooth, 96
Orange Bud, 397
*Orange Judd Farmer*; American Chain, 50; Odd Fellow's Quilt, 20
Orange Peel, 272, 273, 275, 276, 288, 299, 357
Orange Peel Variation, 281, 367
Orange Pekoe, 418
Orange Slices, 288
Oranges, Basket of, 384
Orchid Hemstitch, 230
Order #11, 288
Oregon, 206
Oregon Trail, 268, 269
Oriental Poppy, 391
Oriental Puzzle, 230, 247
Oriental Rose, 397
Oriental Splendor, 352
Oriental Star, 133, 143, 278, 285, 321
Oriental Tulip, 394
Original, 33
Oriole Window, 293
Orion's Wheel, 69
Ornate Star, 25, 27
Orphan Star, 333
Orr, Ann, 222
Ostrich, 373
Our Country, 227
Our Editor, 115, 119
Our Neighborhood, 169
Our Next President Quilt, 131
Our Village Green, 140
Out of This World, 412
Over and Under, 53
Over and Under Quilt Design, 55
Over the Waves, 224, 421, 426
Overall Star Pattern, 343
Owl, 39
Owliver, 234
Ozark Cobblestones, 323
Ozark Diamond, 351
Ozark Maple Leaf, 46
Ozark Mountains, 179
Ozark Puzzle, 270
Ozark Star, 351, 355
Ozark Sunflower, 294
Ozark Tile Pattern, 323
Ozark Trail, 171, 207
Pacific Rail Road, 37
Paddle Wheel, 76, 121
Paducah Peony, 304, 313
*Page, Nancy*; Arizona, 21; Arrow Points, 143; Arrowheads, 156; At the Square, 54; Basket, 383; Beacon Lights, 163; Beggar Blocks, 56; Betty's Basket, 383; Blazing Star, 359; Bluet Quilt, 323; Bouquet's Quilt, 213; Box Quilt, 152; Box upon Box, 359, 419; Brilliant Star, 350; Canadian Gardens, 102; Carmen's Block, 93; Castles in Spain, 175; Cat's Paw, 225; City Streets, 225; Connecticut, 102; Coronation, 135; Criss Cross Quilt, 16; Crooked Path, 268; Cross Bars, 126; Cross Within Cross, 130; Crossroads, 56; Crown of Thorns, 135; Crow's Foot, 187; Danger Signals, 77; Darting Birds, 14; Depression, 214; Dewey, 126; Diamond String, 352; Diamonds, 342; Double T, 16, 29; Empty Spools, 332; Endless Trail, 268; English Wedding Ring, 197; Fish Tails, 336; Flaming Star, 123; Flock of Birds, 82; Flying Birds, 38; Flying Dutchman, 44; Folded Stars, 340; Forget Me Not, 332; Four Winds, 167; Framed Squares, 34; French 4's, 195; Friendship Hexagon, 350; Fruit Basket, 387; Going to Chicago, 36, 100; Golden Wedding Quilt, 110; Green River, 15; Hand Weave, 53; Handwoven, 53; Heavenly Problem, 206; Henry of the West, 24; Hexagon Stars, 350; Hour Glass, 38, 102; Interwoven, 53; Jack and Six, 13; Jewel Boxes, 74; Johnny Round the Corner, 197; Joining Star, 96; Kaleidoscope, 151; Lattice, 110; Lone Star, 24, 359; Lone Star of Texas, 359; Lover's Knot, 272; Lucky Pieces, 136; Maltese Cross, 141; Maud's Album Block, 109; Maud's Album Quilt, 127; Meteor Quilt, 111; Mill Wheel, 197; Mineral Wells, 138; Minnesota, 214; Mixed T, 16; Mona and Monette, 207; Mosaic, 25; Mother's Dream, 58; North Star, 326; Northern Lights, 123; Octagons, 147; Off to San Francisco, 36; Old Grey Goose, 97; Over and Under, 53; Over and Under Quilt Design, 55; Ozark Maple Leaf, 46; Paper Pinwheels, 104; Peach Basket, 385; Pennsylvania, 16; Pershing, 31; Pine Burr, 73; Primrose Path, 148; Quintettes, 412; Rainbow Quilt, 289; Red Cross, 196; Resolutions, 55; Ribbon Star, 12; Rising Star, 329; Round the Corner, 197; Sailboat Quilt, 114; Sally's Favorite, 132; San Diego, 135; Shooting Squares, 95; Signal Light, 123; Spinning Stars, 111; Spokane, 82; Square on Square, 104, 156; Squares and Square, 221; St. Louis Block, 326; Star of Hope, 24, 25; Star of the West, 24; Star Rays, 352; Starlight, 74; Stars and Cubes, 332; Stepping Stones, 153; Steps to the Light House, 203; Strips and Squares, 53; Sugar Bowl, 272, 273; Summer Winds, 39; Sun and Shade, 205; Sunburst, 359; Sunflower, 333; Sunny Lanes, 122, 178; Susannah, 136; Table for Four, 155; Tennessee, 13; Texas, 28; Texas Treasure, 76; Tic Tac Toe, 18; Turnstile, 82; Twinkling Star, 333; Vermont, 153; West Wind, 15; Whirling Squares, 114; Winged Arrow, 113
Painted Snowball, 299
Pale Star, 111
Palm Flower, 393
Palm Leaf, 140, 305
Panama Block, 211
Panama Star, 28
Panda Patch, 381
Pandora's Block, 359
Pandora's Box, 359
Pansy, 391, 392
Pansy Quilt, 397
Papa's Delight, 305
Paper Pinwheels, 104
Paradox, 71
Paragon Quilt Block, 305
Parallelogram, 337
Parallelogram Charm Quilt, 420
Parasol, 138, 172, 182
Parasol Block, 295
Parasol Variations, 172
Parquetry Design for Patchwork, 324
Parquetry for a Quilt, 151
Party Plate Quilt, 316
Party Platform, 227
Patch as Patch Can, 47, 49
Patch Blossom, 399
Patch Quilt Design, 207, 215
Patchwork Accessories & Gifts, 283
Patchwork Bedspread, 20, 49
Patchwork Cushion Top, 247
Patchwork Fantasy, 222
Patchwork Pines, 401
Patchwork Posy, 54
*Patchwork Quilts*; Amish Angel, 310; Fenceworm, 413; Imari Plate, 322; Kite Variation, 308; Orange Peel Variation, 281; Tree of Triangles, 398; Windowpane, 80
Patchwork Sofa Quilt, 324
Path and Stiles, 59
Path of Fans, 267
Path of Thorns, 226, 410
Path Through the Woods, 112, 151
Path to Bethlehem, 166
Pathfinder, 46, 80, 214, 287
Paths to Piece, 125
Patience Corners, 16, 103, 175, 359
Patience Corners Border, 416
Patience Nine Patch, 11
Patio Garden, 122
Patio Tiles, 18
Patriotic Star, 52, 329
Patriotic Star Block, 324
Patriotism design, 156
Patriot's Quilt, 323
Pattern of Chinese Origin, 354
Pattern Without a Name, 178, 201
Patty's Star, 337, 341
Pavement Pattern, 114
Peace and Plenty, 102, 182
Peaceful Evening, 46
Peaceful Hours, 96, 143
Peaceful Valley Quilt, 324
Peach Basket, 385
Peach Blow, 75
Peacock, 382
Peacock Patchwork, 382
Peekaboo, 58
Peekhole, 108
Peeled Orange, 295
Peggy Anne's Special, 224, 302
Penelope's Favorite, 302, 315
Penn's Puzzle, 315
Pennsylvania, 16, 49, 129
Pennsylvania Crossroads, 125
Pennsylvania Hex, 350
Pennsylvania Pineapple, 255
Pennsylvania Tree, 152
Pennsylvania Wheel Quilt, 297
Peony and Forget Me Nots, 150
Peony Block, 398
Peony(s), 226, 300, 315, 335, 339, 395
Pepper and Salt Shakers, 364
Perfume Block, 377
Perfume Bottle, 378
Periwinkle, 123, 323, 325
Periwinkle Variation, 325
Perkomen Valley, 12
Perky Pumpkin, 375
Perpetual Motion, 135
Perry's Expedition, 311
Pershing, 31
Persian, 235, 241
Persian Star, 184
Petal Circle in a Square, 297
Petal Quilt, 272
Peter and Paul, 275
Peter's Quilt, 118
Petit Park, 233
Petronella, 112
Pharaoh, Land of, 418
Pharlemina's Favorite, 77
Philadelphia Block, 194
Philadelphia Patch, 302, 348, 349
Philadelphia Pavement, 194
Philippine Islands Quilt Block, 79
Philippines, 348
Phoenix, 27
Phoenix Star, 346
Photo Bracket Corners with Sashing, 424
Picket and Posts, 196
Picket Fence, 51, 106, 413, 420
Pickle Dish, 317
Picnic Basket, 384
Picture Frame(s), 19, 84
Picture Window, 117
Pictures in the Stairwell, 270
Piecebynumber.com; Ghost, 372; Miss Henrietta, 372; Poinsettia Star, 394
Pieced Basket, 384
Pieced Butterfly, 373
Pieced Duck, 371
Pieced Flower, 169, 392
Pieced Heart, 179, 242
Pieced Heart Block, 199, 217
Pieced Palm Tree, 398
Pieced Pansy, 393
Pieced Pineapple, 235
Pieced Pinwheels, 66
Pieced Pyramids, 418
Pieced Ribbon, 381
Pieced Schoolhouse Block, 406
Pieced Star, 97
Pieced Star Variation, 160
Pieced Sunflower, 283, 294, 311
Pieced Tulip(s), 163, 228, 242, 391
Pierced Star, 97
Pierre, 347
Pierrot's Pom Pom, 272
Pierson, Sandra, 395
Pig Pen, 267
Pigeon Toes, 55, 205
Pigeons in the Coop, 118
Pigs in a Blanket, 97
Pig's Tail, 178
Pike's Peak, 348
Pillar to Post, 125
Pilot('s) Wheel, 278, 285, 294, 299, 307
Pin Cushion, 275
Pincushion and Burr, 280
Pincushion and Cucumbers, 275
Pine Burr, 73, 209, 218, 345
Pine Burr Block, 154
Pine Cone, 346
Pine Forest, 399, 405
Pine Tree, 399, 400, 401, 403, 404, 405
Pine Tree Quilt, 398, 399, 401
Pineapple, 233
Pineapple Cactus, 345
Pineapple Log Cabin Variation, 237
Pineapple Plant, 106
Pineapple Quilt, 111
Pineapple Squares, 224
Pineapple Variation, 135
Pineapple(s), 29, 153
Pines in the Snow, 399
Piney(s), 335, 398
Pink Dogwood, 87, 172
Pink Magnolia(s), 232, 390
Pinwheel Askew, 111
Pinwheel Parade, 168
Pinwheel Quilt, 20, 295, 327
Pinwheel Rose Basket, 234
Pinwheel Skew, 221
Pinwheel Square, 195
Pinwheel Star, 41, 51, 82, 99, 135, 335, 339, 343, 355
Pinwheels & Sawtooth, 33
Pinwheel(s)/Pin Wheel(s), 12, 40, 44, 62, 79, 100, 103, 104, 105, 108, 109, 111, 117, 129, 134, 151, 195, 234, 274, 278, 315, 328, 329, 352, 353, 360, 425
Pioneer Block, 214
Pioneer Braid, 412
Pioneer Cottage Block, 407
Pioneer Patch, 195
Plaid, 191
Plaid Star, 184, 338
Plain Block, 93
Plain Sailing, 108
Plaited Block, 151, 324
Plane Thinking, 51
Platt, Linda, 370
Platter, 378
Pleasant Paths, 89
Plum Island Compass, 181
Poinsettia Quilt, 364
Poinsettia Star, 394
Poinsettia(s), 33, 83, 111, 334
Pointed Ovals, 281
Pointed Tile, 109
Pointing Star, 350, 354, 366
Points and Petals, 314
Points Homeward, 27
Polaris Star, 329
Pole Star, 326, 331
Polka Dots, 268
Polly's Favorite, 204, 213
Pond Lily, 228, 397
Pontiac Star, 124
Poor Boy, 357
Popcorn, 112
Poplar Leaf, 14
Poppy, 390
Pork and Beans, 101
Port and Starboard, 114
Porto Rico, 129
Posey Quilt, 315
Posies Round the Square, 315
Postage Stamp, 16, 122, 230, 247
Postage Stamp Basket, 389
Postage Stamp Block, 61
Posy Patch, 117
Posy Plot, 208
Pot of Flowers, 388
Potomac Pride, 302
Powder Puff, 425
Practical Orchard, 12
Prairie Belle Quilt Block, 78
Prairie Crocus, 345
*Prairie Farmer*, 235
Prairie Flower(s), 42, 308
Prairie home, 30
Prairie Lily, 392, 397
Prairie Queen, 19, 150
Prairie Star, 343, 344
Prairie Sunrise, 200, 202, 213
Precious Gems, 322
Premium Star, 54, 221
President Carter, 41
President Truman, 224
Presidential Armchair, 255
President's Block, 55, 78
President's Choice, 131
President's Quilt, 302, 334
Pretty Kettle of Fish, 84
Pretty Patchwork, 360, 361
Prickly Path, 410
Prickly Pear, 164, 225
Pride of East Kingston, 291
Pride of Holland, 142
Pride of Italy, 228
Pride of Ohio, 128
Pride of Texas, 343
Pride of the Bride, 289
Pride of the Prairie, 273
Primrose, 272, 298
Primrose Patch, 393
Primrose Path, 148, 161
Print and Plain, 184
Priscilla, 110, 124
Priscilla's Dream, 263
Priscilla's Prize, 312
Prism Block, 38
Prisms, 64, 172
Prized Possession, 213
Progressive, 300
*Progressive Farmer*; Autumn Stars, 151; Colonial Garden, 134; Dancing Cubes, 359; Flaming Sun, 302; Four Buds, 139; Galahad's Shield, 32; Garden Spot, 296; Grandma's Fan, 310; Hands All Around, 317; King's Crown, 301; National Star, 337, 341; Smoothing Iron, 352; Star and Cone, 184; Sunrise, 310; Tangled Trails, 279; Wheel(s), 167
Propeller, 194
Prosperity Block, 57
Proud Tree, 402
Providence Block, 149, 193
*Prudence Penny*; Altar Steps, 232; Avalanche Lily, 280; Beaver, 374; Bleeding Heart, 303; Buffalo, 374; Buttercup, 316; Camel, 374; Colt's Corral, 222; Compass, 296; Crocodile, 379; Dogwood, 235; Elephant, 374; Giraffe, 374; Hippopotamus, 373; Indian Paint Brush, 297; Irish Chain, 242; Lone X, 226; Monkey, 374; Ostrich, 373; Queen Victoria's Crown, 229; Reindeer, 373; Rocky Mountain, 316; Saw, 137; Seal, 373; Shooting Star, 186; Silver Maple, 84; Squirrel, 374; Whirl Wind, 295; Wild Iris, 236, 397; Zebra, 374; Prudence's Star, 120
Pudding and Pie, 81
Puff, 425
Puffball, 425
Puffed Squares, 425
Pullman Puzzle, 18, 267, 269, 277
Pumpkin, 375, 378, 379
Pumpkin Vine, 268
Pure Symbol of Right Doctrine, 53, 101
Puritan Maiden, 215
Puritan Star, 328
Puss in the Corner, 16, 18, 19, 53, 54, 58, 109, 325
Pussy in the Corner, 16
Puzzle, 132
Puzzle Tile, 323
Pyramid(s), 32, 136, 361, 413, 417, 418
Pyrotechnics, 297
Quadrille, 61
Quail's Nest, 19
Quarter Turn, 267
Quartered Star, 40
Quarterfoils, 18
Quatrefoils, 315
Quebec, 255
Queen Charlotte's Crown, 194
Queen of May, 56
Queen of the May, 306, 317, 360
Queen Victoria, 97
Queen Victoria's Crown, 35, 226, 229
Queen's Crown, 194, 222, 267, 310
Queen's Delight, 306
Queen's Favorite, 20
Queen's Petticoat, 30
Queen's Pride, 268
Queen's Star, 340
Queen's Treasure, 152
*Quick & Easy Quilting*; Chain Reaction, 424; Scrappy Tree Blocks, 401; Surprise Package, 164
Quiet Love, 72
*Quilt Craft*; Flying Fish, 371; Giraffe, 372; Hexacat, 360
Quilt in Light and Dark, 115
Quilt Mosaic, 23
Quilt of the Century, 329
Quilt of Variety, 110
Quilt Pattern, 317
Quilt Star, 124
Quilt Without a Name, 77
*Quilt World*; American Homes, 48; Bass and Trout, 331; Beautiful Flower Garden, 170; Broken Arrows, 194; Butterfly Migration, 288; Candles of Heaven, 344; Cascade Pride, 401; Cat's Eye, 161; Christmas Basket, 387; Christmas Day, 304; Christmas Star, 339; Country Roads, 152; Country Village, 176; Cupid's Arrows, 88; Dawn, 88; Diamond Rose, 395; Fireball, 273; Fitz's Phenomena, 182; Flower and Fern, 78; Framed Cross, 88; Geometric, 94; Harvest Moon, 308; Iris Rainbow, 395; Jan's Bicentennial Star, 235; Kansas Sunflower, 353; Kansas Whirligig, 100; King's Crown, 64; Leo's Lion, 82; Liberty Star, 116; Lilies, 118; Lily of the Valley, 393; Missouri Corn Field, 71;

Mother's Morning, 172; Moynihan's Crusade, 163; Name Unknown curve pattern, 286; No Name five patch, 233; Over the Waves, 224; Parasol, 172; Parasol Variations, 172; Pieced Flower, 169; Pink Dogwood, 172; President Carter, 41; Prisms, 172; Razzle Dazzle, 172; Ribbons, 234; Rising Star, 174, 328; Saw Blades, 325; Scrap Star Quilt, 336; Snowball, 273; Springtime, 279; Square Block, 130; Square Dance, 160; Squash Blossom, 50; Star in the Window, 79; Stellar Reflections, 183; Sunset Quilt Block, 285; Tahitian Postage Stamp, 242; Tall Ships, 113; Television Quilt, 381; Tiffany, 411; Triangle Quilt, 413; Twinkling Diamond Log Cabin, 356; Twinkling Star, 340; Wheels, 200
*Quilt World Omnibook*; Apple Cores, 305; Autumn Spinning Star, 305; Behold...a Star, 305; Daniel's Device, 307; Dilemma, 172; Ella's Star, 127; Horizon Star, 232; Night and Day, 85
Quiltaholics.com, 377
Quiltalk.com, 376
Quilter's Delight, 210, 242, 270
Quilter's Fan, 281, 287
*Quilter's Newsletter*; Amish Whirl, 65; April Tulips, 164; Arabic Latticework, 46; Autumn Breeze, 336; Autumn Tints Variation, 230; Aztec, 302; Aztec Jewel, 127; Babe Ruth Diamond, 294; Blue for Julie, 224; Bluebirds Flying, 233; Boardwalk, 173; Boat in a Bottle, 377; Bobbin, 50; Bon-Bon, 425; Broken Promises, 108; Buzz Saw Charm, 34; Calico Cat, 170; California Snowflake, 62; Campaign Trail, 168; Cat, 372; Chained Star, 26; Chaos Theory, 87; Charm Packet Odyssey, 363; Chips and Whetstones, 296; Christmas Memory Quilt, 333; City Blocks, 220; City Park, 32; Cobra, 65; Collinsville Rose Star, 353; Crosses and Losses, 40; Crossroads Star, 71; Dandelion Quilt, 315; Delaware Sea Pines, 400; Diamond Bar, 119; Diamonds of Hope, 216; Doreen's Dutch Tiles, 62; Double Pinwheel Whirl, 113; Drucilla's Delight, 234; Ducks in a Row, 371; Eight Point All Over, 114; Equivalents, 312; Father's Fancy, 223; Feathered Log Cabin, 236; Fig Leaf, 46; Finnigan's Wake, 65; Floral Frame, 417; Fort Knox, 65; Friendship Quilt, 272; Fundamental Nine Patch, 53; Grandmother's Flower Basket, 353; Heavenly Stars, 173; Hexagon Snowflake, 355; Hole in the Barn Door, 59; Holland Magic, 65; Homecoming, 328; Hoosier Wonder, 64; Indian Paint Brush, 89; Jacques in the Boat, 288; Land's End, 164; LeMoyne Star, 344; Marigold Garden, 89, 219; Mayflower, 183; Meadow Flowers, 396; Missouri Windmills, 145; Mountain Star, 167; Nativity Star, 220; Nebraska Windmill, 255; Night Vision, 69; Nine Patch Basket, 387; Paradox, 71; Party Platform, 227; Petit Park, 233; Pigeons in the Coop, 118; Pink Dogwood, 87; Poinsettias, 334; Pretty Kettle of Fish, 84; Railroad Crossing, 183; Rhapsody in Blue, 119; Rhododendron Star, 295; Ribbons 'n Pinwheels, 415; Scrap Bag Squares, 177; Six Windows of Sunshine, 166; Skyscrapers, 322; Snake in the Hollow, 301; Snowy Windows, 268, 269; Space Ships, 184; Spice Pink, 316; Spinning Color Wheel, 168; Spinning Stars, 89; Spring Star, 64; Star Bound, 123; Star Chain, 63; Star in Space, 65; Star in the Window, 59; Star of the Decathlon, 313; Star Trek, 77; Stars Galore, 140; Starshadow, 71; Summer Blooms, 230; Sunflower, 40; Sunshine and Shadow, 269; Sunshine Over the Rockies, 86; Swing Your Partner, 119; Taking Wing, 167; Telluride Puzzle, 176; Terrace Floor, 118; Texas Bluebonnet, 394; Thunderbird, 119; Tic-Tac-Toe, 284; Time and Energy, 270; 'Tis the Season, 404; Tulip Garden, 175; Tumbling Ties, 199; Turnabout, 22; Twisted Ribbons, 129; Twisted Star, 340; Unnamed five patch, 191; Unnamed nine patch, 48; V-Block, 69; Westfalen Waltz, 282; Whirling L, 212; Wild Iris, 183; Windy City, 113, 142; Women's Choice, 63
Quilter's Pride, 313
Quilter's Rainbow Charm Quilt, 419
*Quilter's Workbook*; Autumn Leaves, 178; Virginia Reel, 73
*Quilting & Patchwork Dictionary*, 381
*Quilting Today*; Delectable Appalachians, 137; Japanese Scrap Quilt, 42; Pines in the Snow, 399; Sundials, 283
Quilting.about.com; Baby Shoe, 379; Bottle, 377; Lamp, 379; Pumpkin, 378, 379; Tea Pot, 378; Wine Glass, 377
Quiltmag.com, 408
*Quiltmaker*; Arabesque, 410; Butterfly Wings, 215; Calico Grove, 180; Camellia, 395; Cats in the Attic, 371; Charmed Path, 421; Constellation, 218; Desert Blooms, 81; Dutch Dreams, 180; Fields and Fences, 155; French Garden, 211; Garden Shadows, 116; Gem Star, 144; Glory Be, 59; Goin' Home, 421; Harvest Chain, 422; Maypole Dance, 116; To the Moon, 376; Mountain Paths, 241; North Pole, 263; Petronella, 112; Prairie Home, 30; Raspberry Parfait, 174; Skip to My Lou, 59; Stripes and Stars, 183; Summer Rose, 248; Tulip Garden, 394; Tulip Twirl, 145; Victorian Basket, 389; Wedding Basket, 385; Winner's Circle, 371; Woven Fences, 424
Quilts and Co., 218
Quint Five Quilt, 110
Quintettes, 412
Radiant Star, 73, 182, 346, 347
Radio Windmill, 51
Ragged Robin, 214
Rail Fence, 102, 231, 412, 413, 414, 418
Rail Fence Border, 422
Rail Fence Wave, 423
Railroad, 36, 37, 100, 153
Railroad Around Rocky Mountain, 300
Railroad Crossing, 84, 85, 100, 136, 170, 180, 183, 215, 218, 223
Railroad Quilt, 28
Rain or Shine, 211
Rainbow, 81, 282, 284, 300, 301, 317
Rainbow Block, 69, 139, 267
Rainbow Cactus, 162, 383, 387
Rainbow Flower, 94
Rainbow Quilt, 281, 289
Rainbow Square, 217, 219
Rainbow Star, 123, 272, 343
Rainbow Star Quilt, 316
Rainbow Tile, 357, 358
Rainbow Wedding Ring, 317
Raised Patchwork, 425
Raleigh Quilt Block, 306
Rambler, 136
Rambling Road, 136, 164
Rambling Rose, 164
Ranger's Pride, 39
Raspberry Parfait, 174
Ratchet Wheel, 225
Rathjen, Lou, 64
Rattlesnake, 300, 305
Ray, 177
Rays of Sunlight, 219
Razzle Dazzle, 172
Razz-Ma-Tazz, 99
Reardon, Caroline, 85
Rebel Patch, 67
Red and White Crisscross, 146
Red and White Quilt, 369
Red Barn, 407
Red Basket, 385
Red Buds, 277
Red Cross, 11, 85, 107, 192, 196, 197, 199, 201, 225, 323
Red Cross Quilt, 122, 131
Red Schoolhouse, 405
Red Shields, 417
Red, the White and the Blue, 85
Red, White and Blue, 118, 293, 303, 323, 349
Red, White and Blue Criss Cross, 119
Reel, 288
Rehme, Judy; Razzle Dazzle, 172
Rehmel, Judy; Harvest Moon, 308
Reindeer, 370, 373
Reindeer on the Roof, 181
Rejoice, 214
Reminiscences, 144
Reminiscent of the Wedding Ring, 275
Remnant Ovals, 275
Repeat X, 70
Resolutions, 55
Return of the Swallows, 100
Reverse X, 147
Rhapsody in Blue, 119
Rhode Island, 60
Rhode Island Maple, 236
Rhode Island Maple Leaf Star, 255
Rhode Island Red, 174
Rhododendron Star, 295, 310
Ribbon Block, 109
Ribbon Border, 109
Ribbon Bow, 381
Ribbon Square, 87, 236
Ribbon Star, 12, 57, 98
Ribbon Twist, 324
Ribbon(s), 87, 103, 234, 381
Ribbons 'n Pinwheels, 415
Richmond, 21
Richmond Beauty, 317
Right and Left, 95
Right Angle Patchwork, 368
Right Hand of Fellowship, 26
Ring Around the Posy, 127
Ring Around the Rosy, 168
Ring Around the Star, 128, 337
Rink, Nancy, 62
Rising Star, 77, 134, 149, 161, 174, 185, 323, 328, 329, 341, 343, 346, 354
Rising Star Block, 161
Rising Sun, 180, 285, 287, 290, 295, 322, 328, 343
Riviera, 167
Road Home, 270
Road to Arkansas, 36, 37
Road to California, 14, 36, 128, 153, 180, 223, 227, 247, 269, 315
Road to Damascus, 160
Road to Fortune, 327
Road to Grandma's, 33
Road to Home, 219
Road to Jerusalem, 100
Road to Oklahoma, 108
Road to Paris, 126
Road to Tennessee, 125
Road to the White House, 36
Roads to Berlin, 107
Roads to Oklahoma, 169
Roast Rods, 306
Rob(bing) Peter to Pay Paul, 11, 21, 125, 267, 268, 270, 272, 273, 275
Robson, Leslie, 175
Robson, Norma, 305
Rock Garden, 141, 180, 185, 324, 325
Rock of Ages, 127
Rock Wall, 353
Rocket Ship, 159
Rocking Horse, 381
Rockingham's Beauty, 334
Rocky Glen, 114, 137
Rocky Mountain, 118, 316
Rocky Mountain Chain, 193
Rocky Mountain Fan, 310
Rocky Mountain Puzzle, 100
Rocky Mountain Road, 316
Rocky Mountain Star, 310
Rocky Mountain Variation, 310
Rocky Road, 93
Rocky Road to California, 36, 37
Rocky Road to Dublin, 37, 269
Rocky Road to Kansas, 110, 124, 275
Rodriguez, Sheila, 279
Rohrkaste, Rebecca, 312
Rolfe, Margaret, 372
Roll on Columbia, 137
Rolling Nine Patch, 198
Rolling Pin Wheel, 278
Rolling Pinwheel, 41, 42, 48, 284
Rolling Square(s), 40, 66, 195
Rolling Star Quilt, 98, 280
Rolling Star(s), 123, 128, 192, 313, 324, 326, 331, 332, 333, 334
Rolling Stone(s), 40, 59, 169, 192, 202, 282, 325, 334, 356
Roman Cross, 132
Roman Pavement(s), 20, 267
Roman Roads, 215, 221
Roman Square(s), 17, 59
Roman Strip, 60
Roman Stripe, 69, 139
Roman Stripes and Squares, 410
Romance, 116
*Romance of the Patchwork Quilt*; Bread Basket, 388; Colonial Basket, 387; Grandmother's Basket, 386
Rope, 412
Rope and Anchor, 54
Rope Strands, 413
Ropp, Gayle, 283
Rosalia's Flower Garden, 356
Rose, 390
Rose Album, 294
Rose and Trellis, 282
Rose Compass, 81
Rose Dream, 276
Rose Garden, 177, 397
Rose, Helen, 394
Rose in Summer, 184
Rose Mosaic, 28
Rose Star One Patch, 357, 362
Rose Trellis, 112, 395
Rose Windows, 288
Rosebud Patchwork, 396
Rosebud Quilt, 285
Rosebud(s), 28, 31, 45, 122, 225, 280, 304, 396
Rosemary, 88, 215
Rosepoint, 158
Roses of Picardy, 278
Rosette, 398, 425
Rosette of Points, 167
Rosette Quilt Pattern, 306
Rosie's Purina Whirligig, 178
Rough Diamond, 84
Roulette Wheel Star, 356
Round Robin, 309
Round Table, 289, 306
Round the Corner, 197
Royal, 279
Royal Cross, 279
Royal Diamonds, 331
Royal Dutch Tulip/Vase, 388
Royal Gems, 83
Royal Japanese Vase, 388, 392
Royal Star, 59, 109
Ruby Roads, 141
Ruby's Star, 90
Russian Sunflower, 295
Rustic Wheel, 206
Sacramento, 158
Sacramento City, 199
Sacramento Quilt Block, 199
Saddlebag, 120
Sage Bud, 60, 229
Sage Bud of Wyoming, 255
Sail Boat, 117
Sailboat, 15, 74, 106, 113
Sailboat Block, 15, 24
Sailboat Oklahoma, 114
Sailboat Quilt, 114
Sailboats Variation, 89
Sailing Darts, 76
Sailor's Joy, 158, 330
Saint Nicholas' Adventures, 232
Salem, 27, 28
Sally's Favorite, 132
Salt Lake City, 145
Salute to Colors, 132
Salute to Loyalty, 93
Samoa, 306
Sam's Quilt, 366, 367
San Diego, 135
Sandberg, Lyn Peare, 377
Sandhills Star, 23
Santa Fe, 56
Santa Fe Quilt, 110
Santa Fe Quilt Block, 78
Santa Fe Trail, 57, 198
Santa's Guiding Star, 182
Sapphire Net, 88
Sapphire Quilt Block, 75
Saracen Chain, 88
Sarah's Choice, 97
Sarah's Direction, 82
Sarah's Favorite, 132
Sashing Strip or Border, 424
Sassafras Leaf, 236
Satellite, 142, 169
Saturn Block, 79
Saturn's Rings, 303
Savannah Beautiful Star, 274, 316
Savannah Squares, 286
Savannah Star, 274
Save a Piece, 276
Save All Chain, 369
Save-All, 369
Savior's Cross, 248
Saw, 137
Saw Blades, 325, 410
Saw Toothed Star, 177
Sawtooth Circle, 286
Sawtooth Diamond, 251, 369
Sawtooth Patchwork, 20
Sawtooth Puzzle, 138
Sawtooth (Saw Tooth), 14, 31, 69, 83, 105, 114, 202, 346, 356, 369, 415
Sawtooth Star, 347
Sawtooth Triangles, 416, 421
Scallop Border, 424
Scattered Points, 28
Schoenrock Cross, 227
Schoenthal, Carla, 234
School Girl's Puzzle, 99
Schoolhouse, 407, 408
Schumann, Caldelina, 172
Scotch Heather, 58
Scotch Plaid, 127, 158
Scotch Quilt, 93
Scotch Squares, 127
Scot's Plaid, 93
Scottie Dog, 371
Scottie Quilt for Boys, 370
Scottish Cross, 148, 185
Scrap, 156
Scrap Bag (Scrapbag), 61, 139, 213, 222
Scrap Bag Squares, 177
Scrap Basket, 229, 382
Scrap Cats, 370
Scrap Happy, 271
Scrap Patch, 78, 139
Scrap Pyramid, 424
Scrap Quilt Bouquet, 187
Scrap Star Quilt, 336
Scrap Zigzag, 117
Scrappy Tree Blocks, 401
Scroll Work, 123
Scuppernong Hull Quilt Block, 306
Sea & Shadows, 184
Sea Shell Quilt, 301
Sea Shells (Seashells), 270, 421
Sea Star, 42
Seagull, 280
Seal, 372, 373
Seasons, 109, 206
Season's Joy, 181
Secret Drawer, 148
Secret Passage, 176
See Through Block, 356
Seesaw, 112, 115
Segmented Diamonds, 425
Seminole Square, 227
Seminole Star, 133
Semi-Octagon, 147
Sentry's Pastime, 86
September Star, 338
Sergeant's Chevron, 242
Setting Sun, 303
Seven Sisters, 357
Seven Stars, 357
Seven Stars in Cluster, 357
Sewing Circle, 205
Sexton, Carlie; All Hands Round, 330; Around the World, 317; Compass, 288; Dolly Madison's Workbox, 275; Farmer's Wife, 280; Flower Basket, 389; Indiana Puzzle, 268; King Tut, 317; Morning Star, 343; Mother's Delight, 123; Orange Peel, 288; Oregon Trail, 268, 269; Path Through the Woods, 112, 151; Rob Peter to Pay Paul, 11; Scotch Plaid, 127; Simple Star, 328, 329; Solomon's Puzzle, 268; St. Louis, 123; Star of the East, 329; Triangles, 35; Tulips in a Vase, 387; Wild Goose Chase, 200
Shaded Compass, 24
Shaded Crossroad, 130
Shaded Trail, 24
Shadow Box, 15, 105, 118
Shadow Boxes, 95
Shadow Cross, 226
Shadow Quilt, 139
Shadow Star, 251
Shadow Trail, 341
Shadows, 69, 139
Shady Pine, 154
Shamrock, 312
Shasta Daisy, 328, 329, 397
Sheep, 380
Sheep Fold Quilt, 93
Shell, 421
Shell Chain, 421
Shepherd's Crossing, 177
Shepherd's Light, 251
Shepherd's Watch, 86
Sherman's March, 19
Shifting Cubes, 359
Shining Hour, 211
Shining Star, 331
Ship, 101, 114
Ship at Sea, 118
Ship Block, 64
Ship in a Bottle Jar, 378
Ship of Dreams, 117
Ships A-Sailing, 263
Ships at Sea, 106
Ship's Wheel, 343, 344
Shoemaker's Puzzle, 107, 171
Shoo Fly, 19, 59, 114, 200
Shoofly, 12, 24, 94

Shooting Squares, 95
Shooting Star(s), 49, 50, 68, 89, 111, 112, 133, 139, 163, 167, 185, 186, 208, 344
Sickle, 99
Signal, 209
Signal flag patterns, 433–434
Signal Light, 123
Signature, 102, 115, 297
Signature Friendship Quilt, 116
Signature Quilt, 107
Signatures for Golden Memories, 125
Signs of Spring, 156
Silent Star, 25
Silk Patch, 269
Silver and Gold, 329
Silver Lane, 34
Silver Maple, 84
Simple Block, 117
Simple Cross, 16
Simple Design, 67, 120, 202, 218
Simple Flower Basket, 383
Simple Star, 328, 329
Simple Sue, 191
Simplex Star, 11, 12
Simplicity, 12, 114
Simplicity's Delight, 363
Single Chain and Knot, 213
Single Irish Chain, 16, 53, 203
Single Lily, 139
Single Star, 177
Single Sunflower, 283
Single Wedding Ring, 39, 192
Sirius Star Quilt, 369
Sister Mary's Star, 144
Sister Nan's Cross, 147
Sister's Choice, 192, 198
Sitka Quilt Block, 181
Sitka Star, 334
Six and Two Pineapple Variation, 237
Six Point Flower Garden, 355
Six Point(ed) Star, 158, 352
Six Windows of Sunshine, 166
Six-Sided Patchwork, 362
Sixteen Patch, 181
Skinny T Quilt, 198
Skip to My Lou, 59
Sky Rocket, 74
Skyrocket, 42
Skyscraper(s), 322, 357
Slanted Diamonds, 15
Slashed Album, 107
Slashed Star, 284, 298
Slave Chain, 275
Small Business, 132
Small Triangle Quilt, 106
Small Triangles, 101
Small-expressions.com, 376
Smith Autograph Quilt, 71
Smith, Lois; Buzz Saw Charm, 34; Lightning, 116
Smokehouse Block, 67
Smoothing Iron, 352
Snail's Trail, 106, 135, 165, 279
Snake Fence, 417, 418
Snake in the Hollow, 272, 301
Snake Trail, 300
Snow Block, 127
Snow Crystal(s), 332, 351, 357
Snow, Virginia, 330
Snowball and Nine Patch, 18
Snowball Flower, 278
Snowball Variation, 11
Snowball Wreath, 274
Snowball(s), 11, 18, 77, 123, 267, 268, 269, 272, 273, 274, 277, 311, 323, 325
Snowbound, 75
Snowdrop, 390
Snowflake, 127, 200, 362, 366
Snowflake Quilt, 352
Snowy Morning, 126
Snowy Windows, 268, 269
Soldier at the Window, 375
Soldier Boy, 375
Solitaire, 97
Solomon's Garden, 350
Solomon's Puzzle, 268
Solomon's Star, 97
Solomon's Temple, 211, 231
Sombrero Appliqué, 89
Sonnie's Playhouse, 182
Soul Knot, 306
South Carolina, 183
South Carolina Album Block, 222
South Carolina Star, 31
South Dakota, 64, 187
South Jersey Pines, 403
Southern Belle, 95
Southern Moon, 273
Southern Pine, 196, 399
Southern Plantation, 316
Southern Pride, 287
Southern Star, 140, 295, 306, 328, 329
Southside Star, 85
Southwest Cross, 232
Souvenir, 195
Souvenir of Friendship, 199
Space Ships, 184
Space Station, 175
Spanish Squares, 220
Sparkler, 47
Sparkling Crystals, 123
Sparkling Dew, 353
Sparkling Jewel, 124
Sparkling Star, 162
Sparkling Star Block, 26
Specialty Square, 145
Spice Pink(s), 315, 316
Spider, 13, 101
Spider and the Fly, 298
Spider Legs, 38, 157, 419
Spider Web, 52, 108, 141, 148, 150, 153, 183, 234, 248, 300, 322, 329, 351, 352, 354, 361
Spider Web Gone Awry, 141
Spider's Den, 86, 222
Spiderweb Star, 336
Spin Wheel, 17
Spindles, 413
Spindles and Stripes, 133
Spinner, 106
Spinning Arrows, 35
Spinning Ball, 295
Spinning Blocks, 356
Spinning Color Wheel, 168
Spinning Hour Glass, 152
Spinning Jenny, 82
Spinning L, 179
Spinning Star(s), 89, 111, 135, 183, 195, 327
Spinning Tops, 200
Spinning Wheel, 41, 293
Spinning Whirligigs, 273
Spiral, 295
Spiral Log Cabin, 237
Spirit of 1849, 313
Spirit of St. Louis, 17
Split Nine Patch, 11, 14
Split Rail, 316
Spokane, 82
Spool, 15, 107, 145, 196, 422
Spool and Bobbin, 56, 113, 147
Spool Block, 196
Spool of 1966, 299
Spools, 43, 120, 148
Sprecher, Doris, 87
Spring and Fall, 419
Spring Beauty, 136, 311
Spring Blooms, 327
Spring Fancy, 87
Spring Has Come, 129
Spring Is Sprung, 63
Spring Star, 64
Spring Tulip(s), 87, 233, 396
Springfield, 143
Springfield Patch, 143
Springtime, 279, 288
Springtime Blossoms, 272
Springtime in the Ozarks, 342
Sprite, 49
Square & Star, 108
Square and a Half, 213
Square and Circle, 306
Square and Compass, 273, 300
Square and Diamonds, 150
Square and Half Square, 40, 193
Square and Points, 95
Square and Triangles, 150
Square Block, 130
Square Dance, 34, 115, 160, 195
Square Deal, 137
Square Diamond, 156
Square on Square, 104, 156
Square Triangles, 195
Square Up, 112
Square within Squares, 47
Squared Chain, 60
Squared Circle, 293
Squared Star, 85
Squares, 207
Squares and Crosses, 315
Squares and Diamonds, 22, 25, 163
Squares and Oblongs, 221
Squares and Square, 221
Squares and Stripes, 222
Squares Around the World, 247
Squares upon Squares, 93
Squares Within Squares, 93
Squash Blossom, 50
Squire Smith's Choice, 98
Squirrel, 374
Squirrel in a Cage, 39, 40
St. Andrew's Cross, 48
St. Elmo's Fire, 38
St. George's Cross, 38
St. Gregory's Cross, 68
St. John, Judy, 88
St. Louis, 123
St. Louis Block, 210, 326
St. Louis Star, 78, 210, 233
St. Louis Star Variation, 233
St. Paul, 68, 235
St. Valentine, 169
Stacked Bricks, 414
Stacked Stairs, 179
Stained Glass, 412
Stained Glass Star, 235
Stained Glass Window, 339
Stair Step Quilt, 350
Stairs of Illusion, 359
Stairstep Quilt, 359
Stanley, 227
Star, 24, 96, 98, 110, 133, 149, 317, 328, 329, 334
Star & Cross, 191
Star & Crown, 142
Star & Pinwheels, 97
Star & Web, 52
Star A, 63
Star Above the Stable, 86
Star and Arrow(s), 127, 331
Star and Block, 176
Star and Blocks, 355, 356, 368
Star and Box Quilt, 354
Star and Chains, 128, 334
Star and Cone, 171, 184
Star and Corona, 213, 219
Star and Crescent, 42, 167, 271, 300, 353, 367
Star and Cross, 61, 125, 159, 192, 199, 202, 211, 215
Star and Crown, 168
Star and Diamond(s), 110, 124, 333, 369
Star and Dot, 123
Star and Mill Block, 220
Star and Octagon, 197
Star and Planets, 287, 316, 367
Star and Ring, 350
Star and Square, 165
Star and Stripe, 141
Star and Web, 340
Star and Wreath, 343
Star Bed Quilt, 328, 329
Star Bound, 123
Star Bouquet, 251, 341, 366, 393, 394
Star Bouquet Quilt, 350
Star Burst Quilt, 174
Star Center in French Bouquet, 351
Star Chain, 63, 187, 317, 338
Star Crescent, 167
Star Dancer, 325
Star Diamond, 347
Star Explosion, 87, 89
Star Fire, 160
Star Flower, 68, 298, 342, 360
Star Flower Wreath, 394
Star Flowers, 341
Star for Lahoma, 218
Star Garden, 350
Star Gardner, 34
Star Geese, 30
Star Hexagon, 358
Star in a Square, 349
Star in Space, 65
Star in Stripes, 235
Star in the Window, 59, 79, 216
Star Kite, 41
Star Kites, 124
Star Lane, 207
Star Light, 135
Star Mosaic, 73
Star Net, 337
Star of Alabama, 341
Star of Alamo, 42
Star of Bethlehem, 136, 329, 333, 341, 343, 345, 346, 347, 354, 355, 356
Star of Chamblie, 346
Star of David, 365, 368
Star of Diamonds, 317
Star of Empire, 182
Star of Erin, 66
Star of Four Points, 123
Star of Hope, 24, 25, 81, 194, 331, 340
Star of Jerusalem, 340
Star of LeMoyne, 328
Star of Manhattan, 219
Star of Many Points, 24, 141, 334
Star of Mexico, 298
Star of Montana, 353
Star of Mystery, 164
Star of Spring, 32
Star of St. Louis, 210, 326
Star of Stars, 343
Star of Sweden, 328
Star of the Bluegrass, 329, 332
Star of the Decathlon, 313
Star of the East, 117, 133, 322, 329, 333, 343, 356
Star of the Four Winds, 167
Star of the Magi, 333
Star of the Milky Way, 98, 328, 329
Star of the Mountains, 360
Star of the Night, 181, 184, 227
Star of the Orient, 133
Star of the Sea, 42
Star of the West, 24, 111, 118, 167, 171, 220, 284, 349, 350
Star of Virginia, 24, 96
Star of West Virginia, 299
Star of Wonder, 61
Star over the Mountain, 340
Star Pattern, 70
Star Points, 131
Star Premo, 129
Star Puzzle, 97
Star Quilt, 354
Star Quilt Block, 333
*Star Quilts*, 328
Star Ray, 187
Star Rays, 352
Star Sapphire, 277
Star Shower, 337
Star Spangled, 24
Star Spangled Banner, 60, 348
Star Studded Beauty, 352
Star Trek, 77
Star Within a Star, 333
Star X, 25
Starbright Quilt, 333
Starburst, 59, 62, 147, 178, 339
Stardust, 111
Starfish Block, 367
Starfish (Star Fish), 176, 331, 338
Starflower Wreath, 219
Starlight, 74, 212
Starry Compass, 283
Starry Cross, 155
Starry Crown, 329
Starry Heavens, 329
Starry Lane, 207
Starry Mountain Quilt, 332
Starry Night, 115
Starry Nine Patch, 218
Starry Path, 139, 181
Starry Pavement, 184
Starry Sky, 80
Stars and Arrows, 173
Stars and Cubes, 332, 334
Stars and Pinwheels, 134
Stars and Squares, 134, 161
Stars and Stripes, 50, 63, 73, 140, 167, 217, 237, 342, 349
Stars and Stripes Forever, 355
Stars and Triangles, 184
Star's Exhibition Home Quilt Block Pattern, 405
Stars Galore, 140
Stars in a Star, 148
Stars in a Star Variation, 171
Stars in Flight, 87
Stars in the Corners, 336
Stars of Stripes, 329
Stars over Tennessee, 229
Stars over Texas, 158
Star(s) upon Star(s), 340, 343, 344, 350
Starshadow, 71
Stat Shine, 120
State Fair, 48
State Fair Block, 52, 185
State House, 145
State of Arkansas, 231
State of California, 335, 338
State of Georgia, 193
State of Idaho, 64
State of Iowa, 76
State of Maine, 274
State of Massachusetts, 78
State of Michigan, 234
State of Nebraska, 236, 251
State of Nevada, 162
State of New Jersey, 71
State of Ohio, 167
State of Oklahoma, 326
State of Oregon, 215
State of South Carolina, 144
State of South Dakota, 75
State of Texas, 349
State of Virginia, 31
State of West Virginia, 223
Steeplechase, 268, 269, 275
Stehlik, Jan, 175
Stellar Reflections, 183
Stellie, 26
Stepping Stones, 36, 141, 142, 153
Steps to Glory, 121
Steps to the Altar, 37, 43, 194, 359
Steps to the Garden, 81, 82
Steps to the Light House, 203
Steps to the Stars, 124
Steps to the White House, 203
Stevens, Elizabeth, 186
Stiles and Paths, 59
*Stitch 'n Sew Quilts*; Adam's Refuge, 58; Aerial Beacon, 322; Afternoon Shadows, 72; All My Family, 223; Alpha, 166; American Way, 349; Animals Stood By, 214; Autumn Kaleidoscope, 305; Autumn Moon, 124; Away in a Manger, 230; Banded Triangle, 129; Beautiful Crown, 160; Bird Feeder, 372; Bows and Paper, 129; Bricks and Blocks, 199; Bright Star, 234; Bush's Points of Light, 279; Candy Canes, 87; Candy Drops, 304; Center Ring, 304; Chain Bridge, 304; Child is Born, 166; Christmas Spirit, 228; Cookies and Milk, 47; Crowned Star, 231; Cut Diamond, 85; Diamond Cross, 166; Endless Ribbon, 42; Evening Quiet, 211; Expectations, 211; Fantasy World, 155; Fellowship, 132; First Morning Rays, 178; Flamingo's Flight, 172; Fluffy Patches, 155; Flying Kites, 153; Four Mills Variation, 81; Four Seasons, 133; Fowl Weather, 373; Fresh Start, 21; Granddaughter's Flower Garden, 364; Helping Hands, 173; Holiday Crossing, 75; Illinois Corn & Beans, 136; Japanese Friendship Block, 201; Jet Stream, 69; Joshua's Turn, 217; Kiowa Cross, 79; Lasting Blossoms, 204; Little Turtle in a Box, 371; Love Doves, 171; Love Entangled, 64; Love's Dream, 173; McDougall String Quilt, 79; Medieval Castle, 170; Medieval Spirits, 282; Melissa's Pinwheel Log Cabin, 237; Merry-Go-Round, 120; Migration South, 235; Morning Star, 217, 328; Mother's Dilemma, 174; My Tulip Garden, 397; No Name five patch, 233; No Room at the Inn, 18; North Star, 183; Nosegay, 172; Nouveau Lily Quilt, 394; Nova, 172; Owliver, 234; Path to Bethlehem, 166; Perky Pumpkin, 375; Points Homeward, 27; Pride of East Kingston, 291; Quiet Love, 72; Reindeer on the Roof, 181; Rejoice, 214; Reminiscences, 144; Road to Grandma's, 33; Road to Home, 219; Rocky Mountain Star, 310; Rough Diamond, 84; Season's Joy, 181; Shepherd's Watch, 86; Shooting Star, 49; Six and Two Pineapple Variation, 237; Snowbound, 75; Space Station, 175; Specialty Square, 145; Spring is Sprung, 63; Stained Glass Star, 235; Star & Web, 52; Star Above the Stable, 86; Star for Lahoma, 218; Star of Hope, 81; Starburst, 178; Stars and Stripes, 217; Stars and Stripes Forever, 355; Stars in Flight, 87; Straight and Narrow, 29; Streak of Lightning Pineapple Variation, 237; Striped Windmills, 146; Stuffed Stockings, 153; Sweet Buds, 87; This Way 'n That, 79; Thistles in the Mist, 394; Three and Five Pineapple Variation, 237; Three Kings' Journey, 51; Through the Looking Glass, 285; Tracks in the Snow, 150; Tree Top Twist, 68; Tumbling Star, 218; Turkey's Dilemma, 23; Valley Falls Square, 57, 160; Victorian Butterflies, 149; Victorian Fan, 178; Victorian Square, 43; Victorian Star, 212; White Mountain Star, 136; Wisconsin Star, 332; Wishing Star, 284; Yuletide, 78
Stockade, 294, 306
Stockyard's Star, 174
Stockyard's Star for Nebraska, 135
Stone, Clara, 186; Annie's Choice, 97; Aunt Anna's Album Block, 212; Aunt Malvina's Quilt, 60; Aunt Mary's Double Irish Chain, 140; Aunt Nancy's Favorite, 134; Autograph, 51; Autograph Quilt Block, 134; Bachelor's Puzzle, 60; Baltimore Belle, 205; Basement Window, 132; Beauty Block, 85; Black Beauty, 277; Black Diamond, 333; Bride's Fancy, 348; Broken Circle, 303; Broken

Wheel, 40; Chicago Pavements, 132; Colombian Puzzle, 164; Continuous Star, 340; Cross and Star, 221; Cross Plains, 137; Dewey Block, 224; Dewey's Victory, 97; Diamond Ring, 121; Diamond Star #2, 331; Dogwood Bloom, 299; Double Star, 336; Dove at the Crossroads, 229; Dutch Rose, 333; Electric Fan, 117; Elsie's Favorite, 304; Exea's Star, 75; Farmer's Daughter, 202; Fireside Visitor, 54; Fish, 331; Five Cross, 110, 323; Florentine Diamond, 167; Flower Basket, 385; Flying Cloud, 97; Good Fortune, 126; Goshen Star, 144; Grandma's Favorite, 193; Hour Glass, 12; Jack in the Pulpit, 126; Job's Trouble, 323; Kansas Beauty, 130; Kansas Sunshine, 290; King Solomon's Temple, 211; Kite, 110; Ladies' Chain, 327; Lillian's Favorite, 275; Magnolia Leaf, 14; Maple Leaf, 14; Memory, 33; Michigan Beauty, 24; Missouri Puzzle, 59; Mother's Choice, 23; Mother's Own, 220; Mrs. Hardy's Hanging Basket, 386; Mrs. Lloyd's Favorite, 162; Mutual Benefit, 275; New Cross and Crown, 58; Northumberland Star, 330; Papa's Delight, 305; Pike's Peak, 348; Pontiac Star, 124; Queen of the May, 317; Red Cross, 201; Road to California, 315; Round Robin, 309; Round Table, 289; Sailor's Joy, 330; Sam's Quilt, 367; Sarah's Choice, 97; Scrap, 156; Star and Crescent, 300; Star of Bethlehem, 333; Star of Hope, 340; Stockade, 294; Sunburst, 298; Sunflower, 298; Sylvia's Choice, 316; 20th Century Star, 300; Victory, 89; Victory Star, 334; Virginia Reel, 84; Wandering Jew, 329; Washington Snowball, 277; Wheel of Fate, 313; Wheel of Time, 97; Whirligig, 331
Stonemason's Puzzle, 225
Stony Point Quilt Block, 78
Stop Sign, 351
Storm at Sea, 28, 124, 164
Storm Signal, 22
Straight and Narrow, 29
Straight Furrow, 12
Straw Flowers, 46
Strawberry, 285
Strawberry Basket, 43, 383
Strawberry Patch, 70
Strawflower, 80
Streak of Lightning, 16, 105, 237, 413, 414, 416, 417, 418
Streak of Lightning Pineapple Variation, 237
Strength in Union, 197
String Quilt, 84, 90, 327
Stripe Squares, 220
Striped Plain Quilt, 48, 125
Striped Windmills, 146
Stripes and Squares, 216, 220
Stripes and Stars, 183
Strips and Squares, 53
Stuffed Stockings, 153
Sturrock, Wanda, 171
Stylized Eagle, 71
Stylized Flower, 391
Suburban House, 409
*Successful Farming*, 376
Sue's Delight, 181
Suffolk Puffs, 425
Sugar Bowl Block, 138, 163
Sugar Bowl Quilt, 95
Sugar Bowl (Sugarbowl), 104, 272, 273, 383, 386
Sugar Cone, 110, 425
Sugar Loaf, 73, 413
Sugar Scoop, 421
Summer and Winter, 277
Summer Blooms, 230
Summer Fancy, 267
Summer Garden, 82
Summer Rose, 248
Summer Star, 143
Summer Star Flower, 339
Summer Sun, 347
Summer Trees, 415
Summer Winds, 39
Summer's Dream, 128
Sun and Shade, 205
Sun and Shadow, 247
Sun and Stars Quilt, 163
Sun Dial, 56
Sun, Moon & Stars, 273
Sun over Transmountain, 279
Sun Ray, 187
Sun Rays Quilt, 28
Sunbeam, 196, 218
Sunbeam Block, 85
Sunbeam Crossroad, 211
Sunbonnet Sue, 381
Sunburst, 56, 58, 143, 181, 275, 283, 286, 288, 295, 296, 297, 298, 303, 305, 315, 317, 359
Sunburst and Mill, 336
Sunburst Star, 284, 329, 343, 357
Sundance, 84
Sunday Best, 221
Sundials, 283
Sunflower, 40, 81, 158, 283, 289, 294, 296, 297, 298, 303, 305, 308, 317, 323, 333
Sunflower Quilt, 168
Sunlight and Shadows, 69, 98
Sunny Lanes, 122, 178
Sunrise, 283, 284, 310, 315
Sunrise, Sunset, 289
Sunset, 292
Sunset Glow, 292
Sunset Quilt Block, 285
Sunset Star, 284, 312
Sunshine, 137, 290, 302
Sunshine and Shadow, 191, 247, 269, 308, 313
Sunshine and Stained Glass, 274
Sunshine over the Rockies, 86
Sunshiny Day, 109, 117
Surprise Package, 164
Susannah, 94, 136
Susie's Fancy, 36
Suspension Bridge, 284, 303
Swallow at the Window, 336
Swallow(s), 108, 208, 280, 332
Swallow's Flight, 371
Swallows in the Window, 330
Swallow's Nest, 305
Swamp Angel, 25
Swamp Patch, 27
Swasey, Ruth M.; Across the Square, 216; All My Family, 223; American Way, 349; Autumn Moon, 124; Bright Star, 234; Evening Quiet, 211; Fellowship, 132; Flower and Fern, 78; Four Seasons, 133; Fresh Start, 21; Friends & Family, 176; Helping Hands, 173; Holiday Crossing, 75; Lasting Blossoms, 204; Merry-Go-Round, 120; Mother's Dilemma, 174; My Tulip Garden, 397; Points Homeward, 27; Road to Grandma's, 33; Road to Home, 219; Snowbound, 75; Specialty Square, 145; Sweet Buds, 87; This Way 'n That, 79; Tree Top Twist, 68; Turkey's Dilemma, 23; Village Schoolhouse, 407; Whirling Snow, 216
Swastika, 53, 100, 121
Swastika Patch, 53, 71
Sweet Buds, 87
Sweet Clover, 313
Sweet Gum Leaf, 45
Sweetheart Garden, 315
Sweetwater Quilt, 317
Swing in the Center, 20
Swing Your Partner, 119
Swinging in the Center, 20
Swirl Dresden Plate, 307
Swirls, 233
Swiss Patchwork, 425
Swords and Plowshares, 232
Sylvia's Beige and Brown, 426
Sylvia's Bow, 376
Sylvia's Choice, 283, 303, 316
Symmetry in Motion, 113
T Design, 195
T Quartette, 195
T Quilt, 41, 67
Table for Four, 155
Tad Lincoln's Sailboat, 101
Tahitian Postage Stamp, 242
Tail of Benjamin's Kite, 36, 37
Tail of the Covered Wagon, 36
Taking Wing, 167
Tall Pine Tree(s), 398
Tall Ships, 113
Tallahassee Block, 139
Tam's Patch, 93
Tandi Whirl Quilt, 49
Tangled Arrows, 77
Tangled Briars, 31
Tangled Cobwebs, 338
Tangled Garters, 56
Tangled Lines, 84
Tangled Stars, 81
Tangled Tares, 164
Tangled Trails, 279
Taos Treasure, 231
Target, 321, 327
Tassel Plant, 62
Tea Basket, 382
Tea Box, 354, 357, 359
Tea for Four, 29
Tea Leaf, 14, 44, 109, 225, 275
Tea Leaf Strippie, 425
Tea Leaves, 14, 310
Tea Party, 202
Tea Rose, 121, 225
Teapot (Tea Pot), 378, 380, 381
Teddy's Choice, 139
Tee, 68
Teepee Town, 425
Telephone, 379
Television Quilt, 381
Telluride Puzzle, 176
Temperance Tree, 399, 400, 401, 402, 403, 405
Temple Court, 128
Ten patch grid, 258
Tenallytown Square, 132
Tennessee, 13, 329
Tennessee Circle, 301
Tennessee Mine Shaft, 88
Tennessee Mountain Laurel, 326
Tennessee Pine, 403
Tennessee Snowball, 272
Tennessee Star, 335
Tennessee Tulip, 391
Tennessee Waltz, 30
Tents of Armageddon, 195, 418
Terrace Floor, 118
Terrapin, 269
Tete-a-Tete, 45, 177, 196
Texas, 24, 28, 349
Texas Bluebonnet, 394
Texas Cactus, 330
Texas Cactus Basket, 382, 388
Texas Fireside, 66
Texas Flower, 16
Texas Pointer, 288
Texas Puzzle, 200
Texas Ranger, 123
Texas Ranger's Badge, 349
Texas Star, 24, 26, 96, 144, 316, 350, 357
Texas Star Quilt Block, 213
Texas Sunflower, 299
Texas Tears, 80, 82, 275, 280
Texas Treasure, 76
Texas Trellis, 354
Texas Tulip, 268
Texas Two Step, 175, 236
Thelma's Choice, 302
Thirteen Squares, 125
Thirteenth Summer, 282
This and That, 95, 114, 148
This Way 'n That, 79
Thistles in the Mist, 394
Thorny Thicket, 74
Thousand Islands, 84
Thousand Pyramids, 417, 418
Thousand Stars Quilt, 151
Thousands of Triangles, 195, 418
Three Across, 230
Three and Five Pineapple Variation, 237
Three and Six, 13
Three by Three, 17
Three Cheers, 76
Three Crosses, 38, 126
Three in a Corner, 225
Three Irish Chains, 203
Three Kings' Journey, 51
Three Little Kittens, 371
Three Patch, 355
Three Steps, 146
3D Nine Patch, 169
Three-in-One Quilt, 336
Thrift Block, 95
Thrifty, 16
Thrifty Wife, 148
Through the Looking Glass, 285
Through the Years, 210
Thunder and Lightning, 33, 35
Thunderbird, 119, 367, 381
Thunderbird and Sioux Star, 345
Tic Tac Toe, 18, 58, 62, 284
Tiffany, 411
Tiger Lily(ies), 203, 395, 397
Tile Patchwork, 323
Tile Pattern, 367
Tile Puzzle, 55
Tilted Triangles, 153
Timberline, 85
Time and Energy, 270
Time and Tide, 42, 123
Times Remembered, 199
Timson, Joyce, 149
Tin Man, 61
Tin Soldier "T" Quilt, 14
Tinted Chains, 132
Tiny Pines, 404
Tiny Star, 368
Tippecanoe, 113, 407
Tippecanoe and Tyler, Too, 24, 96
'Tis the Season, 404
Tit for Tat, 116, 410
To Market, to Market, 159
To the Moon, 376
Toad in the Puddle, 127
Tobacco Leaf, 273
Tombstone Quilt, 134
Tonganoxie Nine Patch, 234
Topaz Trail, 169
Topeka, 297
Topsy Turvy, 327
Tote a Tote, 196
Totem, 164
Toucan, 372
Towers of Camelot, 26
Town Hall, 409
Toy Soldier, 380
T-Quartette, 45
Tracks in the Snow, 150
Tracy's Puzzle, 263
*Traditional Quilter*; Avian Waves, 86; Cinderella, 138; Circle of Fans, 293; Home is Where the House Is, 408; Home is Where the Quilt Is, 408; Log Cabin Rosebud, 396; Romance, 116; Spring Fancy, 87
*Traditional Quiltworks*; Antique Red and White Quilt, 70; Confetti, 17; Confetti Block, 69; January Thaw, 27; Kite, 49; Rose Compass, 81; Star Dancer, 325; Wild Rose Wreath, 396
Traditional T, 31
Trail of Diamonds, 350
Trail of the Lonesome Pine, 398, 405
Trailing Star, 111
Trails, 101
Train Station, 406
Trapezoid, 365
Travel Star, 139, 167
Treasure Box, 30, 70
Treasure Chest, 26
Tree, 403
Tree and Truth Block, 242
Tree Everlasting, 13, 410
Tree of Life, 66, 400, 401, 403, 404, 405
Tree of Life Basket, 388
Tree of Paradise, 400, 401, 402, 403, 404, 405
Tree of Temptation, 400, 402
Tree of Triangles, 398
Tree Quilt Pattern, 335
Tree Top Twist, 68
Trees in the Park, 22
Trellis, 413
Trenton, 267
Trials and Troubles, 352, 361
Triangle Beauty, 114
Triangle Combination, 101
Triangle Design, 94
Triangle Mosaic, 362
Triangle of Squares, 125
Triangle Puzzle, 72, 209
Triangle Quilt, 413
Triangle Star, 347
Triangle Tiles, 112
Triangle Trails, 72
Triangle Weave, 99
Triangles, 32, 35, 52, 417, 424
Triangles and Squares, 101, 114, 156
Triangles and Stripes, 162
Triangular Trees, 413
Triangular Triangle(s), 170, 413
Tricolor Block, 17
Trip Around the World, 214, 247
Trip to Egypt, 362
Trip to the Altar, 13
Triple Irish Chain, 203
Triple Link Chain, 156
Triple Rose, 62
Triple Square and Double Square, 221
Triple Star, 333
Triple Star Flower, 341
Triple Star Quilt, 337
Triple Stripe, 73
Triple Sunflower, 284, 393
Triple Wedding Ring, 312
Triple X, 100
Triplet, 12
Trout and Bass Block, 331
Truck, 377
Truck Patch, 377
Trucker's Dream, 60
True Blue, 19
True Lover's Buggy Wheel, 278
True Lover's Knot, 142, 195, 236, 241, 275, 276, 326
Trumpet Flower, 390, 396
Trumpet Vine, 410
T-Square(s), 31, 67, 175
Tudor Rose, 235
Tulip and Star, 185
Tulip Basket, 386, 389
Tulip Bouquet, 88
Tulip Garden, 175, 391, 394
Tulip Lady Fingers, 43
Tulip Pattern, 285
Tulip Quilt, 285
Tulip Ring, 342
Tulip Tile, 263
Tulip Time, 390
Tulip Twirl, 145
Tulip Variation, 223
Tulip Wheel, 299, 314
Tulip Wreath, 213
Tulip(s), 109, 154, 157, 163, 390, 391, 392, 394, 395, 396, 397, 398
Tulip(s) in Vase, 387, 388, 392
Tumbler, 375, 412
Tumbleweed, 157, 269
Tumbling Blocks, 193, 359
Tumbling Hexagons, 357, 360
Tumbling Star, 218
Tumbling Ties, 199
Tunnels, 41
Turkey, 373
Turkey Giblets, 161
Turkey in the Straw, 20, 58
Turkey Tracks, 55, 208, 280
Turkey's Dilemma, 23
Turkish Puzzle, 50
Turn About Quilt, 272, 273
Turnabout, 22, 33
Turnabout T, 26
Turnabout Variation, 22
Turning Triangles, 361
Turnstile, 82, 104
Turtle, 337
Turtle on a Quilt, 269
Twelve Crowns, 34
Twelve patch grid, 254
Twelve Triangles, 95
20th Century Autograph Quilt, 230
20th Century Star, 300, 349
Twenty-four patch grid, 250
Twenty-four Triangles, 30
Twilight, 113, 119
Twin Darts, 65, 178
Twin Sisters, 105
Twin Star, 26
Twinkle Star, 328, 329
Twinkle, Twinkle Little Star, 328, 329
Twinkling Diamond Log Cabin, 356
Twinkling Star(s), 42, 76, 77, 110, 123, 185, 230, 271, 331, 333, 340, 346, 347, 351, 353
Twist, 309, 324
Twist and Turn, 193, 277, 278, 286, 412
Twist Around, 202
Twist Patchwork, 131, 175, 324
Twisted Ribbon(s), 50, 129, 231
Twisted Rope, 324
Twisted Spool Box, 185
Twisted Spools, 185
Twisted Star, 340
Twisted Thread Box, 185
Twister, 198
Twisting Spool, 185
Twisting Star, 22
Two Colors, 62
Two Crosses, 193
Two Patch Quilt, 95
*Ultimate Book of Quilt Block Patterns*, 186
Uncle Sam's Favorite, 207
Uncle Sam's Hourglass, 207, 224
Under Blue Mountain Skies, 32
Underground Railroad, 36
Unfolding Star, 322
Union, 34
Union Block, 34
Union Squares, 22, 33, 34
Union Squares, 21
Union Star, 32, 49, 300, 349
Unique Nine Patch, 222
Unknown nine patches, 16, 17
Unknown Silk Block, 36
Unknown Star, 25
Unnamed. *See also* Name Unknown; No Name; border, 426; curved patterns, 270, 290, 300, 314, 315; eight patch, 263; fan, 291; five patch, 191, 223; four patch, 124, 142, 154, 168, 186, 224; nine patch, 30, 44, 48, 51, 72, 74; star, 353, 355; twenty-four patch, 251
Use It All, 176
Utah, 271, 313

5,500 QUILT BLOCK DESIGNS

Utah Star, 139
Utility Block, 32
Vail, Alice; Fowl Weather, 373; Victorian Star, 212
Valley Falls Square, 57, 160
Variable Star, 24, 25, 96, 210, 328, 329
Variable Triangles, 365
Variegated Diamonds, 359, 420
Vase of Flowers, 368, 382
V-Block, 69, 152, 161
Venetian Design, 321, 328
Venetian Quilt, 356, 357
Vermont, 76, 153
Vermont Maple Leaf, 13
Very Old Sawtooth, 346
Vestibule, 173
Vice President's Block, 197
Vice President's Quilt, 235
Victoria Square, 46
Victorian Basket, 389
Victorian Butterflies, 149
Victorian Fan, 178, 291
Victorian Maze, 66
Victorian Square, 43
Victorian Star, 212
Victory, 89, 186
Victory Boat, 15
Victory Quilt, 117, 146, 161
Victory Star, 334
Village Church, 407
Village Green, 23
Village Schoolhouse, 407
Village Square, 94
Vine of Friendship, 268
Vines at the Window, 23
Viola's Scrap Quilt, 217
Violet Blossoms, 282, 311
Virginia, 31
Virginia Outerbacker, 127
Virginia Reel, 73, 84, 101, 135, 178, 334
Virginia Snowball, 277
Virginia Star, 334, 340, 341
Virginia Worm Fence, 17
Virginia's Choice, 272
Virginia's Star, 335, 340
Voiliers, 52
Vortex, 160
Voter's Choice, 55
Wagon Tracks, 35, 36, 37
Wagon Wheel(s), 271, 281, 286, 287, 351, 360
Walk Around, 332, 341, 342
Walk in the Garden, 79
Walker, Mary, 242
Walking Triangles, 51
Walled City, 89, 222
Walls of Jericho, 225
Wampum, 46
Wanderer, 267
Wanderer's Path in the Wilderness, 268
Wandering Diamond, 339
Wandering Flower, 133
Wandering Foot, 280
Wandering Jew, 147, 329
Wandering Lover, 38
Wandering Path of the Wilderness, 310
Wandering Path(s), 140, 356, 357
Wandering Star, 13
Washington, 84
Washington Merry-Go-Round, 311
Washington Pavement, 132
Washington Puzzle, 51
Washington Quilt Block, 210
Washington Sidewalk, 131
Washington Snowball, 277

Washington Star, 160, 174
Washington Tree, 402
Washington's Elm, 402
Washington's Quilt, 302
Waste Not, 103
Waste Not Variation, 130
Waste Not, Want Not, 118
Water Glass, 375
Water Lily, 340
Water Mill (Watermill), 59, 62, 104, 144, 155
Water Wheel (Waterwheel), 40, 88, 104, 105, 130, 180, 322
Water Wiggle, 74
Watered Ribbon & Border, 109
Watermelon, 380
Wave, 414
Waverly Star, 210
Waves of the Ocean, 137
Waving Plumes, 278
Wavy Navy, 419
W.C.T.U., 63
Weather Vane, 164
Weathervane, 39
Weathervane and Steeple, 47
Weathervane Pinwheel, 22
Weathervane Variation, 24
Weaving Paths, 242
Web of Diamonds, 341
Wedding Basket, 385
Wedding Bouquet, 45
Wedding March, 34, 56
Wedding Ring Bouquet, 289, 301
Wedding Ring Chain, 317
Wedding Ring Tile, 323
Wedding Ring(s), 40, 134, 148, 192, 194, 197, 201, 202, 267, 293, 317
Wedding Tile, 356
Wedge and Circle, 53
Wedgewood Tiles, 312
Weeping Willow, 398, 403
Welcome Hand, 19
West Virginia, 79, 130, 143, 182
West Virginia Star, 149
West Wind, 15
Western Spy, 182
Westfalen Waltz, 282
Westward Ho, 337
Whale Block, 276
Whatchamacallit, 227
Wheat Field, 158
Wheel, 297
Wheel of Chance, 192, 278
Wheel of Destiny, 50
Wheel of Fate, 313
Wheel of Fortune, 135, 154, 180, 192, 223, 272, 274, 278, 284, 289, 294, 295, 297, 303, 325, 327
Wheel of Life, 274, 287, 357
Wheel of Luck, 180
Wheel of Mystery, 272
Wheel of Time, 97, 295
Wheeler, Laura; America's Pride, 282; Anchors Aweigh, 83; Ann's Scrap Quilt, 158; Autumn Leaf, 14; Bouquet, 229; Brunswick Star, 330; Carolina Favorite, 277; Chained Star, 212, 323; Crisscross, 315; Daisy Chain, 230; Dogwood, 142; Double Friendship Knot, 234; Double Irish Chain, 69; Double Pinwheel, 309; Double Rainbow, 294; Endless Chain, 140; Feathered Star, 295; Flower of Spring, 300; Flower of the Woods, 292; Flying Geese, 213; Friendship Circle, 309, 328; Friendship Knot, 329; Friendship Ring, 293; Friendship Star, 82;

Garden Beauty, 300; Garden Bloom, 313; Gay Scrap Quilt, 100; Golden Stairs, 166; Grandmother's Pride, 292; Japanese Fan, 290; Joseph's Coat, 356; Leafy Basket, 385; Linked Squares, 314; Lone Star, 88; Lucky Star, 123; Magnolia, 69; Mayflower, 314; Meadow Flower, 322; Melon Patch Quilt, 276; Morning Star, 185, 351; Nine Patch Star, 186; No Name octagons, 328; Noonday Splendor, 298; North Star, 166; Peony, 315; Pine Tree Quilt, 398; Pinwheel, 234; Pride of the Prairie, 273; Priscilla's Prize, 312; Rising Star, 185; Rising Sun, 328; Rose and Trellis, 282; Rose Star One Patch, 362; Rose Windows, 288; Shasta Daisy, 328, 329, 397; Snowball Wreath, 274; Spider Web, 300; Springtime, 288; Star of Spring, 32; Starflower Wreath, 219; Summer Fancy, 267; Sunburst, 58; Sunburst Star, 343; Sunset Star, 312; Three Patch, 355; Turn About Quilt, 272, 273; Twist and Turn, 278, 286; Unnamed curved pattern, 270, 300; Waving Plumes, 278; Whirling Star, 167; White House Steps, 58; Wild Goose Chase, 201; Windflower, 270; Wreath, 330; Young Man's Fancy, 196
Wheeling Nine Patch, 35
Wheeling Triangles, 22
Wheel(s), 39, 100, 167, 200, 301
Whig's Defeat, 317
Whippoorwill, 85
Whirl Wind, 295
Whirlaround, 47, 48
Whirligig Quilt, 165
Whirligig (Whirlygig), 101, 103, 104, 105, 147, 150, 175, 192, 282, 331, 354
Whirling Blade, 101
Whirling Diamonds, 359
Whirling Fans, 301
Whirling Five Patch, 201
Whirling Hexagons, 325, 354, 361
Whirling L, 212
Whirling Pinwheel, 41, 282
Whirling Snow, 216
Whirling Square(s), 114, 160, 198, 236
Whirling Star(s), 52, 68, 85, 111, 167, 186, 286, 330
Whirling Triangles, 354
Whirling Tulip, 339
Whirling Wheel, 294, 316
Whirlpool, 39, 103
Whirlwind, 104, 105, 176
White Cross, 122, 125
White, Helen, 118
White Hemstitch, 135
White House, 72
White House Rose, 72
White House Steps, 58, 121, 241
White Lily, 392
White Mountain Star, 136
White Mountains, 323, 326
White Rose, 289
White Square Quilt, 228
Who'd a Thought It, 369
Wicklund, Mrs. Elmer, 197
Widower's Choice, 206
Wild Duck, 100
Wild Geese, 13, 134, 149
Wild Geese Flying, 412
Wild Goose Chase, 78, 100, 137, 169,

183, 200, 201, 412, 414, 420
Wild Iris, 170, 183, 236, 397
Wild Irish Rose, 186
Wild Lily, 282
Wild Lily, 332
Wild Rose, 332
Wild Rose and Square, 192
Wild Rose Wreath, 396
Wild Waves, 161
Will o the Wisp, 147
Wind Mill Quilt, 97
Wind Power of the Osages, 53, 101
Wind Star for New Hampshire, 255
Wind Wheel Quilt Block, 49, 211
Windblown Daisy, 295
Windblown Lily, 69
Windblown Square, 103
Windblown Star, 361
Windflower, 270
Winding Blade(s), 101, 152, 269, 329
Winding Stairway, 93
Winding Trail, 270, 289
Winding Walk, 133, 136
Winding Ways, 272
Windmill and Outline, 165
Windmill Star, 124
Windmill(s), 13, 44, 58, 62, 95, 103, 104, 105, 106, 107, 108, 112, 124, 138, 147, 149, 151, 179, 205, 272, 274, 325
Windmills All Around, 57
Window, 105
Window Square(s), 48, 186
Windowpane, 80
Windows, 94
Windows and Doors, 214
Windy City, 113, 142, 171, 365
Wine Bottle, 377, 378
Wine Glass, 377
Winged Arrow, 113
Winged Four Patch, 98
Winged Nine Patch, 57, 142
Winged Square, 37, 38, 73, 83, 111
Winged Star, 333
Wings, 279
Wings in a Whirl, 12
Wings of Eagles, 129
Winner's Circle, 276, 371
Winnowing.com, 377
Winter Cactus, 118
Winter Pines, 399
Winter Stars, 329
Winter Trees, 398
Wintery Reflections, 42
Wisconsin, 206
Wisconsin Maze, 83
Wisconsin Star, 332
Wish U Well, 268
Wishing Ring, 50, 195
Wishing Star, 235, 284, 326
Wishing Well, 286, 309
Witches Star, 329
Without Constraint, 283
Woman's Century, 20
Woman's Day; Jacob's Ladder, 359; Old Maid's Ramble, 90; Pennsylvania Hex, 350; Stairstep Quilt, 359; Triangles, 52
Woman's Home Companion, 373
Woman's World; Aeroplane, 195; Cross Patch, 132; Diamond Design, 328; Dragon's Head, 19, 195; Four Birds, 331; Gem Block, 126; Glory Design, 359; Grecian Square, 19; Indian Meadow, 114; Little Saw Tooth, 114; Melon Patch, 276; Peekaboo, 58; Peekhole, 108; Pinwheel Star, 335; Rocky Glen, 114; Rope, 412; Saw Tooth, 114; Sunbeam, 196, 218;

Tennessee Snowball, 272; Whirl-wind, 176; X Quartet, 104; Zig-Zag, 177
Women's Choice, 63
Women's Comfort, 34
Wonder of Egypt, 350
Wonder of the World, 268, 269, 270
Wood Lily, 38, 392, 397
Woodland Path, 205
Work-basket, 309
Workbasket; Delaware's Flagstones, 18; Diamond Solitaire, 167; Knicker-bocker Star, 333; May Time Quilt, 174; New Hampshire Granite Block, 67; Ogden Corners, 323, 326; Party Plate Quilt, 316; Pennsyl-vania Pineapple, 255; Ring Around the Star, 337; Road to California, 269; Ships A-Sailing, 263; Snowflake Quilt, 352; State of Georgia, 193; Vermont Maple Leaf, 13; Wedding Ring Tile, 323; Wishing Star, 326
Workbasket Magazine; Arrowhead, 124; Breeches Quilt, 139; Gem Block, 124; Idaho, 124
Workbox, 379
World Fair Quilt, 151
World Without End, 110, 124
World's Fair, 89, 100, 110, 154, 181
World's Fair Block, 93
World's Fair Puzzle, 137
World's Pride Quilt Block, 144
World's Wonder, 268
Woven Fences, 424
Woven Heart, 140
Wreath, 330
Wreath of Lilies, 330
Wrench, 19, 195
Writer's Block, 339
Wyoming, 298
Wyoming Patch, 299
Wyoming Quilt Block, 310
Wyoming Valley, 33
X Quartet, 104
X-Quisite, 106
Yankee Charm, 18, 182
Yankee Pride, 332, 334
Yankee Puzzle, 100, 101
Yankee Star, 187
Yankee Star Chain, 187
Year's Favorite, 104
Yellow Clover, 212
Yellow Lilies, 235
Yellow Point, 287
Yellow Ribbon, 38
Yellow Square, 94
Yokohama Banner, 114
Yorkshire Daisy, 425
Young Man's Fancy, 196, 222
Young Man's Invention, 301
Your Lucky Star, 174
Yo-Yo, 425
Yreka Square, 214
Yuletide, 78, 273
Z-Cross, 192
Zebra, 372, 374
Zig Zag Blocks, 421
Zig Zag Path, 15
Zig Zag Tile Quilt, 113
Zig Zag (Zig-Zag), 17, 101, 177, 211, 417, 418
Zinnias, 394
Zodiac Stars, 352
Zygocactus, 392